THE
MAGNIFICENT
CONTINENT

THE
MAGNIFICENT
CONTINENT

RAND McNALLY & COMPANY
New York Chicago San Francisco
in association with
Mitchell Beazley Publishers Limited, London

The Magnificent Continent was edited and designed
by Mitchell Beazley Publishers Limited
87–89 Shaftesbury Avenue, London W1V 7AD

Editor: Iain Parsons
Art Editor: Pat Gilliland
Assistant Editor: Marsha Lloyd
Designers: Michael Blore, Roger Hammond
Art Assistants: Pauline Faulks, Carol Johnson
Picture Researchers: Ken Kahn, U.S.A.
Kate Parish, Susan Pinkus

Publisher: Bruce Marshall
Art Director: John Bigg
Executive Editor: Glorya Hale

EDITORIAL ADVISORY BOARD
Photographic Adviser: Arthur d'Arazien
Editorial Advisers: Dorothy Millikan, Paul Tiddens
Art Adviser: Ed Day

The Publishers acknowledge the generous
cooperation of International Paper Company,
whose regard for a priceless heritage
helped make this book possible.

ISBN: 528 81011 1
Library of Congress Catalog Card Number: 75–1928
Printed in the U.S.A.

INTRODUCTION

This book is dedicated to the grandeur of a continent. It is a tribute to North America—to its soaring mountain spires, its stark mesas and gaping canyons; to its rugged shores, haunting lakes, meandering rivers and thunderous waterfalls; to its proud, brooding forests and formidable deserts; to its magical subterranean caverns and vast undulating plains; to its sprawling cities and backcountry hamlets; to the continent's grandiose spectrum of wonderous sites and aspects.

This book is dedicated to the American dream, in which the lure of the land has always been a central theme, fashioning the character and aspirations of Americans, offering visions of eternity, facets of reality transcending human fragility and a retreat to innocence. This book is, for the most part, an exercise in discovery and rediscovery, a quest for elusive dimensions of beauty and truth, for values untarnished by time but often eroded by neglect. Not without wisdom did the Indians endow North America's natural wonders with mystical spirits to be venerated. Not without reason have so many

of these natural wonders now become natural shrines.

This book is dedicated to the moods and meanings of the North American landscape—to the opaque, tangled serenity of the Okefenokee Swamp; to the tempestuous spasms of the sea crashing endlessly over rugged rock formations of the Oregon shore; to the desolate enchantment of Canada's limpid North Woods lakes; to the craggy majesty of the Grand Tetons; to the dazzling polychrome antiquity of the Petrified Forest; to the bleak volcanic glory of Popocatepetl towering over the Valley of Mexico.

This is an expedition through the vestiges of primeval America, touched and transfigured over inconceivable dimensions of time by titanic elemental forces beyond human influence. But it is also an exploration of North America's overlaid tiers, the works and ways which bear the stamp of mankind.

This book is, therefore, dedicated, too, to the people of North America—to the prehistoric men out of Asia who were the first humans to plant roots on the

continent; to the richly diverse and scattered Indian cultures and civilizations which succeeded them; to those audacious explorers who, seeking other realms, stumbled comparatively recently on America's shores and ultimately realized the enormity of their discovery; and to those who followed them and, through toil and ingenuity, built the brave New World they had expected to find.

During his relatively brief tenure on its soil, man has transformed North America. In the process, he has constructed an imposing physical context of his own upon the bedrock of the land. Although not as durable as that which nature molded, it is an integral element in the image of the continent. This book is, therefore, dedicated to the lofty concrete and glass grand canyons of North America's bustling metropolises as well as to the Grand Canyon of Arizona; to the cactus-like totems of the northwest coast Indians as well as to the elegant southwest desert cacti; to down-to-earth small-town main streets as well as to cloud-obscured mountain passes; to graceful bridges spanning yawning waterways as well as to the rivers that flow down to the sea.

This, then, is an excavation as well as a pilgrimage, focusing on visual substance as well as basic significance. The perspective is new, unjaded, fresh; it is that of writers from other lands who went to North America to examine, to explore and to feel uniquely the uniqueness of the continent's prodigious natural and man-made spectacles. Peaks, prairies, plateaus and plazas, the setting is immense, both in size and concept. The continent's splendors are strewn across it like windblown seed. Nevertheless, there is a fundamental underlying confluence—this is North America; its constituent parts comprise a whole. We have sought here to weave together its various threads, to compile a catalog of distinct, vivid impressions, both descriptive and instinctive, and, from those extractions, to construct an image of a magnificent continent.

THE EDITORS

THE FOUR AGES

OF A CONTINENT

AGE ONE
A Continent is Born

North America has been defined and re-defined, discovered and rediscovered, by accident and design, time and time again. It is an illuminating process still unfinished. However, to fix the continent in time and place is an elusive undertaking. Compass readings, statistical tables and this morning's headlines are instructive. But North America's history is a compendium of spectacularly diverse fragments of time, each punctuated by momentous events. Its landscape has been sculptured by a staggering variety of elemental forces and mortal designs. Its mosaic of natural and man-made monuments conveys an infinity of moods—awesome like Death Valley, turbulent like the Colorado River rapids, placid like Canada's Athabasca Glacier, frenetic like downtown New York, luxuriant like the Yucatán jungle, austere like the Dakota Badlands.

The face of North America today is merely the most recent of the many profiles the continent has displayed since the world took shape

AGE ONE: A Continent is Born

from a cloud of celestial gas four and a half billion years ago. What happened so long ago is impossible to determine with certainty; the sequence of events, and the events themselves, are disputed by scholars and scientists. One theory of the origin of the continent suggests that the molten globe, into which the earth was transformed as it grew palpable, cooled unevenly; that North America and the other continents solidified first; and that the remaining, still molten areas subsided before hardening to form permanent oceanbed depressions.

Another theory conceives of North America as originally part of a solitary super-continent —called Pangaea—which was molded from the earth's congealing surface. This enormous landmass was subsequently shattered by terrestrial cataclysms into the various continents, which, in a process begun billions of years ago and still continuing, at a rate of one-half inch a year, drifted into the positions they occupy today. Matching contour traces of their continental shelves still show how Northwest Africa may have slotted into North America's eastern seaboard.

Other theories about how North America began have been advanced and no doubt still more will be propounded. But whatever its origins, the continent was at first, and for a long time thereafter, a lifeless landmass in the explosive process of taking form and shape. Volcanic turbulence thrust up towering mountains, capped with smoldering craters, which spewed forth torrents of lava. The continental crust cooled and contracted. It buckled and buckled again, lifting and shifting mountain spines. Earthquakes shattered and rearranged the void. Primeval seas —inhabited by minute marine creatures, the first living things—repeatedly washed across the continent, obliterating the landscape.

Time is a tease when it comes to contemplating these events. A thousand years is a fleeting instant, barely worth mentioning. A million years is a brief moment, leaving the barest of legacies. A half billion years ago most of North America was inundated. Oceanic intrusions advanced and retreated, eroding and leveling the rock outcroppings they drowned. What is now Arizona was once an island ringed by lapping waters. So was most of Oklahoma. The Great Plains were once totally awash—immense submerged lowlands between higher ground east and west. The high ground was eventually lowered and inundated as well.

Some two million square miles of eastern and central Canada remained untouched by the deluge. This Canadian Shield, the continent's most ancient stable-surface rock formation, a vast storehouse of mineral wealth, took shape more than a billion years ago and, as far

as is known, has never since been submerged. A chain of formidable mountains, snaking down from the shield through eastern America to Alabama, also remained largely high and dry, as did isolated peaks and plateaus elsewhere. But, for the most part, the seas came and went as if there were no continent there.

The submerged areas were not left unaltered. They remained subject to geological convulsions, volcanic eruptions, earthquakes and the folding of the earth's surface. These subterranean regions were also relentlessly veneered with thick strata of sediment. Like coffee grounds settling to the bottom of a pot, countless particles of terrestrial and marine debris sank to the floor of the inland seas and, over a long period of time, hardened into layer upon layer of rock, to be raised, lowered, split asunder and worn down by subsequent upheaval and erosion.

Many such uplifted protrusions as the Grand Canyon and Monument Valley buttes and mesas reveal their venerable sedimentary composition in rainbows of rock stripes, one atop the other, which mark their sides—billions of sand particles, which dropped to the beds of ancient seas and petrified into sandstone layers; mud, which was transformed into shale; and limestone formed from enormous masses of compressed marine skeletons and shells. Each layer, each color, signifies a small eternity which mocks our conventional calendars.

Sediment, often many thousands of feet deep, is the primary constituent of North America's topography, as well as the stuff from which much of its scenic beauty has been hewn. Kentucky's Mammoth Cave, the Carlsbad Caverns of New Mexico and virtually all of North America's underground natural cathedrals are carved from limestone laid down by primal inundations and sculptured by erosion after the seas retreated. The haunting natural arches of Utah were fashioned from sandstone, once submerged. Thick layers of shale which lined the bed of the Niagara River were gradually washed away, undermining a cap of more resistant rock; the resulting collapse produced Niagara Falls. Ancient ranges, like the Nemaha Mountains of Kansas, which once were silhouetted against the horizon, but are now only geological footnotes, were lost beneath the floors of prehistoric seas. They were matched, then buried by accumulating sediment.

A warm, moist climate pervaded the continent during the time of the inland seas. Dense thickets of vegetation sprouted in swamps along the rims of the water and in its shallow reaches. Immense forests also sprang up, to be smothered when the seas advanced and to grow anew when the seas contracted. New woods flourished over the remains of the old,

burying their predecessors and buried, in turn, by their successors. Layer upon layer of dead forest was compressed beneath the surface. The result, after time and the earth's chemistry had done their work, was fossil fuel —the rich coal seams of the Appalachians and of Nova Scotia.

The semitropical swamps and marshes ringing the inland waters were an evolutionary incubator. Higher and higher life forms evolved. The waters teemed with fish and mollusks. Amphibians emerged onto the land. Mammal-like reptiles ranged through the jungles and forests in search of sustenance. The most formidable creatures of all, perhaps of all time, were the dinosaurs, grotesquely huge giants, masters of the continent, and of the earth, for more than a hundred million years—far longer than man's tenure so far.

In the swamps of Connecticut and New Mexico, in the primeval jungles of Missouri and Utah, in the steamy marshes of Alberta and North Carolina, enormous, ferocious carnivores and massive, plodding herbivores hulked across the landscape. The skeleton of a brontosaur, which was ninety feet long and weighed an estimated thirty tons, has been reclaimed from a quarry in northwestern Colorado. Excavations among rock beds near Hell Creek, Montana, have uncovered the bones of *Tyrannosaurus rex*, which stood fifty feet tall, had a thirteen-foot stride and a skull four feet deep, the powerful jaws of which were armed with sharp teeth six inches long. Other explorations nearby have produced the battlemarked remains of its mortal enemy, *Triceratops*, an armored behemoth with long, pointed horns above each eye and another over its snout. The duck-billed *Trachadon*, whose elongated mouth contained two thousand teeth, roamed the marshes of western New Jersey.

There were fifty-ton brachiosaurs, so heavy that they lived most of their lives in water to sustain their weight, having evolved nostrils at the tops of their heads so that they could breathe when almost entirely submerged. There were stegosaurs, tank-like creatures with large, protective, bony plates protruding from their backs and long spikes projecting from their tails. Voracious flying dinosaurs, with fifty-foot wingspreads, dominated the skies. Fifty-foot-long marine reptiles, cousins of the dinosaurs, were lords of the depths of the inland seas.

There were also small, bird-like dinosaurs, as well as the earliest of mammals, diminutive animals, including primitive rodents, which sheltered in high ground. But for no reason yet understood, this was an age of giants, of massive beasts who, despite their size, or perhaps because of it, were destined to disappear forever.

THE DRIFT OF A LANDMASS

The earth's original supercontinent, Pangaea, began to break up about two hundred million years ago. About seventy-five million years ago South America and Africa had separated, but North America and Eurasia still formed one landmass known as Laurasia. North America and Greenland broke away about forty-five million years ago and drifted west to their present positions.

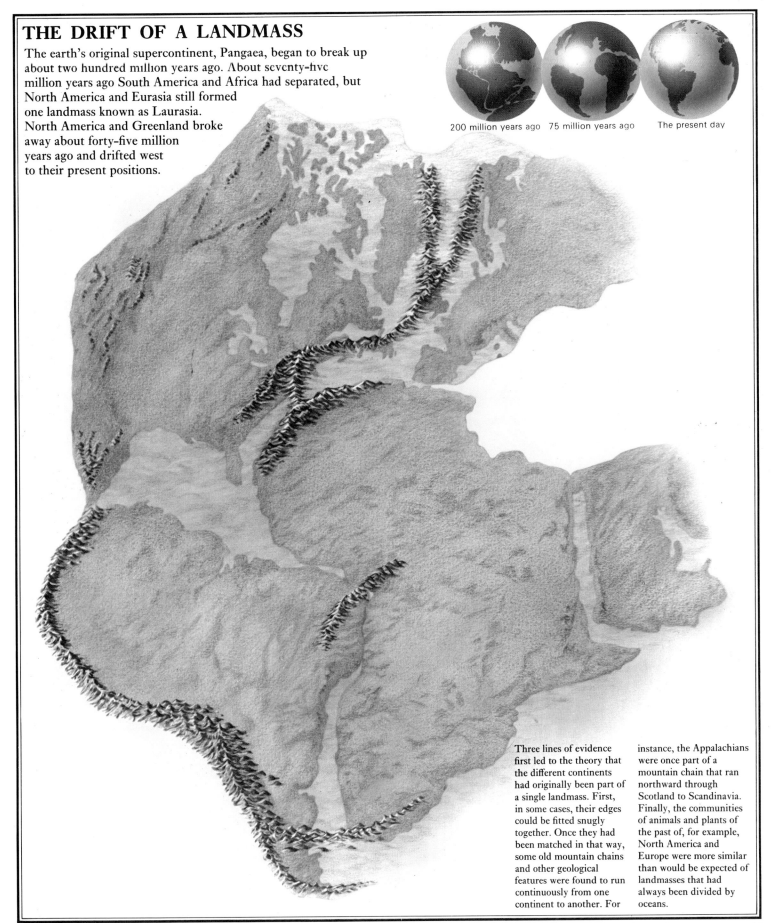

200 million years ago   75 million years ago   The present day

Three lines of evidence first led to the theory that the different continents had originally been part of a single landmass. First, in some cases, their edges could be fitted snugly together. Once they had been matched in that way, some old mountain chains and other geological features were found to run continuously from one continent to another. For instance, the Appalachians were once part of a mountain chain that ran northward through Scotland to Scandinavia. Finally, the communities of animals and plants of the past of, for example, North America and Europe were more similar than would be expected of landmasses that had always been divided by oceans.

NORTH AMERICA IS FORMED

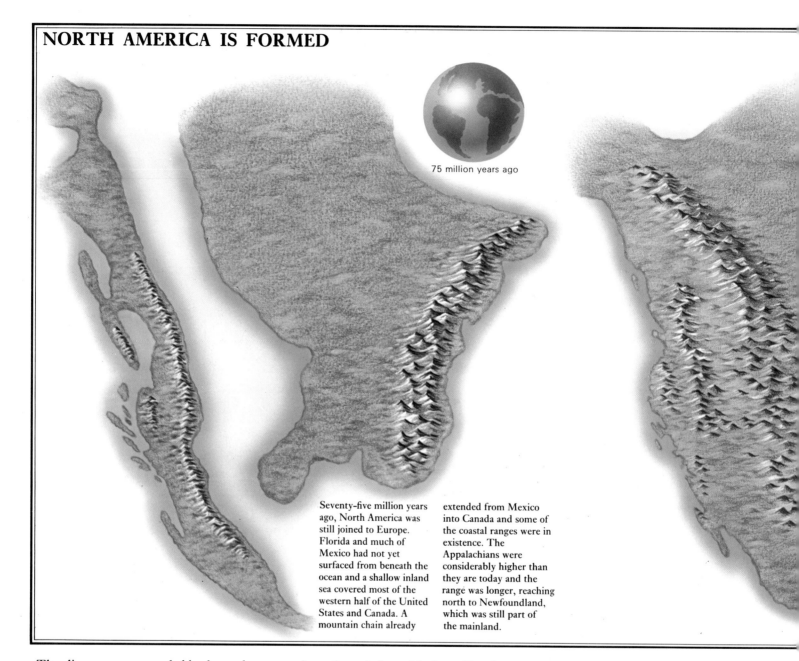

75 million years ago

Seventy-five million years ago, North America was still joined to Europe. Florida and much of Mexico had not yet surfaced from beneath the ocean and a shallow inland sea covered most of the western half of the United States and Canada. A mountain chain already extended from Mexico into Canada and some of the coastal ranges were in existence. The Appalachians were considerably higher than they are today and the range was longer, reaching north to Newfoundland, which was still part of the mainland.

The dinosaurs were probably doomed to extinction by environmental changes. The inland seas slowly withdrew. It grew colder. The swamps and jungles disappeared. Suited only to the conditions in which they had flourished, too ponderous to trudge long distances in search of other subtropical regions, the dinosaurs vanished from the face of the earth.

Their reign was succeeded by long spans of climatic fluctuation. Arid periods turned vast expanses of North America into windswept deserts. There were temperate periods, many millions of years long, during which rainfall wove webs of drainage systems across flatlands and through mountain belts. Wind and water eroded jagged peaks. Enormous forests sprang up, one of which covered most of eastern America. Mammals inherited the continent from their vanished reptilian forebears—among them were giant horned pigs, elephant-like mastodons with shovel tusks protruding from their lower jaws, *Eohippus*, the dawn horse, barely two feet long, and tiny rhinoceroses, almost as small.

A new period of accelerated subterranean disturbance was initiated. Mexico's central tableland was uplifted, as was much of the southern coastal plain, which rose from the sea, Florida last of all, emerging from watery depths a mere forty-five million years ago. Chains of volcanic eruptions threw up the Columbia Plateau in the Pacific Northwest, as well as mountains in Alaska and California. A plateau was raised in northern Arizona from which the mighty Colorado River was later to carve the Grand Canyon. The Rockies were uplifted from a sediment-filled trough in the west and rain-fed streams washed sediment from their cloud-brushing heights into lowlands to the east, laying a bed for the Great Plains, a process duplicated in valleys of mountains great and small across North America.

Still another major force was to be unleashed before the continent took the features that are known today. In the Canadian north, vast ice sheets, as thick as ten thousand feet in places, were accumulating. A million years ago—only yesterday in the continent's overall time scale—these glaciers began inching down over North America, advancing up to one foot a day, pushing forward, scraping and grinding down everything in their paths, fundamentally altering the regions they covered. They chiseled canyons and ravines out of plateaus, redirected river beds, smoothed out plains,

12

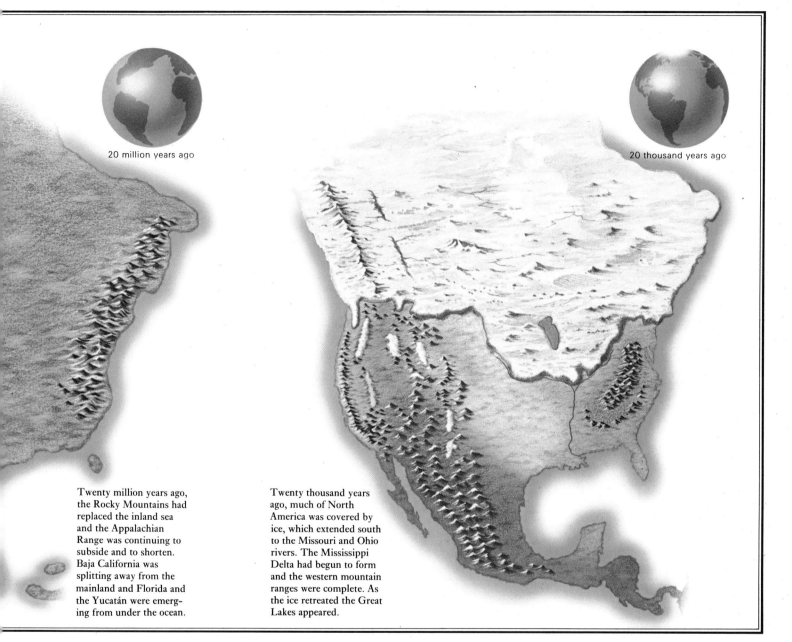

20 million years ago

20 thousand years ago

Twenty million years ago, the Rocky Mountains had replaced the inland sea and the Appalachian Range was continuing to subside and to shorten. Baja California was splitting away from the mainland and Florida and the Yucatán were emerging from under the ocean.

Twenty thousand years ago, much of North America was covered by ice, which extended south to the Missouri and Ohio rivers. The Mississippi Delta had begun to form and the western mountain ranges were complete. As the ice retreated the Great Lakes appeared.

filled in or tore open valleys and pried loose and transplanted huge quantities of soil and stones.

Topsoil was picked up in the north and deposited off the eastern coast to form Cape Cod, Martha's Vineyard and Long Island. California's Yosemite Valley was carved by glacial might. The basins of the Great Lakes and of thousands of lesser lakes were gouged out by the ice walls. Canada, New England and the north were denuded of their rich vegetation and sprawling forests. Tree seeds were carried south by glacial winds to provide the genesis of forests of fir and other northern trees that were to spring up in regions where such trees had never before grown.

There had been earlier glacial periods, lost in obscure recesses of archaic history and geological transformation. But the ice ages which have left their distinct mark occurred within the last one million years—four major glacial periods and several lesser ice ages during which the glaciers crept relentlessly down across the continent, reaching as far south as a line from what would later be New York to St. Louis, then skirting up and stretching to the Pacific just south of the Canadian–American border.

Frigid temperatures created and propelled the ice walls; a warming process brought them to a halt. Each of the ice ages drew to a close (the last one about ten thousand years ago) as the glaciers slowly melted, releasing huge amounts of water to create new rivers and streams and to widen those which had survived the glacial assault. Some glaciers, smaller and less thick, survived; some still do, including those in Canada's Columbia Icefield,

in Alaska and the remnants of ice sheets clinging to the crags and flanks of Mount Rainier and the Grand Tetons.

North America throbbed to life again during interglacial periods. Warm, sometimes subtropical climates nourished new forests and a resurgence of plant life. Fish teemed in swollen rivers, which surged to the sea to unload their glacier-fed rapids, and in the waters of glacier-carved lake basins. Mammals, including giant sloths, camels and saber-toothed tigers, flourished in highlands and lowlands.

Each return of the glaciers spread a white shroud over the continent's life and activity, creating polar deserts wherever they extended. But it was during one of the great ice ages that the most highly developed mammal of all, *Homo sapiens*, already long resident elsewhere, first discovered America.

AGE TWO
The First Americans

The human species, according to all available evidence, is not native to America. Man did not evolve through successive stages from ape-man to human being on the American continent, as he did on other continents in other parts of the world. The first Americans were full-fledged humans, who migrated from somewhere else. But who they were and where they came from has long been disputed.

It has been claimed that the first people to discover America were survivors of lost continents—explorers or stragglers from Mu, which, it is said, sank beneath the Pacific Ocean thousands of years ago, or of Atlantis which, it is contended, disappeared beneath the depths of the Atlantic before recorded history. Others say the Indians are descendants of the lost tribes of Israel, or of Phoenicians, Greeks, Egyptians or others, who navigated uncharted seas on ancient, perilous, forgotten voyages of discovery. However, the evidence of the first Americans—prehistoric remnants and remains, biological affinity and geological probability—points elsewhere, to northeast Asia. It is now generally accepted that the earliest Americans were nomadic stone age hunters who came from Siberia and who left a paper chase of archaeological clues to their identity and to their line of march.

Today, Siberia and Alaska are separated by a fifty-six-mile-wide breach of comparatively shallow choppy water. But, during the ice ages, glaciers which blanketed much of North America, but not Alaska, imprisoned so much water that the sea level dropped as much as three hundred feet, exposing a broad isthmus of land, a bridge more than a thousand miles wide, which linked America and Asia. Wandering herds of animals—including mastodons, long-horned buffalo and musk oxen—which grazed on the Asian side, casually drifted across this fertile landbridge and into Alaska. The nomadic Siberian hunters, following their prey and extending their range of scavenging for wild edible plants, unwittingly found the American continent, too.

Their discovery of America was unintentional and unperceived, an accident neither recognized nor understood by those involved. The first humans to set foot on the North American continent crossed no noticeable frontier. They overcame no natural barriers, contended with no hazards they had not previously encountered and forsook no permanent home to find a new land.

14

It is difficult to determine when this happened. There was at least one, and perhaps several, glacial periods during the era of primitive man when the Alaska–Siberia landlink was above sea level and accessible to the nomads out of Asia, whose heirs were, at least for a time, to inherit America. Bone and stone implements several thousand years old, similar to others found in Siberia, have been uncovered in Alaska. Present-day climatic conditions in both those regions complicate the search for such relics. Radiocarbon tests, however, have shown that a human skull found near Del Mar, California, dates back forty-eight thousand years. Remains of what is believed to be a thirty-eight-thousand-year-old charcoal hearth have been found at Lewisville, Texas. Carved bone implements dating back thirty-two thousand years have been discovered at Tule Springs, Nevada. Near Snake River, Idaho, the bones of bison have been uncovered, which show signs of having been killed by hunters thirty thousand years ago.

It may have taken thousands of years for man to make his way down from Alaska to the North American heartland. It is likely, then, that the first crossing from Siberia took place at least fifty thousand years ago, and perhaps earlier. New discoveries—a human bone here, a primitive tool there—keep pushing the date back in time.

It is probable that the first Americans arrived in trickles rather than in waves, an evergrowing procession of small hunting and plant-gathering bands. The migration may have been halted for long periods by the submergence of the landbridge as glaciers melted and may have resumed when a new ice age drew back the sea and again opened the path from Asia to America.

The first Americans are believed to have had prominent cheekbones, slightly slanted eyes, straight black hair and reddish-brown skin. Some anthropologists, however, suggest that the early migrants may have arrived from Asia before the racial characteristics of *Homo sapiens* became sharply differentiated, in which case the ancestors of the Indians would have developed Mongoloid characteristics over a long period of time subsequent to their arrival from Asia. Later arrivals, including the Eskimos—whose ancestors probably first crossed from Siberia about ten thousand years ago—were more distinctly Mongoloid.

With the glaciers relatively close, the winters were fiercely cold. The first Americans probably wore animal skins and furs and built fires. Perpetually on the move, they lived in easily constructed, readily abandoned homes, probably pit shelters covered with animal skins. They traveled in communities that

IN PURSUIT OF BIG GAM

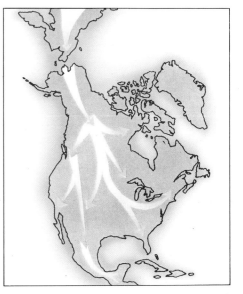

The first Americans came across the land-bridge from Siberia about twenty thousand years ago. They were nomadic hunters who pursued the giant mammals which then roamed North America. Their pursuit of game gradually carried them southward, down the east and west sides of the Rocky Mountains, until they eventually reached the Gulf and Atlantic coasts. Some pushed onward into Mexico and South America. The finds of archaeologists show that these early Americans, armed only with stone-tipped spears and rocks, hunted and killed woolly mammoths, which stood nine feet tall, and giant sloths, which, when they reared, were twenty feet tall.

were tightly knit by the need for numbers to subdue the formidable animals on which they preyed. It is unlikely that individual hunters, armed with stone knives and stone-tipped spears, which they launched from spear throwers, could overcome woolly mammoths, which stood twelve feet tall and weighed several tons.

Early man in America was neither an explorer nor an adventurer. No irrepressible urge led him out of Alaska and across the continent. He was lured on by the same impulse that had brought his forebears across the landbridge. He was a hunter and he followed his prey. No doubt some pursued wandering herds—including camels and horses, which were to become extinct in the western hemisphere—back across the landlink to Siberia. (Spanish conquistadors were later to reintroduce horses in America.)

Although the plains and valleys of Alaska were habitable, a barrier of glacial ice blocked

Excavations in 1952 at a site near Naco, Arizona, where eight projectile points and the bones of a woolly mammoth were found, have proved that early Americans had reached there ten thousand years ago.

Clovis point

Folsom point

The finding in 1926, at Folsom, New Mexico, of flints in the body of an extinct wide-horned bison provided the first proof of Pleistocene Age Americans.

Sandia point

The distinctive stone points found with the remains of a giant sloth in Sandia Cave, New Mexico, are thought to be the oldest weapons found in North America.

Wyoming, Colorado, Arizona, in Oregon and California, in Massachusetts and Alabama, in virtually every region of North America. In 1925, a cowboy rounding up stray cattle near Folsom, New Mexico, found prehistoric spear points embedded in the remains of a long-horned buffalo, an animal that has been extinct many thousands of years. In Gypsum Cave, near Las Vegas, Nevada, a spear shaft was discovered with the bones of a stone age giant sloth.

These weapons were of various degrees of sophistication and of various ages of antiquity. Some were merely chipped bits of stone; others were intricately flaked and fluted. The early hunters grew increasingly skilled at contriving the tools of their survival. As early as ten thousand years ago they had also developed an artistic flair, bringing an eye for beauty to the design of their weaponry.

New migrants drifted south to feed the flow of human streams across the continent. Some were comparatively recent (and more Mongoloid) arrivals from Asia. Some may have been long resident in Alaska or northern Canada before venturing south. With the glaciers in retreat, and a much more agreeable climate taking hold across most of North America, some chose to wander no farther than the Canadian Pacific coast or central or eastern Canada.

The end of the last great ice age was followed by an equally momentous development. Partly because of climatic change, partly because of the growing skill of the hunters, the great mammals that had lured man to and across America gradually died out. Over a period of about three thousand years, beginning with the end of the last glacial spell ten thousand years ago, the giant creatures slowly followed the dinosaurs into extinction. Although not precipitous, their demise had a tremendous impact on the life-styles of the early Americans. They had always supplemented their diets with wild plants and whatever small game happened to cross their paths. But the giant mammals had been their staple. A single mammoth or long-horned bison could provide enough meat to feed many families, perhaps for several days. For them, the end of these creatures was as if a people whose eating habits were based on power-produced refrigeration gradually had its power supply cut off, for good.

New ways had to evolve. The big-game hunters, deprived of their big game, had to adapt more diligently to their environments. New economies had to emerge. A new light began to dawn, the glimmer of embryonic cultures, the first significant traces of those who were to be known as Indians.

Adjusting to circumstances, the forebears of the Indians learned gradually to intensify

further passage into the continent. As the ice caps melted, however, a north–south corridor slowly opened and very gradually the lowlands just east of the Rocky Mountains (and perhaps a narrow avenue to the west as well) became fertile and inviting. The big-game animals roamed into this corridor and, as unwittingly as their predecessors had crossed from Asia, with nothing more compelling than their next meal urging them forward, the early big-game hunters began what was to be the great trek south into the American heartland.

From low-lying regions of Alaska, they pursued their prey into the Mackenzie Valley, along the flanks of the Rockies and through the adjoining lowlands, into what were to become Alberta and Saskatchewan, Montana and North Dakota. There was no date with destiny, no compulsion to maintain a southward momentum. Hunting bands lingered in places, or moved forward, backward or sideways, depending on the availability of suste-

nance. The earliest peopling of America was a random exercise in survival.

Some hunting parties were drawn forward onto the great plateau of the Southwest; others into the fertile expanse of the Great Plains. Some ventured into the dark, sprawling eastern forests; others into the valleys of the Continental Divide's rugged highlands. Like streams branching off from a river, they fanned out across North America. Some hunting bands maintained a southward course to become the forerunners of the great Indian civilizations of Mexico, Central America and Peru, of the still primitive tribes of the Brazilian jungles and of those who, more than eleven thousand years ago, were to reach the southern tip of South America.

Mementos mark their progress down and across the continent—stone and bone implements which have been unearthed or stumbled upon at the Brooks Range in Alaska, in the Yukon, on the plains of central Canada, in and perfect previously marginal skills—for hunting small game and birds, catching fish and gathering edible plants. They became versatile and inventive. They devised traps for catching small animals and made fish spears. They began to mill stones for grinding roots and seeds. They learned to weave baskets for collecting plants and shellfish. Their increasing dependence on berries, edible leaves, roots, nuts and seeds led to closer observation of how they grew and to the first tentative experiments with cultivation. Pumpkins and beans were grown by Indians in northeastern Mexico eight thousand years ago. Primitive forms of domesticated corn (on which the great Indian civilizations of Mexico were to be based) were grown more than seven thousand years ago. Gradually, cultivation of one crop or another spread to arable regions throughout the continent—more quickly to some than to others—and even more gradually, over thousands of years, agriculture became a primary source of nourishment and a key to survival in those regions.

Life became more ordered. Permanent settlements took root and populations expanded. Community structure grew more intricate. Divisions of labor and authority became sharply defined. These developments occurred sooner and with greater thoroughness in more agreeable environments, where improved agricultural and hunting methods made food plentiful and where energy and effort could increasingly be diverted from the pressing problem of sheer survival. Surplus food, material possessions and leisure time became available. Interest and energy began to be devoted to the design and acquisition of decorative and artistic implements and artifacts. Social distinctions based on wealth, skills and heredity developed.

The accumulation by the Indians of the cultural paraphernalia of stable communities was a slow, long-drawn-out process, imperceptible to those involved. About five thousand years transpired between the extinction of the last of the great mammals and the emergence of recognizable Indian cultures. Nor was it a uniform development. There was a blossoming of diversity. Between three thousand and four thousand years ago, communities around the western Great Lakes, in northern Illinois and Wisconsin, were among the first in the world to work with metal, shaping copper into weapons and ornaments. Remains discovered in the Humboldt Cave in Nevada include fishhooks, fishnets and even duck decoys between two thousand and four thousand years old. People in Kansas and Oklahoma used storage pits to put aside food for winter as early as two thousand years ago. Almost three thousand years ago, tribes in northern Mexico built irrigation systems to nourish

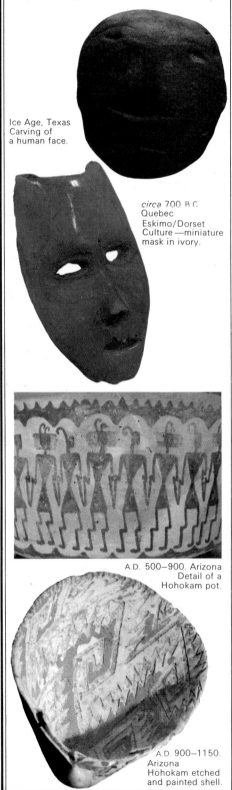

FROM HUNTERS TO FARMERS
As the ice retreated northward, some of the American peoples gradually turned from hunting to farming. This led to more leisure and, as their art illustrates, an increasing interest in their own image.

Ice Age, Texas Carving of a human face.

circa 700 B.C. Quebec Eskimo/Dorset Culture—miniature mask in ivory.

A.D. 500–900. Arizona Detail of a Hohokam pot.

A.D. 900–1150. Arizona Hohokam etched and painted shell.

the growth of their crudely cultivated crops.

Some of the early Indian cultures were still flourishing when explorers from Europe, seeking new worlds, reached North America. Others disappeared before the arrival of the white men, but they left clues to their existence and ways of life—monuments, artifacts and legends passed down through generations.

A belief in the supernatural was a pivotal element in all Indian cultures. There was an overpowering need to control, placate or appease the mysterious, enigmatic forces which governed their existence and their surroundings. Everyday life was played out under the scrutiny and direct influence of an elaborate pantheon of gods, spirits and magical forces, related to the seasons, the harvests, the elements, the earth and the sun, good and evil, life and death. There were ghosts, both friendly and hostile, and shamans, medicine men, who were believed to be capable of interceding with the spirits to induce them to cure illness, to increase the food supply or to punish enemies. Shamans were often also called upon to foretell the future and to interpret dreams.

The Indians often invoked or appeased the gods and spirits through ceremonial tribal dances—sun dances, rain dances, dances to bring good fortune, others to ward off danger, often performed with loud singing and wailing and sometimes continuing, intermittently, for several days.

Supernatural visions were the greatest experience conceivable to young men of the Great Plains tribes, as well as in some other areas. They plunged, heart and soul, into highly prestigious vision quests. Through brief communion with mystical spirits, sometimes induced by fasting and self-mutilation, they believed they acquired lifelong spiritual guidance, powers of endurance and boundless courage.

Many Indian tribes feared and venerated the deceased and went to great lengths to appease departed spirits. The long-vanished but most widespread Indian culture North America ever knew, the Hopewell, was constructed around a cult of the dead. It developed in the Ohio Valley around 400 B.C. and, touching a responsive chord in Indian fears and beliefs, spread through the eastern woodlands, down to Florida and the Gulf Coast and westward to the Rockies. The Hopewellians erected high burial mounds to honor and worship the spirits of dead chieftains and other eminent personages, dome-shaped tombs up to thirty feet high and two hundred feet around, ceremonial centers which were the heart of the communities they served.

This death-oriented culture wove a web of trading links across eastern and central North America that was not to be duplicated north of

Mexico until the arrival of the white man. The enormous range of goods traded testified to its vitality—copper from the Great Lakes, mica from the Appalachians, obsidian from the Rocky Mountains, seashells from the Atlantic coast, alligator teeth from Florida. It was an energetic and lively commerce which welded contact and communications within the trading areas. Many of the items were used as ornamental objects to be buried with, and please the spirits of the dead. This may, in fact, have been the initial and primary impetus for the trading links the Hopewellians spun across so large a part of the continent at a time when most other tribes lived in isolation.

The Hopewellian culture and their lanes of commerce began to draw in and decay around A.D. 400, to be succeeded in some places, particularly along the southern reaches of the Mississippi River, by stockaded villages clustered around pyramids, on which temples were erected. Farther north and east, the heirs of the Hopewellians turned to the erection of effigy mounds, designed in the shape of animals and birds, like the quarter-mile-long serpent mound near Locust Grove, Ohio. The new temples and mounds remained the centers of religious ritual and social cohesion, but the cult of the dead slowly came to an end. Although tribes grew more isolated, populations were expanding. The growing number of dead who deserved veneration and whose spirits required appeasement gradually overwhelmed the capacity of the death-cult Indians to administer the necessary rites and observances.

The Indians did not generally shun violence. Attacks on other tribes—for prestige, plunder and revenge—were common. Men who declined to participate were often ostracized. A warrior's reputation was frequently based on how many scalps he brought back from a raid. Raiding parties, however, tended to be small, less than a hundred warriors, sometimes only six or seven. Judged by modern standards of belligerence, their objectives were usually modest, mere raids or ambushes, virtually never involving actual conquest. War, as it is commonly understood, was rare before the white man arrived.

Despite the alacrity with which warriors of most tribes joined in raids against other tribes, and despite the honor attached to such participation, there were exceptions. Dotted across the Southwest are the remains of a culture more than two thousand years old, whose people, although capable of fighting to defend themselves from outside attack, were profoundly committed to peace and harmony. The Pueblo tribes of today, including the Hopi and Zuni, are descendants of those people, of the Anasazi—the "Ancient Ones" in Navajo language—who abhorred strife and

THE EMERGENCE OF CULTURES

The first farmers were still nomadic, cultivating one area for a number of years and then moving on. When they did settle and form communities their beliefs took on a greater significance and their art became more symbolistic.

A.D. 700–1200. Arizona Shamanistic Anasazi head of unfired clay.

A.D. 1200–1300. Oklahoma Spiro Culture—religious mask.

A.D. 1200–1300. Oklahoma Spiro Culture—wooden deer mask.

circa A.D. 1300 Arkansas Temple Mound Culture—ceremonial pot in shape of human head.

conflict and who left traces of their commitment to harmonious community life in the great pueblos, the cliff houses at Mesa Verde in Colorado, Canyon de Chelly in Arizona and at hundreds of other sites scattered across this sunbaked landscape.

A thousand years ago, the Anasazi were constructing apartment houses up to five stories tall on cliffside ledges and on the roofs of mesas. Pueblo Bonito, the remains of which cover more than three acres of New Mexico's Chaco Canyon, could house more than a thousand people. It was a town made up of a single building, a hive of contiguous rooms, the largest apartment house in the world until a larger one was constructed in New York in 1882.

Anasazi togetherness was a product of the arid, rocky environment of the Southwest. The Anasazi, originally cave dwellers and among the earliest American Basket Makers, had to coax their crops from whatever marginally fertile fields were nearby or through exhaustive dry farming. A high degree of community organization and cooperation was imperative if environmental impediments were to be overcome. There was neither place nor tolerance for such divisive characteristics as aggression, individuality, ambition and hostility; no significant differences in wealth; no social classes. Modesty was a major virtue. Pride, anger and delusions of grandeur were sins. How they were punished is unknown, but among the descendants of the Anasazi, those found guilty of such excesses were deemed witches and were liable to be hung by their thumbs until they confessed and promised to change their ways.

Their rigid moral code may have been at least partly responsible for the decline of the Anasazi. By 1300, migrations southward had left most of the northern section of the culture, including the largest and most advanced of the pueblo communities, deserted. A protracted drought—from 1276 to 1299, according to tree rings—may have undermined the precariously balanced Anasazi economy. It may have been that invading tribes, including the Apache who were sweeping down from Canada, drove the peaceful Anasazi away. It is possible, however, that forces within the culture contributed as well.

In some pueblo communities, there are indications that, for no apparent reason, certain buildings were abandoned before the exodus and new ones erected. In some places, the withdrawal of inhabitants—which might otherwise be attributed to crop failure or enemy attack—was piecemeal, with a succession of small groups leaving the community. It has been suggested that the pervasive taboos against hostility and violence may have left no outlet for the inhibitions and frustrations of closely knit community life and may have hastened the Anasazi decline. Their present-day descendants appear to have channeled aggression into various forms of socially acceptable behavior, including symbolic war ceremonies.

Rank and status in most Indian cultures were based on wealth, heredity or accomplishment. In parts of Nevada and Utah, and of the subarctic region, where life was difficult, where food was hard to come by and where populations were sparse, there were few social distinctions between tribe members. The struggle for survival imposed a large measure of equality. But on the fertile plains, on the prairies where the buffalo roamed, on the shores of waters rich with fish and in forests filled with game, there were distinctions aplenty.

In the Northwest, in what is now British Columbia, Washington and Oregon, the abundance of game, wild plants and berries in the forests, and fish in the ocean and rivers, produced an obsession with wealth so extreme that it often led to a man's status being determined by how much of his possessions—including canoes, hides, copper plates, decorative blankets and slaves—he gave away or ostentatiously destroyed. Gifts were given strictly in order of rank, so that each man knew exactly where he stood in the elaborate pecking order. These gift-giving and property-destroying displays generally took place at a feast called a *potlatch*, during which a wealthy man might pauperize himself while gaining great prestige. His consolation, if he required any, was that others would be shamed by his extravagance into doing the same.

Among many of the tribes of the Great Plains, membership in warrior fraternities conferred special status. These clubs—there were often several to a tribe—had special rites and rituals and sometimes brutal initiation procedures, during which young applicants might be beaten, starved or required to eat filth to prove their worth. Although, like many present-day fraternities, the members were often clownish in behavior, these clubs played important social roles. The members were assigned, in turn, by the tribal elders to the tasks of guarding the community, preserving order, carrying out raids and punishing offenders. Among the Cheyenne, there was a club of "contraries," whose members had a reputation for being the bravest of the brave and who demonstrated their uniqueness by being absurdly contrary—saying no when they meant yes, dressing warmly on hot days and wearing very little in the cold.

In most tribes, the sons of tribal leaders enjoyed distinct advantages and were automatically candidates for high tribal rank them-

18

THE INDIANS CLAIM THEIR CONTINENT

The Indians, all descendants of the same wandering Asian people, never numbered more than a few million north of Mexico. It took them ten thousand years to disperse throughout North America's more than nine million square miles of diverse landscape and climate. Although, in adapting to the different environments, they inevitably acquired regional characteristics, they evolved over a thousand distinct languages and cultures.

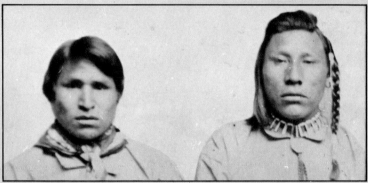

Chinook Indians of the Northwest
The Chinooks lived in the area now known as Oregon and were typical of the Northwest Coast Indians. They used dugout canoes and lived by hunting and fishing. They went barefoot most of the time, even in winter when they wore fur robes over their tunics and skirts of woven plant fiber. Their plank houses had pitched roofs and were similar to those of the Old World.

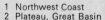

1 Northwest Coast
2 Plateau, Great Basin and California
3 The Southwest
4 Middle America
5 The Plains
6 The Eastern Woodlands
7 Arctic and Subarctic

A Nez Percé of the Plateau
The Nez Percé were Plateau Indians who hunted deer and mountain sheep and fished for salmon. In the cold winters of the high interior, in what is now Idaho, they lived in pit houses.

A Shoshoni of the Great Basin
For the Indians of the Great Basin, where the Shoshoni lived, food was scarce and they existed primarily on plants. Because hides were scarce, their tipis were covered in thatch.

A Hopi of the Southwest
The Hopi, who lived high on the edges of barren mesas, were Pueblo Indians. They spent their summers tending their crops of corn, beans and squash and their winters weaving. Their peaceful way of life contrasted

Navajos of the Southwest
with that of their northern neighbors, the warlike Navajo, who arrived in the area about A.D. 1500 after a migration from northwestern Canada and Alaska that had taken fifteen hundred years.

An Eskimo Family from the Arctic

The Eskimos and other Arctic Indian tribes came to Alaska shortly after 4000 B.C. and spread across the northern coast to Greenland. The igloo, warm and quickly constructed, was perfect for their nomadic hunting existence. The Subarctic Indians, to the south of the Eskimos, reached North America much earlier. They lived mainly on caribou and fish and moved in extended family groups.

Seminoles of the Eastern Woodlands

In most of the Eastern Woodlands tribes it was not uncommon for three or four generations of one extended family to live in one house, which was usually constructed of mud-covered bark built around a rectangular frame. Most tribes lived in towns with up to two thousand inhabitants. The towns of the Five Civilized Tribes, one of which was the Seminole, had streets and squares.

Chief Duck of the Blackfoot

Chief Quannan Parker of the Comanche

A Sioux of the Plains

Kicking Bear of the Miniconjou Dakota

Little is known about the Plains Indians before they acquired their horses from the Spanish ranches in New Mexico. By the middle of the eighteenth century the horse had spread north from the Comanche in southern Texas to the Blackfoot in Alberta. The lands of the Dakotas, also known as the Sioux, lay between the Upper Mississippi and Missouri rivers, and they and the other eastern Plains tribes lived in permanent villages during the growing season, when they raised corn, beans and squash. After storing their harvest, they rode west to hunt the buffalo, living in hide-covered tipis, as did the western Plains Indians, who never farmed.

selves. The same was true for the offspring of the more highly skilled hunters and warriors. Distinction, inherited or attained, tended to perpetuate itself.

Despite their having been lumped together under the name Indian, the result of a bad guess by Christopher Columbus, there were physical differences between Indians of different regions. The people of some tribes were tall; the people of others were not. Some were more roundheaded than others; some more longheaded. Skin coloration ranged from yellowish to copper brown.

There is some dispute as to whether the Eskimos of the far north are really Indians at all, their ancestors having migrated to North America from Siberia long after those of the other early Americans. The Eskimos refer to themselves as *inuit,* which means "people," indicating that they did not know that other people existed, or that they did not care, or that they considered others to be inferior species of creation, thus sharing with many tribes an egocentric view of the world. The Eskimos have always been a self-sufficient, industrious, resourceful people, neither intimidated nor incapacitated by the harsh regions they have inhabited.

Living as they did in small, isolated communities and extracting a living from a stern and inhospitable environment, the Eskimos evolved a system which stressed cooperation. When required or desired, assistance or support from kin was automatically available to any member of a family group, not as a duty or obligation but as a normal response to a normal situation. Denial was unthinkable. Eskimo marriage was based on, and sustained by, a clearly defined division of labor. The husband made the tools, hunted and built the igloo (the word means any kind of house, not only a snow hut). The wife prepared and served the food, dressed animal skins for clothes and other purposes and kept house.

Unlike the placid Anasazi, the Eskimos were, and are, proud and individualistic, but in order to make the most of their bleak arctic habitat, their communities were so efficiently organized that little room was left for disruption. Efforts were made to end, before they caused trouble, quarrels within a group or feuds between neighboring communities. Unlike the Pueblo dwellers of the Southwest, who inhibited open expression of hostility, the Eskimos sometimes organized stand-up, blow-for-blow punching contests and wrestling matches between individual antagonists, to determine the rights and wrongs of arguments. There were also singing duels, in which the rivals sang insults at each other, impromptu ballads of the most personal kind of derision. The contestant judged, through

20

audience applause, to be the most imaginatively insulting was declared the winner.

When such means for defusing disputes failed, and murder took place, the injured community, robbed of a precious hunter, was bound to seek blood vengeance. This could lead to protracted vendettas and, since a man who killed another was often charged with raising his victim's offspring, situations arose in which a foster child would grow up under the protection of his natural father's murderer, and then kill him when he came of age.

Indian tribes developed in different directions, at different speeds and to different levels. Those of the eastern woodlands learned to use more than two hundred distinct wild plants as medicines. Among the inventions and discoveries of various tribes were hammocks, kayaks, tobacco, chocolate, toboggans and rubber balls. However, the Digger Indians of the Great Basin, for example, had few skills, flimsy makeshift dwellings and a meager diet consisting largely of roots, insects and snakes.

Some tribes, like the Eskimos, having mastered their bleak environment, remained comparatively static over the ages. Some, like the mound builders of the Ohio and Mississippi valleys, rose slowly to high levels of accomplishment and then slowly slipped back into the mists of time. Others, like the Aztecs (who rose from wandering tribe to empire in less than two centuries), spurted upward like soaring comets from cultural impoverishment to impressive peaks of achievement, only to plummet into oblivion even more rapidly.

Advanced cultures had developed early in Mexico. The stone age big-game hunters from the north who had penetrated North America at least twenty thousand years ago, turned as readily to agriculture when circumstances demanded as coastal tribes took to fishing. The environment was eminently suited to the cultivation of crops which, in certain respects, may initially have been simply an extension of gathering abundant harvests of wild corn and other plants. The abundance of food encouraged population expansion. Villages sprang up and expanded and trade between them developed, as did increasingly complex cultures.

The Olmecs (400 B.C. to 200 B.C.) of the dense rain forest on the Gulf Coast, slashed clearings for communities gathered around ceremonial centers, where they erected temple mounds, which were embellished with sacrificial altars and sculptured stone slabs. Among the deities they worshiped, and made statues of, was a half jaguar/half human, believed to have been a fertility god, and perhaps one of the earliest American deities to require human sacrifice. Clues to Olmec mechanical skill and

At a time when the rest of North America was peopled by seminomadic tribes of hunters and gatherers, the Mayans created a civilization which paralleled Asian and Mediterranean cultures. With justification they have been called the "Greeks of America." Between about A.D. 300 and 900, in the dense tropical forests of the Yucatán, in conditions which pose problems even for modern engineers, they built fine cities, which were essentially ceremonial and administrative and contained huge pyramids and elaborately carved temples. The Mayans were advanced in mathematics and astronomy and their simple slash-and-burn system of farming is now conceded to be the method most suited to their jungle environment. Their civilization, so organized and so advanced, collapsed suddenly and inexplicably.

The Olmecs, who carved the thirty-ton basalt head, above, had the first sophisticated culture in North America and influenced the formative period of Mayan civilization. The downfall of the Mayans is attributed to the Toltecs, creators of the warrior figure, right, who invaded their cities.

organizational ability can still be seen in the jungles near the gulf—flat-faced, thick-lipped, blank-eyed stone heads, eight feet tall and weighing more than twenty tons, enigmatic remnants of a vanished tribe. They were carved from stone that had been ferried from quarries up to eighty miles away, although the Olmecs, in common with other Indian cultures, neither invented nor used the wheel.

Thirty miles northwest of present-day Mexico City, the people of Teotihuacán (100 B.C. to A.D. 800)—which was later called by the Aztecs "the place where the gods reside" —established the first known American metropolis, more than eight square miles of urban development, occupied by an estimated quarter of a million inhabitants. Dominated, as its

Clay figures, above and below, found on the island of Jaina, show the realism of Mayan art.

The relief carving, left, is typical of the ornate decoration which adorned most Mayan temples. The sheer amount and quality of this work suggests there may have been a class of professional artisans in residence at ceremonial centers.

awesome remains still are, by a huge stepped pyramid called the Temple of the Sun, and by a lesser Temple of the Moon, Teotihuacán was crisscrossed by wide boulevards and punctuated with elegant plazas. Around its ceremonial center, the city was populated in sectors of class identity. Religious leaders and state officials resided closest to the heart of Teotihuacán. Merchants and artisans were congregated in districts of their own, as were laborers. The city was encircled by agricultural villages. As demonstrated by its town-planning system, Teotihuacán had come far from its agrarian origins. It produced and displayed a wealth of jewelry and ornamentation and its merchants traded far and wide across Middle America. Its calendar was based on a fifty-two-year cycle, at the end of which eternal ceremonial flames were extinguished and then relit to commemorate the rebirth of the world.

The Zapotecs, whose civilization (A.D. 300 to A.D. 900) was centered around the pyramid-studded hill town of Mount Alban in southern Mexico, were also skilled builders of temples and palaces—less ornate, but more stately. Their culture employed a written language, but probably only for religious purposes. The Zapotecs also developed an interest in astronomy sufficiently advanced for them to construct observatories to monitor the stars.

The Maya civilization (A.D. 100 to A.D. 1500), straddling the Mexican–Guatemalan border to the south and east of the Zapotec domain, was remarkable both in achievement and location. More than eight hundred greater and smaller serene, dignified Mayan cities were carved from virtually impenetrable jungle. Their temples and palaces were more impressively diverse in design than those of their predecessors or contemporaries. They excelled in mathematical and astronomical sciences and developed a sensitive scale of aesthetic values, still evident in the stone mosaics, sculpture and ceramics recovered from Mayan sites.

The Toltecs (A.D. 900 to A.D. 1224) were a warrior people. But their temple city, Tula, forty miles north of Mexico City, was so splendorous and their skills and achievements —in social organization, architecture, design

21

THE RISE OF THE FIRST NORTH AMERICAN EMPIRE CREATES "THE MOS[

In 1325, the Aztecs, a barbarian tribe from the north of Mexico, established their capital, Tenochtitlán, on a marshy island in Lake Texcoco. Within a century they had built an empire that stretched from the Pacific to the Gulf. With their conquests, they, like the Romans, absorbed cultures which they melded and refined. By 1500, Tenochtitlán, right, had become a metropolis with temples, palaces and plazas. The Spanish thought it "the most beautiful city in the world" but, in conquering it, in 1521, destroyed it.

In the Aztec religion there was a constant conflict between Uitzilopochtli, the sun god who demanded human sacrifice, and Quetzalcoatl, the god of learning and of the priesthood. The turquoise mask with eyes and teeth of white shell, above, is thought to be a representation of Quetzalcoatl.

and agriculture—so refined and diverse, that long after fierce tribes had swooped down from the north to destroy what the Toltecs had built, the very name Toltec was considered synonymous with civilization, breeding and elegance.

Among those who moved into the vacuum created by the destruction of the Toltec culture was a belligerent tribe called the Mexica, later to be known as the Aztecs. According to legend, the Aztecs had originated in a place called Aztlán to the north and had been propelled southward by the antagonism of other tribes and by a prophecy that they would grow and prosper at a place where they came upon an eagle astride a cactus, devouring a snake. They are said to have beheld this vision, in 1325, on a swampy island in Lake Texcoco. Calling upon their innate resourcefulness and the skills they had acquired in their wanderings, the Aztecs drained the swamps of the island, and of others nearby, and proceeded to transform them into the city which

was to make the Spanish conquerors gasp in astonishment.

Alliances were established with neighboring tribes, whom the Aztecs rapidly dominated, as they extended their empire and drew to their coffers the wealth of subjugated peoples. But the Aztecs required more than tribute from those they conquered. No deities had ever been as bloodthirsty as theirs. The sun would not rise, the world would end, the rain would not fall, the crops would not grow, they believed, unless their gods were offered the lives of humans. Ritual sacrifice, sometimes involving many thousands of victims at a time, was the most important event in Aztec life. Their remarkable rise to power and prosperity nourished their belief that sacrifice was effective and necessary and that an ever-increasing number of victims should be offered to the supernatural forces they worshiped.

Wars were often provoked only so prisoners could be taken to be fed to the gods. Pretend wars, called Wars of Flowers, were declared,

games in which prisoners for sacrifice were captured. An individual who felt a god had to be appeased for one reason or another could buy a slave to be sacrificed. Sometimes victims were flayed and their skins worn by priests. Most often, their chests were cut open and their hearts torn out. Their heads were then impaled on skull racks, which horrified the notoriously unsqueamish Spanish conquistadors when they stumbled upon them.

The Aztecs developed elaborate systems of administration and political control. They had an energetic and vigorous merchant class (traders were frequently used as spies by Aztec rulers) and groups of skilled artisans and craftsmen, who banded together in guilds to preserve their professional exclusivity. In agriculture, they employed advanced methods of terracing and irrigation. They had an efficient system of taxation. Aztec rule was strong, confident and untroubled by open internal dissension. Nevertheless, it crumbled and collapsed within five years when it came under

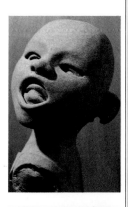

The austere style of the Aztec sculpture, bottom right, is an inheritance from earlier cultures and contrasts vividly with the ferocity which is present in Aztec religious works. The mask of the sorcerer god Tezcatlipoca, above left, was made from an actual skull. The stone head, top right, is of Xipe Totec, the flayed lord. The Aztecs were obsessed with time. In fact even the timing of sacrifices was vital. Their calendars, like the massive stone calendar left, were accurate enough to predict a recent eclipse of the sun.

attack from less than four hundred Spanish soldiers.

So dazzling were the trappings of Aztec civilization that the Spanish conquistadors were astounded when, in 1519, they first came upon Tenochtitlán, the center of the Aztec Empire. Hernán Cortés, who led the Spanish expedition, called it the most beautiful city he had ever seen, "the Venice of the New World."

Tenochtitlán had been built, where Mexico City now stands, on what were then islands in Lake Texcoco. The islands were interlaced with canals and joined to the surrounding countryside by broad causeways over which "ten horsemen could ride abreast." At the center was an enormous plaza in which magnificent structures had been erected, including the imperial palace, a towering temple-capped pyramid, other temples, an armory, an aviary filled with birds of splendid plumage, another for fierce birds of prey and a menagerie for caged wild animals. Around many of these buildings were lush, fragrant gardens.

The emperor, Montezuma, was considered semidivine. The nobles who attended him, and visiting rulers from elsewhere, lowered their eyes and bowed their heads in his presence. He ate alone, choosing from hundreds of dishes prepared for his every meal. His harem was as large as any in tales of ancient Arabia. Nor was this display a mere pretense of power. The Aztec emperor ruled most of Mexico and was more powerful than, until then, any North American ruler had even dreamed of being. His army, many tens of thousands strong, was the largest North America had ever known and his warriors deemed it a privilege to die in battle. His capital city, when the Spanish reached it, had a population of about three hundred thousand, more than London at the time, and the Aztec world was governed and run through intricate social and political institutions, which included courts of law and a complex educational system.

The Aztecs were at first confused by the

Spanish invaders, who appeared to be fair-skinned gods whose arrival had been foretold in their legends. But, after initial paralysis, they did fight back and the rapid disintegration of their culture cannot be easily explained, not even by the fact that non-Aztec subject peoples, who hated as well as feared their masters, joined the Spanish in dismembering the Aztec Empire. The mighty Aztec civilization had, indeed, been very thinly veneered onto the Mexican cultural landscape, in which even sturdier cultures had vanished.

A new age was beginning for all of North America. Its isolation from the rest of the world, which began with the flooding of the landbridge to Asia at the conclusion of the last Ice Age, had come to an end. Heralds of advanced, dynamic cultures, which had matured elsewhere, had begun arriving. Newcomers were to graft different ways onto the American context and were ultimately to find, in the American experience, the makings of a new civilization.

AGE THREE
The Innovators

The explorers who pushed open the gates of the New World were spurred across uncharted seas and into unknown regions by a mixture of incentives. "We came . . . to serve God," said one of the Spanish conquerors of the Aztecs, "and also to get rich." The call of adventure and the thrill of discovery also beckoned them on, as did the whims of chance.

The Vikings were the first whose contact with North America is recorded. In about A.D. 1000 while en route from a Viking colony in Iceland to another in Greenland, a Norse vessel was blown off course. Before it found its way again, its sailors spotted "a flat and wooded country" to the west. Intrigued by their stories, Leif Ericson, son of the Viking founder of the Greenland colony, went in search of this land and found a place—probably Newfoundland, possibly Massachusetts or Rhode Island—where wheat and wild grapes grew. He dubbed this place Vinland and stayed a few months before returning to Greenland.

Some years later, a party of more than a hundred Greenlanders set out to establish a permanent Norse colony in Vinland. The climate they found was milder and more hospitable than that of Greenland; they may have landed as far south as New Jersey. But instead of wild grapes, they found hostile natives, whom they called skraelings (the word could denote barbarians or dwarfs, or a combination of both), whose recurring attacks induced them to abandon their settlement after two years and return home.

Carved stones discovered in Minnesota, Virginia and Oklahoma have been claimed by some to be runic remains of other Viking expeditions to the interior of the continent, but are dismissed by scholars as recently planted elaborate hoaxes. The Norse discovery of America was, however, a passing event, a footnote to history and, in fact, the Vikings may not have been the first outsiders to reach North America.

An Irish community, which had settled in Iceland before the Vikings, was driven out by them in the ninth century. Where these dispossessed Irishmen went is a mystery, but men from a Norse ship blown onto land west of Greenland in the eleventh century said that they were attacked by white men whom they believed were Irish. Whoever they were, they were never heard of again.

Among other tales of early explorers who reached North America, there is a legend of a prince of Wales named Madoc. Madoc is said to have led an expedition of Welshmen which landed at Mobile Bay, Alabama, in the twelfth century, migrated into the interior and, with the passage of time, became the Mandan Indian tribe of the Northwest, which was virtually wiped out by a smallpox epidemic in the nineteenth century. There are ancient Chinese accounts of a strange, fruitful land far out in the eastern sea and, as early as the fifth century, at about the time that Polynesians are believed to have first traveled by canoe from Tahiti to discover Hawaii, the Chinese had vessels which might have managed the Pacific crossing. Similar claims to early landings in America, few of which bear close scrutiny, have been made for Japanese, Roman, Turkish, Basque and other explorers.

Whoever did make the first landing, the opening of America to outside contact was to be a historic juncture, an event to transform the world. But the world was not ready for it until long after the first explorers from across the seas trod American ground, not until the Renaissance in Europe broadened the scope of human curiosity and enterprise, not until the pressure of events set the stage for the great voyages of discovery.

The Ottoman Turks had overrun Asia Minor in the fourteenth and fifteenth centuries, sharply constricting the flow of spices from the Orient to which Europe had grown addicted, as well as pinching off the supply of herbs, silks, dyes, other exotic goods of Eastern origin and trade in general. Despite the prevailing belief to the contrary, astronomers, seamen and others had long before realized that the world was round. If the eastward route to the Orient was controlled by hostile, extortionist infidels, it seemed obvious to Christopher Columbus, an ambitious, strong-willed master sailor, that by heading west he would reach the fabled wealth of the Indies.

With his journey sponsored by King Ferdinand and Queen Isabella of Spain, who sought to replenish their depleted treasury and spread Christianity, "Admiral of the Ocean Sea" Columbus set sail unwaveringly confident. He landed at San Salvador, Cuba and Hispaniola, thereby effectively opening the New World, and believed for the rest of his life that he had reached the Orient. Columbus brought back to Spain a sampling of exotica to prove his contention—a few Indians, named by him for the Indies which he thought he had reached, some spices, tropical birds and some gold. Although he returned with no great wealth, news of his discoveries and adventures, sometimes exaggerated, circulated quickly through the seaports of Europe, prodding others to contemplate westward journeys toward the riches of the East.

Within a decade of Columbus's voyage, the Venetian Giovanni Caboto, known as John Cabot, sailing under the English flag, and the Portuguese Gaspar Corte Real scouted the Newfoundland route to Asia. In 1524, Giovanni da Verrazano, like Columbus a Genoese, sailing for the French, and later to be eaten by Caribbean Indian cannibals, explored the Hudson River, Narragansett Bay and much of the northeast coast. A few years later, Jacques Cartier, also in quest of the Orient, sailed up the St. Lawrence River, stopping at an Indian village that was later to become Quebec and another that was to become Montreal, before regretfully concluding that he could not reach China along that route. French fishermen with more modest objectives were lured by exorbitant stories to the Newfoundland Grand Banks, and discovered that the waters there did indeed swarm with an incredible multitude of fish. On nearby shores, they found the Indians friendly, and furs, for which an eager market existed in Europe, in plentiful supply. Soon French trappers and traders began penetrating inland to plant the roots of modern Canada.

Farther south, the audacious Cortés, a junior official, who had been dispatched to establish a trading post, far exceeded his authority and conquered the Aztecs, thereby setting a standard to which other Spanish explorers, in pursuit of fame and fortune, aspired. De Soto traversed Georgia, the Carolinas, Alabama and much of the rest of the southland before discovering the Mississippi River, on whose banks he succumbed to a fatal fever. Coronado, searching for legendary treasure cities which would dwarf Cortés's celebrated conquest, led a battalion of conquistadors through the area that was to become Texas, Oklahoma, Kansas, New Mexico and Arizona. Some of his men saw the Grand Canyon before he concluded that little wealth could be extracted from those regions, and withdrew. Ponce de León probed the coast of Florida, vainly seeking a fountain of youth. Juan Cabrillo sailed north from Mexico to San Diego Bay and perhaps as far as the Oregon shore, seeking, as did Coronado, cities of gold. Spanish explorers roamed from the Carolina coast to Southern California in the hope of unearthing treasures to match those their compatriots had discovered in Mexico. They found none. But in their explorations and in their colonization of Mexico, they left treasures of their own—horses and cattle brought from Spain, many of which ran wild and multiplied before being tamed again to play a vital role in the transformation of the American West.

None of the early explorers was as gifted as Amerigo Vespucci in describing what they

EXPLORERS FROM THE OLD WORLD

The Old World's discovery of the New World was accidental. Appreciation of its significance was slow and exploration was haphazard. Most of the men who first sailed the east coast of North America sought not to explore it, but to find a way around it. They were searching for a new route to the Indies. The Spanish even conquered Mexico in the belief that it would provide an overland route to the East. Nevertheless, a pattern emerged. The English (brown) and French (lilac) concentrated on the north, the Spanish (yellow) on the south and all three, with the Dutch (green), made occasional landings in the center of the continent.

Christopher Columbus, right, never realized the significance of his discovery of the New World, which was named after another Italian, Amerigo Vespucci, left, who was also in the service of the Spanish crown. Until his death, Columbus remained convinced that he had discovered a new route to the Indies.

In search of the Northwest Passage in the 1570s, Sir Martin Frobisher explored the coast of Baffin Island and charted northern waters.

Sebastian Cabot made two voyages from Bristol—in 1500, to explore Nova Scotia, and, in 1509, Hudson Strait and Hudson Bay.

In the 1530s, Jacques Cartier discovered the St. Lawrence River, sailing as far west as Montreal in the hope of finding a route to China.

During his voyage for France in 1524, the Italian Giovanni da Verrazano is believed to have discovered the harbor where New York now stands.

Juan de Grijalva, exploring the Yucatán coast in 1518, learned of Montezuma's Mexico, which, in anticipation, he named New Spain.

With his conquest of Mexico, Hernán Cortés established Spanish influence in the New World, which was to last for more than three centuries.

In the early 1500s, Hernando de Soto landed in Florida and journeyed through most of the Southeast in a vain search for gold.

In 1515, Ponce de León, a Spaniard, sailed from Cuba and explored the east coast of Florida in search of "the fountain of youth."

Dutch claims in the New World originated with an Englishman, Henry Hudson, who, in 1609, landed on Manhattan Island.

COLONIZERS OF THE NEW WORLD

In the wake of the explorers came the colonizers. The English, who concentrated on the mid-Atlantic coast, proved to be the most influential of all New World colonists, possibly because religious persecution at home often gave them no alternative but to succeed. In 1607, they established their first permanent settlement at Jamestown, Virginia. The Pilgrims, shown right at their first Thanksgiving with the Indians who taught them how to plant and fertilize their crops, followed in Massachusetts. The English founded a total of thirteen colonies, which would later form the nucleus of a new nation.

THE THIRTEEN COLONIES
1 Massachusetts, which included Maine
2 New Hampshire
3 New York
4 Connecticut
5 Rhode Island
6 Pennsylvania
7 New Jersey
8 Maryland
9 Delaware
10 Virginia
11 North Carolina
12 South Carolina
13 Georgia

Until it was relinquished to the English in 1667, the Dutch colony of New Netherlands flourished under Peter Stuyvesant.

In 1681, the Quaker William Penn founded Pennsylvania, which became a haven for religious dissenters.

Walter Raleigh made two unsuccessful attempts to colonize Virginia, where he dreamed of founding a new England.

Captain John Smith played a vital role in establishing Virginia, England's first colony in the New World.

---

found. Vespucci, performing the first major public-relations exercise in American history, wrote so eloquently and engagingly of what he saw when he accompanied Spanish and Portuguese expeditions along the coast of South America, years after Columbus's epic voyage, that a German academician, compiling a revised geography text, chose to call the new land across the sea "America." The name quickly and universally caught on. (Less credence is given to the suggestion that America was actually named after the Englishman Richard Amerike, a merchant sponsor of John Cabot's explorations.)

Well before the English began thinking seriously of North America as anything but a

route to the Orient, Spain had established a lucrative colony in Mexico. Spanish overseers ruled the Aztecs and other subjugated Indians south of the Rio Grande with an iron hand, exploited their labor and shipped home the wealth they extracted from the ground—gold, silver and copper, corn, sugar and cotton, riches which, together with those from its other colonies in South and Central America, seemed to justify Spain's claim to be "Mistress of the World."

The first British effort, by means other than piracy, to tap some of the New World wealth accruing to the Spanish was Sir Walter Raleigh's bid to found an "English Nation" in Virginia, named for Elizabeth, the Virgin Queen. But the settlement, established in

1587 at Roanoke Island, was a grim failure, ending within three years with the disappearance of the settlers, who were probably killed or enslaved by Indians.

Nevertheless, visions of instant wealth lured other Englishmen across the Atlantic. In 1605, in a London stage play, one man describing Virginia to another said, "... golde is more plentifull there than copper is with us. ... Why, man, all their dripping pans and their chambre pottes are pure golde. ... And for rubies and diamonds, they go forth on holydayes and gather 'em by the sea-shore." Joint charter companies, sanctioned by King James I to lay claim to the New World for Britain, had little trouble finding recruits to make the sea crossing.

France's interest in Canada was inspired by the explorations of Jacques Cartier, but its influence, which was to grow to be powerful enough to survive military defeat, can be almost entirely ascribed to one man, Samuel de Champlain. A man of vision, who wanted to do more than simply exploit the obvious abundance of the New World, he was determined to colonize, explore and win the friendship of the Indians. It was Champlain who led the band of one hundred men who, in 1604, established Acadia, Canada's first colony. They started on St. Croix Island, but later moved to Port Royal. In 1608, Champlain settled at Quebec and from there traveled into the interior himself and directed other explorers. These efforts eventually resulted in French control of the lands between the Mississippi and the Rockies. Champlain died in 1635, but not before he had converted other Frenchmen to his dream.

firmed the belief that if wealth was not simply available for the taking in the New World it was there to be found.

Many of the first men to land at Jamestown were motivated by ambition and greed. Other settlers, however, were inspired by loftier pursuits. The Pilgrims, who reached Plymouth, Massachusetts, in December 1620, sought a land where they could worship and live according to their own austere, righteous code of beliefs. Their first winter in America was punishing. Battered by gusts of rain, snow and sleet, the Pilgrims were ravaged by "the great sickness," respiratory diseases compounded by scurvy, which claimed the lives of more than half the Plymouth colony in the first few months. But the coming of spring and summer vindicated their pilgrimage. With the help of friendly Indians—"a speciall instrumente sent of God"—they became aware of the natural abundance of the land they had chosen. They learned, as the Indians had learned long before, how and where to plant corn, gather in "great and fat" lobsters, herrings, eels and clams from the sea and nearby brooks, trap deer and other game and tap maple trees.

The success of the Pilgrims and the Jamestown colony prompted others to seek a haven or a fortune in the New World. Within the next twenty years, English colonies were established along most of America's east coast. Puritans, fleeing from an England they believed corrupted by the Anglican Church, set up the Massachusetts Bay colony. Some who accompanied them found the Puritans too rigid and intolerant and left to establish colonies of their own, in Rhode Island and elsewhere in New England, where religious belief would be a matter of choice. Others who believed the Puritans were not rigid or righteous enough formed a community in New Haven. William Penn led a group of Quakers to Pennsylvania to escape religious persecution in England. Lord Baltimore, founder of the Maryland colony, sought both the material rewards of the New World and shelter for persecuted English Catholics.

Following the lead set by explorer Henry Hudson, an Englishman chartered by the Netherlands, the Dutch, seeking New World rewards as well, transformed a smattering of trading posts and forts, along and near the river and valley that were to be named for Hudson, into the colony of New Netherlands. Its center was New Amsterdam—later to be New York. A Swedish colony—in which American log cabins originated—was established where Wilmington, Delaware, now stands. (Both New Sweden and New Netherlands were soon to be taken over by the English.) Farther south, an English colony, inhabited partly by soldier–farmers, was set up

In 1607, three small, storm-buffeted vessels sailed into Chesapeake Bay, on the shores of which they saw "faire meddowes and goodly tall trees." They cruised up the James River to a spot on the north shore, where 104 men and boys debarked to lay the foundations of Jamestown, the first permanent settlement of England's American colonies, the very beginning of the United States of America. Believing, as so many future immigrants were to believe, that the land was endowed with riches ready for the taking, most of the Jamestown settlers were slow to make serious efforts at planting, harvesting and otherwise sustaining themselves. In addition, the spot they had chosen was swampy and the water impure.

Their first years, during which most of them died, were plagued by hunger, disease, dissension and Indian attacks. To prevent total disaster, rigid discipline was introduced. Men were drummed to and from the fields, and food was made available only to those who worked. A degree of order was established and enough food was grown to save the colony, which was strengthened by the arrival from England of additional supplies, recruits and "young and uncorrupt" women, from among whom the settlers chose wives. But the future of Jamestown was not guaranteed until the colonists learned to grow and cure tobacco and to blend it agreeably. A taste in Britain for Virginia tobacco provided the colony with a firm economic base and con-

A NATION EMERGES

The War of Independence began on April 19, 1775, at Lexington, Massachusetts. The appointment in June of George Washington as commander in chief brought the total commitment of all the colonies to the cause, and the signing of the Declaration of Independence on July 4, 1776, provided the inspiration that sustained it until sovereignty was won in 1783. Two and a half million Americans, without a regular army, had defeated one of the world's most powerful nations.

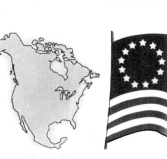

This detail from John Trumbull's painting, below, shows the committeemen who drafted the Declaration of Independence. They are, from left to right, John Adams, Roger Sherman, Robert Livingston, Thomas Jefferson and Benjamin Franklin. Their document was presented to the Second Continental Congress on July 1, 1776, and was approved on the morning of July 4. The first United States flag, above, was adopted on June 14, 1777.

in Georgia as a buffer against Spanish settlements in Florida.

In Canada, Samuel de Champlain, the father of New France, had established the first white settlement at the foot of the Quebec Hills in 1608. He and other explorers probed deeper inland, and missionaries founded the city of Montreal in 1642. But emigration to Canada was slow to build up, and for a long time it remained largely a collection of isolated outposts for the French fur trade. Even when settlers began arriving, few thought of remaining longer than brief periods, partly because of incessant warfare with the Indians.

Crop failure, hunger, disease, fierce winter weather in the north—these were the hazards and problems with which the early North American settlers had to contend. But the threat of Indian attack was most frightening. One newly arrived parson wrote home from New Amsterdam, where the Indians were comparatively friendly, "As to the natives of this country, I find them entirely savage and wild . . . devilish men. . . ." Understandably, the colonists who were claiming the land and the Indians who were losing it rarely understood each other, except as antagonists.

But, as the Atlantic coast colonists overcame their initial difficulties, greater numbers crossed the Atlantic to join them. Family life developed. Communities grew larger and increasingly welded together through defense, churches, schools and markets. Regional characteristics began to emerge.

Austere, pious New Englanders developed egalitarian communities in which a work-and-worship ethic became deeply embedded. In the Middle-Atlantic colonies, flourishing farming communities coexisted with rapidly developing manufacturing, mercantile and financial interests, centered in such growing cities as New York and Philadelphia. In the South, where the first black slaves had been introduced in 1619, the year before the Pilgrims landed, large plantations were established.

The blacks, seized in West Africa and transported to the New World shackled below deck in the cramped holds of slave ships, were at first considered indentured servants, capable of ultimately acquiring their freedom. Indeed, some did. But the availability of great numbers of blacks, brought from Africa by speculating slave traders, stimulated the hitherto gradual development in South Carolina, Virginia and Maryland of large tobacco, rice and, later, cotton plantations, which required great numbers of cheap, controllable, disciplined laborers. The entire Southern economy and way of life, and the course of American history from then on, was to be affected.

To nourish agricultural prosperity, greater numbers of additional blacks were brought to the Southern colonies. The legend of indentured servant was conveniently forgotten and it was decreed that blacks and their offspring would be slaves for life, by virtue of their color and the needs of the plantation economy. By the time American independence was declared, almost one out of every three Americans in the English colonies was a black slave.

By that time, too, the flow of immigrants from other parts of Europe had begun. Germans, including the sturdy Pennsylvania Dutch (a corrupted form of the word Deutsch), who still retain their identity and many of their old ways, Ulstermen, Scots, French Huguenots, Irishmen, Jews; people came from many lands seeking religious or political freedom. They came also to escape poverty and for a bite of the golden apple of opportunity which America was already widely known to offer.

More than a century and a half elapsed between the Jamestown landing and the American Revolution. But the seeds of independence were planted early and deep in the coastal colonies and their inland extensions. Although overall supervision and a measure of assistance was forthcoming from England, and although defiance of the mother country was slow to build, each of the colonies soon proved that it could survive, thrive and govern itself without external guidance.

Independence for Mexico and Canada was to await the unfolding of later developments. In Mexico, the Spanish were trying to superimpose their culture on the subjugated Indians. In Canada, exploration deep into the interior, into what would later be Quebec province, Ontario, Manitoba and Saskatchewan, was not yet succeeded by the spread of permanent settlements. But in the American colonies, new forms and new moods were in the making from the beginning.

Even before landing at Plymouth, the Pilgrims had signed the historic Mayflower Compact "to combine ourselves togeather into a civill body politick . . . to enact, constitute, and frame such just and equall lawes, ordinances, acts, constitutions and officies . . . as shall be thought most meete and convenient for ye generall good. . . ." Ten years after Jamestown was founded, Virginia had a House of Burgesses, at which representatives of the settlers considered matters of common interest. In towns and villages throughout the American colonies, community meetinghouses and local government sprang up spontaneously. The needs of defense and commerce led to consultation between neighboring towns, then to common action and then

to the development of regional assemblies.

Through laws controlling overseas possessions, Britain retained the legal machinery for governing the colonies. Although accepting this jurisdiction, individual Colonial legislatures became increasingly bold in making their own decisions, prompted by local enterprise and by the growing conviction that Americans were, or at least should be, in command of their own destinies.

The Revolution, when it came, was triggered by resentment against taxes and trade restrictions imposed by England. The end of protracted hostilities with France, in 1763, gave the English possession of Canada and virtually all the land as far as the Mississippi River. With such acquisitions, England was prompted to flex its imperial muscles, to the great inconvenience and resentment of the American colonists. But the causes of rebellion ran much deeper. So far from a mother country few of them had ever seen, Americans increasingly questioned the right of the English king, or any monarch, to tell them what they could or could not do. Hardened by their experience in taming a new land, confident in their country's natural abundance, convinced that they could coexist with friendly Indians and defend themselves against hostile ones, aroused by the eloquence of their leaders (Patrick Henry was not alone in declaiming "liberty or death") most Americans concluded that English rule was not only expensive and intolerably unjust, but unnecessary and disposable as well. Although he later reconsidered, Noah Webster even proposed a distinctive American language in which, for example, the English words *bread, give* and *friend* would be spelled *bred, giv* and *frend*.

The Declaration of Independence, promulgated on July 4, 1776, was not merely an act of rebellion. It was to be heard around the world like the shots fired at Concord, Massachusetts, at the outset of the Revolution. Proclaiming the sanctity of human freedom and the "unalienable rights" of life, liberty and the pursuit of happiness, it introduced a daring new philosophy of politics—the right of "the People" to abolish a government of which it disapproved and to choose another. To secure these rights, and independence, the thirteen colonies banded together to form the United States and to provide a fighting force capable of defeating and ejecting British forces, which had strengthened to meet their challenge.

The success of the Revolution was not a foregone conclusion. Many of the colonists, thousands of whom were later to flee to Canada, opposed independence and aided the British forces. There was little money for supplies or to pay the troops. Most of the

American soldiers were ill-clothed; some fought barefoot. Men went hungry and froze. Many left their units to plant and harvest their fields at home, or to make certain that their families—many of whom lived in isolated countryside districts—were well and safe. There were desertions from the field of battle and mutinies at the rear. The Revolutionary army suffered serious military setbacks. "You can form no idea," the Revolutionary commander, George Washington, wrote to his brother early in the war, "of the perplexity of my situation."

But, after early successes, the British found their situation grew even more perplexed than Washington's. Despite their limited training, supplies and discipline, the Americans—the first people in modern times to fight for freedom and independence—proved resilient and tenacious. Shattered state militias re-formed to confound the enemy in a series of key battles. Ragtag troops, whose appearance offended the military sensibilities of British commanders, gradually overwhelmed the splendidly uniformed, impeccably trained redcoats. Frontiersmen and other irregulars, as deeply imbued with the spirit of liberty as the stirring phrasemakers of the Continental Congress, brought the tactics of guerrilla warfare to bear on the shoulder-to-shoulder, stand-and-fight ranks of the king's men. The French, hoping to undermine Britain's growing empire, sent the Americans desperately needed supplies and munitions. As the six years of the fighting wore on, the British position grew untenable. The last major battle ended at Yorktown with a resounding British defeat.

But victory left a residue of problems. Independence had been highly contagious. Many of the thirteen states were reluctant to surrender their sovereignty to a central government, American or otherwise. A British observer commented at the time, ". . . every prognostic that can be formed from a contemplation of their mutual antipathies, and clashing interest, their difference of governments, habitudes and manners, plainly indicates that the Americans will have no center of union among them . . . no common interest to pursue. . . . Their fate seems to be —a disunited people till the end of time." But in the end common interests proved to be more potent than divisive forces. To the consternation of some of the newly independent Americans, one nation, not thirteen, had been molded in the crucible of the Revolution. There was much wrangling, disputation and argument among the Founding Fathers. But they produced a single constitution for the new country, to which a bill of rights was quickly affixed to guarantee that Americans had not exchanged one tyranny for another.

Their independence won, their unity established, Americans began devoting more attention to the little-known land beyond the frontiers of their seaboard nation. The frontier had always been a central focus of New World interest. In Canada, French missionaries, traders and trappers had plunged deep into the interior, and also southward across the heartland of what was to become the United States. A century prior to the American Revolution, Joliet and Marquette mapped much of the upper Mississippi Valley. La Salle reached the mouth of the Mississippi River and claimed Louisiana for France. An arc of isolated French trading posts and forts spread from Quebec to the Great Lakes and down to the Mississippi delta.

For the first English settlers, clinging to the Atlantic shore, the nearby brooding forests were the frontier, the limits of the New World, beyond which lurked fearsome Indians and even, some Pilgrims believed, ferocious lions. But hunters, traders and explorers soon penetrated the fall line, beyond which rivers and streams were no longer navigable. They came to terms with the wilderness and blazed paths for farmers, who sought more open space and more fertile land than was available in the growing coastal settlements. Frontiersmen like Daniel Boone led the way, replete with buckskin leggings, fringed leather shirt, coonskin cap and long-barreled rifle (one of the most accurate weapons ever devised). Boone opened a path which traversed the Cumberland Gap through the intimidating Appalachian heights and up the Wilderness Road to a place that had previously been a land largely reserved for hunting and battle. The Indians called it "The Dark and Bloody Ground"; it is now better known as Kentucky.

Each seeking a world of his own, the frontiersman and the farmer slipped into the Carolina Piedmont region, up the Shenandoah Valley into western Virginia, into the Allegheny foothills, the Mohawk Valley, the Vermont and New Hampshire highlands, the wilds of Maine. Soon the first belt of "back-country" was dotted with log cabins and inhabited by farmers who shed their European garments and habits for clothes and ways more appropriate for clearing and farming virgin soil. Having moved in on Indian country, they always kept their muskets handy.

The frontier had been pushed back a notch, an intolerable development for some pioneers, who, displaying a restlessness that was already part of American culture, left their fields and cabins and pushed with their families still farther west, into Ohio, Indiana and Illinois. Many would continue pressing westward, abandoning homestead after home-

A COUNTRY DOUBLES IN SIZE

At the close of the eighteenth century, the United States consisted of most of the land east of the Mississippi and south of the Great Lakes. In 1803, President Thomas Jefferson concluded with France the treaty known as the Louisiana Purchase, whereby the estimated 909,130 square miles of the Louisiana Territory were acquired. At a cost of fifteen million dollars, Jefferson had bought the land between the Mississippi and the Continental Divide and, virtually overnight, the size of the country doubled. To the west of the Divide, Russia controlled Alaska and Spain the land south of the California–Oregon Line. Both Britain and the United States had vague claims to the land in between, known as Oregon Country. To press these claims and to learn something of the newly acquired territory, Jefferson sent the Lewis and Clark expedition westward to the Pacific. Their epic crossing of the continent, from which they returned in 1806, quickly led to the opening up (and settlement) of the West.

Pacific Ocean

Sacajawea, a Shoshoni girl, above, acted as a guide and interpreter to the expedition. She helped Lewis and

Silver medals showing Jefferson's profile and symbols of peace were given to Indian dignitaries.

stead, repeatedly striking out for new lands, landscapes and fresh starts. In 1835, the bemused French observer Alexis de Tocqueville reported from America, "A man builds a house in which to spend his old age and . . . sells it before the roof is on . . . to carry his changeable longings elsewhere."

Less driven "to break for the tall timber," those who stayed behind welcomed newcomers from the East and from Europe as neighbors. They were soon joined by teachers, preachers, doctors, lawyers and merchants. They banded together for common protection, schooling, church building, country dances and community barbecues, and later to make their voices heard in the councils of the central and state governments.

Agriculture swept westward, keeping pace with the regions of settlement. The wheat belt was to shift gradually from the Mohawk and Hudson valleys to the valley of the Missouri. The center of corn cultivation was to move from Virginia, Kentucky and Tennessee to the Midwest's north central plains. The kingdom of cotton shifted from the southern Atlantic states to the lower Mississippi Valley. The abused, unrotated fields closer to the seaboard were no match for the seemingly inexhaustible prairies of the hinterland.

Victory in the Revolution had not eliminated conflicting state claims to sparsely settled territory to the west of the tidewater. These claims could have caused the fledgling republic much trouble had not the Founding Fath-

Clark to make contact with the Indians
and to understand their customs.

Lewis and Clark's reports of beaver and
muskrat, above, lured trappers westward.

Clarkia pulchella, one of two hundred
new plants discovered on the expedition.

St. Louis

Alexander MacKenzie, an
employee of the North
West Company, was the
first white man to cross
the Rockies and reach the
West Coast overland. His
account of his journey
down the Peace River was
carried by Lewis and
Clark on their trek
west twelve years later.

In 1806, Zebulon Pike,
then a young army
lieutenant, left St. Louis
and traveled west along
the Arkansas River to
locate its headwaters. It
was the first American
attempt to explore the
southern border of the
nation's newly acquired
Louisiana Territory.

Not all the early
explorers of the West
were successful. Major
Stephen Long attempted
to find the headwaters of
the Arkansas, Platte and
Red rivers, but succeeded
only in tracing the Platte.
On the way he branded
the Great Plains as the
"Great Desert."

Although he was called
the Pathfinder, John
Frémont, who led five
expeditions into the West
between 1842 and 1854,
was more important as the
symbol of the expansionist
movement than as an
explorer. More than any
other man, he inspired the
drive to settle the West.

ers worked out a solution as revolutionary as
the struggle for independence had been. Instead of setting up and milking the wealth of
frontier area, as imperial powers had always
done, or permitting individual states to swallow up large chunks of backcountry, Congress
ruled that new territories should have elected
territorial assemblies of their own and could
become fully represented states as soon as
their adult, free populations equaled in number that of the smallest of the original thirteen
states. Vermont became a state in 1791, Kentucky the following year, Tennessee in 1796,
Ohio in 1803. (There would be forty-five
states by the end of the nineteenth century,
awaiting only the formal accession of Oklahoma, New Mexico, Arizona, Alaska and

Hawaii to make up the full complement.)

Before the country had time to digest the
full significance of its independence, it found
itself with inflated geographic dimensions
even more difficult to grasp. In 1803, Napoleon, disillusioned with France's New World
adventures, offered to sell the vast Louisiana
Territory—from Canada to the Gulf of Mexico and from the Rockies to the Mississippi—
to the American Government. His offer was
quickly accepted. Practically overnight, the
United States doubled in size and became
one of the largest countries on earth.

Inspired by the achievements a decade
earlier of Alexander Mackenzie, who crossed
Canada to reach both the Arctic and Pacific
oceans, and excited by America's huge terri-

torial acquisition, President Thomas Jefferson immediately dispatched an expedition to
explore the "Louisiana" area, as well as the
disputed Oregon territory to the west. By the
time Meriwether Lewis, William Clark and
their party of forty-two men completed their
two-year trek over the Rockies to the Pacific
and back, they had mapped and described in
great detail much of the previously unexplored north central and northwest regions
of the United States. The widespread publicity given their expedition offered Americans
a tantalizing foretaste of a nation that would
extend from "sea to shining sea."

Other explorers set out into the western
wilds, either dispatched officially to chart unknown corners and patches, or free agents

THE TRAILBLAZERS OF THE WEST

By 1850 most of the United States east of the Missouri River was officially considered to be settled land. The Great Plains were still thought of as a desert and settlers in search of fertile land to which they could stake a claim had no choice but to migrate west. In one year alone, fifty-five thousand pioneers traveled along the trails blazed by the mountain men, tough trappers who, almost by accident, first explored the West.

Oregon Trail
Mormon Trail
California Trail
Santa Fe Trail
Old Spanish Trail
Gila River Trail

Portland
San Francisco
Salt Lake City
Los Angeles
San Diego
Santa Fe
Nauvoo
Independence

The typical buckskin-clad mountain man, left, carried a heavy-caliber rifle, powder horn, bullet-pouch and knife.

Traveling any of the trails to the West, above, was tougher than the romantic "Crossing of the Rockies," top, suggests.

Jim Bridger was a blacksmith's apprentice before becoming a trapper in 1822. One of the first of the mountain men, he spent nearly fifty years in the wilderness and was responsible for guiding the Mormons to the Great Salt Lake. He died peacefully on a Missouri farm in 1881.

Joe Walker earned the reputation among men of his own kind as the best of the wilderness trailblazers. He roamed the West for fifty years during which he mapped and marked most of the Sante Fe Trail and cut out the route across the Great Basin that eventually became the California Trail.

Brigham Young, the Mormon leader, organized his peoples' one-thousand-four-hundred-mile trek from Nauvoo, Illinois, to the Great Salt Lake, Utah. It was the most meticulously planned and organized of all the cross-country migrations, taking fifteen thousand Mormons to a new life.

driven by a compulsion to see for themselves and perhaps stumble upon a fortune. Zebulon Pike explored parts of the Southwest and the Great Plains and also the Rockies, where he spied the peak that was to be named for him and toward which "Pike's Peak or Bust" prospectors were later to scamper across the broad plains. Stephen Long scouted the Upper Mississippi area. John Colter explored the Grand Teton and Yellowstone scenic wonderlands only to be derided as a teller of tall tales when describing their splendor. John Frémont, with Kit Carson as his guide, traversed parts of Idaho and Oregon before turning south to the then sleepy community of Los Angeles.

The names of explorers on specific missions and of others whose adventures attracted wide attention are known. But a corps of mostly anonymous men, sometimes called the mountain men, also penetrated the unknown reaches of the West. They were a special breed of pioneer, bewhiskered, taciturn, fearless, proud loners who hunted beaver, otter, buffalo and bear, and sometimes stayed on in frontier land for the rest of their lives. They often took Indian wives, always stayed at least one step ahead of the settlers and often served as unsung guides for the explorers who were to go down in history as the people who opened up the West.

As their reports of the glories of the West's wide open spaces filtered back across the continent, people began streaming forward to the Mississippi River, beyond which it had been believed there was nothing but uninhabitable desert. The journey along the two-thousand-mile-long Oregon Trail began to take shape. Travelers gathered at Independence, Missouri, and other nearby starting points, where wagon trains collected. Strangers when they met, they chose leaders from their ranks and hired guides to see them across prairies, deserts and flooded rivers, through Indian country and mountain passes. Canvas-covered "prairie schooners" managed about two miles an hour. Traveling in caravans of up to a hundred wagons, they were often accompanied by herds of cattle. The journey to Oregon's lush Willamette Valley could last six months and more, with courting and marriages, births and deaths along the way.

To the south, traders, and later settlers, followed the Santa Fe Trail through Comanche and Arapaho territory from Missouri to New Mexico. Groups of pioneers moved into Texas, a territory of Mexico, which had seized its independence from Spain in 1821 and had declared itself first an empire and then a republic. The "Texicans" refused to submit to the Mexican Government, rebelled and established their own republic prior to applying for admission to the United States.

Like ocean waves, some mighty movements, some mere ripples, settlers rolled across the West. The Mormons, harassed because of their preference for seclusion and their polygamous habits, fled from the East and set out for a new home where there would be no one to persecute them. Ignoring warnings that they would find nothing but "sand, saltwater, cactus, and rattlesnakes," they veered south from the Oregon Trail, reached their promised land on the shores of the Great Salt Lake and founded what was to be, after years of toil and privation, the State of Utah.

The discovery of gold in California in 1848 touched off a monumental westward rush of prospectors and claim jumpers, honest men and thieves, from Europe as well as from back East. Villages like San Francisco and Sacramento were transformed into gaudy boom towns, complete with boisterous bars, gambling halls and houses of ill repute. Eggs cost a dollar apiece, and the rent for a tiny shack was a hundred dollars a week. Later, many of those who had raced in vain to the Pacific shore found that California's agreeable climate and beautiful natural setting was as much a magnet as the lure of gold had been.

A few years later, the discovery of the Comstock lode of gold and silver in Nevada, and lesser finds in Colorado, sent prospectors and their camp followers scurrying for "pay dirt" into the western mountains, in much the same way as they poured into the Klondike region when gold was discovered in the Alaska–Canada border area in the closing years of the nineteenth century.

But, for the most part, the pattern of haphazard exploration, settlement and development was coming to an end. The tragic, bloody Civil War of 1861–65 proved to be a dividing line in the country's history. Sparked off by regional differences that became crystallized in the issue of slavery, which was abolished as a result of the war, the conflict was a savage bloodletting, which marked the end of national adolescence, the conclusion of the early years of random growth and the beginning of a consolidation of what the land offered.

Few achievements symbolized the confident coming of age of the United States as clearly as the completion in 1869 of the first transcontinental rail line. The Union Pacific Company, employing an army of mostly Irish laborers, built westward from rail links at Omaha. The Central Pacific, with a host of Chinese railhands, built eastward from Sacramento. The final stage of construction, like so much that happened during this period, turned into a race, with both sides prodded forward by mileage bonuses, until Congress decreed that no matter who got there first, the splicing point would be Promontory Point,

THE RAILROADS LINK EAST WITH WEST

On May 8, 1869, the first railroad across the North American continent was completed. On that day the Central Pacific, which had begun building east from Sacramento in 1864, and the Union Pacific, which had built west from Omaha, met in Utah. The men who built it were Civil War veterans, freed slaves, Indian, Irish, German and Chinese immigrants. The new railroad was a triumph, for these men had bridged rivers and canyons, filled ravines and tunneled through mountains, largely by sheer muscle power. Their efforts cut the travel time between the Midwest and the Pacific from twenty weeks to four days. It is little wonder that this was America's most celebrated industrial achievement of the nineteenth century.

Theodore Judah, left, made the first realistic survey for a railroad to cross the Sierras. His route, right, was based on the old Emigrant Trail, but made use of a pass discovered in the 1850s.

Samuel Montague, left, Central Pacific's chief engineer, shakes hands with Grenville Dodge, Union Pacific's top surveyor, as the two railroads link up at Promontory Summit, west of Ogden, Utah.

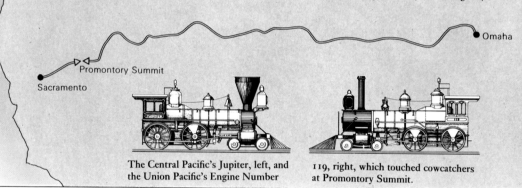

The Central Pacific's Jupiter, left, and the Union Pacific's Engine Number 119, right, which touched cowcatchers at Promontory Summit.

Utah, where railroad executives, on hand for the occasion, swung hammers to drive in golden spikes. To the delight of the Irish and Chinese railhands, they made a mess of the job.

From its outset, the westward movement was the genesis of disaster for the Indians. Although relations between them and the earliest settlers, and with individual trappers and traders, were often friendly, savage acts by one side or the other provoked cruel reprisals, frequently taken against innocent groups of Indians or white men. Vendettas were provoked and undying suspicion was planted. Hostility grew increasingly intense as the settlers crowded the Indians away from the Atlantic shore, and then farther and farther back across the continent.

When the white man arrived, there were more than four hundred Indian tribes scattered across North America. Some consisted of many thousands of people and ranged over wide hunting and raiding regions. A few tribes had only four or five dozen members and rarely ventured outside narrowly confined, secluded tribal areas. The Indians never numbered more than a few million although there were more than three hundred distinct, mutually incomprehensible Indian languages. In the Great Plains and some other areas, tribes developed sign languages to cross the communications barrier. But there was little in their experience to prepare the Indians for the challenge laid down by the claim the white man was to make to their lands.

Early in the nineteenth century, the Shawnee war chief Tecumseh journeyed between the Great Lakes and the Gulf of Mexico to plead with tribal elders to unite to resist the tide of white settlers. They had guns, bought or taken from the French, the English and American traders. The warriors of many of the tribes were superb fighting men, man for man a match for settler or soldier. Some tribes did agree to band together, but too few to make much difference. They were outgunned and outnumbered and they were relentlessly driven back. In the Southeast, the Creeks, Seminoles and Cherokees resisted fiercely, but they, too, were overwhelmed and herded with other tribes along the "Trail of Tears," a long, brutal, forced march. It was part of the removal meant to transplant the eastern Indians forever to the far side of the Mississippi, where the land was then thought to be uninhabitable for white men.

When the tide of settlers swarmed across the Mississippi, too, the process of displacing and dispossessing the Indians began anew. As before, land–division treaties were forced on tribes, and then broken by the settlers and their Government spokesmen. Farmers and cattlemen seized the Great Plains hunting grounds. Miners moved in and parceled out Indian territory among themselves. Wagon trains and railroads brought an inexorable stream of newcomers to claim and fence off Indian land, to destroy the game on which Indians depended for sustenance and clothing, often to shoot Indians on sight. Horror was voiced by many white men appalled by this treatment of the descendants of the very first Americans, but invariably the concern was expressed by people far from the frontier. Their words had little impact on those who were "winning the West" and who were frequently subject to Indian ferocity.

34

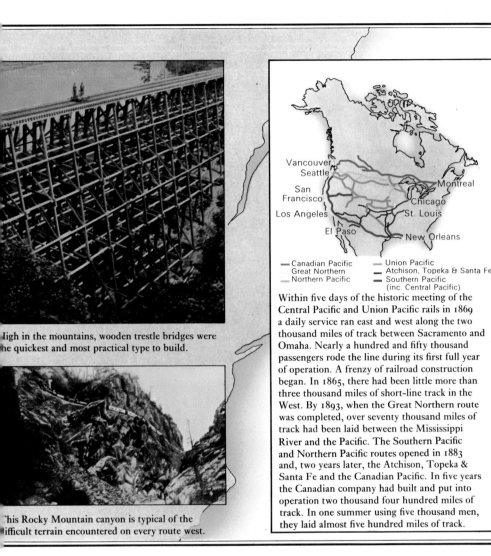

High in the mountains, wooden trestle bridges were the quickest and most practical type to build.

This Rocky Mountain canyon is typical of the difficult terrain encountered on every route west.

Canadian Pacific
Great Northern
Northern Pacific
Union Pacific
Atchison, Topeka & Santa Fe
Southern Pacific (inc. Central Pacific)

Within five days of the historic meeting of the Central Pacific and Union Pacific rails in 1869 a daily service ran east and west along the two thousand miles of track between Sacramento and Omaha. Nearly a hundred and fifty thousand passengers rode the line during its first full year of operation. A frenzy of railroad construction began. In 1865, there had been little more than three thousand miles of short-line track in the West. By 1893, when the Great Northern route was completed, over seventy thousand miles of track had been laid between the Mississippi River and the Pacific. The Southern Pacific and Northern Pacific routes opened in 1883 and, two years later, the Atchison, Topeka & Santa Fe and the Canadian Pacific. In five years the Canadian company had built and put into operation two thousand four hundred miles of track. In one summer using five thousand men, they laid almost five hundred miles of track.

There was no last stand by the Indian nations. There were isolated, bloody spasms of resistance by the Sioux, the Cheyenne, the Apache and others—terrorizing wagon trains and settlers, even taking on the U.S. cavalry, which had established a series of forts (oases of safety for harassed travelers and settlers) across Indian territory. Cavalry General George Custer, who was later to be cut down with his men by Sioux and Cheyenne warriors at Little Bighorn, said, "If I were an Indian, I would certainly prefer . . . the free open plains rather than submit to the confined limits of a reservation. . . ." But after the frontier wars, after being forced to move from one place to another, the last of the tribes was subjugated. Surrendering their lands, the Indians went to live on the reservation compounds to which they were assigned.

Whichever direction one looked across the continent in the last half of the nineteenth century, momentous things were happening. To the indignation of many Americans who considered it a worthless frozen wasteland, the American Government bought Alaska from Russia in 1867. In Canada, that same year, a start was made toward unity and independence through a confederation of the French and English communities. Small, scattered settlements there began developing into thriving agricultural and commercial communities. Roads and railroad lines—soon to reach Vancouver, where once only a sawmill stood—brought increased prosperity, as well as a substantial flow of immigrants from the United States, Britain, Ireland and continental Europe. Wheat flourished on the Canadian Prairies, and Canada itself outgrew the image of being merely a geographical expression.

In Mexico, a shortlived bid by France to establish the Austrian prince Maximilian as emperor, ended with Maximilian's execution and a restoration of the Mexican republic. But mining had declined in the country and poverty was widespread. The development of large, virtually independent, rural haciendas coincided with the growth of revolutionary and reform movements that were to shape Mexico's future history.

In the United States, the frontier was

rapidly vanishing. The immense wealth locked up in natural resources was being hungrily tapped. The invention of the Bessemer converter for extracting cheap steel stimulated the exploitation of iron-ore fields in Michigan and Minnesota. Seemingly inexhaustible veins of coal were worked along the Appalachian backbone at outcroppings from Alabama to Pennsylvania, and new fields were continually discovered elsewhere. The first successful commercial oil well in the world had struck "black gold" near Titusville, Pennsylvania, in 1859, a prelude to the much more substantial later oil finds in Texas, Oklahoma, Louisiana and California. Copper was found in Arizona and Michigan; lead in Missouri and Idaho. Lumberjacks went to work in the forests of the Northwest, Wisconsin and Maine.

But America still remained largely an agricultural country, its vast plains an immense granary. At first, farming the prairies had seemed wildly improbable to small farmers from the East and from the farm villages of Scandinavia, Germany and Bohemia. Aside from being hopelessly thick with untamed grass, they were remote from the eastern markets and seaports. But technological ingenuity overcame the drawbacks. The invention of the steel plow, the mechanical reaper, the harvester, the self-knotting binder and other devices set the stage for converting the Great Plains into the most highly productive agricultural region in the world, serviced by growing networks of railroad lines.

The growth of the cattle empire in Texas was another symptom of America's coming of age. The Spanish had long before brought longhorns to Mexico, from where they had spread across the Rio Grande. But not until the railroads had reached sufficiently far did the beef industry flourish. Cowboys chaperoned their herds up the Chisholm Trail and along other routes from the Texas grasslands to the railroad lines at Abilene and Dodge City. Eight hard-riding, hard-working, hard-cursing, bow-legged men with six-shooters, horses and remounts, and a chuck-wagon canteen drawn by mules could herd up to three thousand head of cattle along the trail while keeping an eye out for rustlers and hostile Indians. They met the big-city beef buyers at the Kansas railheads, and then, as often as not, blew a good part of their earnings in the cow towns before heading back down the trail again. The temptations provided by the vast, lush public grazing lands in the Dakotas, Colorado, Wyoming and Montana spread the cattle realm to the open range farther north, where buffalo were already well on their way to extinction, depleted by the Indians and finished off by railroad company foremen who sent teams of hunters out to bring back bison

MAN MAKES HIS IMPRINT ON THE LAND

North Americans, responding to the special challenges of their vast and underpopulated continent, used their ingenuity to devise new ways to overcome the massive problems of movement within its enormous area, to fully utilize the valuable space within their strategically sited cities, to exploit the rich promise of the land and to harness its powerful natural forces. In so doing they created marvels of their own to match the remarkable natural wonders of their magnificent homeland.

North America's vast agricultural potential has been realized only in the last century and a half. The initial impetus came from inventions like Eli Whitney's cotton gin, above, which helped create the cotton industry, and Cyrus McCormick's reaper, right, instrumental in the cultivation of the plains.

carcasses to feed their track-laying laborers. Where once buffalo roamed, cattle grazed.

The strands of discovery, exploration, settlement and development were diverse and far-flung. The task of weaving them into a cohesive pattern fell to the cities, both long-established and new. Boston, New York, Philadelphia, Baltimore and Charleston had been centers of Colonial economic life. They expanded rapidly as the opening of frontier after frontier created a booming traffic in produce and goods, making greater and greater demands on their trading, manufacturing and financing capacities.

As the frontier rolled westward, inland towns sprang up, usually on waterways along which goods could be shipped. With the spread of railroad lines, cities—such as Omaha, Duluth, Kansas City and Seattle—sprouted at the railheads, bustling termini for both people and goods. Hordes of penniless European peasants and townspeople, first from northern and western Europe, then from southern and eastern Europe, joined many from the eastern states who poured in to start

life anew. They provided an abundant labor supply for factories and mills, and for laying out streets and erecting the buildings of the mushrooming urban centers.

Within forty years, Chicago grew from a village lacking defined boundaries into a city fed by a hundred trains a day. Early settlers saw places like Minneapolis, Des Moines and Portland change from towns to cosmopolitan centers within their own lifetimes. National enclaves of newly arrived immigrants sank roots in various places—Scandinavians in St. Paul and Minneapolis, Germans in Milwaukee, Russians and Poles in Cleveland, Irish in Boston, Italians and Jews in New York.

Across the continent, cities were both servicing surrounding regions and building upon themselves through merchandising, manufacturing, financial operations and land and property speculation which was frequently shot through with corruption. As cities ballooned in size, public transportation systems, including cable cars and elevated train lines, were installed, stimulating even greater expansion.

The urban centers grew too rapidly, often

too frantically, for any but the most occasional practice of urban planning—a park here, a playground there. Grim tenements were raised along grids of parallel streets, which were often laid out with such haste that they were given, and retain, numbers rather than names. No sooner were the tenements up than they were crammed with still more newcomers from abroad, fleeing grinding poverty, political oppression and religious intolerance, "yearning to breathe free" in the crowded slums of their New World. Theirs was to be a frontier as formidable as those crossed by backwoodsmen, with as many hazards along the way.

The adaptation of North America to man's needs, wishes and ambitions inevitably involved major alteration of its physical setting. The face of the continent was lifted, lowered, battered and embellished. Steel ribbons of railroad track were spun out in all directions across its surface, two hundred thousand miles of it in the United States alone. Many mountainous obstructions were totally obliterated and cavities were blasted in others to provide level ground for track beds.

Henry Ford, the man who "put America on wheels," originated the idea of assembly-line production, which still dominates industry today. It was first introduced in 1913, the year that Ford brought out this version of his Model T.

No innovation has transformed the urban environment quite as totally as the skyscraper, which was first conceived and built in Chicago in the nineteenth century by Louis Sullivan, architect of the exquisitely finished Auditorium, above.

The Brooklyn Bridge, which took fourteen years to build and was completed in 1883, had a record-breaking span of 1,595 feet. It was designed by John Roebling, whose new method of cable spinning was so simple and effective that, with modifications, it has been used in the construction of every subsequent major suspension bridge in the United States.

Millions of miles of road were flattened to accommodate the automobile. Henry Ford, who did more than anyone to put people behind the wheels of their own vehicles, conceded that cars, at first, were considered "a nuisance, for [they] made a racket and scared horses." Nevertheless, within the first two decades of the twentieth century, making cars had become America's biggest industry, and getting from one place to another in them had become its most captivating pastime. The soaring number of vehicles led to road widening and highway construction, crisscrossing the continent with an infinity of lines and bends of macadam, tar, asphalt, concrete and just plain country dirt. New designs for resulting mazes produced a variety of road sculpturings, including cloverleaf junctions and futuristic loops, for easier road access and simplified navigation.

Bridges had risen to span inconvenient waterway gaps between road and highway segments and to permit sprawling cities to sprawl even farther, by linking their river-divided sections. Symbols of growth and progress, silhouettes of arches, pillars and cables,

they crossed the Missouri River at Kansas City and many other places, and the Mississippi at St. Louis and elsewhere along its route. They spanned The Narrows of New York Bay, the St. Lawrence River, San Francisco Bay, the Mackinac Straits, Galveston Bay and an untold number of smaller and larger divides up and down the land.

In some key places, the divides were bridged by a different form of link. Dams were planted across mighty waterways to control their flow and reap the neglected harvest of their torrential power. The Hoover Dam on the Colorado River and the Grand Coulee Dam on the Columbia translated the force of mighty rivers, which had run free for millions of years, into colossal quantities of electrical energy, irrigating formerly barren wasteground and making harsh regions habitable. A series of dams was thrown across the Tennessee River and its branches to develop the resources of the Tennessee Valley, control flooding and permit navigation on previously impassable sections. In the process of dam-building, estuaries were diverted, lakes created and the character of nearby regions

modified and sometimes changed beyond recognition.

Up in the air, the Wright brothers had done more on North Carolina's Outer Coast in 1903 than navigate the first flying machine. They had made the initial move toward making air transport the dominant mode of long-distance travel, thus eventually filling the skies with flight paths more diverse and numerous than those of migratory birds.

Even before that aerial overture at Kitty Hawk, rising urban land values and discovery of the use of structural steel had led man to reach toward the heavens in other ways. The realization that a steel cage would support the weight of skyscraping buildings permitted cities to expand upward as well as outward. The first ten-story skyscraper was completed in Chicago in 1889, to be followed the next year by the twenty-six-story World Building in New York and, ultimately, by urban grand canyons of steel, glass and concrete. An architectural movement had been launched, which, in transforming the skylines of all major American cities, kept pace with the alterations made to the natural environment.

AGE FOUR
The New Awareness

The development of the North American continent, and of its people, has been an adventure story, full of deeds of daring, imagination, toil and achievement. Like all adventure stories, it has also been marked by hazards along the way. Among these hazards, comforting but destructive, was the mistaken conviction that the goodness of the land was inexhaustible and invulnerable.

The Indians were the first to be deceived. They venerated spirits of the earth, the woods and the animals. But confident of infinite abundance, they abused all three. They set fire to forests to clear wooded areas for farming and to drive out game sheltering among the trees. They exhausted the fertility of patches of land they cultivated, then moved on to do the same to new ones. They often stampeded herds of buffalo over bluffs to kill the few animals they needed for food.

But their extravagance in the exploitation of nature had no serious consequences. The continent was immense and there were comparatively few Indians in North America, probably about one million, at the time of the white man's arrival. Not until they lost their lands and saw the depletion of the woods and herds they had taken for granted, did they realize, and mourn the fact, that nature's munificence was not infinite.

The realization was also slow to dawn on the settlers, pioneers, farmers and others who set out to conquer the New World wilderness and who, in the process, mistreated the land as casually as the Indians had, but with greater thoroughness and more damaging consequences. Forests were obliterated, plains were broken, nature was subdued, the wilderness was whittled down. There appeared to be no reason not to exploit the land. If some was used up and made barren, there was always more beyond the next ridge; there was always another forest and a new frontier. It was inconceivable that a land so rich in space could possibly run out of fertile soil, trees or clear water.

Each destructive act had far-reaching implications. Chopping down woods let the rain wash away precious topsoil, and the wind swept away much of what was left, leaving wastelands and dust bowls. Farther west, ranchers turned loose more cattle than the open range could sustain. Grasslands were devoured or trampled down so thoroughly that, in many places, instead of new grass

THE NATURALISTS

At the beginning of the nineteenth century, little was known of the land west of the Mississippi and virtually nothing was known of its wildlife. A number of young naturalists, eager to discover and record the many new species of plants and animals, joined the exploration parties that were going into the wilderness. The botanists Thomas Nuttall and John Bradbury and the zoologist Thomas Say were among the most celebrated of those naturalists who sought and classified the flora and fauna of the West, but the most famous was the author, artist and self-taught ornithologist John James Audubon. His books on the birds and mammals of America have become classics of their kind. Working with him were a Lutheran pastor, John Bachman, and Audubon's two sons, John Woodhouse and Victor Gifford, who together painted the portrait of their father, above. Many of the species they described and illustrated, right, were destined to become endangered or even made extinct as the vast natural resources of the continent were used in the pursuit of material progress.

Prairie dogs were described by one early explorer as "a wild, frolicsome, madcap set of fellows when undisturbed." Farmers, who regard them as pests, have been trying to exterminate them and they survive in any numbers only in the Dakotas.

growing, the ground became carpeted with weeds, which attacted colonies of rodents to undermine the soil.

Animal life was also endangered. The beaver may have been saved by the fact that beaver hats, all the rage early in the nineteenth century, went out of style. But other species—including elk, bighorn sheep, grizzly bears, otters, alligators and condors—were brought near extinction by random slaughter.

As cities and industry grew, nearby rivers and lakes seemed ideally suited for simple,

inexpensive disposal of sewage and industrial waste. No one could foresee that they might one day become so totally polluted that some would no longer be able to support marine life and that they might be unsafe for swimming, nor could it be foreseen that environmentalists might one day go so far as to suggest that, because of contamination by chemical refuse, some inland waters should actually be declared fire hazards. It was incredible that the exhausts of millions of cars and the smokestacks of tens of thousands of factories

The American bison, usually called buffalo, epitomized the bounteousness of the Old West, but by 1889 its numbers in the United States, once estimated at fifty million, had been reduced to only 541 animals. Without guns and horses, the Indians had hunted the buffalo for thousands of years without seriously affecting the size of the herds, but the demand for fresh meat created by the opening up of the West and the building of the transcontinental railroads brought in professional hunters. Buffalo Bill Cody alone killed over four thousand in eighteen months. Conservationists saved North America's largest animal, once found as far east as Indiana.

The Eskimo curlew was discovered for science in 1772 by Hudson's Bay Company traders. Bachman, America's first expert on migration, saw the bird in South Carolina in 1830 and realized that it was a migratory species. Audubon saw flocks of the curlews in Quebec in 1833, when he did his famous painting, above. The Eskimo curlew was once common in North and South America. Last sighted in Texas in 1966, it is now one of the world's rarest birds.

The black-footed ferret still has largely the same range, across the Great Plains from the Canadian border to New Mexico, that it had in Audubon's day, but its numbers have been so reduced that naturalists consider it to be on the verge of extinction.

The southern sea otter's range once extended from Washington to Baja California, but heavy exploitation—Audubon was offered one hundred dollars for a skin—was thought to have brought about its extinction in 1911. Rediscovered in 1938 off Bixby Creek in Monterey County, its numbers have since reached over one thousand, although it is still endangered.

might foul the air and hang grim curtains of smog and haze over bustling cities.

But the defacing of the land did not go unnoticed. Long before the worst of the damage was done, George Washington had complained, "Our lands were . . . very good, but use and abuse have made them . . . otherwise." John Chapman, better known as Johnny Appleseed, roamed across Ohio and Indiana early in the nineteenth century, planting apple trees to replenish the land's dwindling resources. It was a modest gesture by a man who, wandering about in a coffee-sack cloak, a long-peaked pasteboard hat and bare feet, was a comic figure to his contemporaries. It nevertheless reflected an undercurrent of concern that was slowly beginning to gather. A century before modern ecologists took up the cry, a Vermont judge, diplomat and farmer, George Perkins Marsh, warned that, unless checked, human excesses could impoverish the environment so completely that mankind might be threatened with extinction. John Wesley Powell, an Illinois school-teacher who had lost an arm in the Civil War, explored large parts of the West, and produced a farsighted program for land and water use to revitalize arid western regions.

But these and other voices were, at first, largely ignored. Proposals to govern the disposal and use of new or sparsely settled frontier territories and to protect natural resources in other areas were vigorously challenged. Some spokesmen for Western states and territories angrily disputed the right of others to retard their growth and prosperity.

THE CONSERVATIONISTS

The peopling of North America is an epic story of endurance, fortitude and energetic opportunism, but it is also one of an early and sadly misplaced belief in the unbounded munificence of natural resources and a later reckless disregard for the sheer magnificence of the land. Among the first successful conservationists was Thomas Moran whose paintings of Yellowstone, including that of the Lower Falls, right, were instrumental in persuading Congress to create the first national park in 1872. As the map shows, many more national parks have been created since then and in North America today there is a new awareness of man's responsibility to conserve, as well as to enjoy, the wild.

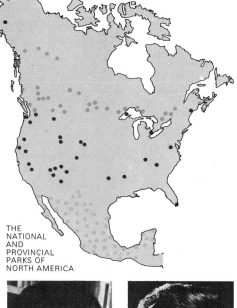

THE NATIONAL AND PROVINCIAL PARKS OF NORTH AMERICA

John Muir was one of the first champions of the conservationist cause. He was largely responsible for the creation of six national parks, Mesa Verde, Glacier, Mount Rainier, Crater Lake, Sequoia and Yosemite.

Theodore Roosevelt, known as the Conservation President, inspired governmental and public interest in conservation at a time when North America's wildlife and wilderness were being abused on an unprecedented scale.

In her book *Silent Spring*, published in 1962, Rachel Carson attacked the irresponsible use of insecticides. She created a worldwide awareness of the dangers of environmental pollution.

During the administration of John F. Kennedy, which ran from 1960 to 1963, there was a great reawakening of public, industrial and government interest in conservation issues and a searching reexamination of land policies.

Land speculators who had acquired substantial tracts of territory lobbied against conservation measures that might keep land values from soaring.

But more was at stake than personal, corporate or regional interests. In 1890, a United States Government report gave the traumatic news that all available land had been spoken for. The land frontier had gone—forever. Abuse of environment could no longer be compensated for by tapping new regions. The first thorough examination of the situation revealed further that two-thirds of the country's forests had been cut or burned down, much of the country's mineral wealth had been wasted through haphazard mining methods, and no serious effort was being made to prevent rich topsoil from being flooded or blown away. The situation called

for a total reassessment of the use of natural resources and bold measures to reverse the tide.

The challenge was taken up by President Theodore Roosevelt at the turn of the twentieth century. Deeply committed to conservation, Roosevelt set aside vast areas of woodland as forest reserves and initiated large-scale irrigation projects for land reclamation. Following his lead, industry and regional conservation commissions became active as well, and representatives of the United States, Canada and Mexico met in 1909 to set the groundwork for continent-wide cooperation in conservation pursuits.

Once begun, the conservation movement gathered momentum. New woodlands were planted where old ones had stood. Forests were reborn in parts of Maine, the Southern

states and other places where they had been eradicated. A national system of tree farming enables owners of small tracts of land to gain assistance in reforestation.

The indiscriminate slaughter of animals and birds was ended by the establishment of wildlife preserves and refuges, by careful game management and by the introduction of restrictions limiting both hunting seasons and the size of each hunter's "bag." As a result, many species which were on the verge of disappearing forever are no longer endangered. Widespread flood control, irrigation and land-reclamation projects were launched, and farmers were taught the advantages of contour plowing and terracing to block the runoff of soil-carrying rainwater. Methods were developed for husbanding mineral wealth. Although much has been irretrievably lost,

tas, Yellowstone was a determined bid to retain an aspect of the frontier, a sense of nature's eternity, where hunting by humans would be prohibited, mining forbidden and forests protected. Yellowstone was the first of the many national parks that were to be set aside for those who chose to sense the splendor of primeval wilderness and for the sustenance of eternal values.

The American parks offer a diversity of scenic spectacles—the mist-shrouded forests of the Great Smoky Mountains, the marsh prairies of the Everglades, the subarctic magnificence of Alaska's Mount McKinley, California's towering Redwood Forest, the mirror-like, glacier-fed lakes at Banff in the Canadian Rockies—a glittering constellation of awesome, untamed realms. Individual natural wonders, set out like gems across the landscape, have also been the subject of renewed attention.

The first Americans—the men who crossed the landbridge from Siberia to Alaska—discovered North America by accident. Columbus discovered it by mistake. The new awareness of its grandeur is a different dimension of discovery, both rational and emotional, both deliberate and desperate. It is the search for a balance of nature and an enhanced quality of life to redeem the erosions of urban pressures, material pursuits and lopsided perspectives. The woodlands are one example. The recognition that trees are a unique, perpetually renewable resource allows a new concept of forest perpetuation to be practiced. It provides greater areas for recreation, watershed and wildlife protection, and yet permits the planned, continuing growth and harvesting of trees to meet man's needs. It is a quest for a sense of proportion, for balance and for permanence.

As early as 1898, the naturalist John Muir wrote, "Thousands of nerve-shaken overcivilized people are beginning to find out that going to the mountains is going home, that wildness is a necessity and that mountain parks and reservations are useful not only as fountains of timber and irrigating rivers, but as fountains of life."

The search for these fountains of life now goes well beyond mountain parks and reservations, although it includes them as well. It has become a widespread and profound reawakening to the call of the countryside, to the lure of the land. A renaissance, both real and symbolic, it has pumped new spirit, meaning, pleasure and reverence into millions who had been in danger of losing contact with earth and skies, with woods and wild creatures, and even with themselves. It is a fresh trail across the continent, a new chapter in the history of North America.

much was also reclaimed from oblivion and ways were devised for preventing a recurrence of the frantic plunder of the land.

The frontier had been, however, so much a part of America during its formative years, had been so crucial in molding the character of its people, that its disappearance evoked an uneasiness that went beyond concern about dwindling natural resources and pollution of the environment. Would there be nowhere to go anymore to escape the frailty of ephemeral things? Could it be that what was left of virgin wilderness would, in time, also be gobbled up by the march of progress, denuded, leveled, asphalted over and crowded with buildings and city dwellers? The poet Walt Whitman warned, "American democracy, in its myriad personalities . . . must either be . . . vitalized by regular contact with outdoor light and air . . . animals, fields, trees, birds . . . and free skies, or it will certainly dwindle and pale." A deep, sad nostalgia for what poet Vachel Lindsay called "lost, wild America" began to rise across the land and began also to elicit a response from elected officials.

As early as 1872, a natural preserve was established in three thousand five hundred square miles of Wyoming and parts of Montana and Idaho. Yellowstone, North America's first national park, was set aside as a "pleasuring ground for the benefit and enjoyment of the people." The object was to protect "from injury or spoliation . . . all timber, mineral deposits, natural curiosities or wonders . . . and their retention in their natural condition." With its geysers, waterfalls, mountain lakes, forests and breathtaking vis-

COAST OF WONDERS

No one was ever in doubt that the land called California was fabulous. Cortés, the conqueror of Mexico, exploring the inland coastline and waters of the Baja Peninsula, gave it the name of a legendary island first sought by Columbus in the Caribbean, and which the sixteenth-century writer Garci Ordóñez de Montalvo had named California in his romance *Las Sergas de Esplandián*. This legendary island was inhabited only by black Amazons with golden arms and lay "at the right hand of the Indies . . . very close to that part of the Terrestrial Paradise." Sir Francis Drake, sailing along the shores of Upper California about thirty years after Cortés, also foresaw a land of plenty and named it New Albion. But after the Portuguese navigator Juan Rodríguez Cabrillo, the first white man to anchor in Californian waters, entered the Bay of San Diego in 1542, the name California stuck. Today, because of the riches in metal, oil, agriculture and the benediction of its climate, California is known as the Golden State.

It is, however, one of the decisive convergences of chance in history that gold was discovered in California at the same time as the territory was ceded to the United States by Mexico, and that the men of the Gold Rush settled on American land. James Marshall picked up a pellet of pure gold from a stream on January 24, 1848; California became American on February 2 of the same year. (It was declared a free state in 1850.) After 1848, the Gold Rush, the greatest migration of the Western World, took place, and where previously a few missions and rancheros had sleepily and pleasantly governed the indigenous Indians, the American spirit, with its grit and vigor and imagination, as well as its brutality and greed, found its fullest expression.

California is the most populous state and one of the richest, but it would be difficult to deduce this from the huge and lovely emptiness of its scenery. Even the sprawling vastness of Los Angeles is lost in the greater vastness of the silent Californian desert and the wave upon wave of majestic ranges behind. Even the stunning coils of the freeways, with their multiple lanes and multiple intersections, fade into insignificance beside the smallest peaks of the Sierra Nevada and into nothingness beside the tall pinnacles of Mount Shasta and Mount Whitney. Even the enormous expanses of citrus orchards and vineyards and cotton fields, interspersed with the rhythmical towers of the oil pumps, look puny against the mighty backdrop of these mountains. Of course the achievements of the boom society, especially its towns and roads, have blighted some of the beauty of this terrestrial paradise. But unlike the landscape of countries like England and Italy, which have been worked and worn and molded by farmers and foresters and builders for generations, California is untamed and indomitable. Everywhere the wild outdoors imposes its vitality on its people. It is active and extrovert, and its most characteristic songs celebrate teenage romance on the beaches.

In California, surfing became a way of life and the dangers of hang-gliding were invented on the bluffs above the Pacific. The body beautiful is mandatory, and some Los Angeles businessmen roller-skate to work to keep fit. Its pleasures are not subtle but flamboyant fantasies—the castles of Disneyland, the concrete footprints and handprints of film stars, the hot dog salesman's van itself shaped like a hot dog. It is not surprising that for its size and energy it has produced relatively few painters or poets. In the war between nature and culture, nature need hardly put up a fight in California. All the frenzy and ferment and success of the human society, which gains its wealth from its buried treasure and remarkable fertility, seems fragile and impermanent beside its gaping canyons, its rolling deserts and its tumultuous shore.

Yosemite

"Elijah's flight in a chariot of fire could hardly have been more gloriously exciting," wrote John Muir of a ride he took on an avalanche of snow in Yosemite Valley. "Being eager to see as many avalanches as possible," he had walked out one fine morning after a heavy snowfall and climbed up to a commanding position over the valley, when the land suddenly gave way beneath his feet. Undaunted, he simply threw himself on his back against the sliding snow and "was swished down to the foot of the canyon as if by enchantment." He later wrote, "This flight, in what might be called a milky way of snowstars, was the most spiritual and exhilarating of all the modes of motion I have ever experienced."

John Muir is the patriarch of American conservation, and the savior and genius loci of

Yosemite Valley. He was born in Scotland, went to America when he was eleven years old and was brought up on a farm in Wisconsin. In 1868, when Muir was thirty years old, he saw Yosemite Valley for the first time, and there began one of the great love affairs between a man and a landscape. "The mighty Sierra" was, he wrote, "so gloriously colored, so radiant, it seemed not clothed with light but wholly composed of it, like the wall of some celestial city. . . . Then it seemed to me that the Sierra should be called, not the Nevada or Snowy Range, but the Range of Light."

Muir built himself a log cabin in Yosemite, and settled there. He was an intrepid mountaineer, as abstemious as a hermit, and his pantheistic passion for the valley's every mood and movement is often Wordsworthian in intensity. To him earthquakes, avalanches, glaciers, blizzards and gales were all "Nature's wild beauty-making business . . . the orderly beauty-making love-beats of Nature's heart." When the great Inyo earthquake of 1872 shook the valley—in the nearby town of Lone Pine several lives were lost—Muir tried to cheer up one of the terrified settlers, saying, "Smile a little and clap your hands, now that kind Mother Earth is trotting us on her knee to amuse us and make us good."

He scampered up the silky granite pinnacles that form the ramparts of Yosemite and clung to rock faces that would defy a bat in order to approach the valley's waterfalls and hear their music roar in his ear. From behind Yosemite Falls one night he watched the dance of the full moon, "now darkly veiled or eclipsed by a rush of thick-headed comets, now flashing out through the openings between their tails." Then the wind suddenly swung the huge cataract against him on his precarious perch. But Muir declared later that he felt "better, not worse, for my hard midnight bath."

Muir's explorations of the valley convinced him that it had been cut out of the rock of the Sierra by glaciers, and that its sheer precipices, so smoothly faceted that they look as if a master gem cutter had worked them out of rough cabochons, had been ground and polished by glacial activity. His theory was ridiculed by professional geologists of the

time, until Muir, in his fearless climbs around Yosemite, discovered living glaciers up on the highest slopes of Mounts Lyell and McClure and Ritter.

John Muir realized very early that the beauty of Yosemite was endangered by the settlers, the herdsmen who overgrazed the valley's alpine meadows and the hunters who pursued the animals who lived there. (Yosemite means grizzly bear, which was last seen there in 1895.) Muir, therefore, left the mountains to campaign in the cities for public ownership and protection of the valley and of other places in the Sierra. He was an eloquent advocate, and founded the Sierra Club, one of the most influential conservation groups in the United States. In 1864, Abraham Lincoln took his mind off the Civil War to sign an act of Congress giving Yosemite Valley and the surrounding mountains to California as the first state park. To prevent further settlement and ruin, the valley was garrisoned by soldiers.

Yosemite Valley hangs high in the Sierra, and the great mountains that form its flanks hang higher still. It has the beauty and authority of enormous scale, of immense, contained energy. The granite battlements challenge each other across the sweet-smelling pines and cedars in the valley below. The helmet of Half Dome meets the rounded cranium of North Dome, while to the west El Capitan rock rises a sheer three thousand feet above the valley floor, itself four thousand feet above the sea. The clouds furl and unfurl around the suspended crags, and the shards of the Mirror Lake, half encrusted with snow, reflect their eddying and drift. Occasionally in winter a fragment of ice breaks free from the frozen cascade of Bridal Veil Fall and crashes down, glancing off the rock with a retort like artillery fire that echoes from the opposing cliffs.

Muir considered Yosemite the finest piece of divine architecture, greater than any human cathedral or palace. From Inspiration Point at the western entrance, where the grandiloquent arrangement of the cliff faces on either side of the deep green canyon can be seen all at once, Yosemite Valley, as Muir wrote, "looks like an immense hall or temple lighted from above. . . . Every rock in its walls seems to glow with life."

Glacier-sculpted Cathedral Rocks rise majestically over the Yosemite Valley. These twenty-seven-hundred-foot-high granite spires were carved from a mountain by glacier flows during the formation of the valley millions of years ago, as were most of the area's distinctive rock formations.

John Muir is most closely associated with Yosemite and the Sierras, which he considered to be his spiritual home, for his extensive studies of horticulture and glaciers took him to Africa, Asia, Australia and across the North American continent from Alaska to the Gulf of Mexico. In 1892, Muir founded the Sierra Club as part of his efforts to secure federal protection for the Yosemite region. Today, Muir's spirit lives on in the work of this important organization dedicated to the conservation of the American wilderness.

Mist covers the higher reaches of Upper Yosemite Fall, which John Muir said had "the richest, as well as the most powerful, voice of all the falls in the valley." The Upper Fall cascades fourteen hundred and thirty feet; the Lower Fall drops a further three hundred and twenty feet to form North America's highest waterfall.

From Dante's View, high on a ridge over the desert ravine of Death Valley, the first chilly rays of the December sun lit up the peak of Mount Telescope, and the snow on it caught the light and glittered. As the sun mounted over the range of the Black Mountains behind, the pall of shadow on the valley floor began to lift and uncover a long lazy swirl of perfect white, a streak of salt which glittered like snow.

These salt crystals encrust the bed of an ancient lake that disappeared eons ago, for little water can survive the sun trap of Death Valley. It is one of the lowest, hottest and driest places on earth. In summer you could griddle cakes on the rocks, and boil water—if you could find it—on the sand. The ground underfoot is a fakir's ordeal, and at night the thermometer does not drop below 100 degrees Fahrenheit.

There are man-made masterpieces, like Stonehenge and Chartres Cathedral, which compress time until the men who built them and the years in which they were built seem within the spectator's grasp. But a natural wonder like Death Valley irons out and stretches time until the spectator feels infinitely alien, and infinitely small. Death Valley in the early morning light seems a place in slow motion, expressionless, silent and deaf. The huge earthquakes and upheavals, eruptions and ice floes that formed it took place far beyond the reach of fantasy. That time expands here is literally true. There are plants in Death Valley which flower every ten years, because a decade has become their natural cycle.

Geologists can read the causes of the valley's formation in the rifts and strata of its mountains and, according to their science, the same forces are still at work, tilting the valley floor and wearing down the hills. Yet, to the uneducated eye, nothing could look more immobile, more immutable than the stiff waves of sand and earth receding from Zabriskie Point over a terrifying distance. In the dawn light it is a bleached, albino landscape that seems to have suddenly stopped stock-still as it churned.

And yet "Death Valley" is a misnomer. It

Wind ripples the sand dunes in the ever-changing landscape of Mesquite Flats. These two-hundred-foot-high dunes form one of the most desolate parts of Death Valley. More than six hundred varieties of plants, however, survive the heat of the valley, including twenty-one species found nowhere else in the world.

SURVIVORS OF AN ANCIENT SEA

A million years ago Death Valley was filled with water, part of the Owens, Amargosa and Mojave rivers' drainage systems. The water remains today only in small aquatic "islands" like Salt Creek and Saratoga Springs, habitat of the Nevada pupfish, one of four species of *Cyprinodon*. These tiny descendants of ancient fish have adapted to the high temperature and salinity of the Death Valley pools. Male, top, and female of three species of *Cyprinodon* are shown, right.

Devil Pupfish

Nevada Pupfish

Death Valley

was a name given by a party of forty-niners who left the charted pass through the mountains to follow a quicker route, or so they thought—to gold. But the map they were given was a hoax and they were soon lost in the harsh Funeral Range. They fell to quarreling among themselves, even stole each other's food, and soon split up. Two families strayed into Death Valley, and on Christmas Day 1849 they camped by a spring now called Furnace Creek. One man died, and when they finally found a way out—they climbed over the huge Panamints, the most arduous route of all—a woman in the party turned and looked down and said, "Good-bye Death Valley."

These prospectors never struck gold in California, but in Western lore they figure as courageous pioneers. They were the first white men to see the valley, which they inadvertently named. With greater poetry the Shoshone Indians who hunted and even lived there called it Tomesha, Ground on Fire.

The name Death Valley is misleading because the land supports many bright desert plants, as well as birds and insects and reptiles and even the rare bighorn sheep. The kangaroo rat has adapted itself to the arid surroundings and no longer needs to drink water, but gets it from the plants it eats.

Above all, the valley's appearance is not always forbidding. In the cool of winter, when the sun has risen in the sky, it mellows the hellish bleakness of the place at dawn, softens its edges and unveils the dreaming pastels of the rocks and mountains. Pistachio, strawberry, vanilla, fudge, toffee—the ranges that enclose the valley are painted and striped as prettily as sugared almonds. In the shadowless noonday sun, the rolling peaks of Zabriskie Point looks like whipped cream and the rounded cliffs like huge helpings of sherbet. Where the earth has thrown a mountain on its side the strata look like candy sticks—the stripes of the earth's crust go right through.

In 1849, to lost fortune hunters, Death Valley was hell on earth. Today, to the visitor who travels there in safety, it looks more like a land where a rainbow came to grief.

vens Valley Pupfish

Sage grows in the cinders of the Ubehebe Crater in the north end of Death Valley. Thousands of years ago, a volcanic explosion in the Panamint Mountains overlooking the valley created this five-hundred-foot-deep crater with thick walls of lava and ash. Younger craters in the area indicate that there still may be some underlying volcanic life.

Pinnacles of salt cover the flat area known as Devil's Golf Course. Alternate flooding and rapid evaporation cause salt crystals to form these rough but intriguingly beautiful shapes. It is almost impossible to walk across this dry and pitted ground, and the flat is nearly devoid of animal life.

The Giant Sequoias

The Big Trees of the High Sierra possess the secret of eternal life, but, like the hero of the myth, they forgot to ask for the secret of perpetual youth as well, and they bear with pride the deeply scored furrows and batterings of the years. In a belt that stretches from the Middle Fork of the American River in the north through the Mariposa Grove of Yosemite Park to the Tule River in the south, the giant sequoia (*Sequoia gigantea*) stands on the heights of the western Sierra Nevada as it has done since before the Ice Age, for the gaps that interrupt its growth along the range mark the pathways of the ancient glaciers. The colossuses of the forest—like the General Sherman and General Grant in the Giant Tree Grove of the Sequoia National Park—were young sprigs when Nebuchadnezzar feasted in Babylon. They were in their prime when Hannibal challenged Rome. When Roland the Crusader fell at Roncesvalles they were already old.

It is not cunning or violence that has made the Big Trees the greatest survivors, but the very quintessence of strength itself, bursting from a seed that is smaller than an orange seed, equipped to withstand almost all onslaught and disease. The old sequoias are bulky, slow and sure, like the heaviest prizefighters. In a single branch from the main trunk of a tree, like the huge Grizzly Giant in the Mariposa Grove, is compacted more muscle, more tonnage than in the whole of one of its neighbors, the noble Douglas fir. The fibrous bark of the sequoia, a rich nutmeg in color that looks surprisingly light-skinned in the snows of the Sierra, is almost fireproof. The forest fires that sweep down can burn out the dead heartwood of the Big Trees, wound the life-giving sapwood, but only lick at the tough bark, the chief source of the tree's moisture and nourishment. When young, the sequoia is more vulnerable to the flames, but bark will heal over the fire scars in time. The tannin in the wood inoculates it against the ravages of fungi and insects, the mortal enemies of other trees.

But the storms of centuries have beaten down on the ancient giants and everywhere in the snowy forests is scattered the evidence of their enduring war. Each of the great trees stands ringed with fallen branches that the winds have torn from them and snows brought down. Lightning has lopped the crowns of all the most majestic trees and gashed the trunks of some from their heads to their hearts. A man can pass inside many a sequoia and look up the hollow shaft to the sky, where a few unvanquished branches still carry their tufted foliage and small trim cones.

Sometimes, weakened by the accumulated attacks of fire and wind and snow, one of the giants crashes to the ground, to lie there, like the weather-polished hulk of a shipwreck, for another century or more. For even in death the sequoia does not crumble or rot. As the naturalist John Muir wrote, "Most of the Sierra trees die of disease, fungi, etc., but nothing hurts the Big Tree. I never saw one

that was sick or showed the slightest sign of decay. Barring accidents, it seems to be immortal. It is a curious fact that all the very old sequoias have lost their heads by lightning strokes. 'All things come to him who waits.' But of all living things, sequoia is perhaps the only one able to wait long enough to make sure of being struck by lightning."

In 1852, one of the first white men to come across the Big Trees of the Sierra could not persuade his companions of the wonder he had seen. Later, he pretended he had killed a grizzly bear too big to haul to camp and led a party of fellow hunters to the grove. In 1855, the bark was stripped the whole way around one of the giants and reassembled in New York's Crystal Palace for exhibition. The Easterners refused to believe it. In Europe, experts argued about the discovery. Some insisted that the mammoth, or mastodon, as the Sierra tree was called, was related to the coastal redwood. Others claimed it belonged to the cypress and juniper family. The leading English botanist, John Lindley, named it *Wellingtonia gigantea* after the Iron Duke, who had recently died. His American colleagues countered with *Washingtonia gigantea*. Finally its kinship with the redwood of the Pacific was confirmed and the Big Tree was also called after the great Cherokee chief Sequoyah who, in 1821, had invented a phonetic alphabet of eighty-six symbols to write down the language of his tribe. Meanwhile, in the forests of the Sierra the tourists were flocking. In order to divert them, a roadway was hacked through one of the sequoias of the Mariposa Grove.

To prevent further desecration, the sequoias of Mariposa Grove were protected "for all time" in one of the earliest forest conservation acts passed by Congress. John Muir's campaign for further conservation led to the creation in 1890 of California's first national park, where the Big Trees can now propagate in safety. The young sequoias stand erect, concealing under silvery-gray trunks and delicate, almost fern-like foliage, the massive musculature that will insure they flourish millennia from now, when man's achievements may well have vanished altogether, just as their ancestors flourished long before man himself was made.

Winter in the Giant Forest, Sequoia National Park. Giant sequoias grow in groves of between six and sixty thousand trees. There are about seventy of these groves, all in a narrow belt two hundred and fifty miles long on the western slopes of the Sierra Nevada, at elevations of four thousand to eight thousand feet.

The world's largest living thing, the sequoia has a massive, gently tapering trunk. The biggest sequoia of all, the General Sherman Tree, has a diameter of thirty-six feet at its base. One hundred and twenty feet from the ground, the trunk is still two feet thicker than the fifteen-foot base of the world's tallest tree, a redwood.

Sequoia National Park was established in 1890 to protect groves of giant sequoia trees from the kind of thoughtless destruction epitomized by the Centennial Stump, right, in adjoining Kings Canyon. In 1876, a huge tree was felled and shipped to the Centennial Exposition in Philadelphia. The stump was polished and used as a dance floor.

A storm had blown up over the Pacific, hurling the ocean against the crags of Point Lobos so that it rose in towering columns of spray and roared like ten thousand lions together. A covey of cormorants, as sober-suited and orderly as Japanese tourists, were sitting it out on the bare rocks of Bird Island and, occasionally, a brown pelican rose in the gale and slowly flapped over the raging sea.

But one cormorant braved the heaving water in a cove and with a sleek movement of its black body dived for fish. For minutes it was underwater, but before it rose again to view, a lovely, sad, wise old face with two round brown eyes and dripping mandarin whiskers broke the surface. For a brief moment it gazed up at the men walking on the shore above, and then, with a practiced flip, turned over on its back, sank beneath the waves and was gone. It was a sea otter, one of the most cruelly hunted animals in the world, which feeds in the icy waters of the Arctic and the Pacific, and, protected now in California, numbers about a thousand strong off Point Lobos.

Point Lobos juts out into the ocean, which has carved it into a hundred spearhead rocks and islets and hewn a hundred gullies and inlets out of it to form a sleepless coastline of such dramatic beauty that as one walks there the greatest enterprises of man—the architecture of Michelangelo or the sculpture of Henry Moore—seem as passing as driftwood.

Curtains of rain sweep down on it, veiling the view in a misty light so that its promontories are blurred, as in a delicate watercolor. When the sky clears, the sun bursts through the reefs of cloud. Then the surface of the sea throws back the light like a mirror and the huge plumes of spray crash in blinding white foam against the rocks. It is a landscape in perpetual motion, the very antithesis of peace, and yet it fills the wanderer there with a peace that is grander than silence, grander than stillness.

The cape was called Point Lobos by the Spanish settlers of California after the "sea wolves"—sea lions—which still bask on its rocks and play in its raging surf. Its beauty was recognized by the Catholic friars, who christened the land up the coast Carmel, after the mountain of the Holy Land, and in 1770 established a mission there. Conservationists saved it from development in 1933, and it became a protected nature landmark in 1968.

Point Lobos forms only a tiny part of the long and magnificent stretch of the Pacific coast of California, but it is unique for its animals and, above all, for its trees. The southern headlands are covered in chaparral shrubs like wild mint, which scents the air, and in its coves, the bull kelp, a whiplike sea-weed, bobs above the water trailing its long tail like a malignant sea serpent. But its northern capes are quite different in character, for they are thickly wooded with fir trees. The light pierces these dark groves with an

eerie glow, catching on the luminous lace lichen that like the hair of a sea witch festoons the branches. The Monterey pine and the Gowen cypress, among the rarest trees in the world, grow here, and so do Monterey cypresses, which Robert Louis Stevenson called "ghosts fleeing before the wind."

Lashed by the elements, the Monterey cypress is making its last tormented stand on the jagged headland above Pinnacle Cove at Point Lobos. The roots of one tree, dubbed the Veteran, grapple with the cliff face, sending down long knotted limbs among the rocks and the star-shaped bluff lettuce for sustenance. Its trunk is crookbacked and twisted by the gales that for nearly three hundred years have waged war on it, but its branches, like arthritic fingers, wear their bright green rings of foliage in triumph. All around the Veteran, skeletons of warriors who have lost the fight raise their gaunt branches to the sky. In another group around the cove, the cypresses are rusted with red algae on their seaward side. And yet they thrive here, one of the only two places where they grow wild.

The poet Robinson Jeffers sang the battle of the untamed Pacific coastline near Carmel all his life. When, after two world wars, he despaired of the humanity of man, he wrote of Point Lobos:

*One light is left us: the beauty of
    things, not men;
The immense beauty of the world, not the
    human world.
Look—and without imagination, desire nor
    dream—directly
At the mountains and sea. Are they not
    beautiful?
These plunging promontories and flame-
    shaped peaks
Stopping the somber stupendous glory,
    the storm-fed ocean?
            Look at the Lobos Rocks
    off the shore,
With foam flying at their flanks, and the
    long sea-lions
Couching on them. Look at the gulls on
    the cliff-wind,
And the soaring hawk under the cloud-
    stream—
... is the earth not beautiful?*

The sedimentary rock at the Slot, a magnificent inlet along the south shore of the reserve, was deposited here about six million years ago. The formation, above, is a marine conglomerate made of pebbles cemented into sandstone.

The Californian sea lion, left, and the Steller's sea lion inhabit the rocky area off Point Lobos. They swim and steer with their flippers and bodies, catching food directly with their mouths. A Californian sea lion swimming underwater has been clocked at over ten miles per hour. This is the species commonly seen at circuses and zoos.

Point Lobos

Brown pelicans visit Bird Island at the south end of the reserve between the end of April and November. The only one of six species of pelican that is restricted to saltwater habitats, these expert divers use their large distensible pouches to scoop up fish.

Sea otters favor the coastal reefs and kelp beds off Point Lobos. They use their forepaws for many purposes—to cradle and play with their young, to shade their eyes from the sun and to secure and eat food, particularly shellfish and crabs. They eat then carefully wash before taking a nap in the same face-up floating position.

Pinnacle Rock, above, and Cypress Point, both located at the northern end of Point Lobos State Reserve, are the only places in the world where the Monterey cypress grows naturally. The area's fog, wind and salt contribute to the tree's slow, natural propagation, as successive wet seasons are required for seedlings to survive.

The California Redwoods

The redwood trees form a living seawall on the Pacific coast of northern California and southern Oregon. They absorb through their beautiful wine-red bark and bright green foliage the moisture that swells the air and loads the sea fogs, and trap in the broad and shallow labyrinth of their roots the gushing creek waters that they help to build and store. Water is the redwood's element, and the huge tree possesses all its mystery.

In the stands of virgin redwood in the deep, damp forests, the silence is as profound as in the ocean depths. Not a leaf rustles or a branch creaks. The springy carpet of rich red needles underfoot muffles all sound, and emerald moss, adorned with brilliant ferns, cushions the fallen trunks and branches. In spring, the purple rosebay rhododendron explodes in gaiety throughout the somber woods. In winter, the sun streams through, but its warmth and its glow is chastened by the solemn, austere giants, and it falls across the colonnades of the trees as in a great cathedral. Sometimes, the waters of a stream splash and dance over mossy boulders, brightening the forest's velvet silence.

Unlike the sequoias of the Sierra Nevada, the redwoods (*Sequoia sempervirens*) grow in serried ranks and their branches interlace overhead, obscuring the sky. They are stately in their every attitude, these trees that grow taller than all living things, that dwarf a village church and that tower over a four-story building. One hundred and fifty feet, sometimes even two hundred feet to the first limb, they seem to have soared heavenward as lightly as swallows, and bear no trace of effort or struggle. Yet their age is immense, and when they fall, each year can be precisely read from the rings in their heartwood—here Christ was born, here William the Conqueror fought at Hastings, and here—very near the rim—Columbus discovered America. Yet redwoods are younger than their kin, the giant sequoias of the Sierra, and they do not live as long.

Although they present a less embattled front to the world, their spirit is irrepressible. As with a rose, shoots spring up from the roots, but these saplings do not weaken the parent tree, which often stands proudly encircled by its smaller offspring. Even when cut down, the tree will not die, but breaks afresh from the stump. When a woodsman built himself a cabin of redwood timber, the logs themselves continued to sprout and he clipped his house regularly, as if it were a hedge.

In spite of this exuberance, redwoods are the gravest of trees. The giant sequoias in the mountains are like the brass section of a military band, but the redwoods, if they were to break their silence, would play a majestic and tragic requiem. John Steinbeck said that in the presence of redwoods, the vainest and most irreverent of men go under a spell of wonder and respect. The great Californian writer was, however, optimistic. Some homesteaders who acquired land in the redwood forests in the nineteenth century lived at peace with the trees, and even kept their animals in hollow trunks they called "goosepens." Some nature-loving hermits built themselves homes in the trees' hearts. But too many settlers thoughtlessly pitted themselves against the titans of the forest and later posed with pride for photographs over the wreckage they had caused. For redwood is the finest timber in the world—soft but durable, uniquely rich in hue and sheen, proof against fire and rot and beetle. Since 1830, ninety out of one hundred trees have been cut down or destroyed by natural forces. In 1918, the Save-the-Redwoods League was formed by some of the earliest conservationists, and gradually it began to buy forest lands in order to create three state parks, Jedediah Smith and Del Norte Coast Redwoods and Prairie Creek Redwoods. When, in 1968, the first national park of redwoods was opened by President Johnson, these three parks formed its core.

Theodore Roosevelt said of the Big Trees of the Sierra, "I feel most emphatically that we should not turn into shingles a tree which was old when the first Egyptian conqueror penetrated to the valley of the Euphrates, which it has taken so many thousands of years to build up and which can be put to better use. There is nothing more practical in the end than the preservation of beauty. . . ." His words still apply to the ancient redwoods of the coast.

In the winter, when the whales are making their annual migration to warmer waters in the south, they can be seen from the land of the Redwood National Park as they rise to the surface, spout a drifting column of spray into the air and then sink back again into the ocean. Thus, within a few miles of each other, the giants of the sea pass the giants of the earth on this part of the Californian coast. Both phenomena have, to some extent, been spared men's destruction, but the conservation of their beauty is still urgent.

Shafts of pale sunlight filter softly through the cathedral-like spires of a redwood grove. These tallest of all living things grew, in an earlier geological era, in many areas across North America. Today, they survive only in California, where they are protected in national parks and a number of state parks.

Early reports of the size of the California redwoods, including the claim of one prospector that he could ride his horse through the hollow trunk of one fallen giant, were largely discounted. Their final vindication came with the discovery that the world's tallest tree, 364 feet in height, was a California redwood.

Delicate rhododendron flower beneath the huge trees in Redwood National Park. These plants thrive in the damp and dark of the redwood forest floor. They bloom throughout the park in early spring, adding fresh, bright color to the splendid forest.

San Francisco Bay cannot be seen from the sea, so, in 1579, Francis Drake sailed past it in the *Golden Hind* and Spanish navigators, searching for just such a perfect landlocked harbor, missed it for nearly two hundred years more. The first white men to behold its level beauty came overland. Missionaries and soldiers sent by the Viceroy of New Spain to settle northern California were struggling north from Monterey when they came across "some immense arms of the sea which penetrate into the mainland in an extraordinary fashion." Seven years later—the year of American independence—a Franciscan monk, Father Pedro Font, realized "the Bay is a marvel of nature . . . the harbor of harbors." He planted a cross on one of the promontories and prophesied, "I think if it could be settled like Europe there would not be anything more beautiful in all the world, for it has the best advantages for founding on it a most beautiful city. . . ."

Two hundred years later, Font's vision spreads itself under a wild and pagan hunter's moon below the heights of Telegraph Hill. Tonight the city of San Francisco is fog-free, and the humps of the hills around the Bay loom sharp and black against the bluer black of the sky. The eucalyptus trees fill the night breeze with their heady, child's sickbed scent, and the gently ruffled surface of the sea blinks black and silver before the metropolis it made rich and powerful and gay.

The lights of Bay Bridge burn on one side; on the other hangs the spider-fine tracery of the Golden Gate Bridge with a mass of metal hurtling over it and two hundred and ten million unbelievable pounds pulling down hard and heavy on the slender threads which sling it from shore to shore. Down on the city slopes in the dark, jazz spills out of dives, touts bark, barrooms throb and the neon lights flash. A semaphore used to stand on Telegraph Hill to signal the comings and goings of the ships in the harbor; long ago the tall Coit Tower was built in its place. The tower is a monument to the San Francisco Volunteer Fire Brigade.

Overnight in the Gold Rush, San Francisco, a collection of huts until then, acquired a population, a branch of Rothschild's Bank and many other sophistications. The price of bread

jumped to seventy-five cents, and an egg cost a dollar. Ships sailed around the Horn to reach it, trains filled to bursting rushed overland. In the last nine months of 1849 over five hundred ships docked at the new boom town, and San Francisco embarked on its dizzy and violent whirl of pleasure. In the words of the ballad, Frisco was frisky. But the citizens stayed hard-headed, and problems or disasters were tackled and swiftly solved. In the 1850s the corrupt politicians were summarily hanged by vigilantes at their headquarters called Fort Gunnybags.

In 1873, when the rapidly expanding population began building on the hills around, Andrew Hallidie invented the first cable cars, which, whirring and ringing, still toil up and down the steep, stacked streets. In 1906, when

San Francisco was gutted after the great earthquake, speculators were soon dining out among the ruins to celebrate new building contracts, and placards in the street read, "Don't talk earthquake, talk business." And in 1937, the Golden Gate was spanned by the world's longest single suspension bridge, a feat of engineering designed by Joseph B. Strauss that remained unsurpassed until the Verrazano-Narrows Bridge in New York was opened in 1964.

But along with the native practical genius goes a streak of plain tomfoolery which applauds and dotes on eccentricity. During the Gold Rush days, Joshua Norton made a fortune which, like so many others, was lost just as fast. Dressed in an old uniform and carrying a sword he reemerged, a few years after his

San Francisco at night, seen from Yerba Buena Island. The illuminated San Francisco–Oakland Bay Bridge spans four and a half miles. Until the bridge was opened in 1936, parts of the Bay Area were linked by an extensive system of ferries. The ferries were abandoned in favor of a highway-bridge transportation system.

Traffic became so heavy, however, especially on the Bay and Golden Gate bridges, that the ferries have been reintroduced and are gaining a new popularity.

San Francisco

ruin, and called himself the Emperor of the United States and the Protector of Mexico. He issued several decrees and made several proclamations. The city's restaurants and bars entertained him free, and the banks let him cash checks—for fifty cents. When he died on the streets in 1880, he was buried at public expense with all ceremonies fit for an emperor.

Today, the spirit of play that is the essence of San Francisco flourishes still. At eleven in the morning the streets of Telegraph Hill are empty, except for a few young couples drinking the best capuccino in America and discussing the merits of different kung-fu champions. The shops' shutters are still up after the late hours of the night before. Only here and there, from the window of one of the sleeping pastel-colored houses, a maid shakes a duster in the bright morning air. Even the docks disguise their huge and serious commerce under an almost idle, toy-like appearance. To the visitor, the people of San Francisco seem to carry on their city's tradition that life is a continuous carnival.

On a corner of Fisherman's Wharf stands "The Only Human Jukebox in the World." On the makeshift booth instructions are daubed and inside, behind the curtains, a wild-eyed young man waits. If you put in your money, he will pop out and blow your selection on his trumpet. He plays badly, but acts a jukebox well and the crowd laughs and claps. Farther along the street, a lamb with a pink ribbon around its neck trots along the pavement, bleating. "Baa, baa," mimic the passers-by, grinning in the sunshine. A sallow young man, carrying a tiny barrel organ painted with flowers, slips out of the throng. He wears a drum major's braided tunic, his top hat is sequined in gold and he smiles and smiles. The lamb spots him, thrusts up its head and bobs up to him with a jaunty step. The young man smiles some more and then squats down, and while the lamb prances beside him begins to turn the handle of the barrel organ. People around are eating shrimps and crab from the wharf. The barrel organ tinkles, and they drop some tinkling money into the young man's box and then move along the edge of the Bay, laughing in San Francisco, in what Jack Kerouac called "the great buzzing and vibrating hum of what is really America's most excited city."

NORTHWEST PANORAMA

For much of the nineteenth century, before the states of Washington and Oregon came into being, the Pacific Northwest was known simply as Oregon Country. Implicit in that name was the acknowledgment that the area had a character separate from the rest of North America. Indeed, until 1846, the year that the American–Canadian border was agreed, Oregon Country had no recognized boundaries.

Only a century ago this wild mountain and forest land was still largely unexplored. It first became known to the Old World in the sixteenth century through the sightings of Spanish navigators. But two hundred years passed before there was any awareness of the area's rich resources. In the course of their voyage in search of the Northwest Passage, Captain James Cook and his crew traded with the Indians for furs, which they sold for huge profits in Canton. This started the fur trade, which brought the first settlers, shipwrecked sailors, to the Northwest. It was not until 1806, however, when Lewis and Clark, who had followed the route of the Missouri and Columbia rivers on their crossing of the continent, returned to the East, that the nation was first awakened to the potential of this far-distant land.

In the 1840s, little more than twelve thousand settlers took the hard and dangerous journey two thousand miles along the Oregon Trail to America's most remote and least-known area. They settled a territory of which very much less than a quarter could be cultivated. The rest was desert or rugged mountain country suitable only for rough grazing or trees. But lumber is a rich resource—in Oregon alone there is said to be enough timber to rebuild every dwelling in the United States—and irrigation schemes can drastically alter the land.

The Northwest now has vast wheatfields, apple and pear orchards, cattle ranches and dairy farms. Fishing, mining, chemicals and the aircraft industry have all brought wealth to the region.

But even today much of the one hundred and sixty thousand square miles of the two states are still uninhabited. And, therefore, every town and even the hearts of the cities are dominated by the sheer magnificence of the landscape. Within sight of great volcanoes plugged with solid ice, beneath some of the world's tallest trees, is the silent, haunting world of the rain forest floor. The backdrop to an unspoiled coastline, where surf seems to beat into the very heart of the forest, is a jagged mountain rim that cradles the still blue waters of a lake. From the indented coastline dense forests of fir and pine flow inland, covering the ground like an evergreen tidal wave, which only runs out of momentum on the upper slopes of the Cascade Range. These beautiful mountains, part of a chain running the full length of both American continents, form a guard of majestic glaciated peaks protecting the verdant valleys and high, dry plateaus of the interior. In this formidable confrontation of mountain, sea and forest lie the lasting riches of the still untamed Northwest.

Mount Rainier

Mount Rainier is a battleground of the powers of fire and ice. The rock of the mountain's volcanic core is superheated to white-hot liquid. Its summit crater, half a mile wide, is plugged by five hundred feet of solid ice and its rugged slopes are supercooled by the largest accumulation of glaciers in the continental United States.

Although Rainier is one million years old, in geological terms it is still young. About ten thousand years ago the summit was a thousand feet higher than it is now. Then an explosive eruption blasted it away. What happened to it is not really known—either it was hurtled some distance away or the top collapsed inward.

Today, except for some hot springs on the lower slopes and steam issuing from fissures at the 14,410-foot summit, there is little outward sign of the great heat deep inside the mountain. No significant volcanic activity has been reported for about six hundred years, but scientists, using infrared aerial photographs, which show the movement of the hot center deep beneath the crater, keep a constant watch for any increase of heat. The slightest rise in temperature might melt the ice in the crater,

allowing thousands of tons of water to break free and roar down the mountain like a dam burst.

Of even greater concern than volcanic activity, however, are the mudflows. These occur when extremely heavy warm rains cause crests of mud and debris, sometimes as thick as cement, to sweep down the slopes, leaving behind a trail of uprooted trees and dislodged boulders. The last major mudflow occurred in the Kautz Creek Valley in 1947, but more recent, smaller mudflows have also left their destructive trails.

At present it is the minus end of the thermometer which has the greatest influence on Rainier's life and conditions. World-record snowfalls for a single season of eighty-six feet and ninety-three feet were received here during two consecutive winters in the early 1970s. National Park rangers had to dig *down* to the second story of their station hut at Paradise, which is on the tree line, fifty-four hundred feet up on the south side of the mountain; tall fir trees in the mountain valleys suffocated under the snow; and the entrance to the famous Paradise Ice Caves, with their incredible

ice formations, was covered by fifty feet of snow.

As you climb from the foothill valleys of Rainier to its wind-whipped summit, the flora and fauna noticeably change. In fact, four of the seven "life zones" of North America can be observed on this mountain. Naturalists use these designations to differentiate between distinctive climatic environments and the animal and plant life which have adapted to them. The lower slopes of the mountain, up to three thousand feet, known as the Transition zone, are densely forested with Douglas fir, western hemlock and western red cedar. These gradually give way to the shorter evergreens—the Pacific silver fir, Alaska yellow cedar and western white pine of the Canadian zone. At Paradise, open meadows dotted with stands of crippled and stunted alpine fir, mountain hemlock and whitebark pine are covered by snow for most of the year. And, for a brief time in summer, they are ablaze with colorful wild flowers. Above six thousand feet is the arctic-alpine zone, a barren, windswept, bitterly cold desert area where vivid dwarf flowers bloom and herds of agile mountain goats roam the rugged crags.

The glaciers are the key to Mount Rainier's beauty. As the largest single-peak glacier system in the United States outside Alaska, it has twenty-six named glaciers, six of which radiate from its crown. Through three, and possibly four, ice ages, glaciers have gouged deep ravines in the mountain's once-perfect cone. Parts of the mountain are still being carried away by avalanches and massive rock slides.

An arctic island in the sky, Rainier creates its own weather system, which is largely independent of the weather affecting surrounding territory. More often than not it is wrapped in cloud as moist Pacific Ocean winds are suddenly deflected by the mountain's bulk. But when the clouds part and the sun washes its deep snow with a delicate pink light, the lone beauty of Rainier dominates the landscape for one hundred miles around. From the coastal cities of Seattle and Tacoma, the mountain seems to be at the end of every street. And, at this distance, its appearance belies its true nature—that of a mountain wracked by the elemental forces of fire and ice.

Captain George Vancouver, an English explorer, was the first white man to see Mount Rainier. In 1792, en route to Vancouver Island for the negotiations that resulted in the withdrawal of Spanish claims to territory as far south as San Francisco, Vancouver explored and mapped Puget Sound and in his log entry for May 7

recorded "a remarkably high, round mountain covered with snow." In his entry for the following day he named the mountain "after my friend, Rear Admiral Peter Rainier."

Mount Rainier's volcanic origins can be clearly seen from the air. Although the last major eruption took place two thousand years ago, warm springs still well from the upper slopes and steam issues from vents near the summit. "Eruptions," reported in the local press in the early 1900s, were probably columns of dust caused by rock avalanches.

Mount Rainier's rocky northeast face looms over a frozen lake on Burroughs Mountain in Mount Rainier National Park, right. The park covers 378 square miles, including the forty square miles of glaciers on Mount Rainier, the largest single-peak glacial system in the conterminous United States.

Crater Lake, relic of an ancient volcanic explosion, is rimmed by fifteen miles of sheer cliffs two thousand feet high and as jagged in outline as the edges of a broken bottle. Nearly round and more than five miles across, the lake is more than a mile above sea level on the crest of the Cascade Range in Oregon—an expanse of water so still and so remarkably pure that it looks as deep and clean and blue as the stratosphere. An eerie stillness seems to trap and intensify the mountain silence. Strangely, after a short time your ears begin to ring as if deafened by reverberations of the cataclysm which consumed a mountaintop.

But what captures the imagination is the specter of that vanished mountain, for it is impossible to admire the lake without reconstructing the phenomenon which created it. While Crater Lake plays tricks with the ears and its diamond brilliance is a feast for the eyes, the mind is busy recreating an event which took place about six thousand years ago.

The geology of the spectacular cliffs surrounding Crater Lake provides clues to the structure of the twelve-thousand-foot-high peak known as Mount Mazama, the name conferred on the area by local Indians long after the mountain was destroyed. Its complex and roughly conical shape was brought into being over hundreds of thousands of years by successive lava flows from the volcano. These layers can still be seen as clearly as the age rings of a log. Entire sections of cliff comprise fun-

nel-shaped masses of lava, showing where the side vents opened in the mature mountain, oozing molten rock down the slopes and indicating that the mountain did not have the geometric outlines of nearby Mount St. Helens and Mount Hood. Harder material forced into cracks in the mountainside from below remain now as buttresses, jutting out sharply and in a variety of colors. These variegations, vents and buttresses give a clear idea of the shape and size of Mount Mazama.

The U-shaped dips in the skyline around Crater Lake show where the side of the mountain was scoured into deep valleys and gorges by glaciers. Scratches in the glacier-polished rocks show the extent and direction of glaciers during successive ice ages. When the explo-

Crater Lake lies serenely amid the mountains of the Cascade Range. The intense blue of the lake is due to its great depth and the rare purity of its waters, which allow all the colors of the sun's rays to be absorbed except for the blue which is reflected so vividly.

SYMBOL OF FREEDOM FOR A NEW REPUBLIC

The eagle has long been a heraldic symbol of freedom, and, appropriately, the majestic American bald eagle was incorporated into the great seal of the republic, designed by William Barton and Charles Thomson, in 1782. At that time this magnificent bird of prey ranged over most of North America. Now it survives only in such remote regions as Crater Lake. The main cause of the eagle's sad decline was the excessive, uninformed use of some pesticides that have so drastically affected the birds' ability to reproduce.

sion occurred the glaciers were in their last period of retreat. The events which reduced the mountain to rubble took place within a matter of days.

The tribes of Indians inhabiting the forests and tundra of the Northwest must have stood in awe and fear as the great clouds of white-hot ash boiled miles high from the top of the mountain. Carried by the wind, it melted glaciers and set forests alight where it fell, covering five thousand square miles to a depth of up to twenty feet. Dust covered the landscape for six hundred miles to the north, far into present-day British Columbia. In modern times, only the destruction of Krakatoa in the East Indies, in 1883, bears comparison, and that was heard three thousand miles away. The Mount Ma-

zama explosion would probably have been heard as far away as Hawaii, Lake Erie and the Gulf Coast.

So much material, over half its height, was blasted from the mountain that the reservoir deep inside could not replenish itself in time to prevent the creation of a vast cavern. Almost eight cubic miles of solid rock shattered into fragments and slid with a crescendo of noise and rising dust into the hole beneath.

When the dust settled, a four-thousand-foot-deep caldera had formed in place of a mile-high peak. The rain and melting snow half-filled the crater to the point where evaporation and seepage balanced precipitation. Later, a minor eruption formed Wizard Island, a small cone of cinders in the lake. The lake

maintains a constant depth of 1,932 feet, making it one of the deepest lakes in the world. Some algae at the lake bottom are the only natural life there. Rainbow trout and kokanee salmon were recently introduced into the lake, but the water proved too pure for them.

Geologically, the great Mount Mazama volcano is now extinct, its energy expended. Crater Lake remains, beautiful and silent. During most of the year the craggy terrain around the lake is covered by deep drifts of snow, the dazzling white enriching the vivid blue of the water. The reflection, blurred here and there by soft breezes, seems unreal, and the imagination is easily stirred to a vivid re-creation of the holocaust that consumed a mountain.

Clark's nutcracker is named for explorer William Clark who first observed it. Unlike most other birds, it stays near Crater Lake all year despite the severity of winter at this altitude. Clark described it as a "new species of woodpecker" but it is classified not with woodpeckers, but with crows. It has the distinctive sedate walk and shape of a small crow, but Clark's mistake is understandable because the nutcracker, like a woodpecker, clings to trees and pecks in the bark for grubs. Using its bill like a crowbar, it pries seeds from evergreens, often storing them for winter. It also robs smaller birds of eggs and young, a crow family trait.

The rock formation known as the Phantom Ship, above, was named by early visitors to Crater Lake, who first noticed the uncanny way in which it became invisible in certain weather conditions.

Oregon Coast

Sea and forest are uniquely confronted on the two-hundred-and-fifty-mile stretch of Oregon's Pacific shore between the Columbia and Siuslaw rivers. It is the ocean, powerfully undermining and scalloping the land into a thousand bays and inlets, that dominates. But it is the contrast of the green tide of conifers, sweeping right to the brink of the windswept, wave-pounded shoreline, that gives the coast its distinctive and unforgettable beauty.

The brilliant sea seems bluer when set against the dark, muted coloring of the forest, which extends inland beyond the far horizon of lofty hills. The sparkle of the water is brighter when glimpsed through the soft gloom beneath the trees. The fragrance of wild herbs and pine resin mingles with the tang of the sea drifting inland on the breeze, while the stillness of the tall fir trees counterpoints the never-ending surge of the surf.

In the forests the silence is so pronounced that the faint whisper of falling leaves seems loud. On the beaches the continuous roar of the Pacific surf maintains such a steady beat that soon, like city traffic, it ceases to be heard.

The coastline displays marvelous variations of landforms. There are precipitous cliffs, in which the sea has carved blowholes, caldrons and canyons, which seethe with white water and foam. Between them are little sheltered bays with beaches of soft sand or small, smooth rocks, like cobblestones. Then there are long expanses of open beach, some stretching out of sight, others curving between bold headlands, seen indistinctly in the haze like ancient forts.

Just offshore the surf churns in fury around scattered rocks and reefs; some domed, like the aptly named Haystack Rock, others drilled by the power of the waves to form rugged archways. One of the most spectacular formations is a group of small islands called Three Arches, one of which is pierced by an immense tunnel. They are a national wildlife refuge inhabited by sea lions, gulls, cormorants, puffins, petrels and guillemots. And mocking the ravaging sea are the one or two gnarled old trees which grow on rocky islets.

In the morning, surf smoke hangs low in the valleys like a mist, drifting inland to mingle with the trees. Unable to rise because of temperature inversion, it forms a pearl-white smog, which gives the coastline the quiet, silky appearance of a Chinese painting. At this time you might see a deer, tiptoeing out of the still, shadowy forest and down to the beach to get salt.

The beach at the high-tide mark and the wide estuaries lying between the forested hills are littered with driftwood—sun-bleached and sand-scoured sticks, huge weather-silvered logs and whole trees, complete with roots, which have been washed down rivers by winter storms. The tidal estuaries attract many birds, including flocks of bad-tempered pelicans. Fishermen's dories dot the deep-water channels at the mouths of the rivers, almost at the place where the current plunges over treacherous sandbars to meet the swirl and surge of the sea.

At the midpoint of the coastline, extending for fifty miles south of the Siuslaw River, the forest gives way to sand. The Oregon Dunes are the most extensive and most spectacular coastal sand dunes in the United States. Reaching inland for up to three miles, they range in crests up to a mile long and three hundred feet high—billowing, wind-sculpted ridges of light-colored sand lying between coppices of scrubby forest and swampy lagoons.

The entire topography of the dunes can change during an overnight gale, which peaks the sand into new crests with steep slip faces like waves about to break. Valleys appear where formerly there had been ridges of sand, sometimes exposing the weathered remains of long-lost trees. And always the sand creeps inland, spilling deeper into the forests. As it advances, at the rate of about six feet a year, the trees die of thirst then stand gaunt and silvered until the wind breaks them and the engulfing sand buries them.

The beach stretches as far as the eye can see, a level runway of hard sand between booming surf and heaps of giant driftwood logs. Each wave deposits on the beach grains of sandstone washed from the cliffs farther up the coast; wind dries the sand and lifts it inland. The roar of the sea is lost in the deep valleys of shifting sands where the soft whistle of flurries of sand leapfrogging in puffs of wind makes an eerie background noise. After a gale has wiped the sand clean, the tracks of a bobcat or mountain lion may remain visible for a time in the open stretches between the clumps of dark green pines.

Far from desolate, the dunes support many forms of life and the Government has protected this sensitive environment by designating it a wilderness area. It is inhabited by 247 species of birds, including such endangered species as the bald eagle and the osprey, which sometimes can be seen hunting over the dunes for small mammals. In the lagoons herons stand motionless as they wait for an unwary frog or salamander to show itself. Two hundred whistling swans winter on one of several rivers that cross the dunes.

Apart from its abundance of wildlife and its dramatic ruggedness, combined with the subtleties of many natural contrasts, this Oregon coast is unusual because so much remains unspoiled while so little of it is officially protected. Man enjoys the meeting point of green forest and blue sea for its swimming, fishing, beachcombing and scenic splendor. The coast is inhabited, but so far it is not civilized. That is perhaps its greatest attribute.

Steller's sea lions bask on the rocks of an Oregon beach. Although in the last three decades there has been an overall decline in sea lion populations along the Pacific coast, in Oregon, where the Steller's sea lion has long been protected, there has been an increase in its numbers.

The potent forces of wind and sea have created two contrasting landscapes along the Oregon coast. In the south, coastal winds sweep a tide of sand as much as three miles inland, sculpting vast dunes. Along the northern coast, above and right, from the Columbia River to the Siuslaw River, dark outcrops of rock and rugged headlands, topped by lonely stands of spruce and pine, resist the surge of the Pacific surf and the power of savage gales.

Olympic Rain Forest

Fallen leaves do not rustle underfoot; they crumple like wet paper. Broken branches bend or tear, but do not snap. Soggy twigs fold rather than crack. It is a wonderland where delicate ferns and mosses flourish in the shade of some of the world's mightiest trees—an enchanting, mysterious and magical wilderness that is quite unlike any other place on earth.

The Olympic rain forest covers three deep glacier-formed valleys on the western slopes of the Olympic Mountains, near the coast of Washington. Technically, a rain forest is an area that receives more than eighty inches of rain annually. Here the moisture-laden Pacific Ocean airstreams are deflected upward so sharply by the mountains that they condense to form an astonishing yearly average of 142 inches of rain.

The characteristic of a true rain forest is perpetual dampness. The sodden, still atmosphere creates a natural greenhouse, where ferns, mosses and lichens cover every twig, branch and stump. Clubmosses trail from branches in long wispy beards. Velvety mosses quilt the rough bark of tall conifers and shroud the pulpy fibers of rotting logs. Ferns form crowns high up in the trees and tiny toadstools grow in the dark, damp hollows of tree stumps.

It is more like an underwater world than a forest. Short flashes of sunlight break through the green canopy of trees like reflections on the sea, while the light at ground level is a dim aquarium-green. The feathery mosses resemble wafting seaweed, and the impression of being underwater is heightened by the sensation of weightlessness you have when you walk on the thick sprung mattress of spongy mosses, ferns and creepers.

The Olympic rain forest is unique, not only in its atmosphere but also as a phenomenon of nature. It is the world's only true coniferous rain forest and the only temperate rain forest. Unlike all other rain forests, which are found in the tropics, it is not a dense tangle of vines and creepers because browsing black-tailed deer and Roosevelt elk keep the undergrowth under control. Consequently, the forest is a delight to walk through, and wildlife abounds. Tiny Douglas squirrels and snowshoe hares scurry about, cougars and coyotes stalk their prey, beavers feed on the bark of alders along the banks of dashing rivers and black bears fish for salmon and steelhead trout. The distant hammering of a woodpecker or the cackling of a jay emphasizes the stillness, and there is always the steady, muffled rustle of water dripping down from leaf to leaf, even when it is not actually raining.

Bastions of the forest are its great trees, which average two hundred and fifty feet in height, some topping three hundred feet. The largest known specimens of four species—western hemlock, Douglas fir, red alder and western red cedar—are found in or near its borders. Strangely, their roots go down only three or four feet, so eventually the giants are toppled by the winter gales, often gusting to more than one hundred miles an hour, that funnel up the forest valleys.

After a tree falls, the process of decay begins. This decay is a particularly potent force on which the renewal of the rain forest depends. Within five years the fallen tree is covered by a dense mat of moss and lichen. Then ferns take root, and in the water-softened bark of the dead tree seedlings of bigger trees spring up as a slowly developing forest in miniature. A twenty-year-old spruce might be only a foot high, yet its roots may have to go down twenty or thirty feet to reach the ground. Once it "pegs in," however, the tree shoots up, reaching its full height in about one hundred and fifty years.

A tree may live as long as eight hundred years, and it may be as many years again before all traces of it have disappeared. Nearly all the trees in the forest have begun life as seedlings on "nurse" logs and, in one of the remarkable features of the rain forest, have grown to create long and grand colonnades. At first the rain forest seems as haphazard as any jungle, but you soon realize that each tree aligns perfectly with several of its neighbors. Often you can sight through tunnels below the arched roots of several trees in succession, showing where the nurse log they shared has completely rotted away.

Every tree soon collects its own colony of mosses, lichens and ferns, called epiphytes because they are supported by other plants. One tree can carry as many as forty species of these delicate plants.

The imagination can run riot in a place such as this, yet the forest is neither oppressive nor frightening. It is mysterious but not ghostly, damp but not chilling. It is silent—yet alive with faint whispers.

The Olympic rain forest is a quiet, lush twilight world where time seems to stand still. Ragged damp club mosses drape the lower limbs of huge trees, left, creating soft cascades of green.

Colonnades of towering spruce and hemlock that began their life before the Revolutionary War straddle fallen nurse logs, above, which stood when Columbus discovered the New World almost five hundred years ago.

In 1879, the naturalist C. Hart Merriam described "a new elk from the Olympics" and named it for Theodore Roosevelt. Fittingly, in 1909, two days before leaving office, the President set aside a large area of the Olympic National Forest as the Olympic National Monument. It was destined to be the last refuge of the Roosevelt elk, then in danger of being hunted to extinction because of the popularity of the elk's-tooth charm. Today the browsing elk help give the Olympic rain forest its special character by preventing the undergrowth from becoming dense and tangled as it is in other rain forests.

Grimly unaccommodating but spectacularly beautiful, the North Cascades Wilderness is an unspoiled terrain of mountains, glaciers, lakes, rivers and virgin forests. Comprising several adjoining protected mountain areas surrounded by vast tracts of national forest, it is situated at the northern end of the Cascade Range. At its widest point, along the Canadian border, the range forms a mountain barrier so high that the mild, wet weather is stopped dead on one side and a new harsh, dry climate is created on the other.

The mountains are such a formidable barrier to the wet winds streaming off the Pacific Ocean that their western flanks trap an average of 111 inches of rain a year, while the eastern side averages only twelve inches. The result is a landscape of wonderful variety, where a dense and lush forest, notable for its tall fir trees and mossy undergrowth, meets an arid, mountainous tundra punctuated with gnarled pines.

On the rainy west side of the mountains temperatures vary only forty degrees between summer and winter, while on the east side the difference between the fierce cold of winter and the blazing heat of summer is one hundred degrees. The eastern slopes also suffer the drying effects of warm winter winds called chinooks, after the Chinook Indians, which suck out what little moisture there is in the soil.

The two tallest peaks, Mount Baker (10,778 feet) and Glacier Peak (10,541 feet), are extinct volcanoes. The other mountains, which face in all directions with no discernible pattern, rose out of swampland millions of years ago, then were gouged into saw-toothed crests and deep valleys by successive ice ages. Now 756 glaciers—nearly half the glaciers in the conterminous United States—blanket more than one hundred square miles of the mountains with solid ice.

So rugged are the mountains that to blast through them to build the North Cascades Highway required twenty thousand tons of dynamite, equivalent in explosive power to an atom bomb. But even the resources and skills of modern engineering are powerless against the forces of the Cascade weather, and the highway is closed by heavy snowfalls and avalanches for up to eight months of the year.

North Cascades National Park was delineated in 1968 in such a way that the North Cascades Highway provides the only major road access, securing the wilderness against the future. To the north of the park there are another eight hundred square miles of unblemished mountain territory, the Pasayten Wilderness, while to the south, almost as extensive, is the Glacier Peak Wilderness.

Eight mountains in the North Cascades rise to more than nine thousand feet above sea level, and dozens top seven thousand feet.

From one of the more accessible summits, such as Slate Peak (7,400 feet), which has a fire-watch tower at the end of a twenty-mile-long, rutted, one-lane gravel track, the sunrise can be seen flooding peak after peak. Between them, still and silent, the forested valleys remain in deep twilight or beneath seas of mist. Sometimes it is midmorning before sunrise comes to the valleys.

Shallow rivers dammed by beavers run over smoothly rounded gray rocks. The banks are lined with aspens, which turn gold in autumn. Where avalanches and rockfalls have torn

FLOWERS OF THE CASCADE MOUNTAINS

The forest flowers of the lower slopes of the Cascades, including mahonia, dogwood and trillium, start to bloom soon after the snow melts in April. The flowers of the trillium are white in spring but turn purple in summer when foxglove, lady's slipper and fireweed also flower. The high country flowers start to bloom in early June when the shooting star is found along streambanks. Aquilegia quickly follows, and in July Indian paintbrush and tiger lily are among the flowers that fill the upper meadows with color.

Shooting Star   Foxglove   Trillium   Mahonia   Indian Paintbrush

North Cascades Wilderness

through the tall timber, the fiery red and yellow autumn coloring of dense ground-covering shrubs spills down the mountainsides and into the valleys.

Hydroelectric dams have flooded some of these valleys, creating long, twisting lakes that give small boats access to part of the wilderness that previously was accessible only to hikers. There is a daily boat service on Lake Chelan, a narrow lake fifty-five miles long. Passing boats are hailed from the shore by hunters and hikers at trail's end after days deep in the heart of the mountain wilderness.

Crystalline lakes and plummeting waterfalls are hidden deep in the mountains. Bobcats and cougars live secretively in the high country. Skunks and porcupines inhabit the forests and shaggy white mountain goats, actually a species of antelope, take refuge on the high crags. Squirrels, including a nocturnal flying squirrel, abound in the woods, and there is a curious little rodent, called a jumping mouse, which leaps away in six-foot bounds when disturbed. Huckleberries grow everywhere, a favorite food of the black bears that live in all parts of the North Cascades Wilderness. In winter

large numbers of bald eagles gather along the Skagit River to feed on salmon.

The Cascades belong to the wildlife, for the area has defied man's efforts to tame it. The mountain wilderness is civilized only to the extent that in a clearing or alpine meadow there will be the acrid smell of wood smoke from a campfire. It is backpack country, where a five-mile trail will go four miles forward and one mile upward. Not territory for the faint-hearted; but for those with the will and strength to brave it, the reward of its wild beauty is unsurpassed.

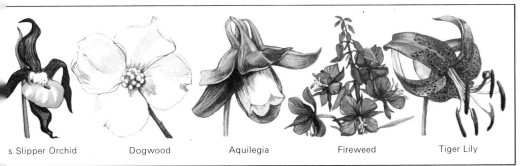

s Slipper Orchid   Dogwood   Aquilegia   Fireweed   Tiger Lily

In summer the high meadows of the Cascade Mountains are aflame with the vivid colors of alpine flowers. Plants growing at this altitude, sometimes over seven thousand feet, deepen their pigmentation to absorb the sun's energy and, to compensate for a short growing season, speed up their life processes.

Most of the huge expanse of America that lies west of the Mississippi was still unexplored when, in 1805, a small band of tired, weatherworn men triumphantly paddled their canoes into the Pacific Ocean. Led by Captain Meriwether Lewis and Second Lieutenant William Clark, they had been charged by President Jefferson to carve a track across the West to the Pacific shore of the continent. They were the trailblazers of a nation, and the last part of their long trek lay through a spectacular sixty-mile canyon—the Columbia River Gorge.

It must have been with mounting excitement, as they swirled downstream in the grip of the current and watched the high basalt cliffs glide silently past, that the adventurers tasted the river water, expecting at any moment to discover a tang of salt. But always there seemed to be more rapids to portage. And then one day there was a change in the character of the riverbanks. The river now was tidal. And salty. They had reached the Pacific Ocean.

Lewis and Clark were not the first to make use of the highway of the Columbia River Gorge. Before them, the Indians had traveled the turbulent river on journeys between the Rockies and the sea. But the river is, in fact, far older than can be imagined and, when the surrounding land was level forest and swamp, it served as a highway for the creatures of prehistory. Then, for millions of years, the Cascade Range pushed its way upward, at a rate of one foot every thousand years, and for millions of years the Columbia River remorselessly cut its way through.

This North American legacy of great geological forces in conflict has resulted here in unparalleled natural grandeur, which even the intrusion of modern man does not diminish. Erosion has prevented the milling mountains from closing in on the river. Cliffs rise abruptly from the shoreline to more than four thousand feet. The imposing snow-capped volcanic peaks of Mount St. Helens and Mount Adams, to the north, and Mount Hood, to the south, stand like portals on either side of the river, their foothills spilling down to confront each other, sometimes barely six hundred feet apart, across the water.

The sheer size of the spectacular Columbia River Gorge too often overshadows the secluded beauty of the secret creeks and waterfalls hidden away along its walls. Their splendor, like that of the deep mossy canyon of Oneonta Gorge, left, is on a different, more private scale.

Columbia River Gorge

Although the Columbia River was a god-send to Lewis and Clark, it was a formidable obstacle to the brave pioneers who determined to follow them to the rich and empty lands of the newfound Northwest. The settlers driving their covered wagons on the Oregon Trail in the 1840s were forced to a halt on its banks. They had to construct rafts and float west on the current.

Twelve logs were required for each raft. Because the rafts floated three inches below the water's surface wheels had to be laid flat beneath the wagons to keep them dry. Many were lost, dashed to pieces or overwhelmed. Halfway down the gorge, the settlers had to take to the land again for five miles to skirt rapids, where scores of Indians could be seen perching on rickety platforms, fishing with scoop nets for salmon.

Today the river is more of a highway than it ever was, but the going is easier. A six-lane freeway hugs the Oregon shore, at one moment curving around precipitous basalt bluffs, then tunneling through the solid rock. Elegantly engineered, the superhighway complements rather than detracts from the rugged grandeur and giant scale of the gorge.

On the Washington side there is a quieter, although more spectacular, highway. The engineers of both states have paid tribute to the beauty of the scenery by constructing many viewpoints, where motorists can pull off the road to enjoy it. Two railroads run through the gorge, following the water's edge, often on causeways. In midstream giant pusher barges and diminutive tugs, towing huge rafts of logs, struggle against the current and the angry whitecaps.

The river continues to be a highway for wildlife, too. Chinook, coho, sockeye, chum and pink salmon still fight the current on their annual sad journeys to the headwaters, where they spawn and die. But as they climb the man-made fish ladders to bypass hydroelectric dams on the river they are counted automatically by television scanner, and are gazed at by rows of people ranged behind windows as if at the theater.

Nevertheless, civilization has had little impact on the beauty of the gorge. The contrast of scenery is as vivid and exciting as when Lewis and Clark first wrote about it in their journals, and when Captain Robert Gray, a Boston trader, recorded his discovery in 1792 of "a large river," which he named after his ship the *Columbia*. The Oregon bank is steep and green, dripping with dew because it gets so little sun. Fir trees cling to precarious root-holds on high rocky crags and dense forests cover the gentler slopes. One of the many beautiful waterfalls spilling down its sheer rock faces is the Multnomah Falls, one of the highest in the country, which drops cleanly out of a forest creek down into a mossy pool.

The landscape opposite is bleached by the sun, drier and rockier. All the colors of autumn can be seen in the scars left by the rockslides; tussocky cheat grass, biscuit-brown in summer but green in winter, covers the steep slopes between outcrops of bare rock and shale.

Because the mountains act as a climatic barrier, freeway travelers can experience in a few minutes the transition between the severe desert-like climate inland and the milder, wet climate of the coast. And when fog creeps stealthily up the gorge to mask the hum of traffic, or you follow one of the many forest trails to some high and lonely vantage point, it is still possible to sense the raw power of this ancient and mighty river—and to appreciate what a challenging barrier it must have been to the gallant Americans, first the explorers, then the settlers, who pioneered the unknown hazards of this great waterway.

The land west and north of the Mississippi, acquired in the Louisiana Purchase of 1803, was largely unexplored. To lead a Corps of Discovery into the region, and, hopefully, find a route to the Pacific, President Thomas Jefferson chose two army officers, one his private secretary Meriwether Lewis, the other William Clark.

Their party, thirty strong, started up the Missouri on May 14, 1804. On November 7, 1805, they reached the Pacific by way of the Columbia River. On March 23, 1806, they started back east to arrive in St. Louis, exactly six months later after covering 7,689 miles.

Lewis

Clark

Sunset in the Columbia River Gorge. The Columbia flows more peacefully now than it did in the days when many of the pioneers lost their lives taking their wagons through the gorge on rafts. Celilo Falls, where the Indians once fished from precarious platforms, and the notorious cascade at the Dalles, where the river raged through the narrow crevasse, disappeared with the building of dams for hydroelectricity. Despite man's harnessing of its power, the Columbia remains the largest river to flow into the Pacific from the North American continent.

LANDSCAPE OF ETERNITY

Moviegoers all over the world are familiar with the dancing dust devils, the deep canyons and the sweeping horizons of this brilliantly colored desert spread flat beneath a perpetually bright sky. Neither a giant saguaro cactus nor a horseman with a six-gun in his holster is needed to identify the film as a Western and the location as the American Southwest.

Endless days of sunshine and clean air are the attractions which bring Hollywood's cameramen to Arizona, Nevada, New Mexico and Utah. Their films have immortalized this landscape, which is hotter, brighter, dustier and harsher than any other and is the most distinctively "Western" in the United States.

What the film action frequently obscures, however, are the wondrous geologic features of the desert, crafted by the meticulous processes of unimaginable time. In the awesome immensity of the Grand Canyon the rock stratas go back far beyond recorded history. In a badlands desert of blistering pink and burnished mauve lie petrified trees that were alive and growing when dinosaurs roamed the land, leaving their footprints fossilized in rock. The oldest living thing, the bristlecone pine, has produced annual growth rings for more than four thousand years in the sparse soil of Wheeler Peak. Erosive rains and chiseling winds have formed the magnificent sandstone arch of Rainbow Bridge and the multitude of spires, mesas and buttes in Bryce Canyon and Monument Valley. Water dripping for millions of years, in the vast underground chambers of Lehman Caves and Carlsbad Caverns, has created limestone formations that rival in delicacy and detail the great masterpieces sculptured by man.

In this desert powerhouse of heat, all life has had to adapt. Cacti have grown spines, with tips which are needle sharp and iron hard, to defend their moisture against burrowing rodents and birds. Animals, like the kangaroo rat, have adapted so that they do not have to drink water, but can derive sufficient moisture from eating the vegetation. The desert slumbers in the noonday heat and, like Las Vegas, springs to life at night. Here, flowers bloom in the dark and most of the animals are nocturnal.

Although it is a land where man does not dominate, the history of the Southwest is enriched by the legacy of its early inhabitants—Indians, Spanish explorers and pioneers. Nomadic Navajos and Apaches roamed and raided throughout the area, while the less transient Pueblos, Hopis, Zunis, Papagos, Pimas and Yumas built adobe and stone dwellings. The five-story community houses of the Pueblo settlement in Taos, New Mexico, remain today as they were when the Spanish arrived in the late sixteenth century. The Spaniards, in search of gold, conquered much of the Southwest, ruling it autocratically as a province of their colonial empire. For the pioneers who came in their wake, the desert, particularly near the Great Salt Lake, was a barrier to westward travel. This desolate and barren land exacted a heavy price from these courageous people.

Gradually, man has learned to adapt the desert to his needs. The people who live in this part of the country are still discovering its potential as well as its limitations. For here the frontier spirit is still very much alive. Americans are building for themselves the oasis "cities of gold" that the Spanish explorers sought but did not find.

The Grand Canyon

Its beauty is astounding, its magnitude overwhelming. At the first sight of this immense abyss, one of the greatest natural wonders of North America, you feel dizzy and elated. Here, unique perspectives mock conventional understandings of distances. From most viewpoints the pinyon and juniper forest continuing on from the brink of the far rim is about eight miles away, but it seems less than half that. The turbid Colorado River, glimpsed between an avenue of vertical cliffs deep enough to conceal the Empire State Building, is incredibly three miles out and one mile down.

You look down on geometric terraces of turrets, spires and cupolas, many of them higher than the highest mountains of the eastern United States. They are banded with differently colored formations, such as the brilliant redwall limestone that forms vertical cliffs three to four hundred feet high about halfway down the canyon, and continues for miles in every direction. Of varying hardness, they have eroded at different rates to form elaborate staircases.

The exoticism of these mystical bare rock structures is evident from their names—Krishna Shrine, Buddha Cloister, Tower of Ra, Cheops Pyramid, Siegfried Pyre, the Hindu, Ottoman and Shinuma amphitheaters and the Temples of Isis, Sheba and Solomon. Below them, three thousand five hundred feet lower than the south rim, there is an intermediate plateau called the Tonto Platform, a semi-desert dotted with clumps of low scrub. Through it twists the narrow slot of the inner gorge, which drops about fifteen hundred feet to the river.

The canyon has many disconcerting contradictions. Its yawning gulf of space is serene, but it is hemmed in by a topography of chilling savageness. Although the rocks are stark and gaunt, their beauty is ethereal. Distances are measured in miles, not feet.

The engineer of this colossal enterprise of Nature was the Colorado, the "red river," named by Spanish explorers in the sixteenth century, which rages through the deepest channel of the canyon floor for 277 miles. Until recently it carried an average half a million tons of sand and silt a day, as much as a five-ton truck passing every one second. The river was the scouring tide of liquid sandpaper that for thirty million years abraded a narrow cleft down and down through the layered rocks of the highlands in central Arizona. Meandering tributaries cut deep side canyons up to thirty miles long. Because the north rim is twelve hundred feet higher than the south rim it gets more rain and snow. Erosion was, therefore, greater and it is now about three times farther back from the river. Torrential summer rainstorms, snow and frost combined to create the fantastic array of mesas and peaks, their summits isolated, their foundations interlinked.

Light is the magician of the canyon. The sinking sun heralds a performance of unique natural splendor. The colored layers of rock burst alight, burning with a ruby and gold light like massive walls of glittering fireworks. The mighty temples are momentarily leafed in rich gold and lacquers. Velvet black shadows emphasize their brilliance, while the depths of the canyon are flooded by an ocean of vermilion dusk.

As you watch, the crisp edge of night advances upward, eclipsing the smoldering colors until there is at eye level only a single band of burnished gold lying across the canyon. Then the narrow light disappears abruptly and the canyon becomes a gulf of darkness. Perhaps a distant campfire, miles away, can be seen glimmering like a fallen star. With the coming of dawn the magnificent performance begins anew, this time in reverse.

Flat, hot daylight bleaches the tints out of the layered rocks and blends them in a haze of delicate blue. Often small thunderstorms take shape before your eyes and travel up the canyon. After the rain, fleecy clouds float upward in small gentle puffs. In winter snow falls upward as flakes are borne out of the canyon on currents of air. On very cold days crystallized snow collected by the wind sparkles as if it were gold dust falling into the canyon. Occasionally the entire canyon is filled with soft cloud and you feel you can walk across it.

The Grand Canyon comes closer to illustrating the realities of eternity than, perhaps, any other natural phenomenon on earth. Apart from its great depth, width and length, it has

"Each wall of the canyon is a composite structure, a wall composed of many walls, but never a repetition. Every one of these almost innumerable gorges is a world of beauty in itself. . . . Yet all these canyons unite to form one grand canyon, the most sublime spectacle on the earth." These words were written in 1874 by Major John Wesley Powell, leader of the first expedition to chart the Colorado River and explore the Grand Canyon. More than one hundred years later, visitors seeing the canyon for the first time are filled with the same sense of awe.

The Grand Canyon

a fourth dimension—time. Hendrik van Loon described eternity as a rock, one hundred miles high, wide and long, where once every thousand years a little bird sharpens its beak. When the rock has worn away, the historian wrote, an eternity will have passed.

Here at the Grand Canyon, entrenching downward through the rocks, the river has revealed a cross section of thirteen layers which were the seabeds, estuaries, sand dunes, deserts and river deltas of prehistory. These chapters of the earth's history go back two billion years. In them can be read the story of the parade of life on earth.

It begins with fossils of algal clumps, a form of the most primitive and earliest life known, found in the vertical cliffs of the inner gorge. It continues with the fossilized casts of soft-bodied undersea animals and the footprints of air-breathing reptiles found just below the rim. Upper layers, where huge dinosaurs roamed two hundred million years ago, have

The Colorado River winds through the narrow gorge of Elves Chasm in the Grand Canyon. The Colorado is nearly fifteen thousand miles long, from its source in the Rocky Mountains to the Gulf of California. Although it has cut nineteen major canyons, the Grand Canyon in Arizona is the most spectacular.

been eroded during recent geological history.

The canyon has a marked effect on present-day wildlife. Its floor is thirty-five degrees hotter than the north rim and receives only five inches of precipitation a year, making it a true desert. And it is the desert, rather than the swift river that is three hundred feet wide, which for millions of years has been a barrier to wildlife. Consequently, species on one side have developed differently from those on the other.

The tassel-eared squirrel, for example, has developed into two distinct subspecies. On the north rim it is blackish, with a white tail, but on the south rim it is gray, with a gray tail and a rust-colored stripe down its back. Isolation of the canyon depths has also played its part in the evolution of such subspecies as the Grand Canyon rattlesnake, which has become a unique salmon pink.

Compared to the immense span of time recorded in its rocky walls, man is new to the Grand Canyon. Three thousand years ago hunters used the remote caves in the canyon as shrines, where they left split-twig figures of deer, antelope and bighorn sheep. But little is known of these early visitors. Two thousand years later Pueblo Indians made their homes in small houses, mainly along the rims. They abandoned the area, probably because of drought, in 1276.

In the twelfth century a small tribe of Havasupai Indians found refuge in a long side canyon. These peaceful Indians continue to live in the riverside oasis of what is now called Havasu Canyon. Accessible only on foot or on horseback, the Indians were provided with prefabricated bungalows delivered by helicopter. Other tribes of Indians, Navajo, Paiute, Hopi and Hualapai, have hunted around the canyon for centuries and their reservations are nearby.

The first official exploration of the canyon was undertaken in 1857 by Lieutenant Joseph Christmas Ives, who wrote, "... after entering it there is nothing to do but leave. Ours has been the first and will doubtless be the last party of whites to visit this profitless locality. It seems intended by Nature that the Colorado River along the greater portion of its lonely and majestic way, shall be forever unvisited

and undisturbed." He could not have been more wrong.

Every year two and a half million people from all over the world visit the Grand Canyon. The first useful move to protect it was made by Theodore Roosevelt in 1908, and since 1919 it has been a national park of 1,052 square miles. But the Grand Canyon is unlike any of America's national parks, for you cannot wander freely through its wilderness. Exploring the Grand Canyon is mountaineering in reverse. Even people accustomed to wild places find it difficult to realize that they have driven directly to the top of a cool and sometimes snowy "mountain" seven thousand feet high, and are overlooking a terrain which is as rugged as the Rockies, but which is also a hot and arid desert.

National park wardens discourage people from wandering into the canyon because the grueling part, unlike ordinary mountain climbing, does not begin until you need to get out of the canyon. You then have to fight gravity, and the effects of altitude, when you are most tired. Every drop of water has to be carried and climbing from the bottom to the top of the canyon takes a full day. Only the most dedicated and fit hikers, armed with water bottles and permits, may tramp down to the campground by the river at Phantom Ranch.

Nevertheless, there are other ways of exploring the Grand Canyon. You can ride down the steep zigzag trail by mule—not dangerous, but terrifying. Or you can ride the two hundred rapids of the Colorado River through the canyon. For decades it was regarded as the fiercest stretch of white water in the world. Every summer sixteen thousand people float through the canyon. And it is they, men, women and children, who probably come nearest to terms with the reality of the canyon.

In large inflatable rafts or small wooden dories they ride the rapids, floating peacefully down the calm stretches and camping on the river's small beaches. Once committed there is no turning back. For ten days, drenched by the water that created the canyon and lulled to sleep by its thunder, they can experience the Grand Canyon, Nature's greatest feat of engineering.

THE CANYON BARRIER Once identical but separated so long by the Grand Canyon that they have evolved into two subspecies of the tassel-eared squirrel, the kaibab, bottom, is found only north of the Colorado River, and the abert, top, is found only on the south side.

Toroweap Overlook on Grand Canyon's North Rim affords a dramatic view of the Colorado River. Here, a visitor can walk right up to the canyon's edge and look straight down on the river some three thousand feet below.

This national park is a still and sterile world of darkness, stone and dripping water. It is a huge museum of geological craftsmanship painstakingly constructed over millions of years in a remote desert basement.

Some of the chambers of Carlsbad Caverns are so vast that when they were first explored they seemed to have no visible dimension. Men standing eight hundred feet below the ground with a bright petroleum lantern—the brightest flashlight available to cave explorers at the turn of the century—could see no walls around them. There was only an immense void of darkness in which fantastic dripstone sculptures seemed to float, disembodied. The ceiling reached many hundreds of feet up into the darkness. Huge, apparently bottomless, crater-like holes gaped in the floor.

Subsequently, the caverns proved to be among the largest in the world. They are probably also among the least claustrophobic, for the sense of spaciousness so deep underground is remarkable. Subdued electric spotlights pick out the vaulted roof, which in the largest cavern is 255 feet high. It is hard to believe that you are deep beneath the hot desert and bright sky of southeast New Mexico. From the moment you walk beneath the ninety-foot arch of pale rock which is the cave's natural entrance, or make the seven-hundred-and-fifty-foot descent by elevator, you embark on a unique adventure.

Before Carlsbad Caverns was made a national park in 1930, visitors were lowered through the entrance two at a time in a cast-iron bucket used for excavating bat droppings. It was bats which led men to the cave early in the twentieth century. For seventeen thousand years a large colony of bats, mainly Mexican freetails, has spent the summer in a chamber near the entrance. At sunset five thousand bats a minute spiral up like grass smoke, forming a seething cloud against the dusky desert sky.

Cowboys investigating this unusual "smoke" found huge deposits of guano in the cave. In twenty years, oné hundred thousand tons of guano were mined for fertilizing citrus trees in California, and it was the miners who first penetrated the deeper parts of the cave. They had already discovered paintings made near the entrance a thousand years before by Indians, who seem to have been afraid of the cave's deeper darkness and mystery.

Today the flight of the bats is a spectacle watched each day by hundreds of people from an amphitheater constructed around the cave entrance. Once the colony numbered about three million bats; now the population is estimated to be one hundred thousand. During the night'they fly about one hundred and twenty miles, consuming nearly a ton of insects. At dawn they dive directly into the cave with loud zipping sounds and spend the day sleeping upside down on the roof—nearly three hundred bats to the square foot.

The outside world is left behind with the last pale shred of daylight as you zigzag down the narrow throat of the cave. The trail winds around and beneath a huge boulder. Then, at the bottom of the cave, nearly nine hundred feet beneath the surface, the rock-strewn narrow and steeply sloping entrance corridor

THE BATS OF CARLSBAD CAVERNS

Many of North America's fifty species of bats have been seen in the caves at Carlsbad, where they are left undisturbed by visitors. The majority of bats there, however, are Mexican freetails, left, a migratory species. The female bats arrive at the caverns in the spring. They soon give birth to their young, which for the first few weeks of their lives cling to their mothers' fur, even during the nightly flight to feed. When they become too heavy, they are left clinging to the roofs of the caves. When the mothers return each

Carlsbad Caverns

leads into chambers of jeweled splendor. Limestone formations decorate suites fit for a royal palace. Chandeliers, dripping with diamond like nodules of crystalline stone, are suspended above a ballroom floor glittering with stalagmites, which take the shape of richly costumed courtiers. Folded draperies and elaborate tapestries cover the walls. Everywhere you look there is a fairy-tale tableau frozen in stone.

Only five percent of the formations are still active, and these grow by the thickness of a coat of paint every ninety years. The great caverns were dissolved from limestone over millions of years. When the land was uplifted the water drained out, and the millimetric accumulation of sediment deposited by water dripping from the ceiling began the interior decoration of the caves.

It was in what is known as the Big Room that the first explorers were so mystified by the cave's spaciousness. The perimeter of the room, which has fourteen acres of floor space, is one and a quarter miles long. It is really a series of interconnecting chambers arranged in a T-shape, which measures eighteen hundred feet one way and eleven hundred feet the other. The deepest of the holes, which the early explorers thought were bottomless, is 138 feet deep.

It is the sheer scale of the Carlsbad Caverns that makes them a subterranean miracle, a wilderness of the great indoors.

morning, rather than seek out their own young, they nurse the baby nearest to them. When the males first return from their winter quarters in Mexico they find other shelter, only rejoining the Carlsbad colony in summer. The population can then reach a peak of over a hundred thousand. In late October or early November the final evening flight occurs. The bats leave the cave at their usual rate of over five thousand a minute, but they will not return until the next spring.

Stone chandeliers adorn the ceiling of the King's Palace, the most ornate of Carlsbad's fifty caverns in the national park area. The glittering formations in the circular chamber are built of cave onyx. The colors in the rock are caused by iron oxides and other minerals.

The icicle-like Lion's Tail stalactite is one of thousands of limestone formations in Carlsbad Caverns. Stalactites, which grow down from the ceiling, and stalagmites, which extend up from the floor, are deposits of calcium carbonate formed by mineral-laden water dripping slowly through the porous rock. Carlsbad Caverns are now primarily dry caves, for the source of water has diminished over the years. Because many of the formations stand on flowstone laid above silts and fossils whose geologic age is comparatively recent, scientists have been able to determine that they have been created within the last one hundred thousand years.

Bryce Canyon

If every pink, red, orange and white flower growing in the world were arranged in a bank twenty miles long and fifteen hundred feet high it might begin to resemble the brilliant colors of bare and crumbling rocks that form Bryce Canyon in Utah. At first glance the canyon gives one instant flashing impression of an engulfing chasm of fire that is on the point of sliding away into the valley beyond. But there is no smoke, no heat; everything is so still. Then individual tones and stripes in the rocks assert themselves and you begin to see the astonishing landscape as a mosaic of separate yet complementary shades and hues.

As if this were not enough there is a second and equally amazing phenomenon of the canyon. Below you is an incredible mass of shaped rocks which look like thousands of sunburned people up on their feet and cheering. The Paiute Indians, who hunted in the canyon, called it "Unkatimpe-wa-wince-pock-ich," Red rocks standing like men in a bowl-shaped canyon. They had a legend that the war-painted throng was turned to stone by the spirits because they fell into degenerate ways.

Some of the hibiscus-hued rocks are nearly three hundred feet high and stand so closely together that you can barely walk between them. Others are capped by amusing shapes. There is the exact image of a disdainful Queen Victoria, another of a wise man and his camel. There are so many pinnacles of varying shapes and sizes that you might have stumbled upon a world congress of chessmen, the teams of red and white intermingled or collected in family groups. Round-topped pawns, thousands of them, stand on slim, waisted pillars. Grim-faced kings look aloof as their bosomy queens flirt with narrow-faced bishops. Turreted castles, invincible atop slender columns rising scores of feet from the canyon floor, stand back in groups, while dashing knights patrol the canyon's rim.

Actually this is not a canyon but a horse-shoe-shaped basin of twenty miles of alcoved cliffs. Geologically it is a badlands scenery. The soft deposits of limestone laid down as silt by rivers millions of years ago are now being carried away again by the combined forces of rain, snow and wind. The rim of the basin retreats about one foot every fifty years.

The marvelous colors, which change with the time of day and the weather, are due to minute quantities of minerals in the rock. White is the natural color. Reds and yellows are pigmented by traces of iron, lavender and purple by manganese.

The combination of color and sculpture of Bryce Canyon makes it one of Nature's masterpieces. But for Ebenezer Bryce, a Mormon farmer who settled near the red rocks in 1875, and after whom the canyon was named, the petrified sunset forever glowing along the boundary of his land had a more prosaic significance. "It's a hell of a place," he said, "to lose a cow."

Bryce Canyon's Wall of Windows. The openings are caused by erosion, as layers of soft rock crumble beneath the stronger arches. Slowly, as the cracks deepen and widen, the windows enlarge. Eventually, the arches will also be worn away and the windows will become deep cracks between sharp spires.

Snow covers the castles and spires of Bryce Canyon, adding a new dimension to the multi-colored landscape. Snow and ice increase the erosional processes, as water which has seeped into crevices in the rocks freezes and expands, widening the cracks and causing some formations to crumble.

Rainbow Bridge

It conveys an overwhelming sense of strength and power, a rock sculpture hewn from the muscle and gristle of the earth yet with a form of great simplicity and beauty. A flame against the bright desert sky, the red rock, varnished with tints of dark lavender, seems electric with energy.

Arching across a canyon in the red rock desert just north of the Arizona–Utah border, Rainbow Bridge, a translation of its Indian name, is the largest known natural bridge in the world. It is an almost perfect quarter circle, reaching upward and outward from the rim of the sheer cliff which forms one side of the canyon. After a short distance it levels off, and, like the trajectory of a stone thrown over a high cliff, curves gradually downward to meet the canyon floor.

The center of the arch is rounded, like a giant cup handle. Its lower end is slab-sided, where massive chunks of rock have fallen away, leaving smooth surfaces that appear to have been shaped by skillful blows of an adz. The entire structure is so beautifully proportioned and elegantly designed that you feel it could only have been constructed by some positive force skilled in artistic geometry; it is hard to accept that this masterpiece of dynamic form is merely the relic of randomly destructive processes.

The red rock originated from a thousand feet of windblown sands which accumulated on an immense desert. They were compacted beneath sediments and finally exhumed by uplifting pressures of the earth which caused the upper layers to erode. Rainbow Bridge is all that remains of an isolated knob left jutting into the canyon, which was carved by a meandering creek. Intense summer heat and night chill caused the sides of the buttress of rock to become thinner until a window was formed. As rubble was carried away by flash floods the opening was made wider, while persistent winds and other erosive forces grad-

ually put the finishing touches to the bridge.

Later the creek was diverted, perhaps by a rockfall, and it cut a small canyon beneath the arch. Today, its small pools of clear water perfectly reflect the brilliant colors of the bridge and provide a narrow oasis of scrub oak, juniper and bright spring flowers.

When Rainbow Bridge was officially put on the map by an exploration party in 1909, it could be reached only by a horseback journey over some of the grimmest territory in the country. But in 1964 the blue water in Glen Canyon Dam began to fill the ninety-one canyons running into the Colorado River, creating a remarkable red rock coastline nearly two thousand miles long. Now boats travel sixty miles up the canyon in two or three hours and berth within yards of the great sandstone bridge. When the dam finally fills to capacity, a narrow arm of water, like a fjord, will lie beneath what the ancient Indians believed was a rainbow petrified in stone.

Rainbow Bridge is the world's largest natural bridge. It forms an almost perfect rainbow-shaped curve, which arches gracefully to a height of 309 feet, high enough for the Capitol in Washington, D.C., to fit neatly beneath it. At the top the bridge is wide enough to accommodate a two-lane highway and it spans a distance of 278 feet. The bridge is situated at the northern edge of the land the Navajo Indians called their own, and it was they who gave it its name, Rainbow Across The Sky.

Prickly pear cactus blooms in early spring, bringing color to the barren desert and dry canyons around Rainbow Bridge. The tunas, dark, pear-shaped fruit, are a favorite food for such animals as the javelina, a wild pig. Tunas were made into a preserve by local Indian tribes.

The desert is a vast three-dimensional kinetic sculpture of bare earth streaked with bands of vibrant color. Constantly shifting shades and hues, combined with tricks of light, cast a hypnotic spell. Clay slopes tinted rosy pink change to geranium red as the sun sinks in the sky, and a delicate shade of lavender instantly becomes deep purple in the shadow of a cloud. The desert has a beauty that is breathtaking in the range and mobility of its colors. Yet this beauty is so subtle that it seems transient, as if the next rainstorm will wash it all into the river.

This geographic mural has been crafted by a one-hundred-and-fifty-mile sweep of the Little Colorado River. For many thousands of years the river has eaten like an etcher's acid through layers of silts and sands, creating a typical badlands canyon ten to fifteen miles wide. The floor of the shallow canyon is flat and scattered with mesas and fissured hills, many not much larger than haystacks. The canyon's meandering rim provides the vantage points from which you overlook the spectacular colors, predominantly pink, gray and purple, banded in the dry earth.

The Painted Desert is on the western edge of the Hopi and Navajo Indian reservations in the center of Arizona. Highways run through it so that suddenly you find yourself driving among hummocky hills that seem to pulsate with hot color. But the most magnificent area of desert finery has been preserved by the Government as the Petrified Forest National Park, insuring that stark roadside telegraph poles and motel signs are kept in their place. Here the wilderness of the Painted Desert is as unblemished as when it was named by the Spaniards who followed Coronado into the area in the sixteenth century.

For most of the year the earth bakes beneath an intense sun, forming a dry and brittle crust that cracks into geometric shapes like the glaze on ancient pottery. It is true desert in that it receives only nine inches of moisture a year, but more than half comes as violent rain. No winged seed landing on the inhospitable slopes is able to withstand the brief summer thunderstorms, which lash down with such force that up to an inch of soil a year is carried away in muddy torrents and trapped behind dams on the Colorado River. By this means the desert palette is constantly renewing itself.

Beneath the bright, flat sunlight at noon the pigments—formed by traces of minerals in the soil—are pale and dusty. In the heat of the day a veil of bluish haze and mirage effects add their own mysterious touches to the interplay of faded color, which after a rainstorm

Nature's artistry is revealed in the subtly colored chips, chunks and logs in Rainbow Forest, one of six areas of petrified trees in Petrified Forest National Park. The tree trunks contain a variety of semiprecious stones, and the ground is strewn with bits of onyx, agate, jasper, carnelian and rose quartz.

The Sonoran coral snake is one of the most venomous reptiles of the Painted Desert. Its brilliant stripes may serve as a warning device to protect the snake from predators and also help to camouflage it. The scarlet king snake, a harmless species, has this same coloration and is afforded the same protection.

Painted Desert and Petrified Forest

take on a new depth and luster. In the soft and diffused glow of sunset and sunrise, the horizontal stripes of saffron, crimson and purple which decorate the bare hills stand out as vividly as the patterns of Navajo rugs.

But the wonder of its color is not the only natural miracle of the Painted Desert. Scattered over part of this unique landscape are the petrified remnants of an ancient forest. The petrified logs of massive trees have been exposed by the gradual erosion of the soft land surface. Some jut from steep slopes or have rolled into gullies. Others lie scattered about like driftwood. They seem real enough to gather for the fire; the debris of broken chips around them is just like the debris surrounding a backyard chopping block. But there is no sweet smell of wood sap. The chips clink noisily underfoot, like pieces of slate, and are five times heavier than natural pinewood. To

pick one up is to step back into the age of dinosaurs, for these "wood chips" have flown before the axes of unimaginable time—they are as much as two million years old.

Once these trees grew majestically two hundred feet above what was a tropical swamp inhabited by primeval creatures. When the trees died and fell, floodwaters heaped them together in logjams, which sank into a marsh and were buried by sediment and then by layers of rock. Deprived of oxygen, the wood did not rot. Instead, mineral-laden water seeped into every pore and cell, turning the wood to stone.

In some logs the detail of the wood was reproduced exactly in stone. In others the log served as a mold in which large crystals formed gemstones of amethyst, citrine, agate, jasper, onyx and rose quartz. Most logs were long ago cracked into even lengths by earth-

quakes, and their exposed butts have been polished by wind and abrasive dust to reveal beautiful swirling colors in the stone. Navajo and Paiute Indians believed the logs were the arrow shafts of their thunder god or the bones of the great giant of their mythology.

The gemstones have a high commercial value and, at the end of the nineteenth century, many petrified logs were destroyed by treasure hunters, who dynamited them to bits. Now, in the national park, it is a felony to collect even the smallest specimen.

When cut and polished by a craftsman the smoky hues of the petrified wood become brilliant. There are coral pinks and mother-of-pearl grays, vivid greens and bright yellows, deep lagoon blues and rusty browns—all the colors of the Painted Desert intensified and crystallized in jewels buried in the desert's own woodpile.

A bobcat rests in a rock crevice after a night of hunting. Rarely seen after sunrise, the nocturnal bobcat sleeps through the intense heat of a Painted Desert day, waking after dark to stalk rabbits, rats, mice and, occasionally, such large prey as deer and antelope.

Colorfully banded buttes reveal the ancient layers of the marsh which once covered the Painted Desert's Blue Mesa, a part of the Chinle Formation of northeast Arizona. The multi-colored sedimentary layers are the result of iron oxides and other minerals, which have tinted the clay a remarkable range of hues.

The water tasted so strongly of salt that perhaps a man could not be blamed for claiming discovery of an arm of the Pacific Ocean. It was in 1824 that Jim Bridger, mountain man, adventurer and explorer, who was gaining his unique knowledge of the unknown western heartland of the continent, made that claim. Clearly, however, he knew little about the sea. For the strangling taste of the soupy green water, lapping a shore of formidably arid desert, was six or eight times saltier than that of seawater. He had found not the ocean, but the largest salt lake in the western hemisphere—the Great Salt Lake.

The lake itself is a liquid desert. Thirteen feet deep and covering fifteen hundred square miles, it offers no value to the surrounding land, where fresh water is worth diamonds. Nothing but tiny shrimps can live in its brine. Only the hardiest plants survive on its shore, much of which is briny mud and extends, desolate and barren, for as far as the eye can see. Even birds nesting on the lake's islands must fly dozens of miles to find food and fresh water. West of the lake's bleak and naked shore the wasteland is so flat and featureless that you can see the curvature of the earth.

To Jim Bridger, however, the wide expanse of glassy water, which perfectly reflected the distant snow-capped peaks, was "paradise." It was probably the magnificent calm emptiness of the area that appealed to this man, who spent most of his life in hostile wilderness.

Despite the railroads and highways that cross the desert as straight as ruled lines, you can stand out in the open and experience today —as Bridger must have done a hundred and fifty years ago—an exciting sense of total isolation. Mountains like silk-screen prints jut up into the sky, sometimes strangely inverted in shimmering mirages, or seem to float on wobbling pillars of mercury. On a hot day the great saucer of desert all around you seems to melt away at the edges.

In the summer of 1847 Bridger fell in with a party of pioneers hurrying west along the migration trail to settle the "paradise" he had discovered twenty-three years before. They were the advance party of a large body of Mormons, who had suffered religious persecution in the East and were now seeking their new Zion in the Salt Lake basin. They were led by a man named Brigham Young who, armed with only a sketchy map and divine inspiration, was pleased to be able to get information from the renowned traveler. But he was less than pleased at Bridger's magnanimity in agreeing to "share" with the Mormons the basin of the Great Salt Lake, and was worried by Bridger's warnings of the difficulties of cultivating crops there.

Before the end of the summer Salt Lake City had been founded and fifty acres irrigated and plowed. For the next twenty-one years migrations of Mormons, from as far away as eastern Europe, flooded across the Great Plains and the Rocky Mountains to the desert city. And they all had to pass Fort Bridger, established by Bridger to supply and support migrants heading for Oregon and California as well as Salt Lake City. The salt desert was Bridger's paradise and Young's promised land. It was not long before the two fell out.

On the pretext that Bridger was inciting Indians to attack, Mormons ran Bridger out of his fort and looted it. When the Mormons, asserting their independence of the United States Government for the last time, evacuated their city during the brief war with federal forces, it was Bridger who rode triumphantly at the head of the cavalry column

THE KINGDOM OF GOD ON EARTH

In 1847, Brigham Young, leader of the Mormons, stood on the shore of the Great Salt Lake with his followers and envisioned a perfect city for his Saints. Salt Lake City was founded the same year, and Young marked off an area for Temple Square, the future spiritual center for the Kingdom of God on Earth. Ground was broken for the gray granite Temple in 1853. Young never saw his cherished project completed. He died sixteen years before it was dedicated on April 6, 1892.

Great Salt Lake Desert

through the empty streets of Salt Lake City.

Today the modern Utah city with its Mormon Temple and world-famous Tabernacle is proof enough of Brigham Young's assertion that "the desert will blossom like a rose." Immediately behind the city, to the east, rise the Wasatch Mountains, which provide its water supply. To the west lies the empty desert and its sterile sea.

Although it often rains in the desert, the raindrops usually evaporate before they reach the ground. The desert gets four inches of precipitation a year, but has the potential to evaporate twenty-four inches. Consequently, the lake, now only a remnant of a huge pre-

historic body of fresh water that filled the mountain-rimmed basin of the desert to a depth of a thousand feet, is constantly diminishing. Over the centuries huge amounts of salts have been concentrated in a reducing amount of water. In 1850, men dangled joints of beef in the water overnight and found it "tolerably well pickled" by morning. The lake is thought to hold at least eight billion tons of salt, and every year about four hundred thousands tons are reaped by solar harvest for the nation's tables and icy roads.

Encrustations of salt have formed dead-level plains so firm that if a car tire blows out at great speed the rim of the wheel will not

dig below the surface. One hundred square miles of these salt flats have been used to topple one speed record after another.

For swimmers in the lake, the seventy-six pounds of salt per cubic foot causes many strange effects. The water is so buoyant that you can sit in it and read a newspaper—although it takes practice to get your feet down far enough. The water stings like soap and it is an old Salt Lake trick to lick your fingers before rubbing your eyes. As you taste the bitter water it is not difficult to put yourself in the place of Jim Bridger, who claimed the Great Salt Lake and its desert as his own particular paradise.

Crystallized salt ridges break the monotonous flatness of the Bonneville Salt Flats. The Wasatch Mountains, rising in the background, were once the shores of an enormous lake. Today, only a small remnant of that vast body of water remains as the Great Salt Lake. The rest has evaporated, forming the Great Salt Lake Desert.

Sagebrush pokes through cracked saline mud in a salt flat of the Great Salt Lake Desert. Many species of salt-tolerant and drought-resistant plants, including salt grass, pickle weed and greasewood, survive in this inhospitable land. The marshes around the Great Salt Lake form America's largest sanctuary for migratory

birds, where some two million birds take refuge each year. Islands in the lake support nesting colonies of great blue herons, great white pelicans, Caspian terns and California sea gulls.

It was John Ford's location. Against its massive backdrop, real or projected, he rolled wagons, tracked Indians, framed hold-ups and shot "the Duke" to stardom. Monument Valley became the familiar landmark of his films, the camera panning across the sagebrush flats and halting, surprised, awestruck, before the sudden eruption of those great buttes from the earth's floor, huge broken molars out of the mouth of time. Then the lens would close in, focusing on Ford's other granite trademark, the figure of John Wayne, pioneer or cavalryman, squaring up to the landscape, the enemy of decay.

Ford first went there in 1939, for *Stagecoach*, his first sound Western, arguably his greatest. The setting was used to telling effect—the big-frame shot of the tiny stagecoach rattling along between the shadows of the giant rocks, a suggestion of menace unseen, of ambush awaiting, then a switch to the hothouse drama in the coach, the wild look in John Carradine's eye and the thud of the first arrow pinning Donald Meek in the shoulder. In the midst of this, John Wayne as the Ringo Kid, coolly twirling his Winchester, gave his first "big" performance in the movies.

Ford and Wayne were to return in partnership to Monument Valley in the postwar years. And nothing could better illustrate Ford's feeling for the actor and the place than the opening and closing shots of *The Searchers*, where Wayne and the valley are seen through a doorway, monumentally framed together. In fact, the director's attachment to the location overcame the logic in choosing it for a particular film. It became, for example, the background to his nostalgic hymn to the cavalry, *She Wore a Yellow Ribbon*, to his jaunty retelling of the Wyatt Earp legend, *My Darling Clementine*, and to his worthy apology to the Indians, *Cheyenne Autumn*.

Although no Cheyenne had ever been within smoke-signal distance of Monument Valley, the apology was appropriate and overdue. More than two dozen movies have been filmed on that location and in almost all of them the Indians have bitten its liberal dust. The irony is that this is Indian land. It belongs to them, the Navajo—The People—owned, administered and inhabited by them.

They call it Among the Red Rocks, and they have given it much of its peculiar mystery.

You feel the mystery from a long way off. Most of the monuments are contained within a comparatively small area, straddling the Arizona–Utah border some sixty miles west of Four Corners, and approaching them from Kayenta, Arizona ("the most remote post office in the U.S.A."), the initial impression, as with so many of the great natural landmarks of the Southwest, is of some magnificent

architectural accident. Following the Navajo Trail through the massive outcrops of red sandstone, you become no more than a weevil in a giant's acropolis. On all sides the vast ruined temples rise, clustered on the grand scale—pillars, spires, columns, enormous rectangular blocks, chimneys, terraces and steps, half-domes, bridges, arches, broken moldings, crazy sculptured pinnacles, battlements on the towering castellations of crimson stone, and between and among them, shaped by an

The Totem Pole is one of the many rock formations that have given Monument Valley its name. Monument is a geological name applied to erosion remnants that are much higher than they are wide and, therefore, often bear some resemblance to living things or man-made structures. Those of Monument Valley, the best-known in North America, are made of sandstone that once covered the area in an unbroken sheet. Over the centuries it has been broken apart, first into terraces, then into mesas, which slowly splintered into monuments. All these successive stages of formation can be seen in the valley.

Monument Valley

unimaginable violence, are the chipped canyons and the chiseled gorges. It is strange, awesome and spectacular, and nothing stays the same for very long because the movement of the sun and the sometimes freakish weather conditions result in a constant play of light and shadow, a cyclorama of color tones subtly changing in a spectrum between raw pink and bruised purple.

El Capitan, Totem Pole, Big Hogan, North Mitten, South Mitten, Sourdough Pass—the names of the monuments are unexceptional, a mixture of cultures, words on a map. But look closely at the markings on their rocky faces and the real mysteries of the valley surround you, impenetrable and pervasive, a private tribal bondage with the past. Marks and signs proliferate, undeciphered picture writings, scattered shells of ancient dwellings tucked into the ledges, and on one adobe ruin, called The House of Many Hands, the imprints of hundreds of hands, pressed onto the cliff long ago in white paint and never washed away.

The Indians who live there today impassively preserve their mysteries. The Navajo shepherdess, silent and rug-encumbered, rides her horse across the arid floor of the valley, gathering her flock of sheep and goats around her like a cloud.

Monument Valley is a monument, for the Indians and for the movies. When the sun sets, the shadow cast by Totem Pole rock stretches thirty-five miles, a black finger on the land.

THE FIGHT FOR NAVAJO LANDS

In 1855, Manuelito, right, was elected chief of the Navajos. In 1859, a wild raid started a bitter war in which troops led by the famous frontiersman Kit Carson, left, pursued a scorched-earth policy. The war ended with the Navajos signing a treaty with General Sherman, far left, in 1868. In 1874, Manuelito and his wife, far right, led a delegation to Washington. They negotiated a reservation which contained much of the traditional Navajo land, including Monument Valley, but excluded their richest pastureland.

Wheeler Peak

There are two scales of time at Wheeler Peak, Nevada. One is the geological clock, the ticking of which is heard in the measured dripping of water in the chambers of the Lehman Caves, deep inside the mountain. The ceilings of the caves have been dripping for one million years, slowly building intricate formations of gleaming white rock that crowd every passageway and vault. A tiny stalactite no larger than a drinking straw, and so fragile that a touch with a finger would crumple it, grows only one inch every one hundred years. Yet the columns of sinewy calcite rising from floor to ceiling like pit props of carved ivory are as thick as tree trunks.

High on the straggling timberline of the mountain there is found another kind of time against which man's span on earth seems equally insignificant. Here grows the oldest-known living thing on earth, the bristlecone pine. The gnarled and twisted trunks of these magnificent trees are as fantastic in their way as the stalactites in the caves. Grotesquely misshapen with very few leaves, but with roots that cling to the mountainside like grapnels, some bristlecone pines have endured the bitter winds of as many as five thousand winters.

The wood of the trees is so hard that even in the extreme conditions of these high desert mountains it does not rot and it is not susceptible to burrowing insects. A thin seam of tissue, building on the column of deadwood like a fin, carries the sap to the leaves. Over many centuries the wood has been eroded by the wind as if it were rock, and the trees have been sculptured into weirdly convoluted shapes. They are like living driftwood.

Wheeler Peak is the highest point of the twenty-six-mile Snake Range, one of many short ranges with steep terrain and short drainages which descend into the arid valleys of the Great Basin. The ranges lie in formation across Nevada, like loaves of bread baking in a dusty oven. From the east, near the mouth of the caves, the peak seems to be a perfect pyramid with matching smaller pyramids on either side. Their slopes are covered with pinyon pine and juniper, which become denser with altitude.

The mountain's double peak, three glacial tarns, a small glacier, aspen and mountain mahogany groves and the stands of bristlecone pine are part of a government-designated twenty-eight-thousand-acre scenic area.

The caves, a national monument, penetrate about half a mile into the mountain in nearly level passageways. Solid marble, the caves were formed by rain and snow which absorbed carbon monoxide from fungi and bacteria in the soil and were changed into a mild form of carbonic acid. This drained through the joints and fractures of the rock and dissolved it away. When increasing aridity of the region caused the water table to drop, a network of passageways remained. Then for a million years spectacular formations grew in the damp darkness as each drop of water falling from the ceiling left behind it a microscopic particle of sediment.

The caves were found in 1885 by Absalom S. Lehman, a local rancher, when his horse stumbled in a hole near the mouth of the caves. Exploring by the light of hissing carbide lamps, Lehman gave predictably romantic names to the incredibly detailed sculptures crafted by the slow touch of time. He named The Wedding Altar, The Pearly Gates, The Cypress Swamp. But every person finds his own visions in the confections of brittle calcite which so cram the passageways that there is hardly room to walk among them.

One rare formation is the shield, or palette. Each shield has two plates, just like clamshells, which do not quite touch. Through the narrow slot between them sweeps the water, gradually building onto the outside rims of the plates. From their undersides trail long draperies of limestone, which are drawn together in tapered pedestals sometimes fifteen feet high.

It is difficult to decide which is the more awe-inspiring—to stand in the caves amid the fantastic geologic craftmanship of millions of years or to stroke the smooth trunk of a tree that has been living since the pharaohs built the pyramids. Perhaps it is the relationship between these two concepts of time that makes Wheeler Peak not only a beautiful wilderness, but a place of intriguing wonder.

Twisted and gnarled bristlecone pines stand amid glacial debris on Wheeler Peak. The bristlecone pine is the world's oldest living thing and several trees have been found which are almost five thousand years old. Found only in the high, barren, wind-swept slopes of the southwestern states, these hardy trees owe their survival to a remarkable ability to curtail their growth during years of drought or exceptional cold. Much of the tree consists of deadwood and the green living part is sustained by a thin lifeline of bark.

The variety of shapes found among the thousands of formations in Lehman Caves seems infinite, but they are all variations of only ten basic formation types. Stalactites, stalagmites and columns, above, are common in Lehman Caves, as they are in most limestone caves. Shields, however, which are extremely rare, abound at Lehman. Shield activity has produced one particularly well-balanced formation known as The Parachute, left, which has become the symbol of these caves.

There have always been two voices in Taos—the inside voice and the outside voice. The outside voice has been heard in many tongues and has often been louder. But the inside voice has tried to remain the same and it is still heard in the Pueblo.

Long before the conquest, the Plains Indians exerted their influence on the Pueblo dwellers. Then came the Spanish, the Mexicans, the Anglo–Americans, the artists . . . and the tourists, who still come. The resistance has been long, and it has been underground, buried in the ancient ceremonies of the kiva, never penetrated. Within the kiva, below the rainbow ladder that joins them to the gods, generation after generation of Pueblo boys has been initiated into the tribal and religious lore, the steps of the dances, the ritual observances, which have sought to keep their people a self-contained and independent tribe.

It is no surprise that the voices from outside have always striven to shout louder. Both in the natural beauty of its surroundings, and in its relationship with those surroundings, the Pueblo of Taos is among the most seductive sights of this world. In 1540, Captain Alvarado, the first European to visit the settlement, reported back to Spain that here was a thriving community of farmers, living in two massive five-story adobe structures, peopled by natives who were skilled at irrigating their fields from the stream that divided their village, producing crops of beans and corn and squash. These Indians, he recorded, appeared to have an organized system of government and a highly developed culture. Alvarado was a member of Coronado's expedition in search of the legendary seven cities of Cibola, which were supposedly overflowing with silver and gold. Instead of Cibola, he had stumbled on Taos.

In 1598, the Spaniards returned, colonized New Mexico, gave the Indian villages the Spanish saint names they have today and demanded homage to the Church. By 1615, Fernandez de Taos was the northernmost frontier of New Spain and the nearby Indian settlement became henceforth the Pueblo of San Geronimo de Taos.

The Taosenos bargained. In exchange for water from their creek, they enlisted the Spaniards to defend them against the raiding Apaches, Navajos, Utes and Comanches. The Spaniards installed Franciscan friars and started a mission. But the native religion was not extinguished, and in 1680 it was fiercely revived. In that year a medicine doctor named Popé came to Taos and talked with three gods in the kiva. The gods instructed him to restore the ancient ways of the Indian peoples and to banish the invaders from their land. All the Pueblos of the region rose. They killed more than four hundred Spaniards and expelled their conquerors from New Mexico. It was short-lived. Plague, drought and marauding Apaches weakened the resistance. Twelve years later the Spanish were back, and Taos became a center for trade and agriculture and a cultural outpost of the Spanish Empire. From their colonizers, the Pueblos adopted their beehive ovens, their silverwork, their sheep and goats and cattle.

In 1821, Mexico won independence from Spain and its flag flew over Taos. In 1847, the American flag replaced it, after another brief and bloody uprising in the Pueblo. Since then the struggle of the Indians has been not so much military as cultural. Taos became an artists' colony, and in 1922 received perhaps its most celebrated visitor—D. H. Lawrence.

The wealthy Mabel Dodge, *patronne* of the artists who had settled there, solicited Lawrence endlessly to come to Taos. Having read his *Sea and Sardinia*, she recognized the voice that would record Taos for history. Lawrence was suspicious: was there not "a colony of rather dreadful sub-arty people?" Were the Indians not dying out and was it not rather sad? But he felt the lure. He believed, he wrote to Mabel Dodge, that "one must somehow bring together the two ends of humanity, our own thin end, and the last dark strand from the previous, pre-white era. . . . Is Taos the place?"

If it was, it can be argued that he never really answered that question. When he arrived he recognized the difficulty. "They are Catholics," he wrote of the Indians, "but still keep the old religion, making the weather and shaping the year: all very secret and important to them. They are naturally secretive, and have their backs set against our form of civilization. Yet it rises against them. In the Pueblo they have mowing machines and threshing machines, and American schools, and the young men no longer care so much for the sacred dance. And after all, if we have to go ahead, we must ourselves go ahead. We can go back and pick up some threads—but these Indians are up against a dead wall, even more than we are: but a different wall."

Yet the impression remains that Lawrence and his wife, Frieda, stayed in New Mexico for its natural beauties. "For a greatness of beauty I have never experienced anything like New Mexico. All those mornings when I went with a hoe along the ditch to the canyon, at the

This pueblo mission at Taos, left, is typical of the churches established throughout the Southwest by Spanish padres. Because of a scarcity of wood, many were built of adobe. Although their facades are plain, their vividly colored interiors contain highly decorated altars and elaborate carvings.

The Taos Pueblo has been occupied continuously for over two hundred years. As the population increased, small rooms were added in a random fashion. Today, it consists of two 5-story terraced community houses. Tall ladders provide the only access to the upper stories; shorter ones are used to gain access to the subterranean kivas.

Taos, New Mexico

ranch, and stood, in the fierce, proud silence of the Rockies, on their foothills, to look far over the desert to the blue mountains away in Arizona, blue as chalcedony, with the sage-brush desert sweeping grey-blue in between, dotted with the tiny cube-crystals of houses, the vast amphitheatre of lofty, indomitable desert, sweeping round to the ponderous Sangre de Cristo mountains on the east, and coming up flush at the pine-dotted foot-hills of the Rockies! What splendour!"

When Lawrence left Taos in 1925 he was dying of tuberculosis. To the end of his life he wished to return, but the disease forbade it.

He had, however, in his time at Taos comple-ted the long short story *St. Mawr* and the novel *The Plumed Serpent*, and the memorial of his stay is enshrined in the chapel at Kiowa Ranch, where Frieda is buried.

Today the beauty of Taos is still truly astonishing. In one gasp it is recognized, best seen in the spring or the autumn, with snow on the Sacred Mountain behind the Pueblo, the river sparkling in the sun and the complex adobe structures stepped mazily back and up and sideways like cubes piled on top of each other and the ladders dark against the sky. At the same time, the eye instantly absorbs the

conflict—the gleaming new truck, parked beside the beehive bread oven, the curio shop selling souvenirs, the notices forbidding photography beyond a certain point, the children in their parkas and the elders in their blankets, the cross on the bright white church set between the ladders on the mud-brown dwellings. The elders voted against electricity, and piping the river into water supplies would destroy its freedom. The two voices.

Outside, in the brilliant air, the cameras whir, for a fee. Inside, in the shadowy kiva, the voices whisper like leaves, preserving and transmitting a private inheritance.

MOUNTAIN MAJESTY

If wealth were measured by scenic splendor alone, the Rocky Mountain states of Montana, Idaho, Wyoming and Colorado would be the treasury of the nation. This is a land of deep valleys and sheer rock walls, of immense peaks revealed through voluminous clouds and silky mists. It is a wild country controlled only by the orderly routine of nature, whose will is imposed on trees, flowers, animals and birds, on the very entity of this royal landscape.

To live with this soaring, rugged wilderness of high granite and deep forest, man must first come to terms with the elemental forces of nature. And nowhere is the ability of man to survive the rigors of his environment put to a sterner test than here, where mountains crown the continent with majestic beauty.

The first white men to challenge this hostile land were fur trappers early in the nineteenth century. They were the epitome of self-sufficiency, for they learned to live off the land and to make the land work for them. They were men who hand-forged their iron traps and hand-molded their bullets over the campfire. They wore homemade buckskin suits that shrank tightly around their bodies from constant immersion in the freezing mountain waters. A hunting knife, both tool and weapon, was always within easy reach in a beaded sheath at the belt. The individualism and independence of these mountain men survive today in the isolated communities which still exist in this immense and lonely territory.

It was in these mountains that the concept of preserving the order of nature took form when, a little more than a century ago, Yellowstone, the first national park, was dedicated. Today, more than half the land in the Rocky Mountains is protected, insuring that the unique beauties of these mountain states are available for all to enjoy—from the steep glacier-formed valleys in northern Montana to the black volcanic scars of Idaho and the centuries-old cliff dwellings at Mesa Verde in Colorado to Wyoming's Yellowstone itself. In the eastern United States, wilderness is preserved in comparatively small but treasured areas. Here, however, in mountain America, cities are large on the maps and small on the ground. Wild country begins at the end of the main street, and people exist in relatively tiny communities surrounded by dazzling, untamed country.

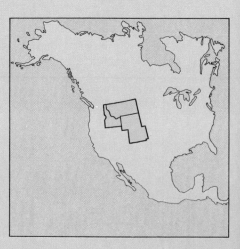

The Rocky Mountains

The map-making priests of New Spain knew them, from reports of wandering adventurers and friendly Indians, as the Shining Mountains. They form links in the mountain chain that extends like a backbone through the Americas from Patagonia to Alaska. In the United States, they stretch for twelve hundred miles from the Canadian border in Montana and Idaho through Wyoming, Utah and Colorado into New Mexico—range after range of magnificent peaks thrusting up into the windy heavens and clothed in a roughcast armor of shining snow and ice.

The Rocky Mountains are a spectacle of immensity, a high-altitude wilderness of hundreds of granite peaks amid formidable, steep, forested valleys and rocky gorges. In the State of Colorado alone, where the United States Rockies attain their most concentrated and imposing mass, there are fifteen hundred peaks over ten thousand feet high—six times as many major mountains as in Switzerland.

But although the Rockies are a great reservoir of untamed and untameable natural wilderness, their remotest peaks have been mapped and climbed. Practically every part of them is utilized for skiing, hunting or camping, and in their vastness Americans can assuage their appetite for backwoods solitude.

The mountains, however, also affect the lives of millions of people who may never see their rugged alpine splendor. Four-fifths of North America gets its drinking water from the streams and rivers of the Rocky Mountains, for all the great rivers of the West rise to maturity in their foothills. They are the nation's domestic hot-air heater, air-conditioner, insulating wall, water tank and oxygen factory. The ranges insulate the Western deserts from the bitter cold of the prairies; they trap moisture which allows the Western desert communities to survive. Consequently, thousands of square miles of prairie east of the mountains are semiarid.

Along the highest peaks and ridges of the Rockies runs the ridgepole of America, the Continental Divide. Theoretically, the divide is the only route by which you could traverse the United States between Canada and Mexico without getting your feet wet. On the east side the country slopes down toward the Atlantic, on the west side toward the Pacific.

The divide also thrusts up into the slipstreams of high-altitude weather and, like a waveswept reef between two tidal races, forms a barrier between the weather systems of east and west. The natural obstacle which the Rockies presents to jet streams coming off the Pacific affects high-altitude weather phases as far east as Great Britain.

Weather over the Rockies is a relentless and dynamic force that explodes around the high peaks like beating surf and rages downward through the valleys, spilling over the Great Plains like waves running up a beach. The life-giving benefits of these winds, called chinooks, are felt right into Iowa. They occur when barometric pressure is lower on the east side than on the west. Air is sucked over the mountains, dropping its moisture and drying as it rises, then compresses and warms as it descends.

The chinook is such a potent force of warmth and power that in the plains it is not uncommon in winter, at midnight, to have deep snow on the ground and an outside temperature which is well below freezing and the next morning a temperature of 40 degrees Fahrenheit with no snow to be seen. Within minutes of the first puff of warm wind reaching the plains from the banks of black, tattered clouds looming over the Rockies, the temperature can jump as much as forty degrees. Without the chinook of the Rocky Mountains, livestock on the Great Plains would not be able to survive the winter.

The high peaks have the climate of Alaska, a spring that lasts only a week and a growing season of less than forty days. As you stand admiring the magnificent scenery, summer thunderstorms can form before your eyes. Electrically charged air causes your hair to stand on end; metal sunglasses begin to buzz. Brilliant lightning flickers, sometimes frightening climbers by snapping along the ground in rivers of deadly fire. Often it starts forest fires. Then, suddenly, all signs of the storm evaporate and the sky is blue again. Sometimes horizontal streamers of cloud trailing from the summits quickly give way to long billowy masses of cumulus clouds, which form over the mountains. Light planes flying east to west across the ranges turn back, because they do not have the horsepower to make headway against the avalanche of wind that comes with a rush and a roar over the Continental Divide.

On the east side there can be winds of eighty miles an hour, whirling snow in a grim whiteout that cannot be braved without protective clothing and face masks. Yet only fifteen miles away, on the west side of the mountains, weather conditions may be absolutely calm. Without the benefit of the chinook, violent though it may be, mountain basins on the west side collect cold; temperatures of − 60 degrees Fahrenheit are common. Because there is no wind, the snow piles into deep drifts and wildlife is unable to graze.

Of the sixty-nine mountain peaks which rise to more than fourteen thousand feet in the continental United States, fifty-four are in the Colorado Rockies. High up in these peaks, the essence of American mountain grandeur, the spectacle of turbulent weather is ever-present. Its potential strength is still largely unknown. On Trail Ridge Drive, the highest highway in the United States, which runs through the Rocky Mountain National Park at about twelve thousand feet for eleven miles, a scientist recently set up a wind-measuring instrument. The Shining Mountains had their vengeance. Not only did the anemometer go off the scale at two hundred miles an hour— the iron pole on which it was mounted was bent double by the wind.

A strict conservation policy protects the big game of the Rockies. The white mountain goat, left, roams inaccessible alpine peaks, where it is safe from predators. Elk, or wapiti, spend winters in the valleys and summers on the higher slopes. During the autumn mating season, male elk, right, spar with pointed antlers.

Alpine flowers bloom on the slopes of the Never Summer Range in Rocky Mountain National Park, above. The establishment of the park was the result of a lifelong campaign by Enos Mills, a local resident, self-educated naturalist and early conservationist. His dream was realized when the national park was dedicated in 1915.

Snowmass Canyon near Aspen in the Colorado Rocky Mountains blazes with gold in autumn when the groves of slender aspens turn to brilliant yellow, right. The evergreen-covered mountainsides are a somber contrast to the flaming canyon, as the trees tremble in the cold winds which precede the first snow.

Yellowstone National Park

Early in the 1830s, the famous trapper and guide Jim Bridger emerged from the wilderness, an Indian arrow in his back and tales of "the place where Hell bubbled up." He was but one of the trappers who, for more than twenty years, had drifted through the plateau region nearly one and a half miles high in the crown of the Rocky Mountains and came back to tell of its thermal wonders. But the men of the mountains were known for fanciful yarns and, therefore, no one took them seriously. The first white man to enter the region was probably John Colter, who had crossed the continent with Lewis and Clark and later, in 1808, came upon it while reconnoitering for good trapping territory. He described a "hot spring brimstone" that was scoffed at as "Colter's Hell."

Bridger, too, was derided, earning national notoriety as "that old liar." Despite corroboration from other wilderness adventurers, his unexaggerated descriptions of boiling water spurting higher than the trees and of rivers flowing so fast that the water became hot at the bottom, were thought to be just too tall to be true. His accounts did, however, seem to become increasingly fanciful over the years. He told of a sour creek so tart that it shrank horses' hooves and of a petrified forest in which even the birds had been turned to stone in midflight. He claimed he had once shot several times at an elk, only to discover that it stood twenty-five miles away, behind a glass mountain perfectly formed into the lens of a telescope.

It was not until 1869 that the first formally mounted expedition entered this little-known territory in what is now the northwest corner of Wyoming with the sole purpose of exploring the area and reporting on it. To the surprise and delight of its three members there was a fundamental truth in Bridger's stories. He had told of a curious spring in which fish caught in the cold water at the bottom were cooked as they were hauled through the hot water near the surface. Here, indeed, were pools of boiling water, beside trout-filled streams and lakes, in which fish could be cooked while still on the end of a fishing line.

The expedition found a stream of mouth-puckering water, later called Alum Creek, and a "glass" cliff of black obsidian with, at its foot, stone chips which glittered like broken bottles. A high ridge of rocks was found to contain the petrified remains of twenty-seven different forests successively overwhelmed by layers of volcanic ash. From swift rivers, steam rose in misty clouds as if it were smoke generated by the friction of its waters racing over the greenish boulders. There were, too, dozens of bubbling mud pots and spurting geysers, just as Bridger and the other trappers had described them.

Jim Bridger's magical wilderness was destined to become a symbol and a showpiece—not only for the United States, but for the world—of practical conservation. In 1870, Henry Washburn, surveyor-general of Montana Territory, took a party of influential businessmen into the area and their enthusiastic reports led to an official expedition, which included scientists, artists and a pioneer photographer. They returned with scientific and visual evidence of the area's curiosities. Members of both expeditions promoted a bill in Washington to set the area apart "as a public park or pleasuring-ground for the benefit and enjoyment of the people." Within five months, on March 1, 1872, President Ulysses S. Grant signed the bill that designated the area as the world's first national park—Yellowstone.

The park, rimmed by the peaks of mountain ranges, is more than three thousand square miles of rolling country, mostly pine-covered but with expansive high-prairie meadows. Near its center is a beautiful lake with a densely wooded shoreline one hundred and ten miles long. At first the country may seem unremarkable. But the surprises of Yellowstone are possibly underrated.

There is the first astonishing sight of a roadside creek steaming as it curves through the woods; its running water is hot. Clouds of steam mushroom like bonfire smoke from the dark forest, marking dramatic hot springs vividly colored by natural chemicals and algae.

Yellowstone is the most concentrated area of hydrothermal activity in the world. More than ten thousand geysers, hot springs, fumaroles and mud pots are set amid the lakes, raging rivers, long cascades and thundering waterfalls which, in their own right, are numbered among the natural wonders of North America. Nevertheless, the combined attraction of spouting geysers and the spectacular natural beauty cannot equal the sheer thrill of being able to observe at close quarters wild animals on their home ground. Here, in the national park, they carry on their lives as if two million visitors a year simply did not exist.

From your car in summer you can sometimes watch wild black bears from the roadside. The park's three hundred grizzly bears are seldom seen, but sometimes they damage tents and property and are given a wide berth.

In spring and autumn massive bison, which are among the last purely wild free-ranging herds in the country, graze in the valley meadows. On the willow flats you might surprise a bemused-looking moose. Elk are common, and wild stags with magnificent antlers will amble through a campground—like all animals in the national park, they have lost their fear of man.

Yellowstone was formed six hundred thousand years ago with a volcanic explosion that some geologists estimate was two hundred times greater than that at Krakatoa, the island in the Dutch East Indies which, in 1883, was destroyed in a blast heard in Australia, three thousand miles away. It was Yellowstone's third and last cycle of volcanic activity. Over a period possibly as short as a week, hundreds of cubic miles of red-hot lava flooded over a wide area, spouting from beneath a dome-shaped mountain, which covered most of the present-day park. Then the entire mountain collapsed inward, forming a giant elliptical caldera forty miles by thirty miles in extent and one mile deep. Into this great caldron, among the largest in the world, seeped more flows of lava, which cooled and, in more recent geological times, were sculpted by glaciers to form the Yellowstone landscape as it is today.

The volcanic forces beneath the park continue to rumble. In 1974, an average of seventeen minor earthquake tremors was recorded every day. The park wardens are accustomed to frequent earthquakes strong enough to set bottles tinkling on shelves, and to give visitors in the park's twenty-two hundred campsites a

An early traveler to Yellowstone described Minerva Terrace at Mammoth Hot Springs as a mountain turned inside out. The terraces, the largest in the world, are built of travertine, a limestone that has been dissolved in hot carbonic acid and forced up through the rocks by thermal pressure. On the surface, the liquid cools and crystalline travertine is precipitated onto the surrounding rock surfaces. When a pool overflows or an edge breaks, the water runs down and begins to form a lower terrace.

Nathaniel P. Langford, a Montana banker, was one of the driving forces behind the Washburn expedition of 1870. He had a financial interest in the proposed Northern Pacific Railway and was well aware that the railroad would benefit if the reported wonders of Yellowstone proved to be a tourist attraction. He was so overwhelmed by the natural beauty of the area, however, that he became one of the strongest advocates of the Yellowstone Park Act. When Yellowstone became the first national park, Langford received the honorary appointment as the first national park superintendent.

Yellowstone National Park

gentle shake in their sleeping bags. Occasionally, the raw power seething below the ground manifests itself more seriously. In 1959, an earthquake outside the park area brought down a mountainside, demolished roads and killed twenty-eight people.

The heat beneath Yellowstone is still sufficient to melt one million tons of ice a day. The primal heat deep inside the planet comes nearer to the surface here than at any other known location. Geologists drilling down through bare ground have measured a temperature of 400 degrees Fahrenheit at a depth of only 265 feet. The distance down from the soles of your feet to the intense heat which extends to the center of the earth is probably less than five miles.

Moisture from rain and melted snow seeps down through the ground, is turned to steam by the heat and then—under pressure—is forced back to the surface. There it may bubble gently into a large, deep pool of hot water, its color brighter than turquoise because the water is so clear. It may burble into a river as a hot waterfall streaked with the psychedelic colors of the slimy algae which thrive in hot water. Smelling of sulfur, it can erupt through pinkish-gray mud with a loud plop. Or the pressure below ground can slowly build up to explode with a roar like that of a wave running up an endless beach. The water flashing instantly to steam expands its volume one thousand times and a plume of boiling water and steam streaks up into the blue sky. A playing geyser is a sublime and exhilarating spectacle.

Old Faithful, named by Washburn in 1870, is famous the world over. Although it is spectacular, it is not the largest geyser in the park. Some would say it is not even the prettiest. But it is one of the most dependable and, for the hundreds of people who see it every day, the most obliging. Intervals between eruptions depend on how hard and for how long the geyser has played previously; they vary from between half an hour and two and one-quarter hours, but can be predicted to within five minutes. The geyser has played more than eight hundred and forty thousand times since it was discovered over a century ago—on average twenty-two times a day.

First, in a series of false alarms, columns of pale green water hiccup from the coral-like font of white rock that forms the geyser's mouth. Then comes the startling eruption, which is over in two to four minutes. Seven thousand gallons of boiling water plume upward in a fountain as high as one hundred and ninety feet. The jet is bent by the wind and, as it loses momentum, the water trails away in feathery traces. As you watch it, you feel you would like to react as Charles W. Cook did, when, in 1869, he and his two companions on that historic first expedition saw the geysers playing, ". . . with one accord we all took

off our hats and yelled with all our might."

There are many surprises at Yellowstone. An entire mountainside seethes with steam issuing from dozens of vents. When you see sulfurous-smelling steam burst up through a caldron of black mud, you realize Jim Bridger understated it when he claimed to have seen hell bubbling up. Boardwalks lead you amid dozens of gulping mud pots and fizzing hot springs. But these curiosities of a mysterious world are almost eclipsed by the sudden transformation, as spectacular as a tropical sunrise, when you step out of the green twilight of the forest to the abrupt rim of

Castle Geyser, one of the oldest of Yellowstone's scores of active geysers, plays in the Upper Geyser Basin. About every eight hours, Castle Geyser erupts in a two-phased pattern, which lasts an hour. After shooting out a seventy-five-foot-high water stream, it changes to a hissing steam phase.

YELLOWSTONE'S FIRST PHOTOGRAPHER
The 1871 Geological Survey expedition into Yellowstone included photographer William Henry Jackson. He took this self-portrait and a photo of expedition leader Ferdinand Hayden sitting by his tent talking to an assistant. But it was the first pictures of such natural wonders as Old Faithful and Lower Falls which awed the nation. Each congressman received a sheath of Jackson's pictures when the historic bill to create Yellowstone National Park was presented and passed in 1872.

the Grand Canyon of the Yellowstone River.

Its steep, fifteen-hundred-foot-deep walls of crumbly soil are a brilliant pale yellow streaked with pink, brown, red, cinnamon, orange and cream. Pillars of colored rock rising like minarets appear so frail that the weight of a bird might topple them, but secure on their chimney-pot summits, rare ospreys build their nests.

At the head of the fifteen-mile canyon the river glides uneasily out of a dark tunnel of brooding pines, curls lazily over the slippery edge and drops more than three hundred feet. Lower Falls, twice as high as Niagara, fill the narrow canyon with booming noise. Spray carried high by updrafts of wind stains the canyon walls with rich, dark colors. Just upstream, hidden around a bend, are the Upper Falls, where the river pours through a narrow cleft with such momentum that it gushes outward in an arc as it plummets over one hundred feet.

Yellowstone has been developed just sufficiently to allow visitors to enjoy with ease its natural splendors. There is a footbridge here, a boardwalk there, discreetly situated campgrounds and car parks, which are always well hidden. Even before the surrounding country had attained statehood, men of vision had set aside this immense area as a place of recreation. It was an innovative concept of conservation that caught the imagination of the world. A century later there were thirty-five national parks in the United States, twenty-eight in Canada and scores more in western and eastern Europe, Africa, Asia and Australasia. More national parks are being created every year in this new age of awareness, but Yellowstone National Park, which established the principle that natural treasures should be maintained, occupies a special place in the hearts of all those who enjoy it.

Geysers are the most spectacular form of thermal activity in Yellowstone, but the hot springs can be the most beautiful. Thermal pools have different colors caused by various algae in the near-boiling waters. Emerald Pool's color is produced by a yellow alga, which reflects green through the deep blue water.

97

Early in the nineteenth century no American gentleman could claim to be well dressed without his beaver hat. For the hat that gave a man stature and style, only felt made from the finest beaver fur would do. And in a roundabout way it was this which caused to be brought to light the magnificence of a mountain range later called the Tetons.

The search for new supplies of beaver pelts to meet the demands of fashion exercised the minds of many traders. In 1808, one group in St. Louis commissioned an adventurer named John Colter to find beaver rivers in unexplored territory west of the Missouri. Colter, who had crossed the continent with Lewis and Clark, and had gone on other expeditions, had not returned to civilization for three years. He now turned back yet again to face the wilderness, this time alone.

It was to be a grueling winter-long trip that led him not only to the splendid Tetons, but also to the mysteries of Yellowstone. Snowshoeing across the plain, a solitary figure depending for survival on his ability to shoot deer and elk, Colter came up to the sawtoothed and spired mountains bunched along what is now the Idaho border of Wyoming.

Although the range is only forty miles long, it includes more than twenty peaks thrusting at least ten thousand feet into the sky. Highest point on the jagged crest is Grand Teton, a 13,766-foot snow-sheathed arrowhead, of which the eastern face is similar in outline to the Matterhorn in Switzerland; and one of a quartet of dagger-blade peaks grouped side by side at the southern end of the Teton Range which, without foothills, soars so abruptly and majestically skyward.

When winter clouds wreathe the peaks and bitter winds stir the lovely glacial lakes on the plain below, the line of mountains has a forbidding and dramatic aspect. In sunshine, the cathedral-like pinnacles seem to have been chiseled from blocks of crystal. But to the lonely mountain man these mountains were only an obstacle blocking his route to the West. He did find a way around them, and, sitting out a blizzard on the west side, he idled away long vigils by the campfire carving on a piece of stone. In 1931, the stone was found, his name and the date still legible, a memento

of one man's experience—the most unusual long expedition of any man in the history of the West. He returned to tell other trappers of his experiences and of the beaver rivers he had found around the mountain range. Indian hostility kept them at bay for ten years, but when resistance faded the trappers moved into the region of the Tetons by the score.

It was French trappers who recognized the resemblance of three peaks—when seen from the west—to the shapes of women's breasts and christened them *Les Trois Tetons*. And it was close to the peaks in 1832 that the mountain men held their most famous and most successful annual rendezvous.

To this place they came from the wilderness, leading packhorses laden with bales of beaver pelts, some accompanied by their Indian wives. They came to trade their furs for guns, ammunition, beads, knives and trinkets brought by pack train from St. Louis, then still a muddy frontier village one thou-

The golden-mantled ground squirrel spends all its waking hours in the summer feeding to store up fat for winter's long hibernation. The tiny rodents, which live in colonies in the Grand Teton area, burrow into the ground before the first frost and do not stir again until spring.

A bull moose feeds on water plants, a favorite food, in a marsh near Jackson Hole. Solitary animals, moose prefer to live alone and rarely share feeding grounds. About two hundred moose live near Jackson Hole all year, and another three hundred come down from the colder highlands of the Grand Tetons each winter.

The Grand Tetons

sand miles back East. The traders profiteered outrageously. Alcohol bought in St. Louis for ten cents a barrel was diluted with water and sold by the drink to trappers for a price that gave a markup of 64,000 percent. But few trappers had had a drink or, for that matter, exchanged a word with another white man for a year. They did not complain.

By 1840 silk hats were in style in the East, and, in any case, good felt could now be made from rabbit fur. The day of the beaver trapper was over. As prospectors, surveyors and settlers moved into the mountains the trappers remained as guides. Today, their spirits remain in the place-names. Jackson Hole, the wide plain below the steep east face of the range, is named after a trapper who worked the rivers and streams in the area. Leigh Lake, which mirrors the beautiful peaks, is named after "Beaver" Dick Leigh, and Jenny Lake after his Indian wife, who died with all her children after bravely giving aid and comfort to a squaw fatally stricken with smallpox.

As a national park the Tetons are preserved for camping and climbing, where modern Americans are able to learn to know and appreciate the wilderness. Today the evergreen forests rimming the lakes abound in small animals and birds. Beaver and other wildlife live unmolested. The mountain and forest trails offer in small measure something of the lonely mountain man's unique confrontation with true wilderness.

Twilight in the Grand Tetons, with the image of the mountains reflected in mirror-like Jackson Lake. The lake, named after Davey Jackson, a nineteenth-century fur trapper, is the largest and one of the most beautiful of the many clear, cold glacial lakes in the area.

The Grand Tetons were the center of the area roamed by the colorful nineteenth-century mountain men. Jim Bridger was one of the most exciting of these characters. In 1822, he answered an ad for "enterprising young men" to join the Rocky Mountain Fur Company. Thus began a sixty-year career as trapper, trader, guide, scout, explorer, Indian fighter and adventurer. Bridger discovered the Great Salt Lake, and his fantastic stories about Yellowstone inspired others to explore it.

Every drop of snowmelt that runs off the south and east faces of Triple Divide Peak eventually finds its way into the distant Mississippi. Water from snow patches only inches away on the north face drains into the Saskatchewan River on the far side of the Trans-Canada Highway. From the west face the water seeps into tributaries of the Columbia River.

Triple Divide Peak is just one of many magnificent mountains in the Canadian border area of Montana, where the Rocky Mountains are at their broadest. In the million acres of Glacier National Park it stands only shoulder-high to grand summits like Little Chief Mountain and Rising Wolf Mountain, but it has a unique significance. For this is the one place in North America from which it is downhill all the way to three of the continent's four coasts. From its 8,028-foot summit you could throw a handful of snow in a wide arc—and hit the Pacific Ocean, the Gulf of Mexico and Hudson Bay.

Cascading water, which radiates to all points of the compass in tumbling streams, glissading rivers and plunging waterfalls, is the dynamic force in this remotest of national parks.

North America could have no more imposing or majestic crown. In Glacier Park there are more than thirty peaks over seven thousand feet high, and several over nine thousand feet high. It adjoins the Waterton Lakes National Park in Canada, another spread of equally magnificent mountains. In 1932, in a gesture of goodwill, the United States Congress and the Canadian Parliament combined the two into an international peace park. Here, in a landscape of stunning ruggedness and grandeur the perfect peace of true wilderness can be discovered.

Glacier Park's only highway cuts through the middle of the park, threading dizzily up the steep face of Going-to-the-Sun Mountain. The road, open only in summer and autumn, provides motorists with a brief glimpse of Triple Divide Peak, the snowcovered pyramid that in a sense is America's center of gravity. Although it is gloriously scenic, the real beauties of the park are best appreciated from the thousand miles of trails which run through the

deep forested valleys, wend up and over rocky saddles and past hundreds of shimmering lakes cradled in the folds of the mountains.

Notices at the beginning of the trails remind campers to pitch their tents near a tree which can be climbed because Glacier Park is one of the two remaining refuges—the other is Yellowstone—of the grizzly bear. Elk and deer abound, and herds of white mountain goats find precarious footholds on the narrow and crumbling ledges.

The massive crests of the mountains jutting high above the tree line have been eroded into sharp pinnacles and ridges as sharp as blades. The peaks form a fabulous geometry of layered rock long ago twisted and molded into crumpled and tilted shapes by subterranean pressures. Each layer of rock forms a terrace, often less than two or three feet thick, which traps the snow, leaving the peaks banded by a fine corduroy of alternating black and white stripes.

Water took over as master of the mountains and valleys when the ice surrendered at the end of the ice age some ten thousand years ago. Until then, for two million years, the great valleys had been filled with grinding rivers of ice—glaciers that fashioned the present landscape from mountains formed sixty million years ago. The ice has now all but disappeared. At the turn of the century there were ninety

glaciers in the park area. Now there are only fifty, the largest covering three hundred acres.

When the ice melted it left steep-sided valleys that sweep around the mountain peaks in graceful curves, banked like bobsled runs. Smaller side valleys which were not gouged out so deeply have been left suspended, their streams dropping precipitously for hundreds of feet. Sometimes the spray is torn away by the wind so that they never reach the ground. Some streambeds are tilted like staircases after an earthquake, and streams course down the mountainside from step to step over the slanted layers of rock. In winter the streams are choked with icicles piled like the tiers of a wedding cake hundreds of feet high.

In the valleys swirling rivers ripple over shallow shelves of gray boulders, their banks edged with dark conifers and the lighter hues of aspens, willows and mountain ash. The flame-yellow autumn colors of the aspens contrast unforgettably with the brilliant blue of glassy lakes. The expanse of Lake McDonald jabs a pointed finger ten miles long into the midriff of grave granite peaks. Smaller lakes and tarns are hidden high in the mountains, and some, like Iceberg Lake, are dotted with chunks of ice even in summer. And always the mountain silence is broken by the splash and swirl of running and falling water—water rushing to join not one but three oceans.

Pure, clear water from melting ice cascades gently down the terraced slope of Clements Mountain in Glacier National Park. Pyramid-shaped Clements Mountain is a glacial horn, a peak formed into a geometric shape by the powerful force of three successive glaciers.

The establishment of Glacier National Park in 1910 insured the survival in the area of species threatened by trappers, who moved into the remote Montana highlands when yields from traditional trapping territories were dropping drastically. The New World mink, left, for example, was highly prized for its thick, soft fur.

One of 210 species of birds found in Glacier National Park, the common loon, left, is a summer visitor. Loons are at their most vocal at night, often shattering the silence with their unearthly laughter and eerie screams, which are frequently taken up far and wide and relayed like distress signals.

The shimmering surface of Hidden Lake reflects the icy face of Bearhat Mountain. Clumps of bear grass, a common plant in Glacier Park, cling to the mountain slopes. When bear grass is in flower, the hillsides are covered with delicate, creamy-white blossoms.

The golden eagle's seven-foot wingspan is but a tiny speck between the cliffs which rise from both banks of the roaring river. The great bird hunts its prey in the high crags, idling in lazy loops with steady wings. Its freedom is enviable, because to soar like an eagle is the only way to encompass the magnitude of North America's deepest gorge—Hells Canyon of the Snake River.

Too deep and vast for its matchless scale to be appreciated from any single vantage point, Hells Canyon is a place that is better experienced than seen. The thin thread of wild water is the only highway and jet boats hammer ninety miles up the Grand Canyon of the Snake River to the lower end of Hells Canyon itself—a thrilling, bone-jarring ride that twists between fountains of white water thrown up by massive boulders in midstream, drives through curtains of spray and fights its way over more than a hundred fierce rapids.

Hells Canyon is an almost perfect inverted mountain. Its Idaho and Oregon rims stand between two and six miles back from the river. But the water is so hemmed in by cliffs and buttresses, themselves at least a thousand feet high, that the higher slopes of the canyon are seldom in view. For about twenty miles the canyon averages a mile in depth—in one place more than one and a half miles—but the impression is not so much of vast depth as of overwhelming size.

From a boat far below, the rims of the Grand Canyon are well defined and visible as great valances of layered rock. The river slithers between drapes of tussocky grass patterned with rock terraces and overhanging cliff faces, which sweep down to brush the water's edge. In some places the slopes level out near the river so the canyon becomes a wide and sunny valley with a mild climate that, even in winter, is kind to stock and wildlife. In summer the water air-conditions the sultry air trapped between the high rock walls, so that in a small boat, nosed into the bank, the air at the stern is ten degrees cooler than at the bow.

In other parts of the twisting river perpendicular walls of rock nearly a thousand feet high come within fifty feet of meeting, forming portals through which the river hurls in seething torrents. Between them dart the boats, slaloming amid plumes of spray, zooming through maelstroms of tossing water. Even above a diesel at full throttle you can hear the mighty roar of the river; it is a sound you never forget.

Impressions of deltas, islands and hidden valleys along the river are fleeting because the boats must travel fast for maneuverability. The downstream journey is a headlong dash, like a bobsled ride, as the river carries you along in its grip. Your eyes are much too busy searching the river ahead for tusk-like boulders to dwell for long on the river's massive bulwarks.

But it always did take a steady nerve to challenge Hells Canyon. At Suicide Point, one of many high bluffs jutting into the canyon, forcing the river into tight hairpin turns, there is a slim ledge high up in the rock. In places it crumbles almost to nothing, yet the first ranchers to settle along the river rode this dizzy trail on horseback. The trick was not to lean inward and hug the rock, or the horse's hooves might be forced over the edge if it stumbled. You had to lean outward, and just try not to look down.

In modern times access may be faster, but it still churns the stomach. One of the ranches is served by a short dirt airstrip pitched at an angle of more than twenty degrees. The wing tip of a plane all but overhangs the churning river. When landing it seems to be flying into

BIRDS OF PREY IN HELLS CANYON

Threatened by pesticides and man, America's birds of prey are moving to remote inland areas like Hells Canyon. The osprey, its talons specially adapted to grip slippery prey, feeds on fish from the Snake River. Swainson's hawk and the prairie falcon both feed on small rodents and birds which they catch on the ground, but they hunt them in different ways. The hawk hovers in wait, while the falcon, a fast flyer, swoops in at high speed.

Osprey

Swainson's Hawk

Prairie Falcon

Hells Canyon

a wall, and on takeoff it has to launch itself into the air as if going down a ski jump.

During floods the river rises thirty feet. Whirlpools suck logs into their vortexes, stand them upright, swallow them whole and spit them out as matchwood miles downstream. Even in the quiet places, where the water is smooth and bottle-green, the river boils gently as it is stirred by boulders and ledges. The speed of the water blurs reflections of the cliffs and sky above.

The river is master of the gorge, yet it is surprising to learn that even here it is governed by man. The depth of water at any time depends not on natural occurrences, such as rainstorms in the mountains, but on how much water has been released from the dam in the upper part of Hells Canyon to meet electricity demands in towns hundreds of miles away.

In spring, when the river is in spate, the water is brown with sand which polishes the rocks. When the level falls again they shine brightly, and the sand is deposited in neat beaches that record the footprints of animals coming down to drink.

Great white sturgeons live in the back eddies, where the rushing water slows down, allowing dead fish and crabs to settle. Pioneer settlers caught these tasty fish by baiting large hooks with calf's liver, weighting them with boulders and tying the line of thick rope to a willow tree. When the tree was seen bending, a horse was hitched up to tow the fish ashore. One sturgeon caught in 1925 is said to have topped fifteen hundred pounds; local people say its head overhung one end of a lumber wagon and its tail the other. Today it is no feat to catch a sturgeon seven feet long, but it has to be put back because now these fish are protected.

After three hours of blasting through walls of white water, suddenly you find that the furious, powerful river, now framed by massive mountains rising close on either side, is reduced to the scale of a woodland creek. This is, perhaps, the most surprising part of the amazing, spectacular experience of the Snake River and Hells Canyon.

The tumultuous rapids of the Snake River pound furiously against the rocks in Hells Canyon. Canadian fur trappers, who were the first white men to travel on the Snake, nicknamed it "Accursed Mad River" because of the raging rapids, which could tear a canoe to pieces.

Hells Canyon is the deepest and narrowest gorge in North America. The average depth is fifty-five hundred feet, more than one mile, reaching seventy-nine hundred feet at its lowest point. The river is less than one hundred feet wide in places, yet the flanking mountains create an air of vast spaciousness. Donald McKenzie was the first man to lead a party through the depths of the canyon. In 1811, McKenzie was employed by John Jacob Astor's fur company as a member of the second expedition to cross the continent. Disaster struck the party when their canoes were wrecked by the rapids on the upper part of the Snake River. The men then struggled through the Idaho desert, only to be faced by the perils of Hells Canyon. Frozen and hungry, some men died and others went mad, but McKenzie managed to lead a small group through the treacherous gorge and down the Columbia River to the Pacific Coast.

Craters of the Moon

It is a landscape of chaos created by a slow leak in the surface of the earth which began twenty-five thousand years ago. Molten rock welled up from thirty miles below the ground and oozed in layers over the surrounding plains. It rippled and folded into waves and ridges, and finally set iron hard. Then fire fountains spurting red-hot liquid rock into the air formed symmetrical hillocks, and globules of molten rock burping upward through fissures fused together in small ragged pyramids called spatter cones. Among them grew sloping cones of cinders, some more than six hundred feet high, with smooth and rounded contours. Thus was formed the unworldly landscape of Craters of the Moon.

These eighty-three square miles of black and bristly lava, which scar the plains of central Idaho like the remnants of some colossal bonfire, have a strange and unexpected magic. At first glance it is a barren outlook of appalling grimness. The rocks are sharp and hostile; a single small cinder is like no ordinary stone, for its edges are razor sharp. Fragments of cones carried away on tides of liquid lava stand in jagged columns like lonely sea stacks. Yet the most remarkable feature of this volcanic wilderness is not its stark bareness but its unusual beauty and the unexpected existence of life.

Like the ocean at night, the blackness of the frozen waves of rock are at first mysterious and forbidding. It seems a contradiction to walk in a landscape as dark as night, yet to feel the sun burning down. But the black lava in certain angles of light can be a beautiful pale shade of lavender. Where it has been chipped away by erosion, the pastry-like texture of the lava crust is peach pink and fluted delicately. The powdery cinders and ashes of the volcanic cones are not really black, but a dark brown dusted with tints of red and amber. The tidal wave of small boulders is splashed here and there with clumps of brilliantly colored orange and yellow algae.

The lava flows extend in all directions beyond the level horizon and into the valleys of the Pioneer Mountains to the north. The slow and steady eruptions which continued to form them until two thousand years ago were the last of the volcanic activity that had been taking place for millions of years. In total, twenty-six thousand cubic miles of lava spread over the plains, forming what is now the Snake River Plain. Much of it has been broken down by erosion, and a gray-green coat of aromatic sagebrush and tansybrush has clothed the ancient black clinker. But at Craters of the Moon there is still desolation and Nature is only just beginning to succeed in her struggle.

More than two hundred species of plants now grow on the black rocks and powdery cinder slopes. They do not grow in profusion, but are well spaced to share what little water can be soaked up before it drains downward through two thousand feet of porous lava. Dwarf buckwheat, for example, forms delicate plate-sized silvery pads that dot the cinder gardens. Although it grows only four inches high, its roots go down four feet.

When pine trees get a hold, their fallen cones and pine needles add nutrients to the soil so that such low shrubs as antelope bitterbrush and rubber rabbitbrush can move in. These plants send long branches through the light cinders and help to catch the soil which blows off the plains. They also provide food and shelter for rabbits, chipmunks, deer mice and mule deer.

The rocky lava flows create such a harsh environment that life is still scarce. Growth is incredibly hard and slow, but somehow plants survive against all odds. One tree that took root soon after the lava cooled can still be seen, proof of Nature's remarkable staying power. During its long struggle for life this limber pine grew only a few feet tall and then doubled over, twisting three times around on its trunk. When it died in 1961 scientists took a core sample of its trunk and counted thirteen hundred and fifty life rings before reaching its hollow center; it was estimated to be about fifteen hundred years old.

It will be many years before this triple-twist tree, which existed for so long in the midst of such barrenness, finally rots away. Meanwhile, it remains to mark the beginning of the new era of order which Nature is imposing, by slow degrees, on this stark landscape of chaos.

The sweet warble of the male mountain bluebird, the state bird of Idaho, can be heard at midday at Craters of the Moon. Turquoise blue with a whitish belly, in fall and winter his plumage has touches of dull brown.

For chemical reasons that are not completely understood, volcanoes produce two types of lava flow, for which geologists have adopted the Hawaiian names aa (ah'ha) and pahoehoe (pah-ho'ay-ho'ay). The surface of an aa is ragged and spiny, covered with clinkers. Pahoehoe, which comprises the lava river, right, near scatter cones in Craters of the Moon, has an undulating, rippled surface, above. This forms because, while the surface of the lava stream hardens, the red-hot liquid beneath is still flowing forward. Its movement gathers the sticky surface layer into waves and wrinkles.

The walls of the small cliff houses blend so perfectly with the pale, smooth sandstone that it takes a long time to spot them at all. Then the first thing you see is a tiny square window, like the entrance to a birdhouse, set in mud-plastered, sandstone bricks, built to form a meager cabin on the brink of a narrow ledge. Nearly one thousand years ago people had to mountaineer from finger-hold to finger-hold up the sheer rock of the seven-hundred-foot canyon wall, first to build and then to live here. But why they had to do it, what language they spoke and why they abruptly abandoned their cliff dwellings is part of the fascinating mystery of Mesa Verde.

The cliff houses of Mesa Verde were last lived in over six hundred years ago and they stood undisturbed for centuries. Although in the seventeenth century Spanish explorers came to the vast Colorado Plateau, there is no evidence that they visited the small area they named Mesa Verde, "green table," which is tucked away in the Four Corners area, where Utah, Arizona, New Mexico and Colorado now meet. Then, in 1888, two cowboys in search of stray cattle came upon these fantastic structures from a lost civilization.

Where rainwater had long ago dissolved long elliptical caverns in the rock walls, incredible apartments and patios, forming cliff "cities," were constructed using only stone axes as tools. The largest of these cities housed about four hundred people. Framed by the majestic cliffs, the ruins are a fascinating geometry of level rooftops with their pole ends jutting out through thick walls, irregularly shaped blank windows, towers and small courtyards. The canyons are so narrow that you can look right into the deserted dwellings from the opposite rim—and wonder why a community of between two and four thousand people made life so difficult for themselves.

There are three main issues in the mystery of Mesa Verde. What suddenly drove a people living comfortably in pueblo-style houses on a green tableland of forest and fertile fields to inhabit what are little more than niches high up in the canyon walls? How did they survive in their dizzy aerie? And, having come to terms with their strange mode of life, why did they abandon their laboriously con-

structed cities and leave the area altogether?

Although archaeologists and anthropologists can provide only half-answers to these questions, they have managed to glean a great deal from the ruins and debris of the ancient dwellings. They know that the people who were to inhabit the two-thousand-foot tableland and its honeycomb of canyons until the fourteenth century arrived as nomads in the American Southwest at about the time of Christ. The Indians sheltered in caves and hunted deer and mountain sheep with stone-tipped spears. Their skill lay in the making of intricate baskets, so closely woven they could be used to carry water and, by dropping hot rocks in, to cook food.

Almost six hundred years later, when they had begun to live in small settlements and to farm, they made their first appearance in the Mesa Verde region, where they grew corn and squash. These still primitive people, known to archaeologists as the Basket Makers, developed a simple architecture. They built pithouses on the mesa. The floors were sunk three or four feet below ground level. Low walls leaned inward and flat roofs were made of mud-covered poles and sticks. A hole in the roof served as chimney as well as entrance. Today the mesa is dotted with traces of hundreds of pithouses, many of which were burned down, either accidentally or in burial rituals. During the two centuries of this Modified Basket Maker Period the people learned to make pottery and to hunt with the greatly superior bow and arrow.

By the middle of the eighth century their houses had become more traditional in design, with vertical walls and flat roofs. They were built completely aboveground and grouped near small courtyards. Circular rooms for ceremonial purposes were built entirely beneath the ground. Anthropologists deduce from similar underground chambers, called kivas, which are used by present-day Hopi and Pueblo Indians, that they were a kind of men's club and had a religious significance. During this Developmental Pueblo Period almost every minor drainage on the mesa was made into garden plots by the construction of hundreds of check dams, which took full advantage of the year's eighteen inches of rain-

fall. Cotton was traded for, probably with deer hides, which were not available to the desert tribes nearby, and the people learned to weave.

The settled and even tenor of their simple lives apparently ended in about the year 1100, when they moved into the cliff-side dwellings, first laboriously building up the floors of the caves and ledges so they could construct their underground kivas. The cities were created to withstand a siege. The city called Balcony House, for example, was reached only by crawling through a twelve-foot tunnel, which was fourteen inches wide and could be easily defended by just one man.

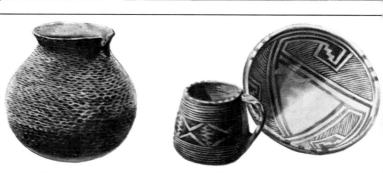

MESA VERDE POTTERY
The women of Mesa Verde fashioned corrugated fireproof vessels, right, which were used for cooking, for storage and for soaking dried beans. During the golden age of their culture they continued to develop and refine their arts and crafts, producing their finest pottery mugs, bowls, jars, pitchers and dippers. Using a paint that was prepared from plants, they executed unique black designs on a glossy white background.

Mesa Verde

It would seem that these people were the victims of constant attacks, yet there is no evidence of any nomadic warlike tribes in the area. And of ninety thousand artifacts which have been discovered in the ruins, only two hundred are the points of spears and arrows. This is hardly what an archaeologist would expect to find if they really did live in fear.

It is possible that the cliff dwellings were winter quarters, colder but more sheltered than the windswept mesa. But the difficulties of living in confined aeries with children, dogs and domesticated turkeys must have been immense. Water was about a quarter of a mile away. Every stick of firewood would have to be carried up.

There is, however, no doubt that the cities were lived in. The overhanging roofs of the cliff caverns are still black from the smoke of cooking fires. The inside walls of many of the small rooms are decorated with reddish pigments and simple patterns. Parts of the sandstone floors are hollowed where men customarily sharpened their stone axes. Below every cave there is a trash heap of turkey bones, broken pottery and rubble.

By the end of the thirteenth century the cliff dwellings were empty. The golden age of Mesa Verde culture had come to a sudden end. It may well have been the bad drought between 1276 and 1299 that drove the people away. Yet the study of growth rings in the poles used as rafters shows that the people had survived extended droughts in the past. If there was internal dissension among the people there is no sign of it. Perhaps an early form of high-rise neurosis, similar to that suffered by some people who live in modern skyscrapers, led the people to seek a different mode of life. Nobody can be certain. The undiscovered secrets of Mesa Verde and its dimly drawn people remain the essence of its enchantment.

Cliff Palace, built about A.D. 1200 under the protection of a high, vaulted cave roof, is the largest cliff dwelling in the Southwest. Containing more than two hundred rooms, there are twenty-three kivas—ceremonial rooms used primarily by men. It is believed that in the Mesa Verde society the women owned the living quarters.

THE ENDLESS RANGE

The level landscape, stretching twelve hundred miles from Canada to the Gulf of Mexico and five hundred miles from the Mississippi River to the foothills of the Rocky Mountains, extends into eight states neatly arranged in the heart of the continent. Far from coast and mountains, the Endless Range is a geometric world. Boundary fences, roads and railroads all intersect at right angles. Immense rectangles of golden grain alternate with areas of black earth, where the turned sod lies fallow for a year to preserve its moisture. The groove of the plow and the track of the harvester create simple geometric patterns, austere but lovely, based on the elegance of the long, straight line.

Nowhere else but on the ocean does the wind have such free play. On this sea of grass there are few trees and no obstacles to break the even tenor of the winds which sweep across to the Rocky Mountains. During their epic crossing of the continent, in 1804, Lewis and Clark set the sails of one of their boats and let it blow across the Great Plains on wheels.

At that time the plains were the homeland of the nomadic Indian tribes, fierce fighters and formidable hunters of the massive buffalo, which roamed the grasslands in their thousands. They fought over hunting territory with the farming tribes living in permanent villages. It was the Lewis and Clark expedition which marked the beginning of the Indians' struggle to keep the white man out of traditional Indian lands. But their war was fought in vain, despite Crazy Horse's celebrated victory at Little Bighorn.

In the wake of Lewis and Clark, a great human tide rolled west. By the 1840s, hundreds of thousands of emigrants had passed through the plains, but they never considered remaining in this desolate ocean of grass, which they inappropriately named the Great Desert.

It was not until the 1850s that the pioneers began to realize that the tall native prairie grasses had to be supported by rich, arable soil. A few families left the crowded Mississippi Valley and started a new life in the plains. The Homestead Act of 1862, which granted ownership of a piece of land to a man if he lived on it and cultivated it for five years, gave further encouragement to settlers to come to these vast, empty spaces.

The early settlers in the plains had to dig for water, the way other men dug for gold. Later they built windmills, using the almost ceaseless winds to pump water for their crops and cattle. In a land without trees, they learned to build houses with sod instead of timber and to make fires with dry grass instead of wood. Life was a constant battle against the elements for the prairie pioneers, but they not only survived, they also succeeded in converting the Great Desert into some of the most productive farmland in the world.

Nevertheless, plainsmen have always had to gamble against nature in this region, and for a period during the 1930s the elements won out. Severe drought and overfarming created huge dust bowls unfit for cultivation, and another great migration westward was undertaken by hungry farmers and their families. Modern plains farmers have vivid memories of those hard times, and, like their pioneer forefathers, they carefully maintain the discipline and ingenuity so necessary for survival here.

The rich farms begin beneath the towering Mississippi Palisades and among the wooded, gentle, green hills of the Ozarks. They stretch from the Rio Grande, sweeping around Big Bend, through the deserts of Texas to the arid foothills of the Rockies and the forbidding Badlands of the Dakotas. But they are most impressive on the level grasslands. There the flatness, the emptiness, the vastness of the Endless Range are unforgettable.

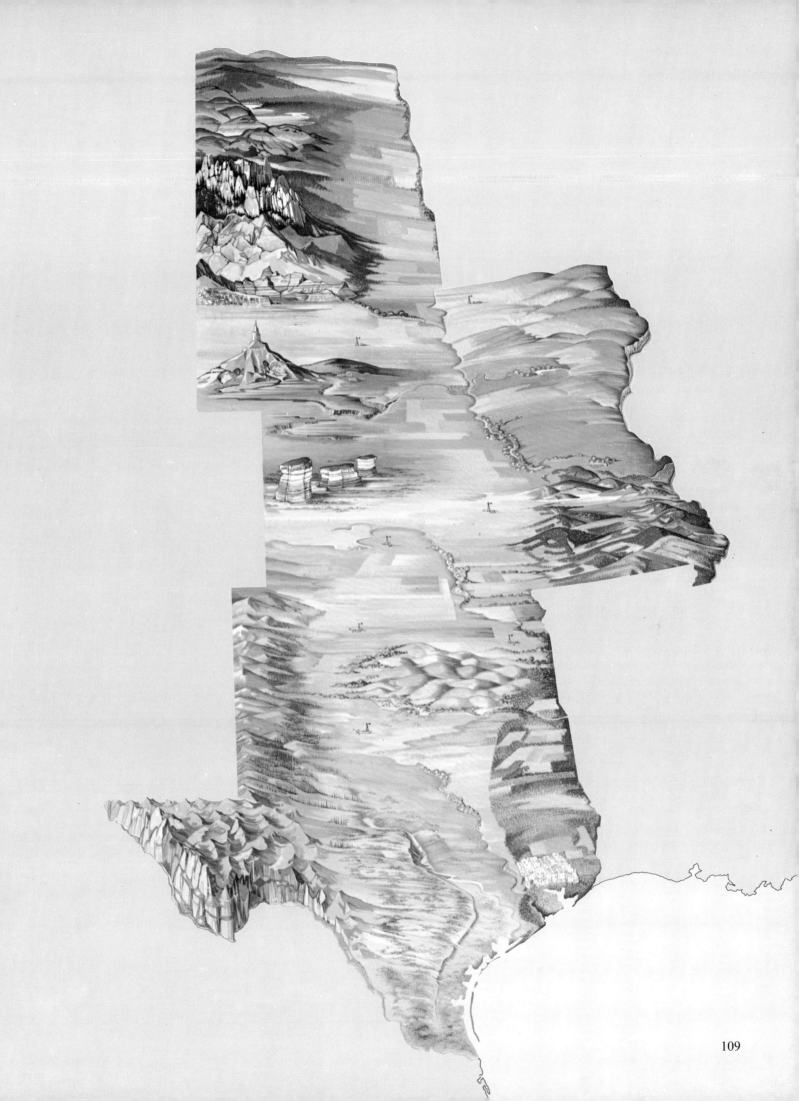

Like towering walls of adjacent castles, these weatherworn cliffs rise steeply from the banks of the Mississippi River. Like sentinels, their peaks and pinnacles look out over the upper reaches of the mighty river as it sweeps past Wisconsin, Iowa and Illinois, forsaking its modest origin in a cool Minnesota lake to become Father of the Waters. The brows of these dramatic bluffs are like camouflaged battlements, fern-clad, wooded and, in summer, disguised with bluebells, violets and wild geraniums.

Stately and magnificent, sturdy and impregnable, the Mississippi Palisades convey a feeling of rock-hard eternity. But it is an illusion, a deception, a trick of time conspiring with nature. Hundreds of millions of years ago, immense inland seas covered the North American interior. There was nothing here but water and strange, tiny aquatic animals—mummy-shaped trilobites, spiral-shelled gastropods, long-stemmed crinoids and a variety of other diminutive marine creatures, which were among the first things that ever lived. The shells and skeletons of billions of them sank to the floor of the inland waters to make soft, shifting layers of sediment which gradually hardened into limestone. Long after the inland waters withdrew, the Mississippi River, probing its way south, began carving its bed through the petrified sedimentary remains, in which prehistoric fossils can still be found.

Now the cliffs rise, in places, more than five hundred feet above the river. It is not surprising that Père Marquette, a keenly observant man who set out from Canada to explore the Mississippi River three hundred years ago, reached this point and was fooled by the Iowa bluffs, noting in his journal, "To the right is a chain of very high mountains."

To look up from the river is a neck-stretching exercise in awe. Looking down from a cliff edge is like peering through a fissure in the sky at the Mississippi in its southward journey. They are visions which evoke and refresh a reverence for nature's magic, modulated here by the transition from the high, sheer bluffs to rolling, tree-covered hills sloping gently away from the palisades, by tributaries winding through craggy ravines to join the river and by thickly wooded valleys.

The Delta Queen, one of the last of the Mississippi paddlesteamers, which at one time numbered more than four hundred, makes her way past the high bluffs of the Mississippi Palisades, which soar up to five hundred feet above this hundred-mile stretch of the meandering river.

This palisades region has been inhabited a long time. For hundreds of years, trails have run along the cliff sides, as the Great River Road now does, and through the adjoining hill country. Arrowheads and other Indian relics, many of which have made their way to museums near and far, are still sometimes found in the vicinity. On the Iowa side, at Effigy Mounds National Monument near the city of Marquette, extensive remains bear witness to the existence here of a long-vanished Indian civilization which mastered the problem of survival and could, therefore, devote time and energy to building, to art and to sophisticated worship. These mound builders constructed animal and bird effigies, some of them hundreds of feet long, sometimes with a surrealistic flavor. They were designed in tribute to the spirits of the forest creatures the Indians venerated. Other, probably earlier, Indians of this region built dome-capped burial mounds to honor their dead, and sur-

Mississippi Palisades

rounded them with protective earthworks. The remains of some of these burial mounds can still be seen near the Illinois palisades.

Later settlers also displayed an impressive measure of imagination and ingenuity. Among them was the Ringling family, which, in the middle of the nineteenth century, produced five sons, four of them born in the Iowa palisades city of McGregor, where, while still youngsters, they planted the roots of the later internationally famous Ringling

Brothers Circus by holding penny shows in their backyard.

Not far to the south is a pleasantly wooded region climbing up from the palisade horizon. It is called Pikes Peak, although, of course, it is not the better-known outcropping of that name which stands at the edge of the Rockies. This peak, however, was found and climbed by explorer Zebulon Pike well before he sighted the Colorado rising that was to make him famous.

The Mississippi cliffs were named after the Hudson River Palisades of New Jersey, an injustice to both. They have also been compared to castellated bluffs along the Rhine in Germany, but the comparison is weak. The Mississippi Palisades are unique in beauty, grandeur and mood. Rugged, proud, serene, incongruously bisecting one of the richest agricultural regions in the world, they mount guard over a mighty river as it gathers momentum for the plunge southward to the sea.

Monument Rocks

It was hope that spurred them on—hope for a new life, hope for a brighter future, hope for a lucky strike in the goldfields of the Rocky Mountains. The Smoky Hill River Trail was the fastest and shortest route between Missouri and Denver, where, in 1858, gold was discovered at Pikes Peak. In their thousands, men headed west with their gold pans, their shovels and their families.

These lonely crags of chalk overlooking the Smoky Hill River in the vast and monotonous emptiness of western Kansas were beacons on that trail of hope. But it was not long before Monument Rocks became a symbol of disillusion, where dreams were dashed. For it was along this part of the trail that many of those optimists traveling west met the disenchanted who were returning east.

These ivory-hued rocks, standing out on the dun-colored prairie, must have sheltered many anxious families who drew up their wagons to get out of the prairie winds and to finally face the awful decision—to return home or to press on to an unknown future, with no hope of gold.

Before long the river valley was dotted with abandoned stoves and other heavy hardware jettisoned from wagons for lightness as disillusioned pioneers turned their backs on the westward trail. Others carried on. Even if there was no gold, perhaps there was at least a better life ahead.

At this time the rocks were also an important stage on the first daily transcontinental mail service by stage line. The Butterfield Overland Despatch carried mail from Missouri to the Pacific in twenty-five days, a three-day improvement on the sea route via Panama. But shortage of water and lack of protection from Indian attack forced the route to be given up in favor of the Oregon Trail.

The rocks, which figured so briefly in the history of the West, are in two main groups on the edge of the wide and shallow Smoky Hill River valley. Gaunt and stark, they seem out of place, like seaside cliffs in search of a beach. Indeed, they are remnants of an ancient seabed. In the stratified layers of deposited chalk are the fossilized remains of tiny creatures that inhabited the Permian Sea,

which covered the plains two hundred and fifty million years ago. As natural forces eroded the surrounding land, the chalk was exposed.

For many thousands of years the rocks were fashioned into pillared and pedimental shapes by chiseling winds and corrosive rain. In places the rocks are now so thin that arches and windows have been formed in their walls. The lower part of each pinnacle is pale gray, merging into a beautiful cream color banded at the top by dark yellow ocher. Each rock, about sixty feet high, is topped by a level brim of grass where pigeons and other prairie birds settle—until the sinister outline of a patrolling hawk appears overhead and they scatter.

Today a straight dirt road connecting far-flung ranches passes between the rocks and cattle roam among them. The lonely rocks flute a low humming note in the prairie winds as, imperceptibly, they are eaten away by weather. Since their brief period of historical importance Monument Rocks have been by-passed. In another few centuries they will have disappeared completely.

The gaunt shapes of Monument Rocks eroded by rain and almost ceaseless wind stand out on the open Kansas plains. For pioneers heading west from Independence, Missouri, along the Smoky Hill River Trail to Denver, the rocks marked the beginning of the difficult trek uphill into the foothills of the Rocky Mountains.

THE TREK WEST

Some pioneers loaded their possessions onto pack animals or two-wheel carts and walked the two thousand miles to the Far West. Most families, however, traveled in wagons. The wagon's cover was made of canvas or heavy cotton twill and was waterproofed with linseed oil. Pucker ropes at either end could be tightened to provide protection and privacy. There was about five feet of headroom inside the usual ten-foot by four-foot wagon, which became home for the twenty weeks that it took to reach California or Oregon.

Chimney Rock

The pencil-thin silhouette became visible through the trail dust at a distance of about thirty miles. So close did it seem across the rolling prairie that horseback riders would often gallop off to inspect it, only to return when they realized how badly they had misjudged the distance. Another two or three days would pass before the lumbering ox wagons of pioneers on the Oregon Trail finally drew abreast of the weird, slender pinnacle known as Chimney Rock. Then, when camp had been made at a nearby spring and the oxen turned out to graze, men would scramble through the sword grass and cacti growing on the rock's conical base to carve their names in the pillar's soft, pinkish sandstone.

Erosion has long since wiped the rock clean, removing all traces of those signatures made during the West's most exciting times. But at least eighty personal journals survive to tell of the rigors and hazards of those covered-wagon journeys undertaken during the middle of the nineteenth century. And all but three of them dwell on the mystery and fascination of this fragile tower of pale rock which was such a distinctive landmark on the overland route to the West.

A quarter of a million men, women and children—trappers, traders, forty-niners, settlers—passed by Chimney Rock during the great migrations across the continent. During 1852, at the height of the California Gold Rush, fifty thousand people stopped here between the bluffs marking the edge of the Wild Cat Hills and the North Platte River three miles to the north. Although the Mormon Trail followed the other bank of the river, many Mormons could not resist the temptation to swim or ford the river for a closer look at the unusual rock standing out from the bluffs like a giant totem pole.

The rock, shaped like an inverted funnel, is actually a remnant of a great plain which was eroded away by the river. Its pinkish clay and sandstone are striped with pale layers of volcanic ash that millions of years ago were carried on the wind from eruptions near Yellowstone. The pillar itself stands about one hundred feet high, its conical base about four hundred feet high. To one seven-year-old trekking west on the Great Migration of 1843 it seemed "to touch the sky." It was described in travelers' diaries in many different ways but was named for its resemblance to the ruins of a house razed by fire.

For the migrants, Chimney Rock was also an ominous landmark. Behind them lay five hundred miles of plains, level and easygoing. Ahead lay mountains, deserts and marauding Indians; nothing but danger and hardship loomed. Many victims of the stoically accepted hazards of the Oregon Trail lie buried in unmarked graves near the rock—people who succumbed to cholera, accidentally shot themselves with unfamiliar firearms or were crushed to death by wagon wheels.

At that time the rock was square in outline and possibly taller. Today it is needle sharp, as graceful and as perfectly formed as a cathedral spire. It presides over the overgrown wheel ruts of the westward trail and is surrounded by ranchlands, but accessible by rough track. It stands as a natural monument to the passing of a nation's exciting era, a forgotten milepost alone with many ghosts.

Chimney Rock, above, was one of the last landmarks on the easier section of the Oregon Trail, which here was passing through the Sand Hills where this small party of pioneers, left, are enjoying their well-earned midday rest. In this section a wagon train could progress up to twenty miles in a day. On the trail a normal day began at four o'clock with the roundup of the teams of oxen and mules and any cattle brought along to provide food. By seven o'clock everyone had breakfasted, the tents had been struck, the wagons loaded, the teams yoked and the trek west resumed. At noon the wagons were unhitched, the stock watered and the midday meal eaten. After a brief rest the train pressed onward until dusk, when the wagons were formed into a circle, more for reassurance than from fear of Indian attack. The stock was turned out to graze, the evening meal eaten and by eight o'clock most people were asleep.

The force which withered and distorted the level grasslands of the prairie and created the spectral canyons called the Badlands is nothing more sinister than running water. Eating into the soft soil like an acid, it has created gaunt vistas of bare ridges, domes and gullies.

Yet there is an eerie fascination about the Dakota Badlands. Despite the air of desolation, this landscape is not without a certain haunting, tingling beauty. When the sun is low the pallid colors of the miniature mountains of bare earth develop warm and rich hues. The grotesque configurations are transformed into a delicate scene with all the rich detail of an old engraving.

The Badlands extend for one hundred miles along the Little Missouri River in North Dakota, and for about the same distance along the White River in South Dakota. The meander-

ing rivers have cut down through the plains, creating flat-floored canyons several miles wide. The canyons are dotted with bare mesas and pinnacles of earth which are in the slow process of being washed away by torrential summer rainstorms. As the grass is undermined, the edges of the canyons eat into the plains, forming walls of imperceptibly oozing landslides which extend far into the distance.

Although they are the result of similar natural processes, parts of the two places—one a national park, the other a national monument—have quite different atmospheres. The starkness of the eroded gorges, buttes and knolls in the North Dakota Badlands is relieved by scrub, grass and juniper trees growing on all but the steepest slip faces, and by bands of brick-red crumbly soil. This brilliant coloring was caused when lightning set alight

thin veins of coal which, as it smoldered, baked the surrounding rock. At sunset the bands of terra-cotta crimson glow ember bright amid the darkening shadows of the canyons. The Badlands, described as "hell with the fires out," glint in the setting sun and you begin to wonder if the fires still burn.

When, in 1883, a young sportsman named Theodore Roosevelt went west to hunt buffalo it was to this neglected frontier that he came. The magical scenery and the opportunity of establishing a cattle industry here so enthused him that he invested as part-owner in a ranch in the Little Missouri Valley. When, two years later, his mother and his wife died on the same day it was on his Elkhorn Ranch in the Badlands that he sought solace in a season's hard riding and work with the cowboys.

"There are few sensations I prefer," he

Theodore Roosevelt first came to the North Dakota Badlands in 1883. He spent a great deal of time there, hunting and ranching, until 1898 when he was elected Governor of New York. He served as President from 1901 to 1908. During his term of office he became known as the Conservation President, setting aside one hundred and thirty-two million acres of forest reserves, and signing the Antiquities Act, which allowed areas of outstanding historical and archaeological values to be set aside as national monuments by presidential proclamation. Under this act, Roosevelt proclaimed fifteen national monuments and obtained Congressional approval for five national parks.

The Dakota Badlands

wrote, "to that of galloping over these rolling limitless prairies, rifle in hand, or winding my way among the barren, fantastic and grimly picturesque deserts of the so-called Bad Lands. . . ." A disastrous loss of stock, caused by overgrazing and the crippling winter of 1887, taught the man who was to become known as the "Conservation President" a practical lesson in conservation that he was never to forget.

Today two of the most beautiful areas of North Dakota's Little Missouri Badlands, totaling one hundred and ten square miles, together with the site of Roosevelt's ranch, which lies between them, form the Theodore Roosevelt National Memorial Park. Americans are able to enjoy the stark beauty just as Roosevelt did when he was forming his first constructive ideas on the importance of con-

serving the nation's natural heritage. As President, he considered historic and scenic, as well as economic, values when he assessed nature's resources.

The Badlands National Monument covers three hundred and eighty square miles of South Dakota's Big Badlands. They are grimmer and bleaker; there is little vegetation. The grassy plain drops abruptly into a confused and contorted moonscape of wizened mountains and valleys, bone-white and gray in color. Only fifteen inches of precipitation occurs in a year, ten inches of it in violent downpours. Rain undermines the brim of the plains, causing the edges to sag. When the covering sods fall, the soft earth beneath is formed into towering pinnacles and sharp ridges from which it gradually oozes downward. Where layers of sandstone have resisted the melting

effect of rainwater and the scouring of winds, they form ledges that protrude several feet from the undercut cliff faces. Everywhere the bare soil is grooved by countless small channels forming intricate patterns.

The etched beauty of the Badlands conceals their treachery. You have only to step off the established trails to discover their true nature and to appreciate how they got their name. Every slope and any bare horizontal surface is covered by a fragile crust only an inch or so deep. Beneath it, the soil is a gummy, sodden mass. Walking in the Badlands is like mountaineering on wet soap. Indians named the slippery valleys and hills *mako sica* and French Canadian trappers, who were the first white men through the area, named them *les mauvaises terres à traverser*, which means much the same thing—bad lands to cross.

The black-footed ferret was unknown to science until 1851 when Audubon and Bachman described it from a pelt obtained from a trapper. Now one of North America's rarest animals, the ferret survives in the Badlands, despite the decline of the prairie dog, its principal prey.

Wind, water and frost worked together to carve this unearthly landscape in the Dakota Badlands. The rocks are richly studded with fossilized remains of the varied prehistoric life forms found in the area as long as sixty million years ago. Fossils of tiny nautiluses have been found imbedded in the same rock as petrified

giant alligator bones. Other past inhabitants of the area include twenty-five species of oreodonts, titanotheres, saber-toothed tigers and ancestors of present-day horses, camels, llamas, pigs and rhinoceroses.

According to the treaty of 1868 between the United States Government and the Sioux Indians, "No white person or persons shall be permitted to settle upon or occupy any portion of the territory, or without the consent of the Indians to pass through the same." Thus the land between the Missouri River and the Bighorn Mountains was granted to the Sioux forever. Satisfied with being able to roam hundreds of miles without seeing a white man, the Sioux hunted the buffalo on which they depended for everything—clothing, food and tents—and kept the peace. But within the territory lay *Paha Sapa*, the Black Hills, most sacred place of the Sioux, where braves went to speak to their gods. To many white men, however, the ponderosa-clad hills, which from a distance looked so strangely black, seemed a likely place to find gold. And in violation of the treaty, prospectors entered the Indians' holy mountains.

By 1874, there were so many rumors about gold in the hills that the Army sent General Custer with one thousand men to reconnoiter the area. Geologists soon proved what everyone had so long suspected—the hills were indeed filled with gold.

So much for treaties. Within two years the pines of the Black Hills were being cut to build crude cabins. Sluice boxes, ditches, dams and hundreds of stamp mills cluttered the small creeks in Deadwood Gulch. When the Sioux exacted their fruitless revenge by massacring Custer and all his men at the Battle of the Little Bighorn in June 1876, the narrow main street of Deadwood was already lined with saloons, stores and hotels. These South Dakota hills had become the richest gold-producing area of North America, and the stage for some of the most colorful sagas in the opening of the West.

The Black Hills Gold Rush made a folk-heroine of a lady in a buckskin suit who scouted for the Army, gambled, worked as a bullwhacker and could swear with a sting that put mule skinners to shame—Calamity Jane. It martyred a law marshal who sat down to a game of poker with his back to the door, much against his better judgment, and was shot in the head—Wild Bill Hickock. The lawlessness of Deadwood when whiskey was cheap and food was scarce has become a legend.

It was an era of such unforgettable characters as Poker Alice, the well-bred young lady from England who became a cigar-smoking cardsharper, "Potato Creek" Johnny, the last of the old-time prospectors, and Deadwood Dick, the hero of dime novels. The pine-shaded Mount Moriah Cemetery above Deadwood is the final resting place of some of these Wild West characters. Here, Calamity Jane, a pistol in each hand, lies buried next to the grave of her friend Wild Bill.

In the wilderness of the Black Hills, these colorful figures of Americana are now associated with four Presidents of the nation. For on Mount Rushmore, a granite bluff towering from the high forest, an artist chiseled and dynamited from solid rock what he considered America's shrine to democracy.

The sculptor was Gutzon Borglum. Born in Idaho, the son of a Danish doctor and rancher, he was a respected artist when, in 1924, Doane Robinson, the director of the South Dakota State Historical Society, invited him to carve such heroic figures of the West as Kit Carson and Jim Bridger in a rock escarpment of the Black Hills. The idealistic Borglum believed, however, that a subject worthy of a mountain should be no less than a monument to the ideals and aspirations of the nation. Over a period of fourteen years, Borglum, and local men whom he trained, chipped away almost half a million tons of rock from the sunny side of the six-thousand-foot peak. Dangling over the sheer rock face in bosuns' chairs, they carved, with pneumatic drills and dynamite, the heads of four great American Presidents.

Borglum's artistry and engineering skill created a memorial not only to the Presidents, but also to the qualities of nationhood which their leadership bestowed—the independence established by George Washington, the rights of the individual as set out by Thomas Jefferson, the integrity of united states preserved by Abraham Lincoln, the right of every American to a square deal as propounded by Theodore Roosevelt. Mount Rushmore is one man's personification of the imagination, intelligence, determination and integrity which has sustained America through two hundred years.

The sculptor died in 1941, just before the sixty-foot-high heads were completed. He created a work that will endure for an eternity, for the granite faces will weather away by only half an inch every ten thousand years.

The sculpture itself, and the vision of its creator, is lent an added significance by its setting in ancient mountains surrounded by thousands of acres of forests and grassland where buffalo roam.

Another giant rock sculpture is nearing completion in the Black Hills. Begun in 1948 by sculptor Korczak Ziolkowski, it is a 563-foot-tall mounted figure of Crazy Horse, a leader of the Black Hills Sioux who, in the struggle to retain their land, won the battles but lost the war.

Cathedral Spires thrusts out above the dark ponderosa pines which cloak the Black Hills. Each spire is made up of columns of granite, which are hard enough to resist erosion, divided by softer rock that is crumbling away.

To the Sioux, the Black Hills were sacred ground barred to white men "forever" by the Treaty of 1868. But in 1874 General Custer, left, with his Indian scouts, led twelve hundred troops into the hills in search of gold, which they found. The Government was unable to force the Sioux to sell their sacred ground and took it by force. But the Indians, under Crazy Horse and Sitting Bull, had the satisfaction of winning the Battle of the Little Bighorn in 1876 at which Custer lost his life.

The figures of Washington, Jefferson, Theodore Roosevelt and Lincoln were carved from the granite rock of Mount Rushmore. Work on the project, one of the largest sculptures ever undertaken, was started in 1927 and completed fourteen years later. The heads of the four Presidents are between sixty and seventy feet high.

Many of the streams and rivers of the Ozarks have cut their way through the soft sedimentary rocks down to the tough old granite rock, which has slowed up the process of erosion and constricted the flow of water into narrow rocky clefts known as shut-ins. Extensive meandering lakes, like this one near Johnson's Shut-In, often build up above these bottlenecks. The lakes and forests of the Ozark region were first explored by Zebulon Pike, who described the country as "one of the most beautiful the eye ever beheld." The Spanish explorers Hernando de Soto and Francisco Coronado are thought to have passed through the Ozarks in the sixteenth century, but the first white men to really penetrate the forests and rivers were French trappers who traded for furs with the Osage Indians. The region was part of the Louisiana Territory acquired for the United States by Thomas Jefferson in the Louisiana Purchase of 1803.

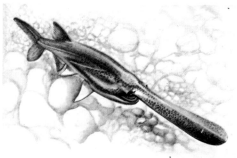

The gravel bars of the muddy Osage River are one of the few remaining spawning grounds of the paddlefish, which can weigh up to one hundred and sixty pounds and is virtually unchanged since prehistoric times. The fish's long snout contains a complex system of sense organs, which help it locate the plankton on which it feeds.

118

Ozark Waterways

There must have been a plan for it. This magical shoreline could not have happened by itself. These strangely shaped miniature peninsulas could not have been accidental —not in this man-made lake. But, in fact, they are accidental; all of them—the duck's head, the pecking chicken, the pointed fingers, the dozens of different human profiles—all etched in green against the crystal blue water, all a whim of nature rather than of man, although it was man who set the stage for this Lake of the Ozarks.

In 1930, the Bagnell Dam was thrown across Missouri's fast-flowing Osage River to provide hydroelectric power for the surrounding area. The rushing waters backed up behind the dam to form the lake, 129 miles long and one of the largest man-made bodies of water in the world. But that statistic does not come close to telling the whole story. Winding, bending, crinkling and poking out fingers of water to shape a profusion of coves, inlets and intriguing figures from the surrounding land, the lake's shoreline measures more than thirteen hundred miles, almost half the width of the continent, meandering like a carefree doodle over the map of central Missouri.

Some of the lake is lined with gaunt limestone fortress escarpments. Elsewhere along its banks, hillocks, wooded with oak, wild crab, elm and hickory and threaded with trails, slope upward toward treetop horizons. Then they descend to the most captivating aspect of this lakescape, the sometimes strange, sometimes quaint land shapes fashioned from the Ozark uplands by the lake and its countless gentle tentacles. This is a panorama of tranquility, a place of enchantment, one of the scenic spectacles of the American heartland.

The land which makes the basin of the lake was once valleys of the Ozark Mountains. The Ozarks are a scenic wonder in their own right, rising and falling wooded highlands stretching between the Missouri and Arkansas rivers. This range is the only large expanse of rugged elevated landscape between the Rockies and the Appalachians.

In prehistoric times, the Ozarks were towering mountains. But erosion, over millions of years, has done its work particularly well here. It has left occasionally stark, mostly graceful, always agreeable rolling countryside, canopied with hardwoods, softened by glades and meadows, dotted with caves, natural arches and precipitous ridges, and alive with color— primrose, wild grape, honeysuckle, heliotrope and hydrangea, plus countless nuances of green. There is also good farmland in the Ozarks and extensive tracts of bluegrass pasture.

This was once hillbilly country, home of clannish, withdrawn mountain people, descended from footloose frontiersmen who went this far but no farther in search of privacy and elbowroom. The hillbillies were, not always accurately, best known for their rabbit guns, hound dogs, family feuds, "moonshine likker," sleeping all day by the fishing hole and their ability to get through life without schools, clocks or shoes. Much fun has been made of them, but much that has been said is untrue or exaggerated—tall mountain tales that got out of hand.

Things have changed, in any case, and if there is still a lot of timeless fishing going on, it is because the Ozarks can be a timeless place and because Missouri waters are an angler's dream, full of goggle-eye, black and striped bass, catfish, crappie and paddlefish.

Although bureaucratic-sounding descriptions can often diminish the splendor of captivating sights, the glories of the Ozark National Scenic Riverways, not far off, have managed to withstand the blunting effects of officialese. More than fifty thousand acres have been marked off here as a natural legacy, a parkland of rushing, babbling and gently flowing streams, of rock-fed crystal-clear springs and of soft early-morning mists hauntingly cloaking the surface.

Trails through the woods lead to the banks of the Current River and its Jack Forks tributary, the core of the Scenic Riverways, as well as to some of their enchanting seminal springs. The most popular way to get around and to capture the mood of the Ozarks is in a flat-bottomed johnboat, a remarkably well-balanced contrivance indigenous to this area. And the johnboat is admirably suited for the great local pastime, float fishing, just drifting through this midcontinent wonderland, with a trailing line to catch what comes.

Five genera of true cave salamanders are known to exist in the United States. One of them, the Ozark, or grotto, salamander, is found only in the Ozarks. As larvae, these salamanders have functioning eyes which atrophy as they grow older, the eyelids fusing almost shut.

One early traveler reported that the Ozarks "abounded in millions of turkeys," but they were threatened by hunting and land clearing. Now they are protected and thrive in the Ozark forests, strutting the clearings in their colorful spring courtship ritual.

The Arbuckle Mountains

The shadows come alive in the late afternoon. The setting sun etches ever-lengthening silhouettes on the craggy rock formations of this cavern-like enclosure. As the light of the day begins its slow retreat, the rocks seem to grow larger and to huddle closer together.

Devil's Den is now a popular attraction, a rugged patch of vacationland, a haven for rock climbers, anglers and sightseers. But it is clear why the Indians believed demons lived here. A whisper in its Dead Man's Cave bounces off the walls and comes back like a murmuring breeze or a mystical incantation. Put your ear to the ground and the rapids of nearby Pennington Creek sound like a bubbling caldron. Duck away from the bright sun, press your back against a shaded rock and a cold shudder will run down your spine.

But perhaps the Indians saw their demons in the strange shapes of the rocks of this boulder-strewn badland. Subsequent visitors also saw images in these formations and gave them descriptive names—Devil's Coffin, Witch's Tomb, Skull Canyon, Devil's Throne. They were once forbidding visions; now they make a gallery of nature in the rough, of waking dreams, of imagination turned loose. Here is an Indian head, there a crouching animal, here an anvil, there a fist.

More fearful of the law than of demons, in the days of the Wild West, outlaws would make helter-skelter for Devil's Den, confi-dent that United States marshals would not pursue them into what was, before it became a state of the union, the Oklahoma no-man's land. Not far away there is an unmarked burial ground for the men who managed to nurse bad wounds only long enough to gallop to safety and oblivion.

Despite appearances, the rocks of Devil's Den were not hurled into position and piled into place by prehistoric giants or even by volcanoes. They are remnants of formations more than a billion and a half years old, a spur of the nearby Arbuckle Mountains, sparsely wooded with blackjack oak, soapberry and red cedar. Over a long span of time, water and wind wore down the rocks to carve out the den and its entrancing rock shapes.

North of Devil's Den, in the gently rolling foothills of the Arbuckle Range, is Platt National Park, only 912 acres, but a welcome relief in the largely barren surrounding countryside. Here there are grass-covered hills and valleys, woods, waterfalls, springs and sparkling streams. Although desert-like, Oklahoma cactus sprouts from hillside rocks and creek beds, pink-flowered cat's claw, Virginia creeper, Spanish larkspur and other wild buds redeem the Arcadian mood of this natural playground.

There is also a special place, a central pasture, set aside for a different sort of redemption. A small herd of shaggy bison, a few of the few saved by man from extinction by man, takes shelter here in a setting reminiscent of the days when these hulking, timid creatures roamed by the millions across the Great Plains.

Man is not the only visitor to Platt Park. The roadrunner, a bird more commonly found in the desert country to the west, finds its way here and sometimes can be seen running its absurd race along park roads. It is a place for birds, a protected sanctuary, and more than one hundred winged species touch down here—including soaring sparrow hawks, stately herons, wrens, cardinals and meadowlarks. Some are in transit on their annual migratory excursions, dropping in, not unlike many human visitors, for a rest and a meal. Other birds spend their winters in the park and, come spring, they can be seen restlessly preparing for a return to their homes in northern climes.

It is said that a treasure may be buried somewhere in the neighborhood, a fortune in ancient coins and gems hidden more than four hundred years ago by Spanish conquistadors to lighten their load when they scouted the region in search of legendary cities of gold. The Spanish found no palaces in Oklahoma, but if they looked out from the crest of Bromide Hill, a steep wooded bluff now within Platt Park boundaries, the view, as now, would have encompassed a different sort of treasure, a panoramic vista of a lush oasis, framed by a gaunt, sunbaked landscape.

The nine-banded armadillo is unable to endure cold and its range extends only as far north as the southeast corner of Oklahoma. Despite its thirty teeth, the armadillo is North America's only edentate, a member of the mammalian order *Edentata*, which means toothless. The name of the species is derived from the nine transverse bands of horn, which give flexibility to the animal's protective shield. When cornered by a dog or coyote, against which its armor plating is inadequate, the armadillo tries first to dig itself into the ground. If it fails it feigns death like the opossum.

The Arbuckle Reservoir, above, nestles among the woods of the Arbuckle Mountains. Oak, hickory, walnut, elm and pine cloak the slopes of the Arbuckles, which were formed some three hundred million years ago by violent earthquakes that folded the rocks into great high corrugations. These were later eroded down into a low range of hills.

The waters of Honey Creek tumble over the Turner Falls, right, in the Arbuckle Mountains. Most waterfalls are the result of rivers eroding away rock layers, but these falls were created by the creek, which built up a precipice of travertine over which it now plunges seventy-five feet into a secluded pool below.

Big Bend is America's last primitive frontier. The desert mountains and rubble-strewn arroyos shimmer in the stillness and the heat. Chalky-green and swift, the Rio Grande glides and ripples in a wide curve between soft banks dotted with scrub. Beyond, the Sierra del Carmen Mountains of Mexico rise in a magnificent purple wall. Villagers with desert-weathered faces punt over in an old boat from Mexico to shop at the general store, once an outpost of the Texas Rangers. The calm scene is immensely grand, yet there is a sense of restrained excitement. You feel that a raiding party of whooping Comanches might appear suddenly among the tamarisk and seepwillow growing along the opposite bank.

The great southward curve of the river, which marks the edge of the United States and is also, for 107 miles, the boundary of Big Bend National Park, is one of the world's most romantic international borders. There are no road crossings in the park and there is little visible evidence of border control. On the Texas side you can hire a burro and ford the river to Mexico. In three places the river cuts through narrow canyons with walls fifteen hundred feet high. Floating through one of them in a boat you can touch the United States with one hand and Mexico with the other.

The eleven hundred square miles of rough lowland desert and jumbled mountains belong topographically to the great emptiness of Chihuahua in Mexico. It was designated a national park in 1935 because it is the only place in the United States where this arid, brittle, fascinating landscape exists. And because the territory south of the river has not been protected, the national park is the finest example of the Chihuahua desert.

It is a desert that is on the same latitude as the central Sahara and the Himalayas. But Big Bend is green with dark-leaved creosote bush, tar bush and dozens of different types of spiny cactus and spear-leaved yuccas. Its ancient and jaggedly heaped mountains are mostly bare rock, but open woodland finds sufficient moisture above five thousand feet where, two or three times a year, there is a light sprinkling of snow. The geology of the Chisos Mountains is so complex that a map showing the different formations requires twenty-five shades of color. Rising to seven thousand feet from rolling scrub desert fluted by dozens of dry watercourses, the mountains are such a picture of haphazard creation that the Indians believed they were heaps of rubble left over from the building of the world.

In this desert a man needs a gallon of water to walk twenty miles beneath the pitiless sun. Water is scarce, except in the summer wet season, when the arroyos become raging muddy torrents for a few hours at a time. Springs are found mainly on the slopes of the mountains, and the roots of shrubs are often larger than their branches. Those who ranched in Big Bend, or mined for quicksilver, quickly learned to climb for water and dig for firewood. Yet a man can find sufficient moisture for survival if he knows how. Like the birds and animals, you can break open the flat pads of prickly pear cactus and suck out the juicy flesh, which slakes your thirst. All species are edible and some are as delicious as strawberries.

The miracle of this desert is its abundance of living things—most of them strange and some not particularly nice, but all of them fascinating. There is the strange plant called ocotillo, which grows everywhere, its stems sprouting out of the ground like ten-foot coachwhips. Among them flutter dozens of brightly colored butterflies, and there are always several varieties of tiny wild flowers in bloom. The sotol, which has a juicy heart tasting of cabbage, grows in spiky-leaved clusters. The century plant, which flowers once every twenty-five years, sends a flowering stalk up to a height of about fifteen feet, using only the food which has been stored in its pulpy leaves. Marooned in the Chisos Mountains by the sea of desert is a species of small, white-tailed deer, which exists only here and in the Sierra del Carmen Range in Mexico.

You might see a tarantula, which in fact is harmless to man, running over the road like a hairy, black dinner plate. It is preyed upon by a brightly colored orange and purple wasp called a tarantula hawk, which paralyzes one of these giant spiders, drags it under cover and lays eggs in its body. As the young hatch they feed on the living spider until it dies. There is the six-inch scorpion called a vinegarroon, because when chased it releases a scent that smells like vinegar. More snakes and lizards are found in Big Bend than in any other part of the Southwest, yet there are also more birds here than in any other national park—three hundred and eighty species.

Today Big Bend is on the road to nowhere, a pocket of Mexican wilderness that has strayed into the United States. For centuries,

Hummingbirds are attracted to the brilliant red flowers of the mountain sage, which is found only in the Chisos Mountains in Big Bend National Park. It blooms in midsummer and it is then that the broadbill, left, and ten other species of tiny colorful birds, known to the Indians as "rays of the sun," can be found in the park.

PLANTS IN BIG BEND NATIONAL PARK

Despite a low rainfall, more than a thousand species of plants have been recorded at Big Bend. Sixty-one species of cacti have been found, most in the dry lowlands, where the prickly pears and chollas predominate. Both are jointed plants. The segments of the prickly pear are flat, while those of the cholla are cylindrical. Among the four species of yucca found at Big Bend is the giant dagger, which blooms only every two or three years. It is rarely found outside the confines of the park.

however, it was on a track that white men hardly dared go near—particularly during the full moon in September, which was known to the Indians as the Mexican moon. At that time, when the water holes were filled by the summer rains, Big Bend became a war trail. First it was the Apaches who annually crossed the Rio Grande to raid the lonely outposts of New Spain. Then, during the eighteenth century, the Comanches swooped into their Texas territory and continued the raids with renewed ferocity. Until the 1860s, toward the end of each year, the war parties came back across the river driving cattle, horses and captives.

Only recently has the road to Big Bend—the old Comanche trail and stagecoach route—been paved. This unique area of desert with its prolific flora and fauna is remote and almost part of another country. But it is a place where the excitement of the West as it was a century ago can still be sensed in the burning sky, the dusty green desert and the murmuring current of the Rio Grande.

Giant Dagger   Prickly Pear Cactus   Staghorn Cholla

Rugged mountains flank the winding ribbon of the Rio Grande. Known in Mexico as the Río Bravo del Norte, the river forms a natural boundary between Texas and Mexico and in one great sweeping hundred-mile curve cradles Big Bend National Park. In 1971, partial skeletons of the largest-known creature ever to have flown were uncovered in the park. Its wing-span is estimated to have been over fifty feet, twice that of the biggest previously known pterosaur, or winged reptile. The creature's unusually long neck suggests that it may have been a carrion-eater, feeding on dead dinosaurs.

LAND BY THE LAKES

At the heart of the American landmass the ships sail out of sight of land on the deep waters of a huge discontinuous inland sea. The Great Lakes are North America's freshwater Mediterranean. Politically they form a frontier. Only Lake Michigan is entirely within the United States, while Canada shares sovereignty over the other four, Lakes Superior, Huron, Erie and Ontario. But geographically the lakes are the bond of unity for a vast American region, its reservoir, the waterway that carries its produce to the outside world, creates its rainfall, controls its climate.

Most of the world's great water systems lie low in valleys, fed by rivers that drain the surrounding landscape. But America's Great Lakes are pent up high on the watershed. Their tributaries are small. The water level of Lake Superior is more than six hundred feet above the sea. Seven hundred miles away, at the eastern tip of Lake Erie, the outflow poises itself for the plunge of Niagara and the eventual rush seaward through the high-walled St. Lawrence Valley. The lakes still form a vast water plateau.

The Great Lakes are a hub, not a divide. Within a few miles of Lake Superior's shores, the rivers begin to fall away northward toward Hudson Bay. From the very outskirts of Chicago the runoff is southward, into the Mississippi and the Gulf of Mexico. The wild birds and animals knew that, long before mankind arrived. The Indians, lugging their canoes across the portages that linked the water systems, showed the first explorers from Europe how the lake waters intermingle and connect with the whole length of the continent.

It is barely two centuries since men began the methodical exploitation of the land by the lakes. By the distant Lake of the Woods, still, there are people who win their livelihood by hunting and trapping, as they did when the first voyageurs, rough traders from France, came up the Mississippi to buy furs from the Indians. On Isle Royale, near the northern extremity of the lakes, something like the primeval struggle for existence has been rescued and perpetuated in a great living laboratory of nature.

But few traces remain of the wild forest that once fringed the lakes' southern shores. Here, the riches are man-made—bustling cities, quiet towns that thrive on the wheat and corn and cattle of the tamed countryside. The lakes are the gateway to the grain basket of the world. On their shores the ports that, through the St. Lawrence Seaway, send grain and ore and timber to the ocean, have grown to be great industrial and commercial communities— Duluth, Chicago, Detroit, Cleveland, Buffalo, Toronto.

There is a quiet confidence about this land by the lakes. Here, America seems sufficient to itself, with wealth enough for anyone who will work for it. History is simple, the story of human advance and progress on the edge of the plains. But if you look closely, the signs are there of how this land was made: the relics of its former masters, the native Americans whose way of life crumbled before that of the Europeans; the rough farms and houses of the first pioneers, who opened the ground with ax and mule plow for the combine harvesters and the railroad tracks that came after; the beginnings of the modern style in cities, with the skyscrapers of Chicago; the first revolt against mechanized city living, in the houses of America's most original architect. Above all, there is everywhere the sensation of a people not yet set in their ways, concerned more with the future than the past, with the infinite hopes and possibilities—and doubtless disappointments too—of an America that is still creating itself.

Lake of the Woods

Like a single handclap in the silent woods, the beaver's short, fat tail strikes the water in a warning to his friends that danger, human danger, is near. The observer catches a glimpse, perhaps an illusion, of cheery front teeth and little shrewd eyes, a disappearing twitch of round, brown fur rump, like a fat lady heading for a subway car, and the beaver is safe again, somewhere in his private tangle of twigs and muddy tree trunks at the bottom of the pool.

All summer the beaver has gnawed away ceaselessly at the surrounding trees, by some secret intuition knowing which will have at its tip just the right sort of woody tangle. The tree's limbs he has dragged down beaten highways, to the water's edge, into the water and under the water, where he has fixed them six feet deep and well below the coming ice of winter. Now in the autumn, they are his refuge and escape route. In winter he will dive with lungs full of air down to that muddy foodstore. His exhaled breath will rise to form air pockets under the surface of the ice. And there, in an emergency, the beaver will have both food and air to breathe, safe from all his enemies.

The enemies are many, in this border country which runs off in an immense plain of rock and water and lost islands toward the frozen desolation of Hudson Bay and the Arctic. To survive here, every creature must make strange, specialized adaptations to the conditions of life—the beaver's mysterious ways are the strangest and most special. Life is a war. Every creature is at some time a potential prey. And the greatest predator is the one that kills not just for food and for survival, but for fun and for cash. The greatest predator of all is man.

Man, on these shores, is nearing the northern limits of his settlement in the center of the North American continent. At the town of Kenora, the northern tip of the Lake of the Woods, the waters tumble out under the Trans-Canada Highway, the great east-west railroad, and through the narrow belt of settled land along those lifelines. Beyond Kenora, the continent runs empty to the far wastes. On the southern shore, in Minnesota, there are prosperous farms and rich land. But between those

extremities it is sixty miles by water, amid reefs and ten thousand wooded, rocky islands, across the shallow glacial scoop of the tree-fringed lake.

Along the shores, the white man has drawn back. The mature timber that once sustained a logging industry has mostly been cut out, and in these latitudes it will be slow to grow again. There remain the Indians, descendants, now often enfeebled by contact with an incompatible civilization they failed to understand, of the men who left their mysterious signs painted on the lakeside rocks, many thousands of years ago.

Those old Indians harvested the lake for fur and pelts to keep warm. French explorers, the voyageurs of the seventeenth century, paddled and hauled their canoes up the Mississippi and across the land to carry back those same furs to the markets of Europe. Today there are few trappers left. Most of the men who come here are seeking sport and the experience of what North America was like before the white man came.

Still on the sandy shore you will see the sharp slot of a small deer's footprint, where he came to drink among the mussel shells. Back in the woods there are moose and caribou, if you can walk far enough to find them. The water teems with fish, great trout and pike and perch, the finest sport fish in the world. Black bears blunder through the trees and swim from island to island in the summertime after berries and wild bees' nests. The great annual bird migrations sweep across the lake and rest on its islands—geese and ducks and swarms of smaller fowl that fly for their nesting to the brief summers of the far north, and back to the softer south for their winter quarters.

The lake is high, a thousand feet above the sea. Its own waters flow north to Hudson Bay, but its tributary streams share their watersheds with other streams that flow west to the St. Lawrence and the Atlantic, and others again that thrust southward to the Mississippi and the Gulf of Mexico.

For the animal kingdom, the lake is a crossroads. To man it is a place of danger. Sudden gales can whip the shallow waters to fury amid the reefs and shoals of the ancient glacier drift. In winter, from a clear sky, the snow drives on the north wind, obliterating every track and sign of life. In summer, beneath the leafy trees, a man who has lost his way is invisible even to searching planes.

Wilderness should, perhaps, be defined as a place where man's technology—his guns, his boats, his seaplanes, his snowmobiles—does no more than give him an equal chance of survival with the animals. At the Lake of the Woods, after all these centuries of man's encroachment, the beasts have survived.

Now peaceful and unspoiled, Lake of the Woods had its share of violence in the eighteenth century when settlers conflicted with the Indian population. In 1736, the son of Pierre de la Vérendrye, who built Fort St. Charles on the lake's northwest angle, was killed by the Sioux on Massacre Island, one of the ten thousand islands which dot the lake. In 1763, the Indians actually destroyed the fort. Another was built by the Hudson's Bay Company in 1836. By then the Indians and trappers were living in peace and the fort was used as a trading post.

FRESHWATER ENGINEERS

The beaver, far right, feeds on bark, especially from willow and birch trees. After stripping a tree, the beaver fells it by gnawing through the trunk. It uses the sticks and twigs to construct the framework for its dam, right. This creates a pond that serves as a moat to protect the beaver's lodge made, like the dams, of sticks, with separate rooms and nests for several beavers.

On the upper floor of the old county jail the prisoners nowadays include the following: one calf with two heads (dusty), one mule plow (rusty), one stuffed eagle (molting), two spinning wheels (that rotate at a touch, like an old Cadillac motor) and an old whiskey still (verdigris-green) whose brother is probably even now at work out there in the woodlands. On their crooked ends the barns of Brown County still carry advertisements for "chew tobacco"; the friendly people still talk with a shut-mouth twang as though they were chewing it.

Brown County is one of those miraculous bits of old America that got left behind in the rush. Steel mills to the north, endless corn in the middle, the flat and prosperous State of Indiana has toward its southern end this exquisite anomaly, this lump, this infertile sandy range where the villages have names like Bean Blossom and Gnaw Bone—and where the quiet beauty of rustic America has survived to enjoy a respected and beloved old age. From the modest peaks mile after mile of folded forest stretches away in every shade of green and brown and gray. Nobody has troubled to tear down and replace with something more convenient the old log cabins of hewn and piled tree trunks, nobody here was sufficiently aware of fashion to melt down the cruel leg clamps in the old log jail house. Now that fashion has come full circle, the true worth and interest of these old things and places has become clear.

Brown County is the triumph of the unsuccessful. Once its hills were prized for their timber—native hardwoods, oak, hickory, black walnut, shining wild cherry—but fifty years ago the forests were worked out. There was no more timber to harvest. The sandy hills eroded into gullies. Almost half the county's people left the area, moving on in search of work and fortune. The state bought much of the land, for about a dollar an acre—it was worth no more—and, for want of anything better, turned it into a nature reserve. They built a big dam and flooded the lowland.

In man's terms, the place stopped dead.

From the 1850s until World War I farming was the major occupation in Indiana. Replaced today in economic importance by manufacturing, the small family farms of Brown County still produce large quantities of corn, soybeans, wheat and oats.

The raccoon, left, has proved to be one of the most successful of all North American mammals since it is found throughout the United States and southern Canada. The woods of Brown County are the ideal habitat for this almost completely nocturnal animal that feeds on nuts, fruit, seeds and, occasionally, fish.

But, left to itself, nature moved on. The eroded sandy slopes grew green from the seeds of the trees that had been harvested. The miraculous colors of the American seasons changed and came around again, year by year, decade by decade. Drawn by the scenery, artists came and, by the early 1960s, once-neglected Brown County was seen to be approaching again its old magnificence. It had attracted a community of painters, craftsmen, lovers of the place, who gave it a special quality.

In an average week now there are likely to be about a dozen exhibitions of paintings and artifacts to be seen in Nashville, the seat of Brown County. By no means all the work would qualify as high art; but that is not the point. The point is that so many of the people who come to live here are seeking actively to make some creative demonstration of their relationship to their new home. They come because this rural place is different from the city. They want, too, to give something to it. In their way they are pressing on to new frontiers, just as the first Brown County settlers did when they came to settle their small family farms, leaving behind them the great plantations (and the slavery system) of the South.

The long-time residents, descendants of those who did not leave when Brown County suffered its period of real poverty, welcome visitors and new residents with a tolerant pleasure. If someone wants to set up an art gallery, or a vegetarian restaurant, or a temple for some little-known Oriental cult, that is fine with the old-timers. It all means work, and a bit of money.

The real danger to Brown County and its special way of life is no longer emigration, but a too-eager influx of outsiders. Much of the land is now maintained in the state park and in Hoosier National Forest, and cannot be built on. The villages remain true villages, intimate in scale, places to walk in not to drive around. For a long time Brown County will remain an oasis, a resting-place from the hardworking world of the prairies that lie so near at hand, cool in the summer, brilliant in fall, sweet with flowers in the spring.

The opossum, left, is the only marsupial—pouch-bearing mammal—in the United States. Their thick fur, thicker in the opossums found in Brown County and the other areas at the northern limit of their range, has led to extensive hunting, but the species has never been endangered, principally because the female generally bears two litters of nine each year. Immediately after birth, the young climb through their mother's fur and enter the pouch, where they remain for the first three months of their lives.

A peaceful creek flowing through Hoosier National Forest epitomizes the tranquility of winter. The creation of this national forest, where oak trees predominate, and of scenic Brown County State Park, insure that this picturesque countryside will remain protected and forever beautiful.

Isle Royale

A splinter of rock cracked from a fault in the earth's surface is moving imperceptibly clear from the face of the world's largest sheet of fresh water. At the rate of one foot a century, Isle Royale is still emerging from the waters of Lake Superior. In geological time, the island is a mere infant, just ten thousand years old—a younger part of the American ecological system even than that notorious latecomer, mankind. Now man has set this island aside for an unrivaled experiment. Here nature is to be allowed to work out its own transient destiny, however harsh or cruel. Man watches; he does not intervene.

On Isle Royale there coexist two animal species that, everywhere else, are hunted or controlled by man—the wolf and the moose, the fierce predator and the largest American mammal that provides the wolf's choice diet. The island, forty-five miles long, eight miles wide, protected from the outside world by at least fifteen miles of water, is a test bed for the interaction of predator and prey. The aim on Isle Royale, carefully observed by the National Park officials who control access to it, is to let whatever happens happen. Man will not intervene, either to introduce a new species of plant or animal, or to protect the moose or to control the wolf.

It is a strange reversal of fortune. For three thousand years or more Isle Royale was plundered by man as ruthlessly as any part of the world's accessible surface. The island was naturally rich in copper and lumber and fur-bearing animals. For all these things the Indians prized it, and left their traces long before the white man came. The Indians feared the place, calling it the Floating Island; they visited, but never settled, there. The white man had no such hesitation.

It took him just two centuries to clear out Isle Royale. By the beginning of the twentieth century it was effectively a desert—there were no deer, no beaver, no workable copper left. There was a lighthouse, to warn men to keep clear, and the summer camps of a few Norwegian fishermen, but nothing else, except coyotes and squirrels and other animals of no commercial value.

But nature abhors an empty space. About 1912 there was a shortage of feed for moose on the Canadian shores to the north. Somehow, probably by swimming about twenty miles—for moose fall over on the ice—the great beasts came back. They prospered—so much so that they almost ate the island out of the sort of undergrowth they like. Then, in another bitter Canadian winter, the wolves, too, grew hungry. Early in 1948 a small pack of half-starved wolves crossed the ice to the island, where they found the too numerous moose herd. The wolves grew fat and multiplied. Since then, moose and wolves have continued their strange coexistence, with man to hold the ring.

When the vegetation prospers, the moose thrive and the wolves in their turn prosper and breed. If the wolves increase too much, the moose decline and the wolves stop breeding. When the moose decline, the vegetation recovers and the whole process starts over again. But is it a balance? Will the pack one day destroy the herd, or the herd destroy the plants and thus, itself disappearing, leave the wolves to starve? Or, will moose or wolves take again to the water or the ice and depart, leaving Isle Royale to new colonizers? While man watches as nature takes its course, other animals, including the beaver and the otter, have reappeared on the island to work out their different destinies.

The island, self-contained, is a United States National Park. Under the law that created it a park it must admit visitors. It offers them no entertainment. Guns are forbidden, as are traps and wheeled vehicles. There are no roads on the island although there are more than eighty miles of foot trails, which lead past the peaceful lakes of the interior and over Isle Royale's easily climbed peaks. If anyone wants to move on the island, he goes on foot or by canoe. On warm days—and 70 degrees Fahrenheit is warm here—the gnats and blackflies and mosquitoes bite like starvelings. On cold days it is usually wet and windy, too. When the lake is not frozen it is infested with leeches, so there is no swimming.

The moose are easy to find. They weigh up to fifteen hundred pounds, and a big bull's horns may be five feet across. If you meet one it is recommended to step smartly behind a tree. There are at the time of writing some twelve hundred moose on the island. The wolves will kill about three hundred in the year: if the feed is good, an equal number will be born. If not, they will diminish.

The wolves, which number about thirty, move in two packs, keeping separate territorial limits. They do not show themselves to visitors—unlike most wild things they even flee from aircraft, with the exception of the plane used by the research team that follows their movements. This they recognize and tolerate as a harmless nuisance.

On Isle Royale the earth's two fierce predators have come to recognize each other's place in the natural order. For mankind, that is a small triumph over his usual habit of interference. For the wolves, of which there are only about three thousand left in the United States, it is a chance—just a chance—of survival in the wild. No more. That is the value of Isle Royale. That value may be incalculable.

THE BALANCING OF NATURE ON ISLE ROYALE

The North American timber wolf, right, with a moose's antlers, the remains of a meal. The moose, far right, largest of all deer, is an excellent swimmer and feeds in ponds off the succulent bottom vegetation. Wolves once thrived over most of the continent, but their numbers dwindled when man began hunting such animals as the moose, on which they lived. On Isle Royale, man does not interfere with nature.

Lake Superior, which surrounds Isle Royale, can be deceptively tranquil, right, and visitors are warned to cross to the island in boats no smaller than twenty feet. Although much nearer the Canadian side of the lake, the island has, at the insistence of Benjamin Franklin, been part of the United States since 1783, when the Treaty of Paris was signed. He believed the island might become a great industrial center because of its copper, a good conductor, which could be utilized in the development of electricity. But the mines were poor. The island's placid inland lakes, above, have their own riches—trout which weigh up to sixty pounds.

The house springs from the hillside as though it had grown from seed. Like the trees on the slopes or the corn in the valley, it belongs in this landscape, is part of it, enriching and crowning the beauty of this quiet, green place by the river. There is no fuss, no drama about this building; just the firm, cool statement of one man's vision of how men could live at peace in their native countryside. This poetic vision—quiet, confident, wholly American—has in the past half century transformed and enlarged the way all men think of houses and landscape and mankind's relation to both.

Frank Lloyd Wright, grandson of a famous Welsh–American preacher, son of a prosperous Wisconsin farmer, was the man who had this vision. He was born near this valley of the Wisconsin River. As a young man he studied architecture in Chicago, in the great days of that city when, piling story upon story, builders first learned to exploit to the fullest the wonderful new techniques of steelwork and concrete and electric power. To design the first towering blocks of the Lake Michigan shore, Wright worked with men devoted to the future—to a future of cities that would reach to the sky. But Wright saw even further ahead, to a time when men would rebel against the machine and seek again the kind of peace he had known as a boy, among the farms that cling to the land of Wisconsin.

Wright was a rebel against the technological revolution. Later he was to declare, "Early in life I had to choose between honest arrogance and hypocritical humility. I chose the former, and have seen no reason to change." He was arrogant in this conviction: "The country, the grass, the green, the living people on the ground—all have to come back. That's why the cities are destroying themselves." Wright stated his rebellion not just in negative words, but in assertions of stone and brick and wood. Taliesin house, standing proudly in the landscape, his own house on his own

Frank Lloyd Wright, far left, was one of the most powerful influences in the modern architectural movement of the 1920s and 1930s, which gave impetus to the young architects who believed in architecture as art. By stressing the elements that constructed the house, Wright made his followers aware of the properties of natural materials. The site, according to Wright, was an inalienable part of the architectural plan, and he sought to reestablish the fundamental links between a dwelling house and the land around it. His ideas are epitomized by his own house, Taliesin East, above, at Spring Green, Wisconsin. He built additional buildings as part of the Taliesin complex, and in 1932 began the Taliesin Fellowship, a residential training program for architects. Twenty to sixty apprentices worked with Wright, left, each year, some remaining with him for decades.

Taliesin East

land for his own use, was a manifesto as well as a place to live. He called it Taliesin after the legendary Welsh poet and prophet.

The first Taliesin was built in 1911. Three years later it was burned down by a crazed employee, leaving seven dead and exposing to the glare of publicity the fact that Wright was living with a woman not his wife. The pastoral escape was turned into nightmare. But the house was rebuilt—and once more it was burned. Taliesin rose again from the ashes.

It stands now in its valley, flanked by the architectural school that Wright built to further his ideas. Nearby, too, is the little country schoolhouse that he designed for the children of his native place and presented to them. A restaurant based on Wright's designs has been built. The centerpiece remains Wright's exemplary house.

The idea that dwelling houses can partake of the nature of their site, and lead their inhabitants into a sharing of the life of the land, now seems obvious. If it is so, it is because Wright made it so. All around the world, in cities as well as in the countryside, his buildings are admired—banks and offices, hotels and factories and art galleries as well as homes. They make use of the most refined and advanced technology: Wright did not seek to turn the clock back, nor to escape from the fact that most men must live in cities, but merely to offer an alternative to the reality of so much bad urban style.

In 1959, at the age of ninety-one, Frank Lloyd Wright died. Personally, he was honored. But his example was, and is, still feared by many of his fellow architects, the men whom he once told as a body, "Gentlemen, you are withering on the vine." Wright's own vineyard flourished so greatly, perhaps, because of the soil it was rooted in—the soil of Wisconsin, rich in corn and cheese, goods that give pleasure and nourishment. Taliesin belongs with those good, natural things. It pleases and nourishes all who come near.

Frank Lloyd Wright was the first architect to dispense with the traditional box-like division of houses and make the interior space into a single flowing unit. His new ideas on designing dwelling houses, in which he linked the inner and outer life of the house by opening up the walls with continuous windows, won him international acclaim. The interior of Taliesin East, Wright's own home, left, exemplifies his use of the open plan, which incorporated new designs in furniture and decoration.

In its earliest days, Chicago was little more than a portage. The completion of canals and the opening of the Great Plains enabled the city to capitalize on its strategic location. Chicago's first railroad was completed in 1848, and within eight years it had become the nation's rail center, which it has remained.

The modern movement in architecture of the 1920s, which utilized structural techniques that made possible the building of skyscrapers, began in Chicago. Two of the most celebrated skyscrapers of the 1920s are the Tribune Tower, far left, with its Gothic revival design, and the Wrigley Building, left, its ornament derived from Renaissance designs.

Chicago

Like a giant's chessmen, the skyscrapers of the Lake Michigan shore stand ranged to move into the checkerboard landscape. On the great central plain of North America, this is where the game begins. To the north the level waters of Lake Michigan stretch for hundreds of miles. To the south, rising imperceptibly from the waters, the flat lands lie dotted with rich farms, the world's breadbasket. Where land and water meet, facing the lakefront, man has erected his palisade of steel and glass and concrete.

Maybe it is just pride, or sheer competitive drive, that makes Chicago the way it is. The Chicago style is to flex the muscles, to do bigger and better than the next man, to build higher, work harder, go faster. Milder communities may deal in reasonable, probable solutions. In Chicago they trade in superlatives, just as they trade in grain and hogs and cattle and hard cash.

At the crossroads of the Great Plains and the Great Lakes, Chicago was bound to be a place of transit. It was literally built on mobility, on the faith that somewhere ahead there must lie something better. Railroads and steamships were its *raison d'être*—and even today its airport is the world's busiest. Chicago became a western terminus in the 1820s when the Erie Canal was opened. In the 1850s it was tied into the westward-bound rail system. By 1870, as the plains behind it were still being opened, Chicago had grown by irresistible bounds to be a great city of three hundred thousand people; a wooden city, built of the cheap and, as it then seemed, inexhaustible supplies of timber which were floated in across the lake. But Chicago never did anything by halves. In 1871, when the legendary Mrs. O'Leary's cow kicked over a lamp and set light to her milking parlor, the entire central city went up in flames.

So Chicago started from scratch. It began exactly at the moment when, in the world's most dynamic society, the new technologies of steel construction and electric elevators made possible for the first time buildings that seemed to scrape the sky. The money was there, the talent of the great innovating architect Louis Sullivan was there, and Chicago set the style that first New York and now all great cities in the world have followed—twentieth-century perpendicular. In Chicago the result along the lakeshore and in the packed business district of the Loop is a complete anthology of modern styles in high buildings, but with each style exaggerated or overemphasized to be the most extreme example of its kind.

From the "renaissance" symmetry of the Wrigley Building, to the Gothic elaborations on the Tribune Tower, by way of Mies van der Rohe's 1950s super-cool and on to the Sears Tower—the tallest office building in the world, until they build a taller—the place is a paragon of energy. In the public squares there is a Picasso sculpture, a Henry Moore, a Chagall, a Calder. Every ornament that money can buy coexists, but nothing blends together. In this, if in nothing else, the buildings of Chicago truly represent its peoples and add to its individuality.

Irish, Italians, Poles, Ukrainians, Greeks, American blacks from the South, Spanish-Americans, even, in a perfect little Chinatown, Chinese—all the elements in America's ethnic jumble are here. Each group guards its identity with care, clinging on to the status of a hyphenated-American, claiming, perhaps, any roots that stretch into any piece of firm soil, for fear of being swept out on the great mobile raft of Chicago. As the city sprawls away along its linking highways, the diverse neighborhoods flash past, with different races, different faces, huge disparities of wealth and poverty.

The tall and warring styles of the Lake Michigan waterfront stand for a place that has not found itself. It has huge energy, riches for many, great art, fine parks, but still not peace. Along the shoreline, as the automobiles roll and jostle between the skyscrapers and the water, clouds gather to northward. The Windy City shakes under the blast that provided its sobriquet. The waves rise. The lake grows angry. But the water that dashes over the highway is fresh, not salt. The ships out there must travel fifteen hundred miles before they reach the open sea. Chicago, in all its big-city splendor and squalor, is right at the heart of the continent, at the heart of the American storm. It is a heart that loves grandeur and show, but it is not yet a heart totally at peace.

The Rookery Building, designed by Burnham and Root in 1886, was one of the first to provide shops and offices around a semi-private square. Cast-iron columns, wrought-iron spandrel beams and steel beams were used to construct its skeleton structural frame. Slender columns and heavy stone-work give it an appearance of grace and strength.

Louis Sullivan's achievements as a designer of ornamental decoration are exemplified by the department store of Carson Pirie Scott & Co. The simplicity of its upper stories is in marked contrast to the lavish decoration of the first two stories, which have rectangular display windows that are like richly framed pictures.

After the Great Fire of 1871, Chicago was rebuilt rapidly. Lake Shore Drive north of the Loop, above, began attracting the city's economic and social elite. By the 1970s, its mansions were being replaced by high-rise luxury apartment buildings, and the drive almost reached from the northern to the southern city limits.

Jaws agape, ready to strike, the snake is coiled on the hilltop. Between his fangs the prey awaits its death. For two thousand years or more they have lain there, killer and victim. From the brown Ohio woodlands a fox yaps, another answers. Time changes the valleys, with the seasons, with the plowing and sowing and reaping of mankind. But on the hilltops the living fox and the snake's doomed prey endure.

For two millennia, until the sixth century of the Christian era, there flourished in southern Ohio a culture whose rise and fall is only now beginning to be traced. The people who lived here then had no writing, and left no legends. The evidence of their existence is in the mounds they erected, sometimes for the burial of their dead, sometimes for more mysterious purposes.

When white people first entered this area, in the early 1700s, they paid no particular attention to the mounds; they plowed under or tore apart whatever stood in their way. But, after a while, the settlers and farmers were followed by scholars and humanists, who understood that in these mounds could lie clues to the dark abyss of the American past. They preserved and excavated and respectfully studied the mounds and their contents. What they found baffled them. Even the scholars, humane men of culture, could not accept that it was Indians—the sad red men they knew, savage and unpredictable—who had done these things. They supposed there had been in the Ohio area a separate "race" which they called the Mound Builders.

But now it is known: two thousand years ago American Indians achieved here a level of culture and prosperity and social organization roughly comparable to that attained at the same period by the rough tribesmen of Germany, Britain and Scandinavia. Then the Indians stopped, while the north Europeans went on to transform the world. It is a stupendous mystery.

Consider this snake. He is a quarter of a mile long, his body up to twenty feet wide and about five feet high. The outline of his body was laid out on the ground in stones, then it was formed with clay and covered with earth. All these materials had to be carried from the valley, five hundred feet below. It was a feat of intense human discipline involving thousands of men over many years. Only a stable society with a strong government or organizing principle could have achieved it. And, strangest of all, the snake cannot be seen in his entirety except from an aircraft, or by mounting a metal viewing platform as high as a tall forest tree. How was it done? What was it for? Who conceived it and carried it through? The answer is lost in time.

About fifty miles from the snake, across

Mound City and Serpent Mound

land marked everywhere with the enigmatic traces of the old Indian cultures, is Mound City. Under the looming watchtowers of the state penitentiary, a five-foot-high embankment—square in form but with rounded corners—encloses an area of thirteen acres. In the enclosure archaeologists have located twenty-three grave mounds. They contain the cremated remains of people. In the graves the survivors placed sharks' teeth from the Atlantic coast, conch shells from the Gulf of Mexico, obsidian, a kind of volcanic glass, from Yellowstone in the Rocky Mountains, copper from Isle Royale in Lake Superior. The Mound City people, who were probably a different group from the Mound Builders—their building techniques at least were different—not only lived in an organized society and made fine works of art, but were also linked into a system of trade relations that reached to the farthest limits of the continent.

But they failed. After the fifth or sixth century A.D. all traces of them disappear. Other Indian peoples buried their dead, from time to time, in the old mounds and the originators were forgotten. They may have been wiped out by disease or, because relative civilization had, perhaps, made them soft, they may have been eliminated by war-like, wandering Indian tribes who looted their farms and raided their villages. But why? What went wrong, when they had already attained so much?

Their use of copper might provide a clue. They imported nuggets of pure copper, found far away to the north. They used it for ornaments, for fishhooks, sometimes for arrows and spearheads. But they never discovered the essence of using metal—that if you heat it and work it and mix it with other metals to make hard alloys, like bronze, it can change the world. The Mound Builders never saw

that. They invented farming, selected wild grain and squash to make better harvests, knew the arts and could construct an object like the serpent, visible not to man but only to a higher Being above. But they used metal only as a specially malleable sort of rock: they balked at the jump into the technology of metal.

Their destruction was accomplished long before the arrival of the white man, who destroyed the way of life of the Indians who came after the Mound Builders. Now white Americans are trying, however confusedly, to make amends for the past. The relics of the former peoples of Ohio are prized, preserved and wondered at, so many centuries after they were made. Standing by the twisted body of the ancient serpent, under the Ohio sky that his creators knew, the ghosts of the first Americans haunt us. And the foxes bark, just as they barked then.

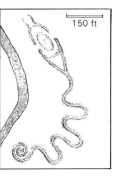

Serpent Mound, left, is the most mysterious of the so-called effigy mounds left by the Indians who lived in the Ohio Valley in the fourteenth century. Nothing has been found in the mound, the length of which can be seen from the nineteenth-century engraving, right, and its purpose remains unknown.

150 ft

The Hopewell Indians roamed from the mid-Atlantic coast to the prairies and from Lake Superior to the Gulf of Mexico, but the Ohio Valley seems to have been the center of their advanced society. Careful excavation of the more than twenty burial mounds of the Mound City site at Chillicothe, above, has yielded

considerable information about their skill as craftsmen in wood, stone, copper and bone, and has revealed the extent of their vast trading network.

The South is another country, surrounded by an intangible frontier. Within it the words of the language remain the same. The sounds and the pace are different. In recent years the Southern personality may well have been analyzed as extensively as anything since the death of Sigmund Freud. Yet the people of the South have resisted the temptation to become introspective or defensive. They remain themselves.

An outsider might venture yet another definition of Southernness: the South is an area in which you are given grits for breakfast, and where the whole household gathers around the table to make sure you enjoy the experience. Southerners feel their way of life is more enjoyable than all other Americans'. They are confident that others will agree. To be included in that belief may be the greatest of all the luxuries that America offers her visitors.

The South, in this psychological sense, is a product neither of climate nor of soil. The Far West is far hotter. The sands of Cape Hatteras are not measurably finer than the sands of Cape Cod. Even the rocks of the Blue Ridge are continuous with the rocks of the Green Mountains to the north. And the Mississippi is unmistakably its grand self from Minneapolis to New Orleans. Southernness is not even directly a product of the South's great historical tragedy, since in Maryland or West Virginia or Kentucky the true Southern quality shines through, although those states did not share in the losing of the War Between the States. And, for that matter, the Latin peoples of Louisiana or Florida are as Southern as the Puritan stock of the Great Smoky Mountains.

What the South has to brew up its peculiar pleasantness may well be an economic experience. Its people were poorer for longer than most Americans, and their experience of poverty is both more recent and more near at hand. But through new industries, such as tree farming, the magnificent land of the South has helped its people to improve their economic lot. In Alabama or Arkansas people take real pleasure in reflecting that things truly are better than they used to be. In Georgia the pleasure becomes pride in what the state has achieved in so few recent years.

Mississippi is awakening from a long, enforced slumber; rejoicing (as who could fail to rejoice) at the splendors of the old plantation homes, but confident, too, that now they are going to do better yet. The man-made lakes of Tennessee are a living memorial to how man in America faced up to the adversities of the 1930s, and conquered them.

In the older cultures of the two Carolinas and Virginia change is coming, perhaps, more slowly. In this great plain between the mountains and the ocean men first established that they could live as stylishly in the Americas as in the old lands across the sea. Laden with history, its people can look back with pride as easily as they can look forward in hope. And yet this blend of old self-confidence and new assurance may augur best of all, in reconciling past and future under the benevolent sway of the all-pervading Southern sweetness.

Puritan and Latin, frontier and plantation, slave and slaveholder, industrial and rustic, seacoast and forest, ancient and modern—all these contrasting experiences of history and of environment have gone to make this special part of America that is the South. That it is beautiful is obvious. That it is full of personal warmth and openness and pleasure is a delight and a cause for happiness.

New Orleans

The fretted iron arabesques of the balcony show double in the relentless sun. As the light strikes direct across the street the chipped black paint sends back an answering glitter from its angles. Behind, against the redbrick wall, the pattern repeated in clear-cut shadow creates a brief illusion of coolness in the heat of evening. The architecture of New Orleans is perfectly adapted to its place and its climate, a style of building that the Spanish learned from the Arabic peoples, who ruled their country for centuries, and carried with them to the Americas. The tradition was carried on in North America by people who spoke French and belonged to an English-speaking nation. It is a muddle, an entertainment, a cultural anomaly that epitomizes the fabric and the spirit of one of the world's great cities.

But New Orleans is more than a city, more even than a state of mind. Many nations in good standing with the international community do not have their own architectural style, their own particular cookery, their own characteristic music. New Orleans, however, with well under a million people, has all these things. Even if it lacks its own language, it has distinctive dialects of both English and French that are peculiar to the native people. And, certainly, there are not many cities in the world where an official census in the mid-1970s could have revealed a population of one alligator for every twenty humans. The Mississippi swamp, which holds the alligators and soaks right into the city limits, has marked the character of New Orleans as surely as did the men who built it.

There are those who criticize New Orleans for being a place of commercial entertainment. They might as well criticize a church for being a place where they talk about religion. The city was founded for the business and the rest and the recreation of tired men engaged in commercial travel. This was where the sea journey ended and the river voyage to the interior of America began. It is still a great commercial and industrial capital. To its old function as an entrepôt has been added the business of a great petroleum industry—an industry which could not be more serious, energetic or relevant to the modern world. But the old, disreputable, well-loved tradi-

tions live on, and the tourists they attract spend the money that maintains the balconied fantasies of the Vieux Carré.

It was in these narrow streets, Spanish in building style, that the sounds of African work songs, Methodist hymns and German marching bands were first blended together in French houses of ill-repute. From New Orleans jazz music traveled on and grew, to become today in its various commercial off-shoots the native music of the entire industrialized world, from Yokohama to Yugoslavia. In New Orleans, even now, you can hear the notes it all began from spilling into the streets. Perhaps the musicians have grown tired, aware that the New Orleans sound itself is the ancestor, the great-granddaddy of all that has come after. But for a few years yet, until the veterans finally hand in their horns and are carried at the head of the parade to the cemetery, youngsters from everywhere will be able to make the pilgrimage, to listen to how it all started in the place where it all began.

Jazz music is undoubtedly one of America's most important and original contributions to the world. It may be no accident that it came first from the American city whose national and racial and religious and cultural and political origins are most confused, and most nearly fused into something original and unique. When the first life consul of France, Napoleon Bonaparte, decided to sell Louisiana to an upstart English-speaking regime in Washington, several obstacles presented themselves. It was doubtful, first of all, whether the United States, a voluntary association of citizens, had any right to buy sovereignty from another ruler. Second, the French had a doubtful title to the property

they wanted to sell. Third, there was the matter of the price. But all ended well. The Spanish waived their rights to the land, the United States Congress swallowed its constitutional doubts and the French were astounded to find that the Americans were prepared to pay more than half as much again than the price they had hoped to obtain.

Napoleon's secret was that he employed a Louisiana lawyer and the sale was completed in New Orleans. The strange and wonderful city had worked its own triumphant magic. A. J. Liebling, a great American writer and lover of New Orleans, supported the theory that "the Mediterranean, Caribbean and Gulf of Mexico form a homogeneous, though interrupted, sea." In spirit, he was absolutely right. New Orleans belongs to an older, wiser, more exhausted world.

When New Orleans was bought by the United States, the Bourbons had temporarily ceased to be kings of France because of the French Revolution. They still ruled Spain and Sicily (which is why the city of Palermo is the place in the world whose architecture most resembles that of New Orleans). It was said of the last Bourbon king of France that his advisers "had forgotten nothing, and learned nothing." As European kings, the Bourbons were great failures. But in America their name survives, commemorated in a type of whiskey and a street of entertainment, the most famous street in New Orleans. Here the crossbreeding of France and Spain, of America and Africa, of shrimps with rice, of Puritan with Catholic, reach a triumphant climax. New Orleans is a blend of deviousness and seduction unmatched in America and unrivaled in the world.

Intricate iron grillwork embellishes a house in the Spanish–French Vieux Carré of New Orleans. The grillwork supports the roof as well as adorning the balcony. This style was created by local eighteenth-century designers and executed by slaves, who were highly trained craftsmen.

The Mississippi River steamboats, which often engaged in much-publicized races from St. Louis to New Orleans, brought prosperity to the Crescent City. The first steamboat reached New Orleans in 1812 and within thirty years there were four hundred boats on the river, and the city had become the fourth busiest port in the world.

New Orleans retains the uninhibited spirit that, at the turn of the twentieth century, made it famous for its gaiety. Marching bands still lead the frequent street parades, just as they did in those days when the bands played an important part in creating the style of collective improvisation that characterized early Dixieland jazz.

141

It was the gale that made it possible. Busting through the beach, the wind and the water cut off the island from its neighboring strip of land. Once again, the barrier reef against the Atlantic was divided by the sea that had created it. Assateague has not always been an island; it has not often been a continuous piece of land. It shifts, breaking, extending, moving with the years. The one enduring presence is that of the wild birds, which ignore the changes in the land, dropping down each spring and autumn on their long flight between the arctic and the tropics.

Assateague is part of a long strip of land that runs down off the coast, from Delaware into the Carolinas, shoved and pushed eternally by the water. In 1933, the ocean, borne on a hurricane, tore a gap between Assateague and the burgeoning little resort of Ocean City which, with its boardwalk and its Big Dipper, serves the people from hundreds of miles around for their summer fun. It was a time of progress and public works. The United States Army Corps of Engineers reinforced and deepened the gap, making a new entrance for pleasure boats to the landlocked shallows of Chincoteague Bay. They cut off Assateague Island for good. In the interest of public recreation and human advance, they insured that the boardwalk of Ocean City could go no farther. Now the island that they set apart is guaranteed for ever as a quiet and separate place of seclusion.

Assateague Island is thirty-seven miles long. Sometimes it is a mile wide, sometimes more; sometimes it is breached again by the storms, as it has been for centuries. All of it is kept open and free for the wild things and for the people who cherish them. At the northern end there is a small public park operated by the State of Maryland for bathing, camping and outdoor recreation. Its southern half, with the brackish bay behind it, is a wildlife refuge, established as a necessary stopover for the wildfowl that travel the coast. Its foundation in 1943 was a decisive step toward saving the Greater Snow Goose, one of the world's most beautiful migrants, from extinction.

For the rest of the island it was touch and go. By the late 1950s a speculative development company had obtained title to the land and parceled it out into 5,850 small lots. They sold quite well. A lot of people did not know about the green-head flies and deer flies and mosquitoes that infest the land until it is drained and sprayed with insecticide. More than three thousand people bought land, and at once started to clamor for drainage and improvements. Assateague was once more on the way to having a boardwalk. Again, the wind intervened. The great March storm of 1962 smashed thirty of the forty-eight homes that had already been built and badly damaged the rest. The wind literally cleared the way for a sudden reversal of policy. In 1965, Congress and the President created by legislative act the Assateague Island National Seashore.

There are still private landowners on the island. There are still difficult problems about what to do with the island and how to do it. The Government's original intention was to open it up for public enjoyment, until they

Indians are known to have camped on Assateague in the 1600s; they gave the island its name, which means Place Across. Today, the largest undeveloped seashore between Massachusetts and North Carolina still retains its wild, primitive character. The combination of salt water and persistent offshore winds affects the type of vegetation on Assateague. Behind its beaches, the sand mounts into dunes that are restrained by beach grasses and low dune plants. The dunes gradually give way to salt marshes, which are filled with widgeon grass and bordered with bulrushes. On higher ground are tracts of pine, oak, myrtle, bay-berry, rose and catbriar.

Assateague Island

found that the necessary road along the dunes would either have to be so high that it dominated the landscape, or it would be swept away by the next storm. Without a road the local people, particularly the sportfishermen, use the dunes themselves as a highway, tearing strips in the soft sand with their four-wheel-drive trucks. But, under the direction of the National Park Service, such problems are being grappled with. Fifteen miles of white sand beach remain apart for wild creatures and for those people who want to take a two-day walk. The island is promised to the future, a blank page of nature.

Wild ponies canter across the sands. Small Japanese Sika deer, introduced almost casually in the past by a group of boy scouts, have made it their home. Fish swarm in the sea between the sands and the perilous offshore reefs that might, someday, themselves become a barrier island. Behind the dunes facing the sea, myrtle and stunted pines struggle to establish their roots before the sea sweeps in again to dig them out. The flat coastal lands of this shore were formed just as Assateague is now being formed and reformed by the sea and wind. Here we can find how it happened, and how it is still happening under the remorseless power of nature.

There is no end yet to the story of Assateague, only a future full of hope and space. It is a marvelous place to see, as the land and the sea and the winds do their work together.

Okefenokee Swamp

The water is bright, clear brown, like tea if you take the tea bag out too quickly. Its surface has a peculiar burnished glitter, reflecting the cypress stems in the windless shade. Look straight down and the depths seem infinite, plunging darkly out of sight. But thrust down with your paddle and the blade hits firm bottom at arm's length. Swing off the main channel into a narrow watercourse behind the trees, across the prairie, and you find that the green grass is not grass but reeds, its roots like the cypress roots springing from beneath that tea-brown flood. A white, seemingly stub-legged bird takes wing and its long legs follow it up out of the shallows—an egret in all its balanced grace.

The Okefenokee is all deception, a place where the wet seems dry, and the dry ground will sink under a man's weight into peat sludge and bubbling marsh gas. Between the tobacco fields of Georgia and the citrus groves of Florida—ordered places, where the land grows green and pleasant for man's profit—it is a lost, indomitable wilderness. It has defied all attempts to make it tame.

In the 1800s there was a plan to drain the swamp, to get rid once and for all of the wetlands and the mosquitoes that stood in the way of progress. It was hoped that the swamp waters could be channeled into a flow that would cut through to the Atlantic. Nineteen miles of drainage canals were cut. But the diggings went down into the native springs that replenish the swamp in the dry season. The springs gushed into the canal and the canal ran backward, into the area it was supposed to drain. The Suwannee Canal Company found that three hundred more miles of deeper canals would be needed before the swamp would begin to do what they wanted. The Company gave up. The swamp had won.

The Okefenokee is not a stagnant bog. It is a living system of shallow, flowing waterways, enclosed on a plateau over a hundred feet above sea level. Its waters and islands, and halfway marshes that are neither wet nor dry, cover about seven hundred square miles of damp territory. Deep down there is the limestone bed, left by an ancient sea; then fine clay, impervious to water; then sand, deposited in lines as the sea withdrew, and forming the occasional firm island. Then there is peat, roots, old rotting stuff, water, fish, marsh weeds, water lilies, jungle, forest, fruit bushes, flowers, bees, bears and a fabulous variety of the frogs, turtles, snakes, alligators, lizards and allied species that inhabit neither land nor water, but the places in between. And there are loons, grebes, herons, ducks, buzzards, hawks, prothonotary warblers, yellow-bellied sapsuckers, Carolina chickadees and, in their thousands, red-winged blackbirds.

Even the waters are alive, rising and falling, always flowing to the sea. The swamp is a single, if interrupted, water surface. But it flows out through two separate rivers, in opposite directions. The St. Mary's River drains circuitously to the Atlantic, the Suwannee River drains to the Gulf of Mexico. If you are wise and take a canoe through the swamp, you will feel the gentle pull of these waters, although you cannot see it by looking. It is a watershed, fed by those underground springs that defeated the canal builders, and the very different seas that it flows to are here, on the apex of the Florida Peninsula, barely one hundred and fifty miles apart. Because it is a watershed, a summit not a destination for water, the Okefenokee's life is utterly its own. It is just far enough from the seas to escape their warmth in the winter: it feels the bite of frost, so it is not truly subtropical. It is like nowhere else in the world.

Only its history in the white man's era is typical of North America. Its native Indians took to attacking the white settlers. (That was how the settlers saw it. The Indians may have felt they were defending their own land, but nobody asked.) So in 1838 an intrepid band of United States soldiers marched across the swamp and, when they returned, claimed that the Indians had left. After that visitation no swamp Indians were seen alive. Trappers and sporadic timber cutters moved in. There followed the farce of the Suwannee Canal. When that failed the big logging firms moved in. They cut the swamp cypresses. At first they found that the trees, growing in water, were too waterlogged to be floated to the sawmills. Consequently, they took to ring barking the trees, so that they died and dried where they stood. Millions of trees died but they were not floated out. Where there was dry ground, the timber firms built small rail lines through the swamp. And so they stripped it, until the native forest was gone, the wildlife almost destroyed and the livelihood of the swamp settlers—trappers and timber workers—wrecked. The wasteland they then sold to the Federal Government as a wildlife refuge.

Out of foolishness may come good. The nature reserve created by this devious process is now once again a mixture of forest and wetlands. The swamp rot has dealt with the railroad piles, the logging camps, the vestiges of human occupation. Where the timber was cut, fires seized the new scrub-and-grass growth, catching hold even to the native peat soil and burning great pits in the earth. But even there, the weeds and the fish and the reptiles have reclaimed the pits for their own. Somehow, breeding couples remained of practically all the wild species. With very few exceptions they multiplied when man left. The Okefenokee is itself again.

Still the islands drift and form, rising on bubbles of marsh gas to form floats of peat that coagulate and divide. Still the fires come, clearing the dry reeds, forming new openings amid the tree stems. Man cannot order this place to stop, go back, be what it once was. The Okefenokee controls itself. Man protects it. He can do no more. It is enough. Go there, if you can. If you can, go there in a boat with no motor, at dawn or in the dusk, and watch the place become.

Frogs and toads are Okefenokee's most common form of amphibian life. The swamp has twenty-two species. The southern leopard frog, right, is an important food supply for predators. The squirrel tree frog, far right, is less vulnerable—it is tiny (one inch long) and can change its vivid coloring at will to camouflage itself.

Stands of cypress trees anchor the floating islands of Okefenokee Swamp, right and above, These islands, known as "prairies," are the origin of the swamp's Indian name, which means "trembling earth." They were created when the roots of water plants, floating in the lakes, wove themselves together to form rafts. Decomposing foliage then made a thin topsoil on their surfaces, in which began to grow large plants and trees. Their roots grew through the rafts and the water beneath to take hold in the firm bed of the swamp. Although firmly anchored, the prairies undulate alarmingly when you walk on them.

The Everglades

In a tangle of mucky roots and wriggling watery life the North American continent peters out into the Caribbean. The long appendix of Florida, a sunny afterthought tagged on to the continental United States, dips down to sea level where it stays for thousands of square miles. Fresh water running off the land flows down to meet and mix with the salt. The result is the Everglades—not land, not water, a world of sparse green dotted with lush islands and fringed with the impenetrable jungle of the mangrove woods, teeming with growth.

The Everglades are subtropical, literally so since the tropic line of Cancer runs across just seventy-four miles to southward, in the Caribbean Sea, which the Everglades run into but do not quite belong to. The Everglades belong nowhere else. They are on their own, blending tropical with temperate life forms, marked and transformed from time to time by the awful force of the hurricanes that swirl up from the south. The Florida Peninsula has never been connected by land with the Caribbean islands. Most of its plants and trees and land animals belong to continental North America. There are bears and possum and raccoon and white-tailed Virginia deer. Here exist the last survivors in eastern North America of the great cat,

the cougar, up to seven feet long and wild to match. Clumps of sparse pine forest on the flat land remind the onlooker that this same coastline, and these same trees, reach right up to Nova Scotia and the far north.

But where a species can be carried by water, or fly on the wind, the Caribbean influence comes into its own. Mangrove swamps, the characteristic seashore growth of tropical regions, stand with their roots like spiders' legs clutching the soil beneath the warm waters. Small patches of true tropic jungle, with orchids and great mahogany trees, stand on the tiny islands. In the salt water lurk crocodiles, distinct from the alligators that live above the tide line. The manatee, or sea cow—a kind of hideous, inefficient walrus, supposed by some to be the origin of the legend of mermaids—blunders along the bays, and pathetically dies of pneumonia in those rare years when the "Yankee wind" comes down with frost into the Everglades. These and myriad other tropical creatures cling on here, at the fringe of the climatic conditions they can endure.

Surprisingly the animals of this fundamentally watery region are confronted each year by the hardships of winter drought. Many of the small animals become dehydrated and suffocate. Others have adapted and wall themselves up in damp chambers under the mud where they await spring.

It is the infinite variety of its living things, land and animal, that makes the fascination of the Everglades. But the character of the region is determined by something far less dramatic in appearance, yet even more extraordinary. For mile after endless mile stretches the flat plain of saw grass, which is not in fact a grass but a low, sharp-edged reed standing with its roots inches deep in water. It is an ocean of green in the wet season, when the water rises and forces the saw grass to grow. In the dry season it turns to brown as the water recedes. And every few years it burns, with a terrible raging speed. The fire flashes in along the pine trees, limiting their spread. It rings around the jungle patches, where they stand on the lumps of organic earth that their own decay has created over the centuries. The fires leave behind them a deposit of potash, that insures an even more vivid growth in the year that follows a

fire. But the fire, along with the hurricanes, insures that the Everglades do not grow into forest or jungle, but remain themselves.

The key to it all is the fresh water that gathers to the north in Lake Okeechobee and flows down in what is really an immensely wide but shallow river, falling just twenty feet in the one hundred and fifty miles from the lake to the southern coastline. The Indians called the Everglades the River of Grass, and that is just what it is, a river that widens from thirty to sixty miles across and is never much more than a few inches deep. The original Everglades covered no less than seven million acres of land—unprepossessing, infinitely flat, mostly impassable except with special equipment, beset with incredible clouds of mosquitoes. (At the old settlement of Flamingo, now a visitor center for the Everglades National Park, they say that after the rainy season you can dip at the air with a quart pot and bring down a full two pints of biting insects.)

So difficult is the terrain that the Everglades were the last real American frontier. Indian peoples have survived here on their own, not the white man's, terms with nature: the Seminoles fly their own flag and have a hearty disregard for Government regulations, including regulations meant to conserve their own habitat. Only in 1928, amid hideous difficulties, was the Tamiami Trail, later to become the first highway, built across the Florida Peninsula. The road and the works to control flooding and provide water for Florida's cities have altered the place, and tamed some of it. Once accessible, the land may be drained, plowed, fertilized and sprayed with water to grow the wonderful year-round vegetables that all Americans regard as their birthright.

Yet a million acres of land, and half a million more acres of coastal waters and low islands, are set aside to remain uninhabited and "unimproved" in the Everglades National Park. Through the park there is a single road, and a few boat and canoe trails. From them may be glimpsed much of the region's unique life, in particular a staggering variety of birds that range at will, with no reason to fear mankind. Running out toward the glittering sea, and the reefs of the Florida Keys, the North American continent ends, as it began, in wildness.

In Fahkahatchee Strand, left, the heart of the Everglades' Big Cypress Swamp, the trunks of the pond cypresses are obscured by air plants. Air plants, or epiphytes, grow on "host" trees, but draw their moisture from the atmosphere. Roseate spoonbills, above, are the most graceful bird inhabitants of the Everglades.

An alligator, left, in Water Lettuce Lake, one of the reptile's favorite spots in the Everglades. The alligators like to bask on the thick carpet of water lettuce which covers the lake's surface. Unlike crocodiles, alligators do not attack humans, but they can eat sizable land animals—catching them by the snout as they drink.

A green anole, left, the Everglades' answer to the chameleon. Changes of temperature or the threat of danger will make it alter its color from green through brown to yellow. Anoles are lizards of the iguana family, not closely related to true chameleons, which are not found in North America.

When the Lord led Moses out of the desert, He took His servant to the top of a mountain and showed the Promised Land spread out below. The mountain was called Pisgah. Moses never entered the land of his people, but he came down from Pisgah and died content.

Looking out from the peaks of North Carolina you can feel still the surge of pride and hope that filled the minds of the first settlers when they named these hills, seeing before them those immense green acres—the mountainsides and the plain at their feet, the plain that is now patched with fields and towns and great cities away beyond the imagination, in the vastness of America.

Even today there are people who choose to see this landscape by the same means as the early explorers, and for that matter as Moses, in another land, before them. They came on foot for mile after mile along the trail, with each far prospect not just a beautiful view, but a hard-won physical achievement, its value measured step by step. About two hundred and thirty miles south of the Pisgah heights, on Springer Mountain in Georgia, begins the marked walking track of the Appalachian Trail. Far off to the north, on Mount Katahdin in Maine, the trail ends. Barring the Kennebec River in Maine, where you have to telephone ahead to arrange a ferry, the trail is an unbroken walk of 2,011.4 miles. The precision of the number is significant. If you are a walker, four-tenths of a mile count. They mean the difference between a blister on the heel or no blister, between finding the ford or swimming the river, between arriving safe or not at all.

The Appalachian Trail is not, in its entirety, something that many people need think about. Unless you find it possible to take five months' vacation, or are exceptionally fit when you reach retirement age, you are unlikely to walk the whole thing at one stretch. But the fact that it exists and is faithfully maintained by voluntary workers, who each year try to clear its fallen trees, remark its worn blazes and refit its occasional shelters, widens the horizons of every two-legged creature in North America. People walk it because the ultimate buzz of adventure is in their ears.

In the Pisgah Forest, indeed, there are many trails, but only the sections of the Appalachian Trail are in serious danger of becoming overcrowded. Both here and in the Great Smoky Mountains, just to the south, overnight camping on the trail is only allowed by permit, and permits are strictly rationed. But crowded, in trail terms, often means meeting another walking party every half hour, and that tends to occur only where the trail crosses a road.

Crossing a highway is certainly the greatest physical danger a trail walker will encounter. Snakes and bears and twisted ankles are less hazardous. Even so, although the trail is so painstakingly marked and signposted, it can be rough and rocky going. The American mountaintops are boulders and slippery clay, and the American forest makes a deep-green tunnel from which, when the trees are in leaf, the view is normally limited to a few yards.

It is just that which makes the Pisgah viewpoints so wonderful. Emerging from the green, the eye must suddenly take on a different focal length; from judging yards to judging miles. There is no foreground. The slope drops away under your feet, reversing far below in the invisible depths into the opposite slope that becomes the facing wall of the valley whose apex you are traversing. In the crystal air perspective is confounded. Everything seems within a stone's throw. Only the map reveals that the next range is as far away as tomorrow's lunchtime.

The Pisgah Forest is traversed, too, by another extraordinary American experiment in bringing the wild within man's reach. Possibly the world's most beautiful road is the Blue Ridge Parkway, which traverses the Pisgah on its 469-mile course from the Shenandoah to the Great Smokies. The parkway is closed to commercial traffic. It is exclusively designed for pleasure, to reconcile the automobile to the countryside, to instruct and entertain its users rather than, as is the case with normal roads, to take them from place to place. From the road you may see views as wonderful as from the trail. You may stop and stroll and get as close to the landscape as a car can take you. On the trail, although you may look at the landscape, you become part of it, too. Mankind reclaims, on foot, the land he was promised at the first Pisgah.

HAWKS OF THE APPALACHIAN FLYWAY

The Appalachian Flyway is one of the major avian migratory systems of North America. Left to right, red-shouldered hawk, red-tailed hawk, turkey vulture and osprey, or fish hawk, are four of the many species of hawks which may be seen in the Appalachian Mountains during the autumn migration. The hawks ride the thermals and up-currents of air from the mountains, enabling them to fly great distances with little expenditure of energy.

The Appalachian Trail

Zionville Valley sleeps under a snowy blanket in the North Carolina Appalachians. Emerging from the wooded Appalachian Trail, many farms and villages like this are encountered. Twenty-five years before the Revolutionary War, small groups of settlers began to move into these mountains, bringing their hopes for a better life and bestowing biblical names like Pisgah and Zion on their new homeland. Two centuries later, the farmhouses, built from the fine Appalachian forest timber, stand untouched by time, and families tend their small, self-sufficient farms in much the same way as their ancestors, who originally built them.

Falling back from the paddle stroke, the drops strike the water with a high singing note that reflects at once and reverberates among the rock faces all around. Idly, the scow moves along the surface three hundred and sixty feet below the top of the hill that enfolds it. By artificial light the water appears oily, unnatural, devoid of the color that normal rivers derive from the sky above. But the boat is on a living river, flowing through its cave in the bowels of the earth through tunnels and crannies, at last to reach the light of day.

Underground they call it Echo River. Where it emerges at last to join the Green River between its forested banks it is called the River Styx, after the stream which, in Greek mythology, barred the way to the Underworld. Almost as amazing as the miracles in Greek mythology is the miracle of Mammoth Cave, this underworld of caverns and mysteries. Here life does not need to be renewed by the sun. There is life all the time and life forms that have renewed themselves without glimpsing sunlight for hundreds of millions of years.

The fish is, to human eyes, the most familiar and thus the strangest of the underworld life forms of Mammoth Cave. There are two distinct fish species: one brownish and one that must be called "gray," although it is almost colorless. Neither species has eyes. Instead where their eyes were, millions of years ago, there now appear unsightly swollen lumps on the sides of their heads. With these organs the sightless fish can discriminate between different kinds of vibrations and pressures in the water, sensing out the other organisms with which they share their dark subterranean world and instantly determining which is suitable for food and which should be shunned.

These fish of the underground rivers are unrelated to any form of fish life in the surrounding lakes and rivers. Biologically, the species to which they are most closely related is the family of sea fish that includes the cod. They are, in fact, in direct line of descent from the salt-sea fish that swam here when the hills of Tennessee were at the bottom of the ocean. That ocean sank, leaving behind it layer upon layer of limestone and sandstone silt where its bed had been. Then the core of the earth thrust and twisted upward, cracking the silt layers into blocks. Vegetation, and eventually great trees, grew where the waters had been. The rotting plant forms decayed into an acid sludge that permeated between the layers and ate them away into caves and underground rivers.

All the time—this geological process took

AQUATIC ANIMALS OF MAMMOTH CAVE

The almost transparent cave fish *Typhlichthys subterraneus* and the crayfish *Procambarus pallidus* are troglobites, living out their entire life cycle in the total darkness of caves. Both are blind and locate their food through their extraordinary sensitivity to vibrations in the water. To avoid undue disturbance, which would confuse their sensory organs, they move slowly through the water, stopping frequently. The crayfish uses its long antennae to locate its food and its short antennae to identify it.

150

Mammoth Cave

about three hundred million years—the fish have survived, adapting themselves, losing the power of sight, developing senses for which we do not have a name, eating, breeding, against all the odds existing.

The Mammoth Cave system is by no means yet fully explored. Men have penetrated along almost two hundred miles of interconnected underground passages here, and there are certainly more to be found. About one hundred and fifty distinctive life forms have been identified as indigenous inhabitants of the cave system. (This does not include certain bats, salamanders and other creatures that use the caves as their base for sorties into the "normal" world outside.)

Mammoth Cave has been from time to time used by man. You may see the body of an Indian who, two thousand years ago, was accidentally crushed by a falling rock when gathering minerals in the cave. A certain Bob Houchins found the cave, in 1799, when chasing a bear he had wounded. (Although one of the local guides claims it was the bear that was after Mr. Houchins.) In the War of 1812, when the British had blockaded the American ports, almost half of the saltpeter used in American gunpowder was derived from the bats' droppings, or guano, found on the cave floor; the ingenious improvised machinery still exists and may be seen.

In Victorian times such popular stars as the Shakespearean actor Edwin Booth and the "Swedish nightingale," opera singer Jenny Lind, would come to the caves and put on a performance as a way of scoring a quick newspaper headline.

Mammoth Cave has for well over a century been a supreme tourist attraction. It is slightly frightening and in its way extremely beautiful. The action of chemical deposits on the soft limestone has created strange phenomena, stalactites, stalagmites, "frozen waterfalls." It is now carefully preserved and most skillfully exhibited by the National Park Service which, as a special bonus, also owns and preserves inviolate a wild area of about fifty thousand acres on the surface above it. There are a large number of other privately owned cave systems in central Kentucky, some of them remarkable and some of them examples of how full-scale commercial exploitation may despoil the thing being exploited.

Mammoth Cave is certainly a showplace. It is also respected and conserved for its genuine scientific interest. It is both spectacular and extraordinary.

Cleveland Avenue Passage, above left, is part of the hundred and fifty miles of explored passages in the Mammoth Cave system, the longest in the world. Many passages remain unexplored and geologists estimate that the cave system is probably over three hundred miles long. During the War of 1812, when the United States was blockaded, the caves were almost the only source of saltpeter, an ingredient of gunpowder. Later they became a tourist attraction which ranked with Niagara Falls. Frozen Niagara, above right, the flowing formation which resembles the Falls, was not discovered until 1923. The last major discovery of new formations was made in 1938.

At night, when the lights go on, there seems to be a great hole in North America—a dark place, fifty-five miles long by almost twenty miles broad, where the glare of civilization does not shine up at the sky. Man has imposed this area of darkness, as he has imposed the lights around it, by his own will. He has set aside this vast area of mountain and wood and falling water in the valleys, to preserve his own sanity, to refresh his body and his mind.

The Great Smoky Mountains rise in vertiginous slopes to their summits above the five-thousand-foot mark. They were for centuries a barrier to settlers. Even after the Indians had been removed, the valleys of the Smokies became a refuge for families whose one endeavor was to keep themselves clear of the law and their children clear of schoolteachers. Old customs, old crafts and old songs lived on in the foothills for long after they had perished elsewhere in the United States, or even in the England from which they had first sprung. The modern world simply could not get into the Smokies.

Establishing a national park here insured that many of the wild species that had been exterminated in the hills by hunters and trappers would be restored. There is one strange addition—the European wild boar. This fierce nocturnal forager, brought from Poland or Germany, has made itself perfectly at home in the remote areas of the park.

Now about eight million visitors a year crowd to an area that is justly a source of pride for all Americans. Around the park's fringes a tourist industry squarely based on the park's attractions is the mainstay of the people's prosperity. In a brief drive across the park you can pass through a range of climates; from the peaches-and-tobacco valleys of the lowlands to the Canadian ecology of the high peaks, with gentians and all kinds of true alpine plants growing on the high ranges, well over six thousand feet. Here mountain maple and mountain ash thrive. Sugar maple and yellow buckeye grow on the slopes, as do conifers, including red spruce and eastern hemlock. Mixed hardwood forests cover the lower slopes.

Inevitably the danger is overuse and congestion. But that is true only of the park areas that can be easily reached by car. Huge spaces

are too far from roads now, and too steep for roads to ever be built. There are in the park, apart from sixty-eight miles of the famous Appalachian Trail, over five hundred miles of foot and horse tracks and countless miles of fishing waters.

The one thing that has gone forever are the people of the Smokies. They can never be replaced or recreated, although they are well commemorated in the park by exhibits and by working farms run on the lines they developed. But time and growing prosperity would have done for them anyway; the six thousand landholders displaced by the park's creation may well now be better off than if they had been left to drift, unguided, to the cities. With the

TREES OF THE GREAT SMOKY MOUNTAINS

The Smoky Mountains lie below the timberline and a great variety of vegetation, including more than one hundred species of trees which span several botanical zones, flourish on the slopes. Mixed hardwood forests thrive on the lower slopes in the Humid Transition zone, along with such conifers as red spruce and eastern hemlock. Sugar maple, native to Vermont and Canada, grows beside such southern species as yellow buckeye in the Transition zone. Mountain maple and mountain ash grow toward the summits.

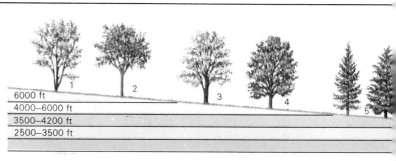

6000 ft
4000–6000 ft
3500–4200 ft
2500–3500 ft

The Great Smoky Mountains

people have gone certain creatures that get on well with man. The little American partridge that scoots so engagingly along the edges of cultivated fields, for example, is no longer there to shout his name, *Bob White*, to tell the stranger he is observed and feared.

By some accounts it is a matter of self-congratulation for man, an example of special human generosity, to have allowed nature to prevail again by pushing back the limits of human settlement. But the chief benefit here is to man himself, as an indivisible part of nature. For those who walk a bit, just a little way off the road, there is a healing goodness in the air that hangs with its puffs of mist gently above the treetops. Despite the name, the mist is not "smoky," but pearly, lit from within by its own watery luminescence, concentrating in patches the opaqueness of the whole sky and leaving the clear view with an especial clarity. From here onward the South becomes the Deep South. In summer the air trembles with heat. But overall, cool and immovable, the wooded mountains preside.

1 Mountain Maple
2 Mountain Ash
3 Yellow Buckeye
4 Sugar Maple
5 Red Spruce
6 Eastern Hemlock
7 Yellow Birch
8 American Beech
9 American Basswood
10 Red Maple

A characteristic haze hangs over the peaks of the Great Smoky Mountains. The "smoke" is always there, shrouding the leaves in summer and the ice-coated branches in winter. A similar light mist covers most of the rest of the Appalachian ranges, but heavy rainfall and location make it thickest in the Smokies. Cold air currents from the Atlantic seaboard mix with the warmer, damper air over these mountains. This air, which contains terpenes—gases from the trees' essential oils—when condensed produces the vaporous mist which cloaks the treetops.

Drunkenly the poles of the power line stagger off toward the indefinite horizon. Their feet are in the mud, which is always moving. The air smells thick and green, like the thick green marsh that spreads flat away into the distance. The seemingly endless fields of sugarcane have ended, the lost lands have begun. No one has taken hold of this place and tamed it. You cannot even really tell where the land is—which is land and which is water.

In truth, the Mississippi mud is neither one thing nor the other. The water is infinitely muddy, the land is the opposite of dry. Even the rise and fall of the wet here, where the Mississippi meets the salt sea, is not orderly and measured by the calendar like the real sea tides. The lift and drop comes and goes, to human eyes at random, raised and lowered perhaps by last week's storm off Cuba, perhaps by last winter's snowfall on the Canadian border. Banks of chocolate silt appear and drown again under these mysterious influences. And even where the green surface looks solid, that, too, may be an illusion; the tropical water hyacinth grows on the water, leaves floating, roots trailing down, a green carpet that remains firm to the eye through all its changes of height. This seemingly delicate plant with its fragile lavender flower once threatened to choke the bayous. Now it is kept under careful control.

Bayou Lafourche was once a supplementary mouth for the great, greedy river. It still opens direct to the waters of the Gulf of Mexico. But in one of the great spasms of human energy that have realigned, if not yet finally tamed, the river, the flow was redirected elsewhere. Now the bayou is stagnant, the levees along its bank crumbling into disuse. But the life along its shores goes on, livelier than ever. Along the hundred miles of waterway from Thibodaux to the sea is an anthology of Louisiana life.

At the seaward end the shrimp boats chug out across the watery desolation of the marsh; the bayou is just a channel in the mud. But even here the men of the bayou find a rich harvest; shrimps and oysters and clams for the exquisite New Orleans cuisine, wild duck for the table, muskrats for their fur. The hunters and trappers of the bayou are understandably contemptuous of the fashion for conservation. If a muskrat has four litters a year, and each litter includes four "kits," how can trapping be harmful to their survival? It is the old, lavish American attitude to wild things, a faith in the inexhaustibility of America that survives among these people. They carry on the traditions of their ancestors, the exiled French, intermarried with Indians, who came here from Acadia, the lost province far to the north in Canada, to find a new home at the mouth of the Mississippi.

As the bayou runs inland the houses begin. This, they say, is the longest street in America, eighty-five miles of continuous village, from Donaldsville to Golden Meadow. The oddity of the street, apart from its length, is that it is a water street. Everything faces the bayou and its boat docks. Behind that line is a road, a grossly crowded and inadequate road, then another more scattered row of houses. Then there are the gardens of okra and tomatoes and swelling Louisiana onions and garlic, trees of figs, plums, peaches, lettuce beds— good things for man's stomach and his heart.

Spanish moss hangs heavily from the trees, catching the sunlight in this solitary place in the bayous. Its grayish-green tendrils fascinated early explorers of these swamps. The French adventurers called it *barbe espagnole*, Spanish beard, while the Spaniards knew it as *peluca francesa*, Frenchman's wig.

Botanically it is *Tillandsia usneoides*, not a moss at all, but a member of the pineapple family. Its tiny, emerald-green flowers look like miniature lilies.

154

Bayou Lafourche

Then, widening gradually as the drained land spreads toward the delta, there is acre after acre of sugarcane. Even deep beneath the earth men have found riches; the pumps and pipes of oil wells stand casually amid the cane fields, and down into the salt flats. At night the gas flares light up the sky. Far out in the Gulf, oil rigs loom dimly in the misted air.

And richest of all is the human life of the bayou. Until the 1940s there were no roads here and no proper schools. Today, the people over forty speak an eccentric and often uncertain English, and many of the young people still speak a French that is preserved in the parochial schools of this almost exclusively Roman Catholic region. It is by no means the French of modern France. (For that matter, the English of present-day Louisiana is not exactly the Queen's English.)

Pirogue à vendre proclaims a rough, hand-painted sign—Pirogue for sale. Pirogue is a word of Spanish origin, which is commonly met in French-speaking West Africa, meaning a dugout canoe. In the United States it means a flat-bottomed swamp boat. But more than that it indicates that these people are the last heirs in Louisiana of an imperial tradition that once brought them under the same flag as peoples in India, in Southeast Asia, in Canada, in Africa, under European rule from Paris. The speech, the religion and the culture of eighteenth-century France live on here on the rich soil of the Mississippi. In all likelihood these things will survive for long after man has pumped the last drop of the oil that has brought brief riches to the bayou. Bayou Lafourche is a monument to the living diversity that, across the centuries, has made the United States what it is today.

Young oaks grow in the tangled forest of Shenandoah National Park. A careful replanting program is replacing the Blue Ridge chestnuts, now destroyed by disease, with a new growth predominated by three species of oak—red, white and chestnut—and the "ghost forest" is slowly returning to a natural state.

Brig. Gen. P. G. T. Beauregard   Gen. Stonewall Jackson

At the crest the forest thins out, giving way to wind-scoured rock. Stand on that ridge when the sun is low in the sky and your shadow falls away into the measureless folds of the valleys, blue and secret far below. From these heights to the ocean the land rolls away in sweet hunched foothills, down across the apple valleys of the Virginia Piedmont and clear to the Atlantic Ocean. To the east, the answering line of the Alleghenies marks the horizon: between the Alleghenies and the Blue Ridge there lies at your feet another plain, fertile and secret, the river, with its melodious name, winding its way to the north in the mist. Shenandoah is as lovely as it sounds.

For a hundred miles the Skyline Drive follows the summits of the Blue Ridge Mountains, linking the high places and forcing out to viewpoints. It may well be the most beautiful road in the world. It was built along the crest in the worst years of the Great Depression, employing men who would otherwise have stood idle. It was socially useful. It was marvelously engineered. Most important of all, it was designed with a remarkable eye for landscape—for the way to see landscape from a highway, and the way to fit a highway into landscape. It runs through what is now a mass of woodland, clothing the already magnificent lines of the hills with shades of green that in the autumn transform themselves into the peculiarly American glory of reds and golds and infinitely various browns. When it was built the hills were a desert.

Primitive farming practices had begun the work of destruction. Then suddenly a strange plague struck, not made by man but brought by him. In the native American forest of the Virginia mountains one tree in three was a chestnut. Chestnut timber and tanbark were the mainstay of the region's human population. Even before men came there the nuts and bark and undergrowth of the chestnut trees had sustained the native wildlife. Early in the twentieth century some chestnut planting stock was casually imported to the port of New York from Asia. It carried with it the spores of a fungus unknown in North America. On new soil the fungus grew, spread and destroyed the trees that were its host.

By 1930 there was not a single mature chestnut tree on the Blue Ridge. They called the bare trunks the Ghost Forest. Some of them still stand, pale and treacherous, breaking in your hand if you pull a branch. From their bases, now and then, spring a few stunted sprouts. Life lingers on among the roots. One day, perhaps, the American chestnut may develop its own immunity to the Asian blight. Meanwhile, from the chaos it left behind a new beauty has been created.

Under careful management and control the long, slim mountain range of the Blue Ridge has grown the lovely wooded cover that may be seen today. Wild creatures have come back to the new woodlands. Only a few signs indicate that the woods are a new creation willed by man. Pale amid the early green of spring, a blossoming, gnarled apple tree shows where a mountaineer had his cottage, before the disaster and the slump drove his family on. A patch of trees on level ground amid the slopes betrays the site of an old logging camp. Here and there the trace of a road can be discerned under the regenerating undergrowth.

Once these hills were full of people, and the people helped to decide the future of America. With the mountaineers' guidance the Confederate armies of the American Civil War were able to use the Shenandoah Valley as a refuge, a place where among a population of their own they could get their fill of bread and meat, and foray through the passes at the Northern soldiers in the Virginia plains. A terrible revenge fell upon the valley; General Grant ordered it so thoroughly devastated "that a crow flying across over the Valley would have to carry its own rations." The era of modern war began with the burning of the barns of the Shenandoah.

But now, it seems, the grimness is all in the past. The hills of Shenandoah are lovely again and accessible; even too accessible sometimes, when the summer cool or the autumn glory brings crowds in their cars. But then there are other hills to see, other beauties to find in the Virginia highlands. Take to your feet. The waterfalls will hurl down their torrents just for you, and the blue jay will flash by, pointing with a scream of color the softest blueness of the mountainside.

THE SHENANDOAH VALLEY CAMPAIGNS

The Shenandoah Valley was the site of one of the most important campaigns of the Civil War. The struggle to control the valley began in 1861, when Confederate troops under General P. G. T. Beauregard routed the first Union invasion of Virginia. Shenandoah was known as the North's "valley of humiliation," particularly after General Thomas J. "Stonewall" Jackson took charge of the Southern campaign in 1862. He not only kept Union troops far from Richmond, but at the same time brought his forces menacingly close to Washington, D.C. The South held the valley until 1865, when Union troops, under General Philip H. Sheridan, crushed their final resistance and devastated the Shenandoah Valley.

Gen. Philip Sheridan

157

Between the crags, the Shenandoah tumbles over its rocks to join the racing water of the Potomac. The valley is narrow, grand and rough, the rocks of its walls tumbled to the bases of the trees that struggle to grow between them. At the point where the rivers meet the little town perches. Thomas Jefferson, returning to his native America from the centers of European taste and culture, thought the view of Harpers Ferry "worth a voyage across the Atlantic." It is as romantic today as it was then. For Harpers Ferry, once the hub of its region, was cut off in midstride and left to wither; it was perhaps the most striking casualty of the ghastly and tragic Civil War.

Through Harpers Ferry and up the Potomac River lay the direct route from Virginia, through the Appalachian Mountains, to the central plains and the Great Lakes. The Shenandoah River, joining the Potomac at the ferry, drains its own fertile valley. In the gorge where the rivers meet, in the space of two miles they fall more than forty feet over the bedrock. Before the days of steam-powered factories and steam-powered railroads, this was an ideal place for a strategic industry. President Washington saw that. He founded at Harpers Ferry the main armaments factory of the new American Republic. Using the rivers to power its machines, and easy to defend if the British got up to their tricks again, it was the ideal place for the new Federal musket factory, which was opened in 1801.

Within twenty years Harpers Ferry was the seat of a uniquely American technological advance. Here, for the first time in the world, breech-loading rifles were made by mass-production techniques; not handmade, gun by gun, but with specialized manufacture of all the finely machined parts, so that the production, maintenance and repair of military weapons reached a level of perfection unprecedented in history. A canal was built along the fast-flowing Potomac to bring raw materials from Washington. In time the railroad arrived. Harpers Ferry was the mainstay of the Federal Army.

That was its downfall. In 1859, a certain

St. Peter's Church, built in the 1830s, stands solemnly on a hill overlooking a row of nineteenth-century houses on Shenandoah Street. St. Peter's is still the parish church of Harpers Ferry, and the houses, along with several other eighteenth- and nineteenth-century buildings, are part of a national historic park.

In 1747, Robert Harper established a mill which was ideally located at the point where the Potomac and Shenandoah rivers meet. Harper also operated a ferry across the river, giving the village its name. The ferry is now replaced by rail and road bridges, but the town retains its charm and tranquility.

Harpers Ferry

John Brown, apparently convinced he had a mission from God to destroy the evils of slavery, raided the Harpers Ferry arsenal in the hope of getting arms to distribute to the slaves of the South. His abolitionist crusade was an appalling failure. Brown was captured and hanged. But his soul, as every English-speaking child in the world knows, went marching on. Seventeen months after his raid the Civil War broke out. It was fought on the very issue that his terrorist raid had almost discredited. The ferry's position on the main access to the Federal capital made it a center of fighting in the war. It was captured, recaptured, devastated with pointless gallantry by soldiers of both sides. Then nature took a

hand in insuring that it would never rise again to provide the deadly weapons of war.

As peace came, the valleys above the ferry were cleared of trees, drained, civilized, planted with corn. When it rained, the water no longer seeped gently into the tributaries of the Shenandoah and the Potomac. It rushed off the farms to the sea, raising the rivers forty feet and more above their summer lows. It ripped through the canyon where the rivers meet. In the 1870s and 1880s Harpers Ferry was washed away again and again. The arsenal was never rebuilt. The town died. Only a few pretty buildings on the hillside survived.

And that is what is there today. The relics of the once-thriving town have been meticu-

lously preserved and restored. They are a memorial to the technological brilliance that set the United States on the road to nationhood, and a terrible reminder of the agony the nation suffered along the way. The first natural beauty of the gorge has survived all; it is even enhanced by the old human settlement in its center. Harpers Ferry is the jewel at the heart of the upland beauty of West Virginia. It is linked with the nation's capital by the quiet waterway of the old Chesapeake and Ohio Canal, now only navigable in part, but preserved for posterity as a triumph of the American conservationist cause. Jefferson, as usual, was right. Harpers Ferry is worth the journey —any journey.

It is strange country, where the last of the eastern hills break down amid cotton fields to the plain of the Gulf Coast. The Little River—little only by American standards; it is a considerable flow of water—is one of the strangest things about this country. The river runs along the top of a mountain, in the great cleft it has carved for itself. It rises up on Lookout Mountain, the heart of the Deep South, from where you may look down for endless miles into Georgia, Kentucky and Alabama. It gathers force and size as it goes southward. And at the falls it plunges into a pit, a thirty-mile canyon with walls that average five hundred feet high, and at one point reach seven hundred feet. It is as though the Appalachian hills, as they end their run down from the Great Lakes and the St. Lawrence River, were playing a final trick. It is also, in its own right, a splendid place, made finer yet by the contrast of its damp, cool depths with the hot Alabama lands to the south.

The daring take boats through the gorge when the waters are just right. If the flow is too great boats are overwhelmed; if it is too low, they cannot pass the rapids which are formed as the river grinds away the stone. Most people walk down into the chasm from the road that runs along its lip. Where the stream deepens into a pool, on the site of one of the old waterfalls that have over millions of years eroded their way upstream, there are great fish. The peculiar climate created by damp river air and shade amid a region where, in summer, there is no shelter, brings a curious and beautiful mixture of plants. The rhododendron glows pink in springtime, as though this were high country. Nearby grow subtropical fruits, dwarf papaw, wild ginger, the mysterious root called "ginseng," which is prized by the Chinese as an aphrodisiac.

A place like this inevitably attracts legends. It is full of mysterious shades and cool distant sounds in the summer heat. More than that, the river today serves as a boundary for Cherokee County, named after the Indian people who, in 1838, were rounded up here by the United States Army and marched off on their terrible journey to deportation in the Far West. At least half of the Cherokee nation perished of hunger or cold or exhaustion on that march. But for almost a century afterward, an Indian warrior would be sighted from time to time on a rocky overlook.

And there are other stories, too. A series of caves high on the rock cliffs, accessible only by a narrow ledge, appears to be defended by a piled stone fortification—something the native Indians never constructed. The Indians themselves are reputed to have claimed that the walls were built centuries ago by white men with beards. From that, and from a few words in the Cherokee language that have a curious resemblance to Welsh, came the belief, held quite seriously by some, that this was the end of the journey for the Celtic sailors who, under Prince Madoc, sailed the

The heavy head and neck of the belted kingfisher, left, absorb the shock of impact when it dives into the water in search of fish. In Little River Canyon these solitary birds, which are seen only in groups during courtship, jealously patrol their own stretches of water, declaiming the boundaries with their characteristic harsh, grating calls.

The distinctive cry of the yellow-shafted flicker, left, heralds the spring in Little River Canyon. This woodpecker, which ranges from Alaska to Florida, has 132 local names, but in Alabama, where it is known as the yellow-hammer, it has a special significance. Its feathers were worn by her soldiers during the Civil War and it is now the state bird.

Little River Canyon

Atlantic in ten ships a thousand years ago.

But the finest thing of all about Little River Canyon is that it has remained almost unaltered by man. From the early 1930s onward most of the valleys of the southern mountains have been dammed and controlled. The dams have provided water for the parched valleys. They have helped regulate the terrible floods off the mountains. They have provided cheap electric power for industry, great lakes that give pleasure to the people, that even moderate and temper the climate of the region. Quite literally, the existence of the new South—which is both an economic fact and a state of mind—has been due to the dams.

But the South also needed a few places untouched by much progress, inaccessible and wild. The Little River, cutting so curiously along the top of its mountain ridge, would, behind a dam, have made an insignificant contribution to Alabama's great need for water and for power. Its existence, as it is, does much for its people's peace of mind.

The Little River races past the trees that crowd its banks, and plunges over broad waterfalls as it surges through the narrow confines of its mountaintop canyon, above. The river flows through five-thousand-acre De Soto State Park, dropping one hundred and ten feet over De Soto Falls before entering the great winding canyon which is the deepest gorge east of the Mississippi River. In spring the canyon is aflame with wild flowers. Honeysuckle, trillium, flameflower, columbine and violets bloom among rhododendron bushes and the beautiful flowering princess trees, brought to America from China.

The pitcher plant, left, is one of the most unusual plants found in Little River Canyon. Insects are fatally attracted to the slippery nectar on its cup of leaves, down which they slide into a fluid containing a protein-digesting enzyme. In this way the plant obtains vital phosphorus and nitrogen from its unfortunate victims.

Natchez Trace

"This road being completed, I shall consider our Southern extremity secured, the Indians in that quarter at our feet, and the adjacent province laid open to us," said James Wilkinson, in 1801, advising President Jefferson on the completion of a footway from Natchez to Nashville.

The United States had barely completed its anti-imperial revolution. Already, with the purchase of Louisiana from the French two years in the future, it was seeking to secure its frontiers and its population. The Natchez Trace was a first and necessary step toward expansion. A *trace*, in the French, was a trail of footprints. This trace ran for four hundred and fifty miles, from the fringes of European settlement on the Cumberland River, at Nashville in Tennessee, right down to the highest point to which boats without power could make their way against the stream of the Mississippi River. It opened the way between the Latin settlements of the Gulf of Mexico and the English-speaking peoples of the new United States. It was used for the subjection of the Indians. Now its course has been laid out as a living monument to the men of all three cultures.

The Indians came first. In the shaggy woods the clearing is clipped and orderly. Children are requested not to slide on the slopes, since that might cause erosion. The vast mound that stands here is respected now, looked after by its official guardians, who understand what it means, looked at by the thousands who come to learn how their country became what it is. It is lucky that Emerald Mound survived. Most Indian mounds along the Mississippi were used by early settlers as nice dry places on which to build houses; when they dug up old Indian bones they would throw them away, to rid themselves of bad luck. But nobody ever wanted to settle here in the forest. The trace went past, up into Indian territory, a few miles to the north.

The Indians used the trace in their mysterious system of trade, swapping conch shells from the Gulf for copper nuggets from the far north. Emerald Mound was a place of worship. They raised it around a natural hill, between the fourteenth and the seventeenth Christian centuries. It is just seven hundred and seventy feet long, one hundred and thirty-five feet wide and thirty-five feet high. On top are lumps, which may have supported structures used in the worship of the sun; nobody is absolutely sure. The Spanish and the French exterminated these Indians.

The trace remained, barely trodden, in the underbrush. Only when the United States got control of their own destiny and tried to develop trade with the Latins to their south—trade which Britain, in Colonial times, had prohibited—did it come back into use. In 1793, the Americans acquired control of the Natchez district, hitherto disputed between French and Spanish (with the British intervening from time to time). Americans with produce from the interior could float their goods down the Mississippi on rafts. When the rafts arrived at Natchez they unloaded; the rafts were then broken up and sold for lumber and the boatmen walked home. That was the use of the trace—that, and military strength. It was the route used by Andrew Jackson, a veteran Indian fighter, and his Tennesseans on their way to victory at New Orleans.

But the route did not remain long in use. On January 10, 1812, the steamer *New Orleans* docked in the city whose name she bore. Within ten years the paddles were churning all the way up the great river. Natchez itself rose to commercial affluence with its cluster of vast and ostentatious palaces built by the new rich merchants and cotton planters. But its wealth came from water transport. The trace fell out of use again. Its taverns and bawdy houses did service for a while as plantation houses for cotton. Then the catastrophe of the Civil War, the War between the States, fell on the slave economy. Under the blazing summer skies, quiet came again.

Today, out of respect for all that historical burden, the Government has almost completed the building of a long-range, slow-speed highway, running the entire length of the old trace across the states of Tennessee, Alabama and Mississippi. On it, cars may be used so that their passengers can enter into, not race across, the landscape. It is designed for stopping.

You may see an old tavern or a field of growing cotton or a quiet ford on the old route, where the heron still stands to fish on his stilt legs in the shallows. In the soft earth, the blown silt of millennia, the old path is sometimes sunk twenty feet or more by the moccasins or boots or plain bare footprints of the men who once used it. Always, on the southern stretch between Natchez and Jackson, there is the ancient forest with its subtropical life, strange birds screeching in the shadows. The modern Natchez Trace is a road that tells a story of America.

Andrew Jackson, seventh President of the United States, got his nickname "Old Hickory" on the Natchez Trace. During the War of 1812, he led his Tennessee Militia down the trace to New Orleans, where an invasion was threatened. General Jackson shared the hardships of the march with his men, his toughness earning him his name.

Emerald Mound, above, is one of many similar burial and ceremonial mounds in Mississippi. Some were made by unnamed prehistoric Indians up to one thousand years ago. Emerald Mound dates from about 1600 and was probably used by the Natchez Indians in their sun-worshiping ceremonies.

Between Nashville and Natchez a ribbon of concrete today follows the Natchez Trace, once a rough path worn by the hooves of buffalo migrating to their feeding grounds. They created a trail which has been used by Indians, explorers, frontiersmen, traders, armies and settlers. Sections of the original trace remain and are carefully preserved.

The Ozark Forests

A kind of miracle is taking place in Arkansas. For generations the Ozark hills of that state were a byword for poverty and deprivation, and for the ultimate devastation that humans can inflict on nature. The rough sandstone hills, cut through by streams, undermined by caves, were never fertile ground. But the growth of centuries had established there, before the white man came, a sparse but strong forest growth that shaded the thin soil from the blast of the summer sun and held the ground when the winter rains tried to wash it away to the Mississippi River.

Men destroyed it all. They cut the trees—the pines, the oaks, the hickories and the walnuts. When they had finished cutting, they burned the unwanted branches and brushwood. They laid the hills naked, and the climate finished what men had begun. "We wasn't no dust bowl, because we hadn't enough dust," an ancient hill man remarked. When the work of destruction was almost complete, the Government took over. Since the loggers had taken all the value from the land, there was no one to raise much objection.

In 1908, the Ozarks became a national forest under the care of the Department of Agriculture. After half a century of work the Ozarks became productive again. The forest covers more than twenty-three hundred square miles. In it, now, the modern timber firms and public officials work together to insure that only the right amount of the right timber is removed, that fire is strictly controlled, that the long-term mutual interests of men and of nature are respected. A great lesson has been learned and acted upon.

The Arkansas hill men have never prided themselves on being law-abiding folk. But they can hardly have been pleased when hillbilly became a term of derision and their poverty became a matter for national concern. They have found a measure of prosperity in the work that their forests, properly managed, bring. They have learned to make the small dirt dams that retain the precious water for their fields and restrain the floods in their rivers. And, after many decades of turning inward on themselves, they have learned to welcome strangers as visitors to what has again become their lovely land.

The national forest has played the leading part in this recovery. Since 1960 the forests have had as a secondary purpose, in addition to the planned renewal of their natural resources, the encouragement of public recreation. The amazing rock bluffs that soar above the timber tops, the lakes and reservoirs and swift rivers, the strange caves of stalagmites and melting, flowing rock forms—some of them, and the strangest, newly discovered in the last few decades—all these things are now being opened to visitors and enjoyed more and more.

The hills are at their best in spring and autumn, between the searing sun of summer and the brief harsh winter. Where the forest is regenerating, the flowering dogwood is the first shrub to reestablish itself, turning whole hillsides white. On the high slopes where the rock has always been too near the surface to permit much growth of trees, the native azaleas flash pink and red. In shady groves, small flowers bloom all year. And, above all, there is the green of the forest, dark with pines, giving shade through the year as the hardwoods renew their leaves. Here, mankind may reflect on a defeat for the infertility he had imposed on the face of the earth, and rejoice in renewal.

The early nineteenth-century explorer Zebulon Pike called the Ozark country "one of the most beautiful the eye ever beheld." Henry Rowe Schoolcraft, another explorer, wrote in 1819 that the Ozarks were "a sort of Rheingau, through which the rivers burst." Today, more than one hundred and fifty years later, this land of trees, rocks and water retains its serene loveliness. Clear, pure, rain-fed streams and rivers flow through tumbled masses of rocks, left, or cascade over boulders into one of hundreds of waterfalls, above.

The delicate milkweed is just one of the fifteen hundred species of plants now native to the Ozarks. Because the area escaped the glaciers of the last Ice Age, northern plants were moved here and survived. As the glaciers melted, some southern species began to migrate north, with many taking root here. Plants have also come from eastern and western parts of North America, making the Ozarks a vast botanical crossroads, a centralized region where vegetation from different areas grows together.

Sea Islands

The land and the sea run into one another and mingle. At low tide the foreshore stretches without a seam to the horizon. Out at sea the shrimp boat seems to be casting its net into a blue beach that shades imperceptibly to gray and then to dry sand at your feet. Slowly the sun moves, the tide rises; with a rustle and no fuss the water advances, and the palmettos and great oaks wreathed in Spanish moss rise straight from the water's edge. By the dry dust road there is a white heron fishing, and with a gurgle among the tomato fields the high tide is here behind the wall.

The mingling of land and sea made these Sea Islands and set them apart. Gaze back across the sound at the great white houses that the planters built in Beaufort. The money that paid for them sprang from the island sands, where there grew in those days the finest and longest-fibered cotton in the world. Ringed around with great trees, dazzling white, artfully constructed to make shade and catch the breeze, these exquisite and entirely American buildings are constructed, on their upper floors, of local timber, while their foundations are of the peculiar local cement known as "tabby," compacted of oyster shells and fossil lime. They are a reminder of a time when Americans lived by their wits, on the produce of their own lands. But they also lived by the labor of others, of men whom they owned. Beaufort grew rich on slavery. It has never quite recovered from its abolition.

For almost three centuries Beaufort County was one of the most prosperous places in North America. The Spanish made a stockade here against the Indians when they landed on these shores almost a hundred years before the Pilgrims left Plymouth. When the French supplanted the Spanish they called their own armed base Beau Fort, beautiful fort, and the British kept the name when they, in turn, expelled the French. But the British planters left to their American successors a system of agriculture that contained the seeds of its own destruction. During the Civil War, in 1861, warships of the Northern states' fleet appeared off St. Helena Island. The slave owners fled, never to return. Their freed slaves volunteered by hundreds to join the fight for their liberty. When peace came the estates were parceled

out among their former workers, or traded like gambling counters among the crooks and speculators who descended like a plague upon the defeated South. Sea Island cotton, the pride of the Carolinas, could not be successfully grown and processed except on big estates. The great days of prosperity were ended.

Where the freed black people took over the land, their descendants live on to this day as small farmers and fishermen, content if not especially prosperous, retaining a particular culture and the particular speech forms of the Gullah dialect that are today recognized as a unique contribution to American life. But many of the islands were cleared of their people in the early years of the present century and set aside by rich Northerners as hunting preserves and playgrounds. Parris Island, one of the largest of these almost unpopulated Sea Islands, was taken over by the United States Marines as a training base. From it come thunderous crashes and the rattle of practice warfare, and it figures large in the history of America's proudest fighting force. Another big island, Hilton Head, has lately been transformed into a discreetly luxurious holiday resort, with hotels, apartment houses and golf courses, all matched as unobtrusively as possible into its landscape of woods and long, sandy beaches.

But the islands are still remote and somewhat inaccessible. Even where bridges have

been built across to the mainland, their central spans have to open and close to accommodate the waterborne traffic of the Intracoastal Waterway, that system of channels and inlets and canals that miraculously allows small boats to travel all the way from Key West in Florida to New York City without ever entering the open sea. Boats take precedence over cars, as they should, and road travelers may have to wait hours to pass over the bridges. The islands live at their own island pace, free and easy and unhurried.

And still, among the Sea Islands, the shoreline is nourished by the silt of the waters that rise and fall with the tides. Fine sand toward the open sea, rich mud on the inlets, the sea's edge swarms with all kinds of amphibious creatures—fish, snakes, shrimps, crabs. It is a place to relax, to walk or to swim or just to do nothing much and enjoy the superlative seafood. In the town of Beaufort itself, the mainland capital of this island region, the relative lack of the past century's particular brand of progress has meant that nobody troubled to tear down or "improve" the great houses that the cotton planters left behind. Now, tactfully and with loving care, the wooden homes and churches are being repainted and restored by their owners, who include black as well as white people. For those who appreciate peace of mind as well as physical beauty, it is a wonderful place to be.

The tidal flats of Cape Romain in the Sea Islands are the largest wildlife refuge on the East Coast. Baldplate ducks, right, and the Canada goose, far right, are just two of the hundreds of species of birds which stop on Cape Romain during their flight along the migratory route to the south known as the Atlantic Flyway.

Spanish moss drapes the ruins of the Chapel of Ease on St. Helena Island. The Church of England chapel was built of tabby, a local building material of crushed shells, lime and sand, when the grand Colonial life-style prevailed in the days before the Civil War. After the war it was

rented by the African Methodist Church and used by the island's large population of Gullah blacks, said to be the purest of African Negroes in North America. The chapel was burned down in the great forest fire of 1886.

Sunset off Sullivan's Island, near Charleston. The island is typical of the Sea Island coast, which stretches south from Georgetown, South Carolina, to Florida. Unlike the reef-like islands to the north, most of the Sea Islands are heavily wooded with longleaf pines, palms, magnolias, myrtles and oaks.

On this great hinge the North Atlantic turns. From this precise point of America the tropical waters flow forever to the northeast, to wash the shores of Spain and to temper the Scottish winter so that even there, in the latitude of Labrador, palm trees may grow by the sea. Surging up from the Caribbean, the warm Gulf Stream meets the cold Virginia Current from the north. They mingle and turn away from land to meet the opposing continent. Where the waters meet they have scored the sandy shores to a point— Cape Hatteras.

The ocean flow from Hatteras carried Columbus home to tell his improbable story of a new India. It was perhaps the greatest of his discoveries that in the stream off Hatteras a ship, however unwieldly and heavy laden,

would be carried eastward into the zone of the trade winds that blew homeward. Off Hatteras, soon, the Spanish treasure fleet would gather in convoy, bearing the incredible gold stores of the Indies. In the inlets behind Hatteras the pirates and marauders learned to lie in wait for their prey. It was as a base for plunder that, in 1585, Sir Walter Raleigh's men set up on Roanoke Island inside the Outer Banks, the first of all English colonies in the New World. It was an ill-prepared venture that ended badly, the people starved or massacred, the fort abandoned, its founder discredited and finally beheaded to placate the Spaniards. But from this inglorious quest for other people's gold stemmed the settlement of the North American continent by men who spoke English and lived by English law.

Hatteras has never been a comfortable place. It is rough, impermanent, inhospitable, good for adventures or escapades or even vacations, not for living. It is the outermost point of the slim broken barrier of islands that runs from Norfolk, Virginia, down to Cape Lookout, North Carolina; a sliver of reefs and sandbars some two hundred miles long. Its weather is ridiculously changeable, ruled now by the northern currents, now by the warmth from the Gulf and always by the rush of the wind between the sound behind and the ocean in front.

It was the clear constancy of the winter winds that made the Wright brothers choose the Outer Banks of North Carolina for their triumphant experiments with flight. At other seasons, however, the storms may rise to fury,

Cape Hatteras Lighthouse warns ships of the dangers along the Outer Bank shoals, the "Grave-yard of the Atlantic." The distinctive black-and-white-striped tower has aided navigators since 1870, except for a fifteen-year period when beach erosion became so severe that waves were washing the base of the lighthouse and, in 1935,

it had to be abandoned. The erosion was finally halted by natural trends, and control work by the Civilian Conservation Corps returned the beacon to Cape Hatteras Lighthouse in 1950.

FISH OF CAPE HATTERAS
Both temperate and tropical fish are found off Cape Hatteras, where warm and cold currents meet. The shoals are the southern limit for the temperate striped drum fish and bluefish, and the northern limit for the tropical pompano, dolphin and blue marlin.

Pompano

smashing across the open sea onto the Banks. In the 1930s the dunes on the seaward side of the sandbanks were built up and stabilized by man. Much more recently a blacktop road has been built all along the ninety miles from Kitty Hawk to Ocracoke. But the storm seas still sweep clear across the barrier, and one day again a hurricane may split the beach as it has done so often before.

Out to sea, under the waves, the sands of Hatteras are still on the move. Twelve miles out, on Diamond Shoals, the far lighthouse flashes its warning. Since written records began the Outer Banks, known to mariners as "The Graveyard," have claimed the wrecks of over five hundred ships, starting with the sinking of Raleigh's *Tiger* in Ocracoke Inlet in 1585. In World War II, U-boats lurked in these waters, earning for the channel off Diamond Shoals the name Torpedo Junction, in recognition of the sinking by enemy action of more than one hundred vessels. Even land-based sailors are not entirely secure here; in 1969, the United States naval facility near Hatteras Lighthouse was almost swept away in a storm.

Now Cape Hatteras, its beach and its long island strip, have been set aside as an immense adventure playground (in 1953 it was established as the first of the national seashores). It may well be the world's best public fishing beach. It contains a vast refuge for the migrant birds of the coastline. It is a place so enormous that solitude still reigns, a place so flat in the bright, damp air that distance becomes an unreal thing, the nearby sand dunes appearing like distant mountains, the far-off boats in the sound looking like toys at arm's length. Where the sand has stayed put enough to let trees and plants grow, the mild Gulf Stream climate makes them resplendent with wild flowers from spring to early winter.

But Hatteras is not tamed. From miles above, the satellite weather cameras show it as it is, a clear pencil line along the coast of America, feathering off to seaward in clouds or currents. To the first astronauts, looking down as men had never looked down before on their own distant planet, Hatteras became a friendly landmark, a recognizable sign that home was still there. Twice in human history, for Columbus and for those modern Americans circling high above the earth, Hatteras has pointed the way.

Dolphin

American Striped Drum

Blue Marlin

Bluefish

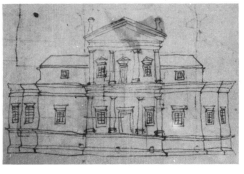

Simple, but elegant, Monticello is one of the most beautiful houses in America. It was the home of Thomas Jefferson, far left, and between 1769 and 1809 he was deeply involved in its construction. He wanted a building unlike the Georgian houses popular then, and the original Monticello was in the style of Palladio, the sixteenth- century Italian architect. Jefferson's sketch for the final elevation of the east front of this house, left, shows a two-story portico, a design feature used by Palladio. During his years as Minister to France, Jefferson visited the great architectural monuments and was most impressed by Roman ruins and by modern French buildings in the classical style. Upon his return he redesigned Monticello, adding a Doric portico to the west front, above, and erecting a dome over the center of the house. It was one of the earliest important neoclassical buildings in the New World.

Monticello

"Here was buried Thomas Jefferson, author of the Declaration of American Independence, of the Statute of Virginia for religious freedom, and Father of the University of Virginia."

Thomas Jefferson wrote his own epitaph. He had been Commissioner of the American Republic during the French Revolution, Secretary of State, Vice-President and then President of the United States. It was not these great public honors that he chose to enumerate on his tombstone, but the triumphs of his mind and his pen. The simple column, in the classical mode, still stands among the family graves in the quiet plot below the house he built for himself. He was anxious that it should remain. He specified that it should be made "of the coarse stone of which my columns are made, that no one might be tempted hereafter to destroy it for the value of the material."

The intellectual, the statesman, remained to the end of his life profoundly aware of the value of a good piece of dressed stone. Thomas Jefferson, in his day, was truly a new kind of man. More than anyone he gave form and force to the ideals of the American Revolution. Yet the chief object of much of his long life was the construction of his own house, for his own enjoyment. The Declaration of Independence will endure as long as men can understand the English language. We are lucky indeed to have the house, too.

Monticello stands precisely on the summit of a clean, sweet hill. From the terrace you may gaze as far as the eye can range over the Virginia plain, or you may turn to the west where the Blue Ridge Mountains close the prospect, with the university that Jefferson founded handsome in the middle distance of the intervening valley. Its image, so familiar in the hand or the pocket on the reverse side of the nickel, is in reality surprisingly intimate and comfortable. Most of all it is beautiful, a copy of the gentlemen's villas of contemporary Europe, themselves derived from Italian models of the sixteenth century, which in their turn were inspired by ancient Greek and Roman designs. Nothing could be less revolutionary. The crucial difference is that this house was not devised by an imported artist and built from costly materials from across the sea. The owner himself did the drawings, supervised the work, conceived and carried through the whole project, with materials grown or gathered or made almost exclusively on his own Virginia estate.

Monticello and its contents are a triumph of ingenuity. Jefferson perfected a device whereby handwriting is simultaneously reproduced on a separate piece of paper, eliminating the need for a copyist for business letters. He elaborated a dumbwaiter to bring up wine from the cellar. He devised a remarkable clock, powered by cannonballs for weights, a ladder that folds up to become a pole, a new design for a wooden plow, a pair of double doors linked by a subterranean chain, so that when one door is opened the other swings wide, too. If the United States can be defined as the land of liberty and labor-saving gadgets, then Jefferson was truly the original American.

Monticello has another even more striking peculiarity. It is surrounded by kitchens, by stables, by workshops, by the inevitable clutter that, before the invention of discreet modern machinery, accompanied the running of a domestic establishment that was also the headquarters of an inherited estate of some five thousand acres of productive land. This is Virginia. Monticello was built and run by slaves, of whom Jefferson usually owned about one hundred and fifty. But nothing of their activity, of their living quarters, of their very presence, could be seen from the great house. All the domestic offices, grouped around the house, are on a lower level of the hilltop. They were invisible. Even in the dining room there is an ingenious device whereby food, brought in from the kitchens through an underground passage, could be placed on shelves on a revolving door, so that only the table servants would be seen by the diners.

Thomas Jefferson's greatness was public and political. His achievements marked the history not just of his own nation and epoch, but of the world and all time. His prose conveys the most exalted ideas, in a form that can still stir the imagination of schoolchildren. But his private life was his own, so personal that scholars still dispute confusingly about its intimate details, which will perhaps never be fully known.

Here on his own estate he lived as a Virginia gentleman of independent means, ruling the people born to serve him with the natural authority of a man of property. Jefferson was an aristocrat, a leader. Yet he used the privileges of his position to advance the cause of those who served him, and of all mankind. Monticello, his private home, reminds us that the American Revolution had its roots not just in a love of justice, but in a love of beauty, too.

Jefferson was intrigued by ingenious inventions, originating some of his own and making clever adaptations to those of others. The polygraph, a device for writing more than one copy of a letter simultaneously, through pens connected together by a mechanical linkage, was invented in England and improved upon by the American painter and scientist Charles Wilson Peale. His first polygraph was sold to the architect Benjamin Henry Latrobe, who showed it to Jefferson. The three men exchanged many letters on methods of improving the device and one of the several polygraphs owned by Jefferson, right, is preserved in good working order at Monticello.

Monticello stands on the summit of a hill surrounded by the thick forests of Virginia. In 1786, Jefferson poetically described the magnificent setting in a letter to a friend: "And our own dear Monticello, where has nature spread so rich a mantle under the eye? mountains, forests, rocks, rivers." Jefferson was the first plantation owner in Virginia to choose such an elevated and inaccessible site for a home. Previously, wherever possible, great houses had been situated on rivers because boats were the major means of transportation.

ATLANTICA

Crammed between the mountains and the ocean, America's Atlantic seaboard was the cradle of its democracy. On this coastline the first free settlers from Europe made their homes, coming of their own free will in pursuit of the civil and religious freedoms that Europe would not afford them. Farther south, the settlement of America was done on the old, imperial principles, with great landlords, royal grants, plantations producing crops for export. From Delaware and Pennsylvania northward this system could not survive. Too many of the settlers were self-sufficient farmers and artisans, Englishmen and Dutchmen whose vision of the world had outgrown their homelands. They did not care that the way westward was barred by hills. There was room enough for freedom by the mouths of the Appalachian rivers.

Now their successors, born here or drawn to America by the freedom they established, enjoy their heritage. The northeast seaboard states have the greatest concentration of people in the United States, in the richest, most extensive, most dynamic complex of cities in the world. And always, at the fringes of the towns, lie the forests and the strands of an older America.

Along the Atlantic coast, the rocky bays of Maine give way to the beaches and barrier islands that stretch from Cape Cod right to the city limits of New York. And the pleasures of the seashore—the boats and the sands and the pretty fishing towns—are matched inland by the pleasures of the hills, where within an hour of any city people may climb or hunt or walk and be alone.

It is a curious accident of geology that gives this form to the northeastern United States. When the continent was forming, it threw up in this corner a great mass of molten rock. In time it has been ground by ice and carved by water, in a process seen at its most dramatic where the thunder of Niagara crashes free from Lake Erie and where the St. Lawrence River drives in its gorge eastward to the sea. But from the St. Lawrence Valley the rivers flow due south, in a series of rifts across the landscape. Millions of years of water flow have carved the parallel valleys between the Alleghenies, the Adirondacks, the Green Mountains of Vermont and the White Mountains of New Hampshire. But each of these ranges once formed part of the undivided Appalachian chain that extends from Canada clear down to its outlying foothills beside the Gulf of Mexico.

Along the valleys the settlers penetrated the country. By the rivers they hunted fur-bearing animals, made their tentative farms amid the forest, established their towns on principles new to the world. Along the hillsides they fought the wars that affirmed their rule over the new continent—against Indians, Frenchmen, British overlords. Water from the mountains powered their first factories. The lakes and rivers and coastal seas made inter-communication possible and nurtured the American trade.

Their genius was political as well as economic. They showed what men could do if once set free. The white-painted churches of New England and the towering cathedrals of commerce of New York City are their physical memorials. And their ideological legacy lives on today, two centuries old and going strong, in the capital city they named after their epitome, George Washington.

Cutting through the
Appalachian Mountains,
the Delaware River flows
dramatically between New
Jersey's Kittatinny Range
to the east and
Pennsylvania's Poconos
to the west. This splendid
view earned the Delaware
Water Gap a reputation,
in the nineteenth century,
as one of North America's
foremost natural
landmarks.

Right through the ancient rocks of the mountain the river has dug its course. Folded green on green over the gray rock that glistens through, the hills slope steeply down to the water, bright, too, with the rock just below its surface. For once in the vastness of North America, the scale of the landscape is human, not gigantic, wild, but accessible. And all this lies within a couple of hours' driving of almost thirty million people in the great cities of New Jersey, Pennsylvania, and even New York City itself. It seems some sort of miracle that it should have remained so unspoiled. Perhaps it is, but it is a miracle brought about by deliberate action to stem and even to roll back the rising tide of human settlement, to leave open a place where the people of the cities may come and be for a while free of the pressure of their fellowmen.

When men from Europe first settled and began to develop the eastern shores of North America, it was by water that they got access to the interior. The great rivers—Connecticut, Hudson, Delaware, Susquehanna—must carve their way to the sea along the parallel north–south grooves carved in the continent by the melting of the glaciers. But of these northern rivers, the Delaware is both the smallest and the least useful to mankind. Running southward, it shoots straight through a great mountain of hard volcanic rock in a bed which, with the years, is still being eroded. At this mountain gap it is either deep and fast, making it difficult for boats, or shallow and fast, making it impossible for boats.

The mountain is called Kittatinny. The pass is called the Delaware Water Gap. From the riverbank the hills rise steeply on east and west to over one thousand feet, forming a narrow gorge. Even where the valley widens upstream from the gorge farming is hard; done by the old methods, it is picturesque but unprofitable. It is a splendid place, but not a useful place for towns or markets. The railroad squeezed through many years ago along the riverbank. A group of artists, attracted by the romantic beauty of the place, came and settled in the nineteenth century and attracted a small but prosperous following. Otherwise there was no development.

The new highways of the 1960s changed all

THE WILDLIFE IN DELAWARE WATER GAP

The success of the bold scheme to create a wilderness area in the Delaware Water Gap can be gauged from the wildlife that chooses to live in the area. Hikers on the long trail up to and around Hidden Lake on the Pennsylvania side of the Delaware River will see a rich variety of animals. Among the smaller ones are, from left to right, in the forests, woodchucks, flying squirrels and red foxes, and, on the open hillsides and among the rocky ledges, poisonous copperheads and timber rattlesnakes.

Delaware Water Gap

that. There was nowhere for the great road direct from New York to Chicago to pass the mountain range, except through the water gap. It swoops right through the valley on its bridge. In itself it is a fine achievement, bold and beautiful. But it brought with it to the valley not just traffic but people. The few remaining farmers, mostly of the old Dutch stock, saw at last a chance to get out with a profit. They began by selling little plots to people for weekend cottages. Then came the land developers and the building firms, the trailer-camp operators, the motel owners. The likelihood was that, if things went on as they were, the water gap would become just another rather hillier dormitory town.

But it has not. A great swath of beautiful land, some forty miles long and spreading back roughly two miles from both the New Jersey and Pennsylvania banks of the river, was designated in 1965 as a National Recreation Area.

It provided that over seventy thousand acres of land were to be acquired, with about three thousand houses on the land. About four hundred of these houses were to be kept for uses connected with the recreation area—either because they are pretty houses or because the park staff need to live there. A dam was to be built on the river, mainly to control the destructive floods that arise downstream when the heavy rains build up a head of water to surge pent up through the water gap. Perhaps, instead of a violent river, there will one day be a narrow lake for forty miles through the mountains.

The valley can never go back to what it was in the days of the old Dutch farmers, any more than it can return to what it was before they built their stone houses, their dikes and their fences. Something new, for a new sort of rural use, is being created; created not for the benefit of landowners or country club members or any specific group, but for anyone who wants to use it.

Already the wildlife is coming back. The deer hang around the houses during the hunting season as though they know that human settlements are places where shooting is not allowed. The beavers build their dams in the culverts under the roads and cause their own brand of damp confusion when suddenly the streams overflow. Occasionally a black bear is glimpsed in the woods near Hidden Lake. The bald eagle has been seen among the hawks gliding gracefully on the wind currents along the ridge tops. Carefully, one farm is being recreated on the old lines as a living piece of American archaeology.

Under Government auspices, artists and craftsmen and students of the countryside are encouraged to live and work in the valley and to share their experience with the visitors. The Appalachian Trail passes along the valley, turning briefly from rock to concrete underfoot as it passes across the highway bridge. A network of other footpaths is being laid out on the hills. And so, in response to the advance of the roads and the increase of population, a uniquely beautiful piece of new America is being evolved to serve the new needs of its people. It is an extraordinarily bold endeavor.

The Delaware River flows four hundred miles from its source, in the Catskill Mountains, to the Atlantic Ocean. Although the southern stretch of the river near Trenton and Philadelphia is heavily industrialized, the northern banks still retain much of their peaceful beauty. The Delaware Water Gap National Recreation Area was established in 1965 to maintain this region in its natural state.

Block Island is named for Adriaen Block, the Dutch merchant and explorer who landed there in 1614 and claimed it for his country. The Dutch, however, had little interest in the island, and the first settlers who arrived in 1661 were English. Hard pressed to make more than a meager living from fishing, they used signal lights to lure clipper ships onto the treacherous submerged offshore ledges, where they were wrecked and then looted. The islanders referred to their few luxuries as having "come by wreck." Today, when the tide is out, ancient skeletons of broken craft are still visible.

NORTH ATLANTIC GAME FISHING

Some of the finest North Atlantic fishing grounds are just off Block Island. Deep-sea fishing for tuna and swordfish, both of which can weigh up to several hundred pounds, requires the heaviest tackle and is a test of endurance. An occasional hazard is hooking a vicious five-hundred-pound porbeagle shark, capable of biting through a steel hook or dragging a person overboard. The small sea bass is also a fierce fighter, a prize catch for surf casters fishing from the beaches.

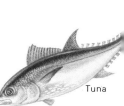

Tuna

Block Island

From the lighthouse, if you turn your back on the ocean, the whole island lies like a jewel on the bright blue showcase of the water. The Block Island light flashes out to ships forty miles at sea. At night, to the southwest, over the water, the light of Montauk Point picks out the tip of Long Island. Turn your back on that and the loom of the Martha's Vineyard lighthouse flashes under the horizon.

Block Island is a punctuation mark in the narrative of the American coastline. On their radios all East Coast Americans have grown accustomed, since childhood, to the storm warnings. "Cape Hatteras to Block Island. Force 8 and rising," says the dispassionate voice of the radio announcer between bursts of music. Against the island the wind and the waves will break their first fury before passing on to the mainland coast and the great cities of the seaboard.

Yet the island is a gentle place when the great winds die down and the everlasting cool breeze tempers the soft sea air. In spring the valleys turn white with the shadbush blossom. In the autumn the hillsides blaze back at the sun, yellow with September-weed whose color lingers on past its due month, to shrivel at last to blackened stems under the renewed gales. Just eight miles long by three and a half miles wide, at no point rising to more than two hundred feet in height, the little island is full of varied surprises. Suddenly among the sand dunes that great white bird is not just another sea gull, but a snowy owl on passage down from the Arctic. A duck skitters off open water to seek refuge; a great sharp-winged harrier is gliding, deadly, through the air.

This patch of earth is a geological relic, the surviving slice of a lost strip of land that once ran from the north end of Cape Cod, through Nantucket, Martha's Vineyard, Block Island and down Long Island to where New York City now stands. It was formed by the sediment of the northern continent, scoured off and ground small by the ice cap and carried to this eastern fringe of the continent, where the last glacier melted. Beneath the Block Island lighthouse the land ends in a soft cliff, one hundred and sixty-five feet high, abruptly cut away into slices and crumbs of erosion. On the cliff face, black and gray and striped with shining quartz, the granite boulders stand out from the gray silt like plums in a rich fruit cake. Below, on the beach at the bottom of the cliff, the boulders lie tumbled on the sand like the fragments left after a birthday party. The sea is eating the cake, tumbling and grinding at the rocks. In time even this hard granite will be smashed and worn down by the winter waves to mingle with the sandy grit of the beach.

Time has transformed the traditional human life of the island, too. Only four hundred people live the year round on Block Island now. Scrub grows where once there were farms. Honeysuckle winds through the unused lobster pots, and the fishing quays have been turned over to pleasure boats. The island lives on its visitors, but it imposes on them a lifestyle which is all its own. Chief among the island's charms, along with its old clapboard houses, its long beaches and its sweet air, is that it contains only a grand total of twenty-two miles of paved roads. Boats or bicycles or a nice slow walk are the ways to get around, to fit into the island rhythm.

The Block Islanders have grown accustomed to strangers, and welcome them more warmly now than they did in the old days when unexplained changes in the navigation lights are reputed to have brought many a lucrative wreck ashore. But strangers are advised to conform to the island's chosen ways for the duration of their visit. Nothing is more resented than "outside" interference. In 1974 the State Supreme Court of Rhode Island ordered the islanders to change the method of election of their chief citizen, the "First Councilman," who had traditionally been both mayor and judge and leader of the island assembly. This system of government was based on a Charter of King Charles II dated 1672. "Don't they understand?" asked a leading citizen. "We've had our First Councilman for a hundred years more than we've had our President in Washington."

Up on the hillside in the cemetery, the names repeat themselves across the centuries, and are the same names as those of the boat builders, repairmen and storekeepers of Block Island today. The first date on a gravestone up there is 1680. The beauty and peace of Block Island today are a bridge back into the American past.

Swordfish

Porbeagle Shark

Sea Bass

By the steps up to the old courthouse, the granite copingstones are worn into smooth grooves. Here, for decade after decade, their backs against the fine iron railings, the men sat sharpening their knives on the stone and waiting for something to happen—for justice to be done, for a steer to be sold, for a hanging or a wedding. Just once in history, the hangers-on had a real event to justify their waiting. In July 1776, rebellious local soldiery "took out of the Court House . . . all the baubles of Royalty . . . set fire to them and burnt them to ashes . . . and a merry day made of it." It made a change from sharpening those knives.

Then, New Castle was a kind of anomalous capital city, the main town, at least, of the three lower counties of the Pennsylvania settlement, which became the State of Delaware, the first State of the American Union. Its merchants were rich and showed their wealth in the building of fine homes and dignified public structures. The bricks that form the sidewalks and run up in mellow tints on the facings of the old houses are larger than American bricks; they traveled here from English brickworks, as ballast in the empty ships that came to return home full of rich American produce. They exemplify the one-way traffic, the system of Colonial exploitation that the American Revolution brought to an end.

The wonder is that, since the Revolution, New Castle has never had the prosperity to repave those sidewalks, replace those buildings, bring itself up to date. It has remained a small town. Its bricks and mortar have been more or less well looked after, not rebuilt, or refurbished, or extensively restored. New Castle's old town center was added to, in a modest way, in the nineteenth century, particularly following the last big event in the town's history, the fire disaster of 1824, which occurred just after they had put the new steeple on the church. The spaces between the grand old houses are sometimes filled in by a decent Victorian store, or a wing added in the 1860s. But almost nothing is out of keeping, nothing breaks the decent plain plan laid out and constructed in Colonial times.

New Castle commands the narrows of the Delaware estuary, on the sea route up to where Philadelphia now lies. It was founded by the traders of the Dutch West India Com-

New Castle, Delaware

pany, who fortified it mainly in order to keep the intrusive Swedes out of their preserves. The Dutch governor Peter Stuyvesant finally drove out the Swedes, laid out the town on its present plan and—being a Dutchman—began to build dikes to control the surrounding marshlands. He called it New Amstel.

When the English drove him in turn out of his American capital at New Amsterdam, they took over its satellite colony, too. Being English, they renamed it New Castle, continued Stuyvesant's admirable town plan, but forgot to go on with draining the marshes. The marshlands were the real victors. They are still there, surrounding the town with their six-foot-high, fronded reed beds. The great industries of the Delaware riverside—oil terminals, refineries, chemical plants—ring the

marshes. But the marshes ring New Castle and have kept it inviolate.

It became, in 1832, the terminus for one of the very first American railroads. But the vast marshes prevented any great progress—and any real damage to the design that William Penn and his Quakers continued on the Dutch pattern.

It was in 1682 that Penn first landed on American soil. Here, at New Castle, a follower recorded: "We did deliver unto him 1 turf with a twig upon it, a porringer with river water and soyle, in part of all." The leader of a new sort of religion was using the magic of an older time to symbolize his seizing of the new lands.

But New Castle and its surrounding counties never quite partook of the spirit of Penn's

Puritan colonizing. Only seven years after his landing, the first parish in the New World of the venerable Church of England was established here. In the graveyard pompous stones in bad Latin record the deaths and the social aspirations of the early ministers and missionaries.

New Castle is on the fringe of the Deep South. Its leading citizens must have had more in common with the planters of the Carolinas than with the hard-working bourgeoisie of the coastal cities to the north. They built their great houses. They conducted their great revolution. Then their town went to sleep. Now, after the years of relative neglect that have accidentally preserved its beauty, it receives from its own citizens the loving care and attention that it deserves.

The peace of The Green in the center of New Castle, left, belies the town's turbulent past. In 1651, Peter Stuyvesant, Governor of New Amsterdam, seized the Swedish colony at present-day Wilmington, which was claimed as Dutch territory. To further establish Dutch dominion in the area, Stuyvesant erected Fort Casimir, the forerunner of modern New Castle. The Swedes captured the fort in 1654, but Stuyvesant recaptured it a year later. While he was there he planned, around a green, the streets for a town called New Amstel. In 1664, fresh from victory in New Amsterdam, the English captured the town and renamed it New Castle. The town changed hands yet again during the Anglo–Dutch war in 1673, but the Dutch withdrew their claims on New Castle in 1674. Under William Penn, the town was left in peace and it prospered. The McWilliam House on the waterfront, above, was built in 1690 during this era of prosperity.

The mountains begin under the sea. Three hundred million years ago a great plug of molten rock forced itself, boiling, from the earth's core up into the light. It cooled to granite, pink and gray, as rough to the touch as sharkskin. Over the granite there formed the world's thrusting northern ice cap, grinding down toward sunnier climates, scoring the new rock hundreds of feet deep in valleys from north to south.

Ten thousand years ago, as the glaciers melted, the waters rose on the face of the earth. Now the sea half fills those ancient scores in the rock. The bays and fjords of the Maine coastland are drowned valleys. The hills slope down to the water's edge and their contours continue on into the depths, below the blackened tidal margin that the algae leave to mark the limit of the land.

Down below the tide, the undersea world has its own fertility. Lobsters and all forms of shellfish thrive. Sardines, mackerel, tuna, bass, cod, all swarm in the pure cold flow of the Arctic currents. Porpoises and seals, warmblooded in the chill waters, prey on the fish and grow fat. And man, too, follows the fish to the sea, which nourishes and cools the rocky shores of Mount Desert Island.

The French called it the deserted mountain. They fished in its rich waters, but they never settled its rocky shores. The island was granted by King Louis XIV in 1688 to his most distinguished servant in the Americas, the Sieur de la Mothe Cadillac, after whom the island's highest summit was named. But Cadillac did not stay. He moved on to Detroit and to Louisiana, for the French in the Americas did not come to settle but to take wealth home. The land that they held they called *Acadie*, a corruption of an Indian name, and a sound suggestive of the mythical paradise of Arcadia. In the end, it was the fortunes of war that drove them out of what is now the northern United States. But their explorations, and the maps they made of their findings, were of inestimable benefit to the English-speaking people who came after them. It is fitting that they should be commemorated here on this rocky coast, in the name of Acadia National Park, which now occupies most of Mount Desert.

The park, the first national park east of the Mississippi, was founded in defense of the beauty of their island, by the rich summer visitors of the early 1900s, whose fashionable "cottages"—in reality immense summer homes—can still be seen on Mount Desert; white elephants now in a day when even the very rich cannot travel around with retinues of servants. Gifts of land and money to public trustees safeguarded the shoreline against the incursions of the rising middle classes, who might have built more numerous but less elegant homes. By 1919 the area contained the first of all the national parks in the eastern United States. Huge private benefactions continued, in particular from the Rockefeller family, who endowed the park with its own system of scenic roads. Bit by bit other pieces of land have been added to the original acreage.

Certain areas of the island are still in use for its original purpose, as a fishing base, by descendants of its original settlers. Today most of Mount Desert Island itself, as well as the nearby Schoodic Peninsula and the wild Isle au Haut, seven miles to the southwest, are protected forever for the people. The particular excellence of this arrangement is variety. Mount Desert Island has bare peaks and slopes rich in flowers, quiet shores and busy fishing ports, the happy little resort town of Bar Harbor, with its bustle of pleasure boats, and the commercial ferry over to Nova Scotia, six hours away across some of the Atlantic's roughest waters.

It is a combination that saves the island from artificial prettiness. There is still a tough rigor about the place, even in the dog days of July when the sun beats down, redoubled by the shimmer off the sea, and the seals bask luxuriously in the glare. The ocean, bright with sun or sparkling with white crests in the prevailing northeast wind, imparts its energy to the land. People come here not to laze on beaches (there are no good sand beaches, anyway) but to walk, or fish, or sail or seek out the wild creatures of shore and mountain. From here southward, with a few carefully guarded exceptions, man has irretrievably marked the Atlantic coastline of the United States. At this point, and northward up the rocky Maine coastline into Canada, the rocks, the trees and the wild things reassert their rule.

Mount Desert Island was discovered in 1604 by Samuel de Champlain, the French explorer. He named it *Isle des Monts Deserts,* Island of Bare Mountains. The first settlement there was a French Jesuit mission, founded in 1613 and destroyed three weeks later in the first incident of the French-English struggle for America.

The North Atlantic surf pounds the rocky shore of Mount Desert Island. Champlain described the island as "very high and notched, so that there is the appearance to one at sea as of seven or eight mountains extending along near each other. The summit of most of them is destitute of trees, as there are only rocks on them."

Mount Desert Island

The river otter's thick dark-brown fur made it a valuable prize for Acadian trappers. During the nineteenth century an otter pelt was worth more than any other fur, and in the eastern United States the animals were exterminated. Otters have been reintroduced in Maine, where strict conservation laws are restoring the population.

Muskrats are one of the most prolific fur-bearing animals. In the nineteenth century their fur was often passed off as more valuable beaver pelts by unscrupulous trappers. Despite extensive trapping, muskrats have never been in danger of depletion because they breed rapidly and produce up to twenty-five kits in a litter.

The land within the Cape Cod National Seashore is slowly being replanted after centuries of erosion. Early settlers overplanted and overgrazed the fertile topsoil. They cut the hardwood forests for shipbuilding. As a result, the soil was loosened, and the Cape began to blow away. Destructive winter tides took their toll of the beaches, and the Cape became a wasteland. However, a carefully planned replanting program has been started, beginning with these hardy species of marsh grass. As vegetation is replenished, further erosion is prevented, and this part of Cape Cod will eventually be restored to its original beauty.

BIRDS OF THE CAPE

Cape Cod provides habitats for sea and shore birds. The osprey takes his prey to a nest built in the rocks or the trees. Terns nest in colonies on the beaches, while piping plovers nest there in pairs. Long-billed marsh wrens and seaside sparrows live in the salt marshes.

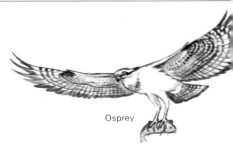

Osprey

Cape Cod

From the thick white blanket that covers the sea comes the blurred honk of a horn. Out there a boat is in trouble, feeling her way through the fog to harbor. In the calm the sea barely tugs at the sharp yellow sand and the only sound is the rustling click of the fiddler crabs' claws as they scurry to their holes as footsteps near. Cape Cod is in its surly mood.

But Samuel Clemens said, "If you don't like the weather, wait a minute." Soon the rising tide will send a breeze ahead of it, the fog will move away, disappearing as fast as it descended, and the fishermen will set off again for Provincetown and home. Cape Cod's weather changes from minute to minute. Its shape changes from year to year, with the twice-daily push and pull of the tide at the soft glacial rubble that makes up this beckoning finger thrust out into the Atlantic. Pounded by storms, shifted by currents, the sands of its beaches have a peculiar grainy roughness to their edge, crushing and rattling underfoot. It is said that it is as hard to get the Cape Cod sand out of your shoes as it is to get the Cape out of your mind.

In 1844, the great American writer Henry Thoreau walked right around Cape Cod. Standing at its tip, looking east from Provincetown, he thought of Portugal and Ireland, about two thousand miles across the water, and reflected that a man may stand there "and put all America behind him." It is appropriate that it was from this outer extremity, on January 18, 1903, that the first wireless message was sent from the United States to Europe. Guglielmo Marconi dispatched, by way of a receiving station at Poldhu near England's southwestern tip, a message of goodwill from President Theodore Roosevelt to King Edward VII of England and all the peoples of his Empire.

The Cape had beckoned its settlers from Europe long before. Gabriel Archer, writer to Captain Bartholomew Gosnold, noted in his ship's journal in 1602, "Neere this Cape we came to Anchor in fifteen fadome, where wee tooke great stoare of Codfish, for which we altered the name, and called it Cape Cod." It was here that the Pilgrim Fathers made their first anchorage in the New World, and drank New England water "with as much delight as we ever drank in all our lives." It was for the cod

and for the great whales that abounded near the coast that the sturdy Portuguese fishermen came and settled here. In Provincetown today Portuguese faces and Portuguese names, and delicious Portuguese fish dishes, are still common. And from England came other fishermen and sea captains and farmers—builders of stout homes to stand against the gales.

But now Cape Cod is a magnet for a population vaster than those old ancestors ever dreamed of. Since the development of the great highways, Cape Cod lies within a day's drive of one-third of the population of the continental United States. There was a clear and imminent danger that the press of people would destroy the very pleasures that they seek on the Cape. The problem was met head-on, in a typically forthright American way. In 1961, more than thirty-five miles of coast, from Provincetown to Nauset, were declared the Cape Cod National Seashore. The people acted to preserve pleasures that are their birthright.

By acquisition and by private benefaction the preserved areas of the Cape are still being extended—natural beaches, wild woodlands, great white houses and clapboard cottages, a whole world that man has made in cooperation with nature. The target is to provide twenty-seven thousand acres of the Cape, to be enjoyed by people today, and by their children and their children's children.

But preserving Cape Cod has by no means sterilized and encapsulated it. There remain tens of thousands of wild acres to enjoy and mile after mile of beach. For it is not possible to solidify or confine this jut of land into the ocean, this shifting piece of living America. Where Marconi's wireless masts once stood the waves are beating now; the sea has advanced one hundred and seventy feet into the shoreline since that historic message went out across the ocean. The melting of the American glaciers formed this Cape. The sea the glaciers left behind is eating it away on the Back Side, the side facing the ocean, and building up with fresh silt the Bay Side, facing in to the North American continent. There is no permanence, just the ebb and flow of the sea, the rush of the wind and the pleasures of the young and the old on the sandy shores of Cape Cod.

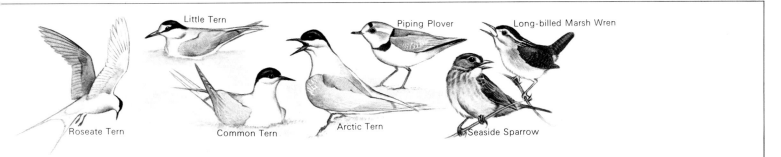

Little Tern
Piping Plover
Long-billed Marsh Wren
Roseate Tern
Common Tern
Arctic Tern
Seaside Sparrow

The White Mountains

The Indians are said to have thought he was holy. Certainly he has some power over men. Down on the valley floor the visitors crane back their necks to see the man's face formed by the tumbled boulders up on the mountain above Franconia Notch. In the bottom of the notch there is barely room for the highway and the tumbling river. The space is all upward, toward the rock and pine and sky of the vertical landscape. The ancient gods of the heights are no longer worshiped here; but they still enforce respect on the beholder.

The Old Man of the Mountains, or the Great Stone Face, as Nathaniel Hawthorne called him in the short story that made him famous, has been known to white men only since the beginning of the nineteenth century. His granite profile was described by geologist Charles Hitchcock, who surveyed New Hampshire in 1870, as being "made of 3 jutting masses of rock in different vertical lines; one piece making the forehead, the second piece making the nose and upper lip; and the third the chin."

Hitchcock was convinced that the Old Man was on the verge of collapse. This point of view, over a century later, seems somewhat alarmist until, that is, you consider the fate of the great boulder which for more than ten thousand years hung suspended in the narrow cleft of The Flume gorge, under nearby Mount Liberty. Thousands of visitors came to see the white-water race through the gloom of the black-walled chasm and they passed beneath the boulder as they walked along the precarious wooden bridges which cling to the sheer rock. Then, in 1883, days of heavy rain culminated in a cloudburst. Water running off the mountain surged through The Flume like a continuous tidal wave. No trace of the huge rock was ever found again.

The Flume is none the worse for the boulder's disappearance and sightseers still throng to see its cascading waters, as they do to gaze up at the Old Man on his mountain. And in the autumn, when the colors on the hillsides span the whole range of the seasons—dark leaf-fall at the summits, gold and scarlet and orange on the midslopes, summer green lingering in the bottoms—they crowd the mountain roads. But it is only a thirty-minute walk up out of sight and sound of cars into the peace of the hills.

From out at sea the first explorers of the New England coastline saw, far inland, the shimmering summits that rise snowbound above the forests. They named them the White Mountains. On the high peaks it is May or June before the snows melt; and it is the torrents off the snowline that carved the narrow notches through the range through which man may enter. For centuries it was the snow that discouraged any extensive human settlement in these mountains. More recently, the snows of the New Hampshire slopes have become a main attraction of the New England winter.

Even before the ski generation, it was the pure quiet of the mountains that brought visitors here. These are by far the highest peaks in northeastern America. As far back as the 1860s, the road—"the carriage drive" they still call it—was built to the summit of the tallest mountain of all. (Since the peaks are each named after a President, the tallest is, inevitably, Mount Washington.) It is a vertiginous drive there, and an even more vertiginous eight miles back down from the peak, at 6,288 feet, far above the tree line in a climate rendered arctic by its height.

It was the weather station on Mount Washington that recorded, on April 12, 1934, the strongest wind ever measured by man—a gust of 231 miles per hour, an unthinkable blast from the northeast. Yet even here, where the climate and the flora resemble those of northern Labrador, there are people who come on foot. Of the two-thousand-mile Appalachian Trail, running from Canada down into Georgia, only one hundred miles are within the State of New Hampshire. But the New Hampshire walkers have a goal that may be even more remarkable than completion of the entire two thousand miles.

The Four-Thousand-Footer Club is for those who have scaled each of the forty-six summits in New Hampshire that rise above that height. The list includes Mount Washington (6,288 feet), Mount Adams (5,798 feet) and Mount Jefferson (5,715 feet). Proudly the New Hampshire climbers concede that members may also claim as achievements the twelve peaks in Maine and the five in Vermont that rise over four thousand feet. The club's organizers are in no doubt that, when it comes

to wildness, New Hampshire cannot be rivaled east of the Rockies.

And so it has come about that the barren mountain wastes, once a barrier confining settlers to the eastern shoreline, have become a magnet for people who seek, each in their own way, an escape from urban America. The point of no return is near. The traffic jams of the "foliage season," and the new highways being built to accommodate that traffic; the lines for the ski lifts on winter weekends, and the vast machines that spray out artificial "snow" when none falls naturally; the neatly carved signposts on the mountain trails; and the regular patrols that retrieve the ignorant climbers who go to the mountain without warm clothes or strong boots—all these things indicate at once the longing of Americans for the open air, and the danger that if all can get to it none will be able to enjoy it. In crowded New Hampshire, so near to the cities by car, so far from the cities in climate and temperament, this modern dilemma of America is working its own way out. On the side of Mount Pemigewasset, to remind us that there is a time limit, the Great Stone Face is poised, ready to disintegrate.

Few creatures can survive the savage weather at the summit of Mount Washington. One which has thrived there for thousands of years is the seemingly delicate White Mountain butterfly. Well adapted to this hostile environment, arctic ancestors of this lovely insect migrated to the area during the last Ice Age.

The unnamed Old Man of the Mountains, above, surveys peaks named after the first leaders of America. The highest peak in the Presidential Range, the largest range in the White Mountains, is called Mount Washington. Other peaks are named Adams, Jefferson, Madison, Monroe, Jackson and Eisenhower.

Vegetation on the slopes of the White Mountains changes with the altitude. Dense forests of maple and birch cover the lowest hills. At thirty-five hundred feet, conifers grow among the hardwoods, in autumn providing a deep green contrast to the bright foliage, right. Toward the summits, there are only dwarfed conifers.

Amid the scarlet and gold of the autumn colors in the valleys, here and there an intruder flourishes still. Between the trunks of oaks and maples, little gnarled apples growing on unpruned boughs show that once there were homesteads here. Lined in defunct hedgerows or squared in one-time orchards, these fruit trees were lovingly tended, and their rough cider fueled many a meeting of the hill men, who played so vital a role in asserting the basic freedoms of the United States. Now the farms are deserted and the ski slopes and the solitude provide the reasons for men to come to the hill country.

"A Vermont year is nine months' winter and three months' damn poor sledding," went the old Green Mountain farmers' saying. And if high hills and hard weather have a toughening effect on the human character, the people of these mountains will serve to prove it. The Green Mountains, rising in peak after peak down from the Canadian border, are among the world's oldest rock formations. They have never been friendly to permanent settlement by man. The French saw them in summer and named them *les monts verts*, the Green Mountains. They hunted and trapped, but did not try to settle in these hills.

The first farmers were English colonists and Dutch squatters, tough and independent men who moved into the mountain frontier to assert their independence of the growing Colonial regimes of New Hampshire and, above all, of New York. "We value not New York, with all their powers; for here we'll stay and work, the land is ours"—ran the song of the Green Mountain Boys, the freebooting militia formed in 1764 by those early settlers. They were against "big government" and the political tradition they established lives on in Vermont, even now that they are gone.

It was, indeed, largely to assert their independence of all government, not just the British Government, that those same Green Mountain Boys launched their famous attack on Fort Ticonderoga in 1775. The expedition was led by Ethan Allen, the true Vermont hero, and only slightly restrained by the representative of the Continental Congress, Benedict Arnold. It was the Vermonters who achieved, at Ticonderoga, the first clear republican victory of the American War of Independence. The one hundred and fifty British cannons that they captured transformed the fighting chances of General Washington's forces. (Less well known, but more immediate in its effect on Revolutionary spirits, was the simultaneous capture of ninety gallons of British Army rum.)

Ethan Allen went on to further exploits, notably in persuading the local Caughnawaga Indians to fight against the British. Allen claimed to have told them, "I know how to shute and ambush just like Indian"; his words were no doubt as true as his spelling was faulty. For having so signally helped the cause of American freedom, the Vermonters then, inconveniently, asserted their own. Led by Ethan Allen's brother, Ira, Vermont, between 1777 and 1791, maintained itself as an independent republic.

Notably, its constitution forbade slavery and gave every man the vote. It was the first American state to go so far toward democracy. Free Vermont conducted its own slightly unconventional diplomatic relations with the outside world, including the newborn United States. At one point it even opened negotiations to rejoin the British Empire. General Washington actually contemplated an invasion of Vermont in 1783. He was deterred in part by hope that even the Vermonters would finally see reason, and in part by military prudence. No good general would invade the Green Mountains if there were any imaginable alternative.

The mountains were in the end too hard even for their own adopted sons. The people moved on to newer lands to the west, or down to the valley towns of New England. The timber houses soon collapsed, gnawed into ruin by porcupines. Even the skiing season is unpredictable, broken from time to time by damp winds from the Atlantic, transforming the crisp surface to slush that freezes hard. The Green Mountains are at their best, still, for the most solitary and independent of occupations. They are a marvelous place to walk.

Under the state's highest mountain, Mount Mansfield (a rugged 4,393 feet tall), there lies a track between towering rock walls, called Smugglers' Notch. Along this route men who knew their footing, and despised government regulations, would travel with goods to trade with the equally lawless French-speaking people across the Quebec border.

The notch, today, is a wonderful point of access to Vermont's Long Trail, which winds for two hundred and sixty miles from Canada

TREES IN THE GREEN MOUNTAINS

More than two-thirds of the land area of Vermont is covered with coniferous and deciduous forests. White pine, hemlock, spruce and fir are the most common evergreens. It is, however, the hardwood trees for which the Green Mountains are famed, particularly in autumn, when they are arrayed with leaves of magnificent color. Left to right, the leaves of American beech in summer and autumn, a lovely autumn maple leaf and black birch leaves in summer.

The Green Mountains

to Massachusetts, traversing forty peaks over three thousand feet. The southern peaks are rounded and softer and the grandeur unfolds as you travel north. There is little grass on the high slopes but green ferns, white wood sorrel, raspberries and blueberries make colorful ground cover. And all along the trail are the dark evergreens of fir and pine and hemlock. In summer the subtler greens of beech, birch and maple cloak the mountains. In the autumn it bursts into glory. It is a walk on the heroic scale, lasting not less than three weeks, but never much more than three hours on foot from inhabited country. And, say the authors of an authoritative Vermont hiking handbook, "We bring along featherweight rainsuits even on the sunniest day." Ethan Allen would certainly have approved.

The chilled nights of late summer paint the Green Mountain slopes near Waterbury varying shades of scarlet, orange and yellow. In winter the slopes become desolate, the bare trees standing dark and somber in the deep snow. In spring they return to the brilliant green for which the mountains are so appropriately named. The forests are Vermont's most valuable natural resource, cherished and carefully protected by conservationist lumbering laws. One-sixth of the state's woodlands are national or state forests.

187

The Adirondacks

Among the white, cold peaks, the sun burns with a redoubled brilliance, striking up from the snow. Everything is bright, hard, crisp. Out on the lakes—the only flat surfaces in a countryside of steep slopes and hard angles—the ice is so thick that men have built, as they build each winter, fishing shacks over a hole chipped through to the water. With a good thick coat, a little stove and, perhaps, a bottle of something for internal warmth, they are quite comfortable. They sometimes claim to catch fish, too.

The Adirondacks are named after the "tree-eaters," a tribe of Indians reputed to sustain life on bark soup in the worst winters. The land is no more friendly now than then. In the entire area of the Adirondack Park, in New York State, one hundred and twenty-five miles from north to south and one hundred miles across,

there is no human settlement of any size—only resorts where people go for the skiing and the open air. It is not one but four ranges of mountains, fold after fold across the vast landscape. On the high ground the soil is thin, shading to bare rock at the peaks, where there are occasional traces of an earlier range estimated to be a billion years old. Even the hardy trees of America's native forest could not grow to any size here, and the timber industry remained confined to the valleys.

There has been no reason for man to penetrate much of this huge, high wasteland. Even today it is only in winter, for the skiing, that many people come here. Wild creatures, bear and deer and beaver, survived and prospered in the Adirondacks even before they were protected by the law. Now, protected, they thrive. The wild coyote, formerly almost unknown in

New York State, howls in the night. The coyote of these parts is a larger creature than in the old days, perhaps through interbreeding with domestic dogs, or even with the few remaining wolves that live on across the border in Canada, where Quebec runs up into the even vaster wastelands across the St. Lawrence River.

In the modern world, there are bound to be pressures by man even on a space as huge as this. An Olympic Village is to be built near the little town and skiing resort of Lake Placid, under the slopes of Whiteface Mountain, where in the frosty mountain air the snow lies long into the spring. The slopes of the Adirondacks will, for a while, become familiar to the world as the site of the Winter Olympics of 1980. There could be no grander place to hold them.

Sheer cliffs of granite, left, are a striking sight in the Adirondack region, where four rocky mountain chains run parallel for over one hundred miles. However, most of the slopes are heavily forested, above. The mountainsides are thick with pine, birch, ash, maple and oak, while the undergrowth abounds with wild flowers and berries. The Adirondack Forest Preserve was created by the State of New York in 1894 to protect this environment.

Once hunted extensively and nearly exterminated, the American black bear now roams the Adirondack forests as a protected animal. Although these small bears prefer their woodland haunts, they have adapted remarkably well to civilization and often wander into inhabited areas to scrounge for food.

Fort Ticonderoga

There are no ships along the lake now. Only the wild geese stay faithful to the old route into Canada, where the valley runs with the lakes in its bed like an ax-cut due north and south through the mountains. At the narrow waist of the lower lake the cars await the chain ferry, clanking back across the water from Vermont eastward. The guns above, on the limestone bastions of the fort, look down in peace, their muzzles stopped forever.

Here, at Ticonderoga, three times the destiny of North America was decisively tipped in a new direction. This was the key to no-man's-land, where warring cultures, rival systems, met and struggled for survival. Native Americans and European intruders, French and English, rebel colonists and imperial soldiers, all met and fought here. The cut in the hills was a highway, the only passable way for troops with guns, between the two great cradles of North American civilization. To the south lay the valley of the Hudson River, and to the north the valley of the St. Lawrence. At the narrows, at Ticonderoga—the place between the lakes—an army could win or lose. Between Lake George and Lake Champlain boats and guns had to take to the land and be hauled across the portage. Whoever held Ticonderoga controlled both lakes and the access to both plains.

Long before the white men came, the Hudson plain was inhabited by the Iroquois, the St. Lawrence Valley by the Algonquins. From north and south, the two tribes paddled along the lakes in search of furs or food. Ticonderoga was the midway mark, the limits of each side's territory and, at about the time Columbus was making his discovery of the New World, their battleground. The Algonquins were slaughtered and the fierce Iroquois settled along the shores of the northern lake.

In May 1609, Henry Hudson, an Englishman with a crew of Dutchmen, sailed up the river that bears his name, and may have heard of the lakes that lay a few miles to the north. In the same month a French explorer was on his way down from the north. Samuel de Champlain, with two French companions and some sixty Indians, paddled south from the French base at Montreal.

At the place between the lakes the invaders met a large force of Iroquois. Loading his matchlock with four balls, Champlain, at the head of his men, marched to within thirty paces of the defenders. With a single shot he killed outright two of the opposing Indian chiefs and wounded a third. Then one of his companions also fired. The Iroquois, amazed at the power of these unbelievable weapons, fled, vowing revenge on the French. That vengeance could only be assured by an alliance of the Iroquois with the British against the French—and that alliance was crucial for the final victory of England over France in this region of America.

But it was half a century before that victory was assured. The French returned and fortified the land narrows of Ticonderoga. It is their fort that stands now above the lake, built in the star-shaped pattern laid down by Louis XIV, the Sun King of France. It was immensely strong. In 1758, it was the center of French resistance against a force of six thousand regular Hanoverian troops and six thousand Colonial irregulars invading from the Hudson Valley. On that occasion King George's army lost two thousand men, including Lord Howe, their most gallant general. It was in 1759, the year Quebec fell, and with it all hope of a permanent empire in America under the French crown, that the British finally took Ticonderoga and insured that the people of this region would speak the English language and live under the common law.

The British thought themselves safe. Fort Ticonderoga was left under light guard. In 1775, the garrison had less than fifty British

troops, under an elderly officer, Captain William de la Place. On May 10, 1775, the captain and his men earned their place in history by being the first British troops to surrender to the American rebels. Ethan Allen, a land speculator from Vermont, and Benedict Arnold, commissioned by the Massachusetts Committee of Safety, led an American force of eighty-three men across the lake by night. At three o'clock in the morning the Americans dashed into the sleeping fortress. "In whose name do you come?" demanded the baffled Captain de la Place. "In the name of the Great Jehovah and the Continental Congress," replied Allen. The War of Independence was truly underway.

With the capture of Ticonderoga, the American insurgents sealed off the gateway from British Canada into their embryo republic. The guns of Ticonderoga, rusty from disuse, but still serviceable, were dragged away to form the main artillery strength of General Washington's army. The war moved on to new battlefields. Ticonderoga saw a few more skirmishes and changed hands twice in the Revolutionary War. But its role in history had been played.

It is a special good fortune that the fort was acquired, in 1816, by William Ferris Pell, a New York businessman, who protected the ruins from total destruction at the hands of farmers in search of the precious building stones that the French had shaped. Mr. Pell's descendants still control the educational trust which has transformed the ruins of the old fort into a memorial and a shrine to the men—Indian, French, British and American—who fought and died there.

It is a lonely place, set amid farmland, overlooking its lake and itself overlooked by the higher hills above. Thoughtless development could have spoiled it. Instead, careful reconstruction has enhanced it. Its museum and its library are of true historical value. And its story is a reminder of the fragile threads, the mere chances of war, on which the existence of a great nation hung—when the Frenchmen killed the Indians, when the redcoats beat the French and when the American farmers with their muskets recklessly took on and defeated the garrisons of the English king.

Fort Ticonderoga was invested for the last time in July 1777, when the British general John Burgoyne and his army took it on their way south from Canada to Albany. The Americans tried unsuccessfully to recapture the fort later in the year, but breached only the outer defenses. This was the last military action to take place at Ticonderoga.

Lake George, dotted with two hundred wooded islands, is a thirty-mile-long finger in the foothills of the Adirondack Mountains; it empties into Lake Champlain. The narrows between the two lakes, the strategic point on the route between the St. Lawrence and the Hudson rivers, were controlled by Fort Ticonderoga.

Fort Ticonderoga, abandoned in 1777 as a military post, still stands silent sentinel over frozen Lake Champlain. The four-sided bastioned structure, now a military museum, is a faithful restoration of the original French fort, Carillon, begun in 1755.

Perhaps the Indians were right to sell off—for a miserable twenty-four dollars' worth of trinkets—this rocky island of Manhattan. It is a very odd piece of real estate, a bizarre place on which to build a capital city. It is just twenty-two square miles in area, a chunk of stone surrounded by brackish water, barren, lumpy, an ill-fitting rock stopper in the mouth of the Hudson River, no use to beast and not much use to man. But see what man has done with it!

Geometrical, the streets and avenues recede in perspective off the island, dwindling to insignificance in the distance. Vertical, the buildings run up at right angles to the sky. From within the city its scale is simply too great to grasp. From without, looking in across what were the marshes and flats of the estuary, you see that there are not just one but two man-made mountains on the island—the towering cluster of midtown, staggering in its size, outmatched only by the giant uprise of the financial district's own separate megalopolis.

Approaching from across the water, from seaward, the sight is almost bafflingly familiar, the backdrop of tens of thousands of movie scenes. But still, however familiar, it surprises and moves the heart by the sheer immensity of its imposition on the landscape. It is New York City's peculiar advantage that, while from close up you cannot conceive the grandeur of the whole, you only have to get off Manhattan Island and the city rears itself up against the sky, not dwarfed by natural hills or enfolded in a valley, but stark and brutal amid its waters, unique, the only place of its kind on earth.

And under all lies the rock. It is the rock that made New York what it is. Only on bedrock could man first have dared to erect these almost blasphemously tall and heavy buildings. It is by hacking into solid rock that the vital arteries of New York were created, with an ease that would have been impossible for a city that had grown more naturally from the soft, yielding soils that are man's more normal habitat. The city could not function at all without the rail tracks that carry its people in and out, each person a corpuscle in the bloodstream of the city. The rock walls of the subway reverberate with the clash of steel on steel that is the peculiar sound of New York.

The rock made the shape and sounds of the city. The sea made its climate—the damp chills of winter, the wet heat in summer. Soft, damp air and hard, sharp noise, sudden gusts of salt breeze cutting the gasoline fumes, abrupt violation of the senses, terrible bursts of energy and of lethargy—all these contrasts are the essence of Manhattan. At its heart is a masterpiece of public art, the green space of Central Park amid its man-made cliffs. Even there, in bowers, where the air is cooled and sweetened by the trees and grass, where the lake waters are laid out in gentle curves, the gray whalebacks of volcanic rock surge out of the man-made landscape to proclaim that they, at least, were here before men. The rock is the root of it all.

Because it was an island rock, the original New York could not grow gradually outward like a normal town. Its expansion took two contradictory forms, once it had filled the whole of Manhattan. Internally it shot upward. Externally it jumped across the water and began again in a different shape.

It is no disrespect to the honorable boroughs of Brooklyn, Queens, Richmond and the Bronx to say that, while very good places in their own right, they are places on a quite different scale of existence from Manhattan. Their surface links with the Manhattan nucleus are expressed in one of the city's most frequently forgotten splendors, its bridges. For a single city to possess two such beauties as the Brooklyn Bridge and the Verrazano Narrows Bridge is simply unfair. That it also has, over to the New Jersey shore and the parallel ridge of the Palisades, the incomparable George Washington Bridge, is really excessive.

But that is the kind of glorious excess that you get if you build a city for easy defense and ready access to deep water, only to find, a couple of centuries later, that nobody is attacking, and most ships prefer to unload elsewhere. The reasons for building a city on Manhattan Island have gone. The city remains. And, looking across at the skyline, it is impossible not to feel uplifted by the impertinence, the sheer verve, that led men to create this alarming city, these piles of brick and cut stone and glass and steel and concrete on the rock. It is, after all, a wonder of the world.

Lower Manhattan, the Wall Street area, above, is the financial capital of the world. The Dutch built a wall across lower Manhattan in 1653 to keep out the Indians. By 1699 the English had dismantled the wall and built Wall Street, an administrative center. The first stock exchange opened in 1792, and the area grew into a major banking and business district, dominated today by the 110-story, twin-towered World Trade Center. High finance is now the main commerce of a city whose economy once depended on shipping. This 1860 view of Manhattan, left, shows a thriving port in the developing city. The docks remain, but shipping is now less important.

Manhattan Island

An enormous rise in population at the turn of the century caused an astronomical rise in New York's real-estate prices. This inspired the trend to build higher and get maximum use from the land. The first large New York "skyscraper," the Flatiron Building, a mere twenty stories, was built in 1902 with a Florentine-decorated steel framework.

Improved methods of construction increased the potential height of skyscrapers, while a zoning law regulated the height in relation to the width of the street. Architecture evolved from the ornate to the vertical, flat, undecorated style of the Chrysler Building of 1930. Its seventy-seven stories made it the world's tallest building then.

Landmark of the city, the 102-story Empire State Building towers over this 1940 skyline. Designed by the firm of Shreve, Lamb and Harmon, this finest example of early skyscraper architecture was completed in less than two years and opened in 1931. The world's tallest building for over forty years, it is now dwarfed by the World Trade Center.

Litchfield County

It looks like the kind of plain white shed you would put the lawn mower in, for the winter, beside the great wooden house, under the shady trees of the broad New England street. But in this little room, in Litchfield, in the Year of the Lord 1784, a gathering assembled that was to make an indelible mark on the growth and the shape of the infant United States of America. Mr. Tapping Reeve, lawyer, of Litchfield in Litchfield County, Connecticut, addressed the first class of the first law school in the new Republic—a place where young men would form their minds to defend by the rule of law the rights of man and of property.

The war was over. The dominance of expatriates from England over the government and the laws of North America was at an end. A new breed of men—tough Yankee lawyers, learned upholders of the revolutionary Constitution—was to emerge from Judge Reeve's school. They were tough in body as well as in mind. Until its closure, in 1833, the wooden law school building never contained a stove to warm its students, even in the hardest New England winters. But out of that school came two vice-presidents of the United States, seventeen United States senators, fifty-three congressmen, ten state governors, twenty-seven judges of State Superior Courts and a host of other worthy and upright men.

Here, in this Connecticut country town, men learned how to make their nation work and prosper for the good of all its free citizens. And the unfree of early America owe a debt to

Litchfield, too. Down the road from the Tapping Reeve law school was born and raised a young girl, Harriet Beecher, whose novel *Uncle Tom's Cabin* was perhaps the most powerful weapon of propaganda in the long campaign against slavery. The people of Connecticut came here to assert their own freedom of life and worship. They defended the rights of others to those freedoms. They changed the world.

The place-names of Litchfield County tell the story. Puritan strongholds from across the Atlantic, names from southwest England and home—Cornwall, Torrington, Bridgwater. God's chosen places in the Promised Land—Goshen, Canaan, Sharon (but *somebody* must have chosen the name for Sodom, Connecticut). Bounding the county to east and west, the river names recall a mistier past—Housatonic, Naugatuck—relics of the people who fled before the Yankees and their God.

It was not until the 1740s that this upper corner of Connecticut colony was parceled out and purchased by the settlers. Even when it was settled, the land was not good enough to let the new farmers thrive. To make a living they turned to crafts, to making clocks or shoes or pottery, using the power of the rivers for small factories. Their oldest sons they sent to the Bar and to the Church. They had no reason to love the tax collectors of the Empire.

When the Revolution began, Litchfield found itself at the crossroads of the war. The route along the coast was endangered by the guns of the Royal Navy. To pass between

Boston and New York, the military and political leaders of the American insurgency traveled back and forth on the highway through Litchfield, resting and refreshing their ideals among the up-country Yankee farmers and craftsmen. In a backyard here, near the law school, they melted down the lead from King George's statue on the New York Battery and turned it into musket balls. The redcoats never penetrated this American hinterland.

Most of the early settlers' families have moved on, into the richer lands to the west, which were opened up by the canals and railroads of the nineteenth century. Outside its one manufacturing town at Torrington, the population of Litchfield County is today little greater than it was two centuries ago. Many of the residents are incomers from New York, writers and artists who enjoy a country peace that is, nevertheless, not far from the cities and the centers of learning of the East Coast.

In Litchfield County the streams run clear between the forest trees. At the center of each village the white-pillared churches still stand, with the massive timber houses amid their lawns, stretching away in decent perspective from the House of God. They were hard, fanatical men who built these communities of order in an untamed landscape. They were hard for the rule of law, fanatical for freedom. Their spirit is not dead in Connecticut. The cause for which those Yankee farmers fought, and the precedents those Yankee lawyers set, were built on foundations as firm as the bedrock beneath Litchfield.

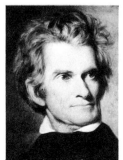

Snow lies softly in a typical New England village in Litchfield County. In the eighteenth century the church was usually the center of a Colonial town and homes were built around it. Wood was the most readily available and, therefore, the most frequently used building material in the Connecticut colony. Wood-framed structures were surfaced with clapboard—thin, wedge-shaped boards about five inches wide and six feet long, laid lengthwise over the supporting walls. Clapboard buildings were warm and could withstand the strong winds of the harsh New England winters.

A simple sign, above, marks the building where Tapping Reeve founded the first American law school. Reeve expounded the doctrine of secession from Britain, and two of his most famous graduates, both vice-presidents, are remembered for their secessionist views. John C. Calhoun, far left, an ardent Republican, called for war with Britain five years before its outbreak in 1812. He did not stop there, however, and historians agree that he, as much as any man, was responsible for the Civil War. Aaron Burr, left, was considered a traitor because he attempted to join the Southwestern states with Mexico, which was fighting for independence from Spain.

A mile off among the bare tree trunks, on the mottled carpet of fallen leaves, the binoculars reveal a tiny spot of unnatural red. Patiently, the archer up there is waiting for a deer. He is dressed from head to toe in green, his face striped like a tabby cat's with paint to break its outline. Only between his shoulder blades shines the giveaway speck of color; it is a folder enclosing his hunting license taped to the back of his jacket. It serves both as a warning to other well-hidden hunters not to shoot him in the back and as a sign to the game warden that he has paid his dues. Light-footed, the buck approaches. The man shifts a mere fraction. There is a flurry among the leaves and the deer starts back from the menace so subtly hidden among the timber.

To kill with a bow, a hunter must get within fifty feet of his target. Absolute quiet, absolute patience are the sport as well as—even more than—final accuracy with the weapon. If the truth be told, not many deer have the bad luck or the lack of fieldcraft to get within killing range of an archer. The Indians learned long ago that if it is meat you want, guns are better. But what matters today is not the death of an animal so much as the experience of moving in wild places on equal terms with wild things. Throughout Pennsylvania, periods are set aside, both before and after the rifle-hunting season, for the archers, the real seekers after wildness.

For them Pennsylvania, with its vast industrial and commercial cities at Pittsburgh and Philadelphia, might seem an unpromising place. In fact the entire northern quarter of the state is high, barren and wild. Of this vast area almost three-quarters of a million acres are set aside as national forest, for the renewal and harvesting of America's wonderful native crop of timber and for the enjoyment of the people. Here you may swim or camp or fish or ski cross-country or simply drive around to look and still be far from the sight or sound of other people.

Here the Allegheny Mountains, the end of the great chain of hills that starts far to the south near the Mississippi Delta, begin their

Just one hundred miles from industrial Pittsburgh lies the peace and tranquility of the Alleghenies. White-tailed deer slip quietly out of the forest to drink from clear woodland streams filled with trout and bass. Black bears, once on the verge of extinction, are now common in these isolated regions, as are foxes, raccoons, skunks, woodchucks, rabbits and squirrels. Several hundred species of birds spend all or part of the year here. A sanctuary for wildlife has been created, as well as the opportunity for people to experience the joys of nature.

The Allegheny Mountains form the western flank of the Appalachian chain, which extends along the East Coast. Millions of years ago, glaciers plowed these peaks into flat-topped ridges, supporting vast tracts of forest. Deciduous and coniferous forests blend on these slopes, where oaks and birches grow beside hemlocks and pines.

The Alleghenies

run down toward the ancient glacial basin of the Great Lakes. (The forest continues in an even wilder but smaller condition across the New York State border. It is spelled Allegany on the New York side, but the hills are much the same.) The ridges of the mountains are distinctively flat, their sandstone covering leveled and worn thin by the same glaciers that diverted the rivers away from the Great Lakes. The forest fades off to the north, the Allegheny River itself turns to the south to join the Ohio, then the Mississippi, and ends in the Gulf of Mexico.

The feeling is rightly there of the vastness of a continent. Behind each crest to the south is another summit. The trees conceal more trees, on and on, seemingly without end. In the air there is a genuine generous spaciousness, a feeling that this land belongs to all Americans and will forever be kept open for the use and the pleasure of all. So that it may be kept open, access to the wild must be organized and controlled. The game laws, the rules on who may cut trees or dam streams are strict.

And under the man-made rules, nature is prevailing again. The streams are stocked with fish. The great reservoir that fills the forest's northern valley is rich in wildfowl. The wild turkey, whose size and clumsy takeoff made it an easy target for hunters, has again become plentiful in parts of the woods.

The hardwood forests are rising again to maturity on the hills. It is because of the rules that the archer has deer to hunt, it is because of the restrictions and the prudent management of the woodlands that there are valuable trees to cut.

America has come to recognize the specialness of her vast open spaces; Americans are getting out of their cars and into the hills. The Allegheny, at its northernmost extremity, is typical of America's hill country, once over-exploited, neglected and despoiled. Now it is open to the people, and the people show their respect for it in the best possible way—by going there and enjoying it. It is the beauty of the hills that tempts America back to its roots.

THE OAKS OF THE ALLEGHENY FOREST

Six species of oak trees grow in the Allegheny Forest, each identifiable by its leaves and acorns. Oak was once the standard building timber in eastern America, and the Alleghenies provided material for farmhouses, fences, ships' hulls, wine barrels, wheel spokes and ladder rungs. Modern technology has ousted oak from many of its traditional uses, but it is still in demand for solid, high-quality furniture.

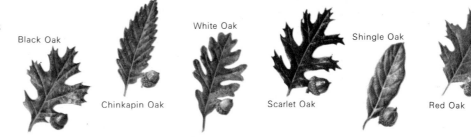

Black Oak

Chinkapin Oak

White Oak

Scarlet Oak

Shingle Oak

Red Oak

Niagara Falls

The clear waters of a quarter of a continent hunch together on a narrow ledge of rock and hurl themselves into the pit that they have dug. The rock trembles under your feet as the greatest expanse of fresh water in the world races toward its destiny in the ocean. There can be no adequate response in words to the overwhelming demonstration of nature's violence that is Niagara: it makes all human activity seem insignificant.

Charles Dickens, a man not often at a loss for words, visited the Falls in 1842 and set the tone for most subsequent writers by devoting much of his account to the indecent inscriptions in the visitors' book kept by the local guide. Niagara, then as now, is highly commercialized, drawing its visitors from all over the world. It is a honeymoon center, a place where conventions are held, ringed by motels, haunted by somewhat run-down exhibitions of curiosities meant to keep the visitor's dollars flowing out of his pocket. It is also, on both the Ontario and New York State banks of the river, a place where factories cluster to take advantage of the cheap electric power from the Falls.

Yet to see and hear and be drenched by the Falls is an experience that wipes away all the razzmatazz of commercial exploitation. The place is invincibly impressive, a frontier of the mind as well as of geography. Even Dickens admitted that they gave him "Peace of Mind, tranquility . . . great thoughts of Eternal Rest and Happiness."

In the old troubled days of dissension, before the freed colonies learned to live at peace with British North America, Niagara was the turning point of conflict, just as it had been earlier when Britain and France fought to control the heart of the continent. Raids and alarms were bitter in this region and the forts and battle sites still remain. The frontier, originally agreed in 1783, runs briefly north and south where the rock shelf that closes off four of the Great Lakes narrows the waters and Lake Erie empties itself through the gut of the Niagara River into Lake Ontario.

The great rock ridge over which the river plunges is a barrier, not just between two nations, but between two climates. The Falls average one hundred and sixty feet in height. But with hurtling rapids above and below the Falls themselves, the waters of Lake Ontario are three hundred and twenty-five feet below those of Lake Erie. On Ontario's lower, milder shores the leaves remain for an extra three weeks in the autumn. Ships on the St. Lawrence Seaway sail across the Niagara Peninsula through the immense locks of the Welland Canal, up to Detroit, Chicago and the world's grain basket, and, like a giant's toys, they loom above a landscape of vineyards and orchards warmed in winter by the great heat store of the lower lake's waters. It is luxurious, flat, gentle land that reminds the European visitor that here he is, after all, on the latitude of the Mediterranean Sea.

Man has tamed the Falls, bypassing them for his ships and harnessing them for electric power. At full flow, the Niagara River carries an average of two hundred thousand cubic feet of water per second. But that full flow is no more. By treaty between Canada and the United States the run of water over the Falls must be maintained at half its full volume during daylight hours in summer, and half that again at night and in the winter. Consequently, most of the time the two countries are diverting three-quarters of the river's power for their own uses, dividing it equally between them.

The United States' share of Niagara's waters would provide enough electricity for a city of a million people. Yet, tamed as it is, there is power and to spare at Niagara: enough to set the heart beating with awe—and enough for the Falls to bring about their own destruction. Geologists claim that cutting the flow over the Falls may, by reducing erosion, considerably prolong their life in roughly their present form. About twenty-five thousand years from now, in a final Samsonian act, the Falls will tear down the pillars of Lake Erie's natural dam, destroying themselves and draining the lake.

DEATH-DEFYING FEATS AT NIAGARA

Niagara Falls has long attracted odd and enterprising stuntmen who have tried to make their fortunes by daring to survive the powers of the Falls. The most famous was Blondin, a Frenchman who became renowned in 1859 for his tightrope escapades across the Falls. On one terrifying occasion, when he was carrying his manager on his back, one of the supporting ropes snapped. Blondin saved them both, but most of the Niagara daredevils were not so lucky. Many attempts to leap over the Falls, ride over them in a barrel or swim the rapids have ended in disaster. One recent incident is, perhaps, the most unusual and miraculous of all. A boy, protected only by a lifejacket, was swept out of a boat and over the Falls to be picked up by a tour boat—alive.

Hundreds of feet in the air, the spray from Horseshoe Falls, on the Canadian bank, drifts over the turbulent waters of the Niagara Gorge, right. The drop from the half-mile-long curving crestline is 162 feet. The American Falls is 167 feet high and more than one thousand feet wide. In the subzero temperatures of a northern New York winter, ice forms and plunges over the cataracts, above, and into the Niagara River. During extremely severe winters, the entire Falls has frozen into enormous icicles.

White marble, green acres of grass, great sheets of water that shine back with the colors of the sky, the capital of the United States of America is on the imperial scale, fitting the worldwide sweep of the decisions that are made here in Washington, D.C. But the men who willed the city into shape were building not in the knowledge of what America's government would mean for the world, but in the confidence that it would mean great things for America. It was a staggering gesture of confidence, the laying-out of this great plan of streets and parks and monuments. It embodies the spirit of its time, the towering aspirations of its people.

The founders of the American nation had launched out on the most daring political experiment the world had yet seen. A number of small Revolutionary governments, defying the age-old principles of human leadership, had decided to merge their individual autonomies in one federation; and they had decided that each citizen's vote should have just the weight of his fellow's, rich or poor, no more, no less. It was a bundle of shocking innovations. The founders believed that it was justified, that it would work and that this was the governmental pattern of the future. They were practical men of business, lawyers and farmers, not ideologists. But they had a dream, too, of a world in which rulers, whose right to rule came direct from the people, should be accommodated in surroundings no less grand than the heirs to the most ancient monarchy of Europe. Washington is the supreme architectural assertion of the faith and the confidence on which America was founded.

The city was built with one purpose alone: to embody, to give effect to and to dignify the daring principles of the American Revolution. The normal practice of American democracy was followed in its founding, too. The marvelous site, where the hills roll sweetly down to the tidal waters of the Potomac, was chosen only after a bitter political wrangle, a deal fixed up in a smoke-filled room, and the striking of a neat balance between the conflicting desires of the North and the South to have the capital on their own ground.

No doubt it was helpful that President Washington himself was a qualified land sur-

veyor who knew a real-estate bargain when he saw one. It was certainly crucial that he engaged a former engineer officer of Lafayette's army to lay out the new capital. Pierre L'Enfant's ideas of town planning were as grandiose, and as untried, as the political ambitions of his employers. They were carried through only partially, by fits and starts, amid constant budgetary crises and recurrent scandals. But the ruling ideas survived and triumphed.

The peculiar beauty of Washington, over and above the individual excellences of its buildings, is that it combines with the usual

grid pattern of American cities a larger network of great boulevards that run at angles across the city. Entering from north or east, you are led through a gradual crescendo to the immensity of the Mall and its monuments. From the west, across the bridges, you arrive with startling suddenness at the great vista up to the white purity of the Capitol dome. It has majesty without monotony, an unerring sense of style.

There are many who claim that Washington has outgrown itself, that its beauty is in danger of being crushed. But Washington has always

The illuminated dome of the Capitol dominates the Washington night sky, above. The original neoclassic building was designed by William Thornton, a West Indian physician and an amateur architect. On September 18, 1793, President Washington laid the cornerstone in a solemn Masonic ceremony, left. Congress moved into the completed building in 1800. Construction of the side wings and the white-painted cast-iron dome began in the 1850s. President Lincoln insisted that work on the dome, a symbol of national solidarity, continue despite the Civil War. Completed in 1863, the dome was crowned with Thomas Crawford's statue "Freedom."

Washington, D.C.

existed on expedients and improvisations. For the first fifty years of its existence it failed to grow beyond the scale of an overgrown Southern borough. During World Wars I and II it suffered an accretion of military encampments that temporarily demarked its open greenness. The peak years of highway construction left Washington with a nightmare maze of access roads unfit for any nation's capital.

But at last the city—which only recently tore up its streetcar network—is acquiring a mass-transit system that should move its citizens more humanely. Along the Mall great new government buildings follow the pattern of L'Enfant's original plan. The Kennedy Center for the Arts and the marvelous new Hirshhorn Museum and Sculpture Garden show at their best the American talent for cultural patronage.

Despite the grandeur of its plan, Washington preserves its small-scale delights, in the unpretentious prettiness of redbrick Georgetown, in the curves of Rock Creek Park, that curl of woodland that runs down through the town, a path for wild raccoons that clatter the trash cans and set the dogs howling in the heart of the city. In fashionable Washington today, legislators and lawyers can look in their backyards and spot a possum teetering gingerly along the fence.

The city has grown beyond even the rash ambitions of its creators. But it remains a city of hope and of faith in the great experiment its foundation celebrated. The great statue of Abraham Lincoln gazes down the Reflecting Pool, between the flowering cherry trees, to Washington's pillar and the Capitol. There for the doubters, in that great work of urban art, is America's answer to the world.

The design for the Jefferson Memorial was adapted from Thomas Jefferson's own plan for the University of Virginia Library. The nineteen-foot-tall bronze statue of Jefferson stands in a marble rotunda whose walls are inscribed with quotations from the writings of this influential architect of democratic thought.

Daniel Chester French's marble statue of Abraham Lincoln gazes silently toward the Capitol from the grand and beautiful Lincoln Memorial. Plans for a building to honor President Lincoln were discussed after his death in 1865, but it took Congress forty-six years to pass the legislation. The memorial was dedicated in 1922.

THE GREAT LAND

It is impossible to write about Alaska without using superlatives, for here, indeed, is an immense land covering as it does 586,412 square miles, almost one-sixth of the area of the continental United States.

It is a harsh land, particularly in winter when the country is blanketed with snow and ice, the air brittle and clear with the biting cold, the sky brilliant with stars and the rippling, dancing lights of the aurora borealis. Even in midsummer, when the Bering Sea may be blue and calm, the tundra carpeted with flowers and alive with the calls of birds, you are always conscious that winter with its iron grip is waiting in the wings.

Alaska is a land of extremes and contrasts. It is a land of great beauty and serenity, but also of frightening magnificence. It is a land where beauty and danger are constant companions, a gigantic stage upon which great dramas are enacted. The props are mountains and lakes, forests and fjords, tundra and glaciers, river valleys and wild coastal cliffs. The characters in this superb setting are an unparalleled assembly of wild animals—from the millions of migrating birds to the famous resident brown bears. Their movements and actions are governed by the rhythms of the seasons.

Everything in Alaska is in keeping with the size of the country. There are nearly thirty-four thousand miles of tidal shoreline, where the scenery varies from the flat tundra bordering the Arctic Ocean in the north to the rugged cliffs that brood over the Bering Sea in the west, and the mosaic of fjords, forests and glaciers that runs down to the Pacific Ocean in the southeast. For much of the year the north and west coasts are locked in by the polar pack ice, home of the polar bear. Within the state are the fourteen highest mountain peaks on the North American continent, dominated by Mount McKinley, 20,320 feet high, in the Alaska Range.

The extreme southeast is the Panhandle, where high coastal mountains trap the warm air from the Pacific to give an average annual rainfall greater than that of the Amazonian forest. Consequently, Sitka spruce, western hemlock and Alaska cedar grow to a height of two hundred feet and more. Throughout Alaska there are one hundred and eighty-six thousand square miles of forest; about fifty-one thousand square miles of glaciers and ice fields; well over three million sizable lakes; and many rivers, the most famous of which is the Yukon, at the turn of the century, one of the routes to and from the goldfields of the Klondike.

Despite his pursuit of minerals, man has made little impact on this vast land. Oil and natural gas are the latest in a series of important finds made since the United States purchased, in 1867, what was known then as Russian America. The population has grown from the thirty thousand estimated at that time, to over three hundred thousand—and yet over 90 percent of Alaska remains uninhabited. The Great Land remains as America's last frontier—a daunting land where the temperature can reach the upper nineties in summer and plunge, as a result of the wind chill factor, to well over one hundred degrees below freezing in winter.

Alaska, the first proving ground in the new commitment to the reconciliation of preservation and exploitation, stands now at a major crossroads in its history. Change is inevitable, and only time will tell how much of this unique wilderness will remain for the benefit of the continent's future generations.

The Alaska Range is a six-hundred-mile-long barrier dividing southern Alaska from the great plateaus of the interior. In the central section of this range, rank upon rank of rugged, parallel, glaciated ridges, up to nine thousand feet high, stand sentinel on the approaches to the massive bulk of Mount McKinley, which, at 20,320 feet, is the highest mountain in North America.

It is a particularly impressive mountain, rising from a base plain only three thousand feet above sea level, its steep north face sweeping upward for fifteen thousand feet. From McKinley, as from all the lofty ice-covered peaks of the Alaska Range, glaciers wind their way down into the valleys below. One of these,

the Ruth Glacier, has carved out so great a gorge that, on each side of the ice, cliffs nearly a mile high rise sheer into the sky

The mountain lies at the heart of a 3,030-square-mile national park to which it has given its name. Much of the park is on the north side of the Alaska Range, where access is gained to the gentler lower slopes by eighty-seven miles of road that end at Wonder Lake; for the first seventy miles it cuts through the five-thousand-foot-high northern foothills to reach the upland tundra. From this road it is possible to backpack into the wilderness: into the forest, across the tundra or up wide, braided river valleys to the foot of the big glaciers. This is truly wild country where

grizzly, wolf and caribou roam at will, and where a man must pit his wits against the elements. But nature's rewards more than repay his efforts.

I well remember one of my first visits to Mount McKinley. It was an August day and I was near Wonder Lake, about thirty miles from the mountain. It had rained for most of the day. Great masses of black clouds boiled down from the high peaks and McKinley had been completely hidden from view. Toward early evening it miraculously cleared and the mountain stood stark and white against a blue sky. Wildlife, which had been remarkably absent all day, suddenly appeared. A golden eagle soared above a distant valley, a grizzly

Snow-covered Mount McKinley, seen from the north across the upland tundra. The tundra vegetation—a mat of lichens, sedges, grasses and dwarf shrubs— flourishes largely because of the protection given from the moisture-bearing south winds by the bulk of North America's highest mountain. The timberline, in the foreground, is at

about three thousand feet, almost seven thousand feet below that of the Rocky Mountains. The trees are small because the subarctic location and frozen subsoil inhibit their growth even at low altitudes.

The sure-footed Dall sheep, the only white wild sheep in North America, live on the high ridges of McKinley Park, where they have few predators. Consequently, their senses of smell and hearing are not well developed. They rely on their acute eyesight and exceptional agility to move at high speed along the steep slopes and deep ravines.

Mount McKinley

stalked down to the Toklat River and a group of caribou trotted over a nearby ridge only sharply to change their course as they caught our scent.

As the sun dropped lower and lower, the great mountain underwent a striking series of color changes—from yellow to orange, then red and, finally, deep purple, with every crag and col etched in sharp relief. The waters of Wonder Lake, far below our vantage point, glowed blood red as the sun finally disappeared behind the distant spruces.

I recall, too, an outstanding autumn day in early September when the landscape was brushed with every conceivable shade of red, with touches of yellow and gold that con-

trasted with the somber green of the spruces. It was a crystal-clear day with just a high scattering of woolly, white clouds over the serried crests of Mount McKinley and its lesser neighbors.

All day small groups of caribou had been moving across the rolling tundra. Moose were browsing on the lower slopes of the hills and flocks of white Dall sheep were clearly visible on far-distant ridges. It was one of those days that no mortal artist could portray, since he could not possibly capture the atmosphere, the vastness of the scene or the myriad of subtle colors that created the splendor of the landscape.

Suddenly, there was a strange, elusive

noise, a clarion trumpeting that seemed to have no definite point of origin. Then, high in the blue dome of the sky, they came from the north—formation after formation of majestic sandhill cranes on their southerly migration, passing over the summit of Mount McKinley itself.

Not many visitors to Alaska will aspire to reach McKinley's summit. But if they do make the climb, they will be able to look down on a panorama stretching for a hundred thousand square miles. Bradford Washburn, one of the first men to see it, wrote that it was "like looking out of the windows of heaven." It is little wonder that to the Indians Mount McKinley was Denali, the Great One.

The two largest animals in Mount McKinley National Park are the grizzly and the moose. Some of the largest moose in the world, weighing as much as seventeen hundred pounds, are found in the brush and woodland areas of the park. Not even this formidable bulk can deter the Toklat grizzly, a blond variety of bear unique to the country around Mount McKinley, from attacking and killing a fully grown moose. The nimble, powerful bear moves at speeds of up to thirty miles an hour, but because it cannot sustain this pace, it can only take such large prey as the moose by stealth or ambush.

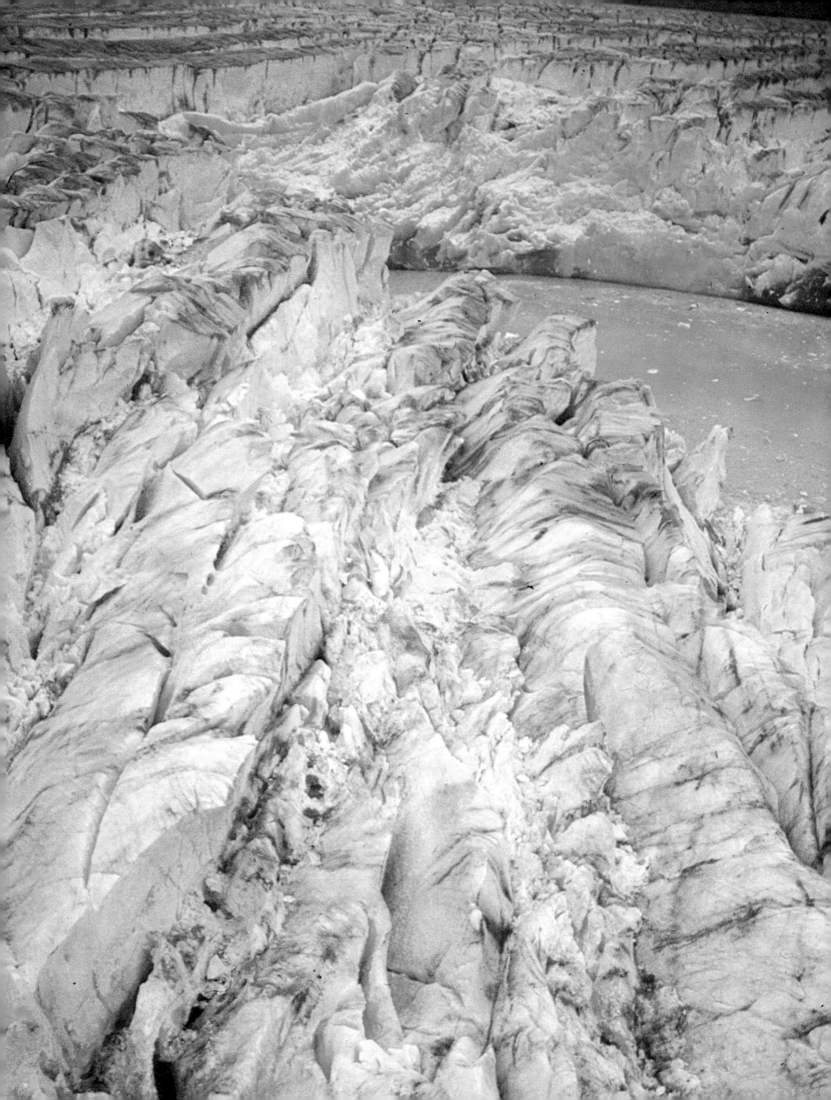

Glacier Bay

Even in Alaska, where spectacular scenery is commonplace, Glacier Bay and its surroundings are in a class apart. It is an area that is wild, savage, primeval and appallingly magnificent. The grandest achievements of modern man pale into insignificance by comparison with this work of nature.

It is impossible for anyone to visit this part of Alaska and not be emotionally affected by it, even if it is only to feel frightened and awed by what has been described as outrageous desolation. Certainly a sense of physical shock must be a common reaction to a first sight of the upper reaches of the bay, which must look the way the northern half of the continent looked ten thousand years ago when the glaciers of the Great Ice Age began their slow retreat.

When the British explorer George Vancouver came to the mouth of Glacier Bay in 1794, he found it blocked by a sheer wall of ice extending from shore to shore and flanked on each side by lofty mountains. By the end of the nineteenth century the ice had retreated considerably, a process which is continuing today in the inner parts of the bay, where a land long imprisoned beneath the ice can be seen gradually coming to life as the glaciers recede. Only the final stage of recovery, when hardy spruce trees yield to elegant hemlock, has not yet occurred.

The setting of Glacier Bay is strikingly beautiful, with massive snow-covered mountains stretching away in almost every direction to a jagged horizon. The bay itself is a massive sixty-five-mile-long fjord carved by the ice from the mountains in which it now lies cupped. High up among these peaks are the enormous ice fields that give birth to the sixteen great glaciers which grind their way down to the blue-green waters of the bay. From the towering perpendicular ice walls that form the front of these glaciers, chunks of ice the size of substantial houses break off and drop into the water with a roar like primitive, booming thunder.

Rain, snow, sleet, fog and mist are all common features of the weather in this extraordinary place. The hulking mountains are usually hidden from view in swirling wreaths of black and gray clouds, and the thunder of ice falling from the glaciers into the sea comes ominously out of the mist. In the late nineteenth century the naturalist John Muir visited Glacier Bay. When the clouds lifted to reveal the berg-filled expanse of the bay he wrote that he gazed upon "a solitude of ice and snow and newborn rocks, dim, dreary, mysterious."

While this is an accurate description of Glacier Bay for much of the time, it is not always so. Occasionally there are exceptional days when the skies are blue, the lowering clouds are banished to the innermost recesses of the mountains and the sun shines down on a glittering landscape. Seals frolic in the cold waters, a bald eagle soars majestically overhead and stately hemlocks march down to the water's edge. These are days to remember, but somehow they lack the aesthetic impact of the wilder conditions. When mist and clouds dominate the scene there are often eerie lighting effects, and an intangible sense of an omnipotent presence and of impending violence.

Indeed, the great power of the ice is everywhere evident. Some of the mountains and ridges have been smoothed and rounded by it, others shattered and splintered. Retreating glaciers have often left long slopes composed of jumbled boulders. In other places, the remains of trees engulfed by the advancing glaciers of past millennia now project through the pebbles of the beaches.

Violence, when it comes, can be overwhelming, as it was in July 1958 when, one evening as the sun was setting, a violent earthquake sent ninety million tons of rock plummeting into Lituya Bay. A colossal surge of water stripped the forest from a steep spur southwest of Gilbert Inlet to a height of more than seventeen hundred feet, and ice to a depth of thirteen hundred feet vanished from the face of the Lituya Glacier. The effects of this catastrophic event are still very evident, and they convincingly illustrate that in the face of natural phenomena of such magnitude, man is helpless.

The extremes of Glacier Bay are fascinating. In the south there is the climax of development in the wake of the ice. Here you can walk in a forest of one-thousand-year-old hemlocks; a damp, dripping world of hairy mosses hanging from the trees, shrouding the boulders and carpeting the forest floor, the whole illuminated by an unearthly green light and pervaded by a great sense of timelessness. At the other extreme, in the innermost parts of the bay, where the land is raw and only recently emerged from beneath the ice, the impression is one of utter lifelessness—an "end of the world" feeling.

Such feelings are not for everyone, but those who do go to Glacier Bay will find its stark, elemental beauty unforgettable.

Most of Alaska's glaciers are in the southeast, in the Panhandle, where moist ocean air meeting cold air over the mountains produces snow. The snow accumulates and turns to ice, which increases in density to form a glacier, left. Sixteen glaciers flow into Glacier Bay and "calve," or break, into huge icebergs.

The mist-shrouded peaks of the St. Elias Mountains, above, surround Glacier Bay. Reaching more than ten thousand feet into the gray clouds, they form the highest coastal range in the world. These mountains and the bay make up the 4,381-square-mile Glacier Bay National Monument, which was established in 1925.

The blue-gray glacier bear is unique to southeast Alaska. This unusual animal is considered to be a color phase, a genetic mutation, of the American black bear, and the blue coloration occurs in only a small percentage of the area's bears.

SALMON-FISHING BEARS
In the summer the largest and oldest brown bears of Katmai claim the prime spots—shallow rapids—to catch salmon as they fight their way upstream to spawn. The bears eat the choicest parts of the fish; the remains are fought over by waiting glaucous-winged gulls.

Valley of Ten Thousand Smokes

There is no smoke, no fire. The Valley of Ten Thousand Smokes is spectacular in its nakedness.

This valley was once green and pleasant and quite unremarkable. Then, in June 1912, to the accompaniment of a thunderous blast heard nine hundred miles away, at the head of the valley a new volcano was born. Great masses of pumice, lava, rock fragments and ash were ejected, and all the trees for miles around were carbonized by blasts of scorching wind. More than forty square miles of the valley were buried under ash and pumice to depths of up to seven hundred feet. For years afterward, steam from the buried streams and springs escaped to the surface through thousands of small vents, creating the "smokes" which gave the valley its name.

Since the eruption the rivers have carved and sculptured their way down through the pumice to their original level. The waters roar through deep and narrow canyons and thunder down waterfalls of huge boulders. Even now, more than half a century after that cataclysmic eruption, petrified tree trunks stand isolated and stark and the pumice plain that forms the valley floor is still almost entirely devoid of plant life. The color effects in the valley change constantly according to the weather. The pumice appears first pink, then deep orange, or almost black as storm clouds and mist roll down from the surrounding somber mountains.

The farther you go up the valley the more menacing it seems to become. When the clouds temporarily lift you realize that the valley is ringed by brooding mountains. Lying at the head are no less than four volcanoes, and between them are extensive ice fields and glaciers. The awesome effect is completed by the steadily smoking volcano of Mount Martin.

The Valley of Ten Thousand Smokes is just the most recent result of the overwhelming volcanic forces that molded the Alaska Peninsula, some four thousand three hundred square miles of which form the Katmai National Monument. Along Katmai's coast a hundred miles of fjords, lagoons and ocean bays are set against a backdrop of snow-covered mountain peaks and glaciers. Beyond those mountains lie extensive forests and lonely valleys, in which, set like gems, are long chains of lakes.

But these numerous attractions are not instantly revealed, for this is a moody area where good weather may occur for barely one-fifth of the year. All too often a fine, sunny morning is the harbinger of a wild and stormy afternoon. Much of the Katmai is still unexplored and some of its most impressive sights, like the volcanic crater lakes tucked away in the mountain peaks, are well hidden from the casual view. There is an air of restrained violence about some parts of Katmai, which may be because there are at least seven active or recently active volcanoes in the area.

The scenery of Katmai is richly varied and the wildlife is abundant. Along the stormy coast seabirds wheel overhead and Steller's sea lions and hair seals laze on the exposed offshore rocks. In the extensive inland forests the deep silence is broken only by the calls of unseen birds.

Because of the high rainfall the forest floor is deeply carpeted with mosses, and winding between the tree trunks can be seen the trails of brown bears for which Katmai is famous. In summer, when thousands of sockeye salmon fight their way upstream to spawn, the huge bears come out of the forest to join the bald eagles and ospreys in exploiting this natural harvest.

Katmai's fame, however, rests not with its fascinating wildlife, but in its scenery, almost overwhelming in its splendor. Fittingly, it is best viewed from Mount Katmai itself. The approach through the Valley of Ten Thousand Smokes and the climb past the glaciers to the mountaintop is hard, but any exhaustion is banished by the amazing panorama.

In the eruption of 1912, the summit collapsed inward, reducing the mountain's height by almost a thousand feet. Inside the resulting crater is a lake, six square miles in area, the encircling snow-covered slopes mirrored in its blue-green waters. To the south, beyond the foothills, are the cold waters of Shelikof Strait and the distant capes of Kodiak Island. To the north are the high peaks of the Aleutian Range and below, past the white ice of the glaciers, lie the vibrant colors of the Valley of Ten Thousand Smokes.

The River Lethe, above, is one of two rivers which wind through the Valley of Ten Thousand Smokes. The valley is a multi-colored landscape of pumice and ash created by volcanic eruption in 1912 and sculpted by powerful winds and fast-flowing rivers. Sand and silt from glacial runoff increase the river's power to erode, and in little more than sixty years they have eaten through to the lowest layer of volcanic ash. The valley appears dead and desolate, yet life has begun again. Once barren rocks now support clumps of green moss, and alders struggle for survival in the sterile land.

The lovely color effects on the floor of the valley are the result of chemical changes in the volcanic deposits as they slowly cooled in the years following the 1912 eruption.

The Yukon River has its origins in Canada, but it soon crosses the border to flow for twelve hundred miles across interior Alaska, pursuing a tortuous course until it empties into the Bering Sea on Alaska's west coast. As it approaches the end of its journey the Yukon parallels the Kuskokwim River, and the two form a vast delta complex covering some twenty-six thousand square miles on the Bering Sea coast.

Throughout the long winter the delta lies flat, white and silent beneath the snow and ice. When spring finally arrives it becomes a watery domain which is best reached by float plane from the little town of Bethel on the southeastern fringe of the delta.

For a seemingly interminable time the small plane drones steadily on across apparently limitless expanses of green tundra, lavishly sprinkled with a sparkling pattern of sloughs and lakes and dotted with the white forms of whistling swans that have recently arrived on these breeding grounds. Then, if it is a fine day, the Bering Sea appears as a blue ribbon on the horizon.

Only after the plane has deposited you at the edge of one of the innumerable lakes near the coast and departed, does the full extent of the immensity of this delta suddenly strike. Out here man is an insignificant mortal in a vast, flat world that stretches away to infinity in all directions. There is no sound except the muted rumbling of the sea and the constant calling of waterfowl. There are no mountains, no forests and no glaciers. There are few elevated vantage points. There is only water and marshy tundra.

The Yukon Delta is unique, one of the few remaining unspoiled deltas of the world. It is a place where man has had little impact. It is a land which, after the long winter, suddenly awakens and becomes the domain of countless thousands of ducks, geese, swans, loons, cranes, gulls and waders. At no time during the day or the almost nonexistent night of summer is it completely silent. Two sounds are particularly evocative of this wild place—the far-carrying trumpeting of the sandhill cranes and the weird wailing and moaning of the loons.

There is a curious, indefinable quality about this vast, remote delta which is created by the tall skies, the limitless horizons, the purely natural sounds and the endless activity of the wildfowl passing in small skeins across the sky. Everywhere there are birds nesting, displaying or feeding with an obvious air of urgency. Even the first wild flowers seem to appear quite suddenly. Not all the summer days are still and sunny, the sky a cloudless blue. Even in summer the Bering Sea can produce wild weather. Cold winds can blow unrestrained across the open landscape, and banks of sea mist or fog will roll in off the sea to enfold everything in a clammy blanket.

The Yukon Delta is a huge waterfowl nursery, where some two million young ducks and geese are born each year. Wildfowl from this delta pass along all four of the great migratory flyways of North America in the course of their

1 Emperor Goose
2 Glaucous Gull
3 Long-tailed Jaeger
4 Sabine's Gull

Yukon Delta

spring and autumn movements. Stand by the Bering Sea in early spring when snow still carpets much of the ground, and you will see a constant procession of birds moving northward to distant breeding grounds. There are sandhill cranes on the way to eastern Siberia; snow geese that will nest in Canada's Mackenzie Delta; black brants and white-fronted geese bound for the Arctic Slope of Alaska.

In the autumn the pattern is repeated as the clamorous hordes pour southward again to escape the freezing grip of winter.

The emperor geese are particularly interesting because they spend their entire life in the Bering Sea area, where most of them winter in the storm-wracked Aleutian Islands. As spring approaches they move north to the breeding grounds in Siberia and western

Alaska. It is to the Yukon Delta that a very large proportion of the population goes.

Soon after the last geese have gone south the pack ice will come down through the Bering Strait, the first snow will dust the tundra and the multitude of lakes will freeze over. The great delta will lie white and silent until, once again, spring arrives and the first emperor geese return.

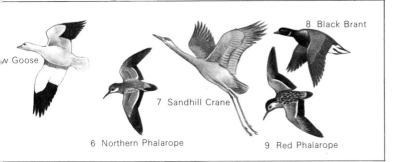

w Goose

8 Black Brant

7 Sandhill Crane

6 Northern Phalarope

9 Red Phalarope

Although it is known as the Yukon Delta, the vast delta complex on the Bering Sea coast of Alaska has been formed over thousands of years from deposits laid down by two rivers, the Yukon and the Kuskokwim. The landscape is a mosaic of meandering channels, lakes, pools and areas of tundra elevated only a few feet above sea level.

On a winter day when it is still dark at noon, when the snow-covered tundra is almost indistinguishable from the frozen sea and the temperature is 40 degrees below 0 Fahrenheit or even lower, the Arctic Slope would seem to many people to be the bleakest place on earth. It is here, where the northern edge of the Arctic Slope is constantly eroded by the pack ice of the Beaufort Sea, that Alaska comes to an end.

The Arctic Slope extends from the Beaufort Sea south to include the northern foothills and slopes of the Brooks Range, an area of 56.5 million acres, slightly over one-sixth of the land surface of Alaska. This is spacious country with tall skies and distant horizons that convey a feeling of freedom.

When the fleeting arctic summer arrives toward the end of May and midday darkness gives way to the eighty-two days of the midnight sun, then the Arctic Slope is transformed from stark winter whiteness to the green of summer. But even before this has happened, the great herds of barren-ground caribou that have wintered in areas south of the mountains have begun their migration north through the snowy passes of the Brooks Range to spread out across the Arctic Slope, where they will give birth to their calves and spend the summer grazing.

As the temperature rises and the snow melts, the grizzly bears emerge from dens in the mountain foothills. Along the northern coast flock upon flock of waterfowl and waders arrive to spend the summer, for this has now become a land of lakes. The level Arctic Slope is underlain by continuous permafrost, frozen ground which prevents the water from draining downward, and an aerial view will reveal thousands of bodies of water. They vary from small pools to the 315-square-mile expanse of Teshekpuk Lake, all glistening in a curious, polygonally patterned landscape—another manifestation of the presence of permafrost.

The exquisite wild flowers bring a variety of colors to the tundra. The ubiquitous cotton grass covers acres with its fluffy white heads. There are also the yellow arctic poppies, the creamy-white blooms of avens and northern windflowers, the tiny pink flowers of the northern primrose and the pale lilac of river beauty on gravel bars in the cold, clear rivers.

Here and there isolated low hills, known as pingos, form islands of dry land. These pingos usually support colonies of arctic ground squirrels and more species of such flowers as the boreal Jacob's ladder. The whole atmosphere at this time is charged with excitement and activity. There are just a few short weeks in which the multitudes of birds can nest and rear their young and the plants can grow and reproduce, for the cold cloak of winter will begin to fall on the tundra by September.

Leaving the coast and traveling southward toward the distant Brooks Range, the flat coastal plain gives way to rolling foothills. New flowers appear, including the alpine shooting star and the showy Richardson's saxifrage. This foothill country is charming. New vistas open up as each fresh ridge is breasted or another bend in the valley is rounded revealing, perhaps, yet another of the beautiful translucent lakes. Civilization could well be a millennium away, and the occasional howl of a wolf evokes the ultimate spirit of the wilderness.

In the mountains themselves, with their razor-backed ridges, nameless peaks and hidden valleys which may have been rarely, if ever, trodden by a white man—something which can be said of but a few places in North America—there is an everchanging pattern of light and shadow as the clouds come and go and sudden, wild storms alternate with brilliant blue skies.

In the northeast, where the mountains approach the coast, lie the 8.9 million acres of the National Arctic Wildlife Range, an area which has seen little of man. It has been subjected only to the forces of nature, which have modeled a land of great physical beauty steeped in tranquility.

In the central Brooks Range there is another area of outstanding beauty and grandeur which may one day be the Gates of the Arctic National Park. Here it is possible to stand on the Continental Divide and look north to where the vast expanse of tundra rolls toward the Beaufort Sea, and south to where the green ranks of spruce march down to the distant Yukon River. The view from this roof of the world is breathtaking beyond imagination.

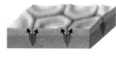

An Arctic Slope summer is short, and manifestations of winter are always present. The subsoil is permanently frozen and only the top foot or so thaws. Alternate freezing and thawing cause the tundra to crack and, because the area can never drain, water seeps into the cracks. It freezes into wedges of ice which gradually enlarge the cracks, left, creating the characteristic polygonal patterning seen in the landscape at Prudhoe Bay, far left.

Few men have ventured into the Brooks Range and many of its peaks remain nameless and unexplored. Geologists are confident that in these mountains lie immense, rich mineral resources, which it will be difficult to exploit because of the rough terrain and hostile climate. Thirteen thousand square miles of the northeastern part of the Brooks Range and the Arctic Slope have, however, already been set aside as North America's largest wildlife refuge, dedicated to the conservation of the flora and fauna of this unique arctic area.

Arctic Slope and Brooks Range

SURVIVAL IN THE ARCTIC WINTER

Some animals of the Arctic Slope go through white color phases. The seasonal camouflage changes of the ptarmigan, for example, give year-round protection from such predators as the golden eagle. Its white winter feathers blend into the snowy arctic land-scape, and its summer plumage of brown and black hides the ptarmigan among the rocks and lichens where it nests. A few animals pass the winter in hibernation, among them the ground squirrel, which sleeps so deeply it seems to be dead.

215

HAWAII

The first navigator to sight the Hawaiian archipelago was the captain of a Spanish galleon who, in 1555, sailed past and did not chart it. Two thousand miles from land in all directions, this handful of flecks on the wide Pacific remained undisturbed until 1778, when the English explorer James Cook saw "tropic birds, boobies, etc. and several turtles" and realized he was near land. He put in at the lush northern island of Kauai, and named the group the Sandwich Islands. The inhabitants he encountered were descendants of Polynesians who had migrated there in swift double-hulled canoes from the Marquesas and the Society Islands in two waves beginning in A.D. 700. They received Cook as the returning God Lono. But after his men, who needed wood to repair their boats, had chopped down a temple precinct and a few idols, and the natives had torn apart a longboat, a fight broke out and Captain Cook was killed.

The conflict of intruder and native continued until, twenty years after Cook's death, the islands were finally united under the warrior king Kamehameha. The king's widow and his heir, in an extraordinary bout of iconoclasm, abolished the taboos that had fettered Hawaiian society and ordered the destruction of the old

gods and their worship. When the first missionaries arrived six months later, in 1820, they encountered a unique opportunity—a people without a religion. But their success was mixed, largely because, as Robert Louis Stevenson pointed out when he lived in Hawaii, "in the course of their evangelical calling they, or too many of them, grew rich."

Fortunes were made in sugar, in pineapples, in whaling. Then, in 1898, Hawaii was profitably annexed by the United States. As the disadvantages of this colonial position became increasingly obvious to Hawaiians, the demand for statehood grew. In 1959, Hawaii was admitted to the union as the fiftieth state.

Even more than the polyglot communities of Chicago or New York, Hawaii represents the concept, the ideal of the Union. For on these islands wave upon wave of immigrants, Chinese and Japanese, Filipinos and Samoans, Koreans and Puerto Ricans and mainlanders themselves are all Americans. One in three marriages is interracial, and the intermingling of styles is the overriding characteristic of the islands.

The Hawaiian strain risked being altogether stamped out in admiration of Americana. But this generation has

turned its eyes with new pride to its islands' past. The hula, the ancient ritual method of storytelling in dance, is being rescued by some from the commercial nadir into which it has fallen. The legends the ancient Hawaiians attached to the caves and valleys, rivers and waterfalls, flowers and trees of their islands are being retrieved from memory. Archaeologists are exploring the burial mounds and abandoned settlements. Above all, acute concern for the islands' beauty hinders the indiscriminate sprouting of more hotels on the beaches and the further destruction of the forests. And because of this awakening, part of the Hawaii Mark Twain recalled nearly a hundred years ago has been providentially saved: "Other things leave me, but it abides; other things change, but it remains the same. For me its balmy airs are always blowing, its summer seas flashing in the sun; the pulsing of its surf beat is in my ear; I can see its garlanded crags, its leaping cascades, its plumy palms drowsing by the shore, its remote summits floating like islands above the cloud wrack; I can feel the spirit of its woodland solitudes, I can hear the plash of its brooks; in my nostril still lives the breath of flowers that perished twenty years ago."

Mauna Loa and Kilauea

To stand on the southern cape of the island of Hawaii is to stand witness to genesis itself. For in 1950 the crater of Mauna Loa, the Long Mountain, disgorged a mighty river of fire, which poured down its broad and shallow slopes until it met the ocean. There the water boiled at contact, the fish died instantly in the caldron and a massive new headland was formed.

In the same way as it first exploded out of the sea millions of years ago, Hawaii is still growing. On all sides this primeval landscape —some of the newest territory on the globe— stretches in midnight desolation, a charred heap of black clinker and rubble, the extinguished hearth of a titanic monster. A few plucky trees claw grimly at its forbidding and shattered surface. The onlooker would hardly start in surprise if a pterodactyl screeched overhead or a brontosaurus lumbered along.

The gigantic caldera of Mauna Loa, the largest active volcano in the world, spectacularly erupted again on December 31, 1974. Fountains of molten lava leaped one hundred to three hundred feet in the air along a three-mile rift. Its sister, the volcano Kilauea, situated only a few miles away, last belched forth in 1960 and added five hundred acres of naked new land to the island. Kilauea has been active ever since, spurting geysers of fire high into the air, or flowing with many-branching deltas of flame down the crater walls in cataracts to form burning and infernal lakes of molten lava.

Like living creatures, the volcanoes of Hawaii inflate before they breathe out their mass of flame. Along a fissure deeply buried in the earth, the magma, or living core of the planet, begins to move, pressing itself upward until it explodes to the swollen surface in a series of fiery fountains. When the magma cools and congeals it builds grotesque cones and stalagmites of lava, mining its own smoky labyrinth and immuring trees that stand in its path in pitch-black tombs.

Yet the lava that flows from Mauna Loa or Kilauea is a gentle enemy compared to the lava of other volcanoes. It oozes at a mere thirty-five miles per hour and its milder gasses do not hurl a sudden hail of brimstone on the world. The Hawaiian volcanoes have rarely taken a human life and they are the only active craters in the world around which you can wander in safety.

When Mauna Loa and Kilauea are not in temper, plumes of steam still issue from the hell cracks in their black surface, and stream across the calderas like the smoke of a barbarian army's fires. And yet this pitiless waste harbors life—flowers and trees and birds. Fragile wands of pale mauve orchids wave under a canopy of giant fern. Underfoot, the red ohelo berry grows sweet and succulent.

In legend, these berries are sacred to Pele, the goddess of the volcano, and no one may eat them until they have tossed her share into the crater that is her home. For in Hawaiian myth, when the goddess of the sea, Na-maka-o-ka-hai, had torn to pieces her sister Pele, goddess of fire, and flung her broken body into the ocean, Pele's spirit rose from the waters and, in revenge, built the volcano Mauna Loa. Her other brothers and sisters became her servants, and each had a separate task in the devastation. One was god of explosions, one of thunder, another of the rain of fire and yet another the cloud bearer. But the crater Pele chose for her palace was not Mokuaweoweo on Mauna Loa but that of Halemaumau on Kilauea, the most active of all, which until 1924 possessed a fiery lake of lava at its heart and is still ringed with sulfurous hot clouds of steam.

In Hawaiian imagination, Pele still rules in her palace of fire, and offerings, particularly gin, are welcomed by the thirsty goddess. Hawaiians swear they have seen her, stalking her grim domain with a hound at her heels. They maintain that she controls the convulsion of the mountains, when the elements are turned inside out and rock courses like water and fire becomes as solid as stone.

Layers of lava flows from Mauna Loa's successive eruptions can be seen near the volcano. Smooth lava from the flow of 1935 covers the pitted and eroded lava from the 1895 explosion. The island of Hawaii is built up from lava flows, and it grows by several hundred acres each time there is an eruption from one of its two active volcanoes.

The Kamehameha butterfly, left, is found nowhere else in the world except on the main Hawaiian Islands. On the slopes of Mauna Loa, the Kamehameha, which has a four-inch wingspan, thrives among the pockets of thick vegetation that have escaped the devastation of recent lava flows, the last of which occurred in 1974.

Plumes of steam rise from the lava lake of Kilauea, the youngest and most active volcano in Hawaii Volcanoes National Park. Congress established the park in 1916 to preserve the environment of this most accessible area of volcanic activity in the world, and volcanologists have since been able to make extensive studies of its geology.

The small bird called the 'o'o is brown and drab, but under its wings and tail it conceals three golden tufts of feathers. For these it was hunted through woodland which the ancient Hawaiian normally shunned for fear of ghosts, and its bright plumage was plucked and woven into the resplendent cloaks and crested war helmets of the princes and the priests. The flashing 'i'iwi and 'apapane were also pursued for their scarlet feathers. Although in theory the birds were set free after their treasure had been pulled, it is no wonder that these unique Hawaiian species were thought to be extinct, for at least three thousand 'o'o birds were needed for one cloak.

But now on the island of Kauai, the Garden Isle and the most ancient of the archipelago, the whistle and calls of the 'o'o, the 'i'iwi and the 'apapane can once again be heard, and they sip again the nectar from the scarlet cheerleader pompom flowers of the twisted ohia lehua trees that thickly cover the rugged reaches of Kauai's mountain country.

Their return marks Kauai's painful rescue from the centuries of neglect and destruction which had almost blotted out its extraordinary natural features. James Cook and, later, George Vancouver, the English explorers calling in at Kauai, introduced livestock to the island. The pigs and goats multiplied in the kindly climate and preyed on the forests. Later, the Chinese desire for sandalwood opened a rich market and the feudal rulers of Hawaii demanded that their subjects pay taxes in the fragrant wood. The sandalwood tree was chopped down ruthlessly all over Kauai and disappeared. Only now has it been replanted. The sugar planters heedlessly bulldozed immense tracts of virgin forest to grow the lucrative cane. This single land-use economy disfigured the natural variety and lush charm of Kauai.

But today a new policy of conservation has been adopted and an active lobby is pressing to create a huge national park, which will pro-

Waimea Canyon

vide effective safeguards of Kauai's special beauty and magnificence. For to this small island, flung in the waste of the vast Pacific, Nature has shown herself at her most lavish, her most uncompromisingly bounteous. A unique duck bobs on Kauai's ponds, a unique species of hibiscadelphus tree flowers in a deep and hidden pocket of its cliffs. The tiny violet, emboldened by the generous climate, grows to a height which overshadows a man. The peak of the extinct volcano Mount Waialeale boasts more rainfall than anywhere else on earth. The golden plover, a speckled bird with spindly legs, gives proof of one of the stoutest hearts in the repertory of the universe, for it

wings its way from Alaska in a mere forty-eight hours to spend the winter on Kauai and other Hawaiian islands. And with a final flourish of incomparable grandeur, the force of wind and water cleaved the island open from the mountain to the sea to create the silent brooding majesty of the Waimea Canyon.

Like the red birds which have returned and the red blossoms of its prolific tree, the mighty cliff face of the canyon is seamed with red. When the sun strikes it, the rich earth beneath the mantle of trees appears to smolder. Streams eroded and worked the plateau until it plunged in sheer curtains of rock to the valley below. The imprint of the waters shows clearly in the

furrows that fork down the canyon's towering cones and their work still continues when, after the rains, they sluice over the edge in a shining veil. Banked clouds spill over the lip of the canyon and steep parts of it in inky shadow. Far below the silver thread of the Waimea River makes its way toward the emerald Kalalau Valley and the ocean beyond.

The graceful white tropic bird glides over the abyss, amusing itself all day on the drifting currents and only at nightfall heading out to sea for fish. The vast canyon is its toy and its nesting place. At worst, man is an interloper in this paradise, at best, its curator and preserver.

Kauai Island's Waimea Canyon, left, the Grand Canyon of the Pacific, is fourteen and a half miles long and twenty-eight hundred feet deep. Like the Arizona Grand Canyon, its steep, multilayered walls are colored in lovely shades of red, yellow and ocher. But, whereas vegetation is sparse in the arid Grand Canyon, the rain-

fall on Kauai, the Garden Isle, justly famed for its hundreds of varieties of flowers, is heavy enough to support lush tropical vegetation in Waimea Canyon.

Morning sun shines across the Kalalau Valley on Kauai Island, and highlights a ohia lehua tree, above. Common throughout Polynesia, these trees flourish particularly well in Hawaii's volcanic ash soil. There are numerous subspecies, ranging from tiny shrubs to enormous trees several hundred feet high, all with scarlet blooms.

Oahu Island Beach

One of the sacred chants of Polynesia, the original home of the Hawaiian people, invokes the creator Tangaroa "of which the universe is but the shell." His name means transparence, and it is as transparence that Hawaii is most aptly described, for on these islands light and vapor and spindrift combine in a ceaseless interplay of rainbows. Mark Twain reproached Captain Cook's lack of poetry when he named the Hawaiian islands after his English patron the Earl of Sandwich, and wrote that they should rather have been called after the many-hued arcs of light that shimmer "like stained cathedral windows" in the azure of the skies, or dance in the cascades that plunge over high ramparts into the valleys below. But the rainbow is never more bewitching than when it plays in the Hawaiian surf, tossed in the spray that blows back from the curling waves to hang magically in the transparence of blue air above.

The coral coast of the island of Oahu booms with the sound of the Pacific breakers. When the arctic ice cap melts, the rolling weight of its waters pours out over the immensity of the Pacific, gathering mass and power until it crashes three thousand miles to the south against the Hawaiian chain. On Oahu in particular, the formation of the reefs catches the blast and forces the ocean upward into mighty waves four, six, sometimes even eight times the height of a man, presenting a living wall of water. It is on this that the surfer flings himself and flies. Then these huge "bluebirds" rip open along their crest and the foam torpedoes sideways, chasing the skimming athlete on his board. Sometimes the sea overtakes him and he falls. For a moment his body hangs in the glassy transparence of the wave's crest, and then he disappears, tumbled in the ocean's suds like so much laundry, while his surfboard spins away high into the air.

The northwest and southeast shores of Oahu have challenged surfers for centuries, for it was the ancient Polynesian settlers of Hawaii who brought the sport with them from Bora Bora. The aristocracy of old Hawaii surfed on *olos*, gigantic and heavy carved wooden boards, but the commoners used smaller and lighter ones. The annual carnival, the *Makahiki*, was celebrated with hula dancing and singing, and with contests of wrestling and sledding, canoeing and surfing. Chieftains staked their livestock and their homes on the prowess of their favorites in the water. But even when it was not carnival time, and the surf was up, the fields and villages stood idle while the Hawaiians, men and women, pitted themselves against the Pacific's fury.

But such hedonism was unpopular with the missionaries, who were horrified, in particular at the mingling of the sexes in the sport. Surfing only narrowly escaped their suppression, and its revival, at the beginning of the twentieth century, can be attributed to a heroic Hawaiian. Duke Kahanamoku was born on Oahu, became champion swimmer of the world at the Olympiads of 1912 and 1920 and introduced the world to his native art of surfing, teaching the Australians and the Californians how to dominate the waves. He is a legend on Hawaii, for in his prime he rode the huge olo board of his ancestors on a single mountainous wave for a record mile and three quarters from the promontory of Diamond Head down to the shallows of Waikiki Beach.

On the shores of his island the international surfing competitions are held, and their most daring event commemorates his name. The waters of Oahu are the world's greatest surfing playground and have been baptized according to their hazards—Avalanche, Himalayas, Shark's Hole and Rock Pile. But the most dangerous of all, the surf that can dash a man to his death on the coral reefs, is the Banzai Pipeline, where the surging waves curl over and enfold the surfer in a translucent tube of rushing water, while above the stiff offshore breeze lashes up the spray in which a rainbow innocently plays.

Koko Head, a promontory of crinkled lava, extends into Hanuama Bay on the windward coast of Oahu. This area was the site of Oahu's last volcanic activity, ten thousand years ago. Hanuama Bay, an ocean-filled crater, is a marine-life conservation district, where hundreds of species of tropical fish are protected.

A surfer's search for the "perfect wave" often takes him to Oahu, where the Hawaiians developed surfing into a competitive sport. Today, Oahu hosts three major international surfing competitions—Makaha, the World Pro-Am and the Duke Kahanamoku—each attracting hundreds of competitors and thousands of spectators.

Canada is bigger than the United States and although peopled by the same sort of immigrant stock as its southern neighbor, it has a population only one-tenth as large. Economically and, in good measure, culturally the two countries are inseparable and Canadians sometimes fret that the rest of the world believes their country is only a northern extension of the United States. This self-deprecating modesty tends to go too far, for Canada's past, present and future, although forged along lines similar to those of the United States, is in no way less vital, less exciting or less interesting. Canada is, quite simply, a New World country whose discovery was exciting and whose development has been dynamic.

Canada has twin pillars of strength—her natural resources and her people. From the rugged shores of the Atlantic Provinces, through the mellow farmlands of Quebec, along the mighty St. Lawrence to the massive seaways of the Great Lakes, across the rich band of the Prairies, up to the frozen and largely virgin territory of the far north, across the majesty of the Rockies to the incomparable forests and fjords of British Columbia in the west, there is a variety of natural beauty that bombards the senses. This natural splendor harbors riches, too—abundant lumber, oil and gas reserves, rushing rivers, which can be converted into power, minerals and metals, fertile soil, great plains for rearing cattle, salt water and fresh water which abounds with fish.

But this is no lush paradise that waited for centuries to bestow its riches on mankind. The Canadian environment, for all its beauty, is also uncompromising. This is an immense land washed on both sides by vast oceans, boasting a terrain that is still difficult to cross, and with a winter that can be savage in its intensity. Exceptional people have, therefore, been needed to

CANADA

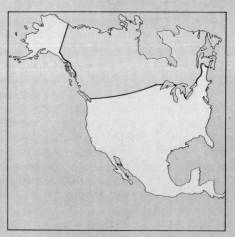

master this environment, to find the key and unlock the doors to the treasure troves within. And herein lies the second pillar of Canada's strength, for it would seem that since before history was recorded, this land has attracted the right people to do the job—the Indians and Eskimos who first came to terms with nature; the great early explorers from Europe, the Bristol merchants, the fishermen, the French colonists, the trappers and agents for the Hudson's Bay Company who pressed ever westward; and the pioneers and immigrants who were prepared to accept the challenges and reap the rewards.

This pioneering determination has not slackened in modern times. Canadians are still performing feats worthy of their ancestors. Be they English, French, German, Italian, Ukrainian or whatever, Canada has been fortunate with its people. They in their turn have been fortunate with their unique and beautiful country.

225

Bonavista Bay, the oldest settled part of Newfoundland, has basically not changed in four hundred years. The physical trappings of twentieth-century society intrude very little. It remains today what it has always been —a place where fishermen go down to the sea in ships, a place where simple folk live simple, hardworking lives, at the mercy of, but also miraculously in tune with, the mighty sea.

The landscape, both natural and man-made, is in reality a seascape. Bonavista Bay and Europe are separated by nothing but thousands of miles of the northern Atlantic Ocean. When the waves roar into the shore, they have behind them the full power of an uninterrupted ocean. As they hit the craggy coastline, with its distinctive mélange of innumerable tiny rocky islands, its shoals and its cliffs, they break off in mountainous columns of spray, fleetingly suspended in midair as if by some heavenly magnet. Sand, that great companion of the sea, is present in abundance, with miles of pristine beaches sometimes rising, just as the surf finally reaches its crescendo, into huge patterns of dunes, spreading over into the wooded countryside behind the shoreline.

This rough environment has its riches in the form of fish. There are tuna, whales, sharks, swordfish, porpoises and, above all, there is the cod, the *raison d'être* of Newfoundland's economic existence. The cod is lured to the waters and banks off the Newfoundland coast by a remarkable natural phenomenon known as the "capelin scull." In midsummer the capelin, a small saltwater fish, only seven inches long, is driven, mysteriously, to the Newfoundland coastline to spawn on the beaches. In its wake it brings millions of greedy cod, happy enough in any case to enjoy the plankton-rich seas where the Gulf Stream and the Labrador Current meet, but unable to resist the easy pickings that the helpless capelin provide. When the capelin scull is out, the waters off Bonavista Bay may be black with fish fulfilling their natural cycle. And this has worked to the advantage of man, who, since the fifteenth century, has been hauling in the cod in Bonavista Bay.

Cabot is popularly supposed to have landed, in 1497, on the tip of the peninsula at what is now the town of Bonavista. Historians doubt this, but there is no doubt at all that before and after Cabot's journeys, Bristol merchants and fishermen had discovered Newfoundland.

The legacy of these early pioneers is still vividly alive today in the small fishing communities that characterize the Bonavista Bay area. It is alive in the place-names, for example, like Witless Bay, Joe Batt's Arm, Peggy's Bag, Seldom-Come-By, but especially in the language, where both names and dialects spring straight from the Devon and Cornwall of three and four hundred years ago. Graplins, starrigans, crunnicks, offers, swiles, bedlamers, drokes, not words of the modern day, are redolent of the sea and the fish in it from time immemorial. And these seventeenth-century terms can still be heard in Bonavista Bay.

The enduring physical mark that man has left on the Bonavista landscape is no twentieth-century product either. Sticking out from what Newfoundlanders call the "landwash," the strip of land between high and low water, are to be seen hundreds of fish-landing stages, ramshackle, spindly wharves made of spring var, above which rise the table-like "flakes," on which the fish are laid out to dry. The stages and flakes seem too frail to endure the rigors of the wind and sea, but they have lasted, essentially untouched, for generations, improved only by the application of an occasional coat of bright paint.

The people who work on the sea and on the flakes and live in white-painted wooden cottages in tiny hamlets on the coast seem even today to be from an earlier, gentler age. The fishing industry now is modern and efficient, but, intriguingly, it does not seem to have much changed either the lives or the methods of those who serve it. For the fisherman of Bonavista Bay is still a man who goes down to the sea in a small boat, braving the worst of the elements, in his blue guernsey sweater and gumboots, a man who is not only more at home at sea than on land, but probably more comfortable in an old wooden fishing smack than he would be in a modern sophisticated trawler. It makes you feel that in four hundred years' time things will not have changed any more than·the surprisingly little they have changed in the last four centuries.

Porpoises, usually moving in groups of five or more, are commonly seen off the Newfoundland coast. These highly intelligent mammals can be taught, in captivity, to fetch and carry objects. They avoid obstacles by emitting high-pitched sounds and listening for echoes in the same way many bats do.

Bonavista Bay

THE ATLANTIC COD

The Atlantic cod, right, is an omnivorous eater, feeding on all kinds of crustaceans, worms and mollusks. It migrates seasonally, heading northward in summer toward shallow waters such as those off Bonavista Bay and southward into deeper waters in late fall.

Newtown, above, is a typical fishing community on Bonavista Bay. European fishermen, attracted to the bay because of its abundance of cod, nevertheless returned each autumn to their native countries. In 1684, the number of permanent residents was only one hundred and twenty, rising substantially in the eighteenth century.

The Cabot Trail is a modern two-lane highway that follows for seventy miles the north, west and east boundaries of Cape Breton Island National Park. It winds its way through remote fishing villages, climbs over mountains, then dips down to skirt sandy beaches and rocky harbors.

ISLAND DISCOVERERS
The Cabots, John, far right, and his son Sebastian, right, set out in 1496 in search of a northwest passage to the East Indies. In 1497, they apparently made landfall on the north coast of Cape Breton Island. Its 184-mile trail is named for John Cabot.

From the lone shieling of the misty island
Mountains divide us, and the waste of seas—
Yet still the blood is strong, the heart is
highland,
And in our dreams we behold the Hebrides

Nowhere in North America is the feel of Scotland more subtly pervasive than in Cape Breton Island. It is not the Scotland of industrial Glasgow or gracious Edinburgh, but the rugged and uncompromising land of the north, of the Highlands and the Western Isles, real Gaelic land where tough people have carved lives out of a beautiful but unwilling environment, with a sheep on every hillside and a loom in every cottage. And nowhere on Cape Breton Island does the spirit of the old Scotland live on more stubbornly than in the territory encircled and served by the winding 184 miles of the Cabot Trail.

At first sight, the topographical resemblance is so uncanny as to lead the outsider to believe that some divine intervention tempted the Scots across the Atlantic to a new home in the New World. Here, as in Scotland, the eye is always, irresistibly drawn to the hills, and, where the uplands meet the coast, to the inevitable spectacular cliffs, often shrouded in mists and sea spray. The trees—spruce, scented balsam fir, maple, birch, poplar and ash— may erupt in the autumn into a blaze of color unique in its intensity to Canada and New England, but for much of the year they look like Scottish trees. And if the heather does not grow quite as abundantly here as it does in the Highlands, the daisies, lupines and wild berries combine to give the same effect.

The climate, too, has a familiar feel. Aptly described by a local writer as "a wonderful summer and fall, a hard winter and a rotten spring," there is nonetheless a fickleness to nature on Cape Breton with which only the hardiest people have come to terms. The western and northern coasts may be iced up in winter. There can be snow in June as well as in January. And, above all, there can be wind, as the fishing people of the island know only too well, for Cape Breton, trapped between two weather systems, is at that precise point in North America where many storms head out into the Atlantic, giving a dying kick before they go.

It was not divine intervention that brought the Scots to their new home but something else that the Highlands and the New World held in common—the salmon. For when John Cabot returned from his great voyage of adventure, which probably saw him land at Cape North in 1497, he brought back tales of great new fishing grounds and of a fish now known as the Atlantic salmon. It might not have been quite the same fish as the revered Scottish salmon, but his description was enough to send the fishermen of Europe—Scots, Basques, Bretons, Normans—heading for their boats.

Of these early settlers, it is the Scots, helped by the fact that the British ultimately beat the French in the war for Canada, who have been the most enduring. But this was not to the exclusion of all others. Among the Gaelic, English, Indian and Portuguese place-names there can be found, like a long-lost tribe, the Acadians, the old French of the sixteenth and seventeenth centuries, who, buffeted around the world, found what may be their final home on the western shores of Cape Breton in the little community of Chéticamp. There still, under the fluttering Acadian flags, the old Acadian language can be heard, a mysterious patois much closer to the dialects of rural western France than to the French of Quebec.

The Cabot Trail is one of Chéticamp's lifelines, just as it is the vital artery for all of the tiny hamlets and villages of north Cape Breton. This is not merely a beautiful road, whisking the visitor up to the Cape Breton Highlands National Park, but a working road, without which the Scots, Acadians and Micmac Indians would be as isolated as they were in the Middle Ages. The road itself was not completed until 1932 and was not fully hard-surfaced until 1961. It is new enough for the visitor still to be able to sense, almost feel, what it was like in the long, hard winters for the farmers and fishermen of Cape Breton, where people worked from dawn to dusk, played the pipes, danced the reels and spoke in the mother tongue of the Gaelic. Even today nearly five thousand people on Cape Breton claim Gaelic as their mother tongue, the highest concentration of Gaelic speakers outside Scotland and Ireland. As the anonymous poet said "the blood is strong, the heart is highland."

The American marten, far left, and the fisher, left, inhabit the coniferous forests of Cape Breton Island. These extremely agile creatures and powerful jumpers stalk squirrels and birds. The fisher also attacks porcupines, however, its name is misleading, as it seldom catches fish.

There are places in Canada, as elsewhere in the world, which conjure up days gone by, but which are, at the same time, very much part of the present era. Bonavista Bay, for example, reminds the visitor of the centuries-old lives of fishing people, but its industry serves a modern need. The Cabot Trail, a beautiful winding road through matchless Highland scenery, is also a functioning road, carrying school buses, logging trucks and vehicles that provide the essential services of modern life. Quebec City is Canada's most famous historical city, but it is also a modern town in which people live and work very much in the twentieth century.

Grand Manan Island, however, is something rather different. It is not so much a place as a mood. Here, the pressures and realities of everyday life can be forgotten and the soul can be revived in an atmosphere where simple, uncomplicated, solid values still apply. Franklin D. Roosevelt loved to withdraw for a while from the pressures of his Presidency to the island of Campobello, part of the Grand Manan archipelago. He would describe Campobello simply but graphically as "this beloved island." The same words could apply to Grand Manan itself.

Grand Manan is situated in the mouth of the Bay of Fundy, the source of the greatest tidal power in the world. Fifteen miles long, six miles across at its widest, fifty-five square miles in all, it is the largest of the three hundred and sixty-five islands in the archipelago. It is part of the province of New Brunswick, although, on a map, it looks as if it should belong to the State of Maine; this is precisely what the American Government thought at the beginning of the nineteenth century, although it finally relinquished its claim to Grand Manan in 1817.

Grand Manan is not an easily accessible island, which, of course, is part of its charm. Even today, ferries take more than two hours to reach the island's rocky coastline across the often violent waters of the Bay of Fundy. It is a place where shipwrecks were rife. Samuel de Champlain, the great French pioneer, ran aground there in 1604. He charted the island and in his 1607 map called it "Menane," apparently borrowed from an earlier explorer,

Stephen Bellinger, who, twenty years before, had first coined the word "Menan," a corruption of the Indian *munan-ook*, or island. Captain Kidd, the great pirate, is, according to popular legend, supposed to have buried two kegs of gold somewhere on Grand Manan. Even the true settlers, the forefathers of the current population of twenty-five hundred, were outcasts of a sort, who left England to find greener pastures in North America.

Thrown ashore on this rocky retreat, they were the United Empire Loyalists, whose allegiance to King George of England was stronger than their feelings for the new independent America.

Things have not changed very much since they came to Grand Manan in 1784. The forbidding black cliffs still repel the outside world, although friendly white lighthouses warn mariners of the trouble they will en-

---

THE SEABIRDS OF GRAND MANAN ISLAND

Over two hundred species of birds have been recorded on Grand Manan Island. Most are subarctic and include, left to right, the Atlantic puffin, common murre, slender-billed murre, Leach's petrel and razor-billed auk. These birds spend most of the year on the high seas, but faithfully return to the island's cliffs to breed. The puffin, slender-billed murre and petrel nest in rock crannies, where their young are hidden; the common murre and razor-billed auk lay their eggs on the bare rock.

Grand Manan Island

counter on the island's rocky frontier. The maritime birds, above all Mother Carey's chickens, who have always flocked to Grand Manan still do so in incomparable variety and numbers. Man, enjoying the most benign climate in New Brunswick, has built himself nice, little tidy villages on Grand Manan and, because the island's settlers were God-fearing people, fourteen churches to make sure the old verities were maintained.

The villages themselves do not have modern amenities like streetlights or road signs, or at least not many of them, simply because they are not needed. Everybody knows everybody on Grand Manan, so much so, the visitor is told, that no one would dream of locking his door. Indeed, it is perhaps appropriate that the only economic activity of significance, apart from amply catering to the visitor and catching lobster, is cultivating dulse, a somewhat leathery but edible seaweed. There were once more than three hundred fish smokehouses on Grand Manan, but now there are barely a couple of dozen. A frenetic commercial existence is hardly Grand Manan's style, and the harvesting of dulse is unlikely to thrust the island into the mainstream of international economic activity. And this is precisely why Grand Manan is unique and so precious.

The lighthouse at North Head warns approaching seamen of Grand Manan's rugged coastline. The relentless pounding of the surf against the foot of the headland has formed such unusual rock shapes as Old Bishop, a mass of trap rock, and Hole in the Wall.

The history of Canada, ancient and modern, is wrapped up in Montreal and Quebec City. In very different ways these two splendid cities proudly symbolize the achievements of the French in Canada.

Quebec, the name was probably adapted from the Indian word *kebec,* which means "the river narrows here," stands at the confluence of two rivers, the mighty St. Lawrence and the St. Charles, and it has been the meeting point, the focus, of people, policies and ideologies in Canada for more than three hundred and fifty years. It has been the scene of the most important, and romantic, battle in Canadian history. It has been the emotional core of the largest French-speaking population outside France, a place where the old and the new have, and still, come together. It is, too, by a miracle of preservation, the most physically attractive city in the country.

Although Jacques Cartier established his winter quarters in 1535 on the site of Quebec, then known as Stadacona, Samuel de Champlain, whose settlement dates back to 1608, was the founding father and the architect of the French colonization of the New World. Champlain never lived to see Quebec flourish, for when he died in 1635 there were still no more than the few dozen hardy colonial families who had come with him. But he left his mark. He first fortified the old town and thus gave birth to a tradition that is still alive; as well as being the oldest city in Canada, Quebec remains the only walled town north of Mexico, although the present fortifications were built only a hundred and fifty years ago.

By the start of the eighteenth century Quebec had become what Champlain dreamed it would be and what, to some extent, it still is today—the social, economic and political center of New France, the seat of the government, the courts and the Church, a seaport of consequence, a trading post and a marketplace for the farmers of the surrounding countryside. It had, therefore, become, when Britain and France went to war in 1756, the most important target on the North Ameri-

can continent for the British Army. The siege and capture of Quebec in 1759, when Wolfe's dramatic storming of the heights of Abraham undermined Montcalm's defenses, were epic and heroic on both sides, worthy antagonists fighting a battle for incalculable stakes. Well aware of the city's preeminence in 1791 the British made it the capital of Lower Canada, which roughly corresponds to the present province of Quebec. And today, although it has ceded much of its regional supremacy to Montreal, Quebec remains the capital city of the province.

In spite of the major role thrust upon it by history, the city of Quebec has remained, in several ways, faithful to Champlain's hopes for it. It is indelibly French; for 95 percent of its inhabitants French is the mother tongue. But more than this, the city still reflects the life-style and attitudes of provincial France, which is just that much slower, more conservative, more relaxed and more religious than its sophisticated, citified counterpart. And this, so true of Quebec City, lends a

Montreal and Quebec City

distinctive atmosphere to the nation's first capital.

For the city not only looks like a provincial French town it also feels like one. It is divided into two separate parts—Upper Town and Lower Town. Upper Town is dominated by the Citadel, the crown of Cape Diamond and the watchdog over the rivers and the Plains of Abraham below. A little lower down, but hardly inconspicuous, lies the massive bulk of the Château Frontenac, yet another extraordinary Victorian Gothic creation of the remarkable people who designed hotels for the Canadian railways in the nineteenth century, and Dufferin Terrace, the wooden promenade, or boardwalk, one of the most striking places for a short stroll in North America. Lower Town, however, is commercial and residential in the uniquely provincial French manner with tiny shops and restaurants, narrow streets, cobbled pavements and the smells and sounds of a French country town. Montreal, too, is French, but in a distinctly metropolitan way. It is the second largest

French-speaking city in the world and, as if in emphasis of its stature as Canada's most important center of trade and commerce, its heart is dominated by wide expressways and the aggressive new architecture of concrete and glass.

Montreal is essentially a series of villages, each with its own individuality, sometimes even with its own language, for this is a truly cosmopolitan city where newcomers from the Old World, from China and from the West Indies retain the customs and idioms of their homeland. These communities are strung out along the St. Lawrence River and around the wooded slopes of Mont Royal, the mountain and the river that have given the island city its shape and its character. The mountain was named by Cartier in 1535 when he visited Hochelaga, the Huron Indian settlement on its lower slopes. By the end of the sixteenth century, Hochelaga had disappeared and in 1642 Paul de Chemedey, sieur de Maisonneuve, founded a settlement there that he called Ville-Marie. The town

became a base for the explorers and voyageurs who opened up the Canadian interior and, in a process that still continues, Montreal grew as Canada grew.

Parts of the old town survive. The narrow streets are redolent of a grander, less impatient time. The buildings are fine and mellow with age. But Montreal is proudest of its sweeping boulevards, its modern Place des Arts, its new subway, Le Métro, and its massive underground complex of shops, theaters and restaurants beneath the towering office buildings and hotels of the city's new center. Montreal is firmly committed to the future.

In the Parisian tradition Montreal flaunts its modernity and its Frenchness. Quebec City is more subtle. It combines its Gallic charm and beauty with historical associations that make it unique in North America. In Quebec one can get a little bit closer to understanding the kind of people who helped to forge the Canadian nation. In Montreal one senses the spirit of the new Canada.

The impressive Château Frontenac dominates the skyline of Quebec City, as seen from Lévis, on the south side of the St. Lawrence River, left. Explorers and voyageurs used the river to reach the interior of Canada, and today it is the vital connecting link between the inland ports of the Great Lakes Basin and the Atlantic Ocean.

Even the skyscrapers of downtown Montreal are dominated by wooded Mont Royal, above. The copper roofs, green with age, mark the old buildings that still survive among the new. Farther from the city center entire streets are lined with period houses, with their distinctive wrought-iron balconies and external staircases, left.

Timmins

Leo del Villano was, on and off, Mayor of Timmins in the 1950s, 1960s and 1970s. Leo used to say that the reason he was mayor so often was because he was Italian, and everyone else in town was either French or English. He was not what could be called a sophisticated man, although he was shrewd enough. He was, in fact, what cockneys would call "a rough diamond." His greatest delight was stunts—to walk in his shirt-sleeves in subzero weather down King Street in Toronto and tell all and sundry that he was Mayor of Timmins, or to organize a bear hunt when he read that the bearskins adorning the Coldstream Guards outside Buckingham Palace were looking a bit threadbare. But, in his own blunt, unique way, he epitomized, in the middle of the twentieth century, something which has been a Canadian characteristic since the time of the first settlers—a willingness to carve, with bare hands if necessary, a living from the most unpropitious surroundings which harbor what has always been Canada's greatest asset, its natural resources.

Timmins is a mining town. More than that it is a town with a feeling that there is always a bonanza hidden under the ground. Copper, zinc, gold, silver, Timmins has known them all in its relatively brief history. The last great rush was only a decade ago. It is not a lovely town in the classic sense. Some people do find a strange, contemporary beauty in the stark profiles of the disused machinery at mine heads, the curious mounds of displaced earth. But this is, perhaps, too esoteric a charm.

Timmins, and many places like it, is a plain town, but underneath its homely exterior is a rugged, determined soul. It reflects the character of the people, immigrants all, who have built it. It reflects the struggles they have met in prizing treasure from a reluctant soil. And that, in its own way, is beautiful.

The town of Timmins was founded in the early part of the twentieth century to house employees of the nearby Hollinger gold mine, one of the world's largest. As a result of copper, zinc, lead and silver strikes, its population has grown so rapidly that it has become the largest town of the Porcupine gold-mining region.

TRAPPING THE ERMINE AND THE WOLVERINE

The country around Timmins was first opened up by fur trappers, and despite the building of the town trapping still continues in the area. The ermine, far right, remains a highly prized catch, particularly during the winter when its coat is completely white. But having the skill to trap the ermine is not always enough; frequently the wolverine, right, will prey upon the trapped animal. The wolverine, also known as the glutton, is clumsy but cunning, often eating the thongs of the snares set specially to trap it.

234

Kitchener

Inside Ontario, Kitchener may not be the precise antithesis of Timmins, but in some respects it comes pretty close to it. For where Timmins is rough and brash and forever seeking the next gold mine, Kitchener, in spite of its broad industrial base, is somehow rooted in a more profound and sober past.

The reason is to be found in the character of the first settlers in Kitchener and in its twin city of Waterloo. They were the Mennonites, the Protestant sect from southern Germany and Switzerland whose teachings are based on the New Testament, particularly the Sermon on the Mount. Hounded from Europe in the late seventeenth century, they set up homes in Pennsylvania and then, just over one hundred years later, moved on, in part to southern Ontario, to become some of the province's earliest settlers.

Kitchener today is very much part of the Ontario industrial heartland. But through their religion and through their Germanic origins, the Mennonites have imposed an additional character on the area. They are the "plain people." They dress in somber colors, often black, and even, in some cases, in the garb of a hundred or more years ago, with long black capes and bonnets. Many refuse to use cars, preferring instead the horse-drawn buggies that can be seen on Kitchener's back streets. The Mennonites themselves remain principally farming folk. On Saturdays, the Kitchener Farmers' Market features their homemade cheeses, sausages, bread, cakes and produce in a manner that is reminiscent of Bavaria. This applies equally to the annual Oktoberfest, when the consumption of beer and mountainous meals assumes truly Germanic proportions.

Their love of music was also transplanted in the New World. The town band was founded in 1856, the musical society was in being by 1875 and today Kitchener supports one of Canada's symphony orchestras.

Somehow it is consoling to realize that, in the midst of the throb of the machines that make cars and shirts, shoes and buttons and furniture, that tan hides and pack meat, there beats another tempo, one that has not changed very much for generations and which will probably go on beating for a long, long time.

Kitchener is in the center of the Niagara Peninsula, which is one of the few places in North America within the ranges of both the native American hare, far right, and the European hare, right, introduced by immigrants in the nineteenth century. The two species are closely related and both undergo a winter color change.

Mennonite men in their broad-brimmed black hats and homemade plain clothes and women in their bonnets, full, simple dresses and capes leave a meetinghouse in Kitchener. Members of the sect founded the city in about 1807. It was first known as Sand Hills, then Ebytown after Mennonite Bishop Benjamin Eby. For over ninety years, from 1824 to 1916, Kitchener was called Berlin, reflecting the origin of the inhabitants, until the wave of anti-German feeling during World War I prompted the adoption of a new name, that of the British general, Lord Kitchener, who had died earlier that year.

As recently as 1965, Toronto, Canada's largest city, could be dismissed, quite simply, as unmemorable. It had some good points, a certain raw vitality stemming from its position as the nation's commercial and financial capital, some pleasant residential areas, quite close to the center of the city, crisscrossed by attractive leafy ravines. But Toronto, its waterfront skyline dominated by the then vast Gothic facade of the Royal York Hotel, seemed to lack an identity. In 1913, Rupert Brooke, the English poet, summed up the city in words that were still valid fifty years later. "It is not squalid like Birmingham," he wrote, "or cramped like Canton, or scattered like Edmonton, or a sham like Berlin, or hellish like New York, or tiresome like Nice; but the depressing thing is, it will always be like it is, only larger."

Today, Brooke's description could not be more inaccurate. In the space of little more than a dozen years, Toronto was transformed. The new face of the city is not merely a product of cosmetic surgery, a form of urban face-lifting, but rather a completely new sculpture, a new image imposed dramatically on a major metropolis. The skyline, the streets and, indeed, the lives and attitudes of the inhabitants themselves have been completely changed by this modern metamorphosis. Downtown Toronto has not only been reshaped but revitalized. People no longer merely work in the anonymous shadows of the Royal York Hotel before fleeing to the comfort of their homes in the evening. Instead they make full use of the new amenities, facilities and pleasures that are now provided.

And it all happened through a combination of luck and management. The fortune lay in the conditions that made Toronto a boom town after World War II—a strong Canadian economy with the city as its hub, a vast influx of migrants from both inside and outside Canada and an almost intangible feeling that after the destruction of war there should be the rebuilding of peace. At first, in the 1950s, this philosophy of growth threatened to get out of hand, as whole communities in suburban Toronto were torn down and replaced with undistinguished apartment buildings. But in 1953, management stepped in with the crea-

tion of a metropolitan local government empowered to direct growth into productive channels. In retrospect, it was probably the wisest decision the city ever made, for the demand to build outstripped all predictable forecasts. In fifteen years, the per capita value of construction in Toronto became the greatest of any major city in the world. Between 1960 and 1970 alone, there was more building in Toronto than had previously existed in its history. The metropolitan management may not have been perfect in those twenty years, it may have made its mistakes, but its perform-

ance still should be the envy of the world.

The jewel in Toronto's modern crown is, fittingly, its city hall. The creation of the Finnish architect Viljo Revell, its twin, elongated clamshell towers almost interlock, but cradle between them a pearl—a perfect little rotunda. The building overlooks an expansive thirteen-acre plaza, where Torontonians stroll, talk, sit and, in winter, skate on the frozen surface of the rectangular pool. In the middle of the plaza, alone but magnetic, stands Henry Moore's magnificent contemporary work "The Archer," which was

Epitomizing Toronto's modern spirit is the new city hall complex with its curved twin towers of twenty-seven and twenty stories, which partially encircle a three-story, umbrella-shaped structure that contains the city-council chambers. A vestige of Toronto's past is the old city hall. This neo-Romanesque structure with its three-hundred-foot tower was built in 1891–99 of Canadian brownstone and granite. It now houses the provincial courts.

purchased by public subscription. Subsequently, the sculptor donated his own private collection of his art for permanent display in Toronto's Art Gallery of Ontario.

Commerce, too, has appropriately stamped its modern imprint on the city. The twin towers of the Toronto-Dominion Centre, now dominate the waterfront skyline, consigning the Royal York to relative insignificance. The larger of the two towers soars over seven hundred feet. Some critics suggested that this creation of Mies van der Rohe's was too overpowering, too much out of scale with its surroundings, but, if this was true, this judgment is becoming less valid with the passage of time as other clean-limbed skyscrapers climb up alongside to give a new, overall dimension to the city. The Commerce Court, the major new hotels and office buildings all play their part in this recreation. And so, too, will the Metro Centre when it is completed, spreading out all around the CN Tower, aptly described by one local writer as the largest celery stalk in the world.

The center is planned as a minicity in its own right, with 197 acres, landscaped and re-plete with office buildings, apartment buildings and underground malls and shopping centers, complementing those that exist under the Toronto-Dominion and Commerce Court towers. These underground facilities, a feature of Montreal, are just as necessary in Toronto, where the winters are hard.

In one sense Toronto has not changed; it remains the business and financial center of Canada. But now it has acquired, through bricks, mortar and steel, not only a new face, but also something it lacked in the past—a sense of identity.

Manitoba is, of course, a prairie province, which conjures up in most people's minds images of endless wheatfields, or great plains dotted with grazing cattle or, more recently, the derricks that sit on top of oil discoveries. However, about 40 percent of the total area of Manitoba is forest and about 10 percent more is water.

It is precisely this almost unexpected combination of wood and water that is Manitoba's greatest charm. Viewed from the air, the southern part of the province appears to be a complex, irregular patchwork with a myriad of little lakes—blue-green, silver and impenetrably dark as the sun plays upon them—scattered willy-nilly among miles and miles of wooded ground, which makes its own patterns of peninsulas and islands in the lakes. Viewed from the ground, the effect is even more impressive, for this is countryside where man has taken very little from nature. Here,

without trying very hard, man can find himself in exactly the same environment as the first trappers encountered three hundred years ago.

The first men from the Old World to penetrate this far inland were Frenchmen, Médart Chouart, Sieur de Groseilliers and Pierre Esprit Radisson, the first of the voyageurs. With the typical independence of men who could survive the hazards of a canoe trip the length of the Great Lakes and the difficult journey north through Manitoba's lakes and rivers to Hudson Bay, the two men quarreled with their own country's government and went to work for the English. Their fur-trading voyages led to the creation of the Hudson's Bay Company, which sent its traders and trappers into Manitoba from the north.

The French continued to use the traditional Great Lakes route into this area, which was still settled only by Indians. Trading posts

and forts were quickly established by both France and England, and the two sides struggled to control the vast wilderness of the North Woods, where the only known riches were the plentiful animals whose pelts were so much in demand in Europe. In 1763, New France was ceded to England, but not even this international accord could bring peace to these hardy backwoodsmen, for a rival English concern, the North West Company, began to compete for the still bountiful North Woods trapping territories. Around its post at Fort Garry the first farming settlement was established and from it, after the two companies had solved their differences by merging, the city of Winnipeg evolved.

As first agriculture and then industry and mining expanded, fur trading dwindled in importance. But the trappers and traders had played a vital part in opening up the Prairies, and most of the rich forests, lakes and rivers

The North Woods

that they traveled are as beautiful and undisturbed now as in their day.

The last Ice Age was responsible for this magical landscape. The melting of the ice scooped out basins, some large, like Lake Winnipeg and Lake Manitoba, some so small that they will never have names, into which water flowed. And as the ice withdrew its blanket from the Canadian heartland, so in its wake the trees came from the south. First came the fast-traveling seeds of the spruce, birch, larch, poplar and willow, then those which penetrated the colder northern climes more warily—pine, maple and basswood. Finally, and only in the most temperate areas, came those seeds which were carried by animals—oak, hickory, walnut and bitternut.

Technically, the Manitoba woods, which fade out on the Precambrian shield north of Flin Flon and which stretch broadly down the province into the State of Minnesota, are boreal forests, by far the largest Canadian forest classification. This, by definition, is principally coniferous and, indeed, the most common trees in Manitoba are white and black spruce, willowy aspen, tamarack, jack pine and balsam poplar and fir. But around the lakes and in the river valleys, these softwoods are joined in pleasing harmony by their deciduous brethren, bur oak, white elm, green ash, basswood, maple and cottonwood, which bring, fleetingly, their gorgeous, rich, autumnal colors to the scenery.

Yet in spite of this mass of natural wooded wealth, in spite of the official statistics which say that some 40 percent of Manitoba's forest land must be considered "productive," the province is not known, as are British Columbia and Quebec, for the commercial use of its forestry reserves. There is logging of course; but it is only a thirty-million-dollars-a-year operation, which may sound a lot, but which is really insignificant and which, even in Manitoba terms, amounts to well under 1 percent of all its economic activity.

There are a variety of reasons for this—economic, conservationist and practical—but the consequence has been that these are largely unspoiled woods and waters, touched but not tarnished by those seeking recreation and relaxation from both sides of the Canadian borderline, and left largely alone by the demands of a modern industrial society. If trees are felled in the Manitoba woods, they are more likely to be brought down by the gnawing teeth of the beaver than the whining, spinning molars of the chain saw. And the best way to get around in the maze of tree-fringed lakes and ponds is to fall back on the good old canoe, the standby and lifeline of the trappers and Indians who first infiltrated the area in search of pelts and fish. For this is quiet country—subtle and unspoiled.

The profusion of lakes and rivers in the province account for an astonishing 39,255 square miles of Manitoba's two hundred and fifty thousand square miles. Living in this vast area are less than a million people, concentrated almost entirely in the more hospitable south, which was first opened up by the voyageurs of the eighteenth century. Then, portaging their canoes around the frequent rapids and waterfalls, like the Brentwood Falls, above, they made their way north from the Great Lakes, eventually reaching the chain of lakes, including Setting Lake, left, that led into the Nelson River, which carried them northeast to Hudson Bay.

The Canadian porcupine, left, is found throughout the Manitoba woods. Leaves and buds are its favorite food, but in winter it is forced to feed on bark, frequently damaging and killing trees. Strong, curved claws help the porcupine to climb and its quills, which detach easily and inflict painful wounds, deter most predators.

Mirages are generally thought to be a desert phenomenon. But the eyes can play tricks in the Prairies, Canada's fertile bread-basket. Stand in an enormous wheatfield in the middle of Saskatchewan and you will not be quite sure if you can believe what your eyes tell you. The sky will somehow seem much bigger, in fact it will be hard to decide where the sky begins and the earth ends. Look toward one of the large grain elevators that dot the landscape or toward the taller buildings in a town if there is one close at hand. Somehow they appear to be floating in midair, detached from the ground on which, logic tells you, they must stand. It is not a place for agoraphobics.

This sense of vast open space is the enduring impression of the Prairies. It is not an entirely accurate impression, for the scenery of Manitoba, Saskatchewan and Alberta has rather more subtlety and variety than this implies. But it is hard to eradicate from your memory the huge fields of waving wheat, the rows of massive combine harvesters majestically dominating the horizon, the roads that run endlessly straight toward destiny or the horizon, whichever comes first, until, for no good reason, unless it be to focus the attention of the car driver, they engage in an eccentric, but gentle, corner.

The Prairies stretch from Lake Winnipeg in the east to the Rockies in the west, cutting a broad swath across the middle of Canada. There are three levels to the Prairies, divided by two ranges of hills along the Manitoba Escarpment and the Missouri Coteau, where the erosion of the sedimentary rocks has created hills that serve as stepping-stones to the second and third levels. The climate is not as benign as the agricultural success of the area might suggest. The summers are hot, but the winters are long and cold, making possible only one major harvest a year. The rains, too, are sparse, averaging little more than ten inches a year in parts of Saskatchewan. Irrigation, both natural and man-made, and a wonderfully fertile soil compensate for the lack of rain, but the fear of drought is real enough. The legacy of it is still there in the hulks of farmhouses abandoned in the Depression-ridden thirties, when not only lack of rain but

also a swarm of locusts decimated the land.

Generally, however, the Prairies have been kind to those who have tilled the soil. Big business has now largely supplanted the original homestead farmers. But, from the best vantage point to appreciate the vastness of the land, an aircraft thirty thousand feet up in the sky, you can still discern the neat symmetry of man's imprint on this rich country. From that great height you see, above all, the precise one-hundred-and-sixty-acre plots, the official

allotment to the first farmers, and the series of little townsites strung out every eight to twelve miles along the ramrod-straight path of the railroad that was built to serve them.

The Prairies, however, are more than just one big wheatfield. Southern Alberta, on the third steppe, is cattlemen's territory, wide plains of short tufted grass, sagebrush and prickly pear cactus, cowboy country where men still ride tall in the saddle and once a year whoop it up at the greatest rodeo in the world,

Between 1877 and 1881, Sitting Bull, leader of the Sioux Indians, lived in the Canadian Prairies with his tribes, trying without success to persuade the Government to grant them a reservation there. Sitting Bull's reputation as the most defiant of Indians had been crowned a decade before at the Battle of the Little Bighorn, or Custer's Last Stand, where General Custer was massacred along with his two hundred and sixty-five men by the chief's superior force. Not one prisoner was taken.

The prairie rattlesnake, left, is a familiar sight in the open plains of Saskatchewan. In daytime it moves considerable distances in search of food, primarily rodents. It uses marmot or prairie dog burrows for its winter hibernation.

The Prairies

the Calgary Stampede. This is Indian country, too, especially in the Cypress Hills on the borders of Saskatchewan and Alberta just north of Montana, the highest land between Labrador and the Rockies, for here was the neutral ground for the Sioux, Nez Percé, Crow, Blackfoot and Cree tribes. And nearby, just as evocative of the Old West, lie the badlands, including the Red Deer River and the Steveville Dinosaur Park, arid, forbidding terrain dominated by grotesque rock piles and

littered with the bones of animals from prehistoric to present times.

In complete contrast to its great open spaces, the Prairies can also boast one quite extraordinary and unexpected gem, the glacial meltwater channel exquisitely called the Qu'Appelle Valley. The deep cut of its path right in the middle of the Saskatchewan grain belt gives it a canyon-like appearance, but, although it is rugged, it is also gentle and peaceful. The valley floor, in places two miles

wide, harbors a meandering river, which itself ties together a string of lovely little lakes. This, too, is Indian territory. It is the place where Sitting Bull sought, and was denied, Canadian sanctuary for himself and his tribe.

The valley is so out of keeping with the popular notion of the Prairies that it perfectly illustrates its true character. It is really not one landscape but many, merging imperceptibly, altering drastically with the seasons and, indeed, with every change and trick of light.

Although the tiny, long-legged, burrowing owl, left, is a tunneler, he usually nests in the disused burrows of prairie dogs, badgers and skunks. Such a habitat gives excellent protection for the young. Once a common sight in the Canadian Prairies, its numbers have been greatly reduced by hunting and large-scale mechanized farming.

The vast grasslands of the Canadian Prairies have been transformed by modern farming methods into one of the great grain-producing regions of the world. The spring-wheat belt forms a crescent across the Prairies, where oats, barley, rye and flax are also planted. Wheat, however, remains the most important single crop.

241

Columbia Icefield

Here, on the roof of the Pacific Northwest, the ice age endures. From this frozen plateau the river networks of half a continent begin their long journeys downward to the three great northern oceans. Westward, the mighty Columbia surges to its meeting with the waters of the Pacific. Far to the north the Athabasca joins with the cold Mackenzie in a rush to the stark seas of the Arctic. Away in the east the strong dark currents of the North Saskatchewan empty at last into the Atlantic wastes of Hudson Bay. Their common birthplace is the fountainhead of North America—the Columbia Icefield.

Through the centuries the icefield lay undetected, the last unyielding vestige of the ice cap which for a million years had clamped itself upon the continent. Cast like a blanket across one hundred and fifty square miles of the Canadian Rockies' loftiest peaks, the icefield impassively crowned the westward-flowing tide of history; a tide which ever was to eddy about its feet, never to engulf it.

The Indians of the plains and foothills never found reason to venture here. Even in summer it remains a scene of desolation—and one of spectacular beauty. Here, eight hundred inches of snow may fall in a year to replenish summer losses from the melting of the icefield's nine great glaciers. In some places, the ice is a carpet four thousand feet deep. Nothing grows here and no animals call it home.

For a hundred and fifty years after Anthony Henday, a fur trader, became the first white man to glimpse the Canadian Rockies, from a hilltop of the Alberta prairies in 1754, the icefield's existence was to remain a barely guessed-at secret. Against its buttresses the great eighteenth-century rivalries of the fur-trading companies broke and swirled to north and south in the race to find the "Great River of the West" of Indian legend. They knew that this river, flowing from the mountains' Great Divide to the western coast, would open up the riches of the Pacific watershed.

Alexander Mackenzie, unknowing, passed the icefield's feet in his long, fruitless quest for the mysterious waterway. Instead he found his way to the Arctic via the river that would bear his name. Later, he reached the west coast, thus making the first transcontinental crossing north of Mexico. But still the river of legend eluded him.

The nineteenth century was ushered in before the young explorer David Thompson, after probing the ranges for eight exasperating years, discovered the vital gap, north of the icefield, which turned legend to reality and engraved his name in the history books of the West. He found the Athabasca Pass, and at its end the fabled river—the Columbia. Upon this swift-running highway the commerce of the West was carried until at last the twentieth century cut its own great trail—the Trans-Canada Highway—through the easier lands of the south.

It was not until 1897, however, that the British explorers Collie and Woolley, on their long odyssey in search of the continent's highest mountains, finally stumbled upon the icefield's secrets. Scrambling up the final ridge of hitherto-unconquered Mount Athabasca, they discovered awaiting them in the light of early evening, a view laying beneath them, which did "not fall often to the lot of modern mountaineers. A new world was spread at our feet, probably never before seen by human eye, stretching mile upon mile before us like a rolling, snow-covered prairie and surrounded by entirely unknown, unnamed and unclimbed peaks. . . ."

Today, the mountains are all named, and a highway runs past the very tip of the Athabasca Glacier on which Collie and Woolley looked down that day. A tourist chalet, too, stands at its base and in summer the cough of the internal-combustion engine mingles with the music of rushing water as snowmobile buses—a novel mixture of ski and caterpillar tracks—scuttle across the glacier with their cargoes of the curious.

Oddities abound. Here, a large slab of flat rock has sheltered the ice beneath from the summer melting, leaving itself poised, a giant natural picnic table on a glacial pedestal. Elsewhere, like fish locked eternally in a petrified sea, boulders are glimpsed deep beneath the surface, where the melting process has swallowed them up. And all around is heard the resounding crash of ice hurling itself from the dark, foreboding cliffs above as the icefield itself expands in the alpine sun.

At the glacier's base, and cast contemptuously to one side, rubble wastelands bear mute testimony to its fearsome grinding power in its inexorable downward march to that point where it must forever lose its battle with the summer sun. Barring the way to the icefield's heart, great crevasses stab the surface. A mere few feet across yet piercing in places almost to the bedrock, a thousand feet below, they provide the adventurous, poised on their lip, with a vision of chilling beauty—walls of translucent blue and green, endlessly reflecting each other down into the depths where light can no longer reach.

Here, the world of the tourist ends. Beyond, the icefield stretches to all horizons, speared at intervals by eleven of the Rockies' highest peaks. Among them is Snow Dome, the very apex of the rivers' fountainhead and meeting point of the boundaries of the national parks of Jasper and Banff and British Columbia's Hamber Provincial Park.

The snow falls early here, and often. Even as in the prairies below the lingering warmth of autumn is being enjoyed, the chalet here is being shuttered; the snowmobiles and other trappings of tourism locked away. Soon the snowplows will begin their struggle to keep open the hundred miles of highway that link the mountain towns of Jasper and Banff. Often they will lose, and at each end the great highway gates will swing shut across this mountain road that ends in the Arctic.

Once more, the icefield's solitude will be complete.

The largest glacier in the Columbia Icefield is the Saskatchewan, left, with an area of twenty-three square miles. Ice depths up to fourteen hundred and fifty feet have been measured in this glacier. Its waters flow down the Saskatchewan River and pass east across the three Prairie Provinces into Hudson Bay.

The Canadian lynx, left, has very large paws with hairy soles, which enable it to travel over the snow and ice of the Columbia Icefield without sinking or slipping, and to creep up silently on its prey before pouncing. It subsists chiefly on snowshoe rabbits, but also feeds on other small mammals, even attacking young deer.

A tributary glacier in the Columbia Icefield. The various parts of glaciers move at different rates. Flow is usually more rapid in the middle part of a glacier than near its head. The brittle zone, or upper one hundred to two hundred feet, fractures easily, and is marked by crevasses— long cracks—and seracs —sharp ridges of ice.

This is the kind of country that makes men into legends and which explains why the legends of the American West, from California all the way up to Alaska, are somehow bigger, better and more vivid than those of anywhere else. It is the kind of country that makes Europeans incomparably envious. Rupert Brooke, the English poet, was quite overcome. "Six Switzerlands in one," he wrote, staggered by his own train journey from Calgary to the Pacific coast shortly before his death in 1915. Then, perhaps still reeling from the impact of so much natural beauty, Brooke felt the need, in the best British traditions of objectivity, to balance his account. But the thrust of his poetic criticism of the mountainous West was simply to note that the Rockies were "this unmemoried land."

In a sense he was wrong. Even at the time that he wrote, and more so since, man had come to terms, at least in part, with these great mountain ranges. Man has driven roads through them, built railroads across them, skied and hiked on them, hunted and fished in them and created just those stories of which legends are made. But in another more profound sense Rupert Brooke was right fifty years ago and would have still been right today, for all man's brilliant ingenuity has but scratched the surface of this magnificent vastness. For every mile of man-made road there are countless thousands of square miles of virgin territory where man's imprint has yet to be felt. And here, the memories are not human but natural. They are not in the mind, but in the bark of the trees and the icy water of the streams.

The Selkirk Mountains are not, as any geologist will confirm, actually part of the chain of the Rockies, but they are the epitome of all that is finest in the North American mountain West. Named after the Scottish earl who first promoted the emigration of his countrymen to Canada, the Selkirks are twice as old as the Rockies to the east of them and date back to the Precambrian era six hundred and fifty million years ago. They form the central range of the Columbia Mountain System, two hundred miles long and eighty miles across, running from just north of the American border to the great curve of the Fraser River, and rising as high as eleven thousand feet in their most spectacular northern section.

It is no accident that, for the modern visitor, his mecca in the Selkirks is called Glacier National Park, for glaciers are perhaps the area's most enduring feature. The park alone contains more than one hundred glaciers in its 521 square miles, from those almost lost in high valleys under the shadow of great peaks and ridges to the marvelous Illecillewaet Glacier, known as the Great Glacier of the Selkirks, and the ice caverns that lie next to it.

And below the glacial peaks, fed by the rain and snow that the westerly winds drop in abundance on the Selkirks, abound the rich wooded valleys, waterfalls, turbulent rivers, canyons and flower-filled alpine meadows of matchless quality. This is, indeed, the virgin territory of the brown and grizzly bears, squirrels, chipmunks and marmots who roam among the hillsides laden with fir, spruce, hemlock and cedar and the huge open meadows of the valleys scattered with white rhododendron.

Yet, miraculously, among all this unspoiled beauty, man has managed to create something quite startling of his own. The ninety-two-mile Rogers Pass section of the Trans-Canada Highway must surely be one of the most spectacular mountain roads in the world. And so it ought to be, not only because of the scenery it crosses, but also because it bears the name of one of the pioneer engineers who managed, sometimes at gunpoint, to achieve, back in 1883, the astounding feat of building a railroad across the Selkirks.

The road swings and swoops along the Columbia and Beaver River valleys, up over the 4,354 feet of the Rogers Pass itself in the northeastern corner of the Glacier National Park, through the Illecillewaet River valley into another jewel, the Mount Revelstoke National Park. Ingeniously protected from the avalanches that the heavy snowfall makes so frequent, today it takes just a couple of hours to cross countryside that the early pioneers spent months—and lost lives—to cover. But even today you can sense the challenge of these mountains and, today, that is no small compensation.

The pika, left, inhabits the rocky slopes of the Selkirk Mountains, where it shelters deep under stones, hidden from hawks and foxes. During the daylight hours in summer and autumn, it cuts and carries quantities of green plants, which it piles in the sun to dry, then stores for winter among the stones it has chosen for a burrow.

To avoid the harsh winters on the remote and wild mountainsides of the Selkirks, the hoary marmot, left, hibernates in a deep burrow, which holds up to fifteen members of a single family. At the first sign of spring, it emerges to feed on green plants and to mate. The cougar, lynx and eagle are its natural enemies.

The Selkirk Mountains

The Columbia ground squirrel, found in the Selkirk Mountains, is one of a number of North American species. It uses its short, strong legs to burrow and to search for small-shelled nuts and seeds, which it stores underground. This tiny squirrel sits on its haunches or stands on its hind legs to look over obstructions.

Many of the peaks in the Selkirk Mountains rise abruptly and spectacularly above green wooded valleys accessible only on horseback or on foot. The mountains are named after the Fifth Earl of Selkirk, a Scottish Lowlander who promoted emigration from the Highlands to Canada and founded a settlement on the Red River, but never saw the mountains which bear his name. The Selkirks are part of the Columbia Range, a massive wedge of rugged terrain that reaches north from the United States border, enclosed on the north and west by the looping Fraser River and on the east by the Rocky Mountain Trench.

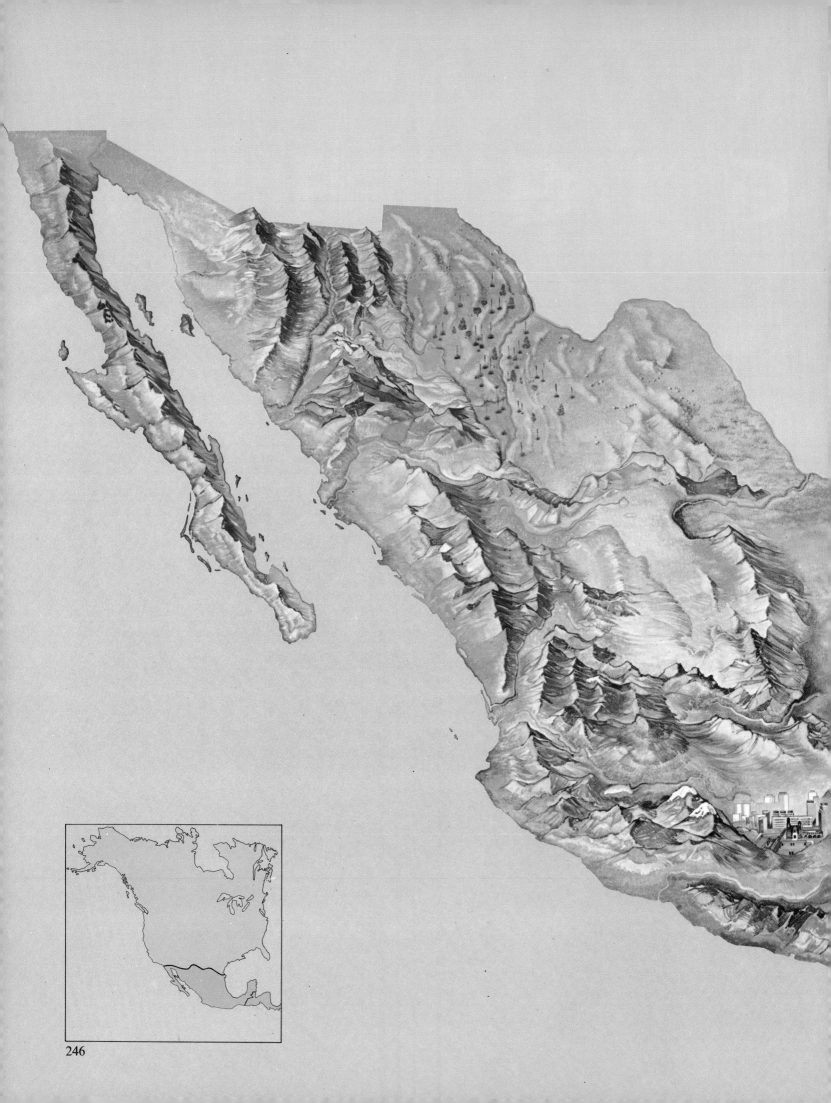

MEXICO

One of the most enjoyable things about Mexico is the way it overacts. Continually, and with utter shamelessness, it sets out to prove itself more Mexican than the unprepared visitor dares to expect. And not just for the tourists, either. The old Spanish-colonial hacienda with its sombreros, ornamental harnesses and high-pummeled saddles hanging in the patio is no more self-conscious than is the ponchoed peasant asleep in the shadow of an adobe wall with a cactus behind him. In the swampy rain forests of Tabasco and Chiapas, the jungle twines its tendrils around the temples of the Maya as sinuously and sensuously as ever it did at Angkor Wat. In the bars of Acapulco, the jet set leaves the "beautiful people" of Cannes and Portofino well behind. Every Mexican cliché is there, and multiplied. The only real surprise is that you should be so surprised to find it, after all, just as you had always been told it was.

Mexico is a country of extremes. First of all there is its size. Tijuana in the northwest is a good deal nearer to Alaska than it is to Chetumal in the southeast. Second, it possesses quite extraordinary variations of scenery and climate, all largely dependent on height rather than on latitude. Drive from Veracruz on the Gulf of Mexico up to the capital. The coastal strip is like being in a greenhouse, only hotter. And it is probably even damper, since in some areas the rainfall can be up to five times that of London or three times that of New York. Then the climb begins. Cocoa and banana give place to oak and elm. You can swim under the shadow of Mount Orizaba in a hotel pool into which a whole wheelbarrowload of gardenias is tipped every morning. A few miles farther bring you to the land of scrub and cactus. These in turn are supplanted by the high pine forests, which continue to the snowline. At last, gratefully, you cross the col by the two splendid volcanoes, Popocatepetl and Iztaccíhuatl, that guard the approaches to the capital, and descend into the giant crater where, at a modest seven thousand feet and under a protective blanket of smog, lies Mexico City.

Its altitude, it must be admitted, is the only modest thing about it. In all other respects Mexico City gives free rein to that other overriding national characteristic—exuberance. Mexican colors are brighter than those of other countries. Mexican music is louder (and so is Mexican traffic). Mexican food is hotter on the tongue. Mexican churches, of the old Spanish style known as Churrigueresque, are more sumptuously decorated. And modern Mexican architecture is among the most adventurous and exciting in the world.

Beneath it all there is an undercurrent of sadness. It is as though, after four and a half centuries, the Mexicans have still not managed to integrate the two great strands of their heritage, the Spanish and the Indian. The country has a long history of bloodshed, and even today you feel that violence is never far away. But the same could be said of Renaissance Italy, and the Mexicans, insecure as they may be, have just that kind of vitality. They like to make things hum. And, triumphantly, they succeed.

Reconstructed Aztec ruins and adjacent modern apartment buildings in the Plaza of Three Cultures, above, emphasize one of Mexico City's charms—the dramatic contrast between old and new architecture. The plaza is the historic focal point of Mexico City. Located here are colonial buildings dating mainly from the eighteenth century: the Palacio Nacional, the seat of federal government, which was the original home of Cortés and the viceregal residence; the Cathedral Metropolitana, which stands nearly on the spot of the main temple of the Aztecs; and the municipal palace, or city hall.

Colorfully decorated boats on Lake Oxchimilco, south of Mexico City, take visitors to see the famous floating gardens. The Aztecs created these gardens by constructing rafts on the lake, covering them with soil and then cultivating fruits, vegetables and flowers. The rafts gradually took root and became lush islands.

Early in the fourteenth century a harsh, warlike, friendless people drifted into the highlands of Central Mexico. They were guided only by a prophecy that somewhere on their wanderings they would find an eagle perched on a cactus with a snake in its talons, and on that spot they would make their home. In the year 1325 that prophecy was fulfilled on an island two miles out in a great mountain lake, over seven thousand feet above the sea. There it was that the Aztecs began to build their capital—the capital which is now known as Mexico City, but which they called Tenochtitlán.

Today, alas, the lake has dried up and the Aztec city is gone, destroyed by a second prophecy and a series of coincidences perhaps unparalleled in history. One day, according to this second legend, the god Quetzalcoatl, the Feathered Serpent, would return to earth in human shape, white-skinned and black-bearded and clothed from head to foot in black, to reestablish his rule. This would occur during a "one-reed year" and would bring much suffering and tribulation in its train.

According to the Aztec calendar a one-reed year fell only once in every fifty-two of our years. One of these rare occasions, however, was 1519, when the Spanish conquistador Hernán Cortés landed on the shores of Mexico. Cortés was noted for his ash-gray complexion, he had a thick black beard and on the day he disembarked he was dressed entirely in black. The Aztecs could not know the reason for this —that it happened to be Good Friday. For them it was simply a "nine-wind day," by another extraordinary coincidence, the one day in the year sacred to Quetzalcoatl. In any other circumstances their huge army would have easily defeated Cortés's four hundred Spaniards and, as was their normal custom, sacrificed them alive. But they dared not defy what the gods had so clearly ordained.

The mutual friendship which grew up between Cortés and the Aztec Emperor Montezuma ultimately failed to prevent the final destruction of Tenochtitlán. Apart from a corner of the great temple pyramid and a short stretch of aqueduct, there is nothing in the modern Mexico City that Montezuma would recognize. Sixth of the world's capitals by population, in terms of sheer decibels it surely yields to none. It is, too, a city of shattering contrasts—wealth and poverty, savagery and sophistication, drabness and flamboyance, sunshine and smog, moldering old Spanish palaces and huge, triumphant explosions of architectural joie de vivre. It claims the longest street in the world—a nightmarish chasm of concrete called the Avenida Insurgentes—as well as one of the noblest, the Paseo de la Reforma, the creation of Mexico's last Emperor, the ill-fated Maximilian of Hapsburg, who reigned for just three years before meeting a heroic death in 1867 before a Republican firing squad.

Maximilian lived in a palace which still stands on a high hill in the middle of the park known as Chapultepec. In his day it was open country, and although it has now been engulfed it remains the most wholly delightful place in the city. It is the place above all where the Mexicans can indulge their insatiable passion for color—in the huge clusters of struggling balloons that nearly lift their vendors off the ground, in the mountains of shocking-pink cotton candy and the boats loaded with laughing children that crowd the ornamental lake. In Chapultepec, too, stands the Mexican Museum of Anthropology (an architectural masterpiece that would be worth the visit even if it were devoid of contents), possessing a thrilling collection of pre-Hispanic works of art. To unite the two as brilliantly as it does is almost overwhelming.

But another corner of Mexico City provides a yet more extraordinary combination—the Plaza de las Tres Culturas, where, as its name implies, the pre-Hispanic, the colonial and the modern streams of Mexican culture all flow together. Here, within the framework of a huge new community development, stands the little Spanish church of Santiago and, a few yards away, what is left of the great Aztec pyramid. Between them, in what was once the marketplace of Tenochtitlán, a marble slab marks the spot where the Aztecs surrendered their Empire and adds the epilogue:

It was neither a victory nor a defeat.
It was the painful birth of the commingled
people that is the Mexico of today.

ARTIFACTS OF ANCIENT CIVILIZATIONS

The National Museum of Anthropology, which opened in 1964 in Mexico City, contains artifacts from almost all the ancient cultures of Mexico. Of particular interest are the rare, life-size funeral mask, center, found among the ruins of a very early civilization at Teotihuacán, and the Mayan sculpture of a human face emerging from the jaws of an animal found at Chichén Itzá, right. In about the sixth century A.D., the Mayans moved to the southeastern Yucatán, where their culture was later enriched by the Itzás, a Toltec tribe.

MUSEO NACIONAL DE ANTROPOLOGIA

Once it was the grandest, the most important and perhaps the most sacred city of the ancient Americas, a city in which nearly a hundred thousand people lived and worked, traded and worshiped. It was the richest, too, capable not only of conceiving huge monumental complexes on a scale never before seen on the whole continent, but of carrying them out in stone, all carved, stuccoed and painted until they glowed like rainbows in the sun. Then, in the seventh century A.D., the city fell victim to a disastrous fire from which it never recovered. When, in the early fourteenth century, the conquering Aztecs gazed at it for the first time, it was abandoned and overgrown. But the Aztecs knew greatness when

they saw it. Such a profusion of pyramids and temples could not, they felt, have been built by human hands. And so they called it, quite simply, the City of the Gods—Teotihuacán.

Still more today, now that it has been cleared and completely restored, it is the sheer size of the place that makes the first impact. Drive out the thirty miles from Mexico City, park your car by the little museum and walk, eyes firmly on the ground, the two-hundred-odd yards southward to the far end of the Street of the Dead. Then, and only then, turn around and look at what lies before you. Even in Imperial Rome itself—which flourished at much the same time, although it did not last as long—there can have been no more tremen-

dous thoroughfare. Sweeping up in an absolutely straight line for nearly two miles, through a succession of steps and staircases (no inconvenience to a civilization without wheels), and across a small ravine, it culminates in a huge plaza, surrounded by twelve similar stepped platforms, above which there rises, in fourteen million cubic feet of concentrated majesty, the Pyramid of the Moon.

Yet progress along the Calle de los Muertos is not a long dramatic crescendo, since it begins with what is already a magnificent architectural statement. The Spaniards called it the Citadel, but they were wrong. It is not a fortress, but a temple complex covering about seventeen acres and dedicated to one of the

The Pyramid of the Moon, left, is one of the most important and best-preserved monuments in Teotihuacán. Unlike the Pyramid of the Sun, this considerably smaller step pyramid, approximately 140 feet tall and measuring 426 feet by 511 feet at the base, has been left undisturbed.

The Temple of Quetzalcoatl, left, is the larger of the two imposing pyramids located in the Citadel within the ancient city of Teotihuacán. It was named in honor of the god of civilization, of the priesthood and of learning, who is represented with only minor variations in appearance and function in almost all Mexican Indian religions.

most powerful gods in the ancient Mexican pantheon, the Feathered Serpent Quetzalcoatl.

Of the temple itself little remains but the pyramidal base, on which, however, part of the original sculpture has, by a near miracle, been preserved. Repeatedly and threateningly, the god's snarling head, framed by a collar of plumes, juts out from the walls, his body coiling in low relief behind and around it, among the shells and snails that symbolize the waters of the earth. There is another portrait, too, which alternates with his and which probably, although no one seems quite sure, represents the rain god, Tlaloc. All are covered with a thin layer of stucco, to conceal irregularities in the stone, on which a few traces of

paint survive—red for the jaws, white for the fangs, green for the feathers of the quetzal bird. And it all reminds you, again, that the purpose of religious art in ancient Mexico was not to delight or to educate, it was to terrify.

About half a mile to the north stands the Pyramid of the Sun, the most massive of the pre-Hispanic pyramids and, with the Pyramid of the Moon, the model on which every other one was based. The temple that once topped it has long vanished. Much of what is seen today is the result of a lamentably inexpert reconstruction. Probably it looks very different from the way it must have appeared when it was first built, shortly before the time of Christ. But its alignment remains as true as

ever, its main facade foursquare to the precise point at which the sun disappears at the summer solstice. Climb it if you must. But keep some energy in reserve for the Pyramid of the Moon. For this is the climax of Teotihuacan.

Here, too, the temple is gone, the summit itself eroded by predators and by time. But it does not matter. Its preeminence is due not to its height but to its position, dominating the city, the focal point of the whole giant perspective. Beneath it extends its own broad plaza. Beyond it, some still undiscovered, some mercilessly laid bare, lie the remains of the once-mighty metropolis and the empty swath of the Street of the Dead, stretching away in desolation to the distant hills.

The Pyramid of the Sun, above, dominates the city of Teotihuacán. Made of large adobe bricks and layers of stone and earth, its five terraces, each sloping at a different angle, rise to a height of two hundred and ten feet. A staircase leads to its summit on the west side. This pyramid was built in one stage about A.D. 800.

The friezes of the Temple of Quetzalcoatl, carved between 0 and A.D. 300, contain 366 heads. These are identical for the six stages of the pyramid. Low-relief masks with staring eyes alternate with high-relief heads of terrifying serpents, which were originally painted in vivid colors and their eyes encrusted with obsidian.

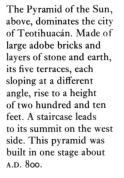

SPANISH SUPREMACY SECURED

A Spanish force led by Hernán Cortés was primarily responsible for the conquest of Aztec Mexico between 1519 and 1521. He landed at Tabasco and then moved up the coast, founding Veracruz. At Montezuma's invitation, he proceeded inland to the Aztec capital of Tenochtitlán. War eventually broke out, forcing Cortés to leave Tenochtitlán. He fled through the ruined city of Teotihuacán to the coast. At the end of 1521 he returned to attack the city, systematically destroying it and securing Spanish supremacy.

Mérida in the evening. Nowhere could be further in spirit from the surge and tumult of the capital than this sleepy, steamy little town. But then Mexico City lies a mile and a half above sea level. In Yucatán even a fifty-foot hill is a major landmark. Here, unquestionably, one is in the tropics; and Mérida, despite the occasional breeze from the Gulf of Mexico only a few miles away, remains very, very hot.

At last the people shake off their siesta, swing themselves out of their hammocks and stroll out for their evening constitutional in the Plaza Mayor. They are proud of their plaza, and rightly so, for it is the model of everything a central square should be.

On one side is the cathedral. Built in the sixteenth century soon after the arrival of the Spaniards, it has about it a sort of massive austerity, a monolithic quality that seems to hark back to something infinitely older, primitive and pagan. Next to the cathedral is what used to be the Archbishop's Palace, now secularized. And beyond that, occupying the center of the south side of the square, is the most remarkable building in Mérida and the oldest continuously inhabited private residence in the Americas—the house of the Montejos.

Francisco do Montejo, the Spanish conqueror of Yucatán, began work on it in 1549 and today it still looks exactly as he left it, with its great thundering facade of twin conquistadors trampling on the heads of howling Indians, flanked by hairy cavemen with clubs. It is, moreover, still occupied by his family, one of whom—a delightful figure, and speaking excellent English—likes nothing better than to show you around.

The principal rooms are monuments not of the violent sixteenth century, but of the prosperous nineteenth century when the family's ships, loaded to the gunwales with sisal, disposed of their cargoes at huge profits in France and returned with the heaviest and most expensive ballast they could find—Carrara marble, Sevres porcelain and Baccarat chandeliers. And yet, despite the trappings of European affluence, the spirit of Europe remains remote. The garden coils its sinuous tendrils through the dining-room windows until it threatens the ormolu clock; the termites have got at the escritoire; mosquito nets hang damply from the valances; and the mahogany bedsteads stand bereft of linen, for in Yucatán no sensible person dreams of sleeping in anything but a hammock. In this house there is even a hammock for the dog.

Outside in the square, strolling beneath the laurels or sitting on the S-shaped stone conversation seats that are such an inspired feature of Mérida outdoor life, the populace is revealed as belonging to a totally different race than that of the high plateau. The men are stocky and inclined to fat, their faces as smooth and hairless as their children's. The women, their long black plaits streaming down their backs, look cool and comfortable in their loose white cotton shifts, embroidered with those explosively colored flowers that would seem impossible anywhere else, but in Mexico are as common as daisies. Both sexes have one remarkable physical peculiarity: their heads are as round as beach balls. A thousand years ago their ancestors would seek to emphasize this defect by further compressing their babies' skulls between splints soon after birth. Much can happen in a millennium, and it is hard to believe that these gentle, easygoing people are the descendants of the Maya, the most prodigiously gifted of all the races of the ancient Americas.

So gifted were they that even today the vestiges of their civilization dominate the green and steaming peninsula of Yucatán. To the Spanish sailors of Hernán Cortés, who

Using its four fingers, and its tail as an extra limb, the spider monkey, left, moves swiftly through the topmost branches in the Yucatán's tropical forests. Spider monkeys, the most northerly of New World monkeys, sleep in bands of up to one hundred, but in daytime split into small groups of between two and eight to look for fruits and nuts.

Thick, wooded country and arid shrubby areas in the Yucatán are the favorite haunts of the jaguar—the largest of the New World cats. At night it preys upon such aquatic and terrestrial animals as tortoises, alligators, horses and peccaries. Occasionally the jaguar becomes a man-eater.

rounded the coast in 1519, the temples and watchtowers of Tulum—their first sight of the New World—seemed to rival, in size and splendor, their own city of Seville. Tulum is smaller now, and deserted but for the iridescent blue butterflies, seven inches across, that flap clumsily like windblown tissue between the encroaching creepers. But it still stands like a fortress guarding the gates of the Caribbean, while behind it in the jungled hinterland lurk the remains of perhaps eight thousand Maya monuments—palaces and pyramids, altars and temples and ballcourts, exquisitely engraved stelae standing alone deep in the rain forest—a few of them cleared of undergrowth and sanitized for tourists, but the huge majority visible only from the air and accessible only by helicopter.

And what monuments they are. The Mayas, like the other pre-Hispanic civilizations, had no wheel, no beasts of burden, no scales or weights or implements of iron. Nor, like the ancient Egyptians or Greeks, did they ever discover the principle of the arch. And yet, using only tools made of the same stone as that on which they worked and only such energy as their own bodies were able to provide, they raised up buildings more sophisticated in design than anything that had ever before been seen on the American continent. They decorated them in a style peculiarly theirs—with innumerable tiny blocks of intricately cut masonry set in such a way as to produce, as the day progresses, endlessly varying effects of chiaroscuro, harsh black shadows slanting and stabbing against the sunbaked stone.

And they had other talents, too. Their knowledge of astronomy and their mastery of mathematics enabled them to compute the transits of Venus with an error of less than one day in six thousand years. No primitive people has ever been so preoccupied with chronology. One inscription contains precise calculations relating to a period four hundred million years ago. Yet their own civilization was tragically short-lived. Arising in about the fourth century—just as, across the Atlantic, Imperial Rome was beginning to crumble after ruling more than one thousand years—it had virtually burned itself out by the time their Toltec neighbors occupied Chichén Itzá in the tenth century. In Europe, this period was known as the Dark Ages. How different things were in Yucatán!

Tulum, a Mayan walled city, is well situated on a cliff overlooking the Caribbean in the Yucatán peninsula, above. The principal buildings—the Castillo, Temple of the Frescoes and Temple of the Divine God—are clustered together near the sea. On the frescoes there are scenes of Mayan gods and female divinities performing rites.

The corbeled, or false, arch, like the one still standing amid the ruins at Labná in the Yucatán, above, is an outstanding feature of Mayan architecture. It was made by gradually bringing together two parallel piles of stones until they met at the top. The arch limited the width of a room, but gave a building massive solidity.

The Red Jaguar Throne, left, a fine example of Toltec sculpture, was found in 1937 in the pyramid of El Castillo in the Yucatán. Carved out of a single block of stone, its inlaid teeth are of white flint and its eyes of jade stones. There are about eighty pieces of green jade, which represent the jaguar's spots, all over its body.

THE GAZETTEER OF GREAT

Included in this gazetteer are almost a thousand of the great places, beautiful and historic, that make North America the magnificent continent. Each place is described briefly and is located on an adjacent map. The entries are grouped by states or regions which are shown on the map on page 255 and listed with their key numbers below.

PLACES

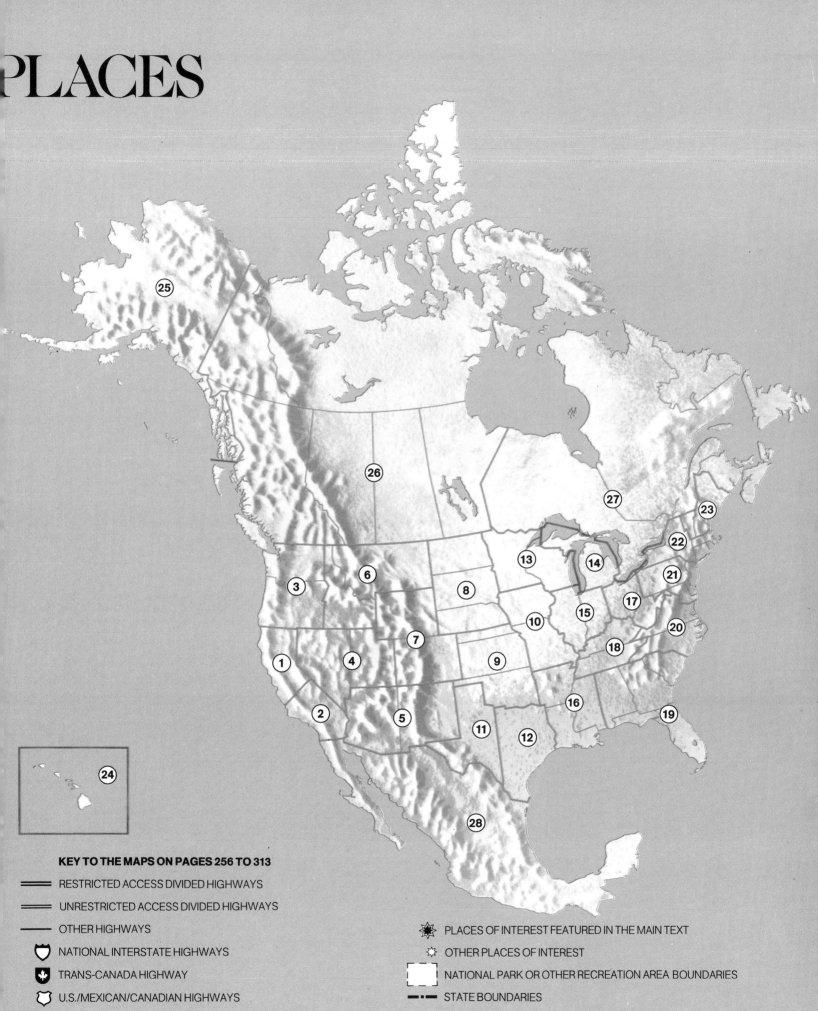

Northern California

Agate Beach, California
For two miles the sand beach curves gently north of Patrick's Point State Park. Winter storms bring driftwood ashore, and high tides and driving winds deposit semiprecious stones on the strand, where they are washed and polished by the ceaseless motion of sand and water.

Angel Island State Park, California
Deer reached this island from the mainland by swimming across Raccoon Strait. The island's exotic flowers were brought by ships' captains from as far away as the Canary Islands and the East Indies.

Año Nuevo Beach, California
The San Andreas Fault cuts beneath the seabed in the area. Earthquakes touched off landslides and exposed fossilized bone and shell specimens dating to the Pliocene Age, over a million years ago. Fossils may be found on the beach. The rocks and reefs offshore are the breeding grounds of seals and sea lions.

Burma Lava Flows, California
Soldiers and Modoc Indians once fought among the brittle rocks and weird cinder cones of the flows, which are in the Modoc National Forest.

Castle Crags State Park, California
Granite spires rise above a primitive backcountry. Polished by glaciers, the crags are made of a granitic material formed 225 million years ago far beneath the surface of the earth and then forced upward. Small animals and mountain lions live in the area.

Clear Lake State Park, California
Peaceful basket-weaving Pomo and Lileek Indians pulled their canoes ashore at Moki Beach. Traces of the Indians can still be seen in the forest that once was their hunting ground.

Coloma, California
James Marshall was setting up a sawmill for Captain John Sutter in 1848 when he discovered gold in the mill race. Thus the great California Gold Rush began. Marshall's cabin has been reconstructed as a state historic monument.

Devils Postpile National Monument, California
Symmetrical columns of basalt rising as high as sixty feet resemble a gigantic pipe organ. The blue-gray rock is the remnant of a lava flow, which was carved into its fantastic form by glaciers.

Donner Memorial State Park, California
Winter closed in quickly in the Sierras and trapped the Donner Party in 1846. Forty-two people died of starvation and exposure in the snows. Today, the site of the tragedy is a quiet forest of lodgepole and Jeffrey pine.

Farallon Islands, California
Desolate, windswept and lashed by waves, the Farallon Islands are a navigational aid to ships bound to and from San Francisco Bay, twenty-seven miles to the east. Sir Francis Drake and the crew of the *Golden Hind* were the first men to step ashore on the islands, which now shelter seabirds, including the rhinoceros auklet.

Fort Ross State Historic Park, California
From 1812 to 1841 the Russian–American Company operated a post and fort here from which hunters slaughtered seal and otter for the fur trade. The buildings, damaged in the 1906 earthquake, have been restored to their original condition. The trace of the Russian wagon road still can be followed to Bodega.

Grover Hot Springs State Park, California
Hot springs boil to the surface along the fault line left when the Sierra Nevada arose millions of years ago. Surface water trickles down into cracks in the earth's crust until it reaches hot rock, from which it rises steaming to form the springs.

Julia Pfeiffer Burns State Park, California
Lathrop Brown, a boyhood friend of Franklin Roosevelt, acquired this beautiful stretch of the Big Sur coastline and his widow presented it to the public as a memorial to pioneer ranchwoman Julia Pfeiffer Burns. Cypress-covered points thrust into the surf and a cool stream ripples down to the sea.

Lake Tahoe, California
Mark Twain acclaimed Lake Tahoe as "the fairest picture the whole earth affords." Sugar Pine Point remains much as it was when Twain saw it. Sugar and Jeffrey pines, quaking aspen, black cottonwood and mountain alder reach to the shore. Trails lead into the Desolation Valley Wilderness, where brown and rainbow trout swim in the tumbling brooks.

Lassen Volcanic National Park, California
The youngest rock in the United States was born on May 19, 1915, at about 9:30 P.M., when the fuming crater atop Mount Lassen roared and spewed the embryo rock to the surface, where it soon hardened. Around the sleeping volcano are bubbling thermal areas, seeping sulfurous gases, and a vast swath cut through the forest by a mudflow from the mountain.

Lava Beds National Monument, California
Collapsed lava tubes, cinder cones and craters make this a volcanic wonderland. There are lava caves, one of which is called the Catacombs. In Merrill Cave there is an ice river and a frozen waterfall.

MacKerricher State Park, California
A herd of harbor seals lives on the offshore rocks and the California gray whale spouts as it passes on its migration from Baja California to Alaska. Anemone, sea urchins, starfish and octopus inhabit the tidepools that dot the shoreline. The wind from the sea keeps the headlands clear of trees, but inland the park is a forest of Bishop and shore pine, tanbark oak and tall Douglas fir.

McArthur-Burney Falls Memorial State Park, California
The park preserves country that has changed little since the days when Hudson's Bay Company fur trappers passed through it along the old Pit River Route. The falls plunge in two equal flows of water over a 129-foot cliff into a pool of emerald water, and streams of frothing white water emerge out of the rocks.

Monterey, California
More than forty Spanish and Mexican period buildings remain in this city, which was the colonial capital of California. Cannery Row was given fame by the novels of John Steinbeck.

Mother Lode Country, California
When the lofty Sierra Nevada thrust up in a titanic upheaval of the earth's crust, molten magma spewed to the surface. Among the elements vaporized in the cataclysms was gold. Settling in crevices and porous openings in the rock, the precious ore awaited the great Gold Rush of 1849. Today, there is still gold to be found, much of it washed down into the placer sands of the rivers.

Mount Diablo State Park, California
Mount Diablo reaches west to the Golden Gate Bridge, north to snowcapped Lassen Peak and along four hundred miles of the Sierra Nevada crest.

Mount Shasta, California
There are five glaciers on beautiful cloud-wreathed Mount Shasta, which towers 14,162 feet high.

Mount Tamalpais State Park, California
When the fog rolls out to sea, the view from the peak of Mount Tamalpais is magnificent. The Pacific Ocean stretches to the west, and to the east there is the broad expanse of San Francisco Bay. The mountain is scarred by deep canyons filled with redwood groves, but there are also grassy ridges and wind-blasted groves of the rare Sargent cypress.

Muir Woods National Monument, California
Redwoods in the grove reach up to 364 feet in height and measure over forty feet around. The giant trees are as much as two thousand years old.

Patrick's Point State Park, California
The Yurok Indians camped in the summers on Abalone Point. Nearby Penn Creek furnished them with fresh water and the woods were rich with game. A broad sand beach lies at the foot of high, steep cliffs. Sea stacks stand offshore amid the surging waves.

Pfeiffer Big Sur State Park, California
Mountains shoulder from the sea in one of the continent's most dramatic meeting places of land and sea.

Pinnacles National Monument, California
Bandits once hid in this volcanic formation. Eruptions thirty million years ago shaped the Pinnacles, which rise to more than one thousand feet. The thick brushy plant cover is a fine example of chaparral.

Point Lobos, California
Gnarled cypress and moss-laden pine grow on the shores of what Robert Louis Stevenson described as "the greatest meeting of land and water in the world." (See page 50.)

Redwood National Park, California
Scenic drives and trails lead visitors through the magnificent groves of giant trees in this recently created national park. (See page 52.)

Russian Gulch State Park, California
A tunnel about two hundred feet long, cut by the sea, collapsed to form the Devil's Punch Bowl on the headland. Wild flowers border the bowl, where waters surge under the influence of the distant sea. In the Pygmy Forest are tiny Mendocino cypresses, trees which usually grow to heights of fifty feet. Russian Gulch Creek Canyon winds inland from the ocean.

Sacramento River Delta, California
The delta formed by the Sacramento and San Joaquin rivers is a forty-mile by twenty-five-mile rectangle of sloughs, marshes and old river channels—literally a thousand miles of tangled waterways. Most of the islands are named for early settlers. Brannan Island, for example, was named for the Mormon colonist Samuel Brannan.

Salt Point State Park, California
Pomo Indians wandered through the area, leaving campsites that still can be identified. Tidal pools along the rocky shoreline are miniscule ecological systems, each to itself, fragile and fascinating. Sheer sandstone cliffs plunge down into the sea at Salt Point and Gerstle Cove. An occasional bear or mountain lion may be seen in the forests.

San Francisco, California
Most cosmopolitan of West Coast cities, San Francisco rises upon its seven hills in misty beauty. (See page 54.)

Sutter's Fort, California
The restored fort established by the Swiss Sutter is now in the capital city of Sacramento, which grew up around it.

Van Damme State Park, California
Lush Fern Canyon is covered with millions of ferns of many different species, ranging from the western sword fern to the five finger, lady, licorice, bird's foot and the rare gold-back fern.

Yosemite National Park, California
Giant trees, meadows carpeted with wild flowers, glaciated peaks and torrential waterfalls are among the many natural wonders of Yosemite. (See page 44.)

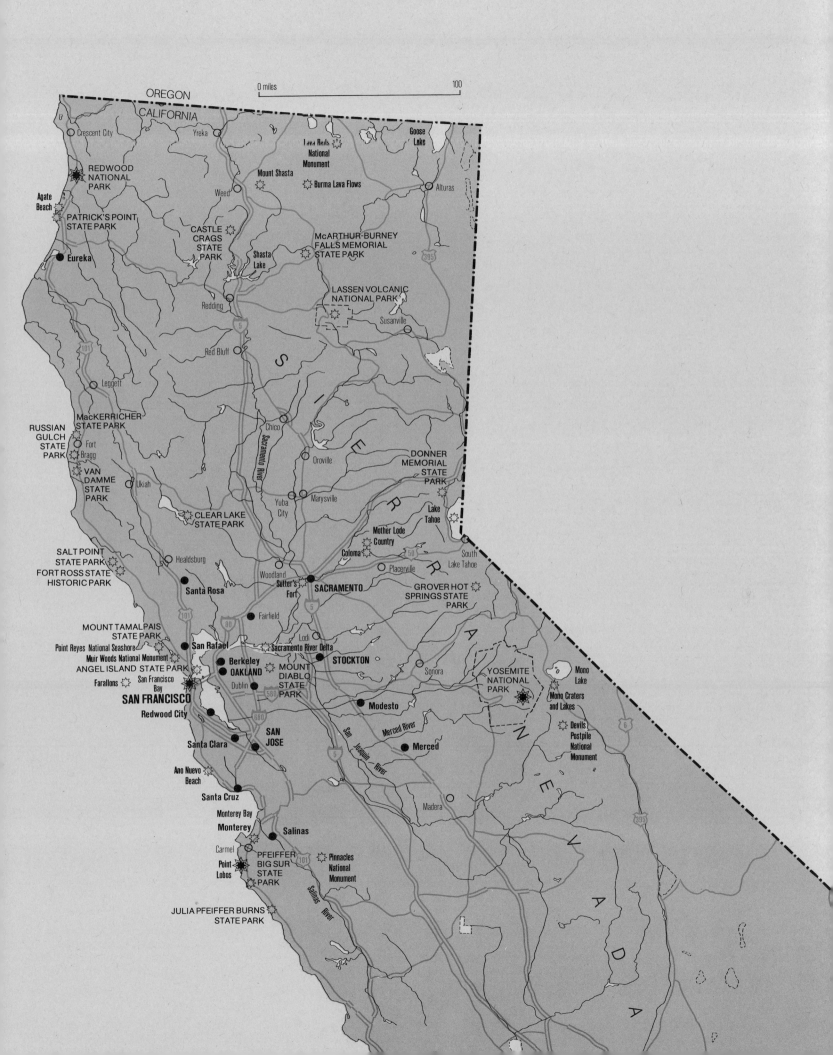

OREGON
CALIFORNIA

0 miles   100

Crescent City   Yreka   Goose Lake

REDWOOD
NATIONAL
PARK   Lava Beds
                                        National
Agate   Monument
Beach   Mount Shasta
PATRICK'S POINT   Burma Lava Flows   Alturas
STATE PARK   Weed

                CASTLE
                CRAGS   McARTHUR-BURNEY
                STATE   FALLS MEMORIAL
Eureka   PARK   Shasta STATE PARK
                        Lake

                        Redding   LASSEN VOLCANIC
                                         NATIONAL PARK

                                                 Susanville

                Red Bluff

                        S
        Leggett   I

                        E
MacKERRICHER   Chico
STATE PARK   R   DONNER
RUSSIAN   MEMORIAL
GULCH   Fort   Oroville   STATE
STATE   Bragg   R   PARK
PARK
VAN   Lake
DAMME   Ukiah   Yuba   Marysville Tahoe
STATE   City   R
PARK
                CLEAR LAKE
                STATE PARK   Mother Lode
                                        Country   South
SALT POINT   Healdsburg   R   Coloma   Placerville Lake Tahoe
STATE PARK   R
FORT ROSS STATE   Woodland Sutter's   GROVER HOT
HISTORIC PARK   Santa Rosa Fort SACRAMENTO SPRINGS STATE
                                                     A   PARK
                        Fairfield
MOUNT TAMALPAIS   Lodi
STATE PARK   San Rafael   Sacramento River Delta
Point Reyes National Seashore   N
Muir Woods National Monument   Berkeley STOCKTON
ANGEL ISLAND STATE PARK OAKLAND   MOUNT   Sonora YOSEMITE   Mono
Farallons   San Francisco   Dublin   DIABLO   NATIONAL   Lake
                Bay   STATE   PARK
SAN FRANCISCO   PARK   E   Mono Craters
                Redwood City   and Lakes
                                Modesto   Devils
                SAN   San   N   Postpile
Santa Clara   JOSE   Joaquin Merced River   National
                               River   Monument
Ano Nuevo   Merced   E
Beach
                                        Madera
Santa Cruz   V
Monterey Bay
Monterey Salinas   A
Carmel   Pinnacles
Point   PFEIFFER   National   D
Lobos   BIG SUR   Monument
        STATE   A
        PARK   Salinas
                River
JULIA PFEIFFER BURNS
STATE PARK

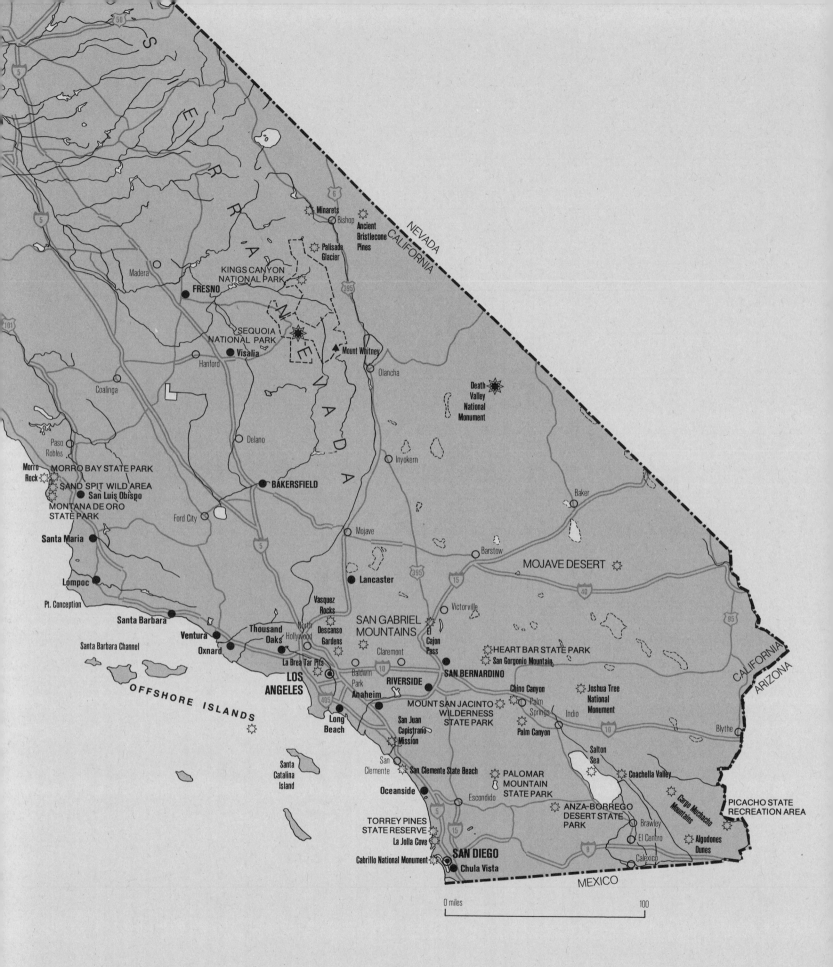

Minarets

Bishop

Ancient
Bristlecone
Pines

Palisade
Glacier

KINGS CANYON
NATIONAL PARK

Madera

FRESNO

SEQUOIA
NATIONAL PARK

Hanford

Visalia

Mount Whitney

Olancha

Death
Valley
National
Monument

Coalinga

Delano

Inyokern

Paso
Robles

Morro
Rock

MORRO BAY STATE PARK

SAND SPIT WILD AREA

San Luis Obispo

MONTANA DE ORO
STATE PARK

Ford City

BAKERSFIELD

Baker

Santa Maria

Mojave

Barstow

MOJAVE DESERT

Lompoc

Lancaster

Pt. Conception

Vasquez
Rocks

Victorville

Santa Barbara

North
Hollywood

Thousand
Oaks

Descanso
Gardens

SAN GABRIEL
MOUNTAINS

El
Cajon
Pass

HEART BAR STATE PARK

San Gorgonio Mountain

Ventura

Oxnard

La Brea Tar Pits

Baldwin
Park

Claremont

SAN BERNARDINO

Santa Barbara Channel

LOS
ANGELES

RIVERSIDE

Chino Canyon

Joshua Tree
National
Monument

OFFSHORE ISLANDS

Anaheim

MOUNT SAN JACINTO
WILDERNESS
STATE PARK

Palm
Springs

Indio

Blythe

Long
Beach

San Juan
Capistrano
Mission

Palm Canyon

Santa
Catalina
Island

San
Clemente

San Clemente State Beach

Salton
Sea

Coachella Valley

Oceanside

PALOMAR
MOUNTAIN
STATE PARK

Escondido

ANZA-BORREGO
DESERT STATE
PARK

Cargo Muchacho
Mountains

PICACHO STATE
RECREATION AREA

Brawley

TORREY PINES
STATE RESERVE

El Centro

Algodones
Dunes

La Jolla Cove

Cabrillo National Monument

SAN DIEGO

Chula Vista

Calexico

MEXICO

NEVADA
CALIFORNIA

CALIFORNIA
ARIZONA

0 miles   100

258

Algodones Dunes, California
East of Holtville, the dunes are a mysterious world of shifting sands, crossed by the weathered boards of the Old Plank Road finished in 1917, but abandoned in the late 1920s. The dunes, which pioneer wagon trails crossed with great trepidation, have been used by Hollywood moviemakers as the location for Sahara Desert epics.

Ancient Bristlecone Pines, California
Judged to be the oldest-known living things, many of these pines were already ancient when Christ was born. The Methuselah pine, for example, is more than forty-six thousand years old. Fire, sand, rock and ice blown by the wind have carved the trees into fantastic shapes. Situated high on the rocky slopes of the White Mountains, the bristlecone forest shelters mountain lions and bighorn sheep.

Anza-Borrego Desert State Park, California
In 1774, Captain Juan Bautista de Anza scouted a trail through the vastness and desolation of the hot lowlands and rugged peaks that are now part of the half-million-acre park. Butterfield Overland Mail stagecoaches later traversed the wastes, and the sites of stations still may be seen.

Cabrillo National Monument, California
Juan Rodríguez Cabrillo, the first explorer to view the west coast of the United States, came ashore at Ballast Point. From December through February, gray whales up to fifty feet long migrate past the point. Spouts ten to fifteen feet high shooting up just beyond the kelp beds tell of their passing.

Chino Canyon, California
Indians camped in this canyon, where hot sulfur and cold springs gush to the surface. The wildlife includes bighorn sheep.

Cargo Muchacho Mountains, California
From these mountains near Winterhaven, old-timers used to bring out gold by the muleload. It was said that even children took out all that they could carry, and so the mountains were named "Cargo Muchacho," or "Boy Load."

Coachella Valley, California
African date palms were introduced into the valley in 1903. The date palm growers gather male pollen in March and April and dust it on the female flowers. Three months after pollination, the bunches of fruits are tied in paper to protect them against rain and birds.

Death Valley National Monument, California
The lowest place in the United States, a point within Death Valley is 282 feet below sea level. (See page 46.)

Descanso Gardens, California
Once part of the Spanish Land Grant from Governor Pedro Fages to Jose Maria Verdugo, the gardens are a floral wonderland that blooms the year round beneath the Southern California sun. There are some one hundred thousand camellias representing more than six hundred varieties.

El Cajon Pass, California
For the early Spanish explorers the difficult El Cajon Pass was the only way over the great barrier of the San Bernardino Mountains. Pioneers cut a trail through the pass, and later a railroad was put through it.

Heart Bar State Park, California
Two Mormon settlers built their cabins on a fork of the Santa Ana River, only to discover it was the wrong fork. They moved away, and their cabins were used by cowhands working cattle in the mountains during the summer. The park takes its name from the brand, a heart over a bar, used on the cattle. A magnificent meadow is the center of the wildlife community.

Kings Canyon National Park, California
Adjoining Sequoia National Park, this mountainous wilderness includes two deep canyons carved by the Kings and Kaweah rivers. Some of the highest peaks in the High Sierra are in the park. In General Grant Cove is the enormous General Grant tree, which has a girth of more than one hundred feet.

Joshua Tree National Monument, California
Not actually trees, Joshua trees are giant desert lilies, which grow up to forty feet in height and forty feet in circumference. This area of half a million acres abounds not only in Joshua trees but also in palm oases and an amazing variety of cacti. Rare Washingtonia palms grow in Twentynine Palms and Lost Palms canyons. After a rare rain the desert is carpeted by miniscule wild flowers.

La Brea Tar Pits, California
Located on Wilshire Boulevard in the heart of Los Angeles, the pits contain the bones of prehistoric beasts trapped in the Ice Age.

La Jolla Cove, California
A submarine canyon twists from the cove's shallow waters out into the sea for seventeen miles, where its floor is thirty-six hundred feet below the surface. Close to the shore is a sunken Indian settlement.

Minarets, California
Towering mountain peaks rise around trout-filled lakes in this spectacular high country, which is part of the Inyo National Forest.

Mojave Desert, California
Legends of lost gold mines and hidden Indian treasures still lure adventurers into the parched desert, which covers one-third of Southern California. Ghost towns and dry waterfalls give the desert a spectral quality.

Mono Craters and Lakes, California
Within this eerie terrain in the Inyo National Forest are twenty craters resembling gigantic heaps of ash. To walk the shore of Mono Lake is to discover a moonscape of delicate tufa formations on an old lake bed.

Montana de Oro State Park, California
Jagged cliffs and headlands reach out of the sea for one and one-half miles, but there are also quiet coves and sandy beaches. Behind the beach is an ancient wave-cut terrace uplifted long ago above the action of the surf.

Morro Bay State Park, California
Opening out into the bay where Los Oros Creek has its mouth is one of the largest areas of natural marshland on the California coast. More than two hundred and fifty species of birds live in the marshes.

Morro Rock, California
Father Crespi mentioned the rock at the entrance of Morro Bay in his journal of 1769. It is a plug-dome volcanic outcropping.

Mount San Jacinto Wilderness State Park, California
Granite peaks, subalpine forests and fern-bordered upland meadows make this 13,521-acre wilderness park one of the most exciting of primitive high countries south of the Sierra Nevada. No motor vehicles are allowed in the backcountry, but there are hiking and riding trails. Mount San Jacinto, at 10,804 feet the highest peak in the San Jacinto Range, reaches over the landscape.

Offshore Islands, California
From the remote Channel Islands lying to the northwest, to the Anacapa Islands and better-known Santa Catalina Island, the Offshore Islands support a variety of sea and birdlife. San Miguel and Santa Barbara islands are home to both seals and sea elephants, and Santa Cruz Island is inhabited by wild boar.

Palisade Glacier, California
The southernmost large glacier in the United States is surrounded by the snow-capped granite peaks of the High Sierras.

Palm Canyon, California
Some five thousand Washingtonia palms grow in the canyon not far from the resort town of Palm Springs. The age of the palms ranges from mere sprouts to a thousand years old. The palms reach a height of seventy feet and wear skirts of dead leaves.

Palomar Mountain State Park, California
Thick forests and rolling mountain meadows lie on the west side of the mountain named Palomar, Place of the Pigeons, by the Spanish. Thousands of band-tailed pigeons nested on the slopes. Pine and fir were cut on the mountain to be used in building Mission San Luis Rey.

Picacho State Recreation Area, California
Picacho Peak, a plug-dome volcanic outcropping, dominates the barren Colorado Desert. Baked dry, the forbidding land still supports such hardy plants as beavertail cactus and ocotillo. Backwater lakes along the Colorado River are lined with Carrizo cane and marsh tule. Tamarisk trees have invaded the flats near the river.

Salton Sea, California
This inland salt lake lies 232 feet below sea level. Although the sea is one of the world's largest landlocked bodies of salt water, it is only a fraction of its ancient extent. Over the millennia, the scorching desert sun reduced the sea to white salt flats. Then in 1905 Colorado River floodwaters broke into the basin for two years and created today's lake in the desert.

San Clemente State Beach, California
Brushy slopes and ravines leading down to the beach shelter gray fox, ground squirrel and opossum. Californian sea lions bask on offshore rocks.

San Gabriel Mountains, California
In the 1850s the bandit Tiburcio Vasquez hid among the rocks that bear his name. Since then the site has been used in the making of dozens of Western movies. The Devil's Punchbowl is a vast crevice in the earth shaped by earthquakes.

San Gorgonio Mountain, California
The 11,502-foot-high mountain is the highest in Southern California. The 34,718-acre San Gorgonio Wilderness surrounds Old Greyback, as the mountain is affectionately called.

Sand Spit Wild Area, California
The sand spit that separates Morro Bay from the ocean has dunes reaching as high as eighty-five feet above the waves. Reached by boat, the spit is an unspoiled world of sea and sand.

San Juan Capistrano Mission, California
Swallows do indeed leave and, at the same time each year, return to this most famous of California missions. The great earthquake of 1812 broke the beautiful stone cruciform. It is one of North America's most poignant ruins.

Sequoia National Park, California
Giant sequoias, some over thirty-five hundred years old, are the largest of the world's trees. (See page 48.)

Torrey Pines State Reserve, California
Pinus torreyana, a relic of the Ice Age, once covered much of Southern California. Today, the tree grows only in the reserve and on Santa Rosa Island, a hundred and seventy-five miles to the northwest. High, broken cliffs indented with ravines remain as in pioneer days. The trees cling to the crumbling sandstone. The Los Penasquitos Lagoon Natural Preserve is at the north end of the reserve.

Vasquez Rocks, California
The rocks in Antelope Valley made a fantastic setting for a bandit's lair during early California days.

Oregon and Washington

Columbia River Gorge, Oregon and Washington
Thirty million years of geological history are portrayed in the great gorge which cuts through the Cascades. Waterfalls and rivers tumble down the small canyons along both rims. (See page 68.)

Crater Lake National Park, Oregon
A lake of incomparable peace cradled in an extinct volcano. (See page 60.)

Deschutes Canyon, Oregon
The eroded escarpments of the canyon look down on the Deschutes River, which flows through a land of sage, juniper and cedar.

Dry Falls State Park, Washington
Glacial meltwater roared over the dry falls ten thousand years ago with a volume a hundred times that of Niagara Falls. Today, the four-hundred-foot sheer rock wall impassively overlooks a dry bed.

Eagle Cap Wilderness, Oregon
Streams flow down from Eagle Cap Mountain toward all the points of the compass. The 220,416-acre Eagle Cap Wilderness includes the Wallowa Mountains. Fifty lakes are hidden in basins on the precipitous slopes. The Wallowa gray-crowned rosy finches, found nowhere else in the world, nest close to snowfields, rocks and in meadow patches.

Fort Clatsop, Oregon
The fort where the explorers Lewis and Clark wintered during the winter of 1805-6 has been rebuilt.

Fort Vancouver, Washington
This fort, founded in 1825 by the Hudson's Bay Company, was the center of all trading activity, as well as the political, military, social and cultural center for the Pacific Northwest. It has been reconstructed.

Ginkgo Petrified Forest, Washington
The largest-known fossil forest lies along the Columbia River. The petrified wood of the strange ginkgo tree takes on blue, crimson, yellow, green and carnelian colors.

Grand Coulee Dam, Washington
One of the largest creations of mankind, the huge dam is four thousand feet long, five hundred feet wide at its base and five hundred feet high.

Granite Falls, Washington
The North Fork of Granite Creek has cut a stairstep channel down through the solid rock in Kaniksu National Forest.

Hells Canyon–Seven Devils Scenic Area, Oregon
According to legend, an Indian brave hunting in this wilderness became lost and met not one, but seven devils. Since then the area has been called Seven Devils. In reality, the devils are weird rock formations. The one-hundred-and-thirty-thousand-acre scenic area lies astride twenty-six miles of the Snake River Canyon. Jagged side canyons and terraced ridges break grassy plateaus.

Hood Canal, Washington
Formed by nature, the canal is a fjord-like arm of water which stretches along almost the entire length of the Olympic Mountain Range. There are sandy beaches between the water's edge and the magnificent rhododendron copses.

Hurricane Ridge, Washington
Mile-high Hurricane Ridge offers a splendid view of the Olympic Range and its glaciers and crags.

Lake Chelan, Washington
Lake Chelan stretches for fifty-five miles from the rolling foothills into the Cascade Mountains.

Lake of the Woods, Oregon
Considered one of the Northwest's most idyllic lakes, it nestles in a setting of pines and firs at the foot of Mount McLaughlin in the Cascades.

Lava Cast Forest Geological Area, Oregon
Lava flowing through the forest several thousand years ago covered trees and fallen logs. As the trees burned out, they left behind casts in the hardened stone. Even the imprint of the tree bark and limbs can be seen today in the now solidified rock.

Lava River Caves State Park, Oregon
Only a few thousand years ago, a huge lava flow boiled down from Lava Butte to form these caves. Lava River Tunnel, the conduit through which the molten rock gushed, is now a mile-long corridor through solid rock. An earthquake broke an opening in the tunnel, and it is possible to descend to its floor and walk through a cool subterranean world where hot lava once roared.

Leadbetter Point State Park, Washington
Dunes, sand packed so hard a car can drive on it, Pacific surf and razor clams, the West Coast delicacy, are features of the park.

Long Beach Peninsula, Washington
One of the world's longest beaches, it stretches uninterrupted for twenty-eight miles.

Malheur Cave, Oregon
The cave contains a mysterious underground lake.

McKenzie Pass, Oregon
The pass is unique in North America for its remarkable views of recent volcanic activity and variety of volcanic forms. Broken lava flows cover seventy-five square miles. Cinder cones, land islands and glaciers can all be seen from the pass. American astronauts have hiked on the lava of the area to accustom themselves to what might be expected on the surface of the moon.

McKenzie River, Oregon
Adventurers float down the river in dories to obtain close-up views of the bears, deer, eagles and ospreys that live along the banks.

Mount Adams Wilderness Area, Washington
The lower slopes of the mountain are rich with trees, shrubs and herbaceous ground cover. On the west side of the mountain there are plants native to moist slopes, and on the east side there are those that grow well on arid slopes.

Mount Baker National Forest, Washington
Captain George Vancouver, the English explorer, named the mountain for his lieutenant, who was first in his crew to spot the peak. In the forest there are glaciers and hundreds of glacial lakes.

Mount Hood, Oregon
Snow mantles the high slopes of this noble 11,235-foot-high peak. The pioneer Barlow Road girdles its flanks.

Mount Rainier National Park, Washington
Mount Rainier's snow-clad peak, 14,410 feet high, is a symbol of the beauty of the Cascades. (See page 58.)

Mount Spokane State Park, Washington
The mountain, the highest in eastern Washington, provides a spectacular view.

North Cascades Wilderness, Washington
Rushing streams, trout-filled lakes and snowcapped peaks characterize this awesome high country. (See page 66.)

Okanogan National Forest, Washington
Liberty Bell Mountain guards the entrance to Washington Pass, a gateway to this jumble of forests and peaks that is Paul Bunyan country.

Olympic National Park, Washington
Elks bugle and, with the crash of antlers, the bulls charge together to determine which is the king of the herd. This forest of towering Douglas fir, western hemlock, Sitka spruce and western red cedar is home to the elk.

Olympic Rain Forest, Washington
Ferns and luxuriant growths adorn the seaward side of the Olympic Mountains. (See page 64.)

Oregon Caves National Monument, Oregon
Elijah Davidson and his dog, pursuing a bear, ventured into an opening in the rocks. Holding up his pine splinter torch, Davidson discovered the sparkling stalactites of the cave, which Joaquin Miller, the poet of the Sierra, later called "The Marble Halls of Oregon." Although called caves, there is actually only one great cave, which contains four different floors and a number of galleries.

Oregon Coast, Oregon
The forest sweeps down to the sea, where dunes, rocky outcroppings and tide pools speak of a primeval world. (See page 62.)

Pacific Crest National Scenic Trail, Oregon and Washington
For two thousand three hundred and fifty miles the trail runs along the mountain ranges from Canada to Mexico. The Oregon section of the trail begins at the Columbia River and follows the skyline of the Cascades on paths first used by game and the Indians. Backpackers take two months to hike this uplands stretch in the two states, where deer are common and in late summer huckleberries are succulent.

Rocky Butte, Oregon
The exposed Clarno and John Day geological formations are a major source of Central Oregon gemstones encompassing a wide variety of the quartz family. Thundereggs may also be found. These are ball-shaped rocks, ranging from less than an inch to several feet in diameter. The exterior is rough, but the interior may be filled with exquisite crystals, agate, jasper or calcite.

Rogue River, Oregon
From Gold Beach, jet boats take the mail and passengers up the Rogue River through the rushing riffles and Copper Canyon. In the wilderness along the banks, deer, elks and bears may be seen. Eagles soar overhead. The names of Rogue points, such as Wake Up Riley Creek and Nail Keg Riffle have a savor of their own.

San Juan Islands, Washington
These jewel-like islands are separated by winding channels. There are hidden coves and lonely beaches. Mount Constitution, the highest point in the 172 islands, is on Orcas Island. Historic sites of English and American camps on San Juan Island, the second largest island in Puget Sound, are associated with the Oregon Territory boundary disputes.

Seattle Center, Washington
The Space Needle towers over the Seattle Center in the cultural center, where the Seattle World's Fair was held in 1962. The Monorail carries passengers between downtown and the Seattle Center.

Silver Falls State Park, Oregon
North and South forks of Silver Creek have sliced deep canyons into the lava rock. The park abounds in waterfalls. Five are on North Silver Creek, one each on its tributaries, Winter Creek and Hullt Creek, and five below the junction of the two forks. The highest is 178-foot South Falls. There are cave-like formations in basaltic rock.

Waldo Lake, Oregon
Glaciers scooped out Waldo Lake six miles long; snowcapped peaks are reflected in its waters.

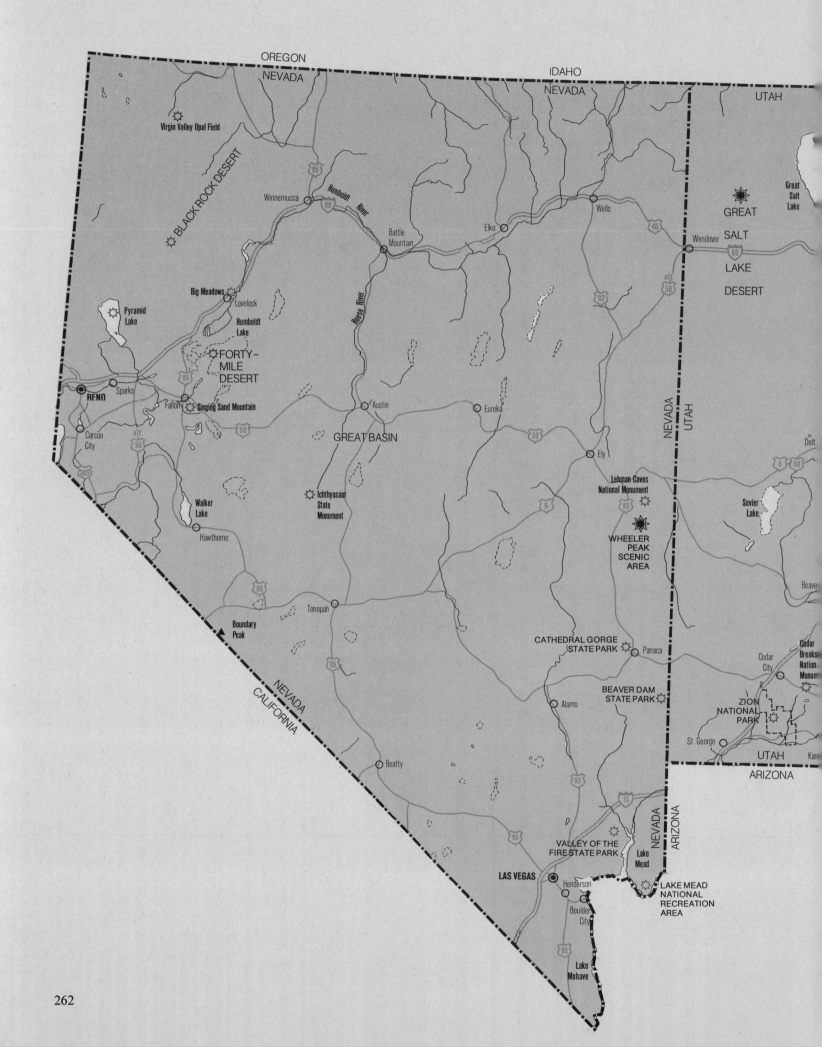

OREGON
NEVADA

IDAHO
NEVADA

UTAH

Virgin Valley Opal Field

GREAT

BLACK ROCK DESERT

Winnemucca

Humboldt River

Wells

Great
Salt
Lake

SALT

Battle
Mountain

Elko

LAKE

Wendover

Big Meadows

Lovelock

Pyramid
Lake

Humboldt
Lake

Reese River

DESERT

FORTY-
MILE
DESERT

RENO   Sparks

Singing Sand Mountain

Carson
City

Fallon

Austin

Eureka

GREAT BASIN

NEVADA   UTAH

Ely

Delt

Walker
Lake

Ichthyosaur
State
Monument

Lehman Caves
National Monument

Sevier
Lake

Hawthorne

WHEELER
PEAK
SCENIC
AREA

Beave

Boundary
Peak

Tonopah

CATHEDRAL GORGE
STATE PARK

Panaca

Cedar
City

Cedar
Breaks
Nation
Monum

Alamo

BEAVER DAM
STATE PARK

NEVADA
CALIFORNIA

ZION
NATIONAL
PARK

St. George

UTAH

Kan

ARIZONA

Beatty

NEVADA   ARIZONA

VALLEY OF THE
FIRE STATE PARK

LAS VEGAS   Henderson

Lake
Mead

LAKE MEAD
NATIONAL
RECREATION
AREA

Boulder
City

Lake
Mohave

262

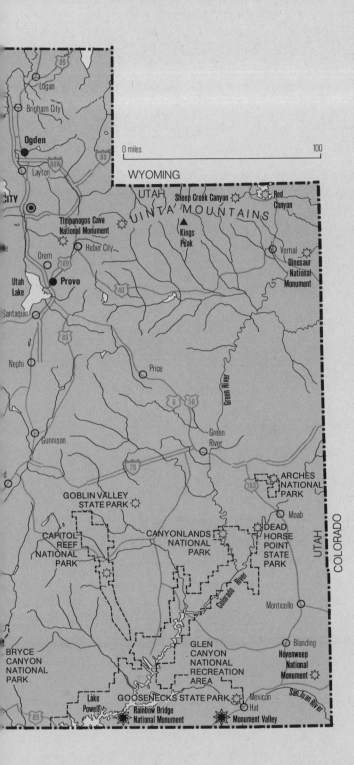

Canyonlands National Park, Utah
It is a hard place to build a road, and Canyonlands, larger than Connecticut, Delaware and Rhode Island put together, did not have its first paved road until 1955. Red-rock gorges and canyons wind dizzily for miles only to end in thousand-foot cliffs. The Green and Colorado rivers twist through the park and placid reaches of water give way to churning rapids.

Capitol Reef National Park, Utah
Erosion has taken millions of years to mold the mammoth sandstone castles, gorges and rock contortions. Butch Cassidy, the desert outlaw, hid in this tumble of strange rock shapes, and Cassidy Arch bears his name.

Cathedral Gorge State Park, Nevada
Rock walls have been carved by nature into spires, domes, caves and lonely sentinels.

Cedar Breaks National Monument, Utah
Massive walls and weird natural statuary strike fire to the imagination.

Dead Horse Point State Park, Utah
Mighty rocks rise two thousand feet above the looping Colorado River.

Dinosaur National Monument, Utah
Prehistoric dinosaur fossils have been unearthed in what was once the vegetation-choked shoreline of a vast inland sea.

Forty-Mile Desert, Nevada
Considered by wagon trains as the toughest part of the journey westward, the desert still contains remains of unfortunate gold-seekers.

Goblin Valley State Park, Utah
Sandstone gnomes and gargoyles lurk in a hidden valley in this state park.

Goosenecks State Park, Utah
The San Juan River meanders below a twelve-thousand-foot-high overlook.

Great Salt Lake Desert, Utah
Mirages dance over this enormous salt wasteland. (See page 82.)

Hovenweep National Monument, Utah
Pueblo Indian dwellings, built nine hundred years ago and mysteriously abandoned, are protected in the monument.

Ichthyosaur State Monument, Nevada
The bones of long extinct ichthyosaurs are numerous in this remote canyon.

Lake Mead National Recreation Area, Nevada
The recreation area, covering more than three thousand square miles in Nevada and Arizona, includes two huge man-made lakes formed by the Hoover and Davis dams from Colorado River waters. Hoover Dam, 726 feet high, is among the highest in the world. Grand Wash Cliffs mark the western end of the high plateaus through which the Colorado carved the Grand Canyon.

Lehman Caves National Monument, Nevada
Ab Lehman, a pioneer homesteader, discovered these caves in the 1870s. The date "1878" found in a side chamber near the entrance may be his scrawl. The Indians used the caves as a burial chamber centuries before he happened upon them. Drip limestone forms rare speleothems called pallettes and floor pools of water have built terraced miniature dams. (See page 86.)

Monument Valley, Utah
The backdrop for many Western films and the valley home of the Navajo Indians lies astride the Utah–Arizona border. (See page 84.)

Pyramid Lake, Nevada
Pyramid is a remnant of Lake Lahontan, which once covered what is now a vast sweep of desert. Broad mud plains called playas that are flooded during rare rains also remain from the ancient lake.

Rainbow Bridge National Monument, Utah
The United States Capitol could easily fit beneath this huge, natural stone bridge. (See page 79.)

Red Canyon, Utah
The Green River helped to form this spectacular canyon in the Ashley National Forest.

Sheep Creek Canyon, Utah
This canyon in the Ashley National Forest has been designated as a geological area by the U.S. Forest Service. A short tour of the canyon takes the visitor through millions of years of geologic development.

Singing Sand Mountain, Nevada
Towering dunes create a Sahara setting.

Timpanogos Cave National Monument, Utah
Translucent crystals encrust the cavern walls beneath Mount Timpanogos.

Uinta Mountains, Utah
The Uintas are the highest east–west mountain uplift in North America.

Valley of Fire State Park, Nevada
Brilliant red sandstone changes hue with the changing light. Elephants, dragons and beehives of natural rock conceal Indian petroglyphs.

Virgin Valley Opal Field, Nevada
Fiery black opals are often found in a field two miles wide and ten miles long.

Wheeler Peak Scenic Area, Nevada
The mountain rises through five vegetative life zones, from the broiling desert of sagebrush and cactus to the alpine zone above the timberline, where moss and lichens flourish. (See page 86.)

Zion National Park, Utah
Two-thousand-foot-high walls of red sandstone tower over the deep canyons and broad mesas.

Arches National Park, Utah
Cowboys looked at these salmon-colored sandstone arches and gave them such descriptive names as "Schoolmarm's Bloomers" and "Dark Angel." There are more natural arches here than in any other region in the world. Awesome Park Avenue is a narrow corridor with vertical sandstone walls rising up to three hundred feet and Fiery Furnace is an intricate maze.

Beaver Dam State Park, Nevada
Lofty cliffs and pine forests give this mountainous park a beautiful setting.

Big Meadows, Nevada
A verdant oasis which afforded wagon trains respite from the cruel desert.

Black Rock Desert, Nevada
The Applegate Road of the pioneers can still be traced through this blistered landscape.

Bryce Canyon National Park, Utah
Thousands of spires, pinnacles and turrets have been cut into fourteen natural amphitheaters along the edge of the Paunsaugunt Plateau. (See page 78.)

Bandelier National Monument, New Mexico
A wilderness of forested mesas, cliffs and plunging gorges surrounds the four-hundred-room Tyuonyi Indian pueblo in Frijoles Canyon.

Capulin Mountain National Monument, New Mexico
A volcanic cone rises in near-perfect symmetry. A two-mile road spirals up to the crater's rim.

Carlsbad Caverns National Park, New Mexico
Beautiful limestone formations in vast underground rooms below the Guadalupe Mountains. (See page 76.)

El Morro National Monument, New Mexico
Travelers dating back to a Spanish party of 1605 carved notice of their passing on Inscription Rock, a sandstone monolith, which also bears Indian petroglyphs.

Fort Apache Indian Reservation, Arizona
North America's largest stands of ponderosa cover the White Mountains, the home of Apache Indians.

Gila Cliff Dwellings, New Mexico
Cliff dwellers lived among the sandstone bluffs that rise from the desert. At Scorpion Campground a "Trail into the Past" shows how the plants of the area were used by the ancients.

Gila Wilderness, New Mexico
The Gila Wilderness was the first wilderness area set aside in the United States.

Grand Canyon National Park, Arizona
Unsurpassed in its natural grandeur, the Grand Canyon is the world's mightiest gorge. (See page 72.)

House Rock Valley, Arizona
A herd of buffalo roams the valley.

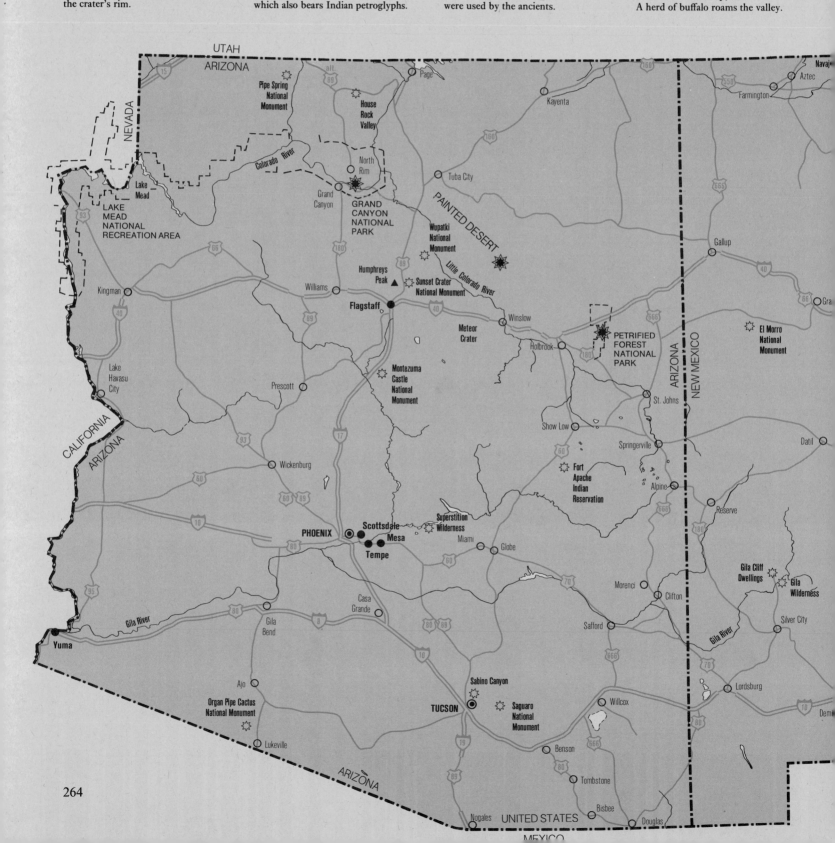

Arizona and New Mexico

Montezuma Castle National Monument, Arizona
Across the streams the long-vanished Pueblo Indians planted corn, beans, squash and cotton in irrigated fields. Here, men and women gathered firewood and dark-eyed children played. The cliff ruin's windows are empty where women once looked down for the return of the hunters. The Indians made meal of the catclaw pods and soap from the gray-thorn berries that grow along Sycamore Trail.

Organ Pipe Cactus National Monument, Arizona
Organ-pipe and senita cacti grow in this 516-square-mile portion of the Arizona–Sonora Desert, which is a land of stark mountains, sweeping plains, rocky canyons, flats and dry washes.

Painted Desert, Arizona
Banded rocks carved by wind and rain stand in a landscape of fantastic form and color. (See page 80.)

Petrified Forest National Park, Arizona
Giant logs of agate lie on the ground amid broken fragments and chips in the monument's six separate "forests." (See page 81.)

Pipe Spring National Monument, Arizona
Nestled at the base of the vermilion cliffs, this well-preserved Mormon fort was settled by the followers of Brigham Young.

Rio Grande Gorge, New Mexico
A sixty-mile-long cleft in the high country of northern New Mexico cuts through volcanic outpourings of long ago.

Sabino Canyon, Arizona
The Sabino Canyon Nature Trail leads up this deep cut in the Santa Catalina Mountains. Creosote bushes and saguaro cacti predominate in this land of dry arroyos and rocky hills.

Saguaro National Monument, Arizona
The giant saguaros live to be two hundred years old and grow up to thirty-five feet tall. The cacti bloom in late May.

Sante Fe, New Mexico
Capital of New Mexico since 1609, the city still reflects the Spanish and Indian ways of life.

Santa Fe Trail, New Mexico
The historic route of traders to Santa Fe still can be followed for hundreds of miles across the ranch country of eastern New Mexico.

Sunset Crater National Monument, Arizona
In 1064, a shattering explosion sent volcanic ash raining down on the homes and farms of the Indians who lived here. When the eruption ended, a new cinder cone a thousand feet high had grown. Jagged lava flows spread out at its base, and black volcanic ash covered hundreds of square miles. Today, the crater and its environs look much as they did then.

Superstition Wilderness, Arizona
Rugged desert dotted by giant saguaro cacti and mountains covered with ponderosa pine make up this wilderness in the Tonto National Forest. Angel Springs is an oasis of mountain laurel and meadows protected by sheer rock walls. Night Hawk Springs was one of the strongholds of Geronimo, the Apache chief.

Taos, New Mexico
Northernmost of the inhabited Indian pueblos, Taos is a multistoried dwelling that still keeps to its ancient ways. (See page 88.)

Wheeler Peak, New Mexico
One of the highest peaks in the state is 13,161 feet tall.

White Sands National Monument, New Mexico
Shifting gypsum sands overwhelm plants and roads alike. Sometimes the sands yield back such things as an ancient Spanish *carreta*, or a suit of armor.

Wupatki National Monument, Arizona
Wupatki Ruin rises from a sandstone spur at the base of a black lava mesa overlooking the Painted Desert. The red sandstone prehistoric pueblos were occupied from about A.D. 1100 to A.D. 1225 by farming Indians. There are more than eight hundred Indian ruins in the monument.

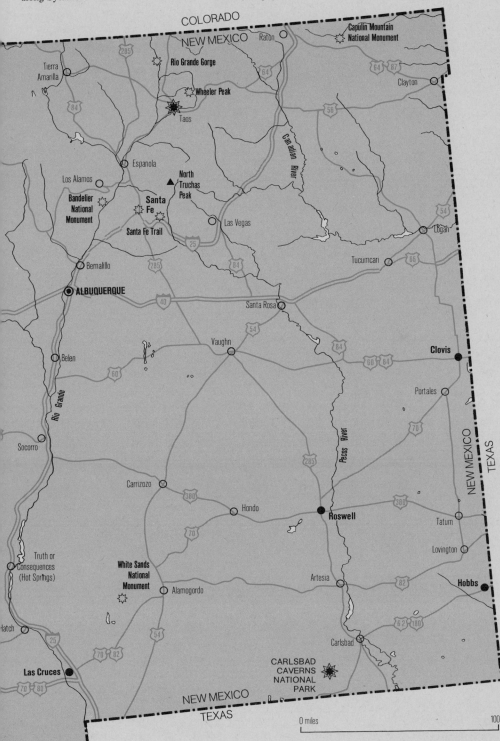

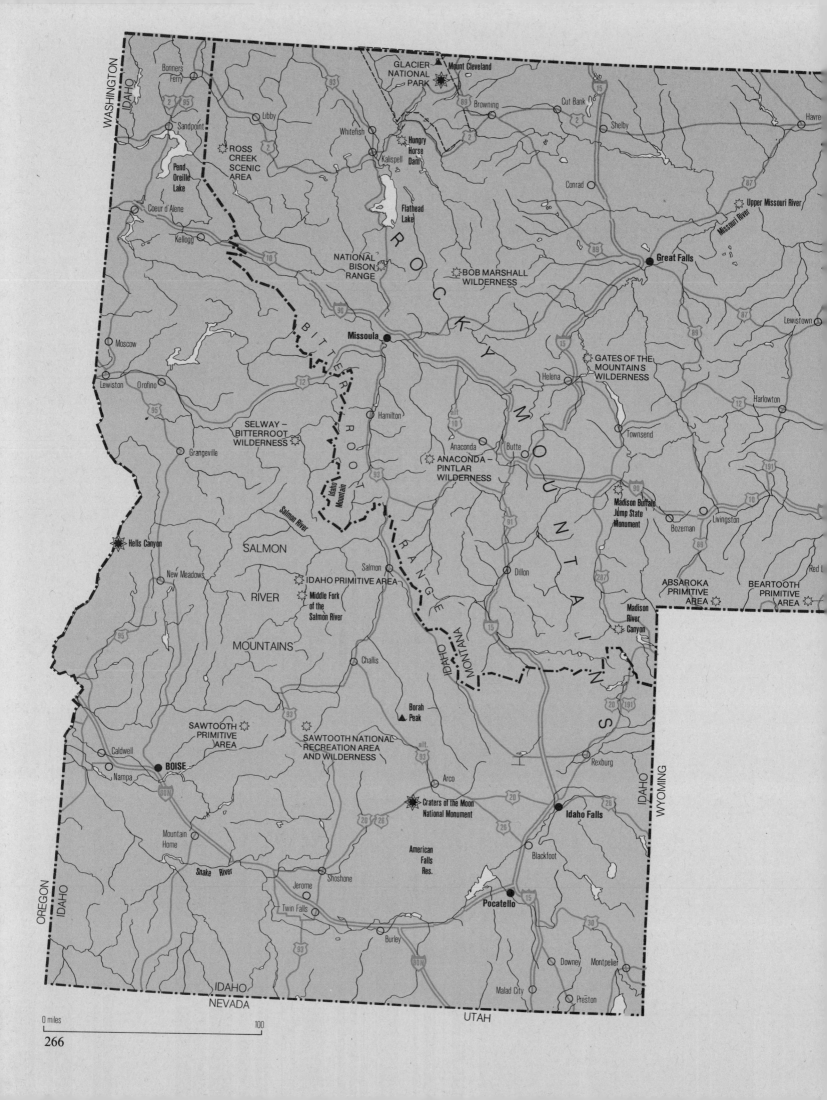

Idaho and Montana

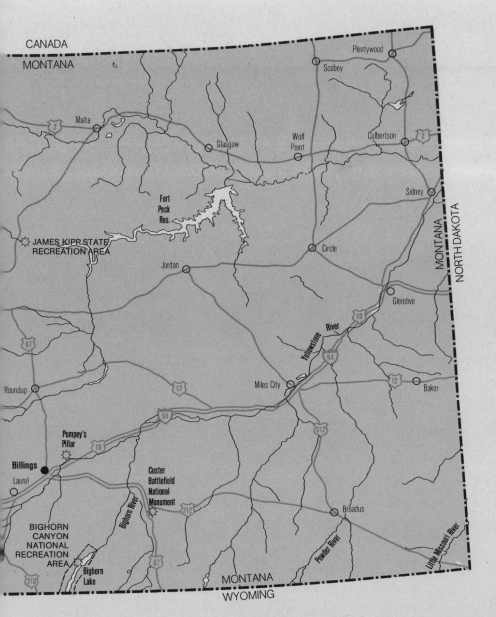

peded buffalo herds over this cliff to obtain a supply of meat.

Madison River Canyon, Montana
On the night of August 17, 1959, about two hundred campers were sleeping peacefully on the shores of the Madison River in the Gallatin National Forest. At twenty minutes before midnight, the earth shook in a gigantic quake that spilled great slides of rock and mud down the slopes, burying campers. The fault scarps and battered terrain still speak of that night of terror.

Middle Fork of the Salmon River, Idaho
For a hundred miles the river rushes through cataracts among crags and wooded canyons inhabited by bighorn sheep and Rocky Mountain goats.

National Bison Range, Montana
About five hundred of the shaggy beasts range the nineteen thousand acres of grassland and timber in the Flathead Valley. Whitetail and mule deer, elk, bighorn sheep and pronghorns share the range.

Pompey's Pillar, Montana
Named by William Clark of the Lewis and Clark expedition for Sacajawea's papoose, Pomp, the tower of rock is a landmark of the Yellowstone River.

Ross Creek Scenic Area, Montana
Giant cedars tower over a rockslide zone in the Kootenai National Forest.

Sawtooth National Recreation Area and Wilderness, Idaho
Alexander Ross of the Hudson's Bay Company came into the country in search of beaver in 1824, and prospectors scoured it for minerals. It is the land of tall peaks, some one hundred and fifty-seven thousand acres of mountains ringed by summer clouds, of rare bighorn sheep, mountain goats and stately elk.

Sawtooth Primitive Area, Idaho
The Shoshone Indians hunted among the glacial lakes and white-water streams that rush among the towering pinnacles of this two-hundred-thousand-acre wilderness domain, which is part of the Sawtooth National Forest. Salmon, which come eight hundred miles from the Pacific to spawn, ascend the Salmon River.

Selway–Bitterroot Wilderness, Montana
There are timbered mountains and sparkling lakes in the largest of the wilderness areas in the lower forty-eight states. Blodgett Canyon, walled by sheer granite spires and massive cliffs, is called the Yosemite of the Bitterroots.

Upper Missouri River, Montana
White cliffs and such rock formations as The Hole in the Wall overlook the river's swirling waters. Old Indian campsites and landmarks of the Lewis and Clark expedition can still be seen. Along cliff rims and wooded bottomland bighorn sheep, deer and antelope live as they did when the first explorers traveled in boats up the river.

Absaroka Primitive Area, Montana
Buffalo and moose roam this sixty-four-thousand-acre primitive area in the Gallatin National Forest. From high points there are breathtaking views of the surrounding peaks.

Anaconda–Pintlar Wilderness, Montana
Virgin forests and snowcapped peaks make up this wilderness through which the Continental Divide, the backbone of North America, passes. Here, streams cascade to bright blue and emerald-green lakes, mountain goats spring about the rocks on the high peaks and glacial cirques and alpine larch grows in dense stands.

Beartooth Primitive Area, Montana
In the two hundred and thirty thousand acres of Montana's most rugged mountain country is the highest mountain in the state, 12,799-foot Granite Peak. Grasshoppers preserved for centuries in the ice can be seen in the glaciers in this high country, where alpine meadows begin above the timberline.

Bighorn Canyon National Recreation Area, Montana
In the heart of the Crow Indian Reservation, Yellowtail Dam backs up the Bighorn River into a steep-walled canyon hundreds of feet deep that cuts through two mountain ranges. The canyon is a geologist's delight of easily read anticlines. Cliffs half a mile high loom over the water.

Bob Marshall Wilderness, Montana
Bold Mountains rise over dark canyons. Grizzly, elk, moose and deer live in this nine-hundred-and-fifty-thousand-acre wilderness. Mountain goats clamber about the Chinese Wall, a spectacular limestone cliff. The Cambrian limestone also contains the fossils of extinct animals a billion years old.

Craters of the Moon National Monument, Idaho
Lava fields studded with cinder cones resemble the craters of the moon. (See page 104.)

Custer Battlefield National Monument, Montana
Sioux and Cheyenne warriors annihilated General George Custer's command in the valley of the Little Bighorn River.

Gates of the Mountains Wilderness, Montana
Lewis and Clark passed among the limestone cliffs and weathered formations that they noted were the gates to the mountains ahead. Brawling streams cut narrow gorges in the limestone. Phlox cover the rocks with an emerald green, and wild flowers bloom in the mountain meadows. The 28,562-acre wilderness is on the Missouri River.

Glacier National Park, Montana
One million acres of rugged mountain splendor. (See page 100.)

Hells Canyon, Idaho
This is the deepest river trench in North America, fifty-five thousand feet deep on the average; it reaches seventy-nine thousand feet in depth. (See page 102.)

Hungry Horse Dam, Montana
One of the highest and largest concrete dams in the world, Hungry Horse backs up the South Fork of the Flathead River to form a reservoir thirty-four miles long.

Idaho Primitive Area, Idaho
The jagged Sawtooth Mountains reach skyward among crystalline lakes and alpine meadows.

James Kipp State Recreation Area, Montana
Blue herons nest in this remote area on the upper Missouri River, where the Black Bluffs overlook the stream.

Madison Buffalo Jump State Monument, Montana
Two thousand years ago, Indians stam-

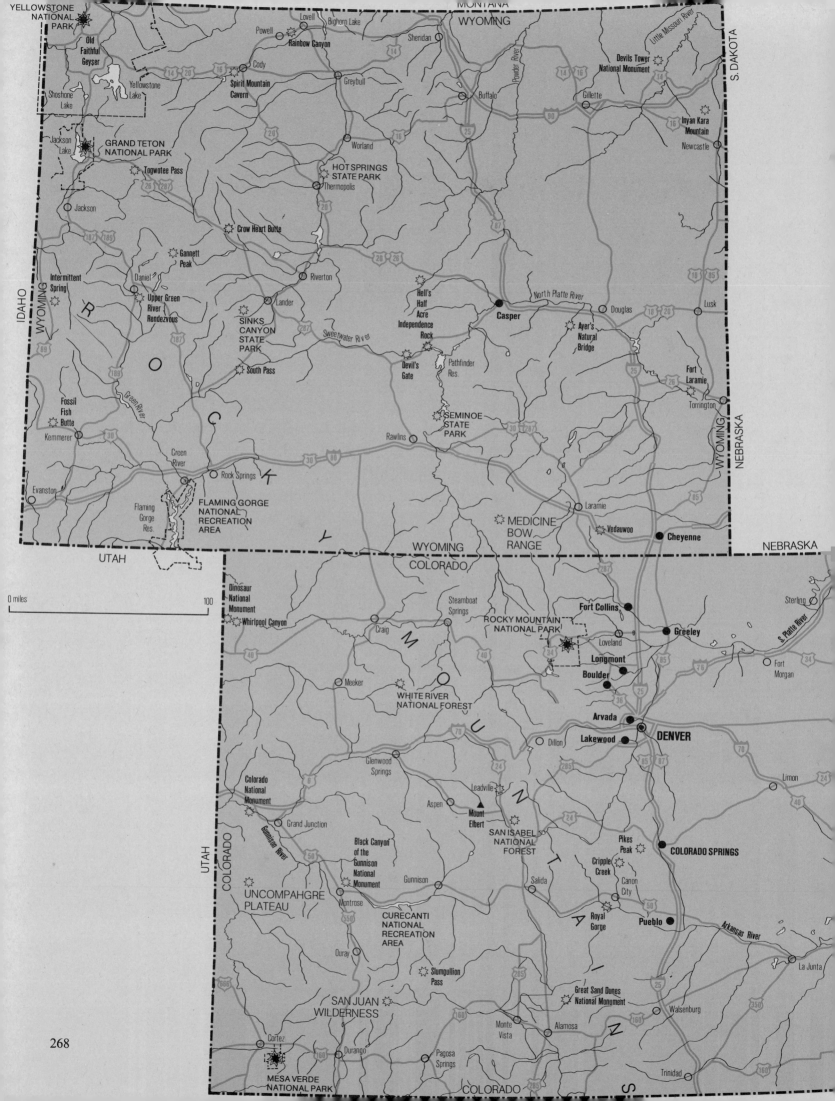

YELLOWSTONE
NATIONAL PARK

☆ Old Faithful Geyser

Shoshone Lake

Yellowstone Lake

MONTANA

WYOMING

Powell ○ Lovell
○ Rainbow Canyon

Bighorn Lake

Sheridan ○

Little Missouri River

S. DAKOTA

Cody ○

Spirit Mountain Cavern

Greybull ○

Buffalo ○

Devils Tower National Monument ☆

Gillette ○

14 16

☆ Inyan Kara Mountain

Newcastle ○

Jackson Lake ★ GRAND TETON NATIONAL PARK

☆ Togwotee Pass

○ Jackson

IDAHO   WYOMING

☆ Intermittent Spring

R

☆ Upper Green River Rendezvous

Daniel ○

Fossil Fish Butte ☆

Kemmerer ○

Evanston ○

Worland ○

20

HOT SPRINGS STATE PARK
Thermopolis ○

☆ Crow Heart Butte

☆ Gannett Peak

O

Riverton ○

Lander ○

SINKS CANYON STATE PARK

287   Sweetwater River

☆ South Pass

C

Green River

Green River

Rock Springs ○

FLAMING GORGE NATIONAL RECREATION AREA

Flaming Gorge Res.

K

UTAH

0 miles   100

WYOMING

North Platte River

☆ Hell's Half Acre
Independence Rock

● Casper

Douglas ○

Lusk ○

☆ Ayer's Natural Bridge

Devil's Gate ☆

Pathfinder Res.

☆ Fort Laramie

Torrington ○

☆ Seminoe State Park

Rawlins ○

30   80

WYOMING
COLORADO

Laramie ○

☆ MEDICINE BOW RANGE

☆ Vedauwoo

● Cheyenne

WYOMING   NEBRASKA

NEBRASKA

Dinosaur National Monument

☆ Whirlpool Canyon

Craig ○

M

Meeker ○

Steamboat Springs ○

ROCKY MOUNTAIN NATIONAL PARK

WHITE RIVER NATIONAL FOREST

O

Sterling ○

Fort Collins ●

Greeley ●

Loveland ○

Longmont ●

Boulder ●

Fort Morgan ○

U

Colorado National Monument

Grand Junction ○

Gunnison River

Glenwood Springs ○

Dillon ○

Leadville ☆

Aspen ○

▲ Mount Elbert

SAN ISABEL NATIONAL FOREST

N

Arvada ●
Lakewood ● DENVER

Limon ○

T

285

Pikes Peak ☆

COLORADO SPRINGS ●

Black Canyon of the Gunnison National Monument

UNCOMPAHGRE PLATEAU

Montrose ○

CURECANTI NATIONAL RECREATION AREA

Gunnison ○

Salida ○

☆ Cripple Creek

Canon City ○

☆ Royal Gorge

50

A

Pueblo ●

Arkansas River

La Junta ○

Ouray ○

666

☆ Slumgullion Pass

SAN JUAN WILDERNESS ☆

Cortez ○

★ MESA VERDE NATIONAL PARK

Durango ○

Pagosa Springs ○

160

Monte Vista ○

Alamosa ○

☆ Great Sand Dunes National Monument

Walsenburg ○

Z

350

Trinidad ○

COLORADO

S

UTAH   COLORADO

268

Ayer's Natural Bridge, Wyoming
Pioneers detoured from the Oregon Trail to camp beneath this magnificent rock formation that spans La Prele Creek.

Black Canyon of the Gunnison National Monument, Colorado
The minarets and shadowy crevasses of the canyon walls are only thirteen hundred feet apart at the narrowest place. The canyon is 2,425 feet deep.

Colorado National Monument, Colorado
Carved by time, this eighteen-thousand-acre natural amphitheater, walled in deep-red sandstone, overlooks a wide valley.

Cripple Creek, Colorado
Bob Womack, a cowboy, discovered a gold mine near the creek. He sold his claim for five hundred dollars and drank it up. Others took four hundred million dollars in gold out of the bare hills. Theodore Roosevelt, riding the Gold Camp Road to Cripple Creek, said, "The scenery bankrupts the English language."

Crow Heart Butte, Wyoming
At a war dance after a victory over the Crow Indians at the butte, Shoshone Chief Washakie displayed the heart of a vanquished Crow on his lance.

Devil's Gate, Wyoming
The Sweetwater River has cut a deep gorge in the Rattlesnake Mountains through which the Oregon Trail passed.

Devils Tower National Monument, Wyoming
A spectacular volcanic neck rises, like a giant tree stump, twelve hundred and eighty feet above the Belle Fourche River. This fifty-million-year-old tower was the first national monument in the United States.

Dinosaur National Monument, Colorado
Cliffs of pale Weber sandstone rise over the riffles, rapids and calms of the Yampa River. The Canyon of Lodore on the Green River lies at the foot of red precipices. The area is the source of dinosaur fossils.

Fort Laramie, Wyoming
Twenty-one original structures remain of the most important outpost in the winning of the American West.

Fossil Fish Butte, Wyoming
Fossilized ammonites, seashells, snails, turtles and palm fronds can be found in the butte, proving that Wyoming's climate was once lush and balmy.

Gannett Peak, Wyoming
The highest mountain in the state, Gannett Peak towers 13,804 feet above a wilderness of lakes and glaciers.

Grand Teton National Park, Wyoming
The upthrust mountains rise above the valley in an exultation of rock, forest and tundra, 310,350 acres of which make up the national park. (See page 98.)

Great Sand Dunes National Monument, Colorado
The highest piled inland sand dunes in the United States parallel the base of the snow-capped Sangre de Cristo Mountains.

Hell's Half Acre, Wyoming
Rock formations have been eroded into canyons which are deep and eerie.

Hot Springs State Park, Wyoming
From one of the world's largest hot springs 18,600,000 gallons of mineral water flow every twenty-four hours at a temperature of 135 degrees Fahrenheit. The water has created striking terraces and mineral cones.

Independence Rock, Wyoming
An isolated igneous rock rises dramatically from the valley floor. Travelers on the Oregon Trail often carved their names in the rock, which was named for a Fourth of July celebration held by fur trappers.

Intermittent Spring, Wyoming
This lovely spring ebbs and flows at regular intervals of about twenty minutes.

Inyan Kara Mountain, Wyoming
General George Custer climbed Inyan Kara on an expedition and carved his name at the top of the mountain which was a symbol of the West to the early settlers.

Leadville, Colorado
The Tabor Opera House, the Vendome Hotel, the Augusta Tabor Mansion and Baby Doe cabin are some of the early structures that survive in this city, which was once the world's greatest silver camp.

Medicine Bow Range, Wyoming
The mountains capped with the snow of winter blizzards wind their way through the Medicine Bow National Forest.

Mesa Verde National Park, Colorado
The fascinating stone cliff houses built by a mysterious people a thousand years ago. (See page 106.)

Pikes Peak, Colorado
"Pikes Peak or bust," proclaimed the drivers of the Gold Rush caravans as they headed across the High Plains toward this lofty peak, which its discoverer, Zebulon Pike, said could never be climbed. In 1893, Katherine Lee Bates climbed the mountain and from its summit wrote the words to "America the Beautiful."

Rainbow Canyon, Wyoming
Colorful badlands that seem to have been created by a sorcerer's wand.

Rocky Mountain National Park, Colorado
This silent world of the high mountains is the rooftop of the continent. (See page 92.)

Royal Gorge, Colorado
The narrow canyon was cut through solid granite by the Arkansas River. The world's highest suspension bridge hangs over the deep gorge.

San Isabel National Forest, Colorado
The wooded wet mountains cradle valleys of flowers. It was along Hardscrabble Creek that the last of the storied mountain men held their final fur rendezvous.

San Juan Wilderness, Colorado
The Needle Mountains range up against the Continental Divide. The Rio Grande has its source in this high country.

Seminoe State Park, Wyoming
Pronghorn antelope abound here. Giant dunes of white sand and miles of sagebrush surround a reservoir.

Sinks Canyon State Park, Wyoming
A river swirls into a cave in the canyon wall only to emerge again as a spring pool.

Slumgullion Pass, Colorado
The pass over the Continental Divide is a rocky defile overhung with fluted escarpments.

South Pass, Wyoming
The Oregon Trail crossed the Continental Divide through this pass. Ruts of the trail still can be followed.

Spirit Mountain Cavern, Wyoming
This natural crystal cave is one of the most beautiful in the American West.

Togwotee Pass, Wyoming
Rocks form a mighty palisade on either side of this high mountain pass.

Uncompahgre Plateau, Colorado
Its corrugated sides rise to nine thousand feet, and steep canyons, sparkling waterfalls and quiet lakes lie in the forest.

Upper Green River Rendezvous, Wyoming
Here, in days of the mountain men, trappers met supply caravans from St. Louis, and it was here that they bartered, gambled, drank and fought.

Vedauwoo, Wyoming
The Indians believed that these strange rocks were created by playful spirits.

Whirlpool Canyon, Colorado
The Green River swings around the base of twenty-five-hundred-foot Harper's Corner and thunders into the canyon, where the walls squeeze in tight and malevolent.

White River National Forest, Colorado
A giant tableland ninety-five hundred to twelve thousand feet above sea level rises like a granite lost world above the foothills. The Devil's Causeway is a narrow basalt ridge over a thousand feet high. Trappers Lake is famed for its high beauty.

Yellowstone National Park, Wyoming
The world's first national park contains both superb mountain scenery and spectacular thermal activity. (See page 94.)

269

North Dakota, South Dakota and Northern Nebraska

Agate Fossil Beds National Monument, Nebraska
One of the world's richest finds of fossils offers mute testimony to the richness of animal life in the area during the continent's early days.

Ash Hollow State Historical Park, Nebraska
At Windlass Hill nineteenth-century travelers across the Great Plains winched their wagons down the steep grade into the valley below. The ruts carved into the prairie by the Conestoga wagons of yesterday still may be seen.

Badlands National Monument, South Dakota
A landscape of fantasy and beauty that covers more than two hundred and forty-three thousand acres. (See page 114.)

Bear Butte, South Dakota
Sacred to the Sioux and Cheyenne, Bear Butte rises eleven hundred feet over the prairies. From atop the butte, which was once a landmark for fur traders, cavalry and gold seekers, there is a fine view of the Black Hills and of the encircling plains.

Big Stone Lake, South Dakota
A glacial moraine rises beside the lake. A U.S. cavalry expedition of four thousand men and two hundred and twenty-five mule-drawn wagons once camped beside the lake, which is the lowest spot in South Dakota.

Black Hills, South Dakota
Called *Paha Sapa*, or "sacred grounds," by the Sioux, the Black Hills are soaring peaks and spires, caves, canyons and ponderosa pines. (See page 116.)

Breaks of the Missouri, South Dakota
The gray-black shale of the breaks west of the Missouri River once was mud at the bottom of a great cretaceous sea that was pushed from the area seventy million years ago when the Black Hills were forming. Fossil shellfish ranging in size from a dime to a large hat may be seen in the shale, together with great marine lizards known as mosasaurs and plesiosaurs.

Buffalo Gap National Grasslands, South Dakota
Eastward from the Rockies stretch the Great Plains, once an enormous sea of grass. Buffalo Gap National Grassland is dedicated to the supremacy of grass. Such wildlife as prairie dogs, bobcats, coyotes and raccoons share the grassland with whitetail and mule deer, pronghorn antelope and rare black-footed ferrets.

Chimney Rock, Nebraska
The once-famous landmark of the Oregon Trail signified the beginning of the mountainous West to pioneers. (See page 113.)

Courthouse Rock, Nebraska
Located on Pumpkin Seed Creek, the rock seemed to pioneers to resemble the courthouse in St. Louis and was so named. Nearby, appropriately enough, is Jailhouse Rock.

Custer National Forest, South Dakota
Hugh Glass, mauled by a grizzly bear in 1823 and more dead than alive, managed to drag himself through the flat and rolling prairies and timbered hills of a land now largely encompassed in the national forest. Glass journeyed for one hundred and eighty miles to safety, and his story remains one of the sagas of the North American continent.

Dells of the Sioux, South Dakota
Craggy rocks overhang the clear waters of the river.

Drift Prairie, North Dakota
The glaciated upland northeast of the Missouri River is one of the continent's most distinctive drift prairies. The rolling, glaciated plateau rises four hundred to six hundred feet above the surrounding plains. Buried from one hundred to two hundred feet beneath the debris left by the glaciers of the Ice Age are the original peaks of the uplift. Devils Lake is the state's largest natural lake.

Fort Niobrara National Wildlife Refuge, Nebraska
Long-horned cattle, deer, elks and buffalo make their home in the refuge.

Fort Robinson, Nebraska
The great Sioux Chief Crazy Horse, victor over both Custer's and Crook's soldiers, rode into the fort to talk with the U.S. Army in the hope of preventing further bloodshed. Vengeful soldiers scuffled with the chief and one stabbed him with a bayonet. Here, in the adjutant's office, with his friend Surgeon McGillycuddy at his side, Chief Crazy Horse died.

Great Lakes of South Dakota, South Dakota
Four huge dams on the Missouri River have created this chain of lakes five hundred miles long, covering seven hundred square miles.

Jewel Cave National Monument, South Dakota
Albert and F. W. Michaud, brothers and prospectors, discovered the cave in a ravine known as Hell Canyon. Thick crystalline calcite lines the galleries that range in color from an unusual light green to darker greens and bronze.

Killdeer Mountains, North Dakota
Two flat-topped buttes indented by erosion and forested with birch, oak and a few cedar rise out of the plains that slope upward from the Missouri River to the west. The Slope is the land of buffalo berry, dogwood and wild rose.

Lewis and Clark Lake, South Dakota
Chalk cliffs, resembling the famed white cliffs of Dover, rise beside the blue waters impounded by Pactola Dam.

Little Missouri Bay State Park, North Dakota
Some of the most rugged lands in the state offer backcountry beauty.

Lower Brule Sioux Indian Reservation, South Dakota
The Indian town is entirely surrounded by the prairie dogs, who perch atop their mounds and bark excitedly at the approach of visitors.

Medicine Rock, South Dakota
The Indians believed that the footprints that are deeply incised into the rock were made by Great Spirit.

Missouri River, North and South Dakota and Nebraska
The muddy waters of the giant river flow past sandbars and tree-studded islands. Lewis and Clark explored the meandering waterway in 1804.

Mount Rushmore National Memorial, South Dakota
Colossal figures representing the heads of four great American Presidents—Washington, Jefferson, Lincoln and Theodore Roosevelt—are carved on the granite face of six-thousand-foot Mount Rushmore. (See page 116.)

Newton Hills State Park, South Dakota
Horse thieves hid out in the wooded hills during pioneer times. Before the thieves, the Indians lived among the hills in cave dwellings that still exist.

Oglala National Grasslands, Nebraska
Named for the Oglala Sioux, who pursued buffalo across these high plains, the grasslands still are the haunt of pronghorn antelope and other game.

Prairie Homestead Historical Site, South Dakota
A sod dugout home is furnished as if the homestead family still lived in it. The beams of the house are of local cottonwood. The homesteader plowed buffalo-grass sod to use for the upper walls of the home, and the original sod still keeps the house warm in winter and cool in summer.

Red River Valley, North Dakota
The beaches and shorelines of what during the days of the great glaciers was Lake Agassiz are the most distinctive features of this flat valley, which is not a river valley at all but the plain of the ancient lake bed. The Red River follows a tortuous course through the wide plain.

Sand Hills, Nebraska
The region called "God's greatest pastureland" is a land of clear air and brilliant stars at night. Between the Loup and Dismal rivers is the Nebraska National Forest, planted by man.

Scotts Bluff National Monument, Nebraska
Hiram Scott, mountain man, dying in the wilderness, dragged himself for sixty miles to expire at the foot of the bluff. To westering families, Scotts Bluff loomed massive as a fortress. Richard Burton compared the rocky formation to the Arabs' City of Brass, that abode of bewitched infidels which appears at a distance to wayfarers in the desert.

Shank's Draw, South Dakota
In 1972, rampaging floodwaters swept out of the Black Hills and scoured out such watercourses as Shank's Draw. The minicanyon slices through geologic ages delineated in white limestone and rocks of yellow, red and maroon fractured with green. The churning waters turned up new gravels laden with placer gold and exposed large pockets of crystals and fossils.

Sioux Indian Reservations, South Dakota
Indian trails lead through canyons with such names as He Dog, Spotted Tail and Crazy Horse. The traditional Indian life exists side by side with modernity. Wounded Knee, where in the nineteenth century blue-coated troopers massacred an Indian band, has taken on new meaning to the Indians after the 1973 confrontation between Indian activists and authorities.

Theodore Roosevelt National Memorial Park, North Dakota
The buttes and canyons of the North Dakota Badlands appear much as they did to Theodore Roosevelt, who established a ranch among them in 1883. (See page 114.)

Valentine National Wildlife Refuge, Nebraska
Waterfowl and other birds find shelter in this refuge.

White Butte, North Dakota
The butte, the highest point in the state, rises 3,506 feet out of the flat plains. It is topped by a massive caprock of sandstone.

Wildcat Hills State Recreation Area and Game Refuge, Nebraska
Buffalo roam the plains that sweep ever higher toward the still-distant mountains. Jagged rocks break the monotonous regularity of the land.

Wind Cave National Park, South Dakota
Tom Bingham stalked a deer in 1881 and heard a curious whistle. The sound was made by wind escaping from a cave. Since then scientists have noted that the wind rushes out when the barometer drops and rushes in when it rises. In 1903, Wind Cave became the first cave park to be established in the National Park System; many of the underground chambers are still unexplored.

Writing Rock Historic Site, North Dakota
Archaeologists still cannot decipher the mysterious hieroglyphics on these large boulders.

miles   100

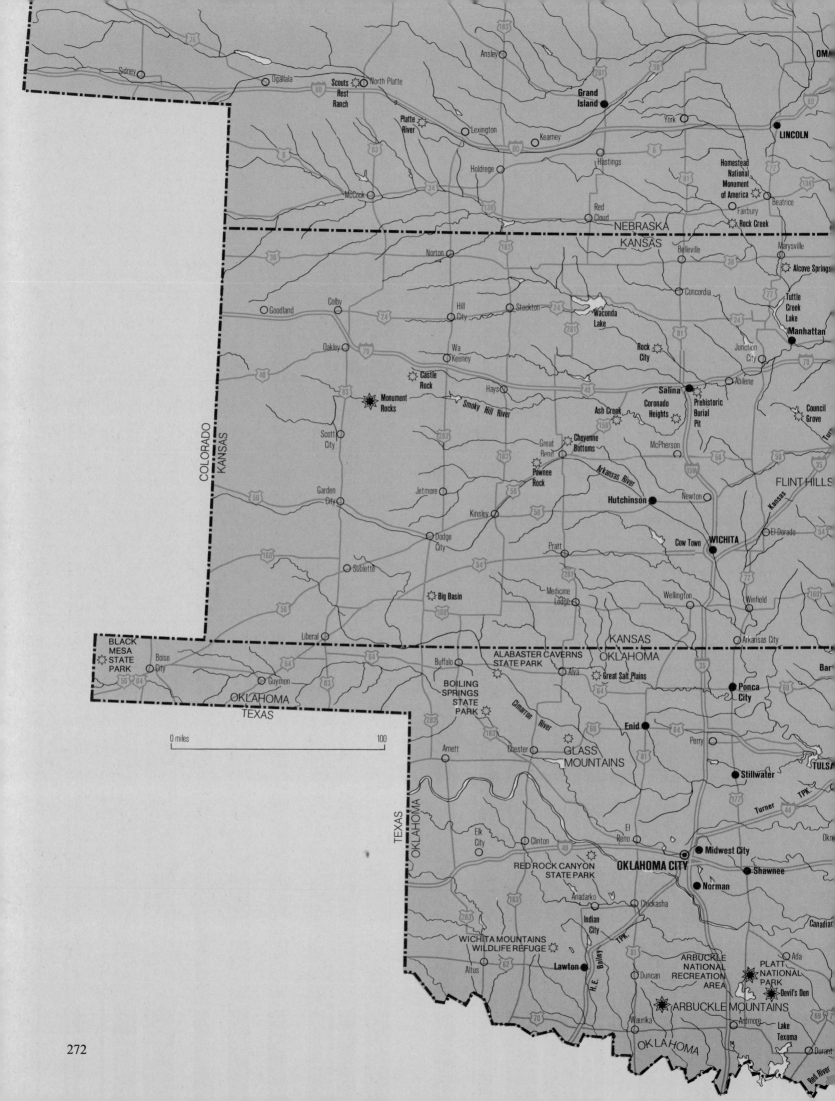

Kansas, Oklahoma and Southern Nebraska

Alabaster Caverns State Park, Oklahoma
Two hundred million years old, the cave contains the world's largest gypsum caverns, stretching for more than half a mile with numerous branches off the main tunnel. Seven species of bats inhabit the cave, and another species lives nearby in the trees of Cedar Canyon. Natural Bridge rises a hundred and fifty feet above the floor of the canyon.

Alcove Springs, Kansas
Fireflies dance about the springs at night as they once danced for the westering Donner Party. "J. F. Reed, 26 May, 1846" was cut deep into the rock beside the springs by a leader of the ill-fated party.

Arbuckle Mountains, Oklahoma
Clear running streams, rocky bluffs and rocky ridges characterize the Arbuckle Uplift. (See page 120.)

Ash Creek, Kansas
The track worn by countless buffalo into the sandstone banks of the stream as they came down to water still may be seen.

Big Basin, Kansas
A mile wide and a hundred feet deep, the depression was formed by underground water dissolving supporting rock strata. Caverns were formed only to collapse. A short distance away is Little Basin, which is smaller, but similar in nature.

Black Mesa State Park, Oklahoma
Dinosaur bones are common at the mesa, the highest point in Oklahoma.

Boiling Springs State Park, Oklahoma
Shade trees shelter several cold-water springs from the hot sun. The springs are called boiling not because they are hot, but because they "boil up" through white sands.

Castle Rock, Kansas
The chalk spire reaches seventy feet high and is visible for miles around in the flat terrain. Fossil discoveries have been made nearby.

Cheyenne Bottoms, Kansas
One of the nation's outstanding migratory waterfowl refuges surrounds a deep central lake and four shallow lakes.

Coronado Heights, Kansas
At the summit, Coronado is said to have camped on his expedition in search of the mythical kingdom of Quivera.

Council Grove, Kansas
Wagon-train people left letters at the Post Office Oak in Council Grove, the last outfitting place on the Santa Fe Trail before the long journey through the wilderness. The tree still stands and so does the Last Chance Store, the Old Hays Tavern, the Cowboy Jail and the stump of still another tree, the Council Oak, beneath which a peace treaty was signed with the Indians.

Devil's Den, Oklahoma
Indians believed that demons lived among the weird rock formations in this boulder-strewn badlands, which was once the impenetrable refuge of outlaws fleeing the Texas Rangers. (See page 120.)

Flint Hills, Kansas
The easternmost major escarpment in Kansas, the Flint Hills are rugged. Upland native pasture grass sweeps over the hills, and eastern red cedar grows in the rocky ravines. Outcrops of limestone and chert accent the terrain.

Glass Mountains, Oklahoma
Millions of selenite crystals on these gypsum-covered buttes sparkle in the sun. The "mountains" are topped by Cathedral Rock, which is three hundred feet tall.

Great Salt Plains, Oklahoma
Flats of gleaming white salt were formed by residue left after salt water evaporated in the heat of Oklahoma summers. The forty-square-mile basin is desolate terrain amid a verdant area. Migrating waterfowl using the Continental Flyway from Canada to Mexico stop here.

Heavener Runestone State Park, Oklahoma
Runes translated as "Nov. 11, 1012" were inscribed, presumably by Vikings, on an upright stone in a deep canyon in Poteau Mountain.

Homestead National Monument of America, Nebraska
Daniel Freeman staked out land in 1862 to become the first homesteader in the United States. Both Freeman and his wife are buried on the land upon which he settled. An authentic settler's cabin and implements remind today's visitors of life on the frontier.

Marais Des Cygnes River, Kansas
Early French trappers found the valley teeming with bird life and named the river flowing between its swampy banks Marais Des Cygnes, Marsh of the Swans. About a hundred and fifty thousand birds still stop over here in the winter and spring, and more than seventy thousand ducks winter on the river banks. About two hundred species of birds have been recorded on the river.

McCurtain County Wilderness Area, Oklahoma
A series of narrow wooded ridges support a rich variety of plants and animals. On the lower slopes there are numerous varieties of trees: holly, sugar maple and red maple, and in the upland areas, shortleaf pine, hickory, post oak and blackjack oak.

Monument Rock, Kansas
Once shale and chalk beds choked the Smoky Hill River Valley, but wind and rain have reduced the formations to rocks sometimes called the Great Smoky Pyramids. (See page 112.)

Parting of the Trails, Kansas
Just west of Gardner is a roadside picnic area, which is one of the most significant areas on the plains. This is where the Oregon Trail separated from the Santa Fe Trail. Planks stretch over a shallow ditch, which becomes muddy in wet weather. The ditch is the ruts of the trail cut into the sod long ago.

Pawnee Rock, Kansas
The rock thrusting up from the plains was a favorite place for Indian ambushes. Sixteen-year-old Kit Carson was on sentry duty at the rock when he thought he heard Indians sneaking up on him. He fired into the dark and shot his own mule.

Platt National Park, Oklahoma
There are thirty-one springs in the woodlands on the prairie. Eighteen of the springs are sulfur, four are iron and six are freshwater. (See page 120.)

Platte River, Nebraska
Mountain men dragging their boats over its shoals during the summer drought said the river was "a thousand miles long and six inches deep," but it remained the easiest road into the West. Sandhill cranes nest along the river.

Prehistoric Burial Pit, Kansas
The pit contains more than a hundred and forty skeletal remains of Indians, who are remarkable in that most were over six feet tall.

Red Rock Canyon State Park, Oklahoma
The tall trees in the canyon have escaped damage from the storms and prairie fires because they are sheltered by the rocky declivity. The Comanche and Kickapoo Indians found this colorful canyon a fine place for their winter camp.

Rock Creek, Nebraska
Wild canaries flit about the creek and bobwhites call. Pioneers called the stream Rock Creek because they found rock salt along its banks. Here, in 1861, young James Butler Hickok, mild of manner and a loner, cut hay for the stock and lived in a dugout. Here, in his first gun battle, Wild Bill Hickok killed a man and wounded two others.

Rock City, Kansas
Large sandstone concretions on the prairie have been named Rock City. Some are nearly perfect spheres with diameters of twelve feet; others are elliptical in shape.

Scouts Rest Ranch, Nebraska
The world knew William F. Cody as "Buffalo Bill." Hunter, scout, showman, he captivated frontiersmen and the crowned heads of Europe. Cody rode for the Pony Express across the Nebraska prairies in the 1860s, and later he built Scouts Rest Ranch where, on July 4, 1882, he premiered his celebrated Wild West show.

Wichita Mountains Wildlife Refuge, Oklahoma
Buffalo and a herd of longhorns graze on the fifty-nine-thousand-acre range. From the top of 2,467-foot-high Mount Scott is a wide view of the surrounding country.

Iowa and Missouri

Amana Colonies, Iowa
The seven villages of the Amana colonies flourish amid their scenic farms in the Iowa River Valley. Founded in 1855 by the German pietists as an experiment in communal living, the Amanas are famed for their superb workmanship and their hearty cuisine.

Backbone State Park, Iowa
A high limestone ridge resembling a backbone looks down on the Maquoketa River. The ridge pines have developed a permanent tilt away from the prevailing winds which sweep across the plains.

Big Oak Tree State Park, Missouri
A pin oak tree stands 127 feet tall and is the biggest oak among the biggest trees in Missouri.

Big Spring, Missouri
The largest single-outlet spring in the United States, each day 846 million gallons of water flow through it.

Bluffton Fir Stand, Iowa
A rare stand of balsam fir spreads beside the Upper Iowa River.

Boneyard Hollow, Iowa
Where Prairie Creek flows into the Des Moines River, the Indians once hunted buffalo, deer and elk by driving them over abrupt sandstone ledges so that they fell nearly seventy-five feet to the gorge floor. Nearby are the copperas beds. The Indians used the copperas powder for war paint, and early pioneers employed it to dye homemade cloth.

Boone's Lick, Missouri
A trail leads past the spring where Daniel Boone's sons, Daniel M. and Nathan, made salt as early as 1805.

Clarksville Bluffs, Missouri
The highest bluffs on the Mississippi look down on the Father of Waters.

Cayler Prairie, Iowa
This virgin prairie contains 219 species of plants.

Coldwater Cave, Iowa
The largest cave in the state, it is entered only through a spring.

Effigy Mounds National Monument, Iowa
On the summits of towering bluffs is the Fire Point Mound Group. The 191 mounds, created by prehistoric Indians for two thousand years between 500 B.C. and A.D. 1400, have the forms of animals and birds. Some of the most beautiful views of the Middle West can be seen from atop the bluffs overlooking the broad sweep of Mississippi River.

Elephant Rocks State Park, Missouri
Huge granite boulders resemble elephants, the largest of which is twenty-seven feet tall, thirty-five feet long and seventeen feet wide. It weighs about six hundred and eighty tons and is judged to be about 1.2 million years old.

Fish Farm Mounds, Iowa
On a wooded terrace there are thirty cone-shaped Indian burial mounds dating from about A.D. 200 to A.D. 500.

Fort Osage, Missouri
Overlooking the Missouri River, the fort is a restoration of the first army post west of the Mississippi. It was established in 1808.

Geode State Park, Iowa
Muddy-looking rocks with hearts of scintillating crystal are dug out of creek banks here.

Gitchie Manitou State Preserve, Iowa
Pink Sioux quartzite outcrops have been dated by geologists at 1.2 billion years old. Amid the quartzite is a beautiful pool.

Graham Cave State Park, Missouri
Indians lived in the cave as long ago as 8000 B.C., according to radiocarbon dating.

Iowa Great Lakes, Iowa
The lakes were formed by glacial action. Spring-fed Clear Lake is one hundred feet higher than the surrounding countryside. This area was the favorite camping ground in the region of the nomadic Sioux and Winnebago Indians.

Kalsow Prairie, Iowa
Prairie flowers bloom here as they did when the first settlers reached the area.

Lake of the Ozarks, Missouri
The lake coves wind among the hills at the heart of Missouri's Ozarks. (See page 118.)

Ledges State Park, Iowa
Nine hundred acres of steep ledges, woods and meadows are laced by a winding stream.

Little Sioux Valley, Iowa
Three glacial advances of the last major glacial period stopped in this valley. Pilot Rock, a huge glacial boulder deposited by an ice sheet, has long been a landmark of travelers on the river, who followed the Little Sioux on their way to the Indian pipestone quarries in Minnesota.

Maquoketa Caves State Park, Iowa
A seventeen-ton balanced rock, limestone caverns and a natural bridge highlight the geological area.

Mark Twain Cave, Missouri
In this cave close to Mark Twain's hometown of Hannibal, Tom Sawyer and Becky Thatcher hid from Injun Joe in Twain's novel of life on the Mississippi.

Meramec State Park, Missouri
In addition to big Fisher's Cave there is another score of caves in the park. In 1865, Thomas C. Fletcher, newly elected Governor of Missouri, held his inaugural ball in the largest room of Fisher's Cave, which is still called The Ballroom.

Mississippi Palisades, Iowa
The broad Mississippi sweeps gracefully between towering wooded cliffs, which provide magnificent vistas over the great river and the gently rolling Iowa countryside. (See page 110.)

Montauk State Park, Missouri
Montauk Springs flows forty million gallons of water daily to form the headwaters of Current River, one of the state's favorite streams for floaters, who glide down the stream in johnboats.

Ocheyedan Mound, Iowa
For generations Iowans thought that the mound was an Indian burying ground, but it is actually a glacial kame. The Indians, however, did use the mound as an observation point. Their lookout proved invaluable in times of trouble, since the mound rises an impressive one hundred and seventy feet above the surrounding floodplain.

Old Spanish Cave, Missouri
Frank Mease obtained a chart and papers from a mysterious Spaniard indicating the presence of a cave near the sleepy village of Ozark, where no cave was known to exist. According to the chart, the cave was filled with treasure. Mease did locate the cave, but there were no signs of treasure in what has since been called Old Spanish Cave.

Ozark National Scenic Riverways, Missouri
The Current and Jacks Fork rivers, down which floaters pole in narrow, flat-bottomed crafts called johnboats, have been included in the national park system. Remnants of an ancient mountain range, the Ozarks are a scenic redoubt within the heart of the continent. (See page 118.)

Pikes Peak State Park, Iowa
Zebulon Pike, leading a party of explorers up the Mississippi, discovered and named the peak, before he went on to discover the much loftier peak in Colorado. There is a view of the confluence of the Wisconsin and Mississippi rivers from the summit.

St. Louis, Missouri
A towering six-hundred-and-thirty-foot-high arch symbolizes the city's position in North American history as the "Gateway to the West." The arch stands on the riverfront in the Jefferson National Expansion Memorial. Nearby are the Old Cathedral and the Old Courthouse, where the Dred Scott decision was made. The original documents of the Louisiana Purchase can be seen at the Jefferson Memorial, a museum of St. Louis and Missouri history.

The Sinks, Missouri
Sinking Creek eroded a wall of solid rock to create a natural bridge, or tunnel. It formed Emerald Grotto from an ancient cave gallery, the roof of which was weakened by water action and collapsed in a heap of rubble.

Washington State Park, Missouri
Hundreds of prehistoric carvings in stone are concentrated in this park.

White Pine Hollow, Iowa
The largest stand of native white pine in the state covers a rough terrain.

Western Texas

Alibates Flint Quarry, Texas
Fifteen thousand years ago, Indians mined this quarry for flint to make weapons and implements. Archaeologists have discovered more than five hundred and sixty quarry pits. Sandia man mined and worked the flints, and since the Indians used the mines long after the coming of the white men, the quarry is the site of the longest-lived industry developed on the continent.

Apache Mountains, Texas
Once these mountains were ocean reefs and floors, and there are marine fossils in their limestone and sandstone flanks. At the foot of the mountains to the east and without an outlet is a lake, which is so salty that nothing grows along its banks.

Big Bend National Park, Texas
Situated where the Rio Grande makes its big bend between the United States and Mexico, the park is a biological island. (See page 122.)

Black Gap Wildlife Management Area, Texas
One hundred thousand acres of brush and mountains have been dedicated to the study of how game can be protected. Bobcat and cougar, mule deer and pronghorn antelope, as well as white-winged dove and quail, are among the denizens of the wilds.

Castle Gap, Texas
Far from any highway the gap now lies deserted, but once it was a busy route for nomadic tribes. The Comanche war trail from the High Plains to the villages of northern Mexico ran through the gap, and later emigrants passed through it on their way to new homes farther west. The trail broken by Indian ponies and cut deeper by wagon trains still may be seen.

Caverns of Sonora, Texas
Crystals make the caverns hauntingly beautiful. The hues of the rainbow sparkle in the light of a torch, and there are translucent and phosphorescent formations. It has been called "the most indescribably beautiful cavern in the world."

Dolan Creek Ranch, Texas
They call it God's country, because, according to West Texans, God gave it to the Indians, who yielded it to the white man, who could not figure out what to do with it and gave it back to God. Austerely beautiful, its cliffs rise abrupt and challenging over the Devils River. The purple sage has a fragrant bloom, a kildeer cries over the river and a golden eagle wheels overhead.

Edwards Plateau, Texas
This is high, broken territory where cattle and sheep forage.

Fort Davis, Texas
Buildings have been restored and furnished as they were when the army was fighting the Comanches and Apaches. An unusual recorded reproduction of cavalry parade sounds ring through the fort at dusk to take visitors on an imaginary trip back to the frontier of yesterday.

Goodnight–Loving Cattle Trail, Texas
Named for rancher Charles Goodnight and his partner, Oliver Loving, the trail followed the route of the Butterfield Overland Mail westward into New Mexico. Texas longhorns were driven over the trail to provision southwestern army posts during the 1870s. Hard-drinking, horse-loving, singing, gun-packing cowboys rode the trail herding the fractious cattle.

Guadalupe Mountains National Park, Texas
The 8,751-foot-high Guadalupe Peak rises over the mountains, but El Capitan is probably the most famous of the mountains in the range because of its sheer two-thous-and-foot cliff. From Bush Mountain a hiker can enjoy sweeping views across the vast plains and salt basins to the south and west. The Pinery is a ruined Butterfield Stage station situated near the top of historic Guadalupe Pass.

Hueco Tanks, Texas
Rainwater is trapped in these natural solid rock basins along the Butterfield Trail. Travelers in this arid region have found the trapped water a godsend since the earliest of times. Indian pictographs dating back two thousand years exist side by side with the names of nineteenth-century pioneers. The pictographs were painted by pre-Pueblos, Pueblos, Apaches, Jumanos and Navajos.

Lower Pecos River, Texas
Streams have cut into the limestone table-land to form canyons, in which there are many rock shelters and caves. These preserve a wide range of rock art dating back as far as eleven thousand years. The smoky smudges on the shelter walls still show where early man built his cooking fires.

Mackenzie State Park, Texas
Chipper prairie dogs have their own Prairie Dog Town in the park, which preserves a piece of the plains.

Medicine Mounds, Texas
Four cone-shaped hills rise some three hundred and fifty feet above the plains. Named by the Comanche Indians, who held them in reverence, the mounds were believed to be the dwelling places of benevolent spirits who could cure ills and insure a successful hunt.

Monahans Sandhills State Park, Texas
Rolling sand dunes make a miniature desert of four thousand acres.

Mount Franklin, Texas
The 7,192-foot-high mountain in the southern tip of the Rockies looks down on the historic pass along the Rio Grande which gave El Paso its name. The rugged mountain is rich in desert flora and fauna.

Muleshoe National Wildlife Refuge, Texas
The oldest national wildlife refuge in Texas protects the migratory waterfowl which fly over the South Texas High Plains.

Paint Rock, Texas
Indian pictographs are inscribed on the limestone cliffs overlooking the Concho River. The fifteen hundred paintings range from prehistoric times to the nineteenth century, when Comanche Indians who hunted in the area painted the last of them.

Palo Duro Canyon, Texas
The cedar-shaded floor of the abyss slices for a hundred and twenty miles through the plains of the Panhandle. Carved by the Red River, the spires and pinnacles of the canyon floor reach toward the brim a thousand feet above. Multihued strata millions of years old have been revealed by the waters.

Permian Basin, Texas
A great underground saucer was formed more than two hundred million years ago by a mountain-girded sea. Today, the sea's swarming life has become petroleum, which is pumped to the surface by more than eighteen thousand producing wells. The countryside is flat and monotonous, broken by flat-topped mesas.

Salt Flat, Texas
Evaporating, intermittent lakes at the foot of the Guadalupe Mountains left broad deposits of salt. In the 1860s, Texas Rangers, army troops and Mexican and U.S. citizens brawled over the salt in what has been called the Salt War. It was a chaotic conflict and killings took place on both sides.

Sand Stone Canyon, Texas
Indian pictographs adorn the walls of the precipitous canyon.

Sierra Diablos Mountains, Texas
The peaks thrusting a mile high are scarred by abandoned copper mines. The last Indian battle in Texas took place in Victoria Canyon.

Staked Plains, Texas
It is said that the Spanish explorer Coronado had to drive stakes waist high to create a trail over which he could retrace his way through the sea of tall grass that covered the plains of what is now the Texas Panhandle. The flat Texas plains are a land of vast cattle herds, and it is here that "Home on the Range" first was sung.

Trans-Pecos Region, Texas
High, dry country is crossed by offshoot spurs of the Rocky Mountains.

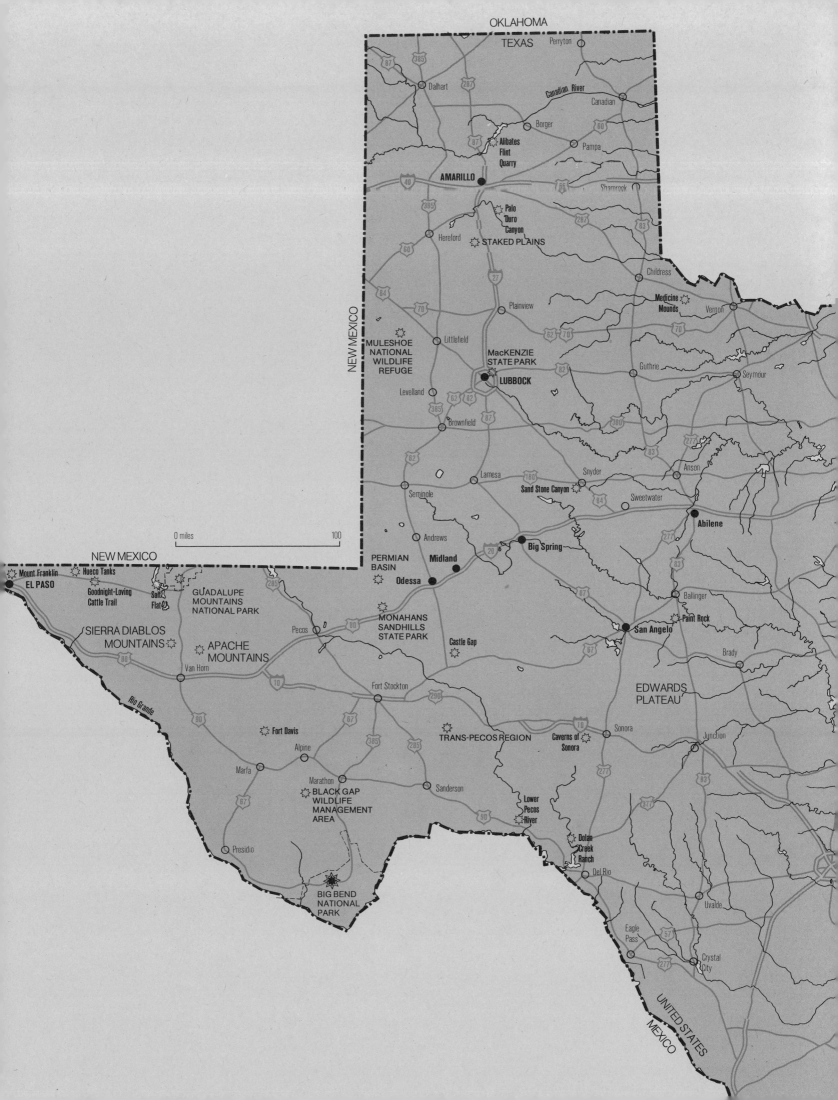

OKLAHOMA

TEXAS

Perryton

Dalhart

Canadian River

Canadian

Borger

Pampa

Alibates
Flint
Quarry

AMARILLO

Shamrock

NEW MEXICO

Palo
Duro
Canyon

Hereford

STAKED PLAINS

Childress

Plainview

Medicine
Mounds

Vernon

MULESHOE
NATIONAL
WILDLIFE
REFUGE

Littlefield

MacKENZIE
STATE PARK

Guthrie

Seymour

LUBBOCK

Levelland

Brownfield

Lamesa

Snyder

Anson

Seminole

Sand Stone Canyon

Sweetwater

Abilene

0 miles   100

Andrews

Big Spring

PERMIAN
BASIN

Midland

NEW MEXICO

Mount Franklin

Hueco Tanks

EL PASO

Goodnight-Loving
Cattle Trail

Salt
Flat

GUADALUPE
MOUNTAINS
NATIONAL PARK

Pecos

Odessa

MONAHANS
SANDHILLS
STATE PARK

Castle Gap

Ballinger

Paint Rock

San Angelo

SIERRA DIABLOS
MOUNTAINS

APACHE
MOUNTAINS

Van Horn

Fort Stockton

Brady

EDWARDS
PLATEAU

Rio Grande

Fort Davis

TRANS-PECOS REGION

Caverns of
Sonora

Sonora

Junction

Alpine

Marfa

Marathon

Sanderson

Lower
Pecos
River

Black Gap
WILDLIFE
MANAGEMENT
AREA

Dolan
Creek
Ranch

Presidio

Del Rio

BIG BEND
NATIONAL
PARK

Uvalde

Eagle
Pass

Crystal
City

UNITED STATES

MEXICO

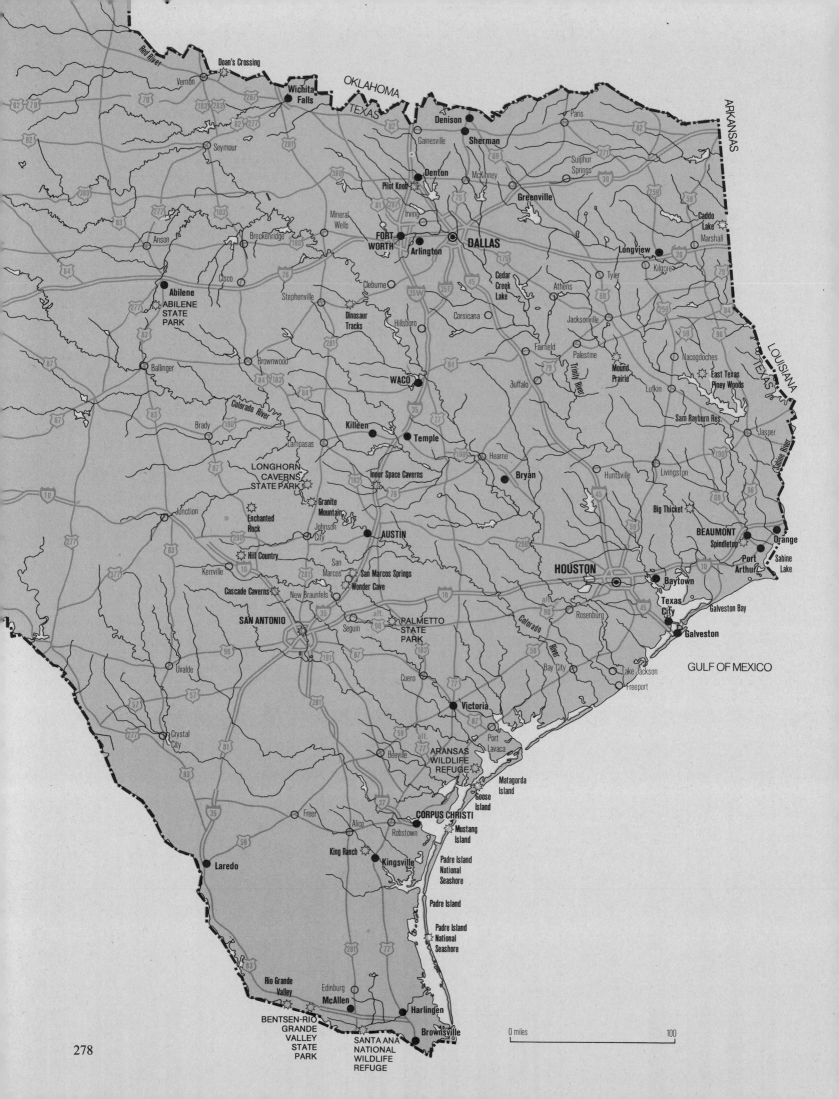

OKLAHOMA

TEXAS

ARKANSAS

LOUISIANA

TEXAS

Red River

Doan's Crossing

Vernon

Wichita Falls

Seymour

Anson

Abilene
ABILENE STATE PARK

Cisco

Ballinger

Colorado River

Brady

Junction

LONGHORN CAVERNS STATE PARK

Enchanted Rock

Hill Country

Kerrville

Cascade Caverns

Uvalde

Crystal City

Laredo

Freer

Alice

Robstown

King Ranch

Kingsville

Rio Grande Valley

Edinburg

McAllen

BENTSEN-RIO GRANDE VALLEY STATE PARK

SANTA ANA NATIONAL WILDLIFE REFUGE

Harlingen

Brownsville

Denison

Gainesville

Sherman

Denton

Pilot Knob

McKinney

Paris

Sulphur Springs

Greenville

Caddo Lake

Marshall

Longview

Kilgore

Mineral Wells

FORT WORTH

Arlington

DALLAS

Irving

Cleburne

Cedar Creek Lake

Tyler

Athens

Stephenville

Hillsboro

Corsicana

Jacksonville

Nacogdoches

Fairfield

Palestine

Brownwood

Lampasas

WACO

Buffalo

Trinity River

Mound Prairie

Lufkin

East Texas Piney Woods

Sam Rayburn Res.

Jasper

Sabine River

Killeen

Temple

Inner Space Caverns

Granite Mountain

Bryan

Hearne

Huntsville

Livingston

Big Thicket

BEAUMONT

Spindletop

Orange

Johnson City

AUSTIN

San Marcos

San Marcos Springs

Wonder Cave

New Braunfels

Rosenburg

HOUSTON

Baytown

Port Arthur

Sabine Lake

SAN ANTONIO

Seguin

PALMETTO STATE PARK

Texas City

Galveston Bay

Galveston

Colorado River

Bay City

Lake Jackson

GULF OF MEXICO

Cuero

Freeport

Victoria

Port Lavaca

ARANSAS WILDLIFE REFUGE

Matagorda Island

Goose Island

Beeville

CORPUS CHRISTI

Mustang Island

Padre Island National Seashore

Padre Island

Padre Island National Seashore

0 miles 100

278

Abilene State Park, Texas
Comanche Indians camped beneath the native pecan trees of this large grove.

Aransas Wildlife Refuge, Texas
The world's only remaining flock of whooping cranes flies here from Canada to winter. There are also about three hundred other species of birds in the refuge, a plashy land of sea marshes and sand spits —the great blue heron, reddish, brown and American egrets, tricolor herons and little blue herons are among them. Bird-watchers take great delight in watching pelicans dive for fish.

Bentsen–Rio Grande Valley State Park, Texas
The native flora and fauna of the lower Rio Grande Valley are preserved in this 587-acre area on the banks of the Rio Grande. Among the two hundred species of birds sighted here are Audubon's oriole, the hooded oriole, the zone-tailed hawk and the red-eyed cowbird. An old military road can still be seen at the edge of the park.

Big Thicket, Texas
Woods and marsh and lazy streams, all are part of the Big Thicket, nearly impene-trable wilds which are the home of an astonishing variety of plants and wildlife. Three of the world's known varieties of carnivorous plants grow here. Canoeists on mysterious Village Creek, a river in any less-watered land, sometimes hear red wolves howling at dusk.

Caddo Lake, Texas
Huge, moss-decked cypress trees rise from the shore waters.

Cascade Caverns, Texas
A hermit lived in the first room of these caverns long ago, but the rest of this under-ground maze was not explored until 1930, when the huge rooms and crystal pools with a dramatic profusion of cave growth were finally discovered.

Dinosaur Tracks, Texas
Eons ago a thirty-ton brontosaur strolled in the bed of the Paluxy River. It left twenty-six-inch imprints, which geolo-gists date back to the Cretaceous Period, the last of the three periods in which the giant reptiles lived.

Doan's Crossing, Texas
Herds of Texas longhorns being driven down the Dodge City Trail from the ranges to the railhead at Dodge City, Kansas, crossed the river at Doan's Crossing. When they forded the Red River, the cowboys knew they were halfway to Dodge.

East Texas Piney Woods, Texas
Wild orchids bloom in the woods where oil was once discovered at Oil Springs. Indians used the oily water as a potion against evil and as an ointment to cure ill-ness. Local folks insist the ghost of a decapitated brakeman may be encountered whirling his lantern in search of his head on the trail of an old railroad right-of-way through the woods.

Enchanted Rock, Texas
A granite mountain, two miles around, rises two thousand feet above the sur-rounding hills. The Indians performed human sacrifices atop the rock, and it is said that on moonlit nights their ghost fires can be seen flickering on its summit. Creaking and groaning noises emitted by the rock at night are said by geologists to be the result of the cooling and contraction of the rock as it releases the day's heat.

Goose Island, Texas
Hugging the coast of the island are wind-sculptured oaks, including a two-thou-sand-year-old giant, the largest live oak in the world.

Granite Mountain, Texas
Texans cut imperceptibly into this huge dome of red and pink granite to take out stone from which they built their state capitol, which is second in size among American capitol buildings only to the U.S. Capitol.

Hill Country, Texas
The Hill Country could also be called wild flower country, cave country or, as one Texan described it, "country of eleven hundred springs," for it is country car-peted with wild flowers in the spring, honeycombed with caves and bubbling with springs.

Inner Space Caverns, Texas
Boring in the rock to determine whether it was suitable for a highway, workmen in 1963 discovered a magnificent cavern re-markable for its stalactites, stalagmites and flowstones as well as the skeletal re-mains of mastodons, giant wolves and other ice age animals.

King Ranch, Texas
The nation's largest cattle ranch, covering nine hundred and sixty thousand acres, is where the Santa Gertrudis cattle were developed. The Santa Gertrudis is the first breed of cattle to be created in North America. The ranch also maintains a herd of longhorns, once the mainstay of the Texas cattle industry.

Longhorn Caverns State Park, Texas
This crystal wonderland is among the largest caverns in the state. Prehistoric cavemen lived in the caverns. During the Civil War a secret gunpowder plant was located within it to produce munitions for the Confederate armies. Later the caverns provided a hideout for bandits.

Mound Prairie, Texas
Hasinai Indians built these ceremonial mounds, two of which are three hundred feet by three hundred and fifty feet.

Mustang Island, Texas
Named for the wild horses that at one time roamed its sandy pastures, Mustang Island has surf and sandy beaches.

Padre Island National Seashore, Texas
The island is a hundred-and-ten-mile scimitar of land stretching along the Gulf

Coast to make up the nation's longest expanse of pristine beach. Some three hundred varieties of fish swim in the Gulf and in the Laguna Madre, which divides the island from the mainland. There are about eighty kinds of shells to be found here, as well as Spanish doubloons from sunken eighteenth-century wrecks, which lie off the coast.

Palmetto State Park, Texas
The ground underfoot is springy. Pal-mettos grow luxuriantly. Located on the San Marcos River, the 179-acre park is equally known for its wild orchids, water lilies, graceful ferns and moss-draped trees.

Pilot Knob, Texas
Outlaw Sam Bass hid in a cave at the foot of this nine-hundred-foot prominence.

Rio Grande Valley, Texas
"Stick your finger in the ground," say valley people, "and it'll sprout." The soil is fertile, and winter never visits this sub-tropical land on the Mexican border, where life and language have a Tex–Mex blend.

San Antonio, Texas
The Alamo, in the heart of the city, is a shrine of democracy, and the city is a happy synthesis of its Spanish–American and Anglo–American heritages. La Villita is old San Antonio as much as is the Alamo. The landscaped river twists through the heart of the business district to provide walkways and gondola paths.

San Marcos Springs, Texas
The springs feed sylvan lakes and streams of pellucid water.

Santa Ana National Wildlife Refuge, Texas
The two thousand acres of the refuge were set aside to preserve birds that are found in South Texas but nowhere else in the United States. The jungle-like growth of the preserve once covered the entire valley.

Spindletop, Texas
At 10 A.M. on January 10, 1901, a gusher blew in and spewed petroleum over the area. Anthony F. Lucas's gusher produced several thousand times more barrels of petroleum than any previous oil well and revolutionized the oil industry. Other wells were soon brought in, and land in the area sold for two hundred thousand dollars an acre and more. The Lucas Gusher Monu-ment marks the historic site.

Wonder Cave, Texas
When nature formed the Balcones Fault, Wonder Cave came into being.

Lake of
the Woods

Karlstad

Thief River
Falls

NORTH DAKOTA

MINNESOTA

75

59

International
Falls

53

71

High Falls
of the
Pigeon Grand Portage
River National Monument

Crookston

Erskine

2

CHIPPEWA
NATIONAL
FOREST

Elv

SUPERIOR
NATIONAL
FOREST

61

TOWER SOUDAN
STATE PARK

Lake Superior
North Shore

Bemidji

169

Hibbing

Virginia

53

BAPTISM
RIVER
STATE
PARK

Lake
Itasca

Cass Lake

Grand Rapids

Gooseberry
Falls

61

Apostle
Islands

Apostle
Islands

Moorhead

59

71

Detroit
Lakes

2

St. Louis River

DULUTH

Canadian
Shield

Lake Superior
National
Lakeshore

94

75

Fergus
Falls

10

Aitkin

SAVANNA
PORTAGE
STATE
PARK

35

Superior

Ashland

SOUTH DAKOTA

MINNESOTA

Brainerd

Little
Falls

Solon
Springs

LUCIUS
WOODS
STATE
PARK

Cable

COPPER
FALLS
STATE
PARK

Mellen

Turtle
Flambeau
Flowage

Manitowish
Waters

45

Eagle
River

Sauk
Centre

59

Hinckley

Glidden

Hayward

83

53

Park Falls

Fifield

Phillips

Rhinelander

Woodruff

Milaca

Dalles of
the St. Croix

Spooner

Chippewa
Lake

Chippewa River

Flambeau
River

8

Prentice

Tomahawk

St. Cloud

169

52

St
Croix
Falls

8

63

Rice
Lake

Ladysmith

53

Merrill

Antigo

51

Tomahawk River

Willmar

12

Anoka

94

35

Chetek

MINNEAPOLIS

Hudson

ST. PAUL

Chippewa
Falls

Wausau

Olivia

212

Bloomington

Prescott

94

Chippewa River

Eau Claire

Marshfield

10

Stevens Point

New
Ulm

71

Northfield

Red
Wing

61

10

Lake
Pepin

Osseo

Black River

Wisconsin
Rapids

Waupaca

Lake

Sanborn

Faribault

52

Whitehall

Black
River
Falls

Petenwell
Flowage

Coloma

Mankato

14

Owatonna

Rochester

Winona

Mississippi River

53

Tomah

Castle Rock
Flowage

Friendship

51

Wisconsin River

Pipestone
National
Monument

Pipestone

169

Albert
Lea

35

14

90

16

Mississippi River

16

La Crosse

90

61

14

Viroqua

Kickapoo River

Richland
Center

Wisconsin
Dells

Portage

16

Worthington

90

Austin

MINNESOTA

IOWA

0 miles   100

Spring
Green

14

Baraboo

Devil's Lake

98

94

Sauk
City

12

Prairie du
Chien

Wisconsin River

Taliesin

Dodgeville

MADISON

Koshkon

Mississippi
Palisades

18

Lancaster

New
Glarus

14

151

Platteville

Monroe

Janesvill

WISCONSIN

ILLINOIS

Belo

280

Alvin Creek Deer Yards, Wisconsin
Evergreen trees protect the deer against the bitter winter winds in the seventy-four thousand acres of deer yards in Nicolet National Forest.

Apostle Islands, Wisconsin
Some twenty-three islands in Lake Superior were home to the Chippewa, then to French and American fur traders. John Jacob Astor's American Fur Company made its headquarters at La Pointe on Madeline Island.

Baptism River State Park, Minnesota
The highest waterfall in Minnesota tumbles down a sheer rock cliff.

Canadian Shield, Wisconsin
The rocks of this billion-year-old formation were once part of the western hemisphere's largest land formation. Created even before there was a continent of North America, the shield was polished and smoothed by four continental ice sheets.

Chippewa National Forest, Minnesota
There are 499 lakes as well as rivers and streams hidden away in the deep forest. Indians harvest wild rice and skim over canoe trails.

Dalles of the St. Croix, Minnesota and Wisconsin
Perpendicular jagged rock walls rise one hundred to two hundred feet above the narrow channel of the rushing river. On the Minnesota shore are the Glacial Gardens, fantastic potholes created by the swirling waters of the river during the Ice Age.

Devil's Lake, Wisconsin
Spring-fed Devil's Lake nestles at the foot of cliffs and bluffs of sandstone and quartzite. There are Indian effigy mounds, which are shaped like an eagle, bear and lynx.

Door Peninsula, Wisconsin
A thumb of land sticking out between Lake Michigan and Green Bay has been likened to Massachusett's Cape Cod.

Gooseberry Falls, Minnesota
The Gooseberry River cascades over three 30-foot waterfalls and through a series of rapids to drop two hundred and forty feet into Lake Superior.

Grand Portage National Monument, Minnesota
The historic nine-mile trail runs from Grand Portage on Lake Superior to Fort Charlotte on the Pigeon River through a rough country of precipitous hills and noble forests.

High Falls of the Pigeon River, Minnesota
The cataract thunders from a height of 108 feet into the bottom of the canyon.

Horicon Marsh, Wisconsin
Thousands of geese and other waterfowl set down in the marshlands. The goose population alone numbers more than a hundred thousand.

Kettle Moraines, Wisconsin
Now part of the Ice Age National Scientific Reserve, the moraines were left by lobes of a glacier, which deposited billions of tons of sand, gravel and rock. Kames formed of the debris rise as high as three hundred and fifty feet.

Kickapoo River, Wisconsin
Twisting among limestone and sandstone bluffs, the river endeavors to live up to its reputation as "the most crooked river in the world." It flows through the non-glaciated driftless area of southwest Wisconsin.

Lake Itasca, Minnesota
The state's only remaining stand of virgin Norway pine grows beside the blue lake, and a trail leads from it to a once-lost village site of the Mound Builders, where the Sioux and Chippewa fought in the seventeenth century. The true marvel of the lake is a small stream that flows out of it, and although children can step from stone to stone across it, this stream is the headwaters of the broad and mighty Mississippi River.

Lake of the Woods, Minnesota
Islands forested with pines and spruce, ankle deep with moss, rise in serenity in this vast wilderness lake. (See page 126.)

Lake Pepin, Minnesota and Wisconsin
The Chippewa River, although small in comparison with the Mississippi, plunges down a steep grade at its mouth so that it has created a natural dam of rock and gravel that backs up the Father of Waters in a twenty-two-mile-long bluff-lined lake.

Lake Superior North Shore, Minnesota
The sweeping hills of the Saw-Tooth Mountains rise from the shore in rocky cliffs. The pounding surf, the soaring gulls, the fishing boats and lighthouses standing on the rugged shore to warn the ships away, all give an oceanic aspect to this coast of the greatest of the Great Lakes.

Lucius Woods State Park, Wisconsin
Indians, voyageurs, explorers and missionaries all paddled over the Brule–St. Croix Canoe Route between the Mississippi River and Lake Superior. An arduous two-mile portage began here at the north end of Upper St. Croix Lake to the headwaters of the Brule.

Mellen Hills, Wisconsin
Once these hills were a mountain range, but they have been worn down by passing millennia so that Mount Whittlesey, the highest point in the hills, is only 1,872 feet above sea level. These ancient hills have both black granite and a low-grade non-magnetic iron ore.

Mississippi River, Minnesota and Wisconsin
High limestone cliffs look down on the channels and sloughs of the Upper Mississippi River. The heron and egret rookeries along the river are among the continent's most extensive. There are deer and fox and sometimes bear in the riverside copses. Giant tows of barges make their way upriver and downriver.

Pipestone National Monument, Minnesota
Longfellow wrote about the pipestone quarries in his *Song of Hiawatha*. To this day only Indians are permitted to mine the red stone from which, for more than three centuries, the tribes traditionally have made ceremonial pipes. Indians chip the red stone from the quarry and carry it back to their own tribes for working.

Rock Island, Wisconsin
This nine-hundred-acre island in Lake Michigan, a mile off the northeast tip of larger Washington Island, looks much as it did when La Salle established a trading post close to an Indian village. Archaeologists have recently excavated the remains of the post and village. The rocky limestone cliffs that rise from the shore give the island its name.

St. Louis River, Minnesota
The torrent rushes and tumbles over the rocky riverbed at the bottom of a deep ravine. Once this was one of the most important trade routes in the North Country, because the Grand Portage on the route between Lake Superior and the Mississippi began at the white water on the St. Louis and ran through the deep forests.

Savanna Portage State Park, Minnesota
Once voyageurs struggled up to their knees in mud for five days over what they called "the worst carrying place in the Northwest." The canoe route was part of the Great Lakes-to-Missippi Trail used during the eighteenth and early nineteenth centuries.

Superior National Forest, Minnesota
The French Canadian voyageurs paddled their way along the water highways of this wilderness in search of fur-bearing animals. Formed during the Ice Age, the lakes in the forest are linked by streams and portages into what were once great arteries of commerce.

Taliesin East, Wisconsin
The studio and school of master architect Frank Lloyd Wright remain amid the Wisconsin hills at Spring Green. (See page 132.)

Tower Soudan State Park, Minnesota
An elevator drops twenty-four hundred feet into the depths of the earth in the state's first and deepest underground iron mine. At the foot of the shaft a tunnel runs through solid greenstone.

Two Rivers, Wisconsin
A walk along the Lake Michigan beach at Two Rivers reveals the remains of a prehistoric forest, which dates back to the glacial era, ten thousand years ago. Ridge and swale alternate to indicate the lake levels when the last Ice Age was drawing to a close.

281

Michigan

Allegan State Forest, Michigan
First an Indian hunting ground, then the scene for lumbering and finally for attempts at agriculture, the land has been allowed to return to forest. Indian Marker Trees, originally saplings bent in a certain direction to show the trail or point to a spring, still may be found.

Big Spring (Kitch-Iti-Ki-Pi), Michigan
Crystal-clear water bubbles from a forty-five-foot-deep spring at the rate of sixteen thousand gallons every minute.

Detroit, Michigan
The automobile assembly lines of Motor City, U.S.A., remain among the production marvels of North America.

Drummond Island, Michigan
In 1828, on this island, the British colors were lowered for the last time over the United States soil.

Fife Lake State Forest, Michigan
Bogs, lakes and forests make up 103,000 acres of state-owned land. About ten thousand years ago, blocks of ice left by the retreating glaciers melted beneath glacial debris to create depressions in which the lakes formed.

Garden Peninsula, Michigan
Ninety-foot limestone bluffs overlook the entrance to Green Bay, where, in the late 1800s Fayette, an iron town, flourished. Now Fayette is one of the largest ghost towns in the nation. Its beehive-shaped charcoal kilns and a lime kiln are deserted, and its opera house, store and hotel are empty. At Burnt Bluff, caves have been eroded into the face of a two-hundred-foot-high cliff.

Grand Sable Sand Dunes, Michigan
Not only the dunes, but sandstone formations, too, stretch along the shore of Lake Superior.

Greenfield Village, Michigan
Henry Ford moved antique homes, shops and other buildings from all corners of the United States to create a remarkable collection of Americana. Thomas Edison's laboratory where the electric lamp was invented, the bicycle shop where the Wright brothers created the first airplane and a courthouse where Lincoln practiced law can be seen here.

Hartwick Pines State Park, Michigan
White and red pines and hemlock woods are a remnant of the vast stands of forest that greeted the first lumbermen in Michigan. The Au Sable River courses through the park.

Huron National Forest, Michigan
The four hundred and seventeen thousand acres of forest contain six hundred and fifty miles of streams and rivers, including the Au Sable, popular with canoeists. Among the animals and birds that live in this vast forest is the Kirtland's warbler, which mates only in this part of Michigan and winters in the Bahamas.

282

Isle Royale National Park, Michigan
The largest island in Lake Superior is a wilderness left to the backpacker, the wolf, the moose and the eagle. There are no paved roads on the island, which was once the site of Indian copper workings and early timber operations but is now thick with hardwood and evergreen forests split by lakes and fjords. (See page 13.)

Jordan River State Forest, Michigan
During logging operations in the early 1900s, cedar and hemlock were floated down the river to the sawmills. Now the logging has ceased, and maple, elm, hemlock and pine have come back.

Kalkaska State Forest, Michigan
Explorer Henry Schoolcraft named the forest Kalkaska from the Indian word *kaskaskia,* meaning a large area of burned-over ground. There are 138,553 acres in the forest, together with a stretch of the Manistee River.

Keweenaw Peninsula, Michigan
Forty centuries ago Indians dug for copper in open pits. It is believed that they built fires on top of the copper-bearing rocks and then splashed cold water on them to break them up. Stone hammers used then to separate the ore from the rock are often found here.

Lake Superior State Forest, Michigan
Sand plains and old beaches support pine trees in this one-hundred-and-seventy-six-thousand-acre forest, bounded on the east by Whitefish Bay and on the north by Lake Superior. Twenty-five miles of rugged Lake Superior shoreline are in the forest. Sand dunes and beaches alternate with rocks. The Two-Hearted River, given fame by Ernest Hemingway, winds through the high pine ridges.

Les Cheneaux, Michigan
Indians and explorers had reason to fear the stormy open waters of Lake Huron and instead canoed through this series of islands and peninsulas.

Mackinac Bridge, Michigan
The bridge, a five-mile-long steel and concrete pathway high over the Straits of Mackinac, links the Upper and Lower peninsulas of Michigan. "Mighty Mac," as the bridge is affectionately called, rests on thirty-three marine foundations that go down to bedrock. The two huge tower foundations are more than two hundred feet below water.

Mackinac Island, Michigan
Old Fort Mackinac, built by the British in 1780–81, looks down on the historic island in the Straits of Mackinac. No motorized vehicles are allowed on the island, so transportation is on horseback, by carriage, bicycle or foot.

Mackinaw City, Michigan
This city, on the southern side of the Straits, was first settled by the French in 1681. In 1793, the fort, by then controlled by the British, was burned and the troops were killed by Indians.

Norwich Bluff, Michigan
Indians climbed to the top of this bluff to signal.

Ottawa National Forest, Michigan
With thirty-six named lakes, noble trees and such birds as the bald eagle and heron, the forest seems unchanged since the Indians lived here. In Sylvania tract there are eighteen thousand acres of virgin forest and significant communities of bog and muskeg.

Pequaming, Michigan
Pequaming is an outstanding example of a tombolo, an island connected to the mainland by deposited sediments.

Pictured Rocks National Lakeshore, Michigan
The multicolored sandstone cliffs, called the pictured rocks, rise perpendicularly to heights of two hundred feet along the south shore of Lake Superior. The forest-topped rocks have such names as Miners Castle, Indian Head, Lovers Leap, Chapel Rock and Battleship Rock. Longfellow mentioned the rocks in *Hiawatha.*

Porcupine Mountains State Park, Michigan
The Porcupines are the highest mountains in the Midwest. A forest wilderness spreads along the shores of Lake Superior. Hiking trails lace the timber. Within the woods there are inland lakes and streams with a number of waterfalls.

Sleeping Bear Dunes National Lakeshore, Michigan
According to Indian legend, a black bear and her two cubs swam from Wisconsin to Michigan. When they had almost reached shore, the cubs lagged behind. The mother climbed ashore and mounted the tall dune where, from a distance, she still seems to wait for her cubs. On closer look the mother bear is actually a vast heap of dark vegetation set against the tawny sands.

Soo Locks, Michigan
The locks, among the busiest in the world, lift boats twenty-one feet from the Lake Huron level to that of Lake Superior. An average of ninety boats a day passes through St. Mary's Falls Canal.

Tahquamenon Falls State Park, Michigan
The river winds through deep swamps and among high hills, the haunts of deer, wolf, bobcat and eagle, to tumble over the beautiful Upper and Lower Falls.

Tahquamenon River State Forest, Michigan
Jack pine and red pine plantations alternate with brushy areas favored by the sharp-tailed grouse. There are impoundments made by beaver and a large peat bog, two miles long and one mile wide, which in summer is matted with blueberries.

Wilderness State Park, Michigan
An almost impenetrable forest fronts on the Straits of Mackinac.

Beall Woods, Illinois
This virgin forest includes both bottom land and upland woods. Wild pecans, standing seventy-five feet tall, bear small but sweet nuts, and there are shagbark hickory trees with nuts as big as golf balls. The largest remaining temperate zone forest in the Midwest, in Beall Woods trees grow to a height of a hundred and sixty feet.

Brown County, Indiana
In Brown County a backwoods atmosphere is still preserved. (See page 128.)

Buffalo Rock State Park, Illinois
Once an Indian stronghold, the rock overlooks the Illinois River.

Cave-in-Rock State Park, Illinois
Indian mounds and caverns are in this park. In one of the caves, Big and Little Harp, grim and murderous bandits, made their lair and lured flatboaters on the Ohio River to their doom with promises of whiskey and wild women.

Chicago, Illinois
The second city of the United States is probably the most American of the nation's cities. (See page 134.)

Clifty Falls State Park, Indiana
The park looks out over the broad Ohio River. Clifty Creek and Little Clifty Creek dash over falls and thrash through boulder-strewn canyons, which are sunless except at noon.

Cranberry Slough, Illinois
In the peat bog are royal fern, purple chokeberry and cranberry.

Dickson Mounds, Illinois
The story of life in this area five hundred to a thousand years ago is pieced together at the burial mounds. More than two hundred Indian skeletons have been found, together with pottery, arrowheads and ornaments.

Dixon Springs, Illinois
The springs are on a giant block of rock that dropped two hundred feet along a fault line. The hilly country sparkles with tiny rivulets and waterfalls.

Ferne Clyffe State Park, Illinois
Tall trees seem tiny in the deep canyons and valleys of this park. Rocky overhangs once sheltered wandering Indian families, and arrowheads are frequently found.

Giant City State Park, Illinois
Huge blocks of stone were moved into position by an ancient people for some obscure reason. Most experts believe they were fashioned into a crude buffalo trap.

Illinois Beach State Park, Illinois
The high waters of Lake Michigan have eroded the beach. There are alternating beach dunes and swales.

Indiana Dunes, Indiana
Along the southern shores of Lake Michigan shifting dunes and woods are home to a vast range of flora including prickly pear cactus and white pine.

Kankakee River State Park, Illinois
A bedrock island in the river gorge is the only place in the world where the Kankakee mallow grows. A tributary, Rock Creek, flows down to the river through a mini-canyon of scarred limestone. The park was once the site of the Indian village called The Little Rock.

Lincoln Boyhood National Memorial, Indiana
Lincoln's boyhood home and his mother's burial site are preserved near two memorial buildings connected by a cloistered walk.

Lower Fox River, Illinois
Miles of cliffs line the river. Cedar and Canadian yew hang from the cliffs, where swallows zoom into their holes.

Lusk Creek Canyon, Illinois
The creek, an unpolluted aquatic environment, lies in a deep gorge which has been eroded through Pennsylvania sandstone.

Matthiessen State Park, Illinois
The Vermilion River plunges over a precipice in the park, where there are canyons, caves and a reconstructed pioneer blockhouse.

McCormick's Creek State Park, Indiana
The creek cuts its way through a limestone canyon to join the White River. In the park there are forests of beech and pine, sinkholes and stone gullies.

Mississippi Palisades State Park, Illinois
Precipitous cliffs rise above the river. The heavily wooded terrain hides a number of deep canyons. Unusual rock formations include Indian Head, Twin Sisters and Bob Upton's Cave. (See page 108.)

Mounds State Park, Indiana
A vanished race of Indians built the mounds. In 1968 and 1969, archaeologists excavated the Great Mound in the southern part of the park and discovered six human burials and valuable prehistoric artifacts, which suggest that the mound was constructed during a transition period from the Adena to Hopewell culture, about A.D. 1050.

New Salem, Illinois
The village of Abraham Lincoln's youth has been restored to look as it did when he was elected to the legislature from Sangamon County in 1834. The log cabin where Lincoln served as postmaster, however, still stands.

Shades State Park, Indiana
Trails lead through beech and white oak forests to striking sandstone formations and scenic overlooks of Sugar Creek and the Silver Cascade.

Shawnee National Forest, Illinois
Towering bluffs, rock outcrops, lush woodlands and cypress swamps are all in this Illinois Ozarks forest. Rim Rock Trail at Pounds Hollow loops along the top of a limestone escarpment. An Indian wall dating back seven thousand years seals the entrance to the escarpment. Williams Hill, 1,064 feet high, is the highest point in the forest.

Spring Mill State Park, Indiana
Donaldson Cave and Twin Caves are eroded into the limestone. In the park there is also a restored pioneer village complete with gristmill and sawmill operated by water power.

Squire Boone Caverns, Indiana
The world's largest rimstone formation, towering columns and three underground waterfalls are in the cave, which was discovered in 1790 by Daniel Boone's brother, Squire. When he died, in 1815, Squire was buried inside the caverns.

Starved Rock State Park, Illinois
The Iroquois Indians surrounded the Illinois Indians on the huge rock rising up beside the Illinois River. The hapless Illinois were reduced to starvation, but they refused to surrender to the vindictive Iroquois. Instead, they jumped into the river to their doom.

Tower Rock, Illinois
The Tower Rock in the Mississippi River was made a national park by President Grant. In the days of the Mississippi riverboats, which once numbered over five hundred, many a boat collided with it.

Turkey Run State Park, Indiana
Sugar Creek twists its way through the solid rock. Deep, rock-walled canyons, virgin timber, abandoned quarries and a covered bridge give the park a special appeal.

Versailles State Park, Indiana
Scenic hillsides with limestone outcroppings rise along Laughery and Fallen Timber creeks. Oak, hickory, tulip poplar, beech and black walnut abound in the varied topography.

Volo Bog, Illinois
A tamarack bog, a floating bog mat and open water area communities make this a place of considerable interest.

Weston Cemetery Prairie, Illinois
The black-soil prairie is representative of the vast prairies that once covered much of Illinois.

White Pines Forest State Park, Illinois
This four-hundred-acre tract preserves the only remaining stand of virgin white pine in the state.

Wyandotte Cave, Indiana
One of the Midwest's largest caves, there are twenty miles of explored passages. The upper level of the Old Cave was discovered in 1798, and the New Cave was found in 1850. Monument Mountain stands 135 feet high in Rothrock's Cathedral, a room that is 185 feet high, 360 feet long and 140 feet wide.

MISSOURI
ARKANSAS

Beaver
Lake
Rogers
Eureka
Springs
Springdale
Fayetteville
WITHROW
SPRING
STATE
PARK
LOST
VALLEY
STATE
PARK
BUFFALO
RIVER
STATE
PARK
Blanchard
Springs
Cavern
Harrison
BOSTON MOUNTAINS
OZARK NATIONAL FOREST
DEVIL'S DEN
STATE PARK
Old Sugar Loaf Mountain

Mountain
Home
Hardy
Pocahontas
Paragould
CROWLEY'S RIDGE
STATE PARK
Blytheville
Jonesboro
Newport

MAMMOTH SPRING
STATE PARK

0 miles   100

Fort Smith
MOUNT
NEBO
STATE
PARK
Russellville
Conway
PETIT
JEAN
STATE
PARK
OUACHITA
MOUNTAINS

OKLAHOMA
ARKANSAS

LITTLE ROCK
Jacksonville

Hot Springs
HOT
SPRINGS
NATIONAL
PARK
Benton

West Memphis
Forrest City
Helena

TENNESSEE
MISSISSIPPI
Corinth
Woodall
Mountain ▲
Holly Springs
Booneville
Senatobia
Sardis
Lake
New
Albany
Batesville
Oxford
Tupelo

Stuttgart
Clarksdale

Pine Bluff
Arkadelphia
CRATER OF
DIAMONDS
STATE
PARK
Fordyce

De Queen

Camden

Cleveland
Leland
Indianola
Greenwood
Winona
Starkville
Columbus

Grenada
Lake
Grenada

Texarkana
Magnolia
El Dorado

Greenville
Lake Village
LAKE
CHICOT
STATE
PARK
LEROY PERCY
STATE PARK
Oxbow Lakes
Anguilla

ARKANSAS
LOUISIANA

Yazoo
City
Durant
Kosciusko
Philadelphia
Natchez
Trace
Pkwy.

Bastrop
Mississippi
River
VICKSBURG
NATIONAL
MIL. PARK
Black
Clinton
Canton
MISSISSIPPI PETRIFIED FOREST
Meridian

Monroe
Ruston
Tallulah
Vicksburg
JACKSON
Forest

Shreveport
Minden

BIENVILLE
PINES
SCENIC
AREA
Laurel
Waynesboro
Hazlehurst
Collins

Mansfield
Grand
Ecore
Winnfield
Natchitoches
Cane River Lake
Many
Port
Gibson
Natchez
Trace
Parkway
Ferriday
Natchez
Bude
Brookhaven
Columbia
Hattiesburg
Beaumont

KISATCHIE
NATIONAL FOREST
Alexandria
MARKSVILLE STATE
COMMEMORATIVE AREA

LOUISIANA
TEXAS
Toledo
Bend
Res.
Sabine River

McComb
PERCY
QUIN
STATE
PARK
Woodville
MISSISSIPPI
LOUISIANA
Lumberton
DE SOTO
NATIONAL
FOREST
Lucedale
Wiggins

De Ridder
CHICOT
STATE
PARK
Opelousas
AUDUBON
MEMORIAL
STATE
PARK
Hammond
Bogalusa
Picayune
Moss
Point
Gulf Coast Biloxi
Pascagoula
Gulfport

BATON
ROUGE
Lake
Pontchartrain
Cat
Island
Horn Island

Lafayette
Jennings
Crowley

Lake
Charles
White
Lake
Avery
Island
New
Iberia
Thibodaux
NEW ORLEANS
CHALMETTE NATIONAL
HISTORICAL PARK
Breton
Sound

ROCKEFELLER
WILDLIFE
REFUGE
Morgan City
Houma
Bayou
Lafourche
Grand
Isle

GULF OF MEXICO
Atchafalaya Bay

286

Audubon Memorial State Park, Louisiana

In 1821, John James Audubon came to Oakley Plantation as a tutor. It was here that he painted thirty-two of his remarkable portraits of Birds of America.

Avery Island, Louisiana

Not truly an island but a salt dome rising out of the tidal marshes along the coast, Avery Island produces oil as well as salt. Pepper plantations grow the Tabasco peppers, which were brought from Mexico. Bird City is a preserve where snowy egrets and other species build their nests, and at dusk the sky is dark with birds returning home.

Bienville Pines Scenic Area, Mississippi

These virgin pines are about one hundred and seventy-five years old. To walk through the forest is to see how Southern pine forests appeared before settlers reached the area.

Blanchard Springs Cavern, Arkansas

This living cave is one of North America's most spectacular caverns.

Buffalo River State Park, Arkansas

The river dashes among the mountain shoulders and is a watery home to goggle-eye and smallmouth bass. Floaters fish as they glide down the river. Every bend in the free-flowing stream brings a view of peaceful bluffs and forest. There are hidden springs and unexpected caves.

Bayou Lafourche, Louisiana

Lined with small Acadian farms, the bayou is at the heart of the Cajun Country, where French-speaking Acadians claim that they can float their pirogues on the dew. (See page 154.)

Cane River Lake, Louisiana

This was the main channel of the Red River until 1832, when the river burst into a new course, leaving the sleepy lake a haunt of fishermen.

Cat Island, Mississippi

This offshore island got its name when French sailors saw raccoons swarming about what was then a forested island and thought they were cats. It is still home to a variety of wildlife.

Chalmette National Historical Park, Louisiana

On January 8, 1815, the last major land battle of the War of 1812 was fought on the Chalmette plantation. The American's victory over the British preserved the United States claim to the Louisiana Territory and prevented the Mississippi River from becoming the western boundary of the United States.

Chicot State Park, Louisiana

Trails descend a high knoll and wind through sylvan ravines, where the sun barely penetrates the forest cover. The plants range from the cucumber tree to the southern magnolia and the grape fern. Armadillos trundle about the brush.

Crater of Diamonds State Park, Arkansas

The only occurrence of diamonds in their natural matrix in North America, the pipe mine has made fortunes for those lucky enough to discover stones. Gems picked up on the ground at the crater range from four to forty carats and include the only black diamonds found in a pipe mine.

Crowley's Ridge State Park, Arkansas

Winds blowing off the Great Plains for thousands of years heaped dust onto what is now a long ridge across the fertile and flat delta region.

De Soto National Forest, Mississippi

Small red flowers grow in the sand hills, and hundreds of yellow butterflies dance among them. There are stands of second-growth timber, grown sturdy since the virgin forest was cut forty years ago.

Devil's Den State Park, Arkansas

The valley nestled among the rugged Boston Mountains is the epitome of Arkansas's beauty spots.

Eureka Springs, Arkansas

Springs gurgle out of crevices in the Ozark Mountains. In Eureka Springs, Village Saint Elizabeth's Church is entered through the steeple from a hill, since the church itself is located in a valley below.

Grand Ecore, Louisiana

A hundred-foot bluff, called by the French the Grand Ecore, looks down on the Red River.

Grand Isle, Louisiana

The island is the plaything of the wind, which blows cowlicks of sand along the beach. Hurricanes have driven the sea right over the island, but in calm weather it is a place of laziness and ease. On the back bay there are three dozen oaks planted long ago by Lafitte and his buccaneers to protect them from the hurricanes.

Gulf Coast, Mississippi

A twenty-eight-mile white sand beach stretches along the coast, a pleasuring ground for people from all over the Middle South and Midwest.

Hot Springs National Park, Arkansas

There are forty-seven bubbling hot springs which de Soto noticed on his journey that resulted in the discovery of the Mississippi River more than four hundred years ago.

Kisatchie National Forest, Louisiana

The antecedents of this ancient forest can be traced back for millions of years. It occupies nearly six hundred thousand acres of wilderness, ranging from flat woods to rolling hills. In the Kisatchie Hills there are caves and small canyons. Long Leaf Vista rises among sandstone outcroppings, and Magnolia Forest is a preserve of huckleberry, beech, blackjack oak, persimmon and red cedar.

Lake Chicot State Park, Arkansas

Once, the Mississippi River's main current flowed through what is now horseshoe-shaped Lake Chicot, Arkansas's largest natural lake. Today, high levees separate the oxbow lake from the river. Cypress trees climb along the lakeshores.

Leroy Percy State Park, Mississippi

Moss shrouds the cypress and sunlight filters down to the leafy forest floor. The French, who were the first to reach the area, called the moss Spanish moss. The Spanish later named it Frenchmen's beard.

Lost Valley, Arkansas

Water tumbles down the mountainside. One fall plunges from a bluff to form a two-hundred-foot foaming column that pours out of the base of a cave. To enter the cave, the stream must be followed to a cone-shaped room about forty feet wide and sixty feet high. Water pours down from the ceiling in an underground waterfall. Lost Valley is now a part of the Buffalo National Riverway.

Mammoth Spring State Park, Arkansas

The spring gushes thirty-six million gallons of water an hour to form an eighteen-acre lake, which is headwaters of the Spring River.

Marksville State Commemorative Area, Louisiana

The mounds here were built by Indians two thousand years before Christ. They have yielded artifacts that give a clear picture of life in the Lower Mississippi Valley in a day long gone.

Mississippi Petrified Forest, Mississippi

Giant petrified logs reveal thirty-six million years of geological history. The logs lie at the foot of a young forest in ravines hollowed out by erosion. Some of the logs are five or six feet in diameter, and they were brought from the north by ancient floods. As they lay in the sand they were changed from wood to stone.

Mississippi River, Arkansas, Lousiana and Mississippi

Behind the levees the great river flows on its unhurried way, coiling lazily past the green woods of Arkansas and the sprawling fertile fields of Mississippi and Louisiana before threading its way through the delta to the Gulf of Mexico.

Mount Nebo State Park, Arkansas

Mount Nebo, eighteen hundred feet tall, is cool even on summer days. From the top, there is a fine overlook of the lush Arkansas River Valley and the mountains surrounding its broad reaches.

Natchez Trace Parkway, Mississippi

Settlers in the Upper Mississippi Valley floated down the Mississippi River on log rafts and flatboats to market their produce in New Orleans and returned home overland on the Natchez Trace, the historic highway of Mid-America. (See page 162.)

Natchitoches, Louisiana

Founded by the French in 1714, the city on El Camino Real has the same Creole roof lines and lacy wrought-iron balconies as New Orleans' Vieux Carré.

New Orleans, Louisiana

The Creole city is proud of its sensuous way of life, of the Vieux Carré and of its exultant jazz. (See page 140.)

Old Sugar Loaf Mountain, Arkansas

A trail leads up a ridge on the south side of the mountain, which rises in the middle of man-made Greers Ferry Lake. From the summit there is a panorama of blue lake, mountains and valleys.

Ouachita Mountains, Arkansas

Pronounced Washita, they are a tangle of mountains and forests, mainly in the Ouachita National Forest. The brawling mountain streams, waterfalls and rocky overhangs have long sheltered mankind.

Oxbow Lakes, Mississippi

The Mississippi River on one of its periodic rampages formed Lakes Ferguson and Washington, classic examples of oxbows, bodies of water left by a great river when it shifts its channel.

Ozark National Forest, Arkansas

The green forest sweeps over the mountains where so-called hillbillies continue their old way of life. (See page 164.)

Percy Quin State Park, Mississippi

Longleaf, shortleaf and loblolly pine all grow on the gentle slopes of this two-thousand-two-hundred-and-twenty-acre park.

Petit Jean State Park, Arkansas

Petit Jean, a winsome girl, disguised herself as a boy to follow her lover into the wilderness. Sentimental Arkansans named the mountain for her. Petit Jean Mountain is distinguished by caves, a canyon and one of the highest waterfalls in the South.

Rockefeller Wildlife Refuge, Louisiana

Scientists are investigating the life cycle of alligators in this plashy region, which is half land and half water. The refuge stretches for 26.5 miles along the Gulf Coast and covers eighty-four thousand acres between the surf and the Grand Chenier Ridge, a stranded beach ridge six miles inland. The refuge is one of the last retreats where alligators can be found in large numbers.

Vicksburg National Military Park, Mississippi

Vicksburg controlled the Mississippi and the taking of the city was a vital part of General Grant's strategy to split the Confederacy by moving in force across the heartland of America. In this semicircular park around the city can be seen memorials and tablets marking the positions of the two armies, defensive fortifications and part of the investment line.

Withrow Spring State Park, Arkansas

A spring rushes out of a small cave at the foot of a bluff to form War Eagle Creek. The creek meanders lazily through the Ozark Mountains.

Ohio and West Virginia

Cathedral State Park, West Virginia
Majestic trees tower over the forest floor in this beautiful area.

Cedar Bog Nature Preserve, Ohio
The northern white cedar still grows in the bog, which was left from the last glacial age. It began with a quaking mat of vegetation over a lake and is now the only remaining alkaline bog in the state. The bog is the home of the spotted turtle and the swamp rattlesnake.

Cranberry Glades, West Virginia
Reindeer moss and other arctic plants grow in this high country in the Monongahela National Forest as if they are in Alaskan tundra. Naturalists have discovered pollen grains in the organic layers of peat that were deposited ten thousand years ago before the last Ice Age. Mountains reach around the glades to an elevation of forty-six hundred feet.

Cranberry Island, Ohio
This unique sphagnum bog floats in the northern part of Buckeye Lake. The flora here includes poison sumac, alder bush, pitcher plants and sundew.

Cranesville Swamp, West Virginia
Plants and animals native to the Arctic Circle thrive in this swamp, which was formed more than twenty-five thousand years ago.

Crystal Cave, Ohio
Situated at Put-in-Bay on South Bass Island in Lake Erie, the cave has the only significant deposit in the United States of strontium sulfate. Some of the strontium crystals are eighteen inches long, which makes them the longest in the world. The side walls of the cave are solid strontium, and the ceilings are arched and hung with prismatic crystals that flash and twinkle.

Delta Queen, Ohio
The historic paddlewheel steamboat makes the Cincinnati waterfront its home port and plies the rivers at the heart of the continent. It is the only remaining overnight steamboat on the rivers.

Devil's Den, Ohio
The caves and sixty-foot waterfall are described by Zane Grey in his book *The Spirit of the Border*.

Dolly Sods, West Virginia
Odd rock formations and windblown flora give this area a primitive beauty.

Harpers Ferry, West Virginia
Here, where the Shenandoah and the Potomac rivers flow together, is the hillside town, which, in 1859, became the scene of John Brown's ill-fated abolitionist raid, a turning point in American history. (See page 158.)

Hinckley Ridge, Ohio
Every year without fail on March 15 turkey vultures return to Whipp's Ledges from their winter quarters in the Great Smoky Mountains. This annual occurrence is celebrated in the region as Buzzard Day.

Holden Arboretum, Ohio
Seven thousand varieties of trees, shrubs and wild flowers grow in this lush forest, which sweeps over twenty-six hundred acres. Guided trails reach deep into the woods and pass many watered lakes.

Hueston Woods State Park, Ohio
President George Washington deeded the woods to Matthew Hueston, who had served in General Anthony Wayne's Indian expeditions of the 1790s, and the woods remained virgin timber. These beech and maple trees are a magnificent part of Ohio's natural heritage.

John Brown's Fort, West Virginia
The firehouse of the old U.S. Armory in which John Brown and his men barricaded themselves during their abortive raid. (See page 158.)

Kelleys Island, Ohio
The glaciers carved grooves on Kelleys Island in Lake Erie.

Mentor Marsh Preserve, Ohio
Prothonotary warblers nest in the marsh, which is also the home of other rare species of birds.

Mound City and Serpent Mound, Ohio
Built by the prehistoric Hopewell Indians, the Serpent Mound curls for 1,335 feet, and when seen from the air it appears that an egg-shaped mound thirty feet by eighty feet is about to be taken into the serpent's mouth. At Mound City there are twenty-three burial mounds built by one of America's first trading peoples. (See page 136.)

Nelson–Kennedy Ledges State Park, Ohio
Huge rocks, deep caves and rushing streams all speak of the great glacier which once locked the area in ice. Rock formations, strikingly carved by glacial action and millions of years of wind and rain, rise abruptly among the peaceful woods.

New River Canyon, West Virginia
The canyon has been cut by the whitewater river deep into the foothills of the Appalachians. Waves in the rapids rear sixteen feet high and smash against the sheer walls, which reach up to 585 feet.

Oak Openings, Ohio
Live dunes, which extend for about twenty-eight miles by five miles, rise up to thirty feet high.

Ohio Caverns, Ohio
Vivid cavern walls are overhung with striking stalactites of pure white and multihued crystals.

Organ Cave, West Virginia
West Virginia is renowned among speleologists for its caverns. Organ Cave is one of the largest in the United States. The Confederates made gunpowder in the cave, and there still are thirty-seven well-preserved saltpeter hoppers in one room. There are forty-three miles of explored passages in the cave.

Perry's Cave, Ohio
A few days before the Battle of Lake Erie in 1813, Commodore Oliver Hazard Perry anchored his fleet in Put-in-Bay and discovered this beautiful cave, which is heavily encrusted with precipitated calcium carbonate.

Pinnacle Rock, West Virginia
The slender rock of quartzite sandstone reaches a height of twenty-seven hundred feet above sea level. Pioneers thought that it looked like an ancient temple.

Schoenbrunn, Ohio
David Zeisberger, a Moravian missionary, founded the settlement in 1772 for his Indian converts. The first church and the first school west of the Allegheny Mountains were here. The historic village has been partially restored on the shores of the Tuscarawas River. The nineteen structures of Ohio's first town include cabins, the schoolhouse and the church.

Seneca Caverns, Ohio
Known as the Earthquake Crack because of their violent origin, the caves are extraordinary. In the caves is an underground stream, Old Mist'ry, which emerges fourteen miles away to feed the Blue Hole, a great artesian spring. On May 14, 1930, three message-bearing bottles were tossed into Old Mist'ry in the fifth level. On June 17, 1930, one bottle emerged in the Blue Hole.

Seneca Caverns, West Virginia
The Seneca Indians hid out in the caverns, which are at twenty-five hundred feet above sea level. The deepest room is one hundred and sixty-five feet beneath the earth's surface.

Seven Caves, Ohio
Deep gorges and waterfalls surround the seven caves.

Shawnee State Park, Ohio
High hills look out over the forest in the Ohio River Valley.

Smoke Hole Cavern, West Virginia
The Seneca Indians used the cavern as a place to smoke meat. During the Civil War it was a storage place for ammunition. The cavern nestles in a little valley amid the mountains.

Spruce Knob–Seneca Rocks National Recreation Area, West Virginia
In Monongahela National Forest are a hundred thousand acres of wilderness preserve, tumbling white-water streams, the head-waters of the Potomac River, Spruce Knob, highest point in West Virginia, Seneca Rocks and the scenic gorges called the Smoke Holes.

Valley Falls, West Virginia
The Tygart River tumbles for one mile through the gorge.

Zane Caverns, Ohio
Stalactites and stalagmites shimmer, and dripping water forms cave pearls of pure white calcite.

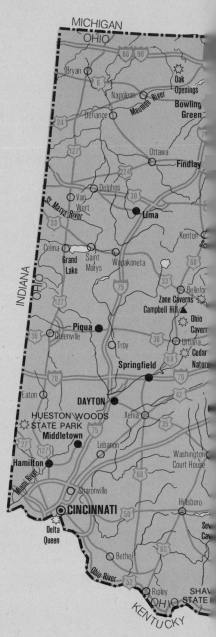

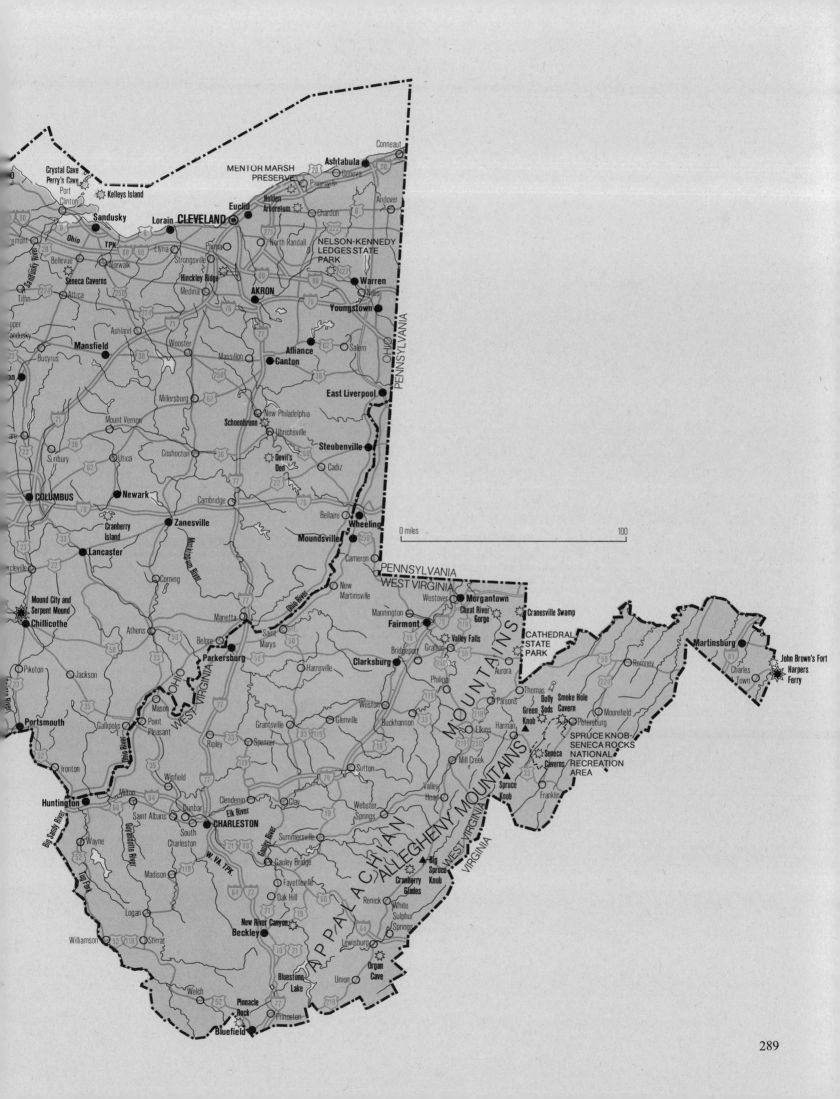

Crystal Cave
Perry's Cave
Port Clinton
☆ Kelleys Island

MENTOR MARSH PRESERVE

Conneaut

Ashtabula
Geneva
Painesville
Andover

Sandusky
Lorain **CLEVELAND**
Euclid
Holden Arboretum
Chardon

Ohio
TPK.
Elyria
Parma
North Randall

Fremont
Bellevue
Norwalk
Seneca Caverns
Attica

Hinckley Ridge
Medina

AKRON

NELSON-KENNEDY LEDGES STATE PARK

Warren
Niles

Tiffin

Ashland
Wooster

Massillon

Youngstown

Mansfield

Bucyrus

Salem

Millersburg

Alliance
Canton

Mount Vernon

New Philadelphia
Schoenbrunn
Uhrichsville

East Liverpool

Sunbury
Utica
Coshocton

Devil's Den
Cadiz

Steubenville

COLUMBUS
Newark
Cambridge

Cranberry Island
Zanesville
Bellaire
Wheeling

Lancaster
Moundsville

Cameron

Corning

New Martinsville

Mound City and Serpent Mound
Chillicothe

Marietta
Athens

Ohio River

PENNSYLVANIA
WEST VIRGINIA

Westover **Morgantown**
Cranesville Swamp
Mannington
Cheat River Gorge

Fairmont

CATHEDRAL STATE PARK

Saint Marys

Valley Falls
Grafton

Belpre
Parkersburg

Bridgeport

Aurora

Piketon
Jackson

Harrisville

Clarksburg

Romney

Martinsburg

John Brown's Fort
Harpers Ferry
Charles Town

Philippi

WEST VIRGINIA

Mason
Point Pleasant

Weston

Thomas
Parsons

Dolly Green Sods
Smoke Hole Cavern

Moorefield

Petersburg

Portsmouth

Gallipolis

Ripley

Grantsville
Glenville

Buckhannon

Elkins
Harman

SPRUCE KNOB-SENECA ROCKS NATIONAL RECREATION AREA

Ironton

Winfield

Spencer

Sutton

Mill Creek

Seneca Caverns

Huntington

Milton
Dunbar
Saint Albans
CHARLESTON
South Charleston

Clendenin
Clay

Webster Springs

Valley Head

Spruce Knob

Franklin

Wayne

Madison

Summersville

W. VA. TPK.

Gauley Bridge

Cranberry Glades
Big Spruce Knob

Logan

Fayetteville
Oak Hill

Renick
White Sulphur Springs

APPALACHIAN **ALLEGHENY MOUNTAINS**

VIRGINIA

Williamson
Stirrat

New River Canyon
Beckley

Lewisburg

Organ Cave

Welch

Bluestone Lake

Union

Pinnacle Rock
Princeton

Bluefield

0 miles   100

289

Kentucky and Tennessee

Big Bone Lick State Park, Kentucky
Salt was manufactured at Big Bone Lick by the Indians before 1756 and until 1812 by the settlers. To make a bushel of salt, pioneers would boil about six hundred gallons of water and then dry and sift the residue. In 1773, James Douglass, a Virginian, discovered ten acres at the licks which were devoid of vegetation and where bones of the mastodon and arctic elephant were scattered about on the ground.

Breaks Interstate Park, Kentucky
This park on the Kentucky–Virginia border has trails that rim the largest canyon east of the Mississippi.

Buffalo Trace, Kentucky
Bull buffalo fought to lead the herd along the Buffalo Trace, which crossed the Ohio River into Kentucky in pioneer days. The trail left by buffalo over millions of years still can be seen cut deep into the Kentucky landscape. The buffalo came to Kentucky from the plains because of salt licks and the lush bluegrass pastures. Their trails are sometimes one hundred feet wide.

Chucalissa Village, Tennessee
Burial mounds and grass huts recall an ancient culture.

Cumberland Gap National Historical Park, Kentucky and Tennessee
Thomas Walker, a doctor, found this gap through the Cumberland Mountains and, in 1769, Daniel Boone blazed the Wilderness Road through it. Trappers and settlers worked their way westward over the road. There is still a lot of wilderness left in the Cumberland Mountains, a region of free-flowing streams, waterfalls, precipitous cliffs and ridges shaggy with forests.

Cumberland Falls State Park, Kentucky
On a moonlit night, a rainbow forms over the majestic falls.

Cumberland Mountain State Park, Tennessee
The largest timberland plateau in the United States spreads over the Cumberland Plateau, two thousand feet above the sea.

Fall Creek Falls State Park, Tennessee
The East's highest waterfall plunges over the brink into a shaded pool. There are deep chasms and gorges and stands of timber which have never been cut.

Falls of the Ohio, Kentucky
The rapids were a hazard to flatboaters descending the Ohio in pioneer times. The river rushes over an enormous fossil reef, an exposed relic of the Devonian era.

Great Smoky Mountains National Park, Tennessee
Fed by fertile soil and nourished by rain and tumbling streams, the plant life of this 512,673-acre park is rich and varied. This is friendly wilderness with few roads, but more than six hundred miles of hiking trails. (See page 152.)

Kentucky Karst Region, Kentucky
Awesome natural wonders lie beneath the earth's surface in the Kentucky cave region. Dozens of caverns include such caves as Mammoth Onyx Cave and Diamond Caverns, a still-growing cave of rare beauty famed for its Hanging Paradise.

Land Between the Lakes, Kentucky and Tennessee
When the Tennessee Valley Authority dammed up the Kentucky and Tennessee rivers to create Lakes Kentucky and Barkley, it was decided to turn the overworked and impoverished backland between the lakes back to its primeval state. Now, decades later, the Land Between the Lakes has emerged as an incomparable recreation area of forests and clearings, streams and lakes.

Lilley Cornett Woods, Kentucky
This virgin forest is a remnant of one of the great forests of the continent which reached its fullest development here in the Cumberland Mountains. Some of the remaining trees are more than four hundred years old.

Mammoth Cave National Park, Kentucky
The huge rooms, yawning pits and fanciful formations make this a fascinating underground world. The scenic hills and peaceful valleys on the surface are part of the park's attraction. (See page 150.)

Natural Bridge State Park, Kentucky
High stone cliffs and arches overhang wooded trails. The Natural Bridge, seventy-eight feet long and sixty-five feet high, was eroded by wind and water over millions of years. The elements cut the softer rock from underneath the hard sandstone cap to create the bridge.

Old Stone Fort, Tennessee
An ancient walled structure stands on the bluffs overlooking the forks of the Duck River. It was already there when the first white settlers reached the area, and it is believed that it may have housed the remnants of a Welsh colony who came to the New World before Columbus.

Red River Gorge, Kentucky
On the floor of the gorge all is cool, even on a hot summer's day, and still except for the sound of running water. The gorge is cut deep into the western slope of the Appalachian foothills. Daniel Boone wintered in a cave in the gorge. There are rare native plants and tall timber.

Reelfoot Lake, Tennessee
In 1811, a violent earthquake caused the Mississippi River to flow backward to form this twenty-three-thousand-acre lake.

Roan Mountain State Park, Tennessee
Hundreds of acres of rhododendron set Roan Mountain ablaze with shades of red during the summer. In late June the spectacular blooms are at their best.

Shiloh National Military Park, Tennessee
At Shiloh, Confederates fell back after bloody fighting in the first major Civil War battle of the western campaign.

Yahoo Falls, Kentucky
On South Fork of the Cumberland River, the falls plunge a misty 113 feet.

291

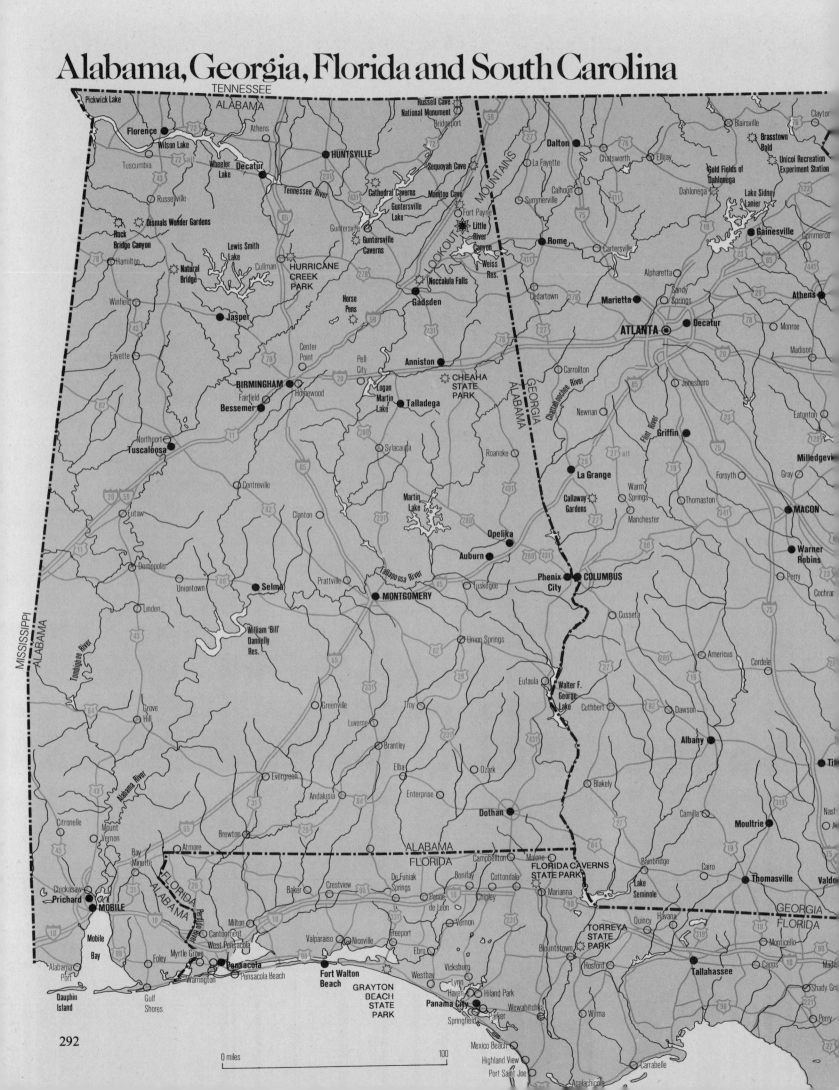

Alabama, Georgia, Florida and South Carolina

ALABAMA

Pickwick Lake

Florence
Wilson Lake
Athens

HUNTSVILLE

Russell Cave
National Monument
Bridgeport

Blairsville
Claytor

Dalton
Chatsworth
La Fayette
Ellijay

Brasstown
Bald

Unicoi Recreation
Experiment Station

Tuscumbia
Wheeler
Lake
Decatur

Tennessee River

Sequoyah Cave

Manitou Cave

Calhoun

Gold Fields of
Dahlonega

Russellville

Cathedral Caverns

Guntersville
Lake

Fort Payne

Summerville
Dahlonega

Lake Sidney
Lanier

Dismals Wonder Gardens

Lewis Smith
Lake

Guntersville

Little
River
Canyon

Rome

Cartersville

Gainesville
Commerce

Rock
Bridge Canyon

Hamilton

Natural
Bridge

Cullman

HURRICANE
CREEK
PARK

Guntersville
Caverns

Noccalula Falls

Weiss
Res.

Cedartown

Alpharetta

Athens

Winfield

Horse
Pens

Gadsden

Marietta

Sandy
Springs

Fayette

Center
Point

Pell
City

Anniston

Carrollton

ATLANTA
Decatur
Monroe

Jasper

Madison

BIRMINGHAM
Fairfield
Homewood

Logan
Martin
Lake

CHEAHA
STATE
PARK

Newnan

Jonesboro

Bessemer

Talladega

Eatonton

Northport
Tuscaloosa

Centreville

Sylacauga

Roanoke

La Grange

Warm
Springs

Forsyth

Gray

Griffin

Milledgevi

Eutaw

Clanton

Martin
Lake

Callaway
Gardens

Thomaston

MACON

Demopolis

Uniontown

Prattville

Opelika

Manchester

Warner
Robins
Perry

Linden

Auburn

Phenix
City
COLUMBUS

Cochran

Selma

Tuskegee

Cusseta

MONTGOMERY

William 'Bill'
Dannelly
Res.

Union Springs

Americus

Cordele

Greenville

Troy

Eufaula

Walter F.
George
Lake

Cuthbert

Dawson

Grove
Hill

Luverne

Albany

Ti

Brantley

Evergreen

Elba

Ozark

Blakely

Citronelle

Andalusia

Enterprise

Camilla

Moultrie

Mount
Vernon

Brewton

Dothan

ALABAMA
FLORIDA

Campbellton
Malone

FLORIDA CAVERNS
STATE PARK

Bainbridge

Cairo

Thomasville
Valdo

Bay
Minette

Atmore

Baker

Crestview

De Funiak
Springs

Bonifay

Cottondale

Chipley

Marianna

Lake
Seminole

Quincy

Havana

GEORGIA
FLORIDA

Chickasaw
Prichard
MOBILE

Milton

Ponce
de Leon

TORREYA
STATE
PARK

Monticello

Cantonment
West Pensacola

Valparaiso
Niceville

Freeport

Ebro

Vernon

Vicksburg

Bloomstown

Hosford

Mobile
Bay

Myrtle Grove
Pensacola

Fort Walton
Beach

Westbay

Hiland Park

Tallahassee

Capps

Dauphin
Island

Warrington
Pensacola Beach

GRAYTON
BEACH
STATE
PARK

Panama City

Parker

Wewahitchka

Wilma

Shady Gr

Alabama
Port
Gulf Shores
Foley

Springfield

Mexico Beach

Highland View

Carrabelle

Perry

Port Saint Joe
Analachicola

0 miles   100

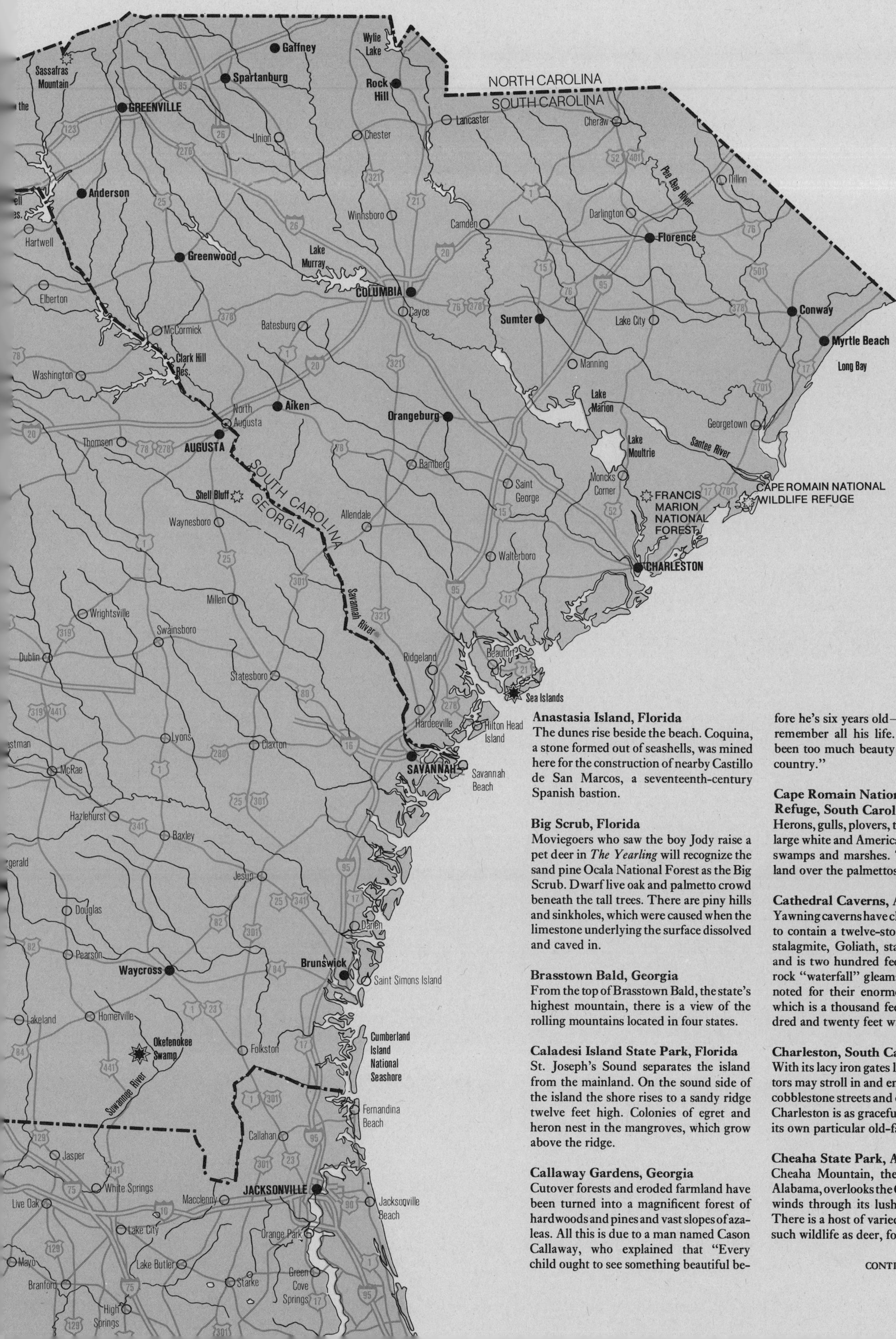

SASSAFRAS MOUNTAIN
NORTH CAROLINA
SOUTH CAROLINA
Gaffney
Spartanburg
Wylie Lake
Rock Hill
GREENVILLE
Anderson
Lancaster
Cheraw
Chester
Union
Hartwell
Elberton
Greenwood
Lake Murray
Winnsboro
Camden
Darlington
Florence
Dillon
Pee Dee River
COLUMBIA
Cayce
Sumter
Lake City
Conway
Myrtle Beach
Long Bay
Washington
McCormick
Batesburg
Manning
Clark Hill Res.
North Augusta
Aiken
Orangeburg
Lake Marion
Georgetown
Lake Moultrie
Santee River
SOUTH CAROLINA
GEORGIA
Thomson
AUGUSTA
Bamberg
Saint George
Moncks Corner
CAPE ROMAIN NATIONAL WILDLIFE REFUGE
Shell Bluff
Waynesboro
Allendale
FRANCIS MARION NATIONAL FOREST
Walterboro
CHARLESTON
Millen
Savannah River
Statesboro
Wrightsville
Swainsboro
Ridgeland
Beaufort
Sea Islands
Dublin
Hardeeville
Hilton Head Island
Lyons
Claxton
McRae
SAVANNAH
Savannah Beach
Hazlehurst
Baxley
Jesup
Douglas
Pearson
Darien
Brunswick
Saint Simons Island
Waycross
Homerville
Cumberland Island National Seashore
Lakeland
Okefenokee Swamp
Folkston
Fernandina Beach
Suwannee River
Callahan
JACKSONVILLE
Jacksonville Beach
Jasper
White Springs
Macclenny
Live Oak
Lake City
Orange Park
Mayo
Lake Butler
Starke
Green Cove Springs
Branford
High Springs

Anastasia Island, Florida

The dunes rise beside the beach. Coquina, a stone formed out of seashells, was mined here for the construction of nearby Castillo de San Marcos, a seventeenth-century Spanish bastion.

Big Scrub, Florida

Moviegoers who saw the boy Jody raise a pet deer in *The Yearling* will recognize the sand pine Ocala National Forest as the Big Scrub. Dwarf live oak and palmetto crowd beneath the tall trees. There are piny hills and sinkholes, which were caused when the limestone underlying the surface dissolved and caved in.

Brasstown Bald, Georgia

From the top of Brasstown Bald, the state's highest mountain, there is a view of the rolling mountains located in four states.

Caladesi Island State Park, Florida

St. Joseph's Sound separates the island from the mainland. On the sound side of the island the shore rises to a sandy ridge twelve feet high. Colonies of egret and heron nest in the mangroves, which grow above the ridge.

Callaway Gardens, Georgia

Cutover forests and eroded farmland have been turned into a magnificent forest of hardwoods and pines and vast slopes of azaleas. All this is due to a man named Cason Callaway, who explained that "Every child ought to see something beautiful be-

fore he's six years old—something he will remember all his life. And there hasn't been too much beauty in this part of the country."

Cape Romain National Wildlife Refuge, South Carolina

Herons, gulls, plovers, terns, ducks and the large white and American egrets live in the swamps and marshes. The birds soar inland over the palmettos and live oaks.

Cathedral Caverns, Alabama

Yawning caverns have chasms deep enough to contain a twelve-story building; and a stalagmite, Goliath, stands sixty feet tall and is two hundred feet in girth. A pink rock "waterfall" gleams. The caverns are noted for their enormous cave opening, which is a thousand feet long and a hundred and twenty feet wide.

Charleston, South Carolina

With its lacy iron gates left ajar so that visitors may stroll in and enjoy its gardens, its cobblestone streets and cavalier way of life, Charleston is as graceful as it is worldly in its own particular old-fashioned way.

Cheaha State Park, Alabama

Cheaha Mountain, the highest point in Alabama, overlooks the Coosa River, which winds through its lush valley far below. There is a host of varied wild flowers, and such wildlife as deer, fox, wild turkey and

CONTINUED ON PAGE 294

Alabama, Georgia, Florida and South Carolina

CONTINUED FROM PAGE 293

wild pig. Birdwatchers can see hawks, owls, crows, doves, quail and redheaded woodpeckers.

Corkscrew Swamp Sanctuary, Florida
Giant bald cypress trees were growing here when King John acceded to the barons at Runnymede. The bald cypress, so-called because it loses its leaves in winter, lives in the ten-thousand-four-hundred-acre sanctuary and provides a nesting ground for the wood ibis. These large wading birds do not nest unless they feel confident that there will be a sufficient food supply for their offspring.

Dismals Wonder Gardens, Alabama
Dismalites are tiny phosphorescent worms that twinkle in the dark in this protected canyon. The entrance to the canyon is a narrow slit in a boulder cracked by an earthquake which has been dubbed "Fat Man's Misery." Grottoes, waterfalls and six natural bridges contribute to the beauty of the natural gardens.

Everglades National Park, Florida
This watery wilderness is an eerie world of dense mangrove forests, alligators, crocodiles, strange vegetarian manatees and plumed birds. (See page 146.)

Farles Prairie Recreation Area, Florida
There is an extensive glade in the forest at the heart of fifty sawgrass-fringed lakes.

Floating Islands, Florida
Fishermen on central Florida lakes pinch themselves with disbelief when an island comes floating by. Lofty maple, loblolly, elder and myrtle rise out of the floating mass. The islands began when matted grass on the lake bed bobbed to the surface. Other plants took hold to form floating islands.

Florida Caverns State Park, Florida
A river disappears within the caverns. This network of caves in the valley of the Chipola River was discovered in 1937, when a tree blew down and revealed an opening where its roots had spread.

Florida Keys, Florida
Floridians say that the keys are "a land that's mostly water and an earth that's mostly sky." The keys curve south and west from the Florida mainland for more than a hundred miles. The Overseas Highway, built on an old railroad trestle, connects the subtropical islands set amid turquoise waters.

Francis Marion National Forest, South Carolina
Named for the legendary "Swamp Fox" of the American Revolution, General Francis Marion, who hid from the King's soldiers in the low country, the forest contains a good part of the coastal plain. Guilliard Lake is separated from the Santee River by a finger of land and is surrounded by cypress.

294

Gateway to the Mountains, South Carolina
Within this district of the Sumter National Forest are spots that seem unchanged since the days when they were Cherokee hunting grounds. The Chattooga River is wild and remote and accessible only on foot.

Goldfields of Dahlonega, Georgia
Preacher's Cut, a deep gorge created by goldmining in the Crown Mountains in Dahlonega, was once owned by a preacher. The site of the 1830s gold rush, gold can still be panned from the sand and gravel.

Grayton Beach State Park, Florida
Full-grown trees, trunks scoured smooth by windblown sand, branches twisted toward the sun, thrive although they are half buried in the drifting sand. Fuchsia clusters vie with yellow trumpet flowers and wild blue lupines in adding color to the beach.

Guntersville Caverns, Alabama
Rich in colorful formations and sea fossils, the caverns also contain relics of an Indian occupation long ago.

Highlands Hammock State Park, Florida
Deer feed among wild orange groves, and alligators bask on logs along the catwalk that leads through this cypress swamp. Sometimes ten-foot alligators may be seen sunning themselves beside huge turtles. Deer emerge from the palmetto thickets in the evening.

Hillsborough River State Park, Florida
The spring-fed river flows among palms, live oaks, pines and hardwoods of great beauty.

Horse Pens, Alabama
The jutting rocks created a natural corral, which the Indians once used to pen their ponies.

Hurricane Creek Park, Alabama
A pool with a white sand bottom lies at the base of a deep gorge. Waterfalls splash beside a trail that winds up a natural spiral stone staircase.

Ichetucknee River, Florida
A tributary of the Suwannee, this wilderness river flows pure and cool over white sand. It has its beginning at a spring of dazzling turquoise color. Cypress trees bearded with Spanish moss crowd the riverbanks. Water oaks and willows dip low over the placid flow. Along the stream other springs boil up and contribute their clear waters.

John Pennekamp Coral Reef State Park, Florida
H.M.S. *Winchester*, a British man-of-war which foundered in a hurricane in 1695, lies half buried in the sand thirty feet below the surface, where skin divers may view it. There are six hundred varieties of fish and twelve hundred kinds of marine plants in this 100,333 acres of underwater wonders. Forty of the fifty-two types of living coral

found on the coast live here, where Audubon studied birds.

Jonathan Dickinson State Park, Florida
Eagles nest high in tall cypress trees. The nests are five feet across and may weigh a ton, since they are built of heavy tree branches and sticks to support the eight-to thirteen-pound adult birds and their eaglets. Mating pairs come to their nests in the autumn and rebuild them in preparation for the eggs.

Juniper Springs, Florida
Through the lush subtropical Ocala Forest flows over eight and one-half million gallons of water a day from the springs, which were visited by Hernando de Soto in the spring of 1539. Bald eagles and Florida's largest herd of deer live in the forest.

Little River Canyon, Alabama
The river flows between steep walls, green with forests, through the deepest gorge east of the Rockies. (See page 160.)

Manitou Cave, Alabama
In the 1890s, people who lived in the vicinity held candlelight dances in the cave, which is notable for its colorful formations and a stream that meanders along its floor. Water dripping from the ceiling forms a cubic inch of stalagmite every hundred years, and the caverns have huge stalagmites that are judged to be at least 186 million years old.

Myakka River State Park, Florida
Hammocks of spreading oaks and lofty sabal palms break the savannah-like marshes along the Myakka River. Florida panthers are sometimes encountered on the lonely trails, but not often, for they are an endangered species. Bald eagle, sandhill crane and alligator—all endangered species—also may be seen.

Natural Bridge, Alabama
Sandstone arches bend across the canyon, where mountain laurels blossom and giant magnolias bear flowers with a span of fourteen inches.

Noccalula Falls, Alabama
The falls drop a hundred feet from a limestone ledge in a region of canyons and mountains called the Alabama Appalachians.

Okefenokee Swamp, Georgia
This half-a-million-acre swamp is called the "land of the trembling earth." (See page 144.)

Rock Bridge Canyon, Alabama
Subtropical shrubs live in the canyon, where there are caves, a waterfall and a sandstone arch overhead. Clay for making pottery was mined from beneath the arch by the Indians.

Russell Cave National Monument, Alabama
The most important archaeological discovery in the Southeast was made in this cave. Layer upon layer of artifacts give

evidence of man's occupation dating back eight thousand years.

St. Augustine, Florida
Founded in 1565 by the Spanish, the city is the oldest European settlement in the United States. There are many historic buildings in the Spanish–Colonial section.

St. Johns River, Florida
The peninsula's greatest river flows north for most of its three hundred miles. From its marshy beginnings the river expands into a three-mile-wide flood; it is a winding waterway lined with pine trees and groves of orange, oak and palm. Since the river is only twenty feet above sea level at its source, it is not only among the widest of the world's rivers, broadening out to form long lakes, but also the laziest.

Sassafras Mountain, South Carolina
At three thousand five hundred and sixty feet, the mountain is the highest point in the state.

Sea Islands, Georgia and South Carolina
Moss-draped live oaks beside sandy beaches and tales of buried pirate treasure are all part of these golden islands. (See page 166.)

Sequoyah Cave, Alabama
Before 500 B.C. Indians lived in this cave, which is situated beneath Sand Mountain. The calcite flowers are brilliantly colored, and the helictites have a rare delicacy. Stalactites and stalagmites shade from cream, salmon, brown and blue to black onyx.

Sanibel Islands, Florida
The tides bring shells in from the sea to this island, whose beaches conchologists consider among the best for shelling in the western hemisphere. A wildlife refuge on the island attracts roseate spoonbills and species of ibis, egret and heron.

Shell Bluff, Georgia
High above the Savannah River, the bluff contains giant oyster fossils twelve to fifteen inches long. The bed was formed when the coastal plains of Georgia were submerged beneath the ocean.

Silver Springs, Florida
More than five hundred million gallons of water a day flow from the springs. They are the largest in a state famed for its springs, which occur in forty-six of Florida's sixty-seven counties.

Torreya State Park, Florida
Tall pines stand on high hills in this piny woods country. The Florida yew grows along the ravines.

Unicoi Recreation Experiment Station, Georgia
The station, operated by the Northeast Mountains Authority, in the Chattahoochee National Forest, is a unique facility of its type. In a wooded hill setting, it offers comprehensive programs and research for the recreation industry.

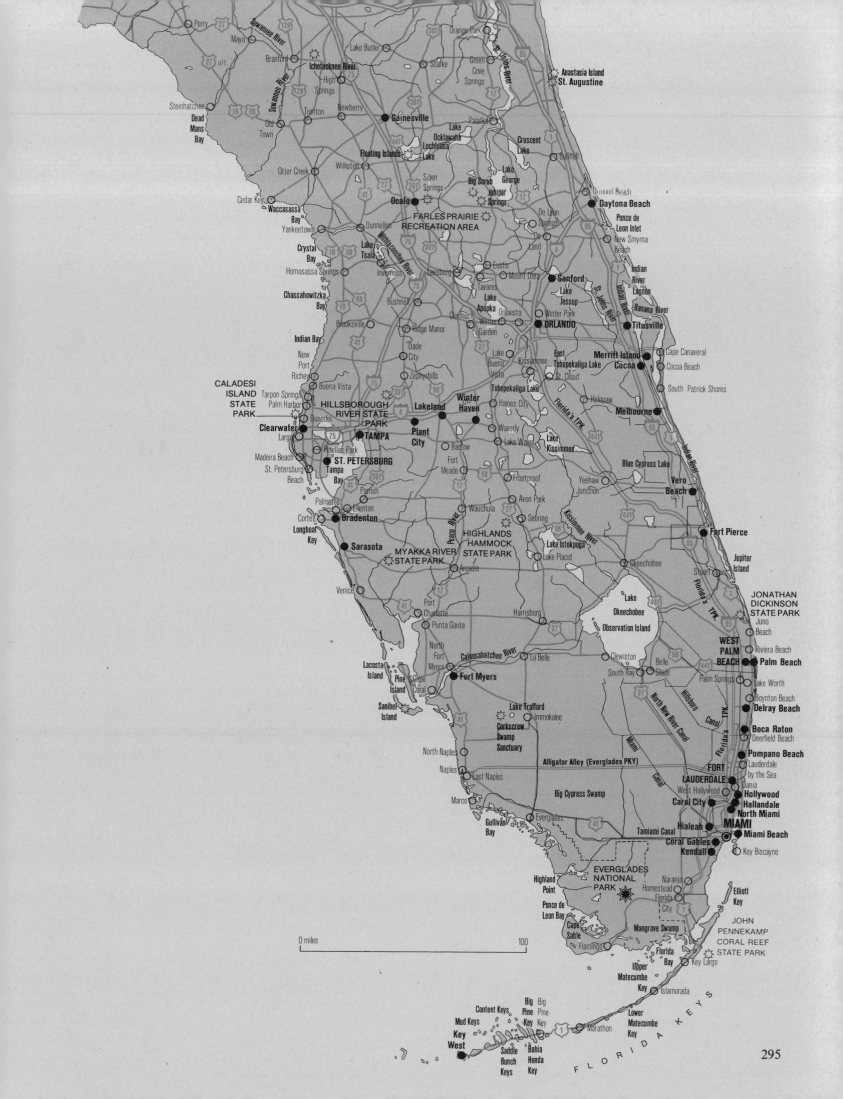

Perry 27
Suwannee River 129
Mayo
Branford
Steinhatchee 19 98
Dead Mans Bay
Old Town
27 alt.
High Springs
Trenton
Newberry
Ichetucknee River
Lake Butler
Starke
Orange Park
Anastasia Island
St. Augustine
Gainesville
Palatka
Crescent Lake
Green Cove Springs
Buttnall
Lake Ocklawaha
Lochloosa Lake
Floating Islands
Williston
Silver Springs
Big Scrub
Lake George
Juniper Springs
Ocala
FARLES PRAIRIE RECREATION AREA
Daytona Beach
Ormond Beach
Ponce de Leon Inlet
New Smyrna Beach
De Leon Springs
De Land
Cedar Key
Waccasassa Bay
Yankeetown
Dunnellon
Otter Creek
Crystal Bay
19 98
Lake Tsala
Inverness
Withlacoochee River
Leesburg
Eustis
Tavares
Mount Dora
Sanford
Lake Jessup
Indian River Lagoon
Indian River
Homosassa Springs
Chassahowitzka Bay
19
Bushnell
Lake Apopka
Oriovista
Winter Park
ORLANDO
St. Johns River
Banana River
Brooksville
Ridge Manor
Clermont
Winter Garden
Titusville
Indian Bay
41
Dade City
Lake Buena Vista
Kissimmee
East Tohopekaliga Lake
St. Cloud
Merritt Island
Cocoa
Cape Canaveral
Cocoa Beach
New Port Richey
Zephyrhills
Tohopekaliga Lake
South Patrick Shores
CALADESI ISLAND STATE PARK
Tarpon Springs
Palm Harbor
Buena Vista
HILLSBOROUGH RIVER STATE PARK
Lakeland
Winter Haven
Haines City
Florida's TPK.
Holopaw
Melbourne
Dunedin
Clearwater
Largo
TAMPA
Plant City
Bartow
Waverly
Lake Wales
Lake Kissimmee
Pinellas Park
Madeira Beach
ST. PETERSBURG
Fort Meade
Frostproof
Yeehaw Junction
Blue Cypress Lake
Vero Beach
St. Petersburg Beach
Tampa Bay
41
Parrish
98
Avon Park
Kissimmee River
Palmetto
Ellenton
Wauchula
Sebring
Fort Pierce
Cortez
Bradenton
Peace River
Sebring
Lake Istokpoga
Longboat Key
Sarasota
MYAKKA RIVER STATE PARK
HIGHLANDS HAMMOCK STATE PARK
Lake Placid
Okeechobee
Jupiter Island
Venice
Arcadia
Lake Okeechobee
Observation Island
JONATHAN DICKINSON STATE PARK
Juno Beach
Port Charlotte
Harrisburg
Clewiston
Stuart
Florida's TPK.
95
Punta Gorda
Belle Glade
WEST PALM BEACH
Riviera Beach
North Fort Myers
Caloosahatchee River
La Belle
South Bay
Palm Beach
Lacosta Island
Pine Island
Cape Coral
Palm Springs
Lake Worth
Boynton Beach
Sanibel Island
Fort Myers
Lake Trafford
Immokalee
Delray Beach
Corkscrew Swamp Sanctuary
North New River Canal
Boca Raton
Deerfield Beach
Hillsboro Canal
Pompano Beach
North Naples
Alligator Alley (Everglades PKY.)
FORT LAUDERDALE
Lauderdale by the Sea
Bania
Naples
East Naples
Big Cypress Swamp
West Hollywood
Hollywood
Miami Canal
Hallandale
Marco
Carol City
North Miami
MIAMI
Hialeah
Miami Beach
Everglades
Tamiami Canal
Coral Gables
Kendall
Key Biscayne
Gullivan Bay
EVERGLADES NATIONAL PARK
Naranja
Homestead
Florida City
Elliott Key
Highland Point
Ponce de Leon Bay
Cape Sable
JOHN PENNEKAMP CORAL REEF STATE PARK
Mangrove Swamp
0 miles   100
Flamingo
Florida Bay
Key Largo
Upper Matecumbe Key
Islamorada
Big Pine Key
Content Keys
Mud Keys
Lower Matecumbe Key
Key West
Saddle Bunch Keys
Bahia Honda Key
Marathon
FLORIDA KEYS

295

North Carolina and Virginia

Appalachian Trail, North Carolina and Virginia
The East's major hiking trail follows the crest of the mountains on its way from northern New England south to trail's end. (See page 148.)

Blowing Rock, North Carolina
Toss a handkerchief off the rock that juts out over John's River Gorge and an updraft blows it back to hand.

Brown Mountain, North Carolina
Mysterious lights appearing over the mountain at night have been attributed to radioactivity, foxfire, St. Elmo's Fire and escaping underground gas that ignites in some fashion. Mountain people say the lights are caused by demons, who inhabit the peak.

Cape Hatteras National Seashore, North Carolina
Sand beaches, waterfowl refuges and seashore villages are all part of the Outer Banks. (See page 168.)

Cowee Valley, North Carolina
The Cowee Valley produces rubies and sapphires.

George Washington National Forest, Virginia
Mountains and valleys are steeped in American history and folklore. The ridges knew the moccasins of the Indians. Pig Iron Trail leads to old Elizabeth Furnace.

Goshen Pass Natural Area, Virginia
Three ridges radiate from the high point of Little North Mountain and drop sharply to the Maury River. The rocks of the pass are tough quartzite, formed when ancient sandstone was fused by powerful pressures. Mountain pine and scrubby bear oak grow on the high, dry ridges.

Grayson Highlands State Park, Virginia
Rugged Mount Rogers thrusts high above the other peaks in this country, where subalpine views are as common as they are unexpected.

Great Smoky Mountains, North Carolina
Most of the highest peaks east of the Mississippi are in these lofty mountains, which the Indians called the "Mountains of the Smokes" because of the mist that hangs over them. (See page 152.)

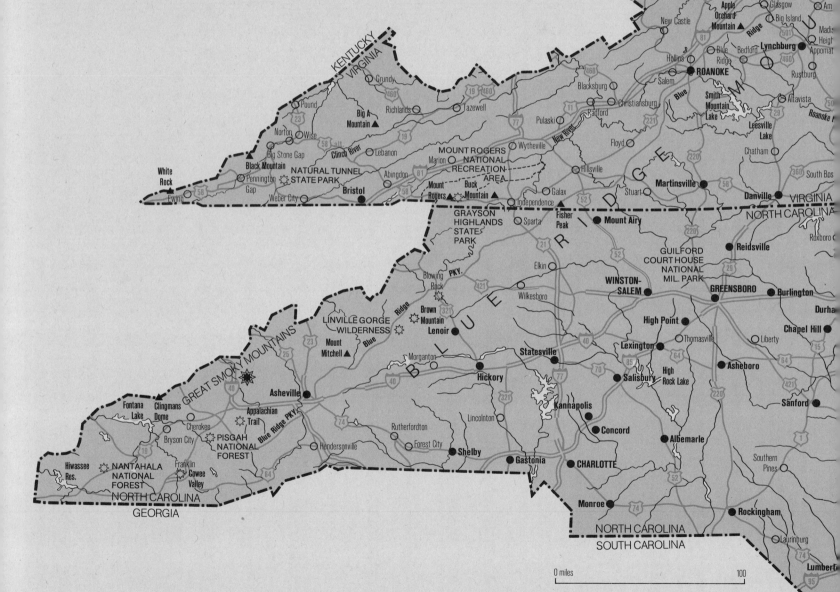

Linville Gorge Wilderness, North Carolina

The Linville River plunges around huge boulders in the gorge, which begins at Linville Falls and stretches some twelve miles to where the river bursts free into the Catawba Valley. The never-cut timber is as varied today as it was when botanist Andrew Michaux visited the gorge in 1802. The area was named for William Linville and his son, who were scalped by Indians here in 1766.

Luray Caverns, Virginia

Vast caves are magnificent with stalactites and stalagmites. The caverns were discovered when Andrew Campbell, a local tinsmith, put his hand over a hole in the ground and felt a draft of air. He made the opening large enough to crawl through, and with rope in one hand and a candle in the other he descended into one of the largest caverns in the East.

Monticello, Virginia

The imprint of statesman Thomas Jefferson's genius as an architect is seen at his home. (See page 170.)

Nantahala National Forest, North Carolina

The forest of 457,627 acres is remarkable for its large number of waterfalls and for the primeval, three-thousand-eight-hundred-and-forty acre Joyce Kilmer Memorial Forest, dedicated to the poet who wrote *Trees*. Some of the poplars, hemlocks, oaks, sycamores and beeches are a hundred feet tall. Decaying logs are all that is left of the American chestnuts, wiped out by blight.

Natural Tunnel State Park, Virginia

A stream has carved a tunnel eight hundred and fifty feet long and as high as a ten-story building through a limestone ridge. Steep stone walls in the area are surmounted by lofty chimneys of rock.

Pisgah National Forest, North Carolina

Gifford Pinchot, the first trained forester in the United States, described the forest as "a great bowl with mountains for the rim, and in the middle the white and rosy blossoms of impenetrable thickets of laurel and rhododendron." Shining Rock Wilderness Area comprises thirteen thousand six hundred acres around Shining Rock Mountain, where white quartz crystals on the high slopes shine like mirrors in the sun

Shenandoah National Park, Virginia

The crests of the Blue Ridge look down on a valley of orchards and nestling towns. (See page 156.)

Williamsburg, Virginia

The Colonial capital of Virginia has been restored much as it was when Jefferson, Washington and Patrick Henry frequented its inns and public buildings. Listening to a harpsichord by candlelight in the Royal Governor's Palace brings the eighteenth century alive.

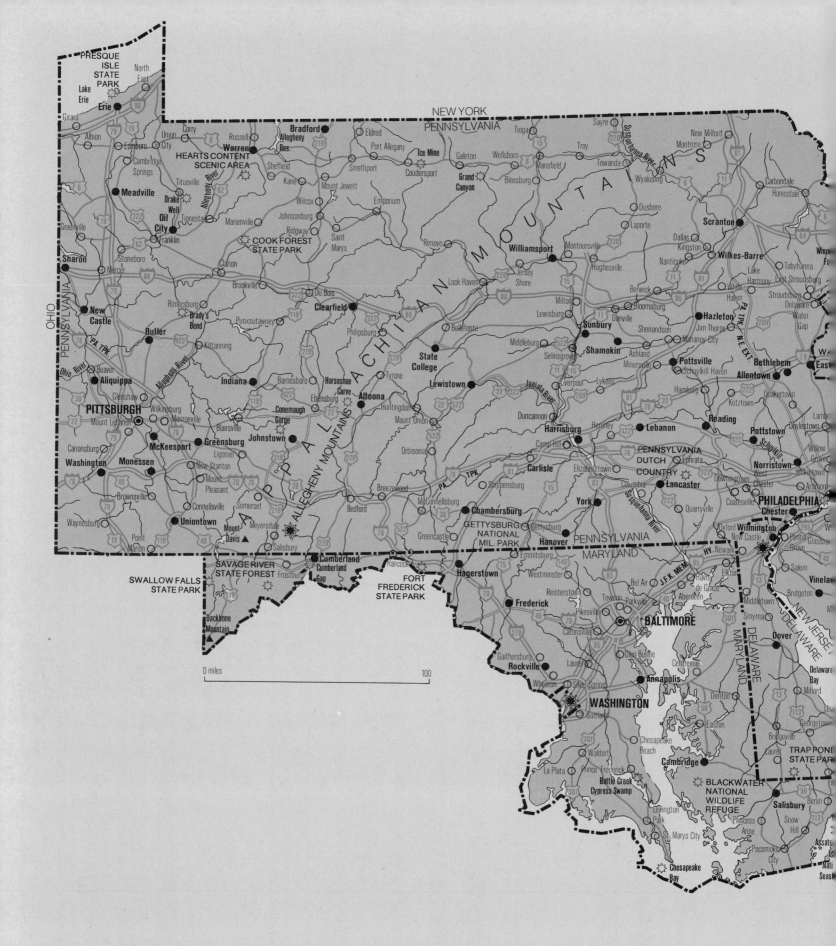

Delaware, Maryland, New Jersey and Pennsylvania

Allegheny Mountains, Pennsylvania
Forested hills, rocky precipices and sparkling mountain streams mark the Alleghenies with beauty. (See page 198.)

Assateague Island National Seashore, Maryland
This almost deserted island of white sand beaches, dunes and stands of pine was created by a hurricane and is still altered by wind and sea. (See page 142.)

Battle Creek Cypress Swamp, Maryland
The northernmost stand of the hundred-foot-tall bald cypress is an important breeding place for the rare pine woods tree frog.

Blackwater National Wildlife Refuge, Maryland
Migrant and wintering waterfowl, using the Atlantic Flyway from Canada to the Florida Keys, stop off in this 11,216-acre preserve of freshwater ponds, marshes, brush and timbered swamps. The wetlands are interspersed with dark stands of loblolly pine trees.

Brady's Bend, Pennsylvania
The Allegheny River makes a horseshoe curve between wooded hills. At the narrowest point in the bend, Captain Samuel Brady won a decisive victory over the Indians.

Bull's Island, New Jersey
The Delaware River on the west and the Delaware and Raritan Canal make an island of this area of luxurious plant growth and interesting species of animals.

Cape Henlopen State Park, Delaware
Early settlers made candles from the waxy bayberries that grow near the cape. Lashed by storms, the cape still supports areas of pine woods, and nearby is a succession of bogs and high dunes.

Chesapeake Bay, Maryland
This shallow and brackish inland sea extends for 195 miles from bay mouth to the Susquehanna River. It is the largest estuary on the Atlantic coast of the United States.

Conemaugh Gorge, Pennsylvania
Glacier-age rocks rise one thousand three hundred and fifty feet above the Conemaugh River to form the deepest water gap in the state.

Cook Forest State Park, Pennsylvania
The magnificent forest spreads over a plain, now seventeen hundred feet high throughout, but once a sea-level plain. Pines and hemlocks give the forest an evergreen beauty in winter and summer.

Cumberland Gap, Maryland
The passage through the mountains, used by early explorers, soldiers and pioneers entering the land beyond the Alleghenies, has great scenic beauty.

Delaware Water Gap, Pennsylvania
The Delaware River slices through the wooded Pocono Mountains to form a beautiful, narrow wooded gorge. (See page 174.)

Drake Well, Pennsylvania
When, on August 8, 1859, oil flowed from Colonel Drake's well, the petroleum industry was born in Pennsylvania.

Fort Frederick State Park, Maryland
The First Maryland Regiment, wearing uniforms of the Revolutionary War era and equipped with period weapons and gear, maneuvers at the fort, which is considered to be one of the best preserved of all pre-Revolutionary stone forts in the country.

Grand Canyon, Pennsylvania
Pine Creek Gorge is fifty miles long and nearly one thousand feet deep. Pines and hemlocks tower over the palisades on both rims.

Hearts Content Scenic Area, Pennsylvania
The white pine was used for the masts of clipper ships. Today, the pine towers over the mixed pine, hemlock and hardwood forest, which has been perpetuated as a living museum.

High Point, New Jersey
The Kittatinny Ridge peaks at High Point, 1,803 feet above sea level, the highest place in New Jersey.

Horseshoe Curve, Pennsylvania
Here the Penn Central Railroad swings in a giant horseshoe curve conceived by railway engineers in the early 1850s.

Ice Mine, Pennsylvania
In a pit measuring forty feet deep by about ten feet square, ice begins to form in the spring. Icicles form in the pit all summer long.

Island Beach State Park, New Jersey
The sand dunes bound the Atlantic Ocean for ten miles. Barnegat Bay is to the west of the park, where there are a botanical zone and a wildlife sanctuary.

New Castle, Delaware
Peter Stuyvesant, the one-legged governor of the Dutch New Netherlands, laid out the central green in this lovely town. (See page 178.)

Palisades, New Jersey
The Palisades rise beside the Hudson River.

Penn Forest, New Jersey
Penn Forest is in the heart of the Pine Belt. What was until recently a cranberry bog is now Lake Oswego.

Pennsylvania Dutch Country, Pennsylvania
The land of rich fields that produces magnificent vegetables for the table, of plain Dutch who wear only the most somber clothes and drive about in horse and buggies and of fancy Dutch who dress in the modern style and drive automobiles, this region is one of the East's most colorful.

Philadelphia, Pennsylvania
The home of Independence Hall, where members of the First Continental Congress gathered.

Presque Isle State Park, Pennsylvania
A sandy peninsula reaches out into Lake Erie and is home to four hundred and fifty species of plant life and two hundred and fifty species of birds, as well as fox, raccoon and muskrat. It is the only peninsula on the southern shore of the lake.

Savage River State Forest, Maryland
The Savage and Casselman rivers begin only two miles apart, but flow in opposite directions so that the Savage River reaches the Potomac and the Atlantic, while the Casselman runs north to send its waters ultimately to the Mississippi and the Gulf of Mexico. The fifty-two-thousand-seven-hundred-and-seventy-acre woodland contains some truly rugged terrain.

Stokes Forest, New Jersey
The forest climbs Kittatinny Ridge. The 14,232 acres of woodlands include Tillman Ravine, a natural gorge. The ravine is kept undisturbed by man as a laboratory where natural forest, rocks and climate can be studied.

Swallow Falls State Park, Maryland
The Youghiogheny River tumbles over a falls and rushes through shaded rocky gorges.

Trap Pond State Park, Delaware
A pinewood surrounds Trap Pond. Just to the west of Trap Pond, Trussum Pond contains a rare stand of cypress. The monarchs of the forest are what William Penn called the "Spanish" oak, the tree now known as southern red oak.

Washington, D.C.
Pierre L'Enfant, a French engineer, was appointed by George Washington to draw up plans for the city by the Potomac which would be capital of the nation. (See page 202.)

Washington Rock State Park, New Jersey
During the Revolutionary War, from the top of the First Watchung Mountain, George Washington looked out onto the New Jersey lowlands to observe the movement of British troops.

Wharton Forest, New Jersey
Containing more than a hundred and fifty square miles of pines, the forest is the state's largest. Batsto Village has been restored to its heyday of 1766 to 1850 when it led in iron and glass production.

Winona Falls, Pennsylvania
The waters cascade through five waterfalls among beautiful woodland settings. There are many other falls in the vicinity, where streams dash through the Pocono Mountains.

Adirondacks, New York
The mountains embrace over 2,488,000 acres of state-owned forests through which canoe routes and hiking trails lead. (See page 188.)

Berkshire Hills, Massachusetts
In the autumn the hills turn vibrant yellow, orange and red on the hardwood trees, and pumpkins, squashes, Indian corn and jugs of cider are piled high at roadside stands. The hills are dominated by Mount Greylock, the highest peak in the state.

Block Island, Rhode Island
The island, which guards the eastern entrance of Long Island Sound, was named after Adriaen Block, the Dutch navigator who discovered it at the beginning of the seventeenth century. (See page 176.)

Boston, Massachusetts
Famous for its Georgian houses, winding Charles River and wealth of universities and museums, historic Boston is where the dramatic opening incidents of the American Revolution occurred.

Cape Cod National Seashore, Massachusetts
Dunes and beaches, cranberry bogs and even the spring from which the Pilgrims first drank in the New World are within the seashore, which stretches for thirty-five miles along the wild Atlantic coast. (See page 182.)

The Catskills, New York
Blue-green mountains broken by ragged crags, ravines and waterfalls make up the land of Rip Van Winkle, the legendary Dutchman who slept for twenty years.

Chappaquiddick Island, Massachusetts
Low sand dunes and a sandy beach reach south from Cape Poge Light for about two miles.

Clark Reservation, New York
Ice and water carved a great stone crescent into the limestone wall of the Butternut Valley. A horseshoe-shaped cliff drops a hundred and sixty feet into a round lake of striking green water. A crescent niche in the wall was scoured by a long-dry waterfall that once rivaled Niagara. Estimates have been made that at one time Ice Age glaciers were three thousand feet deep over the valley.

Crane Beach, Massachusetts
Pitchpine woodlands front on the six-mile beach of fine white sand.

Devil's Hopyard State Park, Connecticut
The origin of the area's name is disputable. Some say that the devil has "a great eye for wild and rugged scenery" such as is found here. Others say a man named Dibble grew hops here for brewing beer, and "Dibble's Hopyard" was corrupted into "Devil's Hopyard." Chapman Falls drops more than sixty feet on the Eight Mile River.

Diamond Hill, Rhode Island
A mile-long mass of veined quartz was deposited by hot water, laden with minerals, flowing along a fracture in the earth's crust millions of years ago.

Dinosaur State Park, Connecticut
The tracks of Eubrontes and Anchisauripus dinosaurs from the Triassic Period, a

Connecticut, Massachusetts, New York and Rhode Island

feet in height. Three falls, one 107 feet high, dash down through the thick forest cover. This is Iroquois country, and an Indian longhouse has been preserved at the park.

Litchfield County, Connecticut
The first law school of the new Republic was founded in this peaceful New England county with its beautiful Colonial churches and homes. (See page 196.)

Manhattan Island, New York
An island of skyscrapers, Manhattan is the heart of New York City, a city which it has been said "gets newer every day." (See page 192.)

Mount Holyoke, Massachusetts
The mountain is the highest peak in the area, and from its summit there are fine views of the Connecticut River meandering through its broad valley.

Mystic, Connecticut
The seaport recreates a nineteenth-century coastal village from the days of iron men and wooden ships. The *Charles W. Morgan*, a whaling ship, is tied up at the historic wharf.

Nantucket Island, Massachusetts
The cobblestoned Main Street in the once-important whaling town on the island still is lined with the mansions of sea captains. The island is thirty miles off the Cape Cod coast.

Niagara Falls, New York
The two hundred thousand cubic feet of water per second that thunder out of Lake Erie into Lake Ontario make Niagara Falls one of the world's natural wonders. (See page 200.)

Plymouth, Massachusetts
The Pilgrim settlement of 1627 has been recreated close to the rock onto which the first English settlers were said to have stepped ashore. *Mayflower II* is a full-scale model of the original ship, which sailed across the stormy Atlantic to the New World.

Purgatory Chasm, Rhode Island
Seawater eroded the narrow cleft in the rock ledges over thousands of years.

Soapstone Quarry, Rhode Island
The quarry was excavated by Indians who used the stone for making jars and pots.

Thousand Islands, New York
There are actually more than seventeen hundred islands in the St. Lawrence River, each set like a gem in the vast waters that reach from Cape Vincent at the eastern end of Lake Ontario to Massena. Channels wind among the islands to create a watery maze for boats.

Watkins Glen, New York
Cliffs rise as high as two hundred feet above a roaring stream, which drops a full seven hundred feet in two miles. Of the nineteen waterfalls, the most beautiful is Rainbow Falls.

hundred and eighty million years ago, may be followed. The imprints, numbering more than a thousand, were turned up by a bulldozer excavating for a new highway.

Fire Island National Seashore, New York
Extending thirty-two miles, this national seashore protects the largest remaining barrier beach off the south shore of Long Island.

Finger Lakes, New York
Located in the central part of New York State, the Finger Lakes region comprises seventy-five hundred square miles of blue fjord-like lakes, deep gorges, rock formations and waterfalls. Indians say that the lakes were made when the Creator pressed his hand down on the earth and created this beautiful countryside.

Fort Ticonderoga, New York
Colonial cannons can still be seen at this important eighteenth-century fort, which is now a museum. (See page 190.)

Howe Caverns, New York
In 1842, a draft of cool air on a hot summer's day attracted Lester Howe, a farmer, to the caverns. He widened an opening in the rocks and, torch in hand, climbed into a huge underground room. The caverns wind for a mile and a half along the banks of a subterranean stream, flowing from a hundred and sixty to two hundred feet below the surface.

Letchworth State Park, New York
New Yorkers call the gorge The Grand Canyon of the East. It writhes along seventeen miles of the Genesee River with precipitous walls reaching up to six hundred

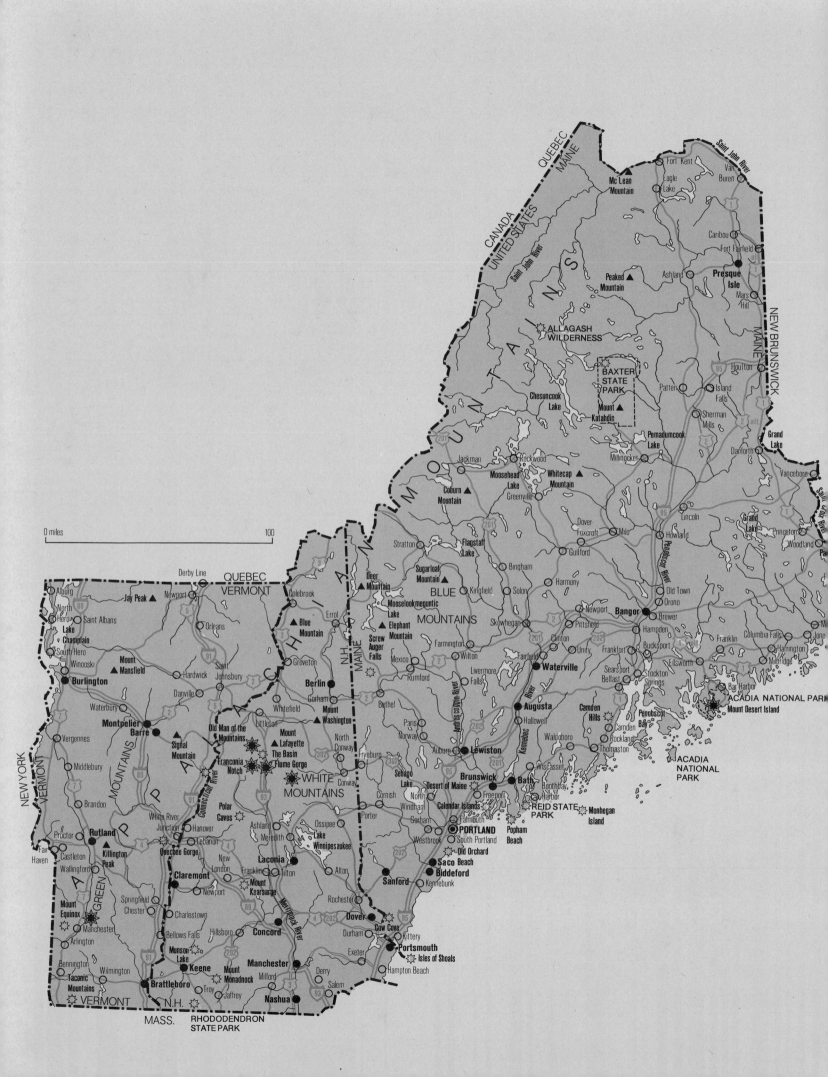

Maine, New Hampshire and Vermont

Acadia National Park, Maine
Established as a national park in 1919, Acadia became the first national park in the East and the only one in New England. Here, surf-splashed cliffs rise to the highest point along the Atlantic coast and are crowned with cool mountain forests.

Allagash Wilderness, Maine
The last great wilderness in the northeastern United States is the land of the Indian, whitetail deer, moose and bald eagle. The white-water Allagash River races through the three-hundred-acre preserve.

The Basin, New Hampshire
A waterfall has bored smooth a deep glacial pothole, twenty feet in diameter.

Baxter State Park, Maine
This wilderness preserve contains more than two hundred thousand acres of mountainous forests, dotted with ponds and streams. Mount Katahdin, Maine's highest point, is within the park. It is upon this peak that the first rays of the morning sun strike the United States mainland. The northern terminus of the Appalachian Trail is in the park, which is the haunt of moose and black bear.

Calendar Islands, Maine
The islands at the entrance to Casco Bay are named for the calendar, since there is at least one for every day of the year. Long promontories and the islands shelter the bay from winter's storms.

Camden Hills, Maine
Mount Megunticook is the highest of the Camden Hills, but from the summit of Mount Battie there is the most outstanding view over Camden Harbor, the ocean, the islands of Penobscot Bay and inland lakes and rivers.

Cobscook Bay, Maine
The bay was named by the Indians. Cobscook means "boiling tide," and the fluctuating water levels make the name apt.

Connecticut River, Vermont and New Hampshire
The Indians called the river Quinatucquet, which means "long estuary." The river, the upper reaches of which are renowned for their beauty, courses among the pine hills and past the farms and apple orchards of northern New England.

Cow Cove, Maine
At this quiet cove in the Vaughan Woods, the first cows landed in the English colonies were brought ashore in 1634 from a boat called *The Pied Cow*. The boat also brought America's first sawmill, and the New England timber industry was born.

Desert of Maine, Maine
This three-hundred-acre miniature desert of shifting sand has engulfed buildings which were in its way.

Flume Gorge, New Hampshire
The chasm reaches along the flank of Mount Liberty. The gorge's fractured Conway granite walls were formed long before the Ice Age. They rise up to seventy feet from the gorge's bottom. (See page 184.)

Franconia Notch, New Hampshire
The deep valley lies between the tall peaks of the Franconia and Kinsman ranges. Trails lead through the six thousand four hundred and forty acres of the valley. (See page 184.)

Green Mountains, Vermont
Samuel de Champlain is said to have taken a look at the mountains across the lake that now bears his name and exclaimed, "*Voilà! Les verts monts!*" and in so doing he christened the range The Green Mountains. (See page 186.)

Isles of Shoals, New Hampshire
Captain John Smith discovered the islands in 1614, and it is believed that Blackbeard, the pirate, buried treasure on them. The windswept isles are five and a half nautical miles off the coast.

Monhegan Island, Maine
Captain John Smith first saw the famed cliffs of Monhegan in 1614.

Mount Desert Island, Maine
The rockbound cliffs of Maine reach their most dramatic point on this island of forests, lakes and fjords in Acadia National Park. (See page 180.)

Mount Equinox, Vermont
On September 19, 1823, Captain Partridge, the director of the American Literary Scientific and Military Academy, led a troop of cadets up the mountain to make barometric observations that indicated the peak was 3,807 feet above sea level. Actually, he was nine feet short of its true altitude.

Mount Kearsarge, New Hampshire
A three-crested, bare-granite summit rears over the highlands.

Mount Monadnock, New Hampshire
The mountain's bald summit of granite reaches 3,165 feet above sea level and almost a thousand feet above the surrounding hills. Early settlers burned off the trees from the mountain to rid themselves of wolves that they believed menaced children and livestock.

Munson Lake, New Hampshire
The lake comes into its own in the middle of winter right after the deer season is over. Ice fishermen, their shacks mounted on runners, thrash their way out through the deep snow and cut holes in the ice through which they fish. The fishermen keep binoculars handy to spy upon their neighbors' luck.

Old Orchard Beach, Maine
This is one of the longest, hardest and smoothest of Atlantic Coast beaches. It runs for eight miles from the mouth of the Saco River to the Scarborough River at Pine Point, and is from four hundred to seven hundred feet wide.

Old Man of the Mountains, New Hampshire
A natural granite profile of a man's face juts from a sheer cliff twelve hundred feet above Profile Lake. When examined closely, the Great Stone Face turns out to be three separate ledges and measures about forty feet from chin to forehead. (See page 184.)

Old Sow, Maine
The Old Sow is a vicious whirlpool that at flood tide forms between Eastport and Deer Isle.

Polar Caves, New Hampshire
The caves boiled under the crust of the earth, were twice buried beneath the sea, uplifted and dropped, and covered and uncovered by ice sheets. Today, they are a deposit of glacial boulders of all shapes and sizes at the base of a granite cliff on the side of Haycock Mountain. Even in midsummer the caves have ice on their floor.

Popham Beach, Maine
Tidal pools, sandy beaches and rocky outcrops make this an appealing place, where the continent meets the Atlantic's surging waves.

Quechee Gorge, Vermont
Vermont's "Little Grand Canyon" is a mile-long chasm through which the Otauquechee River flows.

Quoddy Head, Maine
A lighthouse stands on the easternmost point of the United States mainland. Rock ledges crowned with spruce and fir rise as high as a hundred and ninety feet over the surf. Here, the greatest tides in the United States range from twenty to twenty-eight feet, depending upon phases of the moon.

Reid State Park, Maine
A mile and a half of sand beaches, dunes, marshes, ledges and ocean make this a New England marine beauty spot.

Rhododendron State Park, New Hampshire
More than sixteen acres of wild rhododendron are in full bloom around mid-July.

Screw Auger Falls, Maine
The waters twist and turn their way through the gorge, much like an auger, and in doing so have cut odd forms in the rocks.

Taconic Mountains, Vermont
John Josselyn wrote, in 1672, that Vermont was "full of rocky hills as thick as molehills in a meadow, and clothed with infinite thick woods." In season the mountain laurel flowers on the hills that Josselyn described so well. Blueberries and wild grapes ripen in abandoned pastures.

White Mountains, New Hampshire
"This is the second greatest shown on earth," said P. T. Barnum on reaching the summit of Mount Washington, the highest peak in the White Mountains. Not one to be modest, he left no doubt as to what he considered the greatest show on earth. (See page 184.)

303

Hawaii

Akaka Falls State Park, Hawaii
The falls drop four hundred and twenty feet amid a remarkable variety of tropical ferns.

Black Sand Beach, Hawaii
Black lava sand gleams in the sun against the green of the vegetation and the sparkling blue sea. Coconut palms lift their noble crowns against the sky.

City of Refuge National Historical Park, Hawaii
During the days of the kings of Hawaii, people who broke the law could flee into the City of Refuge without fear of being followed. On a twenty-acre lava shelf dipping into the ocean at the village of Honaunay, this was a guaranteed sanctuary for vanquished warriors and taboo breakers. The Great Wall nearby, built in 1550, is ten feet high and a hundred feet long.

Ewa Forest Reserve, Oahu
The heavy rains nourish the lush growth of this tropical forest, where exotic fruit and flowers may be seen.

Hanalei Valley, Kauai
This tranquil valley, a neat checkerboard of gleaming paddies and fertile fields, nestles peacefully between lush, green mountains. Tumbling waterfalls and frequent rainbows make Hanalei an authentic Pacific paradise.

Haleakala National Park, Maui
The Haleakala Crater is at the end of a tortuous climb to the 9,745-foot-high rim. The volcano is known to the Hawaiians as The House of the Sun. It is a cone-studded remain of a once fiery furnace of the earth that arose millions of years ago from the ocean floor eighteen thousand feet beneath the surface. The volcano has been inactive for a few hundred years.

Hauula Forest Reserve, Oahu
The Sacred Falls plunge eighty-seven feet into a pool among the rocks. There are chimney-like rock formations cut into the canyon wall by water action.

Iao Needle, Maui
The Iao Needle is a volcanic ridge that rises sharply for twelve hundred feet above the floor of Iao Valley, renowned for its native birdlife.

Koolau Range, Oahu
Nuuanu Pali Lookout affords a sweeping view of the cliffs on the windward side of the range, the blue waters of Kaneohe Bay and the buff sands of Kailua.

Laupahoehoe, Hawaii
A finger of lava with a grassy top points out into the sea. On it a plaque tells the tragic story of the great 1964 tidal wave, which smashed ashore and washed a school with twenty-four teachers and children out to sea and to their doom.

Lava Tree State Park, Hawaii
Long ago molten lava coated living trees. When the lava receded, it left trees of stone standing. White, lavender and pink

orchids and fields of papaya grow in between frozen rivers of lava.

Manoa Cliffs, Oahu
Along the cliff trail is an abundance of such plants as maile, ie ie vine, mountain naupaka, kolea, alaa, kapiko, olapua, kolia, ahakea and ohia ai.

Mauna Loa and Kilauea Volcanoes, Hawaii
The smell of sulfur, the inferno of lava in the crater and the nearness of the earth's interior forces at work characterize these great volcanoes that have built Hawaii. (See page 218.)

Mount Waialeale, Kauai
The rainfall over the five-thousand-and-eighty-foot-high mountain is so heavy that seven rivers course down its sides. This is one of the wettest places on earth.

Oahu Island Beach, Oahu
Surfing began as the sport of Hawaiian kings, but it is now a common pursuit on the beautiful beaches of Oahu. (See page 222.)

Pahoa, Hawaii
Anthurium plantations flourish in the shade of giant ferns. The spectacular waxen plants grow in a variety of colors.

Puu O Mahuka, Oahu
The high hill rises above Waimea Bay, and from its peak the ocean can be seen rippling in waves toward the north shore's celebrated beaches.

Puukohola Heiau National Historic Site, Hawaii
Located at Kawaihae Bay on the beautiful northwestern shore of Hawaii, the famous temple built by Kamehameha the Great is closely associated with the founding of the Kingdom of Hawaii.

Queen's Bath, Hawaii
A lava formation encases a pool of cool fresh water. Once Hawaiian queens splashed in the waters set so spectacularly among the black rocks.

Rainbow Falls, Hawaii
The mist of the falls and the rays of the sun combine to create the rainbow for which the falls were named. In the morning the falls are a place of pristine beauty.

Waianapanapa State Park, Maui
A forest of hala impinges on the rocky coast. Secret caves are hidden in the forest, and each has its place in the legends of the islands. There are cave and rock shelters, cairns and graves, and the beach is of black sand. Seabirds nest along the shore, where rock formations include arches, chasms, cliffs and blowholes, where the pounding surf spouts high in the air.

Waimea Canyon, Kauai
The spectacular canyon is an everchanging kaleidoscope of color. High in the canyon the cliffs are orange and red. Where they sweep down to the sea they are a lush tropical green. (See page 220.)

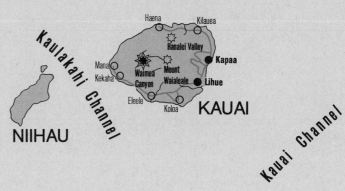

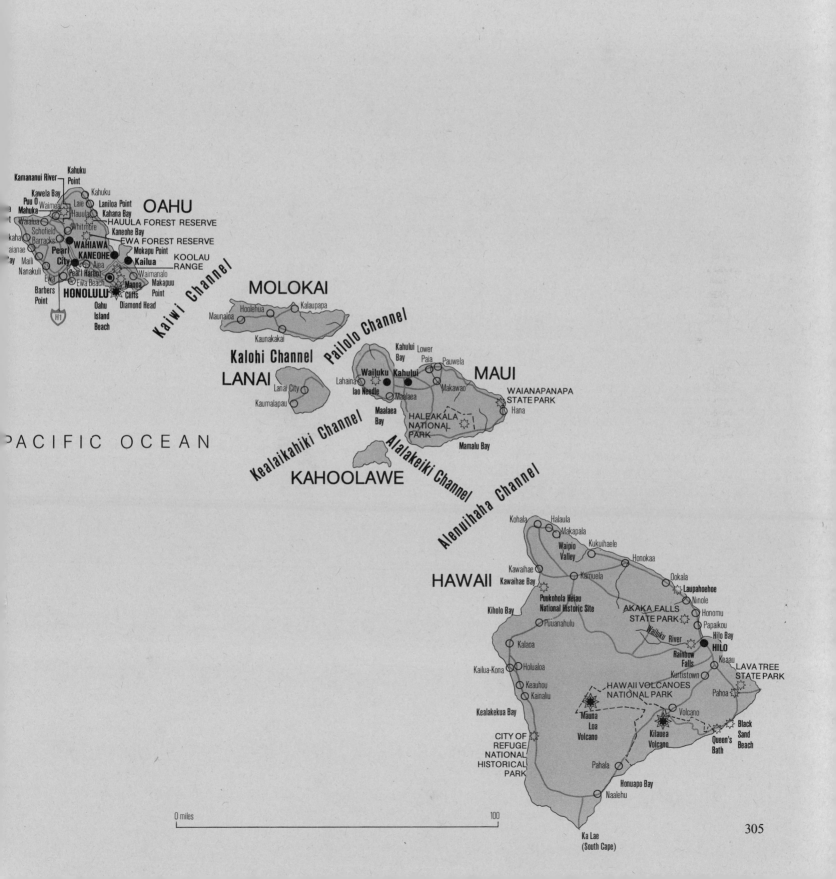

OAHU

Kamananui River
Kahuku Point
Kawela Bay
Puu O
Mahuka
Waimea
Waialua
Schofield
Barracks
Kahuku
Laie
Laniloa Point
Kahana Bay
Haula
HAUULA FOREST RESERVE
Whitmore
Kaneohe Bay
EWA FOREST RESERVE
WAHIAWA
Kaneohe
Mokapu Point
kaha
aianae
Maili
Nanakuli
Pearl City
Aiea
KANEOHE
Kailua
KOOLAU RANGE
Pearl Harbor
Waimanalo
Ewa
Ewa Beach
Manoa
Makapuu Point
Barbers
Point
HONOLULU
Oahu
Island
Beach
Diamond Head
Cliffs
H1

Kaiwi Channel

MOLOKAI
Maunaloa
Hoolehua
Kalaupapa
Kaunakakai

Kalohi Channel

Pailolo Channel

LANAI
Lanai City
Lahaina
Iao Needle
Kaumalapau
Wailuku
Kahului
Kahului Bay
Lower Paia
Pauwela
MAUI
Makawao
Maalaea
WAIANAPANAPA STATE PARK
Hana

Kealaikahiki Channel

Maalaea Bay
HALEAKALA NATIONAL PARK
Mamalu Bay

PACIFIC OCEAN

Alalakeiki Channel

KAHOOLAWE

Alenuihaha Channel

HAWAII

Kohala
Halaula
Makapala
Waipio Valley
Kukuihaele
Honokaa
Kawaihae
Kamuela
Ookala
Kawaihae Bay
Laupahoehoe
Puukohola Heiau National Historic Site
Ninole
Kiholo Bay
AKAKA FALLS STATE PARK
Honomu
Puuanahulu
Papaikou
Wailuku River
Kalaoa
HILO
Hilo Bay
Kailua-Kona
Holualoa
Rainbow Falls
Keaau
Keauhou
Kurtistown
LAVA TREE STATE PARK
Kainaliu
HAWAII VOLCANOES NATIONAL PARK
Pahoa
Kealakekua Bay
Mauna Loa Volcano
Volcano
CITY OF REFUGE NATIONAL HISTORICAL PARK
Kilauea Volcano
Queen's Bath
Black Sand Beach
Pahala
Honuapo Bay
Naalehu
Ka Lae (South Cape)

0 miles   100

305

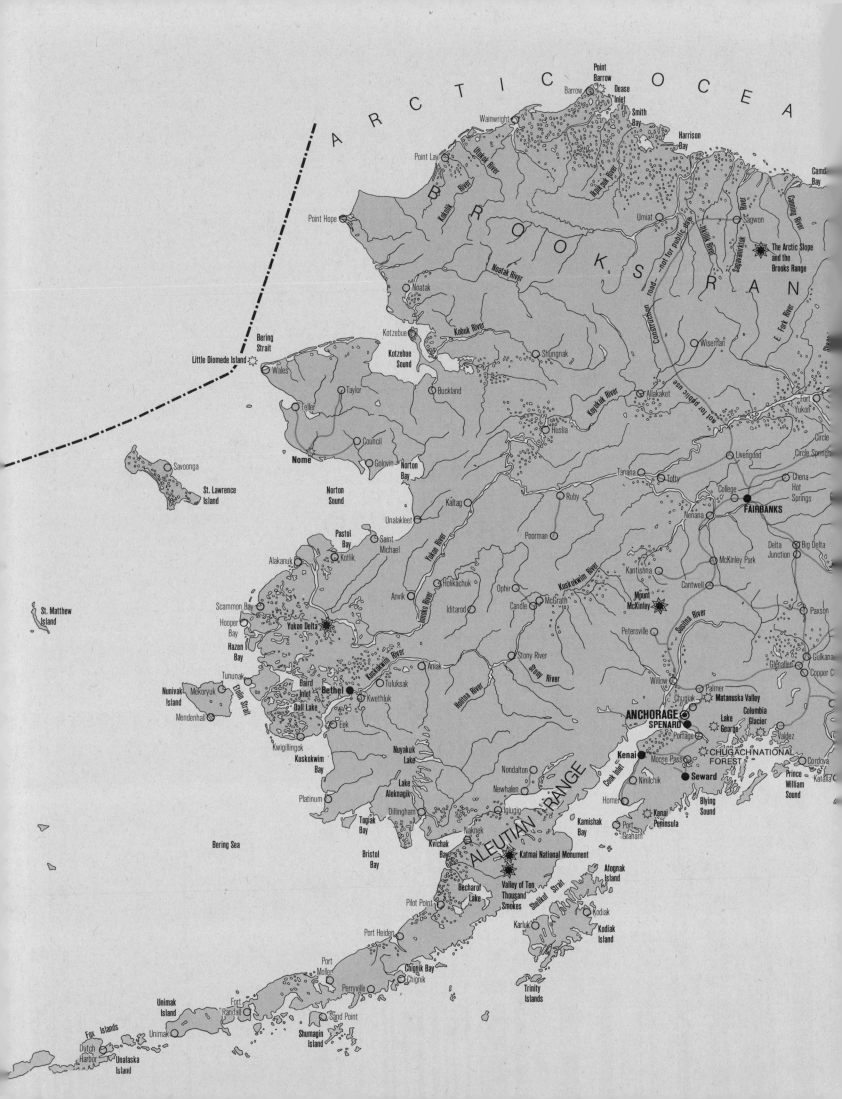

Alaska

The Arctic Slope and the Brooks Range
The Brooks Range, one of North America's few east–west mountain chains, rises behind the petroleum-rich Arctic Slope. (See page 214.)

Chilkoot Pass
The formidable Chilkoot Pass is the gateway from the coast to the Yukon. During the great Gold Rush of 1898, thousands of Stampeders made their fearful way over talus and scree to cross the pass.

Chugach National Forest
Vitus Bering sighted the camps of the Chugach Eskimos on Kayak and Wingham islands, and in so doing discovered Alaska in 1741. The islands are in the forest, a vast domain of Dall sheep, brown and black bear, mountain goat, moose and elk. Portage Glacier is the greatest of the forest's many glaciers.

Circle
Fifty miles south of the Arctic Circle, the town of Circle is the northernmost point on the connected North American highway system.

Columbia Glacier
The nine-mile-long wall of ice reaches three hundred feet in the air. It looks down on Prince William Sound, home of sporting seals, sea lions, porpoises and even schools of killer whales. The seals climb up on the ice floes that break away from the glacier to float down the sound.

Coronation Island
Captain George Vancouver, exploring the northwest coast of the continent, named the island, on September 22, 1793, in honor of the anniversary of George III's coronation. The island, mountainous and evergreen forested, is remarkable for a row of six caves and three arched rock bridges in Egg Harbor. The caves and bridges are cut deep into the limestone.

Glacier Bay National Monument
The great remnants of an ice advance which began about four thousand years ago are fascinating evidence of the changes in the planet's climate. (See page 208.)

Katmai National Monument
Brown bears fish for salmon and sea lions laze on the offshore rocks in the 4,362 square miles of this remote and wild landscape on the Alaska Peninsula. (See page 210.)

Kenai Peninsula
The National Moose Range on the peninsula encompasses two million acres of wilderness.

Lake George
Every winter the Inik Glacier advances until it seals off the stream that drains the sixteen-mile-long lake, which rises until the following summer when the ice is melting. Suddenly, the ice dam collapses into massive pieces as wide as six hundred feet, and the entire lake roars into the valley below, tossing boulders about and raging down to Cook Inlet.

Little Diomede Island
Just three miles away from the Soviet Union's Big Diomede Island, Little Diomede is at the international date line. North America and Asia are continental neighbors across the straits.

Lituya Bay
On July 9, 1958, an earthquake dropped ninety million tons of rock and earth down the steep cliffs at the mouth of the bay and threw up a wave one thousand seven hundred and twenty feet high, which in moments scoured the hills to bedrock. To this day the line of trees shows how high this cataclysmic splash reached.

Matanuska Valley
Long summer days in the land of the midnight sun account for the rapid growth of vegetables in this richest of Alaskan agricultural regions. Cabbages sometimes weigh more than seventy pounds, and a thirty-pound turnip is not unusual.

Mendenhall Glacier
The valleys, channels and fjords of southeast Alaska have been carved by glacial ice. As the Mendenhall Glacier recedes, it reveals great grooves and scratches that it has carved in the bedrock. The ice calved from the glacier is so compressed that it is blue in color. At first the land yielded up by the glacier is bare of life, but in a few years moss and lichens catch hold.

Mount McKinley
The highest peak in North America shoulders above the surrounding mountains and the national park which bears its name. (See page 206.)

Nome
Nome beach sands yielded gold in the great rush of 1899, and gold is still there for the finding. Giant dredges lie idle because there is insufficient gold to make their operation practical. The King Island Eskimos, who left their lonely homes in the King Islands, live at the edge of Nome and carve walrus ivory and the tusks of extinct mammoths found on the tundra.

Point Barrow
The most northerly tip of the mainland thrusts three hundred miles above the Arctic Circle. The Eskimo village at Point Barrow is situated only eight hundred miles from the North Pole.

Tongass National Forest
Following game paths through the mountain barriers, man came to the great forest about eight thousand years ago. This largest of all United States national forests is a wilderness of glaciers, fjords penetrating deep into a mountainous coast, river valleys and interior fastnesses. A fifteen-hundred-square-mile sea of ice reaches northward from the Skagway River to the Taku River.

Valley of Ten Thousand Smokes
The valley, formed by one of the earth's most violent volcanic eruptions, is the centerpiece of the Katmai National Monument. Rivers race through narrow canyons and the vivid colors of the volcanic rock change spectacularly with the weather conditions. (See page 210.)

Yukon Delta
The Yukon and the Kuskokwim rivers spread and wind across this flat, haunting land by the Bering Sea, where two million young wildfowl are born every brief summer. (See page 212.)

Western Canada

Adams River, British Columbia
The Pacific sockeye salmon begins its life cycle on the gravel beds of the Adams River. After two years of wandering in the broad Pacific, the salmon, drawn by some mysterious force, return to their ancestral spot to spawn and die. The largest spawnings of the salmon take place every fourth year.

Banff National Park, Alberta and British Columbia
The majestic peaks, deep valleys and glacial lakes of the park make up 2,564 square miles of awesome scenery. Lake Louise is a crystal mirror that reflects the massive peaks that surround it. Flower-covered alpine meadows, thick forests and high mountain passes far above the frets of the lowland make Banff one of the most appealing places in North America.

Big Hill Springs Provincial Park, Alberta
Buffalo bones are still easy to find on the prairies. They were dropped by hunters, who almost extinguished the species.

Big Muddy Badlands, Saskatchewan
The eroded sandstone hills and buttes reveal seams of coal. Around alkaline Big Muddy Lake the sandstone cliffs support native grass and cactus and a plentiful population of rattlesnakes.

Bowron Lake Provincial Park, British Columbia
This wilderness park of 304,155 acres is a land inhabited by wolves, mountain caribou and a score of other species over whom the grizzly bear rules. The silt-laden Cariboo River washes through the mountains.

Buffalo Pound Park, Saskatchewan
An old buffalo pound was used by the Indians, who lured the animals into it and then killed them with bows and arrows.

The Bugaboos, British Columbia
Rushing streams, untamed glaciers, rolling alplands covered with miniscule flowers, clear lakes and towering peaks make the Bugaboos extraordinary in a province where great and impressive mountains are everywhere.

Cariboo Country, British Columbia
From Cache Creek to Barkerville the old goldfields still have an atmosphere of high adventure.

Chilcotin Watershed, British Columbia
The milky glacial flow of the Taseko boils into the clear waters of the Chilko River, where it emerges from a deep laval canyon. The Chilko flows down through lodgepole pine and bunch-grass country where deer, grouse and bear are common. It debouches into the Chilcotin, where Indians still use either a dip net or a jigging hook to fish for salmon. Farwell Canyon is the home of the California bighorn sheep.

Columbia Icefield, Alberta
The seemingly endless sheet of ice feeds thirteen rivers. (See page 242.)

308

Cypress Hills, Saskatchewan
The craggy hills rise out of the ranchlands to a height of four thousand five hundred and sixty feet. The plants and animals found in the hills are more common in the mountains much farther west.

Dinosaur Provincial Park, Alberta
Badlands yield up dinosaur fossils and petrified wood.

Elk Island National Park, Alberta
Elk, moose, mule deer and a herd of some six hundred buffalo roam this seventy-five-square-mile park, the largest fenced wild animal preserve in Canada. The buffalo once neared extinction in North America. The herd at Elk Island was built up from about forty animals discovered there in 1907. There are also fifty of the rare wood buffalo that date back to the Ice Age.

Fort Walsh National Historic Park, Saskatchewan
Built in 1875 by the North West Mounted Police, the fort insured law and order on the Canadian frontier. The Royal Canadian Mounted Police are still very much part of the Canadian scene.

Fraser River Canyon, British Columbia
The river roars through a canyon that is more than three thousand feet deep in places. Two million salmon fight their way upstream through such rapids as Hell's Gate to spawn.

Goldstream Provincial Park, British Columbia
Old shafts and tunnels made by early miners are all that is left of the gold strike made on the Goldstream River by Peter Leech in 1885. The forest in this south Vancouver Island park is tall with six-hundred-year-old Douglas fir and western red cedar, which have never heard the sound of the logger's ax.

Great Sandhills, Saskatchewan
The semidesert area is home to the sharp-tailed grouse, the pocket mouse and the unusual kangaroo rat, which does not need to drink water, deriving from plants sufficient moisture to survive.

Jasper National Park, Alberta and British Columbia
Jasper Hawes was the clerk in the first trading post at Brule Lake about 1813, and his Christian name has been given to this forty-two-hundred-square-mile slice of the Canadian Rockies, including the lofty Ramparts, Mount Edith Cavell and Whistlers Mountain.

Kluane National Park, Yukon Territory
Canada's highest mountain, Mount Logan, and the St. Elias Range, the country's highest mountain chain, are both within the eighty-five hundred square miles of this park. High tundra country in the mountains is flecked with arctic flowers. There are odd regions of sand dunes and dust storms traced to glacial action.

Kootenay National Park, British Columbia
Sinclair Canyon's copper-colored walls rise 4,875 feet. Marble Canyon has been eroded out of gray-white marble limestone. To these natural wonders must be added the curious Ochre Beds, or "paint pots," and the hot springs at Radium.

Last Mountain Lake, Saskatchewan
The north end of the lake is a refuge for the sandhill crane, and thousands drop in there on a single day between mid-August and early September.

Manning Provincial Park, British Columbia
A divide cuts off the interior of the park so that its foliage has the softer hues of a drier climate, while the coastal portion of the peak has the dark hue of seaside forests. There is arctic vegetation on the high slopes. Tiny plants with huge blooms huddle between the weathered rocks.

Miracle Beach Provincial Park, British Columbia
The forest sweeps down to the sea. In the shadow of the tall trees fragile ferns grow.

Mystic Writing-on-Stone Park, Alberta
Indian writings on the stone fascinate anthropologists. The Milk River, so-called for its color, meanders through the park and empties eventually into the Missouri River.

Nahanni National Park, Northwest Territories
To the north are tundra-clad mountains, the haunt of the Dall sheep and mountain goats, looking down on a valley where Rabbitkettle Hotspring flows. Virginia Falls is twice the height of Niagara Falls. It roars down into a canyon where rapids and whirlpools churn through Hell's Gate.

The North Woods, Manitoba and Saskatchewan
North of the prairies is this pristine world of crystal lakes edged with sandy beaches and deep forests. (See page 238.)

Pacific Rim National Park, British Columbia
The west coast of Vancouver Island is a beautiful meeting place of the Pacific and the North American continent. Welling up from the ocean floor, the cold waters bring with them nutrients so that the coastal waters team with marine life. In the summer, Wickaninnish Bay is the feeding ground for fifty-foot-long gray whales. The beach supports razor clams and beach hoppers.

The Prairies, Manitoba and Saskatchewan
The golden prairies seem to run to the world's end. (See page 240.)

Riding Mountain National Park, Manitoba
The vast plateau of Riding Mountain reaches two thousand feet over the prairies.

Selkirk Mountains, British Columbia
More precipitous than the Rockies, spiked with peaks, the Selkirks are clad with snow and glaciers. (See page 244.)

Sunshine Coast, British Columbia
Steep mountains rise beside the inlets sheltered by offshore islands. Octopuses, who despite their ugly appearance are usually gentle and harmless, live together in the water with dangerous wolf eels, who have jaws like steel traps. Bald eagles nest high in the trees on the cliffs and eat young sea gulls and gull eggs.

Victoria, British Columbia
The most English of Canadian cities, Victoria caused Rudyard Kipling to remark, "To realize Victoria, you must take all that the eye admires in Bournemouth, Torquay, the Isle of Wight, the Happy Valley at Hong Kong, the Doon, Sorrento, Camp's Bay, add reminiscences of the Thousand Islands, and arrange the whole around the Bay of Naples with some Himalayas for the background."

Waterton Lakes National Park, Alberta
Glaciation has made this upland park renowned among geologists for its cirques, tarns, U-shaped valleys, hanging valleys and waterfalls. Mountains arise abruptly from the prairies.

Wood Buffalo National Park, Alberta and The Northwest Territories
The continent's largest single buffalo herd of about twelve thousand animals live in the enormous wilderness preserve. The whooping cranes, saved from virtual extinction, nest in the remote regions of the park. The calliope hummingbird, weighing one-tenth of an ounce, is among the world's smallest birds.

Wells Gray Provincial Park, British Columbia
This primitive wilderness ranges over 1,300,000 acres of the Caribou Mountains. There are five large lakes, glaciers and major peaks so numerous that they have never been given names. Mule deer feed along Hemp Creek, and caribou inhabit the wild country. Grizzly bear prefer the high mountains of the north, away from their enemy, man.

Yoho National Park, British Columbia
Ever since the Alpine Club of Canada held its first climbing camp in the mountainous park, the peaks of Yoho have challenged mountaineers. The park is rich with plant life, and botanists have identified more than six hundred alpine and subalpine plants. There are fossil beds, canyons and the tumultuous union of the Yoho and Kicking Horse rivers. "Yoho" is the Indian word for "how wonderful!"

Beaufort Sea

Mackenzie
Bay

Old Crow

Tuktoyaktuk

Cape
Parry

Inuvik

Amundsen Gulf

Fort
McPherson

UNITED STATES

YUKON

Peel River

Dawson

Horton River

Beaver
Creek

Keno Hill

Fort Good Hope

NORTH WEST TERRITORIES

Mount
Logan

Destruction Bay

Pelly
Crossing

Mayo

Norman Wells

Great
Bear
Lake

Carmacks

Haines
Junction

Fort Norman

KLUANE
NATIONAL
PARK

Alaska Highway

Ross River

Whitehorse

BRITISH COLUMBIA

Wrigley

Back River

UNITED STATES

Watson
Lake

Liard River

Utikuma Lake

Thelon River

Fort Nelson River

Fort
Simpson

Fort
Providence

Rae

Yellowknife

Dubawnt
Lake

Baker
Lake

Stikine River

NAHANNI
NATIONAL
PARK

Great
Slave
Lake

Snowdrift

Fort Reliance

Chesterfield
Inlet

Kotcho
Lake

Hay River

Fort
Resolution

Prince
Rupert

Williston
Lake

ALBERTA

NORTH WEST territories

Pine Point

ALBERTA

SASKATCHEWAN

Kasba
Lake

Eskimo Point

Queen
Charlotte
Islands

Skeena River

WELLS
GRAY
PROVINCIAL
PARK

WOOD BUFFALO
NATIONAL PARK

Nueltin
Lake

Thlewiaza River

Seal River

BOWRON
LAKE
PROVINCIAL
PARK

Queen
Charlotte
Sound

Ocean
Falls

Prince
George

Grande
Prairie

Peace River

Lesser Slave
Lake

Lake
Athabasca

Woolaston
Lake

Hudson Bay

Churchill River

MANITOBA
ONTARIO

MIRACLE
BEACH
PROVINCIAL
PARK

Vancouver
Island

Quesnel

Chilcotin

BANFF
NATIONAL
PARK

Fort
Saskatchewan

Reindeer
Lake

Cariboo
Mountains

JASPER
NATIONAL
PARK

YOHO
NATIONAL
PARK

Lac la Biche

ELK ISLAND
NATIONAL
PARK

Lac la Ronge

Southern
Indian
Lake

PACIFIC RIM
NATIONAL
PARK

Lake
Chilko

Watershed

Edson

EDMONTON

Churchill River

Campbell
River

Powell
River

Cariboo
Country

Vegreville

Montreal
Lake

MANITOBA

Port Alberni

Sunshine
Coast

Kamloops

Columbia
Icefield

Vernon

Camrose

Lloydminster

Flin
Flon

Cedar
Lake

GOLDSTREAM
PROVINCIAL
PARK

Nanaimo

Duncan

VANCOUVER

New Westminster

Revelstoke

Ponoka

Lacombe

Red Deer River

Prince
Albert

Nipawin

The Pas

Victoria

Kelowna

Red Deer

Wainwright

Stettler

North
Saskatchewan River

Melfort

Lake
Winnipegosis

RIDING
MOUNTAIN
NATIONAL
PARK

Summerland

Penticton

Sullivan Lake

Saskatoon

Humboldt

Adams
River

Nelson

CALGARY

Drumheller

The Prairies

Big Quill Lake

Swan
River

Dauphin

The North
Woods

MANNING
PROVINCIAL
PARK

Kimberley

Lake
McGregor

South Saskatchewan River

Kamsack

Yorkton

Last
Mountain
Lake

Lake Manitoba

The Bugaboos

Trail

Lethbridge

Moose Jaw

SELKIRK
MOUNTAINS

Cranbrook

Taber

Medicine
Hat

Melville

Virden

Portage
La Prairie

Selkirk

BIG HILL
SPRINGS
PROVINCIAL
PARK

Cardston

Milk River

Swift
Current

Old
Wives
Lake

Regina

Weyburn

Brandon

WINNIPEG

Steinbach

KOOTENAY
NATIONAL
PARK

MYSTIC
WRITING-
ON-STONE
PARK

Cypress
Hills

DINOSAUR
PROVINCIAL
PARK

Estevan

UNITED STATES

WATERTON
LAKES
NATIONAL
PARK

Great
Sandhills

BUFFALO
POUND
PARK

FORT WALSH
NATIONAL
HISTORIC
PARK

Big Muddy
Badlands

0 miles   100

309

ATLANTIC
OCEAN

NEWFOUNDLAND
QUEBEC

NEWFOUNDLAND

NEWFOUNDLAND

Hudson Strait

Ungava
Bay

Povungnituk River

George River

Caniapiscau River

Lake
Melville

Hamilton River

Goose
Bay

Lobstick
Lake

Lake
Michikamau

GROS MORNE
NATIONAL
PARK

Notre Dame
Bay

White Bay

Bonavista Bay

Trinity Bay
Conceptio

St. J

MANITOBA
ONTARIO

Hudson Bay

Lake
Mintô

Eau Claire
Lake

Bienville
Lake

Atikonak
Lake

LONG RANGE MOUNTAINS

Grand
Lake

Grand
Falls

Meelpaeg
Lake

Corner Brook

Red
Indian
Lake

Grande Baleine River

Moisie River

Anticosti
Island

St. Georges
Bay

TERRA NOVA
NATIONAL
PARK

La Grande River

James
Bay

Sakami
Lake

Rupert River

Ottardes River

Lake
Mistassini

KOUCHIBOUGUAC
NATIONAL PARK

Percé
Rock

GULF OF
ST. LAWRENCE

Bonaventure Island

Cabot Trail

Mount Albert

Chaleur Bay

St. Lawrence River

Sydney Mines

Glace Bay

Sydney

Bras d'or
Lakes

PRINCE EDWARD
ISLAND NATIONAL
PARK

RAINBOW
FALLS
PROVINCIAL
PARK

Albany River

ONTARIO
QUEBEC

LAURENTIANS

Campbellton Dalhousie

Miramichi
Bay

Chatham

PRINCE
EDWARD ISLAND

Charlottetown

THE ROCKS
PROVINCIAL
PARK

Geraldton

Ontario
Northland
Railway

Lake
Abitibi

La Sarre

Kenogami
Chicoutimi

Jonquiere

Bathurst

Amherst

Springhill

New Glasgow

Edmundston

Moncton

Truro

Winnipeg
River

Dryden

Lake
Nipigon

PUKASKWA
NATIONAL
PARK

Timmins

Kirkland
Lake

La Tuque

Rivière du Loup

Fredericton

Saint
John

Dartmouth

QUETICO
PROVINCIAL
PARK

Lake
of the
Woods

Lake Superior

UNITED STATES

Sault St.
Marie

Sudbury

MONT
TREMBLANT
PARK

Shawinigan

Trois Rivières

QUEBEC

Levis

Ile D'Orleans

Thetford Mines

Drummondville

Sorel

Saint John
River

Bay of
Fundy

Saint
John

Grand
Manan
Island

Halifax

KEJIMKUJIK
NATIONAL
PARK

Yarmouth

NOVA SCOTIA

ALGONQUIN
PROVINCIAL
PARK

Espanola

North
Bay

Bonnechere
Caves

Pembroke

St. Jerome

Joliette

Hull

Sherbrooke

St. Hyacinthe

MONTREAL

NEW
BRUNSWICK

FUNDY
NATIONAL
PARK

Lake Huron

Owen
Sound

Georgian
Bay

Opeongo Line

Orillia

Kingston

OTTAWA

Renfrew

ST. LAWRENCE
ISLANDS
NATIONAL
PARK

Georgian
Bay
Islands

Niagara
Escarpment

Peterborough

Barrie

Guelph

Belleville

Trenton

Oshawa

TORONTO

Lake Ontario

KITCHENER

HAMILTON

LONDON

Stratford

Woodstock

Brantford

St. Thomas

Niagara
Falls

Chatham

WINDSOR

Lake Erie

POINT PELEE
NATIONAL
PARK

0 miles

310

Algonquin Provincial Park, Ontario
There is a large population of timber wolves in the park, and on moonlit nights they set up a spine-tingling howling. The two-thousand-nine-hundred-and-ten-square-mile park straddles the highlands at the southern edge of the Canadian Shield. The call of a loon over a lake at sundown is as much of the park's lure as is the howl of the wolf.

Bay of Fundy, New Brunswick
Rising and falling twice each day, the tides in the bay are the highest in the world. Because of the bay's unique shape and size they reach heights of up to fifty-three feet. At low tide people stroll along the tidal flats at Alma, Point Wolfe or Herring Cove to see the small pools alive with periwinkles, limpets and sea anemones. The rising tide floods the flats.

Bonaventure Island, Quebec
The island is a high-rise bird sanctuary. All kinds of seafowl make their nests on the rocky ledges, where the sea spray is flung with the crashing waves.

Bonavista Bay, Newfoundland
Harbor seals and whales sport among the icebergs in the blue water. (See page 226.)

Bonnechere Caves, Ontario
Five hundred million years ago the limestone of the caves lay at the bottom of a tropical sea. Passages twist through the rock to reveal fossils of coral and sea creatures, who lived before the age of the dinosaurs.

Cabot Trail, Nova Scotia
The trail reveals seascapes and rocky hills and valleys reminiscent of the Scottish Highlands from where the ancestors of most of the area's inhabitants came. (See page 228.)

Fundy National Park, New Brunswick
Steep cliffs rise above the bay broken at intervals by deep valleys cut by streams. The plateau, eleven hundred feet higher than the sea, is the remains of an ancient mountain range, cut by deep valleys with rocky walls and given charm by waterfalls.

Georgian Bay Islands, Ontario
The bay contains an archipelago of thirty thousand islands. Flowerpot Island at the tip of the Bruce Peninsula is named for its shape. It was eroded from sandy dolomitic limestone. The ice of the Pleistocene epoch polished and rounded the ancient bedrock, but the waters of the bay have made little impact on it so that to this day the grooves in the rocks made by the ice can be seen.

Grand Manan Island, New Brunswick
Island of the lobsterman and of lighthouses blinking out to sea, car-free Grand Manan lies in the Bay of Fundy. (See page 230.)

Gros Morne National Park, Newfoundland
The Long Range Mountains rise dramatically from the low coastal plain, and the scenery ranges from shifting sand dunes beside the sea to fjord-like lakes set in dense forests.

Ile d'Orleans, Quebec
Champlain called it the "Isle of Bacchus" because of its wild grapes. Today, it is renowned for its strawberries and waterfalls. There are six villages on the island, each virtually unchanged since the eighteenth century, each with its gilded church and stone houses. Past this *habitant* island the great ore carriers and transatlantic ships make their way down the St. Lawrence.

Kejimkujik National Park, Nova Scotia
Micmac Indians cut pictographs into the slate rocks for seven miles along the shore of Lake Kejimkujik, and they employed beavers' teeth to do it. The Indian trail runs for four miles to Honeymoon Cove, where the Micmacs set up a wigwam for newlyweds.

Kitchener, Ontario
German settlers named the town "Berlin," but during World War I they changed it to "Kitchener," in honor of Lord Kitchener. (See page 235.)

Kouchibouguac National Park, New Brunswick
Serene lagoons and bays and a fifteen-and-a-half-mile stretch of offshore sandbars are in the park.

Laurentians, Quebec
The mountains worn down by the passing millennia contain some fifty thousand lakes and dashing streams. The mountains usually are soft and gentle, but in a few spots they remain jagged and steep.

Montreal, Quebec
Second largest French-speaking city in the world, Montreal is the great seaport and business heart of Canada. Forested Mount Royal rises in the center of the city, towering higher than the man-made forest of skyscrapers. (See page 232.)

Mont Tremblant Park, Quebec
This enormous nine-hundred-and-ninety-square-mile park represents the great outdoors to many Quebecois. The Diable River meanders through the park below Lac Chat.

Mount Albert, Quebec
The mountain at the heart of the Gaspé Peninsula reaches 3,775 feet above the sea. Caribou frequent the mountain fastnesses, where there is a high plateau around the bald summit. On this twelve-square-mile plain lichen, moss and alpine flowers grow.

Niagara Escarpment, Ontario
The rugged upthrust lip of rock runs from the tip of the Bruce Peninsula at Tobermory about 435 miles to Niagara Falls. Along its crest is the Bruce Trail, a favorite of backpacking North Americans.

Niagara Falls, Ontario
The Canadian Falls thunder in splendid competition with the falls on the American side. (See page 200.)

Ontario Northland Railway, Ontario
The Polar Bear Express snorts out of Cochrane with its mixed cargo of passengers and freight on its way to where Moose River flows into James Bay, deep in the north country. It puffs through a land of muskeg and scrub brush and stops whenever somebody flags it down.

Opeongo Line, Ontario
Pioneers began at Farrell's Landing on the Ottawa River and headed northwesterly to Lake Opeongo over the sixteen-foot-wide road cut through the primeval forest. The historic road still can be followed.

Ottawa, Ontario
The copper-roofed Parliament Buildings are an appropriate offspring of the mother of Parliaments in London, but Ottawa is a New World capital city despite its daily changing of the guard and colorful traditional ceremonies.

Percé Rock, Quebec
Towering out of the sea, 288 feet high and 1,420 feet long, the rock has a gap pierced into the end through which the tide rushes. It was Jacques Cartier who in 1534 rounded the Gaspé Cape, discovered the rock and named it Percé.

Point Pelee National Park, Ontario
A remnant of subtropical deciduous forest covers a V-shaped spit of land jutting out into Lake Erie. Aquatic plants and animals live in a two-thousand-acre marshland, which is called "between land" since it is neither water nor land. This is the southernmost tip of the Canadian mainland. Since the time of the glaciers ten thousand years ago, the lake has shaped the sandspit.

Prince Edward Island National Park, Prince Edward Island
The pink sand beach stretches for twenty-five miles along the north shore. Islanders and visitors alike dig clams on the beach. The waters off the park are infamous for their destructive storms. In 1851, the Yankee Gale wrecked more than seventy ships along the coast, and the graveyard in the Dalvay section contains the graves of the drowned mariners and fishermen.

Pukaskwa National Park, Ontario
Bays, beaches, rocky points and islands on the north shore of Lake Superior are features of the park. Set back from the shore are wild rivers and waterfalls and lakes. It is a land of caribou, moose, lynx and wolves.

Quebec City, Quebec
The oldest walled city in North America preserves its battlements and the Citadel, sometimes called the "Gibraltar of America." (See page 232.)

Quetico Provincial Park, Ontario
The forested canoe country contains the historic waterways that linked Canada's East and West during the days of fur trappers. The portages, streams and lakes are much as they were in the time of the trailblazing voyageurs.

Rainbow Falls Provincial Park, Ontario
The Selim River plunges over a series of falls and cascades as it races down a rocky gorge on its way to Lake Superior.

The Rocks Provincial Park, New Brunswick
The rocks have been likened to giant flowerpots. At low tide it is possible to walk among them and explore the dark caverns in their entrails. The formation of the rocks at Hopewell Cape began three hundred million years ago, when swift streams carried pebbles, boulders and sand to the shore. Thick beds of conglomerate formed only to be carved by the pounding waves of the Bay of Fundy.

Saint John River, New Brunswick
Tides rushing up the river cause the Reversing Falls to reverse the direction of their flow. The Grand Falls is a cataract two hundred and twenty miles from the sea.

St. Lawrence Islands National Park, Ontario
Some of the thousand islands in the Canadian waters of the St. Lawrence River have been set aside in a national park. The ancient rocks eroded before and during the last Ice Age rise from the river's current. The islands are a northeastern redoubt of the North American deciduous forest.

St. Lawrence River, Quebec
The entire Great Lakes system empties out into the Atlantic through this mighty river, which in its lower reaches resembles a sea. Soaring capes rise above sandy coves, and gentle meadows sweep back to the mountains.

Terra Nova National Park, Newfoundland
The northeastern extremity of the Appalachian Mountains is in the park together with fjords reaching inland like long arms from the sea. Arctic icebergs drift by in the wind and ocean currents. The many bogs are matted with wet sphagnum moss. Seaweeds and kelp wash up on the beaches.

Timmins, Ontario
The mines crowd around the town, which has expanded out of the sandy plain between the original mine and the river. (See page 234.)

Toronto, Ontario
Once known as "Toronto the Good" because of its conservative laws and attitudes, Toronto has emerged as one of the continent's most exciting cities. (See page 236.)

Acolman, Edo. De Mexico
Nuestros Pequenos Hermanos, the hacienda of Our Little Brothers is the home of a remarkable social experiment that promises much, not only for the succor of orphans, but for a new approach to social organization.

Alamos, Sonora
Once the richest silver town of the entire Spanish Empire, this colonial city is a national treasure of architecture.

Baja California
The peninsula is a natural paradise of deserts, fertile valleys, mountains capped with winter's snows and dramatic rocky promontories. The wild cimarron, deer and the mountain lion are at home on the peninsula. There are caves with mysterious prehistoric paintings.

Barrancas de Cobre, Chihuahua
The vast labyrinth of canyons extends for a thousand miles. They are coppery in color and beneath the canyon lips are caves, the homes of the Tarahumara Indians, a tribe that avoids other people as much as possible. The Tarahumara are among the world's great runners. It is said that they can run a hundred miles without stopping and hunt deer by chasing them on foot.

Cacahuamilpa Caves, Moreloa
One stalagmite is taller than the towers of the cathedral in Mexico City.

Cholula, Puebla
Once the holy city of the Toltecs, this great archaeological area contains the ruined Tepanapa Pyramid, located a short distance from the main plaza. The pyramid exceeds in volume that of Cheops in Egypt. About five miles of tunnels run through its interior.

Citlaltépetl, Puebla
The snowcapped volcanic cone is the highest peak in Mexico. It reaches 18,851 feet.

Cola de Caballo, Nuevo Leone
Cola de Caballo, or Horse Tail Falls, tumbles down from the rocky formation known as Chipinque Mesa into a crystalline pool, a cool respite in a desert.

Cuernavaca, Morelos
Surrounded by spruce-clad mountains that reach nine thousand feet, the valley in which Cuernavaca nestles waves with the feathery white tassels of sugarcane. Banks of fuchsia and jacaranda line the roads. Because of its equitable climate the valley is known as the land of eternal springtime.

Desert of the Lions, Edo. de Mexico
This desert is not a desert at all, but a dense wood around the ruins and gardens of a Carmelite monastery built in 1602.

El Canon Del Zopilote, Guerrero
Vulture Canyon contains some of the earliest silver mines worked by the Spaniards.

Guadalajara, Jalisco
Four great plazas surround the colonial cathedral. As a band plays in a plaza in the evening, boys walk one way and girls the other and exchange amorous glances as they pass. Guadalajara is the home of the mariachis, the troubadours of Mexico, who sing of its beauty and its heartfelt way of life.

Huasteca Canyon, Nuevo Leone
The Santa Catarina River, flowing along the foot of Saddle Rock Mountain, has cut the canyon deep into the rock. The odd rock formations rival those of Yosemite in the United States. The river flows through cactus, sage and groves of flowering anachuite trees.

Hill of the Star, Edo. de Mexico
Aztec priests considered this volcanic cone to be sacred, and once every fifty-two years they built a fire at its peak to mark a cycle in the Aztec calendar.

Inner Gorda Banks, Gulf of Cortés
Pelicans fly slowly overhead, porpoises arch gracefully out of the blue sea, sperm whales break surface and blow. The massive whales breed in these warm waters and come to rub their barnacles off on the reef. They rise out of the sea and slowly sink again with long lazy flicks of their tails, leaving only circles of boiling white water.

**Ixta-Popo National Park,
Edo. de Mexico**
Popocatepétl, Smoking Mountain, towers 17,887 feet into the sky, and its neighbor volcano, Iztaccíhuatl, Sleeping Women, reaches 17,343 feet. Cortés dug sulfur from the volcanic craters to make gunpowder.

Juxtlahuaca Caves, Guerrero
An archaeologist from the United States explored the caves in 1966. They are said by local people to be the center of a fearful witch cult. There are Olmec paintings in the cave dating to 500 B.C., the oldest-known paintings created in the western hemisphere.

Manila Galleon Road
The ancient road can still be made out following closely beside the modern highway that runs from Acapulco to Mexico City. Pack trains of burros still follow the trail over which the spices and incense of the Orient and bars of silver and gold that had been brought ashore from galleons at Acapulco were transported in Spanish colonial times.

Mexico City, D.F.
The stones of the Cathedral of Mexico City were cut long before the Spanish reached the New World, for once they were part of the towering Aztec Temple to the Sun. Mexico City, capital of the Republic, is the enduring child of two cultures—Spanish and Indian. (See page 248.)

Nevado de Toluca, Edo. de Mexico
The fourteen-thousand-nine-hundred-foot volcano rises above the city of Toluca. The crater contains two lakes, the Lake of the Sun and the Lake of the Moon, which are renowned for their silent, unruffled beauty.

Querétaro, Querétaro
The mighty arches built over two hundred years ago by the Spanish still carry the aqueduct into the city. Many visitors take one look at the aqueduct and are certain that the Romans visited North America. Father Hidalgo met with patriots in this city to plot the independence of Mexico.

Sea of Cortés
Zane Grey called the sea the "World's greatest fish trap," and it does have a remarkable population of fish. The youngest sea in the world, it was formed only fifteen million years ago when the Baja California Peninsula was ripped off the mainland by a cataclysm along the San Andreas Fault, which lies at its bottom. Whales breed in its isolated coves.

Sierra Madre Occidental
In the highlands of Mexico, the peasant says, "a poor man's cloak is the sun." Even in winter the sun is bright and warm. The massive mountains cut the west coast off from the Mexican east.

**Sonora Desert, Sonora and
Chihuahua**
Vaqueros drive dusty herds of cattle across the arid plains studded with mesquite and cactus. Sun-baked villages of adobe houses and crumbling mission churches, built long ago by Father Kino, can be found in the desert.

Teotihuacán, Edo. de Mexico
The Pyramids of the Sun and of the Moon are at Teotihuacán, once the metropolis of the Americas. (See page 250.)

Tequila, Jalisco
Behind rock walls, silver-green agave plants stretch in rows. Between their eighth and twelfth years they are harvested so that tequila can be made from their huge hearts, which resemble giant pineapples weighing from fifty to two hundred and fifty pounds.

Volcan Ceboruco, Guerrero
The extinct volcano is surrounded by lava flows and forests of twisted tropical trees.

Yucatán
An archaeological treasure house where the present draws meaning from the past. (See page 252.)

O miles 100

Rio Lagartos

MERIDA

Puerto Juárez

Santa Elena

Yucatán

Bahiá de la Ascencion

Campeche

Champotón

Bahiá del Espiritu Santo

Ciudad del Carmen

Escárcega

Bahiá de Chetumal

Laguna de Terminos

Ciudad Chetumal

GUATEMALA

Tapachula

INDEX

314

315

INDEX

Klondike, 204
Kodiak Island, 210
Koko Head, Oahu, 223
Krakatoa, 61, 95
Krishna Shrine, Grand Canyon, 73
Kuskokwim River, 212

L

La Salle, René-Robert, 30
Labná, Yucatán, 253
Labrador Current, 226
Lady's slipper, 66
Lake Champlain, 190
Lake Chelan, 67
Lake Erie, 124, 200
Lake George, 190
Lake Huron, 124
Lake Manitoba, 238
Lake Okeechobee, 147
Lake Ontario, 124, 200
Lake Oxchimilco, 248
Lake McDonald, 101
Lake Michigan, 124
Lake of the Woods, 124, 126-7
Lake Shore Drive, Chicago, 135
Lake Superior, 124, 130
Lake Texcoco, 22, 23
Lake Winnipeg, 238
Land reclamation schemes, 41
Land speculation, 39-40
Langford, Nathaniel P., 95
Languages
    American, 29
    dialects in New Orleans, 141, 155
    in Quebec, 232
    of Newfoundland, 226
    see also Indians
Larch trees, 238
Larks, meadow, 120
Larkspur, Spanish, 120
Las Vegas, 70
Latrobe, Benjamin Henry, 171
Laurasia, prehistoric landmass, 11
Lava flow, types of, 60, 104, 218
Law school, Litchfield, 197
Lawrence, D. H., 88-9
Lawrence, Frieda, 88-9
L'Enfant, Pierre, 202, 203
Leeches, 130
Lehman, Absalom, 87
Lehman Caves, 70, 87
Leif Ericson, 24
Leigh, Dick ("Beaver"), and Jenny, 99
Leigh Lake, Grand Tetons, 99
León, Ponce de, 24, 25
Lethe River, 210
Lewis, Meriwether, 30-1, 31-2, 57, 60, 68-9, 95, 98, 108
Lewisville, Texas, 14
Lexington, Massachusetts, 28
Liebling, A. J., 141
Life, evolution of, 10; see also Prehistoric times
Lily, tiger, 66
Limestone formations, 10, 70, 76-7, 87, 151
Lincoln, Abraham, 44, 116, 117, 202, 203
Lind, Jenny, 151
Lindley, John, 49
Lindsay, Vachel, 41
Lion's Tail stalactite, 77
Litchfield County, 197
Little Bighorn, Battle of the, 35, 108, 116, 117, 240
Little Chief Mountain, 101
Little Colorado River, 80
Little Missouri River, 114
Little River Canyon, 160-1
Lituya Bay, Alaska, 209
Lituya Glacier, 209
Lizards, 122, 144
Llamas, 115
Lobster, fishing for, 180
Locust Grove, Ohio, 17
Locusts, 240
Lone Pine, Yosemite Valley, 44
Long, Stephen, 31, 33
Long Island, 13, 177
Long Trail, Vermont, 186
Lono, Polynesian deity, 216
Lookout Mountain, 160
Loon, Hendrik van, 74
Loons, 144, 212
    common, 101
Los Angeles, 32, 35, 43
Louis XIV, King of France, 180, 190

Louisiana
    bayous of, 154-5
    ethnic groups in, 138
    French exploration, settlement, 30, 141, 155, 180
    oilfields, 35
    purchase by United States, 30, 31, 69, 118, 141, 162
Lower Falls, Yellowstone, 40, 96, 97
Lower Yosemite Fall, 44
Lupines, 229
Lynx, 244
    Canadian, 243

M

McCormick, Cyrus, 36
McGregor, Iowa, 111
Mackenzie, Alexander, 31, 243
McKenzie, Donald, 103
MacKenzie Delta, 213
MacKenzie River, 243
MacKenzie Valley, 15
Mackinac Straits, 37
McWilliam House, New Castle, 179
Mackerel, 180
Madoc, Prince in Wales, 24, 160-1
Magnolia trees, 166
Mahogany trees, 147
    mountain, 87
Mahonia, 66
Mail services, by stagecoach, 112
Maine
    coast of, 172, 180
    end of Appalachian Trail in, 148
    exploration by frontiersmen, 30
    exploitation, restock of forests, 35, 40
Makahiki, Hawaiian carnival, 223
Mako sica (Badlands), 115
Mall, The, Washington, 202, 203
Mammals, prehistoric, 10, 12, 13, 14, 15
Mammoth Cave, Kentucky, 10, 150-1
Mammoth Hot Springs, Yellowstone, 95
Mammoths, woolly, 14, 15
Man
    concept of, as predator, 127
    early, hunting skills, life-style, 14-15
    early migration across continent, 13, 14-15, 19, 20, 213
    evolution, 14
Man-eating jaguars, 252
Manatee (sea cow), 147
Mandan Indians, 24
Mangrove swamps, 147
Manhattan Island, 24, 192-5
Manitoba
    exploration, 29
    glaciers, 243
    scenery, 239, 240
    woodlands of, 238-9
Manitoba Escarpment, 240
Manuelito, 85
Maple trees, 186, 187, 188, 229, 238, 239
    mountain, 152
    sugar, 152
Marconi, Guglielmo, 183
Mariposa Grove, 49
Marmots, 240, 245
    hoary, 244
Marquesas Islands, 216
Marquette, Père, 30, 110
Marsh, George Perkins, 39
Marshall, James, 43
Marshlands, of Delaware, 179
Marten, American, 229
Martha's Vineyard, 13, 177
Maryland
    early settlements, 27
    force of storms on coast, 142-3
    founding colony, 26
    plantations, 28
Massachusetts
    founding colony, 26
    possible Viking colony in, 24
    prehistoric remains discovered, 14-15
    see also Pilgrim Fathers
Massachusetts Bay Colony, 27
Massacre Island, 127
Mastodons, 12, 14
Mauna Loa, 218
Mauvaises Terres à Traverser, Les, 115

Maximilian, Emperor, 35, 249
Maya civilization, 20, 21, 247, 249, 250-1, 252-3
Mayors, election system, 177
Medicine, Indian skills in, 20
Menane see Grand Manan Island
Mennonites, 235
Mérida, Yucatán, 252
Merriam, C. Hart, 65
Mesa Verde
    cliff dwellers of, 17, 90, 106-7
    conservation of, 90
Mesa Verde National Park, 40
Mesquite Flats, Death Valley, 46
Metro Centre, Toronto, 237
Mexica people see Aztec Empire
Mexican Moon, 122-3
Mexican Museum of Anthropology, 249
Mexico
    advanced nature of early cultures, 20-3
    cession of California to United States, 43
    coastal strip, 247
    contact with southern Texas, 122
    cooperation in conservation schemes, 40
    early agricultural communities in, 16
    extremes of life, 247
    failure of French policy in, 35, 249
    geological history, 12, 13
    independence from Spain, 29, 88, 197, 249
    internal problems, 35
    introduction of longhorn cattle, 35
    migration of early man into, 14, 15
    Spanish conquest of, 24, 25, 26, 249, 251, 252
Mexico City, 23, 247, 248-9, 252
Mica, early trade in, 16-17
Michigan, mineral resources, 35
Micmac Indians, 229
Migration routes, migrant birds, 127, 148, 166, 169, 177, 204, 207, 212-13, 214, 221
Milkweed, 165
Mills, Enoch, 92
Milwaukee, 35
Mineral resources, overexploitation conservation, 40, 41
Minerva Terrace, Mammoth Hot Springs, 95
Miniconjou Indians, 19
Mink, New World, 101
Minneapolis, 35, 36, 138
Minnesota
    farmlands of, 127
    iron-ore resources, 35
    possible Viking ruins, 24
    source of Mississippi in, 110
    woods of, 239
Mint, wild, 50
Mirror Lake, Yosemite Valley, 44
Mississippi Delta, 13
Mississippi Palisades, 108, 110-11
Mississippi River, region, 17, 20, 24, 30, 33, 37, 101, 108, 110, 124, 127, 138, 139, 141, 154-5, 162, 199
Mississippi, State of, 162
Mississippi steamboats, 110, 139
Missouri Coteau, 240
Missouri River, region, 13, 30, 37, 56-7, 69
Missouri, State of,
    prehistoric creatures, 10
    sources of lead, 35
Mobile Bay, Alabama, 24
Mohawk Valley, 30
Mokuaweoweo, Hawaii, 218
Mojave River, 46
Monkey, spider, 252
Montague, Samuel, 34
Montana
    cattle rearing, 35
    conservation areas, 90
    extent of Rocky Mountains in, 90, 101
    first national park in, 41
    prehistoric creatures, 10
    wildlife, 101
Montauk Point, 177
Montcalm, General, 232
Montejo, Francisco de, 252

Montejo family, 252
Monterey, California, 1, 320
Montezuma, 23, 25, 249, 251
Monticello, 170-1
Montreal, 28, 35, 232, 233, 237
Monument Rocks, Kansas, 112
Monument Valley, Cover, 10, 70, 84-5
Monuments, geological definition of, 84
Moore, Henry, 135, 236-7
Moose, 95, 98, 127, 130, 206, 207
Moran, Thomas, 40
Mormon Trail, 32, 113
Mormons, 32, 33, 82-3, 113
Mosquitoes, 130
Mother Carey's chickens, 231
Mound City, Ohio, 136-7
Mounds, burial, ceremonial, 16-17, 20, 110-11, 136-7, 162
Mount Alban, Mexico, 21
Mount Adams, 68, 184
Mount Athabasca, 243
Mount Baker, 66
Mount Desert Island, 180
Mount Eisenhower, 186
Mount Hood, 60, 68
Mount Jackson, 186
Mount Jefferson, 184
Mount Katahdin, 148
Mount Katmai, 210
Mount Liberty, 184
Mount Lyell, 44
Mount McClure, 44
Mount McKinley, 204, 206-7
Mount McKinley National Park, 41, 206
Mount Madison, 186
Mount Mansfield, 186
Mount Martin, 210
Mount Mazama, 60-1
Mount Monroe, 186
Mount Moriah Cemetery, 117
Mount Orizaba, 247
Mount Pemigewasset, 184
Mount Rainier, 13, 58
Mount Rainier National Park, 40, 58
Mount Revelstoke National Park, 245
Mount Ritter, 44
Mount Rushmore, 116, 117
Mount St. Helens, 60, 68
Mount Shasta, 43
Mount Telescope, 46
Mount Waialeale, 221
Mount Washington, 184
Mount Whitney, 43
Mountain men, 32, 33, 95, 98, 99
Mouse, deer, 104
Mouse, jumping, 67
Mu, lost continent of, 14
Mudflows, on Mount Rainier, 58
Muir, John, 40, 41, 44, 49, 209
Multnomah Falls, Columbia River, 69
Munan-ook see Grand Manan Island
Murre
    common, 230
    slender-billed, 230
Music, Mennonites' support for, 235
Musk ox, 14
Muskrat, 31, 154
My Darling Clementine (John Ford film), 84
Myrtle trees, 142, 143, 166

N

Naco, Arizona, 15
Na-maka-o-ka-hai, 218
Nantucket, 177
Napoleon, 31, 141
Narragansett Bay, 24
Nashville, Brown County, 128-9
Nashville, Tennessee, 162
Natchez (town), 162
Natchez district, 162
Natchez Trace, 162
National Arctic Wildlife Range, 214
National Forests, 187
National Monuments, 114
National Parks, Park Service, 40, 41, 95, 97, 114, 143, 151; see also individual parks
National Recreation Areas, 174

National Seashores, 142, 169
Nature reserves, 128, 144
Naugatuck, Connecticut, 197
Nautilus, fossilized, 115
Nauvoo, Illinois, 32
Navajo Indians, 18, 70, 74, 79, 80, 81, 84-5, 88
Navajo Trail, 84
Negroes
    Gullah population, 166
    transportation into slavery, 28
    see also Slavery
Nelson River, 239
Nemaha Mountains, 10
Nevada
    desert landscapes, 70
    early civilizations in, 16
    gold rush in, 33
    prehistoric remains discovered, 14, 15
Never Summer Range, 92
New Albion see California
New Amsterdam, 27, 28, 179
New Brunswick, 230
New Castle, Delaware, 178-9
New England
    geological history, 13
    importance of churches, 172, 197
    Puritan settlements, 27
    regional characteristics, 28
New France, 28, 232, 238
New Hampshire
    Appalachian Trail in, 184
    exploration by frontiersmen, 30
    founding colony, 26
    Green Mountain Boys, 184
    physical characteristics, 172
New Haven, Puritan settlements, 27
New Jersey
    access to countryside in, 174
    founding colony, 26
    possible Viking landfall in, 24
    prehistoric creatures of, 10
New Mexico
    acquisition by United States, 31, 88
    Anasazi culture in, 17, 20
    desert landscapes, 70
    geological history, 10
    prehistoric creatures of, 10
    prehistoric remains discovered, 15
    pueblo communities, 70
    Spanish exploration, settlement of, 88-9
New Netherlands, 26, 27
New Orleans, 35, 138, 139, 141-2, 154
New Orleans, navigation of Mississippi by, 162
New Spain, 25; see also Mexico
New York, 9, 13, 25, 26, 27, 35, 36, 37, 54, 166, 172, 174, 177, 184, 192-5
Newfoundland
    discovery, exploration, 24, 226
    fishing grounds, 24, 226
    languages, 226
    place-names, 226
    prehistoric link with American continent, 12
    Viking landfall in, 24
Newtown, Bonavista Bay, 227
Nez Percé Indians, 18, 241
Niagara Falls, 10, 124, 172, 200-1
Niagara Peninsula, 200, 235
Niagara River, 10, 200
North Carolina
    Appalachian Trail in, 148, 149
    early Spanish exploration in, 24
    founding colony, 26
    prehistoric creatures of, 10
North Cascades Highway, 66
North Cascades National Park, 66
North Cascades Wilderness, 66-7
North Dakota
    Badlands of, 114-15
    creation of canyons in, 114-15
    grazing lands, 35
    prehistoric migration of man through, 15
North Dome, Yosemite Valley, 44
North Head, Grand Manan Island, 231
North Mitten, Monument Valley, 85
North Platte River, 113
North Saskatchewan River, 243
North West Company, 238

317

319

INDEX

ACKNOWLEDGMENTS

GENERAL ACKNOWLEDGMENTS

A great many individuals, organizations, institutions and state and federal agencies have given invaluable help and advice during the preparation of this book. The publishers wish to extend their thanks to them all, and in particular to the Chief Park Naturalists of the National Park Service; the Directors of State Tourism Departments; the Head of the New York Port Authority; the Mexican Government; Gillian Abrahams; Joyce Born; Don Brothwell; Richard Brun; Canadian Pacific Limited; Barry Cox, University of London, King's College; Malcolm Hart; Jacqueline Sarsby.

SPECIAL ACKNOWLEDGMENTS

From "De Rerum Virtute" (page 50) Copyright 1954 by Robinson Jeffers. Reprinted from *Selected Poems*, by Robinson Jeffers, by permission of Random House, Inc.

From *The Collected Letters of D. H. Lawrence* (page 88), edited by Harry T. Moore. Copyright © 1962 by Angelo Ravagli and C. M. Weekley, Executors of the Estate of Frieda Lawrence Ravagli. All rights reserved. Reprinted by permission of The Viking Press, Inc., and Laurence Pollinger Ltd.

From *Phoenix I*: The Posthumous Papers of D. H. Lawrence (pages 88–89), edited by Edward D. McDonald. Copyright 1936 by Frieda Lawrence, Copyright © 1964 by the Estate of the late Frieda Lawrence Ravagli. All rights reserved. Reprinted by permission of The Viking Press, Inc., and Laurence Pollinger Ltd.

Index prepared by Brenda Hall M.A. Registered indexer of the Society of Indexers.

ILLUSTRATORS

Arka Cartographics, maps and studio services 14–41, 254–313; Norman Barber/LINDEN ARTISTS 152–53; Dateline Graphics 42, 57, 71, 90, 108, 124, 138, 172, 205, 217, 225, 246; John Davies 42–43, 90–1, 108–9, 246–47; Brian Delf 172–73, 204–5; Gerry Embleton/LINDEN ARTISTS 32; Shireen Faircloth/ARTISTS PARTNERS 106–7, 216–17; Ronald Lampitt/ARTISTS PARTNERS 124–25; Annabel Milne 118, 227; Richard Orr/LINDEN ARTISTS, animals 14–15, 65, 74, 115, 150, 168–69, 176–77, 209; Charles Pickard/CREATIVE PRESENTATION 56–57, 70–1, 224–25; Maurice Pledger/LINDEN ARTISTS 102, 182–83, 212–13; Cristen Rosenberg/SAXON ARTISTS 31; Sally Slight, retouching 22–23, 35; Michael Woods, stone points 14–15, 34; Sidney Woods 11–13, 138–39, 184, 218; Elsie Wrigley/JOAN FARMER 66–67, 123.

PHOTOGRAPHIC CREDITS

Cover: Monument Valley, Utah, Shelly Grossman/WOODFIN CAMP & ASSOCIATES
Half-Title page: Monterey, California, Richard Beattie
Title page: Cape Lookout State Park, Oregon, Ray Atkeson/SHOSTAL
Contents page: Cedars Breaks National Monument, Utah, Shelly Grossman/WOODFIN CAMP & ASSOCIATES
Introduction page: Humboldt Redwoods State Park, California, Dan Budnik/WOODFIN CAMP & ASSOCIATES
8–9: Grand Canyon National Park, Arizona, Inez & George Hollis/PHOTO RESEARCHERS
16–17: Stone head from Malakoff/Courtesy The Texas Memorial Museum; Eskimo miniature mask/WERNER FORMAN ARCHIVE/National Museum of Man, Ottawa; Detail showing Shamanistic dance/WERNER FORMAN ARCHIVE/Tuscon University Museum, Arizona; Etched painted shell, Head of unfired clay/WERNER FORMAN ARCHIVE/ Spiro culture masks/WERNER FORMAN ARCHIVE/Heye Foundation; Ceremonial pot, head-shaped/WERNER FORMAN ARCHIVE/State Museum,

Chicago; 18–19: Chinook Indians, Nez Percé Indian, Navajos, Sioux, Seminoles/POPPERFOTO; Washakie, Shoshoni Indian chief/WESTERN AMERICANA/Courtesy Smithsonian Institution National Anthropological Archives; Hopi Indian, Eskimos, Kicking Bear/WEIDENFELD & NICOLSON Archives/Courtesy Smithsonian Institution National Anthropological Archives; Chief Duck/BARNABY'S PICTURE LIBRARY; Chief Quannah Parker/WESTERN AMERICANA/Courtesy Smithsonian Institution; 20–21: Olmec carving of a head/ROBERT HARDING ASSOCIATES; Toltec warrior figure/Photo Janet Chapman: MICHAEL HOLFORD LIBRARY; Mayan temple relief, Jaina figures/ WERNER FORMAN ARCHIVE/Museum of Anthropology, Mexico; 22–23: Aztec turquoise mask, Aztec mask/MICHAEL HOLFORD/ British Museum; Reconstruction of temple/Courtesy of the American Museum of Natural History; Figure of Xipe–Toltec/WERNER FORMAN ARCHIVE/National Museum of Anthropology, Mexico; Aztec figure/Ianthe Ruthven; Aztec calendar/SALMER/Museum of History of Science, Florence; 24–25: Vespucci, Cabot, Verrazano, De Soto, De Leon/ WESTERN AMERICANA; Columbus, Cortés/BETTMANN ARCHIVES; Sir Martin Frobisher, Cartier/RADIO TIMES HULTON PICTURE LIBRARY; Grijalva/MARY EVANS PICTURE LIBRARY; Detail from "Hudson's Last Voyage" by J. Collier/ALDUS ARCHIVES/ Courtesy Tate Gallery, London; 26–27: John Smith, Sir Walter Raleigh/BETTMANN ARCHIVES; Peter Stuyvesant/ALDUS ARCHIVES/Courtesy New York Historical Society; William Penn/ALDUS ARCHIVES/Courtesy Historical Society of Pennsylvania; Detail from "The First Thanksgiving" by J. L. G. Ferris/ALDUS ARCHIVES/Courtesy Archives of 76, Ohio; Samuel Champlain/RADIO TIMES HULTON PICTURE LIBRARY; 28–29: "Signers of the Declaration of Independence" by John Trumbull/Jack Zehrt/SHOSTAL ASSOCIATES; 30–31: Sacajawea guiding the Lewis & Clark Expedition/BETTMANN ARCHIVES; Lewis & Clark medal/Oregon Historical Society; Muskrat/WESTERN AMERICANA; Alexander Mackenzie/ALDUS ARCHIVES/Courtesy Provincial Archives of British Columbia; Zebulon Pike/ALDUS ARCHIVES/Courtesy Independence National Historical Park Collection, Philadelphia; John Frémont/ALDUS ARCHIVES/Courtesy Denver Public Library; 32–33: "Crossing the Rockies"/WEIDENFELD & NICOLSON/Reproduced by permission of the American Museum in Britain, Bath; Jim Bridger/ALDUS ARCHIVES; Portrait of Captain Joseph Reddeford Walker/ALDUS ARCHIVES/ Courtesy Joslyn Art Museum, Omaha, Nebraska; Brigham Young/ALDUS ARCHIVES/Courtesy Information Service of the Church of Jesus Christ of the Latter Day Saints; 34–35: Laying last rail/Courtesy Central Union Pacific Railroad Museum Collection; Building the CPR/POPPERFOTO; Denver & Rio Grande Railroad/Denver Public Library; 36–37: Whitney's Cotton Gin/WESTERN AMERICANA; Reaper/ International Harvester Company of Great Britain; Brooklyn Bridge/RONAN PICTURE LIBRARY; Auditorium Hotel, Chicago/ BETTMANN ARCHIVES; 1913 Model T Ford/Ford Motor Company; 38–39: Detail from Audubon portrait/American Museum of Natural History; Curlew, Prairie marmot squirrel, Black-footed ferret, American bison, Sea otter/paintings by Audubon/all Courtesy Victoria & Albert Museum/Photos: Flemings; 40–41: John Muir/BETTMANN ARCHIVES; Theodore Roosevelt/POPPERFOTO; Rachel Carson/ASSOCIATED PRESS; John F. Kennedy/CAMERA PRESS; "Lower Falls of Yellowstone River" by Thomas Moran/WEIDENFELD & NICOLSON/Courtesy Thomas Gilcrease Institution of American History & Art, Tulsa.

Pages 44–254: Major photographs are designated by numbers only; smaller photographs, appearing along the bottom of a page, read from left to right and are coded a to d.

Art d'Arazien 55, 134, 135, 196, 197 (left); ARDEA PHOTOGRAPHICS: E. Burgess 80a, 165a; K. W. Fink 51a, 61a,

79a, 92a, 210c; P. Morris 81a; S. Roberts 231a; W. Stribling 60a, 101b; W. Weisser 122a; Bettmann Archives 44a, 82a, 114a, 132a, 134a, 159b, 193a, 193b, 193c, 197a, 202a; Dean Brown 107; Fred Bruemmer 230a; T. Callaghan 214a; CANADA WIDE: S. J. Krasemann 131, 244b; Brian Milne 126; R. Barry Ranford 231b; T. Willock 245a; Canadian Pacific 244; BRUCE COLEMAN INC.: G. Ahrens 61, 78a; B. Brooks (Public Archives of Canada) 228a; J. M. Burnley 188, 189; L. R. Ditto 120a; K. W. Fink 244a; M. P. Gadomski 187b; K. Gunnar 58, 65, 67; J. L. Hout 230b; M & S Landre 144; L. Riley 119b; L. M. Stone 119a; J. Van Wormer 68; BRUCE COLEMAN LTD.: G. Ahrens 186a, 187a; J & D Bartlett 128a; Bruce Coleman 234a; J. Dermid 174b, 175b, 186b; F. Erize 50a, 252a; M. P. L. Fogden 81; J. Foott 51b; O. S. F. 230c; H. Reinhard 234b, 235a; D. Robinson 243a, 252b; L. Lee Rue 101a, 127a, 129a, 160b, 161a, 175a, 181b, 210b, 229b, 239a; J. Simon 166a, 240b; N. Tomalin 174a, 250b; C. J. Ott 127b, 174c, 181a, 215a, 215c, 235b; G. D. Plage 241a; J. Van Wormer 62a, 104a, 148c, 149a, 229a; Colour Library International 233; Richard Cooke 194–195; Christopher Davis 88; John DeVisser 243; Mary Evans Picture Library 49a, 53a, 82b, 137a, 141a, 156c, 159a, 180a, 197b, 200a; Walter Grishkot 190; Hedrich-Blessing 132b, 133a, 133b, 135a, 135b; Jerry L. Hout 213; JACANA: Marc Lelo 189a; Thomas Jefferson Memorial Foundation 170b, 171a; Peter B. Kaplan 49, 64, 102, 141, 156, 164, 165; FRANK W. LANE: R. Austing 160a; Michael J. Lutch 128, 129, 197 (right); MAGNUM N.Y.: Charles Harbutt 163; Mansell Collection 58a, 162a; MILLER SERVICES: E. Jones 233a; E. Otto 230; NATURAL HISTORY PHOTOGRAPHIC AGENCY (TSA = TOM STACK & ASSOCIATES): M. Brandow/TSA 98b; J. H. Carmichael Jr. 146, 147, 147a, 147b, 184a; E. R. Degginger/TSA 103, 185, 198; B. Hawkes 207b; B. Noel Kleeman/TSA 98a; C. Mundt/ TSA 130a; T. Myers/TSA 62; J. Tallon 92b; 226a; John Norris Wood 144a, 144b; PHOTO RESEARCHERS INC: J. Amos 152; J. Barkin 130; L. Bartlett 209; L. E. Battaglia 202; R. W. Brooks 87, 87a, 104; V. Bucher 136, 137, 145, 159c, 160 (top & bottom), 178; Colurychrome Photo System 235; D. Davis 248a, 250a; D. Durrance 171; C. Frank 251; T. D. W. Friedman 200; L. J. Georgia 112, 120; P. W. Grace 181; D. Guravich 155, 162; D & J Hadden 193; G. Holton 253a; D. James 223; L. Jossel 252; R. Kinne 60, 76, 130b, 150, 151, 191; R. Macia 184a; R. Mason 215; B. Mays 74; F. J. Miller 148; P. Miller 187; MN Dept. of Econ. Dev. 127; Porterfield-Chickering 69, 83a; P. Rowan 208; J. L. Stage 176; D. D. Sullivan 182; T. Webb 75; L. S. Williams 179; PICTOR: Fred H. Ragsdale/FPG 80, 148b, FPG 166b; RAPHO GUILLUMETTE: Bill Belknap 82; Dick Hyman 83; Ianthe Ruthven (both courtesy Anthropological Museum, Mexico City) 249b, 249c; Bryan Sage 206, 207a, 210, 210a, 211a, 215b; Scala (Uffizi Gallery) 251a; SHOSTAL ASSOCIATES: 166, 170, 248; G. Ahrens 221; B. Allen 145; R. Atkeson 53; E. Carle 118, 140, 199, 249c; E. Cooper 167; R. Gildea 219; L. Gilpin 253; P. Heisleman 168; G. Hunter 201, 227, 228, 234, 237, 238, 239, 241, 242; Malak 232; R. Manley 79, 89; J. C. Maycock 159; D. Muench 44, 45, 46, 47 (both), 48, 50, 51, 52, 59, 63, 72, 76, 78, 86, 92, 93, 94, 96, 97, 98, 100, 101, 105, 114, 116, 117, 123, 218, 220, 222; R. Pinney 175; W. Pote 157; P. Reddin 174; C. Reyes 250; B. Vogel 111; J. Zehrt 113; SPECTRUM: 203a, 203b; Ezra Stoller Associates 132; W. Stribling 206a; Western Americana 85a, 85b, 85c & 85d (both courtesy of Smithsonian Institution), 112a, 112b (Courtesy American Museum, Bath), 113a (Denver Public Library, Western History Dept.), 117a, 156a, 156b, 157a, 190a, 192a, 228b, 240a (US National Archives); WOODFIN CAMP & ASSOCIATES: Shelly Grossman 4–5, 85; Yellowstone National Park 95a, 96a, 97a, 97b, 97c, 99a.

STUDIO SERVICES: Advent Graphics, Focus Photosetting, Summit Art Photography.